MICROECONOMIC THEORY

MICROECONOMIC THEORY

David G. Luenberger

Stanford University

McGraw-Hill, Inc.

New York St. Louis San Francisco Auckland Bogotá Caracas
Lisbon London Madrid Mexico City Milan Montreal New Delhi
San Juan Singapore Sydney Tokyo Toronto

This book was set in Lucida Bright by Publication Services, Inc.
The editors were Scott D. Stratford and Lucille H. Sutton;
the production supervisor was Friederich W. Schulte.
The cover was designed by Hermann Strohbach.
Project supervision was done by Publication Services, Inc.
R. R. Donnelley & Sons Company was printer and binder.

MICROECONOMIC THEORY

 This book is printed on recycled paper
containing 10% postconsumer waste.

1 2 3 4 5 6 7 8 9 0 DOC DOC 9 0 9 8 7 6 5 4

ISBN 0-07-049313-8

Library of Congress Cataloging-in-Publication Data

Luenberger, David G., (date).
    Microeconomic theory / David G. Luenberger.
        p.   cm.
    Includes index.
    ISBN 0-07-049313-8
    1. Microeconomics.   I. Title.
    HB172.L945   1995
    338.5—dc20   94-40073

INTERNATIONAL EDITION

Copyright 1995. Exclusive rights by McGraw-Hill, Inc., for manufacture and export.
This book cannot be re-exported from the country to which it is consigned by
McGraw-Hill. The International Edition is not available in North America.

When ordering this title, use ISBN 0-07-113465-4.

To the memory of
William K. Linvill

CONTENTS

Chapter 6   ECONOMIC EFFICIENCY   168

Chapter 7   GENERAL COMPETITIVE
EQUILIBRIUM   206

PREFACE

This book is intended to serve as a basic textbook in microeconomic theory, primarily at the beginning graduate or advanced undergraduate levels. Like any book at this level, this book has several interacting objectives, all of which are important. Most obvious, of course, is the presentation of the broad range of topics that make up the subject of microeconomics, including the theories of production, consumer choice, efficiency and equilibria, externalities, welfare, and uncertainty. This material is extraordinarily rich in conceptual content, making the subject quite exciting and challenging both to teach and to learn. This book has, then, as one objective to present a comprehensive treatment of the basic concepts of the subject as well as to present a sampling of advanced and specialized topics that enrich the field. The book also points to the history of the subject by providing notes and references to important works.

In addition to presenting the vast assortment of economic concepts, a course in microeconomic theory at this level also faces the challenge of having to teach advanced methods of mathematical expression. Frequently, it is in this course that students learn to represent economic concepts using the formalism of sets and mappings, to use global analysis methods, such as convexity and fixed point theorems, to construct proofs, and to sharpen their skills in moving between mathematical expression and economic interpretation. This leap to a new level of scientific and mathematical sophistication is perhaps the most important aspect of a course of this nature. It is this skill that will enable students to continue to absorb and create economic concepts throughout their careers. This text is intended to facilitate this leap.

Another objective of a text in this area is to show how microeconomics can be applied to real situations. However, it is recognized that application occurs in two fundamentally different modes. In one mode, microeconomic concepts are used to gain understanding and to suggest broad outlines of possible policy changes. For example, the fact that a competitive equilibrium is Pareto efficient might suggest that free markets are more desirable than a regulated distribution of goods. The second mode of application is more specific. In this mode one considers a specific situation, such as the problem of a specific firm, and attempts to work out a specific solution, such as a pricing policy. For the first mode of application, an understanding of concepts is often sufficient. For the second, it is also necessary that one possess a mastery of the techniques for implementing the concepts. For example, one might need to know how to compute an equilibrium as well as know that one exists. This text attempts to teach this aspect of economics by including several examples of both modes.

A final aspect of microeconomics that must be recognized is that microeconomics is a science, and as such its theories must be tested. Sometimes this can be done by direct experimentation. However, the nature of the subject makes it difficult to conduct controlled experiments on a scale large enough to evaluate many aspects of the theory meaningfully. Accordingly, the methods for systematic testing of economic theory make up a large special subject, typically treated in other courses. This text attempts to point out important established results whenever possible, but it does not provide detailed coverage of this aspect.

The text was designed according to a particular weighting of the general objectives outlined above. First priority is given to a mixture of the first two: presentation of the subject itself and development of the skills necessary for students to make the leap in sophistication with respect to rigorous expression of and use of concepts. Once students understand the fundamental principles and make the leap in sophistication, they are prepared to delve deeply into any particular topic, even if it is not included within the text.

A special technical feature of this book is the introduction of the benefit function and related concepts. This material arises in many portions of the book and serves as a kind of unifying theme. This material was in fact not contained in the early versions of the text, for the topic evolved gradually as I worked through the chapters. It seemed clear all along that Pareto efficiency and equilibria should each be related to some general optimization principle. Ultimately, I found that this idea could be expressed as the *zero-maximum* principle and its dual, the *zero-minimum* principle. In various forms these principles actually have roots that go back a long time in economic thought, but I believe that this is the first general textbook that includes significant discussion of them.

The exercises are a major part of the text. Some are versions of standard exercises in texts of this type, but many are original, being developed with the help of many individuals. The exercises emphasize the objectives of the text. Hence they are intended to illustrate the theory, present extensions of the theory, help students develop facility in mathematical expression of economic ideas, and show how the theory can be applied. (A solutions manual is available to instructors.) Several exercises are classroom demonstrations. I have found that inclusion of one or two of these each semester can help make the material come alive—and they are a lot of fun!

Some of the sections, subsections, and exercises are marked with a star (an asterisk *). For sections and subsections a star indicates that the material is rather difficult or perhaps tangential. Generally, it is safe to skip over starred sections at the first reading. Starred exercises are more difficult than others.

The organization of the book is, I think, relatively standard. The theory of production and of the firm are presented first in Chapters 2 and 3. This material requires relatively few behavioral assumptions, is a good introduction to the kind of mathematical technique that is important, and can be used to address numerous economic applications. Next, in Chapters 4 and 5 the theories of individual preferences and demand are presented. These require somewhat more profound behavioral assumptions, and expand on the mathematical methods (especially those of duality), but they have fewer direct economic applications.

In Chapters 6 and 7 the two previous segments are linked by consideration of overall efficiency and competitive equilibrium. This material is perhaps the heart of modern microeconomic theory, it contains the central theorems relating Pareto efficiency to equilibria and establishing the existence of competitive equilibria.

Chapter 8 is devoted to a fairly brief introduction to game theory. Game theory is a fundamental tool for modern economic analysis, and this chapter develops the tools and concepts that are required for the subsequent chapters.

Chapters 9 and 10 are devoted to externalities and welfare, respectively. Both of these are important topics that go beyond standard competitive analysis, and they are an integral part of any microeconomics course.

Finally, Chapters 11 and 12 discuss uncertainty and information. These are modern topics, for textbooks of a decade or two ago rarely included more than a few sections on uncertainty and information. Now these subjects are considered to be essential to a full course on microeconomics.

The writing of this book spanned approximately 10 years, and the book itself went through several evolutionary stages as I continued to learn new things about economics and as the concepts related to the benefit function developed. It is perhaps obvious that many people contributed to this project, either directly through reading drafts or suggesting exercises or indirectly by providing comments on benefit function theory. I would like especially to thank Kenneth Arrow, Hanan Bell, Pamela Brown, David Cariño, Mark Cronshaw, Darrell Duffie, Stephen Fan, Philip Hanser, Robert Maxfield, Scott McKeon, Maria Luisa Petit, Neal Stoughton, Robert Welch, and Andrew Yates for their comments and help. The final text was improved by the suggestions of the following reviewers: Scott Atkinson, University of Georgia; Gauttam Bhattacharya, University of Kansas; David Card, Princeton University; Kevin Cotter, Wayne State University; Roy Gardner, University of Indiana—Bloomington; Richard Jensen, University of Kentucky; John Pencavel, Stanford University; and Al Slivinski, University of Western Ontario.

My editors, Scott Stratford and Lucille Sutton, had continuing faith in this project and provided every resource possible to complete it in excellent fashion. Support for much of the research that accompanied this project was provided by the National Science Foundation, to which I am very grateful.

One special person who has been with this project from the beginning to the end, who entered the text in the word processor, corrected the grammar, and kept the manuscript in order through all of its transmutations, is Nancy Florence. I thank her especially. I offer special thanks to my family members, especially my wife, Nancy. This project would not have been accomplished without their understanding of lost weekends and their continuing encouragement and support.

This book is dedicated to the memory of Professor William K. Linvill, who was inspiration, teacher, friend, and colleague to many of us at Stanford and elsewhere. He passionately advanced the vision that analytic methods could contribute significantly to the understanding and solution of a broad assortment of important world problems and issues, and he long ago convinced me that microeconomic theory represents an important class of analytic methods ideally suited for that purpose.

Finally, I want to thank all the students who endured the many early versions of the text. Perhaps these students felt that they were contributing to the welfare of future generations of students, for their suggestions were marked by wonderful enthusiasm and support. I thank them for all they taught me!

David G. Luenberger
Stanford
October 1994

MICROECONOMIC THEORY

Chapter **1**
INTRODUCTION

1.1   What Is Microeconomics?

It is not easy to give a concise definition of economics, but almost every-one has a general notion of what it is. It is, at least in part, the study of how scarce resources are distributed, including how they are employed for the production of other goods and services and how goods and services are chosen for consumption by individuals. Economics also includes the study of possible institutional mechanisms for facilitating and guiding this distri-bution, such as various market structures, incentive plans, tax mechanisms, and regulations. Finally, the field of economics studies the relation between individual desires and societal objectives—how these can be reconciled, and how the economy can be structured to be best in some sense. These themes are discussed further in this introduction, and they run throughout the text; but as for any richly complex subject, a list of the main themes can only be an overview, not a real definition of the subject. As one studies the subject, a deeper understanding of its very definition is obtained.

Economic theory is divided into *microeconomics* and *macroeconomics*. The division is a bit arbitrary, since both are concerned with the broad sub-jects outlined above. Actually, the distinction between the two relates more directly to the methods employed than to a partitioning of the overall sphere of economic problems. Nevertheless, the two methods do lend themselves to different kinds of problems.

Microeconomics describes economic activity at the level of individual agents, such as consumers, investors, or managers of firms. Microeconomic theory is founded on the premise that these individuals behave rationally, making choices that are optimal for themselves. Under this premise, the theory can deduce the choices that would be made in various situations if the choice criteria of an individual or a firm are known.

Microeconomic theory also describes production and trade of elemental commodities, such as bread, automobiles, haircuts, ski trips, and so forth. In a specific analysis, groups of commodities might be aggregated, to reduce dimensionality, but the theory does not rely on such aggregation. At the most general level, microeconomic theory describes production processes

1

in detail, listing all inputs and outputs and accounting for all possible ways that inputs might be combined to produce outputs. In principle, therefore, microeconomic theory can consider a detailed tracing of commodities: from the source of underlying raw materials, through production, through distribution, and finally to use (consumption) by individuals—all on the basis of choices.

There are two distinct ways to use microeconomic theory. First, it can be used *specifically*, to represent specific situations. For example, a firm might use microeconomics to design a pricing policy by modeling its production processes and product demand; the firm thus solves a specific problem to get specific numerical results. For more ambitious problems, larger models, encompassing a greater number of agents, might be constructed. Although there are obvious limits to this type of analysis, it can be extremely valuable when used appropriately.

The second way microeconomic theory is used is *generally*, to describe and analyze broad economic concepts. In this use, the theory is applied abstractly. For example, the production possibilities of a firm might be represented by an abstract set with certain properties. One might then deduce general properties of an optimal production plan, without calculating specific details. In this way, the theory can build up general conclusions from elementary assumptions. These conclusions add substance to the theory and can serve as guidelines for both individual and societal action.

Macroeconomics, by contrast, deals principally with large aggregates of agents and commodities—for example, total consumption (in monetary units), total production, and total investment. Macroeconomic methods are usually used to obtain results and insights for an entire economy, painting a broad-brush picture of the aggregates rather than a detailed picture of individual agents as in microeconomics. The dichotomy of the two subjects is not rigid, however. Modern macroeconomic theory is progressing by adding detail, and modern microeconomic theory is successfully bridging the difference in theory between individuals and aggregates. The focus of this text is microeconomics, which approaches the vast scope of economics by building upward from individual action to aggregate behavior.

1.2   The Elements of Microeconomics

As stated above, microeconomics looks at the problems facing economic agents—the problem of selecting an appropriate action or making an appropriate decision. It considers the range of alternatives available to an agent and evaluates them in terms of economic consequences. This viewpoint can be applied to a wide variety of agents (including managers, workers, bank presidents, and homemakers) in a whole spectrum of problems. But primarily, microeconomics selects two prototypical economic agents, namely, producers and consumers who are both part of a market economy, where goods and services are produced and purchased under a price system. In simplest terms, the producer needs to determine how much to produce and the best method for doing so; the consumer needs to determine what to buy given a budgetary constraint. The problems facing these two prototypical agents are addressed in some detail in microeconomics.

Production

To study producers, one first studies the technology available to a firm—a description of the technically possible transformations of inputs into outputs. This description can take many forms: it might be a simple list of the possibilities, it might be a mathematical expression giving output quantity as a function of input levels, or most generally, it might be described simply as a *set,* a set of permissible inputs and outputs. Whatever the form, the description of physical possibilities is the foundation for analysis.

A firm must also understand its economic environment—the demand for its products, the structure of its competition, and the market for its input. A description of this economic environment may be more difficult to obtain than that of its technical structure, but it is just as important.

A firm must make several important decisions. Some are purely technical, such as selections of plant facilities, production levels, and input combinations. Some are purely economic, such as the setting of product prices and bids for resources. All these decisions interact and depend on both the technical and the economic environment. How are the decisions made?

According to the general framework of microeconomics, a firm is considered as being governed by a rational economic agent (or agents). Most frequently this is understood to imply that a firm is operated to maximize profit, although other possibilities can be considered. The rational agent assimilates all available information, both technical and economic, and finds the optimal overall plan. Production theory shows how this is to be done and expresses the consequences of such rational behavior on overall market behavior.

Preferences and Consumption

In microeconomics, consumption decisions are traced down to the level of individuals. The theory therefore attempts to explain how such individual consumption choices are made. To develop such an explanation, one looks first, just as when studying production, at what is feasible—the set of choices that the consumer could actually make.

Imagine a wealthy consumer faced with an array of goods available for purchase. The goods include a large variety of foods, different types of shelter, a selection of automobiles, various sporting and cultural activities, and a truly vast assortment of other items. Let us imagine a budget cycle of, say, one year during which this well-to-do consumer will purchase a collection (or bundle) of these items using the income that is available during that period. In a perfectly competitive market, each item will have a well-defined price; let us suppose this price remains constant during the period. Determining the bundles that are feasible for the consumer is quite straightforward. The consumer can purchase any bundle of these goods that, under the given prices, can be purchased with the available budget. So determining feasible bundles is relatively easy. The hard part of the theory is determining which will be chosen from among the feasible possibilities.

Modern consumer theory resolves this by assuming that each consumer has a preference structure for bundles of commodities: Given any two commodity bundles, the consumer is able to say which is preferred (or whether he or she is indifferent to them). Hence, the wealthy consumer we considered above, when presented with any two different bundles of food goods, shelter types, automobiles, and so forth, can say which complete bundle is preferred (or whether they are equivalent). The theory then posits that when faced with a choice between two bundles that are both feasible, a consumer will select the bundle that is most preferred. The modern theory of the consumer, then, is based on *individual preference maximization*: individuals have preferences over entire bundles of goods and always select the most preferred bundle from those that are feasible.

The theory of individual preference maximization has surprisingly great power. It explains many properties of consumer choice, and it provides a foundation for welfare theory, as discussed later in this section. It can be put to practical use by firms to develop advantageous pricing policies, design profitable products, or determine a response to a competitor's policy change. The theory can be extended to treat consumer choices over several time periods or when there is uncertainty. Hence, the theory is flexible enough to treat an extensive array of real economic choice problems; yet, it is inherently simple in concept.

Markets

Although it is possible (conceptually) to allocate resources mechanically, real economies typically allocate resources through trade. Agents arrange mutually beneficial trades among themselves, increasing profits or preferences. In a fully functioning economy, however, the trades actually consummated are not merely the result of one-to-one bargaining, for many agents are aware of the terms of other similar trades. In other words, trading takes place in an environment of information exchange, and this environment influences the terms of trade. The composite of procedures for trade including the informational environment is (loosely) termed a *market*.

In one idealized version of a market, everyone is aware of all other trades (or at least aware of the most favorable terms of trade available), trading is unrestricted (so that identical terms are in fact available to everyone), and each agent's trades represent a vanishingly small fraction of the total. Such markets are termed *perfect,* or *perfectly competitive,* and are characterized by the fact that all trades (of identical items) use the same terms. The idealized situation may never be achieved exactly in a real market, of course, but it is a convenient reference point for study.

In a perfectly competitive market, commodity prices are meaningful, indicating the relative values of the commodities as evidenced by the trades. This greatly facilitates the planning of trades, for rather than thinking in terms of a multitude of pairwise (or more complex) trades, agents can simply plan purchases and sales according to market prices.

Closely related to the concept of perfectly competitive markets is the concept of a *competitive equilibrium*. A competitive equilibrium is a condition of the overall economy such that no agent has an incentive to trade further, and all agents are small relative to the whole economy so that individually no agent can influence prices.

There is no guarantee, in general, that such an equilibrium exists. One of the major achievements of modern microeconomic theory is the proof that a competitive equilibrium does in fact exist for a perfectly competitive market (under certain assumptions). This theory is considered major, for it brings together the separate theories of production and consumer choice, showing that they are in a sense consistent with competitive markets.

Not all markets approach the idealization described by perfect competition. Monopolies, imperfect information, and a host of other "abnormalities" can and do occur in real markets. Microeconomic theory addresses these markets as well, although the theories are not as complete as for perfect competition.

Welfare

Earlier we said that economics is the study of how scarce resources are employed and the resulting products allocated to individuals. Welfare theory addresses two main questions about this overall process. First, it asks how one can measure the quality of a given allocation. Second, it examines whether given *mechanisms* of allocation, such as perfect competition, will produce high quality results.

A central concept for assessing quality is *Pareto efficiency.* An allocation of resources is Pareto efficient if there is no other allocation that everyone prefers at least as well to the first one and which at least one person strictly prefers. This is an *efficiency* concept because if it is satisfied, it is impossible to find an improved allocation, as measured by individual preferences. For example, if an economy consists of two people and six apples, the allocation of three apples to each person is Pareto efficient; but so is the allocation of all six to one person and none to the other. In either case, there is no way to improve the situation for both people simultaneously. If, on the other hand, three of the six apples were given to one person and just one to the other person, that would not be Pareto efficient because two apples are wasted—each person could be given an additional apple, which they both would like. In a complex economy, inefficiencies can be much harder to detect than in this simple example, but the principle is the same. The Pareto efficiency concept is a first step toward welfare analysis.

It can be shown that the mechanism of perfect competition does (under certain conditions) lead to Pareto efficient allocations. Conversely, any Pareto efficient point can (under somewhat more restrictive conditions) be maintained by perfect competition. Hence, the mechanism of perfect competition leads to high-quality allocations as measured by Pareto efficiency.

Situations involving imperfect competition, such as when there are monopolies, are inherently inefficient. A goal of welfare theory is to develop mechanisms and procedures (such as introducing special taxes) to obtain efficiency in these cases. This is an important application of welfare economics.

The other aspect of welfare analysis is *equity*—how trade-offs between the desires of different individuals are evaluated. Equity is vastly more difficult and controversial than efficiency. Yet this aspect of welfare is at the heart of the kind of important social choices faced regularly: Should a city build a highway that would decrease traffic congestion but disturb nearby residents? Should national defense be increased at the expense of welfare payments to the poor? These questions must be decided by the members of society. What process should they use—majority voting, perhaps? It is not surprising that welfare theory formally ratifies our intuitive belief that these difficult questions cannot be satisfactorily relegated to a mechanistic procedure, even a voting procedure. Society is forced to look beyond mechanisms and instead analyze issues by blending a variety of principles and calculations through a political process. In other words, microeconomic theory can assist the decision process, but the theory itself acknowledges that these decisions cannot be reduced to quantitative calculation. In decisions involving societal values, analysis must remain a servant, not a master.

1.3   Methods

We preview here some of the mathematical methods used in later chapters. This serves partially as general preparation for what is to come, but also shows how the methods relate to each other and to the structure of microeconomics.

Calculus?

The tables of contents of microeconomics textbooks are all remarkably similar. They all list production theory, consumer theory, welfare, and something about markets and equilibrium. Typically, of course, more topics are included as the level of the text increases, but at the core, the subjects are nearly identical. The presentations differ primarily in the analytic tools that are used.

Beginning textbooks use *no* calculus. Instead, analysis is based on verbal discussion and graphs. Microeconomic concepts can be effectively introduced this way, and this method has the advantage of focusing on the broad interpretation of concepts rather than details of analysis.

Texts at the lower intermediate level use *some* calculus. This provides more analytic power, which in turn allows for deeper probing of the issues. Calculus, however, is basically a tool for analysis of local properties of functions. Hence, when using calculus, one must express relations in terms of functions, and analysis tends to address *marginal* (that is, local) quantities. There is a possibility that the greater analytic power of calculus is accompanied by a loss of broad perspective.

Texts at the upper intermediate and graduate level, such as this one, use *less* calculus (at least, calculus is less dominant). Instead, calculus is replaced in many arguments by the even more powerful methods of sets, optimization, equilibrium, and game theory, which are discussed below. These methods emphasize global rather than local properties and are not tied to representations in terms of functions. Using these methods, a more complete and more intuitive perspective can be attained. The objective is one of directness and clarity, similar to the objective of beginning-level texts, but much greater depth is achievable.

Finally, one can imagine a really advanced text that, again, like beginning texts, would use *no* calculus. But we do not go *that* far.

Sets

Like any theory, microeconomics expresses relations, partitioning what is true from what is not true. And there are many ways to represent relations. For example, there are many ways to express the relation defining the feasible input-output combinations in a firm: as a graph of input versus output, as a mathematical expression giving output as a function of input, or as a list of the possibilities (perhaps in the form of a table). All of these methods might work for a particular case. However, the underlying entity that each of these methods describes is a *set* of feasible possibilities. The different methods are just alternate ways of describing the same set.

It is therefore most general, and really most natural, to develop microeconomic theory directly in terms of sets rather than in terms of a particular form of set representation, and this is the approach taken in this text. Particular representations are, most surely, used as well—we use plenty of graphs, functions, and tables—but the use of sets for general theoretical development leads to a far more powerful theory than that which would evolve from the use of just one kind of representation.

Most of the sets used in microeconomics express relations between quantities that can vary continuously, such as pounds of meat or ounces of gold. Hence most sets are defined in a finite-dimensional space and are *connected,* as opposed to consisting of several isolated points. These connected sets are easy to visualize, and indeed, when drawn as two-dimensional shapes, they have the same visual power as a graph. The difference between the two is that a set is more general and is easier to work with notationally. But because sets share the visual properties of graphs, a theory based on sets frequently yields more insight than a comparable theory based on functions.

Set representation also blends naturally with the other principal methods employed in microeconomic theory. This fact, together with the advantages of generality and visualization, makes the use of sets very compelling.

Optimization and Duality

Optimization is fundamental to modern microeconomic theory because it is used to express the rationality of individual agents: an objective is defined, constraints are identified, and finally an optimal point is determined that represents a specific decision or action. The idea of optimization is used to describe a firm's production decisions (determined by profit maximization), consumer choice (through maximization of preferences), and often government policy as well. For this reason optimization permeates the entire text, and the reader should consult Appendix C for necessary background.

Closely related to optimization is duality. Duality is somewhat difficult to define exactly, for it takes many forms and plays many roles. Frequently, it appears in surprising and subtle ways. One simple definition of duality in the context of microeconomics is that it expresses relations in terms of prices rather than quantities—so whenever a function is defined with respect to prices one might suspect that it is a *dual* concept. On the other hand, functions defined in terms of quantities are called *primal*.

Duality is related to optimization because generally, if one defines an optimization problem with respect to quantities, there is a corresponding problem defined with respect to prices that has the same value. One example of this relation is that to achieve a competitive equilibrium, society should allocate resources (i.e., quantities) to maximize a quantity called *benefit,* and alternatively, the equilibrium prices will minimize another quantity, called *surplus.*

Optimization and duality have a natural affinity for microeconomics, for the economic interpretation of dual results is usually very helpful both for understanding the mathematics and for clarifying the economics.

Equilibria and Fixed Points

One of the central concepts of microeconomics is that of equilibrium. However, the term really has two interpretations: the first as an economic phenomenon, a kind of rest state for an economy as discussed earlier, and the second as a purely mathematical principle, a solution point of a system of equations.

A simple version of the mathematical concept is a fixed point of a function that maps vectors into vectors. A fixed point of such a function f is a solution $\mathbf{x}$ to $f(\mathbf{x}) = \mathbf{x}$. The vector $\mathbf{x}$ is *fixed* in that it does not move if f is applied.

In an economic context, the term *equilibrium* describes a state where there is no incentive to change individual decisions. Each agent is satisfied with the current choice. We can relate this economic definition of equilibrium to the fixed-point concept by considering the function that from a given state produces the aggregate response. If the new state is equal to the old, it is an economic equilibrium, and it is also a fixed point of the function that defines new states in terms of old ones.

Equilibrium is a powerful concept for structuring general theory. It is used to model oligopolies, to treat bargaining, and to look at incentive issues. It can be applied to simple static situations, to sequences of decisions extending over time, and to situations involving uncertainty. Various recent modifications of the basic definition give it even wider applicability and realism.

Game Theory

Game theory addresses situations where a group of individuals make separate decisions, but individual rewards are determined by the collective, interactive effect of all their decisions. The theory can be applied, as the name itself suggests, to well-defined real games, such as tick-tack-toe, poker, or even (in theory at least) chess. It can also be applied with good result to economics, as demonstrated in the later chapters of this text.

Game theory embraces equilibrium theory as a major component concept. The equilibrium results of game theory have been used to study perfect competition, auctions, contracts, bargaining, and various forms of imperfect competition. It provides a coherent superstructure for the study of a vast collection of important economic problems.

Game theory also addresses cooperative situations, where individuals are able to share information and jointly select strategies for mutual benefit. This aspect of game theory also has many economic applications. In particular, it encompasses social choice issues, in which a group of individuals, each having individual preferences, jointly determine the best way to allocate resources.

These general methods (sets, optimization and duality, equilibrium, and game theory) are introduced more or less sequentially in the text. Sets arise first, since they are required for expressing structure. Optimization and duality enter next, since they form the basis for individual action, whether of firms or consumers. Equilibrium theory enters later as the principle for coordinating individual actions. Finally, game theory is introduced to study complex forms of competition and to provide a framework for studying cooperative as well as noncooperative interactions. While progressing through the subsequent chapters, the reader will witness the development of these methods. Working together, these methods build microeconomic theory and provide the means for its application.

Chapter **2**
PRODUCTION AND COST

Economic activity can be partitioned into production, trade, and consumption. Production should be interpreted very broadly, however, to include production of both physical goods—such as bread or automobiles—and services—such as medical care or financial services. When studying the theory of production, it is simplest to imagine production in the first interpretation, that of physical goods. However, most of the concepts developed apply to the production of services as well.

The first part of this chapter presents a general framework of production technology. By itself, this framework, however, does not describe how production choices are made. It only defines what choices *can* be made; it does not specify what choices should be made, for that depends on many other (nontechnological) factors. The early sections of the chapter describe production possibilities in physical terms. Later, in the second part of the chapter, this description is recast into economic terms—using cost functions. Chapter 3 expands the economic description and discusses what choices *should* be made.

The framework for describing production technology presented in this chapter is general and somewhat abstract. This generality is a source of power, for the framework is capable of describing a wide diversity of technologies and processes. On the other hand, it is important to see how this abstract framework can accommodate concrete representations of real processes. The chapter therefore presents several illustrations of particular, but simple, processes.

Part I
PRODUCTION

2.1 Technology of Production

A firm's technology consists, roughly, of methods for transforming inputs into outputs. Typically, inputs consist of labor, capital equipment, raw

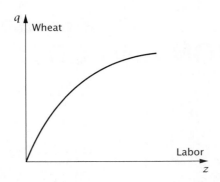

z **FIGURE 2.1   Wheat production.**

materials, and intermediate goods purchased from other firms. Outputs consist of finished products or services, or intermediate goods to be sold to other firms. Often alternative methods are available for producing the same output, using different combinations of inputs. The final choice of which method to use is made on economic grounds, but for the purpose of describing the technology, all methods are included.

We illustrate some of the various ways technologies can be described through three examples.

Example 2.1 (Wheat production).   Consider a farm that produces a single commodity, wheat, using only a single input, labor. (In this simplified example we are admittedly neglecting other inputs, such as seed, machines, and other water than that obtained naturally from rain.) As more labor is employed, more wheat can be produced. But the increase in production resulting from additional labor falls off at higher levels, because when a great deal of wheat is growing, additional labor has a small influence on the final output. As a specific example we suppose that the maximum quantity, q, of wheat that can be produced from an amount z of labor is

$$q = 3z^{1/2}.$$

See Fig. 2.1. This expresses the output quantity q as a function of the input quantity. (Such a function is termed a *production function*.) This method of describing production processes by expressing output as a function of input is used frequently, and we consider it in more detail later in this chapter.

Example 2.2 (Seamstress).   A seamstress makes dresses in her home. She uses cloth and labor as inputs. Each dress requires 3 yards of cloth and 5 hours of labor. The seamstress obviously cannot substitute between these two inputs. She must have 3 yards of cloth and 5 hours of labor for every dress. Additional labor without additional cloth will not yield more dresses. Her production of dresses as related to inputs can be shown by a table, as in

		Labor (hours)				
		5	10	15	20	25
	3	1	1	1	1	1
Cloth	6	1	2	2	2	2
(yards)	9	1	2	3	3	3
	12	1	2	3	4	4

FIGURE 2.2 Dress production.

Fig. 2.2. Such a table is a useful way to describe the production possibilities for discrete quantities.

Example 2.3 (Oil refinery). An oil refinery produces three products: gasoline, heating oil, and jet fuel. These products are produced from two types of crude oil: light crude and heavy crude. Each type of crude yields different amounts per barrel of the three products, as described in the table below. For example, one barrel of light crude yields 0.3 barrels of gasoline, 0.2 barrels of heating oil, and 0.3 barrels of jet fuel. In addition, there is a maximum capacity of the refinery: only 10,000 barrels of crude can be processed per day.

	Gasoline	Heating oil	Jet fuel
Light crude	0.3	0.2	0.3
Heavy crude	0.3	0.4	0.2

Since there are three outputs and two inputs, it is not possible to express the output as a single function of input, but we can write down the constraints on production. Let z_1 and z_2 denote the amounts of light and heavy crude, respectively, used as inputs, and let q_1, q_2, and q_3 denote the produced amounts of gasoline, heating oil, and jet fuel, respectively. Then from the production table and that capacity constraint, it follows that

$$
\begin{aligned}
0.3z_1 + 0.3z_2 &\geq q_1 \\
0.2z_1 + 0.4z_2 &\geq q_2 \\
0.3z_1 + 0.2z_2 &\geq q_3 \\
z_1 + z_2 &\leq 10{,}000.
\end{aligned}
$$

In addition,

$$
q_1 \geq 0, \quad q_2 \geq 0, \quad q_3 \geq 0
$$
$$
z_1 \geq 0, \quad z_2 \geq 0.
$$

The left side of the first inequality above is obtained by adding up the total possible production of the first product using the two types of crude oil available. This total must be at least as large as the amount of the product actually produced. (Actually, in practice the refinery would operate to obtain equality rather than inequality, so as not to waste resources; but we allow for the possibility of waste here.) The second and third inequalities have similar meanings, and the fourth is the capacity constraint.

Any set of values satisfying the above inequalities represents a feasible set of inputs and outputs for the oil refinery. Hence the set of inequalities describes the refinery's technology. We shall find that, in general, a system of inequalities is a very useful method for representing technologies.

2.2   Production Possibility Sets

The most general way to describe the technology of a firm is in terms of a set. Such a representation includes as special cases descriptions in terms of production functions, graphs, or systems of inequalities. If a firm uses and produces a total of m different commodities, the technology can be described by a set in m-dimensional space.

The distinction between inputs and outputs is not always clear, since a firm may have the choice of producing some of the intermediate goods it requires (in which case these intermediate goods are potential outputs) or purchasing them from other firms (in which case they are inputs). Therefore, to be as general as possible we suppose that there are m commodities under consideration that can be used by the firm—some as inputs, some as outputs, and perhaps some as either. These commodities are indexed in a fixed order, from 1 to m. A particular production plan can be represented by a vector $\mathbf{y}$ in $\mathcal{R}^m$, corresponding to various amounts of these commodities. If a component of this vector is positive, say $y_i > 0$, then a net amount y_i of the ith commodity is produced. If a component y_j is negative, a net amount $-y_j$ of the jth commodity is used. The vector $\mathbf{y}$ is called a *netput vector*, each component of $\mathbf{y}$ equals the net amount produced of the corresponding commodity, which can be either positive, negative, or zero. This leads to the formal definition of the production technology of a firm.

Production possibility set.   The *production possibility set* of a firm is a subset $\mathcal{Y}$ of the space $\mathcal{R}^m$. A firm may select any vector $\mathbf{y} \in \mathcal{Y}$ as its production plan.

The production possibility set of a complex firm such as an automobile manufacturer would be difficult to describe in detail. A netput vector would contain, as components, all inputs, including all plant and machinery, all intermediate parts, which might be either purchased or made internally, all raw materials, all labor and management, and all final products. The corresponding production possibility set would include all such feasible netput vectors. It would include plans that are wasteful or otherwise unlikely to be chosen by the firm as well as reasonable and efficient ones. For purposes of a general theory, however, it is enough that we are able to conceptualize the existence of this set. For purposes of a specific analysis, one would probably develop a simplified version.

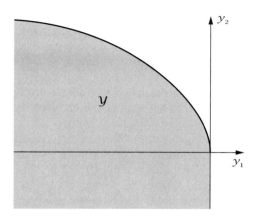

FIGURE 2.3   A production possibility set.

As an example, consider again the wheat farm described by the production function $q = 3z^{1/2}$. In this case we define a netput vector having two components $\mathbf{y} = (y_1, y_2)$ with $y_1 = -z$ and $y_2 = q$. The first component corresponds to an input, so it will have a negative value. In the general description, we also allow inequality in the relation; giving $q \leq 3z^{1/2}$, which allows for wasteful use of the input. In fact, if we allow the farm to acquire wheat, we can have negative values of q in the production possibility set.

The resulting production possibility set is shown in Fig. 2.3. Note that the set is located on the negative y_1 axis, since labor is consumed rather than produced by the process. It extends below this axis because $y_2 = q$ can be negative as well as positive. Explicitly,

$$\mathbf{y} = \left\{ (-z, q) : q \leq 3z^{1/2}, \ z \geq 0 \right\}.$$

As another example, consider again production by the seamstress. In this case production levels jump whenever enough additional inputs are gathered to produce another dress. The corresponding "jumpy" production possibility set is shown in Fig. 2.4.

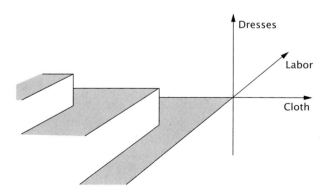

FIGURE 2.4   Production possibility set for seamstress.

This example illustrates that even commodities that are produced in discrete quantities can be handled by the production possibility framework. And it is easy to see that discrete input commodities can also be handled by having isolated points in the set.

Generally, if a commodity can be meaningfully measured in continuous units, it is said to be *infinitely divisible*, or simply *divisible*. Commodities such as wheat or water are most naturally considered as being divisible. Others, like dresses or battleships, may be most naturally treated as indivisible. However, the appropriate classification depends on the scale of production and the focus of analysis. If the quantities are large, it is usually appropriate to consider discrete commodities as being divisible. This smooths out the production possibility set.

The above examples only begin to illustrate the range of structures that can be accommodated by the general definition of a production possibility set. Others will be explored in later sections.

Common Properties

Although the production possibility sets of different processes can differ widely in structure, many technologies share certain general properties. If it can be assumed that these properties are satisfied, special theoretical results can be derived. Six of the most important properties are defined below.

Closed.   A production possibility set $\mathcal{Y}$ is *closed* if whenever a sequence of netput vectors $\mathbf{y}_i$, $i = 1, 2, \ldots$, are in $\mathcal{Y}$ and $\mathbf{y}_i \to \mathbf{y}$, then the limit netput vector $\mathbf{y}$ is also in $\mathcal{Y}$. (This says that $\mathcal{Y}$ satisfies the standard definition of a closed set as stated in Appendix A.)

Closedness is illustrated in Fig. 2.5. It is a technical assumption, in that its main purpose is purely mathematical. It guarantees that points on the

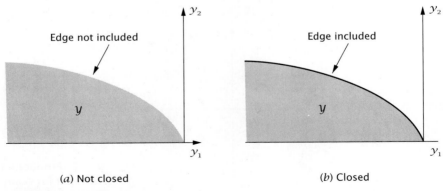

(a) Not closed   (b) Closed

FIGURE 2.5   Closedness.

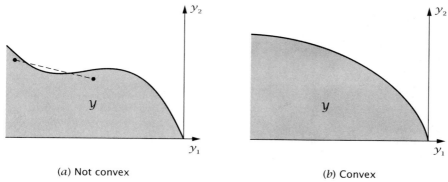

(a) Not convex   (b) Convex

FIGURE 2.6 Convexity.

"edge" of y are feasible. It has little economic significance, for even if y were not closed, feasible points arbitrarily close to the edge of y could be found. However, for mathematical convenience, we almost always assume that y is closed.

Convex. The set y is *convex* if whenever $\mathbf{y}_1$ and $\mathbf{y}_2$ are feasible netput vectors, the vector $\alpha\mathbf{y}_1 + (1 - \alpha)\mathbf{y}_2$ is also feasible for any α, $0 \le \alpha \le 1$. (Convexity of y is equivalent to the standard definition that y be a convex set, as described in Appendix B.)

Convexity is illustrated in Fig. 2.6. y is convex if given any two points in y, the line segment joining them is also in y.

There is often strong economic justification for an assumption of convexity of y. If all commodities are divisible, it is often reasonable to assume that two production plans (netput vectors) $\mathbf{y}_1$ and $\mathbf{y}_2$ can be scaled downward and combined. If, for example, two production plans for growing crops on a farm are known, it is likely that by scaling each plan down by one-half—by allocating half the acreage, water, labor, and so forth to each plan—a combined plan equal to the sum of the half-plans can be implemented. If this is true, it means that $(\frac{1}{2})\mathbf{y}_1 + (\frac{1}{2})\mathbf{y}_2$ is also a feasible plan. Nonequal proportions α and $1 - \alpha$ could also be used. Hence, the convexity assumption derives from the basic notions of divisibility and the additivity of scaled-down processes.

Free disposal. If $\mathbf{y} \in y$ implies that $\mathbf{y}' \in y$ for all $\mathbf{y}' \le \mathbf{y}$, then the set y satisfies the condition of *free disposal*.[1]

Free disposal implies that commodities (either inputs or outputs) can be thrown away. This property does not always hold. In graphical terms free disposal means that if $\mathbf{y} \in y$, then y includes also all vectors in the

---

[1]$\mathbf{y}' \le \mathbf{y}$ means that $y_i' \le y_i$ for each $i = 1, 2, \ldots, m$. See Appendix A.

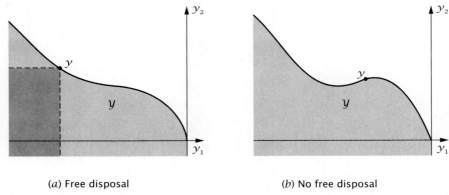

(*a*) Free disposal   (*b*) No free disposal

FIGURE 2.7   Free disposal.

negative orthant translated to **y**. In Fig. 2.7*a* the free disposal condition holds, because at any point **y** all vectors with components less than those of **y** are in $\mathcal{Y}$. For the particular **y** shown, the set of these other vectors is shown as the darkly shaded area. In Fig. 2.7*b* the condition fails at the indicated point. For two dimensions this means, in particular, that the upper boundary of $\mathcal{Y}$ always has a nonpositive slope.

Example 2.4. Consider the oil refinery again. Its production possibility set is defined by the system of inequalities

$$
\begin{aligned}
0.3z_1 &+ 0.3z_2 &\geq q_1 \\
0.2z_1 &+ 0.4z_2 &\geq q_2 \\
0.3z_1 &+ 0.2z_2 &\geq q_3 \\
z_1 &+ z_2 &\leq 10{,}000
\end{aligned}
$$

$$
q_1 \geq 0, \qquad q_2 \geq 0, \qquad q_3 \geq 0
$$
$$
z_1 \geq 0, \qquad z_2 \geq 0,
$$

where here we put $y_1 = -z_1$, $y_2 = -z_2$, $y_3 = q_1$, $y_4 = q_2$, and $y_5 = q_3$. This is a closed set. (It is closed because the inequalities are not strict but include equality.) It is also easy to verify that this technology is convex (because the inequalities are linear). The technology does not satisfy free disposal because of the inequalities $q_1 \geq 0$, $q_2 \geq 0$, and $q_3 \geq 0$. If oil could be acquired as an input and then thrown away (which is unlikely), these constraints could be eliminated and the technology would satisfy the free disposal property.

Inputs and Outputs

The general theory of production is developed in terms of netput vectors. However, an important special case is when inputs and outputs are clearly defined. In that case, we partition the netput vector into two parts: the input and output components. A netput vector then is a composite vector $(-\mathbf{z}, \mathbf{q})$ where **z** denotes the vector of inputs and **q** denotes the vector of outputs.

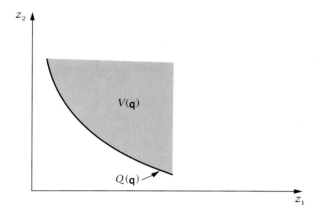

FIGURE 2.8 Input re-
quirement set and iso-
quant.

The various inputs used in production are frequently referred to as *factors* of production. If there are n inputs and m outputs,[2] the production possibility set $\mathcal{Y}$ is then a subset of $\mathcal{R}^{m+n}$.

One advantage of the formal distinction of inputs and outputs is that one can hold output levels fixed and examine what input levels are required to produce those outputs.

Input requirement set.   The input requirement set corresponding to any output vector $\mathbf{q}$ is the set

$$V(\mathbf{q}) = \{\mathbf{z} : (-\mathbf{z}, \mathbf{q}) \in \mathcal{Y}\}.$$

Physically, the input requirement set is the set of all possible input combinations that can produce the output vector $\mathbf{q}$. Input requirement sets have the pictorial advantage that, in a drawing, dimensions are not wasted on outputs. Hence, a process with two inputs can be illustrated in just two dimensions, as in Fig. 2.8.

Under free disposal, we see that if $\mathbf{q}' \leq \mathbf{q}$, then the inputs that produce $\mathbf{q}$ can also produce $\mathbf{q}'$. Thus, in this case $V(\mathbf{q}) \subset V(\mathbf{q}')$. Therefore, $V(\mathbf{q})$ can be thought of as the set of inputs that can produce *at least* $\mathbf{q}$. It is also useful to define the set of points that can produce exactly $\mathbf{q}$ and no more.

Isoquant.   The *isoquant* associated with output $\mathbf{q}$ is the set

$$Q(\mathbf{q}) = \{\mathbf{z} : (-\mathbf{z}, \mathbf{q}) \in \mathcal{Y}, (-\mathbf{z}, \mathbf{q}') \notin \mathcal{Y}$$
$$\text{for any } \mathbf{q}' \geq \mathbf{q}, \mathbf{q}' \neq \mathbf{q}\}.$$

The isoquant $Q(\mathbf{q})$ is usually the boundary closest to the origin of the input requirement set $V(\mathbf{q})$, as shown in Fig. 2.8.

---

[2]The letter m gets double use in production theory, first as the dimension of a general production possibility set $\mathcal{Y}$ and second as the number of outputs when this decomposition is used. The context should always clear up the potential confusion.

2.3   Transformation and Shortage Functions

Our first examples of technologies were represented by a production function, a table, and a system of inequalities, respectively. Although the most general representation of a production possibility set is in terms of a set, it is in fact frequently possible to describe this set as the solution to a *single* inequality of the form $T(\mathbf{y}) \leq 0$. That is, $\mathcal{Y} = \{\mathbf{y} : T(\mathbf{y}) \leq 0\}$. This form of representation is sometimes convenient since it gives specific structure to the abstract concept. A function T that describes $\mathcal{Y}$ this way is called a *transformation function*.

If a transformation function T exists, it is not unique. Any other function of the form $T^*(\mathbf{y}) = g\,(T(\mathbf{y}))$ will also work if g is any continuous function on the real numbers (that is, $g : \mathcal{R} \to \mathcal{R}$) with $g(\xi) > 0$ for $\xi > 0$ and $g(\xi) < 0$ for $\xi < 0$. That is, g can be any sign-preserving, continuous function.

The transformation function representation is useful for general arguments, since it enables a firm to be described by a single function. However, in a specific case an alternative representation such as we have seen in the examples may be most natural.

Shortage Functions

The shortage function is a special function associated with the set $\mathcal{Y}$ that often serves as a transformation function. It will be convenient to use this function, since it is related to a firm's profit, which will be discussed in Chapter 3.

Shortage function.   Let $\mathbf{g} \in \mathcal{R}_+^m$ with $\mathbf{g} \neq 0$ and let $\mathcal{Y} \subset \mathcal{R}^m$. The *shortage function* σ of $\mathcal{Y}$ (with reference $\mathbf{g}$) is defined by

$$\sigma(\mathbf{y}) = \begin{cases} \min\{s : \mathbf{y} - s\mathbf{g} \in \mathcal{Y}, \text{ if there is an } s \text{ such that } \mathbf{y} - s\mathbf{g} \in \mathcal{Y}\} \\ +\infty \quad \text{otherwise.} \end{cases}$$

We assume that the minimum indicated in the definition is achieved, or that there is no feasible s for the definition, in which case $\sigma = +\infty$.

The construction of the shortage function is illustrated in Fig. 2.9. Fig. 2.9a shows the case where the minimum in the definition is well defined. In that case the shortage function measures how far "short" $\mathbf{y}$ is from being in $\mathcal{Y}$ (measured in terms of $\mathbf{g}$). Figure 2.9b shows the case where $\sigma = +\infty$ because it is not possible to get to $\mathcal{Y}$ by moving in the direction $\mathbf{g}$ (either forward or backward). It is easy to see that $\mathcal{Y} \subset \{\sigma(\mathbf{y}) \leq 0\}$. This is because $\sigma(\mathbf{y}) > 0$ implies that $\mathbf{y} \notin \mathcal{Y}$. If $\mathcal{Y}$ satisfies free disposal and $\sigma(\mathbf{y})$ is always finite, then $\mathcal{Y} \supset \{\sigma(\mathbf{y}) \leq 0\}$. This is because $\sigma(\mathbf{y}) \leq 0$ implies $\mathbf{y} - \sigma(\mathbf{y})\mathbf{g} \in \mathcal{Y}$, but by free disposal $\mathbf{y} - \sigma(\mathbf{y})\mathbf{g} +$

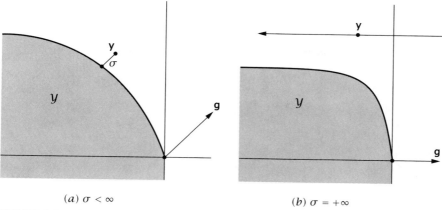

(a) $\sigma < \infty$ 　　　　　　　　(b) $\sigma = +\infty$

FIGURE 2.9　The shortage function.

$\sigma(\mathbf{y})\mathbf{g} = \mathbf{y} \in \mathcal{Y}$. Thus, under these conditions σ serves as a transformation function.

The shortage function has a number of interesting and important properties, some of which are discussed in Exercise 5.

2.4　Efficient Production

Firms usually want to produce as much output as possible for given levels of inputs or, equivalently, use the smallest levels of inputs necessary to produce a given output. To do otherwise would be wasteful. This idea is formalized by the definition of efficient netput vectors.

Efficient points.　A point $\mathbf{y} \in \mathcal{Y}$ is *efficient* if there is no $\mathbf{y}' \in \mathcal{Y}$, $\mathbf{y}' \neq \mathbf{y}$, with $\mathbf{y}' \geq \mathbf{y}$.

Note that the inequality applies to all netput components, both outputs and inputs. Clearly a netput is inefficient if output can be increased. It is also inefficient if input can be decreased; since an input is represented by its negative in the netput component, that the input can be decreased means that the netput component can be increased. In either case, an increase in netput signals inefficiency.

The definition is illustrated in Fig. 2.10. For a given $\mathbf{y}$, the points $\mathbf{y}' \geq \mathbf{y}$ correspond to those that lie in the nonnegative orthant that is attached to $\mathbf{y}$ (that is, the nonnegative orthant is translated so that its origin is $\mathbf{y}$). If $\mathbf{y}$ is efficient, there is no other point in $\mathcal{Y}$ in this translated orthant. Intuitively, an efficient point must be on the upper boundary of the set $\mathcal{Y}$, although if the upper boundary of $\mathcal{Y}$ has dips or flat spots, not every upper boundary point is efficient.

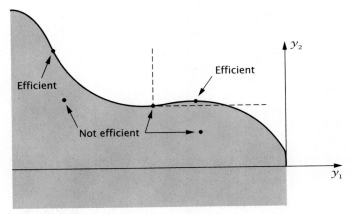

FIGURE 2.10   Efficiency.

   The following proposition states the intuitively obvious result that if y is described by a transformation function T, then $T(y) = 0$ is a necessary condition for efficiency.

Proposition 2.1 (Efficiency).   *Suppose* y *is defined by a continuous transformation function* T; *that is,* $y = \{y : T(y) \leq 0\}$. *Then* y_0 *efficient implies* $T(y_0) = 0$.

Proof: Suppose $T(y_0) < 0$. Then by continuity there is a (small) spherical region around y_0 such that $T(y) < 0$ for all y in that region. In particular, there is $y' > y_0$ with $T(y') < 0$. Hence, y_0 is not efficient. ∎

2.5   Production Functions

An important class of technologies are those having a single output whose maximum level can be described by a production function. Such technologies are frequently assumed in both theoretical discussions and empirical work because they are easy to manipulate analytically.

   The netput vector of a single-output technology has the form $(-z, q)$ where q is the output. If the technology has a transformation function, the production possibility set is the set of netput vectors satisfying $T(-z, q) \leq 0$. And, under certain regularity conditions, it is possible to solve the equation $T(-z, q) = 0$ for q in terms of z (for $z > 0$) leading to an equivalent equation

$$q = f(z).$$

The function f is the *production function*, and the equation $q = f(z)$ gives the upper boundary of y. The quantity $q = f(z)$ represents the maximum output level that can be achieved with input z. That is, $f(z) = \max \{q' : T(-z, q') \leq 0\}$.

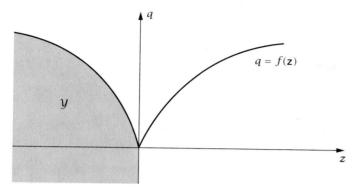

FIGURE 2.11   Production function.

In terms of the graphical representation of the production possibility set, the graph of the production function is simply the reflection about the q axis of the upper surface, as illustrated in Fig. 2.11. This is because positive input levels now correspond to positive values of **z**.

Although a production function is an especially convenient representation of a technology, it must be recognized that if it is to accurately represent the underlying process, it might be a very complicated function. Nevertheless, there are certain classical forms of production functions that are simple but useful. We introduce two of the most important below.

Example 2.5 (Cobb-Douglas technology).   Consider a single-output technology using two inputs. The inputs might represent machinery and labor, for example. In general it will be possible to substitute more of one input for less of the other while maintaining constant output level. The Cobb-Douglas technology has this substitution property. The simplest version of this technology is defined by the production function

$$q = z_1^\alpha z_2^{1-\alpha},$$

where α is a fixed number such that $0 < \alpha < 1$. The production possibility set is the set in $\mathcal{R}^3$ defined by

$$y = \left\{ (-z_1, -z_2, q) : q \leq z_1^\alpha z_2^{(1-\alpha)},\ z_1 \geq 0,\ z_2 \geq 0 \right\}.$$

The corresponding isoquants are smooth curves, as shown in Fig. 2.12. Tracing along such an isoquant shows how the two inputs can be varied to maintain a constant output level.

Example 2.6 (Leontief technology).   A Leontief technology uses inputs in fixed proportions, and the production process can be scaled up or down arbitrarily. The fixed-proportions property means that there is a single fixed formula, or recipe—just like a cooking recipe—for production: one unit of

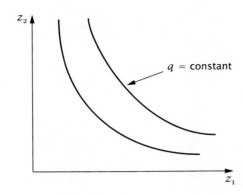

FIGURE 2.12 Isoquants for Cobb-Douglas technology.

output requires exactly a_1 units of input 1, a_2 units of input 2, ..., and a_m units of input m. If some inputs are in oversupply, they cannot substitute for others, but are merely wasted, just as having extra eggs alone does not allow one to make two cakes instead of one. The maximum amount that can be produced from a given input vector $\mathbf{z}$ is found by scaling the recipe up as high as possible until one or more inputs are used up. It is the minimum of the ratios z_i/a_i, $i = 1, 2, \ldots, m$, that determines the maximum possible output, since that is the maximum scalar multiple of the basic recipe that is contained in $\mathbf{z}$. Therefore the maximum output level q associated with $\mathbf{z}$ is

$$q = \min\left\{\frac{z_1}{a_1}, \frac{z_2}{a_2}, \ldots, \frac{z_m}{a_m}\right\},$$

and this is the production function of the Leontief technology.

As we shall see, the Leontief technology represents a fundamental building block for many other technologies, since many complex processes consist of several fixed-proportions subprocesses. As shown in Fig. 2.13, a

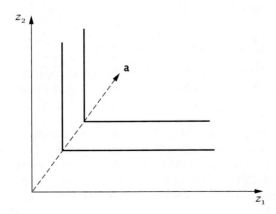

FIGURE 2.13 Isoquants for Leontief production function.

Leontief technology does *not* have smooth isoquants. This points out that procedures of analysis based, at least implicitly, on differentiability may not always be adequate.

Returns to Scale

Some production processes can be scaled up or down to produce greater or lesser output levels, proportional to the input levels employed. A Leontief technology has this property, for example. For single-output processes, we introduce a definition of this scalability property in terms of production functions.

Constant returns to scale.   A technology with production function f has *constant returns to scale* if for every $t > 0$ and every $\mathbf{z}$, $f(t\mathbf{z}) = tf(\mathbf{z})$.

Many processes at least approximately satisfy the property of constant returns to scale, especially processes that inherently work with small quantities, because perfect multiples of the input-output combinations can be created through complete duplication of the process. However, constant returns to scale is really an idealization. In practice there are difficulties with scaling upward and scaling downward. These difficulties motivate us to introduce two other definitions as well.

Decreasing returns to scale.[3]   A production function exhibits *decreasing returns to scale* if for every $t > 1$ and $\mathbf{z}$, $f(t\mathbf{z}) < tf(\mathbf{z})$.

Processes exhibit decreasing returns to scale when increasing the scale of production leads to new difficulties. A commonly cited such difficulty is management: it becomes increasingly difficult to manage an operation as it is enlarged, and hence upward scaling of inputs does not yield a proportionate increase in output. Another difficulty is the frequent impossibility of replicating key inputs. When growing a crop, for example, if the inputs of land, labor, water, machinery, and fertilizer could be scaled up together, one should be able to expand output proportionately. In practice, however, the amount of land of given fertility and within a given climactic zone is limited, so in the attempt to expand a farm operation, production rates fall off because the new land is inferior to that used before. Of course, if the *same kind* of land could be obtained, the output would in fact increase proportionately; but if we simply measure the land in acreage units, we will observe decreasing returns to scale.

Decreasing returns to scale is also observed when the list of inputs in the production function is really not complete. When ones tries to scale up a cooking recipe, for example, production will not increase in proportion

---

[3]Sometimes this case is distinguished as *strictly* decreasing returns to scale.

to a (large) increase in all food ingredients. This is because other implicit inputs, such as ovens, pans, and labor, although not formally in the list of inputs, are necessary for the process and must also be scaled. The production increase actually observed is the returns to *some* factors—and this is almost always less than full proportionality.

Increasing returns to scale.[4]   A production function exhibits *increasing returns to scale* if for every $t > 1$ and $\mathbf{z}$, $f(t\mathbf{z}) > tf(\mathbf{z})$.

Increasing returns to scale means that a scaling up of inputs leads to a greater than proportionate increase in production. It is exemplified by the phrase "two heads are better than one." In an industrial setting, it arises when a larger operation is not merely a pure expansion of the original process, but involves new, more efficient processes. Manufacturing facilities often have this characteristic. As production increases, from a few units a month to many thousands, larger machines are used and tasks are organized differently, leading to more efficient production. Increasing returns to scale also occurs when learning influences productivity. For example, if you require 20 hours to prepare one tax return, you probably can prepare two in less than 40 hours. Finally, increasing returns to scale is also observed in networks, where interactions between components is the primary measure of production. Examples include telephone and mail service.

The concept of returns to scale can be generalized to arbitrary production possibility sets. A producton possibility set $\mathcal{Y}$ is said to exhibit *nonincreasing returns to scale* if $\mathbf{y} \in \mathcal{Y}$ implies $t\mathbf{y} \in \mathcal{Y}$ for all t with $0 \leq t \leq 1$. This means that any feasible netput vector can be scaled down. Likewise $\mathcal{Y}$ exhibits *nondecreasing returns to scale* if $\mathbf{y} \in \mathcal{Y}$ implies $t\mathbf{y} \in \mathcal{Y}$ for all t with $t \geq 1$. Finally $\mathcal{Y}$ exhibits *constant returns to scale* if it satisfies both the above conditions.

Elasticities

Consider an arbitrary function y of a single variable x. If this function is differentiable, the value $y'(x) \equiv dy(x)/dx$ is a measure of how fast y changes with respect to changes in x. This measure, however, depends on the units used to define both x and y. So, for example, if y represents apples and x represents money, a different numerical value of the derivative would be obtained in the two cases: (*a*) y is measured in bushels and x in dollars, and (*b*) y is measured in tons and x in pesos. To simplify communication, it is convenient to measure the slope of functions in a way that does not depend on the units selected. This can be done by using percentages; that is, by giving the percentage (or fractional) change in one variable due to a

---

[4]Again, this is sometimes called *strictly* increasing returns to scale.

one percent change in the other. Since the percentage change of a variable is independent of the units used for that variable, the resulting description is unit free. The resulting measure of the slope is termed an *elasticity*. The elasticity of y with respect to x is defined by

$$e \equiv \frac{dy}{y} \bigg/ \frac{dx}{x} = \frac{dy}{dx} \cdot \frac{x}{y} = \frac{d \ln y}{d \ln x}. \tag{2.1}$$

We may apply this idea to the concepts we have used in the discussion of production. For example, associated with the production process defined by $q = f(\mathbf{z})$, the *elasticity of scale* at point $\mathbf{z}$ is defined as

$$e(\mathbf{z}) = \frac{df(t\mathbf{z})}{dt} \cdot \frac{t}{f} \bigg|_{t=1} = \sum_{i=1}^{n} z_i \frac{1}{f} \frac{\partial f}{\partial z_i}.$$

Elasticity of scale greater than, less than, or equal to one corresponds to locally increasing, decreasing, or constant returns to scale.

Other elasticity quantities are discussed in the exercises and in other chapters.

2.6 Linear Programming and Production Technologies

Smooth production functions, such as the Cobb-Douglas function, with broadly defined aggregate commodities, such as capital and labor, are frequently proposed for the study of production issues. But while useful for broad characterization, such functions do not always adequately reflect the structure of the underlying production processes. A real firm's technology frequently consists of a number of alternative processes, leading to kinked production functions, each kink corresponding to a switch from one process to another. These technologies are best studied with a more structural representation of the underlying processes.

A Single Production Process

Let us consider again the special production process known as a Leontief process, or fixed-proportions process. In this process, a single commodity is produced by combining inputs in given fixed proportions. Production of one unit of output requires an m-dimensional input vector equal to $\mathbf{a} = (a_1, a_2, \ldots, a_m)$. Given an arbitrary bundle of inputs $\mathbf{z} = (z_1, z_2, \ldots, z_m)$, the maximum amount of output that can be produced corresponds to the maximum multiple of the vector $\mathbf{a}$ that is contained in the vector $\mathbf{z}$. Specifically,

$$q = \min\left\{ \frac{z_1}{a_1}, \frac{z_2}{a_2}, \ldots, \frac{z_m}{a_m} \right\}, \tag{2.2}$$

which is the Leontief production function.

There is an alternative way to express (2.2) that is less compact but generalizes to multiple processes; namely,

$$q = \max\ x$$
$$\text{sub to } a_1 x \le z_1$$
$$a_2 x \le z_2$$
$$\vdots$$
$$a_m x \le z_m.$$

This form shows explicitly that the output level q is equal to the maximal multiple x of the **a** vector contained in the given vector of inputs **z**.

Multiple Processes

The representation above can be extended to the case where several production processes are available, each of the type discussed above but with different coefficients.

Example 2.7 (Carpet manufacturing).   Consider a carpet factory that has two processes for converting yarn into carpet. The carpets produced by the two processes are indistinguishable. One process uses hand looms, and the other uses an automated loom. Both processes use the same amount of yarn to produce a carpet, but they use different amounts of labor and electric power, as shown in Table 2.1.

   Let x_1 and x_2 be the levels at which the two processes are operated, and let z_1, z_2, and z_3 denote the levels of the three inputs. Then the maximum possible output for given input levels is

$$q = \max\ x_1 + x_2$$
$$\text{sub to } 5x_1 + 3x_2 \le z_1$$
$$x_1 + 2x_2 \le z_2$$
$$x_1 + x_2 \ \le z_3$$
$$x_1 \ge 0, \quad x_2 \ge 0.$$

The constraints correspond to the fact that the total use of each input cannot exceed what is given. The total output is the sum of the levels at which the two processes are operated.

TABLE 2.1   Inputs for carpet production.

	Hand loom	Automated loom
Labor	5	3
Power	1	2
Yarn	1	1

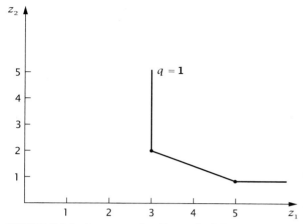

FIGURE 2.14 Isoquant for Example 2.7.

The production function is again, as in the single process case, expressed as a maximization problem (a linear program). An isoquant for this process (corresponding to $q = 1$) is shown in the space of the first two inputs in Fig. 2.14. (It is not necessary to show z_3 since the amount used is always equal to q.) The two dots represent the two pure processes. We can then obtain the line between them or, by throwing away inputs, any point above these.

If there are n separate processes, this type of technology can be defined by an $m \times n$ matrix $\mathbf{A}$. Each column of $\mathbf{A}$ corresponds to one of the processes; the jth column, $\mathbf{a}_j = (a_{1j}, a_{2j}, \ldots, a_{mj})$, indicates the fixed amounts of the m inputs necessary to produce one unit of output with the jth process. An efficient point is determined by optimally apportioning available inputs to the n individual processes. Specifically, the maximum output is given by the solution to the linear program

$$q = \max \ \mathbf{1} \cdot \mathbf{x}$$
$$\text{sub to } \mathbf{A}\mathbf{x} \le \mathbf{z}$$
$$\mathbf{x} \ge \mathbf{0},$$

where $\mathbf{1} = (1, 1, \ldots, 1)$.

An isoquant of such a process looks like that shown in Fig. 2.15, where the dots indicate the corner points of the individual processes. As shown in the figure, some processes may be inefficient relative to the others, and these would never be used. As more processes are incorporated, the composite isoquant looks smoother. A general constant returns-to-scale technology with smooth isoquants can therefore can be regarded as a collection of infinitely many fixed-proportions processes.

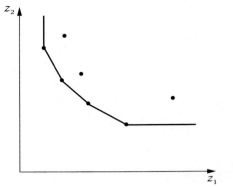

FIGURE 2.15   Isoquant for many processes.

2.7   Production over Time

In simple discussions of production, production is considered to take place within a single, well-defined time period. A set of inputs is employed in that period to yield a set of outputs in that same period, and then, perhaps, the process is repeated in the next period. In reality, of course, production cannot always be described this way. For example, consider the various production processes on a farm. Eggs might be produced daily but wheat only every six months, showing that different products have different natural periods. Capital improvements on the farm enhance production for several years, showing that one input can influence many production periods. And crop rotation procedures show that production procedures in one year influence production possibilities in other years. Clearly one must have a more general view of the role of time in production.

The concept of production possibility sets is rich enough to include the situations described above, but for it to do so, the notion of commodities must be somewhat expanded. The key idea is that of *dated commodities.* We pretend that a date label is attached to every commodity, and commodities with different date labels are considered different even if they otherwise look identical. Thus wheat produced this year is considered different from wheat produced last year, and the associated input commodities, such as seed, labor, or even tractors, must also be dated. The dated commodities make up the components of (an expanded) netput vector. The corresponding production possibility set consists of all such netput vectors that are feasible.

Example 2.8 (Oil well).   Let us consider the pumping of oil from a well as a production process. Suppose the well reservoir holds an initial quantity r_1 of oil, which is extracted over a period of N years. The amount of oil pumped in any year cannot exceed some known function $f(r, z)$, which depends on input effort, z, and the amount of oil remaining, r. We may assume that

$f(r, 0) = 0$. Specifically, if z_k is the input effort expended in year k, then q_k, the amount of oil extracted in year k, must satisfy

$$q_k \leq f(r_k, z_k), \qquad k = 1, 2, \ldots, N$$
$$q_k \geq 0,$$

where r_k is the quantity remaining at the beginning of period k; that is, $r_k = r_1 - \sum_{i=1}^{k-1} q_i$. It would be impossible to treat this process using isolated periods, because production in one period affects the reserves available for later periods. However, the process can be treated as a unit, spanning all N time periods. The corresponding production possibility set $\mathcal{Y}$ is the set of netput vectors $(-z_1, -z_2, \ldots, -z_N, q_1, q_2, \ldots, q_N)$ satisfying the above inequalities.

Part II
COST

2.8   The Cost Function

The first part of this chapter presented a general framework for describing the technology of a firm based on a set of feasible netput vectors. It was argued that firms will usually choose efficient points, but beyond that no specific criterion was proposed for selecting a particular netput vector. This choice will be governed largely by economic considerations, which this section begins to address.

We assume that input combinations are chosen on the basis of *cost minimization*. That is, if an output level **q** has been selected, we assume that the firm will select inputs to produce this **q** at minimum cost. This assumption concerns only the choice of input **z** for a given output **q**. The choice of **q** is based on other considerations.

It should be fairly clear that if a firm operates to maximize profit, it will, after selecting an output level, select inputs to minimize cost. (This is the case if profit is sales revenue minus cost, and revenue depends only on output.) The assumption of cost minimization is therefore consistent with that of profit maximization, but somewhat weaker. For example, not-for-profit enterprises usually also wish to minimize costs. The difference between such an enterprise and a profit-maximizing firm is in how the choice of output is made. Cost minimization is concerned only with the choice of input.

Production cost depends directly on the cost of input factors. If there are fixed (nonnegative) prices $w_1, w_2, \ldots, w_m$ for the m input factors, the cost for input levels $z_1, z_2, \ldots, z_m$ is $w_1 z_1 + w_2 z_2 + \cdots + w_m z_m$. We can also consider the case where prices depend on the amount purchased, but for the present we assume that cost is a linear function of input factor levels, with coefficients equal to factor prices. This assumption leads us to the following definition:

Cost function.   The *cost function* of a firm is the function

$$c(\mathbf{w}, \mathbf{q}) = \min \ \mathbf{w} \cdot \mathbf{z}$$
$$\text{sub to} \ \mathbf{z} \in V(\mathbf{q})$$

defined for $\mathbf{w} \geq \mathbf{0}, \mathbf{q} \geq \mathbf{0}$.

This function is defined only for $\mathbf{q}$'s such that $V(\mathbf{q})$, the input requirements set, is nonempty. Further, we generally assume that the minimum in this definition is well defined.

Example 2.9.   Consider a technology described by the Cobb-Douglas production function

$$q = K^{1/2} L^{1/2}.$$

Here K is capital and L is labor. The cost function is

$$c(w_1, w_2, q) = \min_{K,L} \ w_1 K + w_2 L$$
$$\text{sub to} \ q = K^{1/2} L^{1/2},$$

where w_1 and w_2 are the input prices.

We can evaluate $c(w_1, w_2, q)$ in two steps. First, we substitute for L from the production function. This gives

$$c = w_1 K + \frac{w_2 q^2}{K}.$$

Second, we minimize this with respect to K. This gives

$$K = q \sqrt{\frac{w_2}{w_1}}$$

and

$$c(w_1, w_2, q) = 2q \sqrt{w_1 w_2}.$$

2.9   Short-Run Costs

Production processes normally do not last for just one period. Rather, as discussed earlier, cycles of production are repeated: new materials and labor are purchased each period, but equipment and land, for example, are used repeatedly. A complete evaluation of cost in such situations would require use of the expanded production possibility set based on dated commodities. But for many purposes a simpler procedure is adequate.

In the simplified approach, inputs are broadly classified into two groups: those that are variable in the short run, within a single production cycle (such as material and some labor costs), and those that are variable only in the long run (such as capital equipment and executive salaries). The costs associated with input variables in the short run are termed *variable costs*. The costs associated with input variables that are variable only in the long run, and hence are fixed in the short run, are referred to as *fixed costs*, or sometimes as *sunk costs* because they have already been paid or committed. Fixed costs should not influence decisions regarding short-term operations. Of course, this classification of costs into two groups is only a simplification. There is often no definitive partitioning of time into short- and long-run periods, and costs normally considered fixed can sometimes be reduced even in the short run if extreme measures are taken. Nevertheless, the distinction of short and long run helps clarify thinking and form a basis for analysis.

For a firm with a single output q, we may plot the short-run cost as a function of q, assuming that input prices are constant. The resulting short-run cost curve typically looks similar to that shown in Fig. 2.16c. The short-run total cost is divided into short-run *variable* cost and short-run *fixed* cost as shown in Fig. 2.16a and b. The fixed cost is the cost at $q = 0$ and corresponds to the cost of inputs, such as capital, that cannot be varied in the short run.

As indicated in the figure, short-run variable costs are typically concave (bending downward) for low values of output corresponding to increasing returns to a factor; then there may be a region of linear, constant returns-to-scale; and eventually there is a convex (bending upward) region corresponding to decreasing returns to a factor. As output is increased from very low values, efficiency improves, but eventually decreasing returns set in because short-run variable inputs cannot efficiently substitute for the long-run variable inputs such as capital.

Example 2.10 (Capital and labor).   Consider again Example 2.9, where the technology was described by the production function $q = K^{1/2}L^{1/2}$. In the

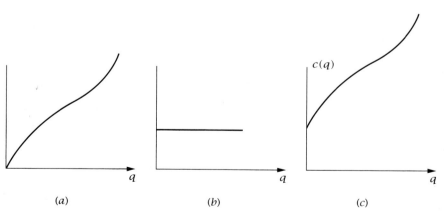

(a)   (b)   (c)

FIGURE 2.16   Short-run costs: (a) short-run variable costs; (b) fixed cost; (c) total cost.

first step of that example, we calculated the cost when K was held fixed and L was chosen to meet the output specified. This cost is

$$c = w_1 K + \frac{w_2 q^2}{K}.$$

This is the short-run cost. As a function of q, it is a quadratic function.

Example 2.11 (Standard cost model).   Suppose a young entrepreneur sets up a cold-drink stand near a stadium. He has fixed costs F due to the cost of the stand, rental of equipment, and his own time. He has variable costs equal to the cost of the drinks and cups, which is proportional to the number of drinks sold, say Vq. The short-run cost is therefore $c(q) = F + Vq$. This is a standard model used for many simple analyses.

2.10   Average and Marginal Costs

Firms are very interested in the *average* costs of production—averaged over the quantity of output units. This gives a measure of what each unit costs, and hence the selling price minus this average cost is the profit per unit sold. Firms often strive to minimize their average cost.

There are three types of average cost: average variable cost, AVC, average fixed cost, AFC, and average total cost, ATC, which is frequently termed just *average cost,* AC.

First consider average fixed cost, AFC. It is simply FC/q where FC is the (constant) fixed cost. This function, shown in Fig. 2.17a, is a monotonically decreasing hyperbola reflecting the fact that as output increases the fixed cost decreases relative to the size of production.

Next consider average variable cost, AVC. Typically, in the short run it has the shape shown in Fig. 2.17b, which is referred to as U-shaped. The curve initially decreases, corresponding to the fact that variable costs usually exhibit increasing returns, and ultimately it increases, reflecting the fact that variable cost exhibits decreasing returns for large values of output.

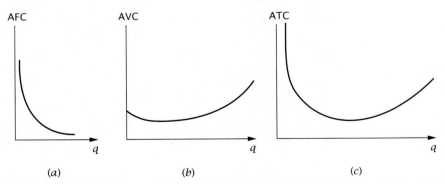

FIGURE 2.17   Average costs: (a) average fixed cost; (b) average variable cost; (c) average total cost.

Finally consider the average total cost, ATC, which is the total cost divided by the output level, q, or equivalently, the sum of the AFC and AVC curves. Typically, this curve will also be U-shaped. In this case, however, the U shape does not depend on an initial region of increasing returns. Instead the initial bend of the U is due to the sharp fall in AFC.

The minimum point of the ATC curve occurs at a larger output level than the minimum point of the AVC curve, if this latter curve has a minimum point. This can be shown by the following simple analysis. The minimum point is found by setting the derivative equal to zero. We have

$$\frac{d}{dq}\text{ATC}(q) = \frac{d}{dq}\text{AVC}(q) + \frac{d}{dq}\text{AFC}(q).$$

The last term is always negative. Hence at a point where the left side vanishes, the first term on the right must be positive. This means that AVC is already beyond its minimum point.

Marginal cost (MC) is the slope of the total cost curve. It can be interpreted as the cost of producing one more unit of output beyond the current level (provided, of course, that one unit is small compared to the total output). It is therefore the added cost due to the marginal extra unit. Marginal fixed cost is always zero, and therefore marginal total cost is always equal to marginal variable cost. Hence, the term *marginal cost* without the adjective *total* or *variable* is unambiguous.

The marginal cost curve will also typically be U-shaped, reflecting the increasing returns at low output levels and decreasing returns at high levels of output. The minimum point of the marginal cost curve, however, will be to the left of the minimum point of the AVC curve. In fact, the MC curve must pass through the minimum points of both the AVC and ATC curves, as shown in Fig. 2.18. This can be derived analytically, but it can also be seen by inspection of the total cost curve, as shown in Fig. 2.19. The ATC is the slope of the line drawn from the origin to the total cost curve. The minimum ATC point therefore corresponds to a point where the slope of this line is minimized; and it is clear that this must be a point where the

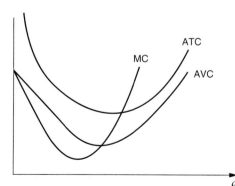

FIGURE   2.18   Relation   between   cost curves.

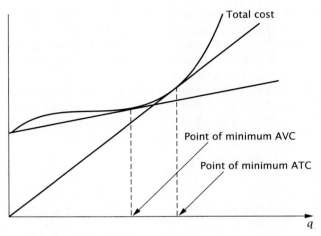

FIGURE 2.19   Total cost curve.

line is in fact tangent to the total cost curve. At this point ATC will equal MC because both are equal to the slope of the tangent line.

The average variable cost is, in a similar way, the slope of the line from the initial point on the cost axis to the point on the total cost curve. Again, minimum AVC corresponds to the minimum slope of such a line and must correspond to a point of tangency. The value of the slope at that point is again both the MC and the AVC. It is also easy to see from this diagram that $AVC(0) = MC(0)$.

2.11   Long-Run Costs

Over the long run a firm can usually change the levels of all of its inputs. Additional land can be purchased, new plants can be built, and more managers and workers can be hired. Or, conversely, these resources can be laid off or sold. The production possibility set of the firm can therefore be regarded as being larger in the long run than in the short run. Correspondingly, for a fixed level of output, long-run cost may be less than short-run cost since there is more flexibility.

There is a simple way to derive a long-run cost curve. One begins by constructing short-run total cost curves for various values of the inputs that are fixed in the short run. For example, a short-run total cost curve could be constructed for each of several assumed plant capacities. The resulting family of short-run cost curves might look something like that shown in Fig. 2.20a. Once the firm has decided on an output level q, it will select the particular plant capacity that yields the least total cost at q. In general, there will be a continuum of short-run cost curves corresponding to all the possible values of long-run variables. The overall long-run total cost curve is the lower envelope of these curves.

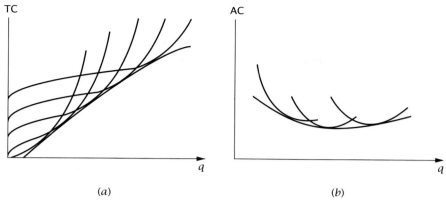

TC

AC

q

q

(a)

(b)

FIGURE 2.20   Long-run cost as envelope of short-run costs: (a) total costs; (b) average costs.

The construction of long-run costs can be carried out in terms of average costs as well as total costs. As illustrated in Fig. 2.20b, the overall long-run average cost curve is the lower envelope of the individual short-run average cost curves corresponding to various values of the long-run input variables.

By definition, the long-run total cost curve must always be no higher than any particular short-run total cost curve. Also, typically, the long-run average cost curve initially decreases with output level q, it is then fairly flat, reflecting the nearly constant returns to scale that are expected when all input factors can be varied, and it finally increases, reflecting decreasing returns to scale, which is often attributed to inefficiencies in managing a large organization.

Example 2.12 (Machines).   Suppose a firm can, in the long run, adjust the number of machines it uses to produce its product. When it uses y machines, it has the quadratic short-run cost curve (see Exercise 10)

$$c(y,q) = ya + bq + \frac{d}{2y}q^2,$$

with $a > 0$, $b > 0$, and $d > 0$. Let us assume that y can take on continuous values. Then the long-run cost, with y chosen optimally for a fixed q, is

$$c(q) = \min_{y}\left\{ya + bq + \frac{d}{2y}q^2\right\}.$$

One can easily find

$$y(q) = q\sqrt{\frac{d}{2a}},$$

$$c(q) = q\left\{\sqrt{2ad} + b\right\}.$$

Hence the long-run cost is linear in q, corresponding to constant returns to scale.

2.12   Multiperiod Costs

We usually think of costs as associated with a given period, correspond-ing to production in that period. A sequence of production cycles is then thought to generate a sequence of costs. However, in the general theory, production that takes place over several periods actually corresponds to a single point in a production possibility set involving dated commodities. Correspondingly, there should be just a single cost value associated with such production. It is essential, therefore, that we know how to transfer cost definitions back and forth between the period-by-period and aggregate viewpoints.

Suppose there is a stream of expenditures $c_1, c_2, \ldots, c_n$ occurring over n periods. How does a firm assign a single value to this stream? The answer is found by looking beyond the production technology to the *financial market*, where the firm borrows and lends money. Through borrowing and lending, expenditures or receipts in any period can be reflected back (or *discounted*) to equivalent expenditures or receipts in the first period. This provides a common standard for cost comparison. To evaluate the stream of expen-ditures, we determine how much money must be on hand in period 1 to cover these expenditures over the n periods. This money could be placed in an interest-bearing account, and withdrawals made each period to pay the then current expenditure. If the interest rate is fixed at i per period, one deposited dollar would become $(1 + i)$ dollar after one period, $(1 + i)^2$ af-ter two periods, and so forth. Said another way, in order to have one dollar available at the second period, it is only necessary to have $(1 + i)^{-1}$ dollar at the first period, to have one unit at the third period it is only necessary to have $(1 + i)^{-2}$ unit at the first period, and so forth. Hence, the total amount necessary in the first period to pay the expenditure stream is

$$C = c_1 + \frac{c_2}{1 + i} + \frac{c_3}{(1 + i)^2} + \cdots + \frac{c_n}{(1 + i)^{n-1}}.$$

This value C is called the *present value* of the expenditure stream. The present value of a cost stream can be used as a consistent method for as-signing a single value to a multiperiod production process.

2.13   Cost Functions and Input Prices

In the previous few sections we examined how cost functions vary with out-put $\mathbf{q}$. However, a general cost function $c(\mathbf{w}, \mathbf{q})$ depends on the input prices $\mathbf{w}$ as well. Therefore in this section we emphasize the $\mathbf{w}$ dependency and calculate an explicit expression for the cost function corresponding to some important technologies.

Example 2.13 (Cobb-Douglas).   A general Cobb-Douglas production function with m input factors has the form

$$q = \prod_{i=1}^{m} z_i^{\alpha_i},$$

with $\alpha_i > 0$, $i = 1, 2, \ldots, m$.

The associated cost function is

$$c(\mathbf{w}, q) = \min \sum_{i=1}^{m} w_i z_i$$

$$\text{sub to } q = \prod_{i=1}^{m} z_i^{\alpha_i}.$$

The first-order necessary conditions can be found by using a Lagrange multiplier λ for the constraint. This yields

$$w_i - \lambda \alpha_i z_i^{\alpha_i - 1} \prod_{j \neq i} z_j^{\alpha_j} = 0$$

for $i = 1, 2, \ldots, m$. Or more compactly,

$$w_i - \frac{\lambda q \alpha_i}{z_i} = 0$$

for $i = 1, 2, \ldots, m$. Dividing the ith such equation by the jth, we obtain

$$\frac{w_i}{w_j} = \frac{\alpha_i z_j}{\alpha_j z_i}$$

for all i, j. This equation means that

$$\frac{w_i z_i}{\alpha_i} = \frac{w_j z_j}{\alpha_j} = b$$

where b is a constant. Hence

$$z_i = \frac{b \alpha_i}{w_i}.$$

From the constraint we may then find

$$b = q^{1/\alpha} \prod_{i=1}^{m} \left(\frac{w_i}{\alpha_i} \right)^{\alpha_i / \alpha},$$

where $\alpha = \sum_{i=1}^{m} \alpha_i$. This leads to

$$c(\mathbf{w}, q) = \sum_{i=1}^{m} w_i z_i = \alpha q^{1/\alpha} \prod_{i=1}^{m} \left(\frac{w_i}{\alpha_i} \right)^{\alpha_i / \alpha}.$$

Example 2.14 (Leontief, or single-activity, technology).   Consider the Leontief technology

$$q = \min \left\{ \frac{z_1}{a_1}, \frac{z_2}{a_2}, \ldots, \frac{z_m}{a_m} \right\}.$$

It is easy to determine the associated cost function. We have in general

$$c(\mathbf{w}, q) = \min \; \mathbf{w} \cdot \mathbf{z}$$
$$\text{sub to } \mathbf{z} \in V(q).$$

In this case it is clear that for any nonnegative input factor prices $\mathbf{w}$, the least expensive way to produce output level q is to use the inputs in *exactly* the fixed proportions dictated by the vector $\mathbf{a} = (a_1, a_2, \ldots, a_m)$, since additional amounts of just some inputs will add to the cost but not contribute additional production. Thus the cost for a unit of output is $\mathbf{w} \cdot \mathbf{a}$; and since this is a constant-returns-to-scale technology, the cost of output level q is

$$c(\mathbf{w}, q) = q \, \mathbf{w} \cdot \mathbf{a}.$$

Example 2.15 (CES technology). The *constant elasticity of substitution* (CES) production function for two inputs and with constant returns to scale has the form

$$q = (az_1^\rho + bz_2^\rho)^{1/\rho},$$

where $a > 0$ and $b > 0$. It can be shown that this form contains several important cases of production functions as special cases.

(1) $\rho = 1$ corresponds to a *linear production function, $q = az_1 + bz_2$.*

(2) $\rho \to 0$ corresponds to the Cobb-Douglas production function, $q = z_1^\alpha z_2^{1-\alpha}$ where $\alpha = a/(a + b)$.

(3) $\rho \to -\infty$ corresponds to the Leontief production function $q = \min \; (z_1, z_2)$.

The cost function is

$$c(\mathbf{w}, q) = \min \; w_1 z_1 + w_2 z_2$$
$$\text{sub to } az_1^\rho + bz_2^\rho = q^\rho.$$

The first-order necessary conditions can be found as in the Cobb-Douglas case to be

$$\frac{w_1}{w_2} = \frac{az_1^{\rho-1}}{bz_2^{\rho-1}}.$$

Then after a fair bit of algebra, it is found that

$$c(\mathbf{w}, q) = \left[\left(\frac{w_1}{a} \right)^r + \left(\frac{w_2}{b} \right)^r \right]^{1/r} q$$

where $r = \rho/(\rho - 1)$ for $\rho \neq 1$.

Example 2.16 (Multiprocess cost functions). Consider the production function corresponding to the multiple constant-proportions processes of Section 2.6:

$$q = \max \ \mathbf{1} \cdot \mathbf{x}$$
$$\text{sub to } \mathbf{A}\mathbf{x} \le \mathbf{z}$$
$$\mathbf{x} \ge \mathbf{0}.$$

The production function is defined by a linear program. It follows immediately from the definition of a cost function that in this case $c(\mathbf{w}, q)$ is also defined by a linear program. Specifically,

$$c(\mathbf{w}, q) = \min_{\mathbf{x}, \mathbf{z}} \ \mathbf{w} \cdot \mathbf{z}$$
$$\text{sub to } \mathbf{A}\mathbf{x} \le \mathbf{z}$$
$$\mathbf{1} \cdot \mathbf{x} = q$$
$$\mathbf{x} \ge \mathbf{0}.$$

This linear program can be interpreted geometrically as in Fig. 2.21. Given a price vector, one finds the point in the input requirement set $V(q)$ corresponding to minimum cost. As is clear in the figure, this solution will occur at one of the extreme points (that is, one of the corners) of the set. This means that one particular process is most economical (although sometimes there are ties).

This example illustrates that both production functions and cost functions may not have simple analytic representations. Rather, in general, both are defined as solutions of optimization problems.

General Properties of Cost Functions

Cost functions inherit certain structural properties from the basic definition. These fundamental properties are summarized by the propositon below. In this proposition it is understood, as always, that $\mathbf{w} \ge \mathbf{0}$ and $\mathbf{z} \ge \mathbf{0}$ if $\mathbf{z} \in V(\mathbf{q})$.

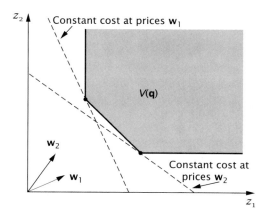

FIGURE 2.21 Cost function for two fixed-proportions processes.

Proposition 2.2.   *A cost function is*

(a) *Homogeneous of degree 1 in w:* $c(\alpha w, q) = \alpha c(w, q)$, *for* $\alpha > 0$.

(b) *Nondecreasing in w: if* $w' \geq w$, *then* $c(w', q) \geq c(w, q)$.

(c) *Concave in w:* $c(\alpha w_1 + (1 - \alpha)w_2, q) \geq \alpha c(w_1, q) + (1 - \alpha)c(w_2, q)$ *for*
$0 \leq \alpha \leq 1$.

Proof

(a) By definition $c(\alpha w, q) = \min \; \alpha w \cdot z$, subject to $z \in V(q)$. Clearly the α can be taken outside the minimum if it is positive.

(b) Suppose $w' \geq w$, and let $z' \geq 0$ be the minimum point corresponding to w'. Then $c(w, q) \leq w \cdot z' \leq w' \cdot z' = c(w', q)$.

(c) We have

$$
\begin{aligned}
c(\alpha w_1 + (1 - \alpha) w_2, q) &= \min_{z \in V(q)} (\alpha w_1 + (1 - \alpha)w_2) \cdot z \\
&\geq \min_{z \in V(q)} \alpha w_1 \cdot z + \min_{z \in V(q)} (1 - \alpha)w_2 \cdot z \\
&= \alpha c(w_1, q) + (1 - \alpha)c(w_2, q). \quad \blacksquare
\end{aligned}
$$

The first two of these properties is quite intuitive. Since cost is proportional to prices, it is clear that multiplying prices by a constant also multiplies the cost by the same constant. Also it is quite clear that cost increases if prices increase. The concavity of the cost function is less apparent, but it follows directly from the fact that the cost function is defined by a minimization process.

2.14   Conditional Factor Demand

Consider the cost function

$$
c(w, q) = \min \; w \cdot z
$$

$$
\text{sub to } z \in V(q).
$$

The *conditional factor demand* $z(w, q)$ is the value of z that achieves the minimum. It is the vector of inputs that the firm will demand at prices w, conditional on the outputs being q.

This demand may not always be unique. Two examples are shown in Fig. 2.22 (a) and (b). In the first example, the input requirement set $V(q)$ is smooth and strictly convex, so the conditional factor demand (the solution point) varies continuously as the price vector w is changed. The second case represents two fixed-proportions processes. In this case the factor demand jumps discontinuously from one corner point to another as the price vector w changes, and for a certain w the demand is not unique. Discontinuities in

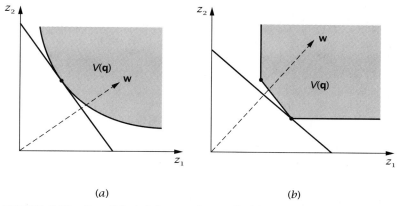

(a)   (b)

FIGURE 2.22 Conditional factor demand: (a) smooth input require-ment set; (b) nonsmooth input requirement set.

conditional factor demand can also arise if the set $V(\mathbf{q})$ is smooth but not convex.

In the examples of the previous section, in fact, we first found the conditional factor demand in order to evaluate the cost function. It is possible to go in the other direction, using the structure of $c(\mathbf{w}, \mathbf{q})$ as a function of $\mathbf{w}$, to determine $\mathbf{z}(\mathbf{w}, \mathbf{q})$. In the case where $c(\mathbf{w}, \mathbf{q})$ is differentiable, the conditional factor demand is given by a simple formula.

Shephard's lemma. *Let the cost function $c(\mathbf{w}, \mathbf{q})$ be differentiable with respect to $\mathbf{w}$ at a point $(\mathbf{w}, \mathbf{q})$, $\mathbf{w} > 0$. Then the conditional factor demand at this point is*

$$z_i(\mathbf{w}, \mathbf{q}) = \frac{\partial c(\mathbf{w}, \mathbf{q})}{\partial w_i}, \qquad i = 1, 2, \ldots, m.$$

Proof: Let $\mathbf{z}^*$ be an input vector that minimizes the cost function at $(\mathbf{w}^*, \mathbf{q}^*)$. Let

$$g(\mathbf{w}, \mathbf{q}^*) = c(\mathbf{w}, \mathbf{q}^*) - \mathbf{w} \cdot \mathbf{z}^* .$$

Then by definition of $c(\mathbf{w}, \mathbf{q}^*)$ as the minimum cost required to produce $\mathbf{q}^*$, we have $g(\mathbf{w}, \mathbf{q}^*) \leq 0$ for all $\mathbf{w}$. However, $g(\mathbf{w}^*, \mathbf{q}^*) = 0$ and thus g is maximized at $\mathbf{w}^*$. This implies that

$$0 = \frac{\partial g(\mathbf{w}^*, \mathbf{q}^*)}{\partial w_i} = \frac{\partial c(\mathbf{w}^*, \mathbf{q}^*)}{\partial w_i} - z_i^*,$$

completing the proof. ∎

The economic interpretation of this lemma is worth considering. Suppose that there were only a single input, and it was used at level z^*. The total cost would be wz^*. As w varied, the total cost would vary proportionately at the rate z^*. A similar interpretation holds for several inputs. If the price of the ith input were increased, the total cost would increase, at least to first order, in proportion to the amount z_i used. The fact that the input levels themselves would also change is a second-order effect, since these inputs are already optimized.

Example 2.17 (Cobb-Douglas, decreasing returns to scale). Consider the Cobb-Douglas production function

$$q = z_1^\alpha z_2^\beta$$

where $\alpha + \beta < 1$ (implying that there are decreasing returns to scale). The corresponding cost function is

$$c(\mathbf{w}, q) = (\alpha + \beta)\left(\frac{\alpha}{w_1}\right)^{-\alpha/(\alpha+\beta)}\left(\frac{\beta}{w_2}\right)^{-\beta/(\alpha+\beta)} q^{1/(\alpha+\beta)}.$$

The conditional factor demands can be found from Shephard's lemma to be

$$z_1 = \left(\frac{\alpha}{w_1}\right)^{\beta/(\alpha+\beta)}\left(\frac{\beta}{w_2}\right)^{-\beta/(\alpha+\beta)} q^{1/(\alpha+\beta)},$$

$$z_2 = \left(\frac{\alpha}{w_1}\right)^{-\alpha/(\alpha+\beta)}\left(\frac{\beta}{w_2}\right)^{\alpha/(\alpha+\beta)} q^{1/(\alpha+\beta)}.$$

Since factor demands depend on prices, it is possible to investigate the effect of small changes in factor prices. Such effects can be characterized by the derivitives $\partial z_i/\partial w_i$. The study of such derivatives is termed *comparative statics*. The reader may wish to consult Appendix D (especially the section on duality), which shows how to carry out the analysis in this case.

2.15   Exercises

1. A craftsman spends the first part of every day sharpening his tools and the second part working with these tools. His total output is $q = z_1^{1/4} z_2^{3/4}$ where z_1 and z_2 denote the number of hours devoted to sharpening and use, respectively. What is the efficient way for him to divide his time between these two activities? Hint: $z_1 + z_2$ is fixed.

*2. Let $\mathbf{y} = (-\mathbf{z}, \mathbf{q}) \in \mathcal{Y}$. Show that

   (a) $\mathcal{Y}$ convex $\Rightarrow V(\mathbf{q})$ convex;

   (b) $\mathcal{Y}$ closed $\Rightarrow V(\mathbf{q})$ closed.

3. (Combining two processes) Suppose a single-output firm has two identical production facilities, each of which can be described by the production function $q = f(z)$, which satisfies decreasing returns to scale. Show that the aggregate production function of the firm is $q = 2f(z/2)$.

4. Suppose a firm's output is governed by the production function $q = f(\mathbf{z})$. In the netput space of $(-\mathbf{z}, q)$'s, select $\mathbf{g} = (\mathbf{0}, 1)$ with the 1 being the component corresponding to output. Show that the shortage function is $\sigma(-\mathbf{z}, q) = q - f(\mathbf{z})$.

5. Let $\mathcal{Y} \subset R^m$ and $\mathbf{g} \in R^m_+$, $\mathbf{g} \neq \mathbf{0}$. Show that the shortage function satisfies

   (a) $\sigma(\mathbf{y} + \alpha\mathbf{g}) = \sigma(\mathbf{y}) + \alpha$ for all α.

   (b) If $\mathcal{Y}$ is a convex set, then $\sigma(\mathbf{y})$ is a concave function with respect to $\mathbf{y}$. (Draw a picture.)

   (c) Suppose $\mathcal{Y}$ is closed and convex and $\mathbf{0} \in \mathcal{Y}$. Assuming $\mathbf{g} \geq \mathbf{0}$, and $\mathbf{g} \neq \mathbf{0}$, show that if $\sigma(\mathbf{y}) = -\infty$ for some $\mathbf{y}$, then $\mathbf{g} \in \mathcal{Y}$. Hence if $\mathcal{Y}$ satisfies no free production, $\sigma(\mathbf{y}) > -\infty$ for all $\mathbf{y}$.

6. Suppose a firm produces a single output according to $q = f(z_1, z_2, \ldots, z_n)$. The elasticity of return to the jth input is

$$\mu_j = \frac{z_j}{f(\mathbf{z})} \frac{\partial f(\mathbf{z})}{\partial z_j}.$$

Show that $\sum_{j=1}^n \mu_j =$ elasticity of scale.

7. As stated in the chapter, a technology with production possibility set $\mathcal{Y}$ is said to have nonincreasing, constant, or nondecreasing returns to scale if $\mathbf{y} \in \mathcal{Y}$ implies $t\mathbf{y} \in \mathcal{Y}$ for all t with $0 < t < 1$, all t, or all $t > 1$, respectively. Suppose a technology has netput vectors $(-\mathbf{z}, \mathbf{q})$ corresponding to inputs and outputs.

   (a) If the technology has nonincreasing, constant, or nondecreasing returns to scale, show that $c(\mathbf{w}, t\mathbf{q}) \leq tc(\mathbf{w}, \mathbf{q})$, for t with $0 < t < 1$, all t, or all $t > 1$, respectively.

   (b) If q is one-dimensional and there are constant returns to scale, show that $c(\mathbf{w}, q) = qc(\mathbf{w}, 1)$.

   (c) If $\mathcal{Y}$ is convex and $\mathbf{0} \in \mathcal{Y}$, show that there are nonincreasing returns to scale.

8. A hen's egg production depends on her age. Typical production is roughly as follows: no eggs are produced during the first six months of life, 60 eggs per month are produced during the next two years, and then no eggs are produced after that. Assume that all hens die after N months. A henhouse can therefore be considered as a process that produces two kinds of dated commodities: eggs and hens. Let $h(k, i)$ denote the number of hens in month i that are k months old. Let $u(i)$ denote the number of new female chicks added to the henhouse in month i. Develop a description for the production possibility set.

9. (Profit maximization implies cost minimization) Assume that the prices for a firm's output are fixed at $\mathbf{p}$, so that the firm's revenue is $\mathbf{p} \cdot \mathbf{q}$ where $\mathbf{q}$ is its production level. Show that if the firm selects $\mathbf{q}$ and input vector $\mathbf{z}$ so as to maximize profit, its choice of $\mathbf{z}$ will minimize cost with respect to all other $\mathbf{z}$'s that can produce $\mathbf{q}$.

10. Suppose that for fixed input prices the total cost function for production using a single machine has the quadratic form

$$c(q) = a + bq + \tfrac{1}{2}dq^2,$$

with $b > 0$, $d > 0$. Find the cost function for a facility having n of these machines.

11. Suppose a firm can produce a product with either of two facilities, with the quadratic cost functions

$$c_1(q_1) = a_1 + b_1q_1 + \tfrac{1}{2}d_1q_1^2$$
$$c_2(q_2) = a_2 + b_2q_2 + \tfrac{1}{2}d_2q_2^2,$$

where $d_1 > 0$, $d_2 > 0$. Find the cost function of the combined facilities (which is also quadratic).

12. An executive course is being planned. A mailing of 30,000 brochures will cost $30,000. Payments to lecturers and other fixed operating expenses will amount to $15,000. The marginal cost per course member will be $500. The tuition for the course is $2,000 per person. Find the break-even number of attendees. If an insufficient number of people enroll, the course can be canceled, saving all but the original $30,000. What is the cutoff number of enrollments for cancellation?

13. (Artificial sweetener).[5] Aspartame (a sweetener) is produced continuously in large plants. The costs associated with a 10-million-lb/year plant operated at full capacity are shown in the table. Of these, operations, overhead, and administrative costs are considered fixed costs. Raw materials are variable in direct proportion to production. Utilities are intermediate in that the savings for reduced production level is only 60 percent of what it would be if it were strictly proportional. Hence utility costs themselves contain fixed and variable components. Find the total cost for production if the plant is operated at 100 percent, 75 percent, 50 percent, and 0 percent of capacity.

Aspartame—10 million lb/yr

Production Costs		377.09
Raw materials	268.17	
Utilities	39.22	
Operations	69.70	
Overhead		129.63
Plant overhead	40.71	
Taxes and insurance	14.82	
Depreciation (10 percent of capital)	74.10	
Administrative		172.99
Total cost (cents/lb)		679.71

[5] Source: SRI International PEP Yearbook 1987, Process Economics Program, SRI International, Menlo Park, California.

14. (Two production facilities) Suppose a firm produces a single product but has two production facilities with cost functions $c_1(\mathbf{w},q)$ and $c_2(\mathbf{w},q)$, respectively. Assuming that the best way to operate has $q_1 > 0, q_2 > 0$, show that the facilities should be operated so that the marginal costs are equal.

15. A production function f is *strictly homothetic* if $f(\mathbf{x}) = h(g(\mathbf{x}))$ where h is a strictly monotonically increasing function on $[0, \infty)$ and g is homogeneous of degree 1 (see Appendix A). Show that if a production function f is strictly homothetic, its cost function can be written in the form

$$c(\mathbf{w}, q) = k(q)c(\mathbf{w},1)$$

where k is a strictly monotonically increasing function on $[0, \infty)$.

16. A firm has several different fixed-proportions, constant-returns-to-scale production processes capable of producing its output. These processes are described in the table below. The firm can use one process or any combination of processes.

Process	Labor (hours)	Capital (machine hours)	Units of output
1	28	18	100
2	40	10	100
3	80	5	100
4	14	33	100
5	70	8	100
6	20	20	100
7	30	12	100
8	50	6	100

(a) Draw on graph paper the various input combinations that can be used to produce 100 units of output. That is, draw the input requirement set for a given output of 100 units.

(b) If the prices of capital and labor vary, what production processes will be used under which price combinations? What processes will never be used?

(c) Assume that the price of labor is $4.00 per hour and the price of capital is $12.00 per machine-hour. Plot as a function of output the following curves: total cost, average cost, and marginal cost. These are the long-run cost curves for this firm.

(d) Assume that the firm owns 40 units of capital equipment and that it can neither buy more of these specialized machines nor sell those that it owns. Draw the production function for capital held fixed and labor varying from 0 to 800 hours.

17. (Parallel arrangement) Suppose there are M distinct production operations, each of which is essential to the production of a common product. The operation of each unit is described by a production function

$$q_i = f_i(\mathbf{z}_i) \qquad i = 1, 2, \ldots, M$$

where q_i represents the level of final product that that unit can sustain and z_i is the corresponding input vector. The overall production function is then

$$q = \min\{f_1(z_1), f_2(z_2), \ldots, f_M(z_M)\}.$$

Find the overall cost function in terms of the cost functions of the individual units.

18. (Series operations) Suppose two production units are connected in a series. The first produces a single output using a constant-returns-to-scale technology. The second uses this output, together with additional inputs, to produce a final product. Find the overall cost function in terms of the cost functions of the individual units.

*19. (Cost allocation of joint products) Often a single input factor is used to produce several products. For example, through refinement and combination with various additives, crude oil simultaneously yields various grades of oil and gasoline. The cost of the common factor is typically allocated among the final products for accounting purposes. Ideally, this cost allocation method should allow the overall decision of input level to be decentralized to lower levels, with the aggregate of these individual decisions being optimal for the firm.

Suppose a firm produces n outputs $q_1, q_2, \ldots, q_n$ each using a different factor $z_1, z_2, \ldots, z_n$ and a single common factor x. We assume that the production functions $q_i = f_i(z_i, x)$, $i = 1, 2, \ldots, n$, can be inverted to have the form $x = g_i(q_i, z_i)$. Define $z = (z_1, z_2, \ldots, z_n)$. Let w be the vector of corresponding factor prices and let v be the price of the common factor. The cost function then can be written as

$$c(w, v, q) = \min_{z,x} w \cdot z + vx$$

$$\text{sub to } x = g_i(q_i, z_i), i = 1, 2, \ldots, n.$$

Let $\lambda_1, \lambda_2, \ldots, \lambda_n$ be the Lagrange multipliers of the cost minimization problem. We propose to assign a price λ_i for use of the common factor by the ith product.

(a) Show that this method completely allocates the cost of the common factor; that is, show that $v = \sum_{i=1}^{n} \lambda_i$.

(b) Based on this allocation method, construct a decentralized cost minimization problem associated with each output and show that these problems lead in aggregate to the correct overall solution.

(c) Suppose each output is produced according to a Leontief technology $f_i(z_i, x) = \min \{z_i, x\}$. Find the total cost function and determine how the cost of the common factor should be allocated.

*20. Suppose a firm produces output in each of two periods according to the Cobb-Douglas production function

$$q = L^{1/2}K^{1/2}$$

where L is labor and K is capital. The interest rate is zero, but the firm produces q_1 in the first period and q_2 in the second. The price of labor is

w in both periods, and the price of capital is 1. Capital is purchased only once and is used in both periods.

(a) How much capital is purchased, and how should its cost be allocated to the two periods? Hint: use Exercise 19.

(b) Repeat part (a) for the technology $q = \min\{L, K\}$.

21. A farm produces corn using the production function

$$q = \left(L^{1/2} + K^{1/2}\right)^{4/3},$$

where L and K are the amounts of labor and capital used. Let w_L and w_K denote the prices of labor and capital, respectively.

(a) Find the cost function $c(\mathbf{w}, q)$ (and in the process find the conditional factor demands $L(\mathbf{w}, q)$ and $K(\mathbf{w}, q)$).

(b) Use Shephard's lemma to verify the formulas for the conditional factor demands.

2.16 References

2.1–2.12   The main body of this material is quite standard. Some suggested general references (roughly in increasing order of difficulty) are Quirk (1982), Nicholson (1985), Hirshleifer (1984), Malinvaud (1985), Nadiri (1982), Kreps (1990), Varian (1992), and Samuelson (1947).

2.13–2.14   The study of the general properties of cost functions and of their role as a dual description of a technology is fairly recent. See Varian (1992) for a good textbook exposition and Diewert (1982) for a survey of duality results. See also Shephard (1953).

2.15   Cost allocation methods such as that of Exercise 19 are important for proper decision making. See Kaplan (1984).

Chapter 3
BEHAVIOR OF THE FIRM

The previous chapter presented a framework for describing the technology of a firm based on the production possibility set. Although any point in the production possibility set is feasible, the two criteria of efficiency and cost minimization were introduced to help select particular plans from all those available. But these criteria alone are not sufficient to select a single netput vector; they merely reduce the set of contending choices. This chapter focuses on the specific choices that a firm must make and how it makes them. This constitutes the behavior of the firm.

The choices made by a firm are influenced not only by the firm's technology but also, clearly, by external market conditions. However, the relevant market conditions can encompass a whole complex of external factors. Certainly, for a start, a firm must know the prices of its product and of its input factors. And it should also have some knowledge of how these prices change with quantity produced or purchased. In addition, a firm may find it advantageous to know and account for demand characteristics broken down by various geographic areas, economic classes, and time periods. A firm that is part of an oligopoly will in addition want to understand the technology of competing firms, as well as its own technology, so that it can develop suitable competitive strategies. The decisions of a firm are also influenced by financial markets, including the market for its own stock. Finally, there is a whole collection of other factors—such as community relations, political considerations, stockholder relations, and working conditions—that influence the behavior of a typical firm.

3.1 Profit Maximization

In addition to the technology of a firm and the external market environment, there is another very important determinant of firm behavior, namely, the firm's fundamental business objective. This objective together with the firm's decision processing determine action once the alternatives and their economic consequences are known.

The objective that is postulated most frequently is maximization of profit, where profit is defined simply as the total revenue minus the total cost. That is, it is assumed that a firm selects the netput vector in its production possibility set that corresponds to maximum profit. There are some subtleties and ambiguities involved in calculation of profit in specific cases (and we shall discuss some of them later), but within the theoretical framework, the operation of a firm based on profit maximization is generally well defined.

The profit maximization postulate can be viewed both *normatively* (what a firm *should do*) and *descriptively* (what a firm *actually does*), and there is continuing controversy from both perspectives. From the descriptive perspective, it can be argued that firms do not act solely to maximize profit. There are other important concerns, including those of the managers and workers in the firm and those of society as a whole that influence decisions. In fact, explicit criteria alternative to that of profit maximization have been proposed, such as preservation of the firm, maximization of the firm's growth rate, or maximization of the personal wealth and comfort of managers. But market forces are strong. The stock market urges a public firm toward profit maximization, especially if only a small fraction of the firm is owned by managers and other employees. If managers deviate too far from the profit objective, the owners (either existing or new, as in the case of a takeover) may replace them. Furthermore, none of the alternative criteria has stood up to the test of empirical verification nearly as well as the simple criterion of profit maximization.

Profit maximization is also subject to debate from a normative viewpoint. Presumably, each firm should be operated in such a way that its actions promote overall, collective efficiency and welfare. Profit maximization does seem justified in this context when a number of idealized conditions hold, including the following: (1) a firm's operations are not technically influenced by the actions of other firms (no externalities), (2) there is no uncertainty, (3) there are no taxes, and (4) ownership consists of a large pool of stockholders with small individual holdings. When these assumptions are relaxed, the issue of how firms should be operated can become quite clouded. However, if we stay within the simple setting where the above conditions are met, profit maximization is efficient for society as well as for owners of the firm (as is discussed in Chapter 6). Therefore, because of its simplicity, its good descriptive accuracy, and its reasonable normative justification, we assume throughout this chapter that firms are managed so as to maximize profit subject to the physical constraints of production and the realities of the marketplace.

Finally, it is important to point out that profit as we define it is *economic profit* as opposed to *accounting profit*. Economic profit is equal to the total revenue minus the total economic cost, which includes appropriate wages for labor and rent for property, even if these are on hand and not actually paid for, and it includes an appropriate return on investment. Accounting profit, on the other hand, is generally constructed to conform to tax law, is based on costs actually paid, and does not include the above items. Hence, it is quite possible for a firm to operate continuously at zero profit in the economic sense, whereas under the imposed accounting definition, zero profit would not be acceptable to the firm's owners, who would take steps, such as liquidation, to free up their resources to be used in other opportunities.

3.2   The Basic Production Law

To determine the best level of production, a firm must have a description of the market for its product. This market has two key ingredients: the underlying consumer demand for the product, and the structure of the supply as determined by the number and size of competing firms. In a single-product market, the underlying consumer demand is summarized by a *demand function* $D(p)$, which gives the amount of this product that consumers will buy as a function of its price. Usually the demand function decreases as price increases.

If the firm we are studying were the only firm in the industry, that firm would be a *monopolist*, and the overall demand function $D(p)$ would be the demand function for its output. Most firms are not monopolists, since they face competition from other firms producing the same or similar products. The presence of other firms means that at any price p, the demand supplied by a given firm will be smaller than the total demand $D(p)$. If one firm increases price even a small amount and the other firms do not, many customers may shift their demand to other firms, greatly reducing the demand for the one firm's product. In general, then, the sales of a single firm will be more responsive than $D(p)$ to price changes.

We let $d(p)$ denote the demand for a given firm's product as a function of that firm's price. This is the *effective demand function* faced by the firm, and for the reasons stated above, it is generally different from the overall demand function. We usually omit the adjective *effective* since, from the firm's viewpoint, it is the one demand function that really matters.

If a firm produces m commodities, the effective demand function is an m-dimensional function $\mathbf{d}(\mathbf{p})$, which depends on the m-dimensional price vector $\mathbf{p}$. This accounts for the fact that the demand for any one of a firm's products might depend on the prices of others, not just on the price of the given commodity. The demand for an automobile maker's large cars may depend on the price of its small cars, for example.

We usually assume that the effective demand function $\mathbf{d}(\mathbf{p})$ is invertible. That is, the equation $\mathbf{d} = \mathbf{d}(\mathbf{p})$ can be solved for $\mathbf{p}$ for any value of demand $\mathbf{d}$. The resulting inverse function $\mathbf{p} = \mathbf{p}(\mathbf{d})$ is called the *(effective) inverse demand function*. For many purposes the inverse demand function is more convenient than the direct demand function.

Conditions for Maximum Profit

Consider a firm that produces a single product and faces inverse demand function $p(d)$. If the firm produces the amount q, the price will be $p(q)$, since we assume that all units are sold and hence $d = q$. The *revenue* derived from sale of this output is $r(q) = p(q)q$. We assume that the firm's cost of production depends on the level of output and is described by a cost function $c(q)$. The firm's profit π is revenue minus cost, or

$$\pi(q) = r(q) - c(q) = p(q)q - c(q). \tag{3.1}$$

We can consider the choice of q as the basic decision faced by the firm. Accordingly, we assume that the firm selects q so as to maximize profit. If this maximum occurs at positive output, the first-order conditions for profit maximization are found by setting the derivative of profit equal to zero. Hence the first-order condition is $\pi'(q) = 0$, or

$$r'(q) = c'(q). \tag{3.2}$$

The left side of this equation is marginal revenue, and the right side is marginal cost. Hence, we may state the following general economic law:

Production law.   *If output is positive at maximum profit, marginal revenue is equal to marginal cost, or, equivalently,* MR = MC.

The economic interpretation of this law is that at an optimum point the revenue derived from one additional (small fractional) unit of output must equal the cost of producing it. If the additional revenue were greater, it would be advantageous to produce more. If it were smaller, it would be advantageous to produce less.

Marginal revenue is $r'(q) = p(q) + p'(q)q$. The first term on the right side of this expression is the direct additional revenue derived from selling an additional unit at price $p(q)$. This term is positive, since prices are positive. The second term is the indirect change in revenue due to the fact that all output q that would have been sold at price $p(q)$ will, if a change in q is made, be sold at a slightly different price. This term is usually negative, since demand usually decreases with increasing price. Hence marginal revenue will be less than $p(q)$. This is indicated in Fig. 3.1 where the marginal revenue curve, MR, is shown lying below the inverse demand curve.

The solution of the profit maximization problem for a single commodity is represented graphically in Fig. 3.1. The optimal level of production occurs at the point q^*, where the marginal cost curve intersects the marginal revenue curve. The price at which the commodity is sold, however, is the corresponding value, p^*, on the inverse demand curve.

Total revenue is equal to p^*q^*, which is the large rectangular area shown. Total cost is the average (total) cost at q^* multiplied by q^*, so it is

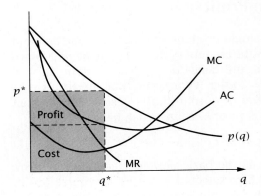

FIGURE 3.1   Profit maximization.

equal to the area of the lower rectangular region. Profit is therefore equal to the area of the upper small rectangular region. In the case shown, the profit is positive. It is also possible, if fixed costs are high, for the maximum profit to be negative. The reader may wish to draw the diagram for this case.

The second-order sufficient condition for maximum profit is $\pi''(q) < 0$. This means that the derivative of marginal revenue must be less than the derivative of marginal cost. Graphically, this means that the marginal cost curve must cross the marginal revenue curve from below, as shown in the figure.

Example 3.1 (Linear demand function). Suppose the inverse demand function for a firm's product is $p = a - bq$ and the firm's cost function is $c(q) = F + mq$. Let us compute the profit-maximizing output level. The profit is

$$\pi(q) = (a - bq)q - F - mq,$$

and the first-order necessary conditions are accordingly

$$a - 2bq - m = 0.$$

Thus,

$$q = \frac{a - m}{2b}.$$

This solution is valid for $a > m$. If $a \le m$, then the optimal solution is $q = 0$. The second-order condition requires $b > 0$; otherwise there is no finite maximum.

Multicommodity Case

The extension of profit maximization to the multicommodity case is straightforward. (Recall that repeated production in different time periods is really multicommodity production.) The revenue associated with production of **q** is $r(\mathbf{q}) = \mathbf{p}(\mathbf{q}) \cdot \mathbf{q}$ where $\mathbf{p}(\mathbf{q})$ is the inverse demand function. The profit maximization problem is then

$$\max \ \pi(\mathbf{q}) = \max\{r(\mathbf{q}) - c(\mathbf{q})\} = \max\{\mathbf{p}(\mathbf{q}) \cdot \mathbf{q} - c(\mathbf{q})\}. \tag{3.3}$$

Assuming that the solution has $\mathbf{q} > 0$ and that the functions $\mathbf{p}$ and c are differentiable, the first-order necessary conditions are

$$\sum_{i=1}^{m} \frac{\partial p_i(\mathbf{q}^*)}{\partial q_j} q_i^* + p_j(\mathbf{q}^*) = \frac{\partial c(\mathbf{q}^*)}{\partial q_j}, \qquad j = 1, 2, \ldots, m. \tag{3.4}$$

These equations set marginal revenue equal to marginal cost for each of the m commodities. They comprise a system of m equations in the m unknowns consisting of the components of **q**.

*3.3   Practical Pricing Methods

The theory of the previous section is not in a form that can be readily used in practice. Most firms set product prices rather than quantity to be sold. However, we can develop an alternate form of analysis that considers price as the decision variable.

Markup Pricing

One of the main difficulties a firm faces when attempting to establish price or quantity logically is that the effective demand function $d(p)$ is usually not known or is known only very roughly. It is therefore not possible for the firm to know the optimal quantity to produce (or price to set) exactly. Therefore a simplified or approximate method for making the appropriate decision is typically used.

   Many firms employ some variant of *markup pricing,* where price is some factor above average cost. The markup factor is the firm's profit margin for the product, which may vary from a few percent up to a hundred percent or more. The markup factor is usually related to the characteristics of the industry, as revealed by experience and comparison with similar industries. This approach to pricing can, however, be related to the theoretical structure of the previous section, and it can in fact be regarded as a logical and practical way to implement the theory.

   The starting point for analysis of the method is the alternate form of condition (3.2) for profit maximization based on price. We first denote by $\varepsilon(p)$ the *price elasticity of demand,* given by

$$\varepsilon(p) = \frac{p}{d(p)} d'(p). \tag{3.5}$$

This elasticity is normally negative since $d'(p)$ is normally negative. Now condition (3.2), that marginal revenue equals marginal cost, can be written in the form (substituting q for d)

$$p(q^*)\left[1 + p'(q^*)\frac{q^*}{p(q^*)}\right] = c'(q^*).$$

Since $d(p(q)) = q$, we have $d'(p^*)p'(q^*) = 1$ and hence $p'(q^*)q^*/p(q^*) = 1/\varepsilon(p^*)$. Therefore the above optimality condition can be written

$$p(q^*) = c'(q^*)\left[1 + \frac{1}{\varepsilon(p^*)}\right]^{-1}. \tag{3.6}$$

Since $\varepsilon(p^*)$ is negative and marginal cost is positive, it follows that the optimal price is a markup over marginal cost, with the markup factor being a function of the price elasticity. If the magnitude of elasticity is large, corresponding to a nearly horizontal inverse demand function, the markup will be small. If, on the other hand, the magnitude of price elasticity is small, as it might be for a monopoly of an essential commodity, the markup will be large. However, the relevant elasticity is that of the effective demand curve for the firm, not the demand curve for the industry. As an example, the overall demand function for food has a moderately low elasticity, but its effective elasticity, as seen by a specific firm, is high because of competition. Therefore markups of food products tend to be low.

Equation (3.6) is a helpful recasting of the optimality conditions, but we can tie it even more directly to the practical pricing procedure of a firm. When faced with a pricing decision, especially for a new product, a firm may not know the demand function. To make a profit, however, it must set price above average cost. Hence, as a feasible starting point, the firm might begin with a certain output level q and set price as a markup over short-run average cost; that is, it might set

$$p = (1 + m)AC \tag{3.7}$$

for some markup factor m. Once this price is set, the firm will find a new level of q from the market, and it may then adjust its fixed factors and perhaps also the markup. Ultimately, if its long-run average cost curve is essentially flat, MC will be close to ATC and the firm will adjust its fixed factors so that AC equals ATC. Then the policy (3.7) will correspond exactly to the optimal policy (3.6) for appropriate m.

Evaluation of Local Demand Properties

Increasingly, firms are in fact using the theory of the previous section to help set prices. A key ingredient of this approach is some estimate of the demand or inverse demand curves. These estimates are derived in part from market surveys, from econometric studies (which study historical data over an industry), or most directly, through subjective evaluation by managers familiar with the industry. It is argued that one of a manager's most important responsibilities is to understand the market for the firm's products, and this understanding should be translated into numerical form. Usually, estimates are made of just the local slope of the demand curve, near the current point of operation. This estimate may be in elasticity or direct form.

Elasticities

In the multiproduct situation, elasticities are defined that relate the demand of one commodity to the price of another. These are termed *cross elasticities.* Specifically,

$$\varepsilon_{ij} = \frac{\partial \ln d_i(\mathbf{p})}{\partial \ln p_j} \equiv \frac{\partial d_i(\mathbf{p})}{\partial p_j} \cdot \frac{p_j}{d_i(\mathbf{p})}$$

is the cross elasticity of demand for good i with respect to p_j. These elasticities and others are frequently used in applications.

Example 3.2 (Telephone pricing model). A small telephone company serves an isolated community. It uses a simple economic model based on elasticity information to determine its pricing structure.

Table 3.1 shows the basic structure. There is a fixed access fee per month for a telephone line. Calls are priced at $.15 during daily business hours (8:00 A.M. to 5:00 P.M.), but there is a discount for calls during nonbusiness hours. We only consider local calls in this model. The first column of Table 3.1 shows the existing situation.

In order to determine the impact of price changes, the company could use the four elasticities involving combinations of daytime and nighttime prices. As a shortcut method the company estimates two elasticities: the *share elasticity* (the share of the total calls that are made during nonbusiness hours divided by the relative change in nighttime price) is −0.1; the *price elasticity* of total calls per month with respect to average price is −0.2.

Based on this information, the phone company can examine the effect of proposed rate changes. For example, the second column shows the effect of

TABLE 3.1 Telephone pricing.

	Night Discount	
	40%	70%
Lines	5000	5000
Access fee per line per month	$11.00	$11.00
Calls per line per month	100	101.45
Day (percentages of calls)	80%	79%
Night (percentages of calls)	20%	21%
Rate	0.15	0.15
Revenue	$124,000	$119,893

changing the discount during nonbusiness hours to 70 percent. This column is computed as follows.

Let S and P denote the share and price of night calls. The change of nighttime price is $\Delta P/P = (0.6 - 0.3)/(0.6) = 0.5$. Hence

$$(\Delta S/S) = (-0.1)(\Delta P/P) = (-0.1)(-0.5).$$

Therefore, $\Delta S = 0.20\cdot(-0.1)(-0.5) = 0.01$, and the new share is 21 percent. The original average price of a call was $0.80(0.15) + 0.20(0.15)(0.6) = 0.138$. The new average is $(0.79)(0.15) + 0.21(0.15)(0.3) = 0.128$. Hence if V is the total volume of calls, we have $\Delta V/V = (-0.2)(-0.01/0.138) = 0.0145$. This gives a new volume of 101.45.

Some phone companies do use models of this type, although realistic models are much more complex than the one of this example.

3.4   Perfect Competition

Perfect competition is an important idealization of the market. It is defined by the condition that the effective inverse demand curve of a firm is constant; that is, there is a constant product price p, independent of the quantity produced. In other words, perfect competition corresponds to $p(q) = p$, a constant. This idealization is approximately realized when an industry has many independent firms each producing an identical product and every firm's production is equally accessible to consumers. The firms are assumed not to collude, and each produces only a small portion of the total production. Under these conditions, the price charged for a product must be the same for every firm, since no firm can charge a higher price than others without losing all sales, and no firm can influence the price. In this perfect competition case, each firm is a *price taker;* it can only take the market price as given and fixed. Or, as said before, the firm's effective inverse demand function is constant.

Examples of markets that are essentially perfectly competitive include the large markets for agricultural products such as grain and corn and the markets for financial instruments such as bonds. Indeed any large, diffuse, and unrestricted market is likely to exhibit the characteristics of perfect competition.

Given the competitive price p, the problem of profit maximization for a single-product firm is

$$\max_{q} \pi = \max_{q}\{pq - c(q)\}.$$

If c is differentiable, this leads to the first-order necessary conditions (for a finite solution)

$$
\begin{aligned}
p &= c'(q) &&\text{if } q > 0 \\
p &\le c'(0) &&\text{if } q = 0.
\end{aligned}
\qquad (3.8)
$$

The first of these is a special case of the general production law that marginal revenue should equal marginal cost, since marginal revenue is just p in the case of pure competition. The second condition states that if the optimal solution is $q = 0$, then price is below (or perhaps equal to) marginal cost.

Note that if $p > c'(q)$ for all q, the "optimum" would be achieved at $q = \infty$. What this means realistically is that the ideal of perfect competition breaks down and that the firm will produce a high enough output to significantly increase total industry supply, thereby forcing the price to fall to a value $p^* = c'(q^*)$ for some q^*.

In the finite case, the corresponding second-order necessary condition takes the especially simple form

$$c''(q) \geq 0 \quad \text{if } q > 0, \tag{3.9}$$

which states that an optimal point must be a point where marginal cost is nondecreasing. If marginal cost were equal to p but decreasing, it would pay to increase production.

It is straightforward to extend the first-order conditions to the m-product case. If the prevailing prices are given by $\mathbf{p} = (p_1, p_2, \ldots, p_m)$, the optimal output vector $\mathbf{q} = (q_1, q_2, \ldots, q_m)$ must satisfy

$$p_i = \frac{\partial c(\mathbf{q})}{\partial q_i} \quad \text{if } q_i > 0$$

$$p_i \leq \frac{\partial c(\mathbf{q})}{\partial q_i} \quad \text{if } q_i = 0, \tag{3.10}$$

$i = 1, 2, \ldots, m$.

3.5   The Supply Function

In perfect competition, the market environment of a firm is completely described by prices. It is therefore meaningful to define a function $\mathbf{q}(\mathbf{p})$ that describes the optimal production levels as functions of prices. This function $\mathbf{q}(\mathbf{p})$ is called the *supply function* of the firm.

The supply function for a single-commodity firm can be determined explicitly by use of the necessary conditions (3.8) and (3.9) and by reference to the original problem definition. We assume, for simplicity, that the marginal cost curve is *unimodal*; that is, it has a single relative minimum point at some positive (or zero) value of q, as shown in Fig. 3.2.

The first-order necessary conditions state that, in general, $p = c'(q)$ or $q = 0$. To tell which of these conditions applies, we can simply compare the corresponding profits and select the largest one. A point with $q > 0$ can be a solution only if

$$pq - c(q) \geq p \cdot 0 - c(0),$$

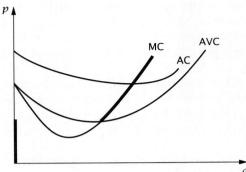

q **FIGURE 3.2   Inverse supply curve.**

or equivalently, if

$$p \geq \frac{c(q) - c(0)}{q} = \text{AVC}(q). \tag{3.11}$$

Therefore, the optimal solution will be positive and have marginal cost equal to p only if p is greater than or equal to average variable cost at that output.

The supply curve is shown as the heavy line in Fig. 3.2. (Actually, what is shown is the inverse supply curve, since p is shown as a function of q.) At any $q > 0$, the corresponding supply price is equal to the marginal cost. Therefore, the inverse supply curve corresponds exactly to the marginal cost curve for such points. However, at any price below the minimum of the average variable cost curve, q must be zero because there is no $q > 0$ that can satisfy condition (3.11).

A supply curve can be derived either for short-run production decisions or for the long run. One simply uses the appropriate cost functions. For example, for the long run, fixed costs might be zero, while for the short run, they are not.

The structure of the supply curve has strong intuitive meaning. A firm will not produce positive output if the derived revenue will not cover the associated variable costs. Why should it take an action that by itself loses money? It will produce positive output if revenue covers the variable costs, even though revenue may not cover total cost, because the fixed costs are incurred even at zero production level. Hence, these fixed costs should be ignored when a firm is deciding whether to operate, since they must be paid in any event. (It is for this reason that such costs are often called *sunk costs:* they are already committed and hence already sunk into the business.) Thus, as shown in the figure, the supply curve may lie below the average (total) cost curve for some output levels. Profit is negative at such levels, but it is less negative than it would be if the firm did not produce.

Under perfect competition, if a firm does operate at a positive level, it should operate where marginal cost equals price. Otherwise each incremental unit will produce incremental profit or loss, pressuring the firm either to increase or to decrease production.

Example 3.3. Suppose a firm has the Cobb-Douglas production function

$$q = K^{1/2}L^{1/2}$$

where K represents capital and L labor. Suppose, however, that K is fixed at some value K^*, as it would be in the short run. Then if output level q is produced, the required labor input is

$$L = \frac{q^2}{K^*}.$$

If the input factor prices are p_K and p_L, respectively, the total cost is

$$TC = p_K K^* + p_L L$$

$$= p_K K^* + \frac{p_L q^2}{K^*}.$$

From this we easily compute

$$MC = 2\frac{p_L}{K^*}q$$

$$AVC = \frac{p_L}{K^*}q.$$

In this case marginal cost is always greater than average variable cost, so the supply curve is equal to the marginal cost curve; that is, the inverse supply curve is

$$p = \frac{2p_L}{K^*}q$$

where p is the price of output.

Constant Returns to Scale

Consider a firm that produces a single commodity using a constant-returns-to-scale technology (which might be appropriate for the long run). Since the optimal bundle of inputs scales up in proportion to output with such a technology, we see that $c(q) = qc(1)$. Hence both average cost and marginal cost are constant (and equal). This means that the inverse supply function is also constant and is equal to this same value. The situation is shown in Fig. 3.3.

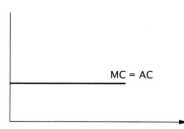

MC = AC

q **FIGURE 3.3   Constant returns to scale.**

The inverse demand curve can be read directly from this figure. First, suppose p is greater than the value corresponding to MC (or AC). Then if the firm operates at level $q > 0$, it will make positive profit equal to $(p-AC)q$. In theory, therefore, the firm could make infinite profit by selecting $q = \infty$. This is not consistent with the assumption of perfect competition, so such a p cannot really arise. Next, suppose p is less than the value corresponding to MC (or AC). If the firm operates at level $q > 0$, it will make negative profit equal to $(p - AC)q$. Hence in this situation the firm should select $q = 0$ and attain $\pi = 0$. Finally, suppose $p = MC$. Then the firm can operate at any level $q \geq 0$ and the profit will be zero. In fact, any level $q \geq 0$ is optimal for the firm in this case, so the scale of operation is indeterminate. Hence, in this case the level of output is determined by other factors, such as overall demand and the competitive structure of firms. We see, therefore, that under constant returns to scale and perfect competition (both of which are idealizations), the optimal profit is either ∞ (which is inconsistent) or 0.

Now let us generalize this result to the case of a firm producing several outputs using a constant-returns-to-scale technology. Assuming fixed input prices, the cost function of the firm then satisfies the identity $c(t\mathbf{q}) = tc(\mathbf{q})$ for all $t > 0$ (see Exercise 7, Chapter 2). This means that

$$\pi(t\mathbf{q}) = t[\mathbf{p}\cdot\mathbf{q} - c(\mathbf{q})].$$

Hence, if $\pi(\mathbf{q}) > 0$ for some q, then $\pi(\mathbf{q}) \to \infty$ as $t \to \infty$, which means that the original assumption of perfect competition is inconsistent. The best that can be done, therefore, is to find $\mathbf{q}$ such that $\pi(\mathbf{q}) = 0$. Hence, again, finite operation using constant returns to scale implies zero profit.

Decreasing Returns to Scale

Now consider a firm producing a single product using a decreasing-returns-to-scale technology. This means that the average cost curve is increasing,[1] and this implies that there is no fixed cost. Hence AC = AVC as shown by the solid curve in Fig. 3.4. Since average cost is increasing, it follows that marginal cost is greater than average cost since

$$AC' = \frac{d}{dq}\frac{c(q)}{q} = \frac{c'(q)}{q} - \frac{c(q)}{q^2} \geq 0$$

implies that $MC = c'(q) \geq c(q)/q = AC$. The inverse supply curve is therefore equal to the MC curve, and profit will be positive. If the output level is q^*, the profit π is equal to the area shown in the figure.

The profit associated with a decreasing-returns-to-scale technology can be interpreted as rent derived from some feature of the production facility,

---

[1]Remember that we are referring to the long-run cost.

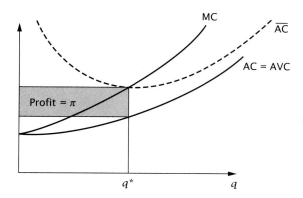

FIGURE 3.4 Decreasing returns.

usually land, capital, or personnel, that is not explicitly included in the original list of inputs. This interpretation of profit can be seen in Fig. 3.4. If we assume that the cost of the special factor, treated as a fixed cost, is π, the actual average cost curve is $\overline{AC} = AC + \pi/q$, shown as a dashed line in the figure. The MC curve will remain the same. In this interpretation the firm operates exactly at its point of minimum average cost and profits are zero.

It should be recalled that, as discussed in Section 3.1, an enterprise can be economically healthy even if the profit is zero. Labor costs and normal return on investment are included in the costs. The profit π is measured above these.

Example 3.4 (Skyscraper economics). Construction of office buildings requires land L and construction K as inputs. The amount of office space in a building is equal to the area per floor (which we take to be L) times the number of floors F. The amount of construction K required is proportional to the area per floor, but each floor requires y times as much construction as the floor below it ($y \approx 1.02$ for some common types of construction). Let us examine this construction process under the assumption of perfect competition.

The office space q in a building can be regarded as the output of a production process with L and K as inputs. Let us assume that it takes one unit of construction to construct a one-floor building on one unit of land. Building F floors requires

$$K = 1 + y + y^2 + \cdots + y^{F-1} = \frac{y^F - 1}{y - 1}$$

of construction. The total office space in this case is $q = F$. Hence we may solve for q as

$$q = \frac{\ln\left[1 + (y - 1)K\right]}{\ln y},$$

which is the production function for office space on a piece of land with $L = 1$. Note that this exhibits decreasing returns to scale.

For $L \neq 1$, we have $K/L = (\gamma^F - 1)/(\gamma - 1)$ and $q = LF$, which yields the general production function

$$q = L\frac{\ln\left[1 + (\gamma - 1)K/L\right]}{\ln \gamma},$$

which exhibits constant returns to scale (because all factors are accounted for).

Now assume that the price of office space is p per unit area of floor space and the price of construction is w per unit. For $L = 1$ we can calculate the optimal level of construction K by maximizing $pq - wK$. This yields

$$K^* = \frac{p}{w \ln \gamma} - \frac{1}{\gamma - 1},$$

and because the production function with $L = 1$ has decreasing returns to scale, there will be positive profit. This profit is

$$\pi = \frac{p}{\ln \gamma}\left\{\ln\left[\frac{p(\gamma - 1)}{w \ln \gamma}\right] - 1\right\} + \frac{w}{\gamma - 1}.$$

This value is the implied value of a unit of land.

Increasing Returns to Scale

In the case of increasing returns to scale, the average variable cost decreases. This implies that marginal cost is below average variable cost, and hence there is no finite, nonzero solution to the profit maximization problem under the assumption of fixed prices. See Fig. 3.5. Increasing returns to scale is therefore *inconsistent* with perfect competition. In reality, industries that exhibit increasing returns to scale are usually characterized by monopoly, oligopoly, or heavy regulation, or the firms in such industries operate at such a large scale that decreasing returns to scale does in fact set in.

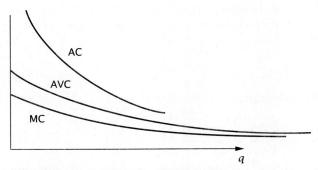

FIGURE 3.5   Increasing returns to scale.

3.6 Perfect Competition over Time

The above method of analysis is useful for obtaining qualitative descriptions of long-run behavior in a competitive industry. A complete analysis of a firm under perfect competition, however, would explicitly account for production in each of several periods and could be based on the concept of dated commodities. An analysis over time then is equivalent to an analysis of a multiproduct firm.

Example 3.5. A high-tech manufacturing firm enters a new product market where price is declining. We analyze the firm over two periods.

The firm uses a technology that has variable cost in each period

$$VC = c(q,k) = bq + \frac{eq^2}{2k},$$

where k is the level of capital and q is the level of production. The cost for capital k is ak and this is purchased in the first period. The product prices in the two periods are p_0 and p_1. The overall problem of the firm is to maximize profit π. Hence

$$\pi = \max_{k,q_0,q_1} \{-ak + p_0 q_0 - c(q_0,k) + \rho[p_1 q_1 - c(q_1,k)]\},$$

where the second period profit has been discounted by the factor ρ. If k is considered fixed, the single-period supply function of the firm is found by solving MC $= p$, or in this case,

$$b + \frac{eq}{k} = p.$$

Hence,

$$q_0 = \frac{(p_0 - b)k}{e}, \qquad q_1 = \frac{(p_1 - b)k}{e}.$$

The resulting profit can be found by substituting these values into the profit expression, leading to

$$\pi(k) = -ak + (p_0 - b)^2 \frac{k}{2e} + \rho(p_1 - b)^2 \frac{k}{2e}.$$

This is homogeneous of degree one in k, reflecting the constant returns to scale of this technology (in the long run). Therefore, if the market is perfectly competitive, we must have $\pi(k) = 0$ for all k. Hence, the prices must satisfy

$$(p_0 - b)^2 + \rho(p_1 - b)^2 = 2ae.$$

Although the total profit is zero, the profit accrued in each period separately will depend on how the capital cost is allocated to the two periods. From the equation above, it is clear that perfect competition implies a relation between the product prices in the two periods; they cannot both be arbitrary.

3.7   Equilibrium

We can now combine the information about all the firms in a perfectly competitive market to determine the equilibrium price and quantities produced in the market. Suppose there are n firms, each of which produces a common good. We assume that n is large, so each firm acts as if it were a price taker. Let $q_i(p)$ be the supply function of firm i, for $i = 1, 2, \ldots, n$. The *industry supply function* is then

$$Q(p) = \sum_{i=1}^{n} q_i(p).$$

Suppose also that there is an industrywide demand function $D(p)$. Equilibrium is obtained by setting overall demand equal to overall supply. That is, we set

$$D(p) = Q(p).$$

The solution to this equation gives the equilibrium price in the industry.

Associated with this price is a set of individual firm outputs. Given the price p, each firm i will produce the corresponding $q_i(p)$. Under the assumption of perfect competition, no firm has any incentive to change from this production level, and for this reason the result is termed an equilibrium. Note that in computing the equilibrium, each firm considers the price as fixed, but our computation of the equilibrium price actually accounts for how price changes influence aggregate supply and demand.

This equilibrium analysis is called a *partial equilibrium* analysis because it focuses on one market only, implicitly assuming that changes in this one market do not change prices of other goods and upset the equilibrium that (already) holds in those markets. A *general equilibrium* analysis treats all markets simultaneously; this is the subject of Chapter 7.

3.8   Monopoly and Oligopoly

We now consider two important market structures that are not characterized by perfect competition.

Monopoly

The term *monopoly* describes an industry in which there is a single firm. A firm that enjoys a monopoly is not a price taker, for it knows that its actions directly affect the price of its product; it is a price setter.

A monopoly firm will set output level q to maximize profit. That is, it will solve

$$\max_{q} \; p(q)q - c(q),$$

where $p(q)$ is the inverse demand function.

This is just a special case of the analysis of Section 3.2. Here the actual industry-wide function $p(q)$ is equal to the effective inverse demand function for the firm—since there is only one firm!

As a general rule the profit obtained by a monopoly (if it elects to produce) will be positive, as illustrated in Fig. 3.1. A monopoly can operate under decreasing, constant, or increasing returns to scale. It can make positive profit in each case, provided demand is sufficiently great.

Oligopoly

The term *oligopoly* describes industries that consist of relatively few firms, each producing an identical product. Such an industry usually does not exhibit the characteristics of perfect competition, since individual firms' actions can in fact influence market price. For example, if a firm that initially produces a significant share of total output suddenly reduces its production and other firms do not change their production, the market price will tend to increase, and the profits of the other firm will consequently increase even though they did not change output. Hence, production planning of all firms is intrinsically intertwined.

In the analysis of oligopoly, it is usually assumed that firms do not explicitly collude, since collusion is often illegal or impractical. (However, collusion certainly can be considered; it will be discussed in Chapter 8.) Even given this assumption, it is not evident how the final configuration of production will be determined. A new concept is required.

Cournot Equilibrium

A fundamental concept for the analysis of oligopoly was introduced by Cournot. A *Cournot equilibrium* is a special set of production levels that have the property that no individual firm has an incentive to change its own production level if other firms do not change theirs.

This equilibrium concept is somewhat different than that used in perfect competition (although as we shall see in Chapter 8, the two are closely related). The Cournot equilibrium is not a single price that coordinates supply and demand. Rather, a Cournot equilibrium is a complete set of production levels, one for each firm, that balance their profit interactions in the market. This equilibrium concept and its generalizations are a basic foundation of a substantial part of the microeconomic theory. The subject is discussed in much greater detail in Chapter 8, but here we present a brief introduction since it is an important aspect of the theory of the behavior of firms.

To formalize the analysis of oligopoly and this equilibrium concept, suppose there are m firms producing a single homogeneous product. If firm i produces output level q_i, the firm's cost is $c_i(q_i)$. There is a single marketwide inverse demand function $p(q)$. The total supply is $q = q_1 + q_2 + \cdots + q_m$.

Cournot equilibrium. A set of output levels $q_1, q_2, \ldots, q_m$ constitutes a *Cournot equilibrium* if for each $i = 1, 2, \ldots, m$ the profit to firm i cannot be increased by changing q_i alone.

In other words, a set of production levels is a Cournot equilibrium if there is no incentive for unilateral change by any firm.

The profit to firm i is

$$\pi_i = p(q_1 + q_2 + \cdots + q_m)q_i - c_i(q_i).$$

To determine the equations that describe a Cournot equilibrium, we set the derivative of profit equal to zero or, equivalently, equate marginal revenue to marginal cost for each firm. This leads directly to the following set of simultaneous equations

$$p'(q_1 + q_2 + \cdots + q_m)q_1 + p(q_1 + q_2 + \cdots + q_m) = c_1'(q_1)$$
$$p'(q_1 + q_2 + \cdots + q_m)q_2 + p(q_1 + q_2 + \cdots + q_m) = c_2'(q_2)$$
$$\vdots \qquad\qquad (3.12)$$
$$p'(q_1 + q_2 + \cdots + q_m)q_m + p(q_1 + q_2 + \cdots + q_m) = c_m'(q_m).$$

In general the above system of simultaneous equations must be solved as a unit (assuming that a solution exists.)

An important question is how the above system can be solved in practice by the firms participating in the market. To study this, and for theoretical reasons as well, it is useful to define a firm's *reaction function*. Consider the ith equation. For any value of the sum of the other outputs, denoted by s_i, this equation can be solved for q_i . The resulting solution, denoted $Q_i(s_i)$, is a reaction to the total output produced by the other firms. In practice, firms might continually respond to the actions of the other firms, according to their reaction functions, so that the outputs are successively adjusted. Eventually, this process *might* lead to equilibrium, but special conditions are required to assure that it does.

Reaction functions give a direct characterization of a Cournot equilibrium: a set of q_i's, $i = 1, 2, \ldots, m$, is a Cournot equilibrium if each reaction function gives $q_i = Q_i(s_i)$; that is, the q_i's form a Cournot equilibrium if the reaction functions imply no change in the production levels.

An important special case is that of *duopoly*, an industry with just two firms. In this case the reaction function of each firm is a function of just the

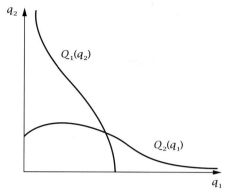

FIGURE 3.6 Reaction functions.

other firm's output. Thus, the two reaction functions have the form $Q_1(q_2)$ and $Q_2(q_1)$. The reaction functions of two firms are shown in Fig. 3.6. In the figure, if firm 1 selects a value q_1 on the horizontal axis, firm 2 will react by selecting the point on the vertical axis that corresponds to the function $Q_2(q_1)$. Similarly, if firm 2 selects a value q_2 on the vertical axis, firm 1 will react by selecting the point on the horizontal axis that corresponds to the curve $Q_1(q_2)$. The equilibrium point corresponds to the point of intersection of the two reaction functions.

Stackelberg Equilibrium

There are alternative methods for characterizing the outcome of an oligopoly. One of the most popular of these is the *Stackelberg equilibrium* concept.

Consider the special case of a duopoly. In the Stackelberg formulation one firm, say firm 1, is considered to be the *leader* and the other, firm 2, is the *follower*. The leader may, for example, be the larger firm or the firm with better information. If there is a well-defined order for firms committing to an output decision, the leader commits first.

Given the committed production level q_1 of firm 1, firm 2, the follower, will select q_2 using the same reaction function as in the Cournot theory. That is, firm 2 finds q_2 to maximize

$$\pi_2 = p(q_1 + q_2)q_2 - c_2(q_2),$$

where $p(q)$ is the industrywide inverse demand function. This yields the reaction function $Q_2(q_1)$.

Firm 1, the leader, accounts for the reaction of firm 2 when originally selecting q_1. In particular, firm 1 selects q_1 to maximize

$$\pi_1 = p(q_1 + Q_2(q_1))q_1 - c_1(q_1).$$

That is, firm 1 substitutes $Q_2(q_1)$ for q_2 in the profit expression.

Note that a Stackelberg equilibrium does not yield a system of equations that must be solved simultaneously. Once the reaction function of firm 2 is found, firm 1's problem can be solved directly. Usually the leader will do better in a Stackelberg equilibrium than in a Cournot equilibrium. See Exercise 14.

Monopolistic Competition

Many industries consist of several firms that produce similar, but not identical, products. Consumers may switch purchases from one product to another, depending on relative prices, but the prices of the different (but similar) products do not have to be equal. Each firm is thus a monopolist with respect to its own product, but faces competition from similar products. This situation is described as *monopolistic competition*. It generalizes the notion of oligopoly because the firms that compose the industry do not produce exactly the same product.

To analyze monopolistic competition, we assume that each firm produces a single product. The inverse demand function for firm i's product depends not only on its own level of output, but also on the output level of all other firms in the industry. We represent this inverse demand function as $p_i(q_i; \mathbf{q}_{-i})$, where $\mathbf{q}_{-i}$ denotes the vector of output levels of all firms except firm i. (That is, $\mathbf{q}_{-i} = (q_1, q_2, \ldots, q_{i-1}, q_{i+1}, \ldots, q_m)$.) Firm i's profit is

$$p_i(q_i; \mathbf{q}_{-i})q_i - c_i(q_i) \tag{3.13}$$

and it is this quantity that the firm wishes to maximize. However, this profit depends on the behavior of the other firms who are in turn affected by the behavior of firm i. Hence, in general, the determination of optimal output levels is a set of interrelated problems.

We define a solution approach by appealing again to the equilibrium concept introduced by Cournot. The general definition is the same as before: a set of output levels $\mathbf{q} = (q_1, q_2, \ldots, q_m)$ is an equilibrium if for each $i = 1, 2, \ldots, m$ the profit to firm i cannot be increased by changing q_i alone.

This concept is formulated in equation form by maximizing the profit (3.13) with respect to q_i. This leads to

$$\frac{\partial p_i(q_i; \mathbf{q}_{-i})}{\partial q_i} q_i + p_i(q_i; \mathbf{q}_{-i}) = c_i'(q_i), \tag{3.14}$$

$i = 1, 2, \ldots, m$. There are m equations and m unknowns from which the vector $\mathbf{q}$ of outputs can be determined. This structure also falls into the general category considered in greater detail in Chapter 8.

*3.9   Unconditional Factor Demand

So far in this chapter we have focused on a firm's choice of production levels and how that choice is influenced by the market for products. The production levels influence the level of input factors employed by the firm, but we have treated this variation implicitly, assuming fixed input prices. In the next three sections of the chapter we explicitly consider the choice of input factor levels and how these are influenced by the markets for these factors.

In Section 2.14 we studied conditional factor demand—a function of input prices giving the firm's demand for input factors conditional on a given level of output. The *unconditional factor demand* is a function of input prices giving the firm's demand for input factors when output is allowed to vary. This demand takes account of the fact that output will be adjusted to maximize profit, and accordingly, this demand function depends on both input and output prices.

Output and Substitution Effect

When factor prices change, the resulting change in demand can be thought of as corresponding to two distinct effects. First, the firm will adjust its output level to a new point of profit maximization, and this change itself will induce a change in the level of inputs required. This is termed the *output effect*. Second, even if the output is not changed, the input levels will change if there is a factor price change. This effect is termed the *substitution effect* and is determined by the conditional demand function. The two effects can be combined to yield a method for computing the unconditional factor demand.

If we assume that the firm faces an inverse demand function $\mathbf{p}(\mathbf{q})$ for its output, its profit maximization problem is

$$\max_{\mathbf{q}} \ \mathbf{p}(\mathbf{q}) \cdot \mathbf{q} - c(\mathbf{w}, \mathbf{q}).$$

The necessary conditions are (assuming an interior solution)

$$\sum_{i=1}^{m} \frac{\partial p_i(\mathbf{q})}{\partial q_j} q_i + p_j(\mathbf{q}) = \frac{\partial c(\mathbf{w}, \mathbf{q})}{\partial q_j}, \qquad j = 1, 2, \ldots, m. \qquad (3.15)$$

Now (assuming appropriate regularity conditions) we may solve (3.15) for $\mathbf{q}$ in terms of $\mathbf{w}$. The resulting function $\mathbf{q}(\mathbf{w})$ gives the profit-maximizing level of output as a function of factor prices.

The overall (unconditional) factor demands are then found by substitution of this value of $\mathbf{q}$ in the expression for conditional factor demands as given by Shephard's lemma (see Section 2.14). Thus,

$$z_i = \frac{\partial c(\mathbf{w}, \mathbf{q}(\mathbf{w}))}{\partial w_i}, \qquad i = 1, 2, \ldots, m.$$

Example 3.6. Let us consider the Cobb-Douglas production function $q = z_1^\alpha z_2^\beta$, with $\alpha + \beta < 1$. We assume that the firm faces perfect competition in the output market at price p. The cost function was found in Example 2.13 in Section 2.13. The necessary condition (3.15) then becomes

$$p = \frac{\partial c(\mathbf{w}, q)}{\partial q}$$

or

$$p = \left(\frac{\alpha}{w_1}\right)^{-\alpha/(\alpha+\beta)} \left(\frac{\beta}{w_2}\right)^{-\beta/(\alpha+\beta)} q^{\gamma/(\alpha+\beta)} \tag{3.16}$$

where $\gamma = 1 - \alpha - \beta$. This can be easily solved for q in terms of w_1 and w_2. The result can then be substituted into the conditional factor demand equations determined in Example 2.17 in Section 2.14. This yields

$$z_1 = \left(\frac{\alpha}{w_1}\right)^{(1-\beta)/\gamma} \left(\frac{\beta}{w_2}\right)^{\beta/\gamma} p^{1/\gamma}$$

$$\tag{3.17}$$

$$z_2 = \left(\frac{\alpha}{w_1}\right)^{\alpha/\gamma} \left(\frac{\beta}{w_2}\right)^{(1-\alpha)/\gamma} p^{1/\gamma}$$

as the unconditional factor demands.

Example 3.7 (Constant returns to scale).   If $\alpha + \beta = 1$ in Example 3.6, then $\gamma = 0$ and (3.16) cannot be solved for q. This will happen whenever the firm has a constant-returns-to-scale technology and faces a perfectly competitive output market. The output level is then not determined by the conditions of profit maximization alone, and an unconditional factor demand cannot be defined without making additional assumptions.

An alternative method for computing unconditional factor demands is given in the next section. This method is more concise and leads to strong comparative statics results, as shown in Appendix D.

3.10   The Profit Function

We now return to the general framework where a firm is described by a production possibility set $\mathcal{Y}$. During the past two chapters we have opened up the set $\mathcal{Y}$ for a detailed view; we have explored its structure and determined how a firm can make intelligent decisions based on knowledge of $\mathcal{Y}$ and the economic environment. It is useful now to "close down" our view of $\mathcal{Y}$ once again and fold the details into the general framework. All of this can be done for a perfectly competitive economic environment (where markets for *all* goods, inputs and outputs, are perfectly competitive) through the *profit function*. This function provides a compact summary description of a firm and is one that is used frequently in later chapters.

We therefore return to the general framework where $\mathcal{Y}$ consists of the set of feasible netput vectors, typically denoted by $\mathbf{y}$. We denote the price vector associated with netputs by **p**. That is, **p** contains component prices for *all* netputs: inputs, outputs, and quantities that can be either input or output. (Earlier, in our more detailed discussion of output choice, **p** was used as the price for outputs, but now in this aggregate view the use of this symbol is expanded.)

The profit associated with a netput vector **y** and price vector **p** is easily seen to be **p·y**. This will add the revenue terms (associated with outputs) and subtract the cost terms (associated with inputs). We then introduce the following definition.

Profit function. Let $\mathcal{Y}$ be a production possibility set. The corresponding *profit function* is

$$\pi(\mathbf{p}) = \max_{\mathbf{y} \in \mathcal{Y}} \mathbf{p} \cdot \mathbf{y}.$$

We assume, for now, that the indicated maximum exists.

In the above definition $\pi(\mathbf{p})$ is the maximum profit that can be made under prices **p**. The construction of $\pi(\mathbf{p})$ is illustrated in Fig. 3.7. A price vector defines a family of hyperplanes corresponding to equations of the form $\mathbf{p} \cdot \mathbf{y} = c$, for various values of c. (See Appendix B.) These hyperplanes can be called *isoprofit planes* since profit is constant on each of them. (In Fig. 3.7 they show up as lines perpendicular to **p**.) The highest such hyperplane touching $\mathcal{Y}$ corresponds to the greatest possible profit. The value $\pi(\mathbf{p})$ is the value of c in the equation $\mathbf{p} \cdot \mathbf{y} = c$ describing that hyperplane.

The construction of the profit function is analogous to the definition of the cost function. The difference is that the cost function is a minimum over the input requirement set, rather than a maximum over $\mathcal{Y}$. Because

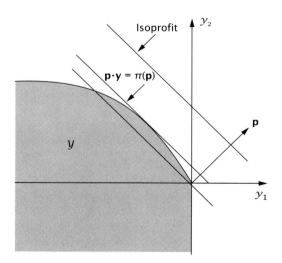

FIGURE 3.7 The profit function.

of this similarity, the following properties of the profit function are easily established by the same methods as used to prove the analogous properties of the cost function.

Proposition 3.1.   *The profit function $\pi(\mathbf{p})$ is*

(a) *Homogeneous of degree 1: $\pi(t\mathbf{p}) = t\pi(\mathbf{p})$ for $t > 0$;*

(b) *Convex in $\mathbf{p}$.*

Example 3.8 (Cobb-Douglas).   Consider the Cobb-Douglas production function $q = z_1^\alpha z_2^\beta$, with $\alpha + \beta < 1$, $0 < \alpha$, $0 < \beta$. Let p_1 and p_2 be the prices for the two inputs and let p_3 be the price for output. The profit function is

$$\pi(p_1, p_2, p_3) = \max_{z_1, z_2} \; p_3 z_1^\alpha z_2^\beta - p_1 z_1 - p_2 z_2.$$

It can be easily shown that this has the value

$$\pi(p_1, p_2, p_3) = \gamma \left(\frac{\alpha}{p_1} \right)^{\alpha/\gamma} \left(\frac{\beta}{p_2} \right)^{\beta/\gamma} p_3^{1/\gamma},$$

where $\gamma = 1 - \alpha - \beta$.

Example 3.9 (Skyscraper economics).   In Section 3.5 we deduced the production function

$$q = \frac{\ln[1 + (\gamma - 1)K]}{\ln \gamma}$$

for construction of office space on one unit of land using construction K. We also found the maximum profit associated with construction price w and output price p to be

$$\pi(w, p) = \frac{p}{\ln \gamma} \left\{ \ln \left[\frac{p(\gamma - 1)}{w \ln \gamma} \right] - 1 \right\} + \frac{w}{\gamma - 1},$$

which is the profit function for this technology.

Hotelling's Lemma

The profit function contains a great deal of information about $\mathcal{Y}$. Indeed, to find the function $\pi(\mathbf{p})$ it is necessary to find the maximizing value of $\mathbf{y}(\mathbf{p}) \in \mathcal{Y}$ for each $\mathbf{p}$ and then evaluate $\mathbf{p} \cdot \mathbf{y}(\mathbf{p})$. The following lemma shows that the process can in a sense be reversed: starting with the function $\pi(\mathbf{p})$, it is possible to find the corresponding optimal netput vectors $\mathbf{y}(\mathbf{p})$. This process is analogous to that of Shephard's lemma.

Hotelling's lemma.   *Let* y(p) *be the function that gives the point of maximum profit as a function of* **p**. *Assume that the profit function* $\pi(\mathbf{p})$ *is differentiable at a point* **p** > **0**. *Then at that point*

$$y_i(\mathbf{p}) = \frac{\partial \pi(\mathbf{p})}{\partial p_i}, \qquad i = 1, 2, \ldots, m.$$

Proof: The proof parallels that of Shephard's lemma and is left to the reader. ∎

Example 3.10.   The profit function for the Cobb-Douglas production function was found above to be

$$\pi(p_1, p_2, p_3) = \gamma \left(\frac{\alpha}{p_1}\right)^{\alpha/\gamma} \left(\frac{\beta}{p_2}\right)^{\beta/\gamma} p_3^{1/\gamma}$$

where $\gamma = 1 - \alpha - \beta$. Hotelling's lemma leads immediately to

$$z_1 = \left(\frac{\alpha}{p_1}\right)^{(1-\beta)/\gamma} \left(\frac{\beta}{p_2}\right)^{\beta/\gamma} p_3^{1/\gamma}$$

$$z_2 = \left(\frac{\alpha}{p_1}\right)^{\alpha/\gamma} \left(\frac{\beta}{p_2}\right)^{(1-\alpha)/\gamma} p_3^{1/\gamma}$$

$$q = \left(\frac{\alpha}{p_1}\right)^{\alpha/\gamma} \left(\frac{\beta}{p_2}\right)^{\beta/\gamma} p_3^{(\alpha+\beta)/\gamma}.$$

The expression for q agrees with (3.16), which was derived directly from the necessary conditions (or the basic production law). The expressions for z_1 and z_2 are the unconditional factor demands. These agree with (3.17), which was obtained by combining the output and substitution effects.

CRTS Technologies

A simple, two-dimensional, constant-returns-to-scale (CRTS) technology together with some isoprofit lines is shown in Fig. 3.8. It should be evident from the figure that $\pi(\mathbf{p})$ can take only two values for $\mathbf{p} \geq 0$. It is either infinite (as for $\mathbf{p}_1$ in the figure) or zero (as for $\mathbf{p}_2$), in agreement with our earlier discussion of CRTS technologies and perfect competition in Section 3.5. We can prove this conclusion holds generally very simply. A production possibility set $\mathcal{Y}$ is CRTS if $\mathbf{y} \in \mathcal{Y}$ implies that $t\mathbf{y} \in \mathcal{Y}$ for all $t > 0$. (See Exercise 7, Chapter 2.) Suppose $\mathbf{p} \cdot \mathbf{y} > 0$ for some $\mathbf{y} \in \mathcal{Y}$. Then since $t\mathbf{y} \in \mathcal{Y}$ for all $t > 0$, and since $t\mathbf{p} \cdot \mathbf{y} \to \infty$ as $t \to \infty$, it follows that $\pi(\mathbf{p}) = \infty$. Hence either $\pi(p) = 0$ or $\pi(p) = \infty$.

There are two ways to treat the potentially infinite value of the profit function. One way is to allow infinity as a legitimate value of an *extended* profit function. The properties stated in Proposition 3.1 (homogeneity and convexity) formally still hold for these extended functions. Of course, Hotelling's lemma will not apply at points where $\pi(\mathbf{p}) = \infty$.

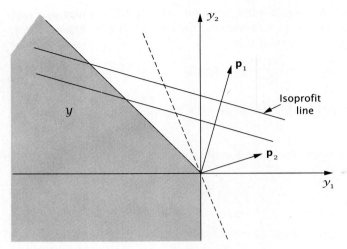

FIGURE 3.8 $\pi(\mathbf{p})$ for CRTS technology.

The second way to treat such technologies is to restrict the domain of the function π to those $\mathbf{p}$'s that yield finite values (which for CRTS technologies will be the value zero). In this treatment the domain must accompany the definition of the function.

The two methods are, of course, equivalent since in either case, for a CRTS technology, one must state where $\pi(\mathbf{p}) = 0$. For notational convenience the extended approach is often preferred since the single function π is a complete statement.

Example 3.11 (Leontief).   Consider the production function

$$q = \min\left[\frac{z_1}{a_1}, \frac{z_2}{a_2}, \dots, \frac{z_m}{a_m}\right].$$

We know that the corresponding cost function is $c(\mathbf{w}, q) = \mathbf{w} \cdot \mathbf{a}q$. Letting p denote output price and $\mathbf{w}$ input prices, it follows that

$$\pi(\mathbf{w}, p) = \max_{q \geq 0}\{pq - \mathbf{w} \cdot \mathbf{a}q\}.$$

This will be finite (equal to zero) if and only if $p \leq \mathbf{w} \cdot \mathbf{a}$. Hence in extended form

$$\pi(\mathbf{w}, p) = \begin{cases} 0 & \text{if } p \leq \mathbf{w} \cdot \mathbf{a} \\ \infty & \text{otherwise}. \end{cases}$$

Comparative Statics

A comparative statics analysis follows directly from the definition of the profit function. The general approach is discussed in Appendix D, but we shall sketch the details here for this particular case. From Hotelling's lemma we have

$$y_i = \frac{\partial \pi(\mathbf{p})}{\partial p_i}.$$

Hence

$$\frac{\partial y_i}{\partial p_j} = \frac{\partial^2 \pi}{\partial p_i \partial p_j}.$$

Since $\pi(\mathbf{p})$ is convex with respect to $\mathbf{p}$ the Hessian matrix of partial derivatives $[\partial^2 \pi / \partial p_i \partial p_j]$ is positive semidefinite. Therefore we obtain the following:

1. *The own price is nonnegative.* That is,

$$\frac{\partial y_i}{\partial p_i} \geq 0.$$

   This is certainly in accord with the intuition that if an output price is increased, more of that good will be produced, whereas if a factor price is increased, less of that factor will be demanded.

2. *The cross effects are symmetric.* That is, for all i and j

$$\frac{\partial y_i}{\partial p_j} = \frac{\partial y_j}{\partial p_i}.$$

3. *The average price effect is nonnegative.* That is,

$$\mathbf{dp} \cdot \mathbf{dy} \geq 0.$$

3.11 Duality and the Shortage Function

A basic feature of price vectors is that their scale is arbitrary. We can measure prices in any units at all, as long as we are consistent. Thus we can use U.S. dollars, British sterling, Japanese yen, and so forth. Converting prices from one set of units to another is accomplished by multiplying all prices by the appropriate conversion factor.

One way to establish a suitable set of units for prices is arbitrarily to set the price of a certain bundle $\mathbf{g}$ of goods equal to 1; that is, we can scale prices so that $\mathbf{p} \cdot \mathbf{g} = 1$. For example, we might take $\mathbf{g}$ to be the bundle consisting of an ounce of gold, in which case prices are all measured relative to gold.

If a reference bundle is chosen to scale prices, it becomes simpler to determine profit directly from a figure showing the production possibility set, such as shown in Fig. 3.9. Let us take $\mathbf{g} = (1, 0)$, meaning that prices $\mathbf{p}$ always have $p_1 = 1$. Consider a hyperplane (which in the two-dimensional case is really a line) defined by $\mathbf{p} \cdot \mathbf{y} = c$, for some constant c. Consider also

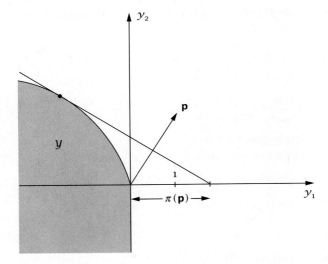

FIGURE 3.9   Profit when prices are normalized.

the point of the form $\mathbf{y} = (y_1, 0)$ on that line, which is the point where the line crosses the y_1 axis. For that point we have $\mathbf{p} \cdot \mathbf{y} = p_1 y_1 = y_1 = c$. That is, for this setup the value of y_1 where the line crosses the horizontal axis is equal to the constant c.

Let us apply this fact to the determination of profit. Given a price vector $\mathbf{p}$, the profit $\pi(\mathbf{p})$ is the maximum value of $\mathbf{p} \cdot \mathbf{y}$ for $\mathbf{y} \in \mathcal{Y}$. Hence when $\mathbf{p}$ is normalized with $p_1 = 1$, the value of $\pi(\mathbf{p})$ equals the y_1 intercept of the line tangent to $\mathcal{Y}$, as shown in the figure. This makes it easy to determine $\pi(\mathbf{p})$ graphically.

The Shortage Function

Recall that the production possibility set $\mathcal{Y}$ can frequently be represented in terms of a transformation function with the representation being of the form $\mathcal{Y} = \{\mathbf{y} : T(\mathbf{y}) \leq 0\}$. A convenient way to construct such a transformation function is to select a reference vector $\mathbf{g}$ and use the corresponding shortage function $\sigma(\mathbf{y})$. This shortage function is intimately related to the profit function, as shown by the following proposition.

Proposition 3.2 *Suppose* $\mathcal{Y}$ *is closed. Suppose* $\mathbf{p} \in \mathcal{R}^m$ *with* $\mathbf{p} \cdot \mathbf{g} = 1$. *Then*[2]

$$\pi(\mathbf{p}) = \max_{\mathbf{y} \in \mathcal{R}^m} \{\mathbf{p} \cdot \mathbf{y} - \sigma(\mathbf{y})\}.$$

---

[2]Throughout we assume that all maxima are achieved (or are infinite). If this assumption is not true, the proposition can nevertheless be made to hold if the maximization operations are replaced by supremum operations.

Proof. Fix $\mathbf{p} \in \mathcal{R}^m$ with $\mathbf{p} \cdot \mathbf{g} = 1$. Select $\mathbf{y} \in \mathcal{R}^m$. We shall first show that the inequality $\pi(\mathbf{p}) \geq \mathbf{p} \cdot \mathbf{y} - \sigma(\mathbf{y})$ holds. There are three cases: (*a*) $\sigma(\mathbf{y}) = +\infty$, (*b*) $\sigma(\mathbf{y}) = -\infty$, and (*c*) $-\infty < \sigma(\mathbf{y}) < +\infty$. In case (*a*), clearly $\pi(\mathbf{p}) \geq \mathbf{p} \cdot \mathbf{y} - \sigma(\mathbf{y})$. In case (*b*), for arbitrarily large β we have $\mathbf{y} + \beta\mathbf{g} \in \mathcal{Y}$, and correspondingly $\pi(\mathbf{p}) \geq \mathbf{p} \cdot (\mathbf{y} + \beta\mathbf{g}) = \mathbf{p} \cdot \mathbf{y} + \beta$. Thus $\pi(\mathbf{p}) = +\infty$, and again the inequality holds. In case (*c*) we have $\mathbf{y} - \sigma(\mathbf{y})\mathbf{g} \in \mathcal{Y}$ and hence $\pi(\mathbf{p}) \geq \mathbf{p} \cdot (\mathbf{y} - \sigma(\mathbf{y})\mathbf{g}) = \mathbf{p} \cdot \mathbf{y} - \sigma(\mathbf{y})$, which again is the desired inequality. Thus, since $\mathbf{y} \in \mathcal{R}^m$ was arbitrary, we have

$$\pi(\mathbf{p}) \geq \max_{\mathbf{y} \in \mathcal{R}^m} \{\mathbf{p} \cdot \mathbf{y} - \sigma(\mathbf{y})\}.$$

To prove the converse, we note that for $\mathbf{y} \in \mathcal{Y}$ there holds $\sigma(\mathbf{y}) \leq 0$ and thus

$$\pi(\mathbf{p}) = \max_{\mathbf{y} \in \mathcal{Y}} \mathbf{p} \cdot \mathbf{y} \leq \max_{\mathbf{y} \in \mathcal{Y}} \{\mathbf{p} \cdot \mathbf{y} - \sigma(\mathbf{y})\} \leq \max_{\mathbf{y} \in \mathcal{R}^m} \{\mathbf{p} \cdot \mathbf{y} - \sigma(\mathbf{y})\}. \quad \blacksquare$$

The relation between the profit function and the shortage function given by Proposition 3.2 is shown graphically in Fig. 3.10. We again take $\mathbf{g} = (1, 0)$ and normalize prices so that $\mathbf{p} \cdot \mathbf{g} = 1$. For any $\mathbf{y}^1$ we can evaluate $\mathbf{p} \cdot \mathbf{y}^1$ easily when $\mathbf{p}$ is normalized this way. We first form the line perpendicular to $\mathbf{p}$ that represents the set of solutions to $\mathbf{p} \cdot \mathbf{y} = c$ through $\mathbf{y}^1$. The constant c is equal to the y_1 intercept of this line, and hence this intercept is equal to $\mathbf{p} \cdot \mathbf{y}^1$. This is shown for a particular, but arbitrary, point $\mathbf{y}^1$ in the figure. Likewise, the profit $\pi(\mathbf{p})$ corresponding to $\mathbf{p}$ is the y_1 intercept of the line orthogonal to $\mathbf{p}$ but tangent to the set $\mathcal{Y}$ as shown. The shortage value

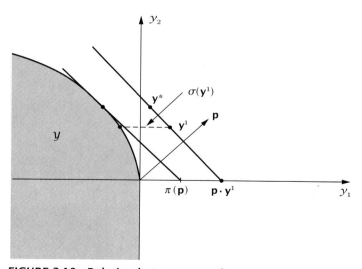

FIGURE 3.10   Relation between π and σ.

$\sigma(\mathbf{y}^1)$ on the other hand is the horizontal distance from $\mathbf{y}^1$ to the set $\mathcal{Y}$. This is shown as a dashed line in the figure. It is clear that in general

$$\pi(\mathbf{p}) \geq \mathbf{p} \cdot \mathbf{y}^1 - \sigma(\mathbf{y}^1).$$

If $\mathbf{y}$ is chosen just right—namely, as the point $\mathbf{y}^*$ in the figure—then

$$\pi(\mathbf{p}) = \mathbf{p} \cdot \mathbf{y}^* - \sigma(\mathbf{y}^*).$$

The formula $\pi(\mathbf{p}) \geq \mathbf{p} \cdot \mathbf{y} - \sigma(\mathbf{y})$ has a simple economic interpretation. Since $\mathbf{g}$ (for example, gold) is established as a reference, the term $\mathbf{p} \cdot \mathbf{y}$ measures the value of $\mathbf{y}$ in terms of $\mathbf{g}$. Likewise, $\sigma(\mathbf{y})$ measures how short $\mathbf{y}$ is from feasibility in terms of $\mathbf{g}$; that is, it measures how much $\mathbf{g}$ would have to be supplied in addition to $\mathbf{y}$ in order to obtain feasibility. The difference $\mathbf{p} \cdot \mathbf{y} - \sigma(\mathbf{y})$ is therefore the net value (in units of $\mathbf{g}$) for selecting $\mathbf{y}$ but restoring feasibility. To maximize profit, one finds $\mathbf{y}$ that maximizes this net quantity. This relation provides a direct connection between the purely physical characteristics of $\mathcal{Y}$ (which are captured by σ) and the economic characteristics (which are captured by π).

3.12 Exercises

1. XYZ Computer makes a small personal computer with a number of special features. XYZ's total cost function over the next year is

$$TC = 2.5 \times 10^6 + 2000q + \tfrac{1}{2}q^2.$$

XYZ sells in two distinct markets: domestic and foreign. The inverse demand functions in these two markets are

$$P_D = 9000 - 6q \quad \text{and} \quad P_F = 6000 - 3q,$$

respectively, where q is XYZ's sales in the market.

(a) If XYZ uses a common price in both markets, what is the overall effective inverse demand function? (Ignore complications due to end effects of the demand curves; i.e., assume that linearity applies even for nonpositive values.)

(b) What price will XYZ set for its computer, and how many units will be sold?

(c) Suppose now that XYZ decides to set two different prices, one for the domestic market and one for the foreign. How many units will be produced, and what will be the price in each market?

(d) Antidumping laws prohibit selling in the foreign market at a price that is below average cost. Would the solution found in (c) violate these laws?

2. (Learning curve) Because of learning, the marginal cost of production often tends to decrease as a function of total past production. We illustrate this with a firm producing a single product in each of two periods in quantities

q_1 and q_2, respectively. Costs are incurred at the end of each period according to the following cost functions:

$$c_1 = aq_1^{1/2}$$
$$c_2 = a(q_1 + q_2)^{1/2} - aq_1^{1/2}.$$

Assume that the revenue earned by the firm in period i is equal to $b \ln q_i$.

(a) Determine the firm's period one average and marginal cost as a function of q_1.

(b) Suppose the firm thinks it will go out of business after period 1. What is its optimal first-period output?

(c) Now suppose the firm decides to make its first- and second-period production decisions simultaneously by maximizing the sum of first- and second-period profits. What are the new optimal production decisions for periods 1 and 2?

(d) Using the results of part (c), compare the marginal revenue and period-1 marginal cost of the last unit produced in period 1. Explain why this relation holds.

3. (Innovation) Consider a perfectly competitive industry where all firms have constant marginal cost of, say, M. One firm has developed an innovation that reduces its marginal cost to $m < M$, and the firm has perfect patent protection for this innovation. The firm may license the innovation to other firms and receive a royalty L on each unit produced.

(a) Show that the innovating firm can make at least as much profit by licensing as by not licensing.

(b) Assume that $p'(q_0)q_0 + p(q_0) > 0$ at the original perfectly competitive solution, where $p(q)$ is the industry inverse demand function and q is the total demand. Show that for a sufficiently large innovation (m sufficiently small) the innovating firm can achieve complete monopoly profit either by acting as a monopolist or by licensing.

4. A producer of oil owns two kinds of oil fields. The cost function of field F is

$$C_F(q) = 2q^{3/2}$$

and the cost function of field G is

$$C_G(q) = 2q^2$$

where q is the production level. Find the supply function of this firm.

5. (Revenue function) A firm produces outputs $\mathbf{q}$ from inputs $\mathbf{z}$. The set of all possible $\mathbf{q}$'s that can be produced from a given $\mathbf{z}$ is the *conditional possibility set* $U(\mathbf{z})$. The *revenue function* is defined to be

$$R(\mathbf{p}, \mathbf{z}) = \max \mathbf{p} \cdot \mathbf{q}$$
$$\text{sub to } \mathbf{q} \in U(\mathbf{z}).$$

(a) Suppose output prices are fixed at $\mathbf{p}$ and there is only a single input, labor. Define $R(z) \equiv R(\mathbf{p}, z)$. Assume that the labor market is perfectly competitive at a wage rate w. Set up the firm's operating problem and, assuming interior solutions, find the firm's inverse demand function for labor $w(z)$ in terms of the revenue function $R(z)$.

(b) If average revenue per unit of labor is increasing, is average revenue above or below marginal revenue?

(c) Assuming that the average revenue function $R(z)/z$ is shaped like an upside-down U, sketch the firm's demand function for labor. Will the demand be positive at all wage rates?

(d) In the general, multidimensional case, is the revenue function $R(\mathbf{p}, \mathbf{z})$ convex or concave with respect to $\mathbf{p}$?

(e) Find a formula analogous to Shephard's lemma for the conditional supply $\mathbf{q}(\mathbf{p}, \mathbf{z})$ in terms of $R(\mathbf{p}, \mathbf{z})$.

6. (Airline operation) The cost of many industries has the approximate form

$$c(q, K) = \begin{cases} mq + bK & \text{for } q \le tK \\ \infty & q > tK \end{cases}$$

where K is a level of capital and q is output level. The number tK is the capacity supplied by capital K. An example is an airline, where K is the number of airplanes and q is the number of passengers. Find the supply function $q(p)$ for such a firm, and calculate the corresponding functions $K(p)$ and $r(p)$ where $r(p)$ is the load factor (i.e., $r = q/tK$). Assume that the cost of capital is 1.

7. The AE Brick Company has been operating two plants, A and E, in a region. Both plants have been profitable until recently, when a slowdown in the housing market caused a decrease in demand for bricks. In particular, E has higher labor costs, and although profitable when first opened, it now appears to be barely able to cover its variable costs. Management fears that a further drop in the price of bricks may force the closing of E, which would cause great hardship to the many employees who would be laid off.

The market for bricks has been competitive, although there are only four regional suppliers: AE and three other firms, B, C, and D, who operate one plant each. An operating plant principally incurs labor and material costs, which are variable costs, and can produce output up to the designed capacity limit for that plant. In addition, a firm incurs recurring annual fixed costs (mortgage, insurance, property taxes, etc.).

An analyst has provided the following estimates of costs and capacities of the five plants:

Plant	Fixed cost (dollars/unit capacity)	Variable cost (dollars/brick)	Capacity (thousands)
A	0.60	1.80	100
B	0.60	2.00	50
C	0.40	2.60	50
D	0.20	2.70	50
E	0.15	3.00	75

(a) Sketch (fairly accurately) the short-term industry supply curve.

(b) It is estimated that the current inverse demand curve for bricks is $p = 5.75 - q/100$ where q is in thousands. Because of the slowdown, the analyst believes that the inverse demand curve in the coming years will be $p = 5.40 - q/100$. What is the current equilibrium price? Can this price be sustained with the projected new demand curve?

(c) A consultant has suggested the following aggressive (and perhaps illegal) strategy for AE to consider. Instead of shutting down E, cut the price to try to cause other suppliers to shut down. It is felt that any firm will shut down permanently if it sustains a loss of at least $10,000 in one year. After some firms drop out, the price could be raised to a level at which E is again profitable. If this strategy were implemented, at what level should the interim price be set? Which firm(s) can be expected to drop out? What will be the new pure competitive price? Will E in fact be profitable at the new price? (Assume that all firms sell at the price set by AE.)

(d) Assuming now that AE and only one other company are in the market, what is the oligopolistic price you would expect? What would be the profit for E at this price?

8. (Class demonstration) Divide the class into six teams and give each team $40 of play money. Each team may operate a factory with production function $q = GL$. Factor prices are $p_G = \$4$ and $p_L = \$1$. Teams can purchase these factors with their money and thereby produce according to the production function. Total output determines the price according to the industrywide inverse demand function $p = 70/q^{3/4}$ for one period. Teams are then paid for their production at this price.

   Using previous profits, teams operate for a new cycle (new G and L are purchased, new output levels are determined, and new output prices are found from the inverse demand function). This is continued for several cycles. Teams try to accumulate as much money as possible. (Negotiation between teams is allowed.) Discuss what characteristics of this situation lead to the observed results.

9. Let $c(\mathbf{q})$ be the cost function of a decreasing-returns-to-scale technology. Let p be the output price and let π be the maximum profit. Define a new technology that replicates the first one by a factor z. This technology can produce $\mathbf{q}$ for a (variable) cost of $zc(\mathbf{q}/z)$. The quantity z can be thought of as the capital associated with the decreasing returns. If a price (or rent) r is assigned to z, the total cost of operating at scale z is $rz + zc(\mathbf{q}/z)$. Find the value of r (in terms of π) that makes $z = 1$ the optimal scale.

10. (Price discrimination) Suppose a firm with constant marginal cost sells in two markets with demand functions

$$q_1 = A_1 - B_1 p, \qquad q_2 = A_2 - B_2 p.$$

The firm may either use a single price or discriminate by using a different price in each market. Let π_1 and π_2 denote the profits obtained in these two cases, respectively. Assume that the parameters are such that in every case the optimal solution is interior (i.e., $q > 0$, $p > 0$).

(a) Show that the total amount sold is the same in both cases.

(b) Show that

$$\pi_2 - \pi_1 = \frac{(A_1 B_2 - A_2 B_1)^2}{4 B_1 B_2 (B_1 + B_2)}.$$

11. (Edison's invention)[3]

> I was the first manufacturer in the United States to adopt the idea of dumping surplus goods upon the foreign market. Thirty years ago my balance sheet showed me that I was not making much money. My manufacturing plant was not running to its full capacity. I couldn't find a market for my products. Then I suggested that we undertake to run our plant on full capacity and sell the surplus products in foreign markets at less than the cost of production.
>
> Every one of my associates opposed me. I had my experts figure out how much it would add to the cost of operating the plant if we increased this production 25%. The figures showed that we could increase the production 25% at an increased cost of only about 2%. On this basis I sent a man to Europe who sold lamps there at a price less than the cost of production in Europe.

Suppose Edison's plant had constant marginal cost and fixed costs were $2,875 per month. Suppose his original production level was 10,000 lamps per month and that a 25% increase corresponded to full capacity.

(a) Find the marginal cost of a lamp.

(b) Assume now that the marginal cost was 2.5 cents and the domestic price was 30 cents. If only the domestic market was served (with 10,000 lamps), what was the profit and average cost?

(c) Suppose an additional 2500 lamps were then sold in the foreign market at 20 cents each. What was the total profit and average cost?

12. A product has a marketwide linear inverse demand curve $p = A - Bq$. There are n producers of this product, each of which produces with constant marginal cost m. We have $A > m > 0$, $B > 0$.

(a) What price and total amount produced would prevail under perfect competition?

(b) Suppose total supply is determined by conditions of Cournot equilibrium for the oligopoly consisting of the n producers. Find the total amount produced Q, the price p, and the total profit π as a function of n.

(c) What are these values in the limit as $n \to \infty$?

13. Each oil well in an oil field with N wells operating from a single reservoir produces at a rate

$$q(N, t) = q_0 e^{-D(N)t}.$$

(a) Show that the decline rate $D(N)$ is linear in N if the total amount of oil Q_T that can be recovered from the reservoir is a constant independent of N. Thus, drilling more wells leaves Q_T unchanged but allows quicker recovery.

(b) Assume that an oil producer is a price taker. Find the present value of profit as a function of N, given an annual discount rate r continuously compounded. (That is, profit rate at t is multiplied by e^{-rt} and the result integrated over t.) Include start-up costs C and operating costs W per year for each well. Disregard the discounted abandonment costs.

(c) Suppose you are considering the purchase of such an oil field. There are already fifteen wells each producing at a rate of 61 barrels per day at an annual decline rate of 15 percent. The price of oil is $10 per barrel. Find the market value of the oil in the field (neglecting extraction costs).

(d) Assume that the price of oil will remain at $10 per barrel and assume a discount rate of 10 percent. Also assume that $C = $80,000 per well and $W = $23,000 per well-year. Find the present value of the field and the optimal number of wells. (It may be beneficial to install additional wells.)

14. (Stackelberg equilibrium) Suppose there are two firms in an industry with profits defined, respectively, by

$$\pi_1(q_1, q_2) = (a - q_1 - q_2)q_1 - b_1 q_1^2,$$
$$\pi_2(q_1, q_2) = (a - q_1 - q_2)q_2 - b_2 q_2^2.$$

(a) Find the Cournot equilibrium and the corresponding profits.

(b) Find the Stackelberg equilibrium and corresponding profits when firm 1 is the leader.

(c) What will the firms' profits and outputs be if they set output levels by collusion so as to maximize their joint (total) profits?

15. A firm has the cost function

$$c(\mathbf{w}, q) = q^2 \left(\frac{1}{w_1} + \frac{1}{w_2} + \frac{1}{w_3} \right)^{-1}.$$

(a) Find the conditional factor demands $z_i(\mathbf{w}, q)$, $i = 1, 2, 3$.

(b) Find the unconditional factor demands $z_i(\mathbf{p}, \mathbf{w})$, assuming that the firm faces a purely competitive market with output price p.

16. (Transfer pricing) Large firms are often organized into several divisions in such a way that the outputs of one division are used as inputs to the next. For example, engines and chassis components may be produced at different plants, but are combined in final assembly to produce automobiles. It is possible for a firm to coordinate the activities of its various divisions by means of a price system, granting each division a certain degree of autonomy while furthering the overall objective of the firm. These internal prices at which one division will "sell" its output to another are called *transfer prices*.

(a) Suppose a firm produces a final product q and an intermediate product x. The final assembly division combines x with other factors (which are fixed for the purposes of this problem) to produce q by means of the production function $q = f(x)$. The intermediate product division has a cost function $c(x)$. Let p be the price of the final product. What is the necessary condition for maximization of the overall profits of the firm?

(b) Suppose corporate management allows each division to make production decisions independently, but requires the assembly division to pay a price w per unit of x obtained from the intermediate division. The intermediate division receives w per unit of x it produces. State the necessary conditions for profit maximization by each division individually. How should management set the transfer price w (expressed in terms of $c(x)$)?

(c) Assume now that $f(x) = x^{3/4}$, $c(x) = \frac{3}{5}x^{5/4}$, and $p = 4$. What value of w should management choose? What levels of x and q will be produced?

(d) Suppose there is a market for x external to the firm, in which the firm can either buy or sell any amount at the market price. If the market price for x is 2, what should the transfer price w be, and how much q should the firm produce?

17. (Law of supply and demand) Let $\mathcal{Y}$ be a production possibility set. Assume that the profit function $\pi(\mathbf{p}) = \max\{\mathbf{p}\cdot\mathbf{y} : \mathbf{y} \in \mathcal{Y}\}$ exists for all $\mathbf{p} \geq \mathbf{0}$. Let $\mathbf{y}_0$ correspond to $\mathbf{p}_0$ and $\mathbf{y}_1$ correspond to $\mathbf{p}_1$ in the maximization. Show that $(\mathbf{p}_1 - \mathbf{p}_0)\cdot(\mathbf{y}_1 - \mathbf{y}_0) \geq 0$. Interpret this result in the cases where only a single input or single output price changes.

18. (a) Suppose a firm's technology is described by a transformation function $T(\mathbf{y})$, and suppose $\mathbf{y}^*$ is the feasible netput vector that maximizes $\mathbf{p}\cdot\mathbf{y}$. Show that

$$\frac{\partial T(\mathbf{y}^*)}{\partial y_i} \Big/ \frac{\partial T(\mathbf{y}^*)}{\partial y_j} = \frac{p_i}{p_j}$$

for all i, j.

(b) Suppose the transformation function is the shortage function $\sigma(\mathbf{y})$ relative to $\mathbf{g}$ and suppose $\mathbf{p}\cdot\mathbf{g} = 1$. Show that

$$\frac{\partial \sigma(\mathbf{y}^*)}{\partial y_i} = p_i$$

for all i. (Hence prices are marginal shortages, directly, without requiring ratios.)

(c) Suppose output is governed by $q = f(\mathbf{z})$. Let $\mathbf{g} = (\mathbf{0}, 1)$ and evaluate profit for this special case using Proposition 3.2, showing that this formula reduces to the standard formula.

3.13 References

3.1–3.7 Most of the material is quite standard. See the general references listed for Chapter 2. For an interesting early discussion of perfect competition see Robinson (1934).

3.8 For more material on price discrimination see Phlips (1983a) or Phlips (1983b). For a detailed survey of market structure and for a discussion on the legal constraints of price discrimination, see Scherer (1980).

3.9 The Cournot equilibrium was proposed in Cournot (1897) and later generalized by Nash (1954). In this form it is one of the main tools of microeconomics. The concept of monopolistic competition was devised by Chamberlain (1950).

3.10–3.11 The profit function was introduced by Hotelling (1932). For a detailed overview of duality see Diewert (1982). The duality between the shortage function and the profit function was shown in Luenberger (1992b).

Chapter 4
INDIVIDUAL PREFERENCES

A fundamental ingredient of microeconomic theory is a description of how individuals make economic decisions, that is, how individuals select certain alternatives from all those that are available. Modern theory postulates that each individual is able to order all available alternatives according to relative preference. Then, when faced with a choice, the individual selects the alternative that ranks most highly from among those that are feasible. This chapter develops the theoretical framework associated with the preference concept. It shows how preferences can be described in general, introduces utility functions, and presents several associated concepts and special cases. This framework is used in later chapters for analysis of decision-making situations. Specifically, the next chapter explores the implications of this preference framework for consumers selecting goods for purchase.

Part I
BASIC CONCEPTS

4.1 Individual Preferences

Assume that you are considering a collection of n alternatives. These may be n different objects that you can own, n different candidates for a public office whom you can vote for, or n different baskets (or bundles) of goods. Whatever the situation, if you list the n alternatives in order, from most desired to least desired, you have expressed a preference ordering. There may be ties, with some alternatives occurring at the same level in your list; this expression of indifference is allowed. However, there are two essential properties of your list. First, it is possible to compare any two alternatives, saying which of the two is higher, and hence the more preferred, or whether they are at the same level. Second, by its very nature, the list is noncyclic, or in other words, if one alternative is higher than a second, and that higher than a third, the first is also higher than the third.

Now, once this ordering is established, if only some of these alternatives are feasible, you will be able to select a most preferred feasible alternative, by running down your list until you reach the first feasible entry. Therefore the list provides a basis for making choices involving the alternatives on the list.

A general preference ordering is an extension of this idea to sets that may contain an infinite number of elements. In this case a list cannot be made, but nevertheless an ordering of elements can be established.

Formal Definition

Assume that there is a set X of possible alternatives to be considered by an individual. The set X may be simply a finite set of alternatives, or in the case of a consumer, it may represent the set of available consumption bundles. At this point, no restrictions need to be placed on X.

In general, a *binary relation* on X is a subset R of $X \times X$, the set of ordered pairs (x, y) with $x \in X$ and $y \in X$. Pairs in the subset R are said to *satisfy* the relation. A *preference relation* is a special case, and we write $x \succsim y$ if $(x, y) \in X \times X$ satisfies the relation. If $x \succsim y$, we say that x is *preferred* to y, although it is intended that *preferred* be interpreted in the weak sense of "at least as good as" rather than the strict sense of "better than." The symbol $\succsim$ is analogous to the numerical relation $\geq$. We write $y \precsim x$ to mean $x \succsim y$.

In order to qualify as a preference relation, the relation $\succsim$ must satisfy three fundamental properties:

Completeness.   For all elements x, y in X, either $x \succsim y$ or $y \succsim x$ (or both).

Reflexivity.   For all x in X, $x \succsim x$.

Transitivity.   For all x, y, and z in X, if $x \succsim y$ and $y \succsim z$, then $x \succsim z$.

Actually, the second of these follows from the first, but it is useful to include it since later we shall consider relaxing completeness.

The meaning of these properties should be quite clear. The first property simply says that any two elements in the set X can be compared. The second says that any element is preferred (in the weak sense, remember) to itself. The third property, that of transitivity, prevents circular preference relations and is really the heart of the preference concept.

It is useful to extend our notation somewhat. We write $x \succ y$ and say that x is *strictly preferred* to y if it is not true that $y \succsim x$. Finally, we write $x \sim y$ and say that x is *equivalent* or *indifferent* to y if both $x \succsim y$ and $y \succsim x$ are true.

A preference relation on X is also termed a *weak ordering* or simply an *ordering* of X. This is because the relation $\succsim$ has many of the properties of the relation $\geq$, which establishes an ordering of the real numbers. It is termed a weak ordering because it is possible for $x \sim y$ with $x \neq y$. An ordering in which ties of this kind do not occur in called a *strong ordering*. We use the terms *preference relation, ordering,* and *preference ordering* interchangeably.

Example 4.1 (Finite set).   In the case where X consists of a finite set of elements, a preference relation can be described, as discussed above, by making a list of equivalent elements, beginning with the most preferred group. One first finds an element over which no element is strictly preferred. Then all elements equivalent to this element are listed together in the first group. The process is then repeated with the set of remaining elements to determine the next group, and so forth. The result of this process is, for example, a list of the form

$$\begin{array}{llll} x^1 & x^2 & x^3 & x^4 \\ x^5 & x^6 & x^7 \\ x^8 & x^9 & x^{10} & x^{11} \\ x^{12} \end{array}$$

where x^1, x^2, x^3, and x^4 represent the elements of the most preferred group, $x^5, x^6,$ and x^7 the next, and so forth. The preference relation $x^i \succsim x^j$ is satisfied if x^i is at least as high on the list as x^j.

Example 4.2 (Summation ordering).   We shall illustrate the ordering concept by a purely mathematical relation, not intended to convey any "preference" interpretation. Let $X = \mathcal{R}^m$; that is, X consists of all m-tuples of the form $\mathbf{x} = (x_1, x_2, \ldots, x_m)$. Define the ordering $\mathbf{x} \succsim \mathbf{y}$ to mean that $\sum_{i=1}^{m} x_i \geq \sum_{i=1}^{m} y_i$. This is clearly a complete, reflexive, and transitive relation. It can be interpreted as "$\mathbf{x}$ is preferred to (ranked at least as high as) $\mathbf{y}$ if the sum of the components of $\mathbf{x}$ is at least as great as the sum of the components of $\mathbf{y}$."

Example 4.3 (Lexicographic ordering).   An interesting ordering on $X = \mathcal{R}^m$ is the lexicographic ordering, based on the way one orders words alphabetically. It is defined as follows: $\mathbf{x} \succsim \mathbf{y}$ if there is a j, $1 \leq j \leq m$, such that $x_i = y_i$ for $i < j$ and $x_j > y_j$, or if $x_i = y_i$ for all i, $1 \leq i \leq m$. Essentially the lexicographic ordering compares the components one at a time, beginning with the first, and determines the ordering based on the first time a difference is found; the vector with the greater component is ranked highest.

The lexicographic ordering could actually represent a preference ordering. For example, a voter may rank-order issues and then compare candidates by examining their records on those issues, one issue at a time.

Given a preference relation, a few other definitions and observations are useful. Corresponding to an element $x \in X$, we define the *indifference set* $\mathcal{I}(x) = \{y : y \sim x\}$, the set of all elements that are indifferent (or equivalent) to x. It can be easily shown (see Exercise 3a) that every x belongs to a unique indifference set. Also, corresponding to x we define the *preferred set* $\mathcal{P}(x) = \{y : y \succsim x\}$, alternatively called the *upper contour set*. Similarly, the *lower contour set* is $\{y : x \succsim y\}$. It is easy to see that the preferred sets are nested in that if $y \in \mathcal{P}(x)$, then $\mathcal{P}(y) \subset \mathcal{P}(x)$. Indeed there is a direct connection between a family of nested sets and a preference relation (see Exercise 7). It is useful to visualize a preference relation in terms of its preferred sets, especially in a continuum space such as $\mathcal{R}^m$, and this is emphasized in the next section.

Individual preference relations are central to the theoretical structure of microeconomics. However, the assumption that individuals possess preference relations that they use consistently is debatable. Experiments have revealed situations where either completeness or transitivity is not satisfied. Nevertheless, the assumption of the existence of individual preference relations is usually maintained because it is appealing, leads to a rich general theory of behavior, and does neatly explain much, but not all, observed decision-making behavior.

4.2 **Preferences on** $\mathcal{R}^m_+$

Preference relations are most frequently used in microeconomics to characterize a consumer's desires for various combinations of goods. The distinct goods are indexed from 1 to m and might range over everything from soup to automobiles, from tennis balls to vacuum cleaners. A *bundle* of goods is a collection of various amounts of these m goods. The amount of each good in a bundle is a nonnegative real number; hence, a bundle can be represented as an m-dimensional vector of nonnegative numbers. Here, we are essentially assuming that the goods are divisible, so that the m components can be any nonnegative numbers. It is therefore natural to take $X = \mathcal{R}^m_+$, the nonnegative orthant of $\mathcal{R}^m$. In this setting a preference relation can be visualized graphically, as shown in Fig. 4.1 for the two-dimensional case. Usually, in a well-behaved case, the indifference sets are curves and are called *indifference curves*. (The conditions for this are discussed later in this subsection.) In m dimensions, well-behaved indifference sets are surfaces of dimension $m - 1$. The upper contour sets are the sets above (and including) the indifference curves, and one such set is shown in the figure.

The shape of the indifference curves shown in Fig. 4.1, with curves flattening as one component gets large, reflects a general property that is expected to hold for preferences for bundles of goods. Specifically, imagine that the two components represent two different goods, such as bread and cheese. Suppose you have a relatively large amount of bread and not very

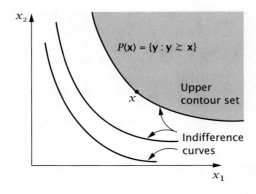

FIGURE 4.1   **Preferences in two dimensions.**

much cheese. Then a small further decrease in cheese must be compensated by a large increase in bread in order for you to be indifferent between the new and old positions. The same holds for the reverse situation. Thus ultimately, as the magnitude of one good is increased relative to another, the corresponding indifference curve tends to flatten.

In order to obtain strong theoretical results, certain additional, more precise assumptions concerning the nature of preference relations on $\mathcal{R}^m_+$ are introduced at various points in our development. Hence we introduce several standard definitions of additional properties. A most important property is that of continuity.

Continuity.   A preference relation on $X = \mathcal{R}^m_+$ is said to be *continuous* if for all $\mathbf{x}$ in X the sets $\{\mathbf{y} : \mathbf{y} \succsim \mathbf{x}\}$ and $\{\mathbf{y} : \mathbf{x} \succsim \mathbf{y}\}$ are closed.

With reference to Fig. 4.1, continuity assures that points on the boundary of $\mathcal{P}(\mathbf{x}) = \{\mathbf{y} : \mathbf{y} \succsim \mathbf{x}\}$ are equivalent to the element $\mathbf{x}$. (Note, however, that continuity does not rule out the possibility that indifference surfaces or curves may be "thick" closed sets, protruding within the corresponding preference or upper contour set.)

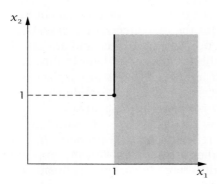

FIGURE 4.2 **Preferred set for lexicographic ordering.**

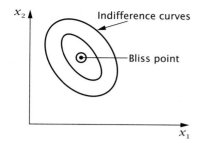

FIGURE 4.3 Bliss point.

Example 4.4 (Summation ordering). It is easily verified that the summation ordering defined in the last section is continuous.

Example 4.5 (Lexicographic ordering). The lexicographic ordering defined in the last section is *not* continuous. This is easily seen for the two-dimensional case by considering the upper contour set corresponding to the element $\mathbf{x} = (1, 1)$, that is, the set of elements $\mathbf{y} \succsim \mathbf{x}$. This set is shown in Fig. 4.2. It is clearly not closed because the boundary of the set below $(1, 1)$ is not contained in the set. For example $(1, \frac{1}{2}) \prec (1, 1)$ while $(1, 1\frac{1}{2}) \succsim (1, 1)$.

Nonsatiation. A preference relation $\succsim$ on X is *nonsatiated* if for all $\mathbf{x} \in X$, there is a $\mathbf{y} \in X$ with $\mathbf{y} \succ \mathbf{x}$.

The converse to the above definition is that there *is* an element $\mathbf{x}_0$ in X that is preferred to every other element. Such an element is often termed a *bliss point*. (See Fig. 4.3.) The existence of such elements is excluded in many theoretical developments.
A property slightly stronger than nonsatiation is the following.

Local nonsatiation. A preference relation on $X = \mathcal{R}^m_+$ satisfies *local nonsatiation* if for any $\mathbf{x}$ in X and any $\varepsilon > 0$ there is a $\mathbf{y}$ in X with $||\mathbf{x} - \mathbf{y}|| < \varepsilon$ such that $\mathbf{y} \succ \mathbf{x}$.

This means that for any point $\mathbf{x}$ there are nearby points that are strictly preferred to $\mathbf{x}$. This property together with continuity is sufficient to ensure that the preference or upper contour sets are closed, are infinite in extent, and do not have thick boundaries.
The next property is sometimes paraphrased as the "goods are good" property, for it implies that additional amounts of any component of the vector are always preferred.

Strong monotonicity. A preference relation on $X = \mathcal{R}^m_+$ is *strongly monotonic* if $\mathbf{x} \in X$, $\mathbf{y} \in X$, $\mathbf{y} \geq \mathbf{x}$, $\mathbf{y} \neq \mathbf{x}$ implies that $\mathbf{y} \succ \mathbf{x}$.

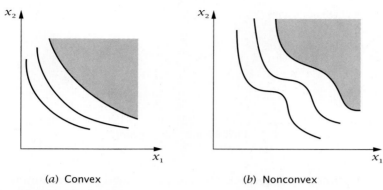

(a) Convex   (b) Nonconvex

FIGURE 4.4   Convexity.

Strong monotonicity implies local nonsatiation, and hence it is often used as a replacement for it. Strong monotonicity also has an important implication regarding the shape of the preference or upper contour sets. Consider any point $\mathbf{x}$ in X, and imagine that the positive orthant (in two dimensions this is the positive quadrant) is translated to the point $\mathbf{x}$; that is, consider the set $\{\mathbf{y} : \mathbf{y} \geq \mathbf{x}\}$. If the preferences are strongly monotonic, the upper contour set $\{\mathbf{y} : \mathbf{y} \succsim \mathbf{x}\}$ must contain this set. In two dimensions, this implies that the indifference curves slope downward, as depicted in Fig. 4.1.

Convexity.   A preference relation on $X = \mathcal{R}_+^m$ is *convex* if given $\mathbf{x}$, $\mathbf{y}$, and $\mathbf{z}$ in X such that $\mathbf{x} \neq \mathbf{y}$, $\mathbf{x} \succsim \mathbf{z}$, and $\mathbf{y} \succsim \mathbf{z}$, then for all α, $0 < \alpha < 1$, $\alpha\mathbf{x} + (1 - \alpha)\mathbf{y} \succsim \mathbf{z}$. Preferences are said to be *strictly convex* if the last relation is replaced by strict preference.

Convexity of preferences simply means that the upper contour sets are convex, as illustrated in Fig. 4.4. Convexity can be interpreted economically by considering two equivalent (equally preferred) elements, $\mathbf{x}_1$ and $\mathbf{x}_2$. An element of the form $\overline{\mathbf{x}} = \alpha\mathbf{x}_1 + (1 - \alpha)\mathbf{x}_2$, with $0 < \alpha < 1$, is a weighted average of the two, lying on the line segment between them; the convexity assumption states that it is at least as preferred as the original elements, $\mathbf{x}_1, \mathbf{x}_2$. In Fig. 4.4$a$ the preference relation is strictly convex. The contours could have some flat (straight line) segments and still be convex.

Even though we have incorporated some additional structure by considering orderings on $\mathcal{R}_+^m$ rather than on an arbitrary set X, it must be stressed that a preference ordering is an *ordinal*, rather than *cardinal*, concept. The relation $\mathbf{x} \succ \mathbf{y}$ means only that $\mathbf{x}$ is ordered higher than $\mathbf{y}$; it says nothing about how much higher.

Utility Functions

It is usually awkward to express preferences in the most general form of set relations. A great simplification is obtained when a preference relation can be represented numerically by a *utility function*. A utility function is a real-valued function u defined on the set X such that preference rankings over X are preserved by the magnitude of u. That is, a utility function u has the property that given any two elements $\mathbf{x}, \mathbf{y}$ in X, $u(\mathbf{y}) \geq u(\mathbf{x})$ if and only if $\mathbf{y} \succsim \mathbf{x}$.

Not all preference relations can be represented by utility functions, but it can be shown (although it is difficult) that any continuous preference relation on $\mathcal{R}_+^m$ can be represented by a continuous utility function. Rather than prove that general result here, we focus on a somewhat simpler result, but one that can be proved constructively. The idea of the construction is illustrated in Fig. 4.5. We select a fixed line that cuts all of the indifference curves (or, in general, indifference surfaces). Once utility is defined along this line, the utility of any other point is found by tracing the appropriate indifference curve to the line and using the utility value there. The assumption of strong monotonicity guarantees that the indifference curves exist and that any line of the form $\alpha\mathbf{e}$, $\alpha > 0$, with $\mathbf{e} > \mathbf{0}$, cuts them all.

Although the basic idea of the construction is simple, the detailed proof is a bit complicated. The reader can safely skip over the proof if the general idea is clear.

Existence of a utility function. *Suppose a preference relation is continuous and strongly monotonic on $X = \mathcal{R}_+^m$. Then a continuous utility function exists that represents that preference relation.*

Proof: Let $\mathbf{e} \in \mathcal{R}^m$ satisfy $\mathbf{e} > \mathbf{0}$. For any $\mathbf{x} \in X$ let $A = \{\alpha : \alpha \geq 0, \alpha\mathbf{e} \succsim \mathbf{x}\}$ and $B = \{\alpha : \alpha \geq 0, \mathbf{x} \succsim \alpha\mathbf{e}\}$. Both sets are nonempty by the assumption of strong monotonicity: A because $\alpha\mathbf{e} \geq \mathbf{x}$ for large α; B because it contains 0.

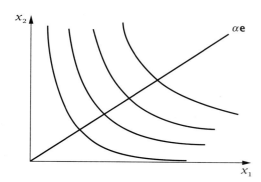

FIGURE 4.5 **Construction of utility function.**

Both A and B are closed by the continuity assumption. Every $\alpha \geq 0$ belongs to one of these sets by the completeness property of the preference relation. It follows that there must be a common point, say α, with $\alpha \mathbf{e} \sim \mathbf{x}$. This point is unique by strong monotonicity. We set $u(\mathbf{x}) = \alpha$.

Next we show that the function u represents the original preference relation. Suppose $\mathbf{x}, \mathbf{y} \in X$. By definition $\mathbf{x} \sim u(\mathbf{x})\mathbf{e}$ and $\mathbf{y} \sim u(\mathbf{y})\mathbf{e}$. If $u(\mathbf{x}) > u(\mathbf{y})$, then by strong monotonicity $u(\mathbf{x})\mathbf{e} \succ u(\mathbf{y})\mathbf{e}$. By transitivity (see Exercise 3), it follows that $\mathbf{x} \succ \mathbf{y}$. Conversely, if $\mathbf{x} \succ \mathbf{y}$, then by transitivity $u(\mathbf{x})\mathbf{e} \succ u(\mathbf{y})\mathbf{e}$, which again by strong monotonicity implies that $u(\mathbf{x}) > u(\mathbf{y})$. Similarly, it is easy to show that if $u(\mathbf{x}) = u(\mathbf{y})$, then $\mathbf{x} \sim \mathbf{y}$ and conversely. Therefore, $u(\mathbf{x}) \geq u(\mathbf{y})$ is equivalent to $\mathbf{x} \succsim \mathbf{y}$.

Finally, we show that the function u defined above is continuous. Suppose $\{\mathbf{x}_i\}$ is a sequence with $\mathbf{x}_i \to \mathbf{x}$. We want to show that $u(\mathbf{x}_i) \to u(\mathbf{x})$. Suppose not. Then we can find $\varepsilon > 0$ and an infinite number of i's such that $u(\mathbf{x}_i) > u(\mathbf{x}) + \varepsilon$ or an infinite set of i's such that $u(\mathbf{x}_i) < u(\mathbf{x}) - \varepsilon$. Without loss of generality let us assume the first of these. This means that $\mathbf{x}_i \sim u(\mathbf{x}_i)\mathbf{e} \succ u(\mathbf{x})\mathbf{e}+\varepsilon\mathbf{e} \sim \mathbf{x}+\varepsilon\mathbf{e}$. So by transitivity (see Exercise 3) $\mathbf{x}_i \succ \mathbf{x}+\varepsilon\mathbf{e}$. But for large i in our infinite set, $\mathbf{x} + \varepsilon\mathbf{e} > \mathbf{x}_i$, so $\mathbf{x} + \varepsilon\mathbf{e} \succ \mathbf{x}_i$. This is a contradiction, and hence u is continuous. ∎

The role of the utility function is to efficiently record the underlying preference ordering. The actual numerical values of u have essentially no meaning: only the sign of the difference in the value of u between two points is significant. This somewhat arbitrary nature of a utility function can be characterized explicitly by considering the ways one can transform a utility function without destroying its underlying relations. Specifically we can show that a utility function is unique only to within an arbitrary, strictly increasing transformation.

In what follows we let $\mathcal{U}$ denote the range of u; that is, as $\mathbf{x}$ varies over X, the values $u(\mathbf{x})$ vary over $\mathcal{U}$.

Proposition 4.1. *If a preference relation is represented by a utility function u over $\mathcal{R}^m_+$, then any function of the form*

$$v(\mathbf{x}) = f(u(\mathbf{x})), \tag{4.1}$$

where f is a strictly increasing function on the range $\mathcal{U}$ of u, is also a utility function representing the same preference relation. Furthermore, if u and f are continuous, then v is also continuous. Conversely, all utility functions representing that preference relation are of the form (4.1).

Proof: First let us check whether v of the form (4.1) is also a utility function. If $\mathbf{x} \succ \mathbf{y}$, then $u(\mathbf{x}) > u(\mathbf{y})$. Since f is strictly increasing, it follows that $f(u(\mathbf{x})) > f(u(\mathbf{y}))$. Hence $v(\mathbf{x}) > v(\mathbf{y})$. This argument can be reversed, so we have $v(\mathbf{x}) > v(\mathbf{y})$ if and only if $\mathbf{x} \succ \mathbf{y}$. Since the composition of two continuous functions is also continuous, v is continuous if u and f are continuous.

To prove the converse, let v be any utility function representing the same preference relation as u. It is clear that $u(\mathbf{x}) = u(\mathbf{y})$ if and only if $v(\mathbf{x}) = v(\mathbf{y})$ for either case implies $\mathbf{x} \sim \mathbf{y}$. It is also clear that $v(\mathbf{x}) > v(\mathbf{y})$ if and only if $u(\mathbf{x}) > u(\mathbf{y})$. Therefore we may write $v(\mathbf{x}) = f(u(\mathbf{x}))$ where f is strictly increasing. ∎

The foregoing proposition is a strong reminder that the utility value associated with a point $\mathbf{x}$ has no intrinsic meaning. That is why utility can be scaled arbitrarily, and even nonlinearly. As said before, only the sign of the difference of utility between two points matters.

Example 4.6 (Lexicographic ordering). Given a continuous utility function u the set $\{\mathbf{x} : u(\mathbf{x}) \geq \bar{u}\}$ must be closed for each value of u. It follows that the lexicographic ordering on $X = \mathcal{R}_+^m$ discussed earlier cannot be represented by a continuous utility function because its upper contour sets are not closed.

Example 4.7 (Cobb-Douglas utility). A utility function that is used frequently for illustrative and empirical purposes is the Cobb-Douglas utility function,

$$u(x_1, x_2, \ldots, x_m) = x_1^{\alpha_1} x_2^{\alpha_2}, \ldots, x_m^{\alpha_m}$$

with $\alpha_i > 0$, $i = 1, 2, \ldots, m$. This utility function represents a preference ordering that is continuous, strongly monotonic, and strictly convex.

The Cobb-Douglas form is popular because it is simple and it exhibits the general properties associated with many preferences. In particular, the associated indifference curves (or surfaces, in dimensions greater than 2) bend smoothly from nearly vertical to nearly horizontal. Also, as we shall see in later examples, the Cobb-Douglas form admits to rather easy analytic manipulation. It therefore frequently serves as a good concrete example to illustrate other concepts, and it provides a simple structure for approximating actual preferences in empirical investigations.

The important properties of a preference relation are reflected into analogous properties of any associated utility function—and these properties are then easy to verify by examination of the utility function. For example, an ordering is strongly monotonic if and only if any associated utility function is strongly monotonic as a function, that is, if $\mathbf{x} \geq \mathbf{y}$, $\mathbf{x} \neq \mathbf{y}$, implies $u(\mathbf{x}) > u(\mathbf{y})$. Likewise, if a utility function is continuous, the underlying ordering is continuous. Convexity of preferences is reflected as quasiconcavity of the utility function, as defined below.

Quasi-concavity. A function u is *quasi-concave* if $u(\mathbf{x}_1) \geq c$, $u(\mathbf{x}_2) \geq c$ implies that $u(\alpha \mathbf{x}_1 + (1 - \alpha)\mathbf{x}_2) \geq c$ for all α, $0 < \alpha < 1$. The function u is *strongly quasi-concave* if $\mathbf{x}_1 \neq \mathbf{x}_2$ and $u(\mathbf{x}_1) \geq c$, $u(\mathbf{x}_2) \geq c$ implies $u(\alpha \mathbf{x}_1 + (1 - \alpha)\mathbf{x}_2) > c$ for $0 < \alpha < 1$.

It should be noted that a function is quasi-concave if and only if for every real c the set $\{\mathbf{x} : u(\mathbf{x}) \geq c\}$ is convex.

See Appendix B for a bit more about quasi-concave functions. Since a utility function is quasi-concave if and only if every upper contour set is convex, a preference relation is convex if and only if any associated utility function is quasi-concave.

The Benefit Function

We now introduce an auxiliary function, derived from a utility function, that converts preferences into a numerical function that has some cardinal meaning. This function, the benefit function, is based on a reference commodity (or bundle) $\mathbf{g} \in X$ and uses this reference for utility comparison. The benefit function $b(\mathbf{x}, u)$ is defined for $\mathbf{x} \in X$ and values $u \in \mathcal{U}$. It measures how many units of $\mathbf{g}$ an individual would be willing to give up to move from a utility level u to the point $\mathbf{x}$. The formal definition is stated below.

Benefit function.   Let $\mathbf{g} \in X = \mathcal{R}_+^m$ with $\mathbf{g} \neq \mathbf{0}$. The *benefit function* with reference $\mathbf{g}$ is defined for $\mathbf{x} \in X$ and $u \in \mathcal{U}$ by

$$
b(\mathbf{x}, u) = \left\{ \begin{array}{l} \max\{\beta : u(\mathbf{x} - \beta\mathbf{g}) \geq u, \ \mathbf{x} - \beta\mathbf{g} \in X\} \\ \qquad \text{if } \mathbf{x} - \beta\mathbf{g} \in X \text{ and } u(\mathbf{x} - \beta\mathbf{g}) \geq u \text{ for some } \beta \\ -\infty \quad \text{otherwise.} \end{array} \right.
$$

The definition is illustrated in Fig. 4.6. Fig. 4.6a shows the normal situation where it is possible to move to the indifference curve defined by the value u in the direction $\mathbf{g}$. To find $b(\mathbf{x}, u)$, we gradually increase β, subtracting $\beta\mathbf{g}$ from $\mathbf{x}$, until we find the largest β that keeps $\mathbf{x} - \beta\mathbf{g}$ above the contour. That value of β is $b(\mathbf{x}, u)$. In the case shown, the benefit is positive, since the utility at $\mathbf{x}$ is greater than u and it is possible to give up some $\mathbf{g}$ in order to get back to utility level u. If $\mathbf{x}$ were below the indifference curve, the benefit would be negative. Fig. 4.6b shows a case where the benefit is positive, but it is not possible to get all the way back to the indifference curve. Finally, Fig. 4.6c shows a case where it is not possible to get a utility level of at least u by movement in the $\mathbf{g}$ direction. This corresponds to a benefit value of $-\infty$.

The reference bundle might, for example, be taken as a unit of gold. Then if you initially had a bundle of goods that yielded a utility level of u, the benefit function $b(\mathbf{x}, u)$ would measure how much gold you would be willing to trade for the opportunity to receive the bundle $\mathbf{x}$ rather than the one that you had initially. The benefit function therefore assigns a gold equivalent to every point $\mathbf{x}$. However, this gold equivalent amount depends on the value u taken as a reference point.

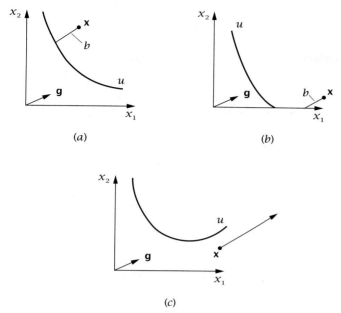

FIGURE 4.6   **The benefit function.**

Example 4.8 (Cobb-Douglas).   The general m-dimensional Cobb-Douglas utility function is

$$u(\mathbf{x}) = \prod_{i=1}^{m} x_i^{\alpha_i}, \qquad \alpha_i \geq 0, \quad i = 1, 2, \ldots, m.$$

Let us set $\mathbf{g} = (1, 0, \ldots, 0)$. Then

$$b(\mathbf{x}, u) = \max \ \beta$$
$$\text{sub to } (x_1 - \beta)^{\alpha_1} \prod_{j \neq 1} x_j^{\alpha_j} \geq u.$$

Hence we solve the equation

$$(x_1 - \beta)^{\alpha_1} \prod_{j \neq 1} x_j^{\alpha_j} = u$$

and the resulting β is $b(\mathbf{x}, u)$. Accordingly,

$$b(\mathbf{x}, u) = x_1 - \frac{u^{1/\alpha_1}}{\prod_{j \neq 1} x_j^{\alpha_j / \alpha_1}}.$$

The reference bundle $\mathbf{g}$ is arbitrary, but it would typically be selected as a bundle that individuals like. This idea is made precise by the following definition.

Good bundles.   A bundle $\mathbf{g}$ is said to be *good* (that is, $\mathbf{g}$ is a good bundle) if $u(\mathbf{x} + \alpha\mathbf{g}) > u(\mathbf{x})$ for all $\mathbf{x} \in X$ and all $\alpha > 0$. A bundle is *weakly good* if $u(\mathbf{x} + \alpha\mathbf{g}) \geq u(\mathbf{x})$ for all $\mathbf{x} \in X$ and all $\alpha > 0$.

Note that if preferences are strongly monotonic, any $\mathbf{g} \in \mathcal{R}_+^m$, $\mathbf{g} \neq \mathbf{0}$, is good.

The reader has perhaps noticed that the benefit function is constructed in a manner very similar to the shortage function for production possibility sets (see Section 2.3). Indeed, the two are related, but the benefit function is actually more useful than the shortage function, since it provides a convenient way to represent preferences, which are by their nature difficult to quantify meaningfully.

We now show that the utility of a point can be recovered from the benefit function by solving $b(\mathbf{x}, u) = 0$.

Proposition 4.2

(a) *If $\mathbf{g}$ is good, then $u(\mathbf{x}) = u$ implies that $b(\mathbf{x}, u) = 0$.*

(b) *If $\mathbf{x}$ is in the interior of X, then $b(\mathbf{x}, u) = 0$ implies that $u(\mathbf{x}) = u$.*

Proof

(a) Suppose $u(\mathbf{x}) = u$. Then clearly $b(\mathbf{x}, u) \geq 0$. However, since $\mathbf{g}$ is good, if $\mathbf{x} - \beta\mathbf{g}$ is feasible then $u(\mathbf{x} - \beta\mathbf{g}) < u(\mathbf{x}) = u$ for any $\beta > 0$. Hence, $b(\mathbf{x}, u) = 0$.

(b) If $\mathbf{x}$ is an interior point of X, then $b(\mathbf{x}, u) = 0$ implies that $u(\mathbf{x}) \geq u$ and $u(\mathbf{x} - \beta\mathbf{g}) < u$ for $\beta > 0$. By continuity $u(\mathbf{x}) = u$. ∎

The benefit function has a number of important properties (which are similar to those of a shortage function). Some of the main properties are stated below.

Proposition 4.3.   *The benefit function satisfies*

(a) *$b(\mathbf{x}, u)$ is nonincreasing with respect to u.*

(b) *If $\mathbf{x} \in \mathcal{R}_+^m$ and $\mathbf{x} + \alpha\mathbf{g} \in \mathcal{R}_+^m$, then $b(\mathbf{x} + \alpha\mathbf{g}, u) = \alpha + b(\mathbf{x}, u)$.*

(c) *If $u(\mathbf{x})$ is quasi-concave with respect to $\mathbf{x}$, then $b(\mathbf{x}, u)$ is concave with respect to $\mathbf{x}$.*

Proof: Parts (a) and (b) follow immediately from the definition. To prove (c), assume that the function u is quasi-concave. Let $\mathbf{x}_1, \mathbf{x}_2 \in \mathcal{R}_+^m$ be given. Select $u \in \mathcal{U}$. Suppose first that $b(\mathbf{x}_1, u)$ and $b(\mathbf{x}_2, u)$ are finite. Then, by definition,

$$u(\mathbf{x}_1 - b(\mathbf{x}_1, u)\mathbf{g}) \geq u$$
$$u(\mathbf{x}_2 - b(\mathbf{x}_2, u)\mathbf{g}) \geq u.$$

By quasi-concavity of the function u, it follows that

$$u(\alpha\mathbf{x}_1 - \alpha b(\mathbf{x}_1, u)\mathbf{g} + (1 - \alpha)\mathbf{x}_2 - (1 - \alpha)b(\mathbf{x}_2, u)\mathbf{g}) \geq u$$

for any α, $0 \leq \alpha \leq 1$. This means that

$$b(\alpha\mathbf{x}_1 + (1 - \alpha)\mathbf{x}_2, u) \geq \alpha b(\mathbf{x}_1, u) + (1 - \alpha)b(\mathbf{x}_2, u),$$

which shows that b is concave. If either $b(\mathbf{x}_1, u) = -\infty$ or $b(\mathbf{x}_2, u) = -\infty$, it follows (always) that $b(\alpha\mathbf{x}_1 + (1 - \alpha)\mathbf{x}_2, u) \geq -\infty$ and hence the concavity relation holds. ∎

The interpretation of these properties is quite straightforward. Part (a) simply states that benefit decreases (or does not increase) as u is increased. This is because benefit is measured relative to a given utility level u. If this reference level is increased, the benefit must decrease.

Part (b) is a translation property. If an individual is willing to trade an amount b of $\mathbf{g}$ for the opportunity to move from utility level u to $\mathbf{x}$, then that individual is willing to trade $b + \alpha$ for the opportunity to move from u to $\mathbf{x} + \alpha\mathbf{g}$. Since benefits are denominated in units of $\mathbf{g}$, the incremental benefit in moving from $\mathbf{x}$ to $\mathbf{x} + \alpha\mathbf{g}$ must be α.

The concavity property means that the benefit of an average is always at least as great as the average of the benefits; specifically, $b(\alpha\mathbf{x}_1 + (1 - \alpha)\mathbf{x}_2, u) \geq \alpha b(\mathbf{x}_1, u) + (1 - \alpha)b(\mathbf{x}_2, u)$. Concavity of the benefit function holds if the underlying preferences are convex—or equivalently, if the underlying utility function is quasi-concave. We frequently assume this property of preferences, and it is quite convenient that the corresponding benefit function reflects this property in the form of concavity.

We shall use the benefit function in much of our further development. It is an especially useful tool for combining preferences of different individuals, something for which utility functions are poorly suited.

4.3 Prices and the Basic Consumer Problem

There is strong interplay in microeconomic theory between quantities and prices of goods, with prices often being dual to quantities. This is evident in the theory of production, and it arises also in the theory of preference relations. It leads us quickly to the concept of indirect utility.

To appreciate the motivation for the introduction of prices, let us briefly describe the basic problem of the consumer—a problem that will be treated in greater detail in the next chapter. Assume that there are m commodities, which are infinitely divisible. A consumer selects a bundle of these commodities, described by the m-vector $\mathbf{x} = (x_1, x_2, \ldots, x_m)$, where x_i, $i = 1, 2, \ldots, m$, represents the amount of commodity i. The consumer's

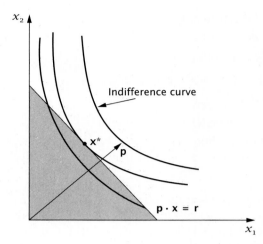

FIGURE 4.7   Consumer's choice.

preferences for the various possible bundles is represented by a preference relation on $\mathcal{R}_+^m$.

Associated with each commodity is a unit price (measured in some monetary measure) $p_i \geq 0$, so that the cost of choosing x_i is $p_i x_i$. The total cost of the bundle $\mathbf{x} = (x_1, x_2, \ldots, x_m)$ is therefore $\sum_{i=1}^m p_i x_i = \mathbf{p} \cdot \mathbf{x}$. The consumer is assumed to have a budget of r monetary units. (The letter r can be associated with the word *resources*.) Thus the consumer's choice is restricted by the budget constraint

$$\sum_{i=1}^m p_i x_i \leq r$$

or in vector notation

$$\mathbf{p} \cdot \mathbf{x} \leq r.$$

The situation is depicted in Fig. 4.7. The budget constraint defines the shaded triangular region. The diagonal edge of this region is perpendicular to the price vector $\mathbf{p}$ as indicated. If the budget r were changed, the edge of the region would move outward (for increasing r) or inward (for decreasing r) but would remain parallel to the original edge.

A consumer acting rationally on the basis of this information will select a bundle that is preferred to all others within the triangular region defined by the budget constraint. The above process thus determines a particular (not necessarily unique) preferred bundle, indicated by $\mathbf{x}^*$ in the figure. The solution shown is on the indifference curve of highest value that just touches the set of feasible bundles.

When preferences are described by a continuous utility function u, the basic consumer choice problem described above can be expressed as below.

Basic consumer problem.   Given prices $\mathbf{p}$ and budget r, the consumer solves

$$\max_{\mathbf{x}}\ u(\mathbf{x})$$

$$\text{sub to } \mathbf{p}\cdot\mathbf{x} \leq r \qquad\qquad (4.2)$$

$$\mathbf{x} \in X,$$

where $X = \mathcal{R}_+^m$.

We assume that this is a well-defined problem with a (possibly nonunique) solution $\mathbf{x}^*$. (If $\mathbf{p} > \mathbf{0}$, the problem is well defined because u is continuous and the set defined by the constraints is closed and bounded. For $\mathbf{p}$'s having some, but not all, zero components, some additional assumptions on u will ensure a solution.)

Note that the solution does not depend on the choice of utility function used to represent the preference relation, since all such utility functions have the same indifference surfaces. Use of a utility function merely provides a convenient way of expressing the consumer choice problem as a constrained maximization problem.

The Indirect Utility Function

Associated with problem (4.2) is a maximum utility value, achieved by the solution. This value is expressed by a special function.

Indirect utility function. Corresponding to a utility function u of $\mathbf{x} \in X = \mathcal{R}_+^m$ is an *indirect utility function* v depending on prices $\mathbf{p}$ and income r defined by[1]

$$v(\mathbf{p}, r) = \max_{\mathbf{x}}\ u(\mathbf{x})$$

$$\text{sub to } \mathbf{p}\cdot\mathbf{x} \leq r \qquad\qquad (4.3)$$

$$\mathbf{x} \in X.$$

The function v is termed the indirect utility function since it indirectly measures the utility associated with a given price and budget level. However, the indirect utility function does have significant meaning of its own. For instance, if $\mathbf{p}$ is decreased, normally a consumer will like the change, and that change is translated directly into utility terms by the indirect utility, indicating the new utility level that can be achieved with this $\mathbf{p}$. The indirect utility function (with r fixed) is illustrated in Fig. 4.8.

The indirect utility function satisfies several important properties.

Proposition 4.4. *The indirect utility function $v(\mathbf{p}, r)$ is*

(a) *Homogeneous of degree zero in $(\mathbf{p}, r)$: $v(t\mathbf{p}, tr) = v(\mathbf{p}, r)$ for all $t > 0$.*

(b) *Nonincreasing in $\mathbf{p}$ and nondecreasing in r.*

---

[1]The maximum will be achieved if $\mathbf{p} > \mathbf{0}$. In general we can replace the maximum operation by supremum, or *sup*. See Appendix A.

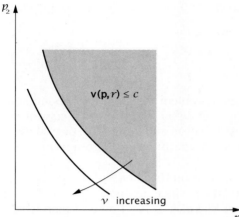

p_2

$v(\mathbf{p}, r) \le c$

v increasing

p_1 **FIGURE 4.8   Indirect utility.**

(c) *Quasi-convex with respect to* **p***: the set* $\{\mathbf{p} : v(\mathbf{p}, r) \le c\}$ *is convex for every* $r > 0$ *and* c.

Proof: Part (a) follows from the fact that multiplying both **p** and r by any $t > 0$ does not change the constraint region.

Part (b) follows from the fact that if $\mathbf{p}' \ge \mathbf{p}$, the corresponding constraint sets satisfy $\{\mathbf{x} : \mathbf{p}' \cdot \mathbf{x} \le r\} \subset \{\mathbf{x} : \mathbf{p} \cdot \mathbf{x} \le r\}$, and hence the maximum of u over the first of these is no greater than the maximum over the second. Hence $v(\mathbf{p}', r) \le v(\mathbf{p}, r)$. The argument for r is similar.

To prove part (c), let c be real and suppose $v(\mathbf{p}_1, r) \le c$ and $v(\mathbf{p}_2, r) \le c$. Then for any α, $0 < \alpha < 1$, let $\mathbf{p} = \alpha \mathbf{p}_1 + (1 - \alpha)\mathbf{p}_2$. Define the constraint sets $C_1 = \{\mathbf{x} : \mathbf{p}_1 \cdot \mathbf{x} \le r\}$, $C_2 = \{\mathbf{x} : \mathbf{p}_2 \cdot \mathbf{x} \le r\}$, and $C = \{\mathbf{x} : \mathbf{p} \cdot \mathbf{x} \le r\}$. We can show that $C \subset (C_1 \cup C_2)$: Given **x** with $\mathbf{x} \notin C_1 \cup C_2$, we have $\mathbf{p}_1 \cdot \mathbf{x} > r$ and $\mathbf{p}_2 \cdot \mathbf{x} > r$. Therefore $\alpha \mathbf{p}_1 \cdot \mathbf{x} + (1 - \alpha)\mathbf{p}_2 \cdot \mathbf{x} > \alpha r + (1 - \alpha)r = r$. Hence $\mathbf{x} \notin C$. Therefore $C \subset C_1 \cup C_2$.

Now $v(\mathbf{p}, r) = \max\{u(\mathbf{x}) : \mathbf{x} \in C\}$. But by the above, any $\mathbf{x} \in C$ must belong to either C_1 or C_2. Hence $v(\mathbf{p}, r) \le \max\{v(\mathbf{p}_1, r), v(\mathbf{p}_2, r)\}$. Therefore $v(\mathbf{p}, r) \le c$. ∎

The first property, homogeneity, is clear mathematically, as shown in the proof, but it also has an important economic interpretation. Prices are always subject to a scale-factor change, as, for example, a change of monetary unit from dollars to pounds. This will have no influence on the consumer's problem as long as both income and prices are changed together.

The second property, that $v(\mathbf{p}, r)$ is nonincreasing in **p** and nondecreasing in r was discussed above. This property has a clear economic interpretation.

The third property, the quasi-convexity of $v(\mathbf{p}, r)$, is not as simple to interpret economically. It is a result of the fact that $v(\mathbf{p}, r)$ is defined by an optimization problem. It is a very important property, and it should be noted that it holds even without the assumption that $u(\mathbf{x})$ is quasi-concave with respect to $\mathbf{x}$.

Note also that the indirect utility function is measured in units determined by the original utility function u and hence is defined only to within a strictly increasing, continuous transformation.

Example 4.9 (Cobb-Douglas). Consider again the m-dimensional Cobb-Douglas utility function

$$u(\mathbf{x}) = \prod_{i=1}^{m} x_i^{\alpha_i}, \quad \alpha_i \geq 0, \quad i = 1, 2, \ldots, m. \tag{4.4}$$

We define $\alpha = \sum_{i=1}^{m} \alpha_i$.

The corresponding indirect utility function is the value

$$v(\mathbf{p}, r) = \max \prod_{i=1}^{m} x_i^{\alpha_i}$$

$$\text{sub to } \mathbf{p} \cdot \mathbf{x} = r$$

$$\mathbf{x} \geq \mathbf{0},$$

where we have used equality in the budget constraint since for $\mathbf{p} \geq \mathbf{0}$ that clearly will be optimal for this utility function. The maximum is found by introducing a Lagrange multiplier λ and setting to zero the derivative of the Lagrangian with respect to x_i. This yields

$$\alpha_i x_i^{\alpha_i - 1} \prod_{j \neq i}^{m} x_j^{\alpha_j} - \lambda p_i = 0$$

for $i = 1, 2, \ldots, m$. Multiplication by x_i then yields

$$\alpha_i \prod_{j=1}^{m} x_j^{\alpha_j} - \lambda p_i x_i = 0$$

for $i = 1, 2, \ldots, m$. Using $\alpha = \sum_{i=1}^{n} \alpha_i$, summing these equations over i then gives

$$\alpha \prod_{j=1}^{m} x_j^{\alpha_j} - \lambda \mathbf{p} \cdot \mathbf{x} = 0$$

from which it follows that

$$\lambda = \frac{\alpha}{r} \prod_{j=1}^{m} x_j^{\alpha_j}.$$

Using this in the second equation above we find $\alpha_i = \alpha p_i x_i / r$, or

$$x_i = \frac{\alpha_i r}{\alpha p_i}, \tag{4.5}$$

which explicitly gives the optimal x_i in terms of p_i. Note that $p_i x_i = (\alpha_i/\alpha)r$, which says that commodity x_i is always allocated the portion α_i/α of the budget.

The indirect utility function is now easily found to be

$$v(\mathbf{p}, r) = \prod_{i=1}^{m} \left(\frac{\alpha_i r}{\alpha p_i} \right)^{\alpha_i} = \left(\frac{r}{\alpha} \right)^{\alpha} \prod_{i=1}^{m} \left(\frac{\alpha_i}{p_i} \right)^{\alpha_i}. \qquad (4.6)$$

This also has the Cobb-Douglas form (although with negative coefficients for the prices).

Example 4.10 (Leontief utility).   An interesting utility function is the Leontief fixed-proportions, or perfect complements, utility function

$$u(\mathbf{x}) = \min\left\{ \frac{x_1}{a_1}, \frac{x_2}{a_2}, \dots, \frac{x_m}{a_m} \right\}$$

where $\mathbf{a} = (a_1, a_2, \dots, a_m) > \mathbf{0}$. This represents a preference based on an ideal composite commodity $\mathbf{a}$. Utility increases only if there is an increase in the amount of this composite in the bundle $\mathbf{x}$. An example might be utility for coffee and cream, which an individual drinks only in fixed proportions. Additional cream without more coffee is of no value.

The indirect utility is found as

$$v(\mathbf{p}, r) = \max_{\mathbf{x}} \ \min\left\{ \frac{x_1}{a_1}, \frac{x_2}{a_2}, \dots, \frac{x_m}{a_m} \right\}$$
$$\text{sub to } \mathbf{p} \cdot \mathbf{x} = r$$
$$\mathbf{x} \geq \mathbf{0}.$$

The Leontief utility function is not differentiable, so the maximum must be found by a direct argument. Assume that $\mathbf{p} > \mathbf{0}$. Then, as should be clear from Fig. 4.9, $x_1/a_1 = x_2/a_2 = \cdots = x_m/a_m$ holds in an optimal solution.

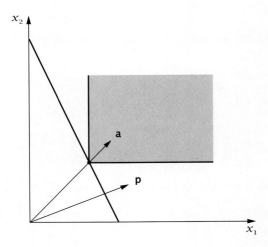

FIGURE   4.9 Leontief preferences.

Equivalently, $\mathbf{x} = \lambda\mathbf{a}$ for some λ. The budget constraint then produces $\lambda\mathbf{p}\cdot\mathbf{a} = r$, or $\lambda = r/\mathbf{p}\cdot\mathbf{a}$. Thus

$$\mathbf{x} = \frac{ar}{\mathbf{p}\cdot\mathbf{a}}. \tag{4.7}$$

We then calculate the indirect utility function to be

$$v(\mathbf{p}, r) = \frac{r}{\mathbf{p}\cdot\mathbf{a}}, \tag{4.8}$$

which by continuity holds for all $\mathbf{p} \geq \mathbf{0}$, $\mathbf{p} \neq \mathbf{0}$.

The Expenditure Function

A function closely related to the indirect utility function is the *expenditure function*. It is obtained by reversing the objective and constraints of problem (4.3) defining $v(\mathbf{p}, r)$.

Expenditure function. Corresponding to a utility function u, *the expenditure function is*[2]

$$
\begin{aligned}
e(\mathbf{p}, u) = \min\ &\mathbf{p}\cdot\mathbf{x} \\
\text{sub to}\ &u(\mathbf{x}) \geq u \\
&\mathbf{x} \in X.
\end{aligned} \tag{4.9}
$$

The value of the expenditure function is the minimum expenditure required to achieve utility level u. Note also that this is a well-defined problem if u is continuous and $\mathbf{p} > \mathbf{0}$. For if r is any upper bound on the value of $\mathbf{p}\cdot\mathbf{x}$ (which can be found by finding any value of $\mathbf{x}$ that satisfies the constraint), the constraint $\mathbf{p}\cdot\mathbf{x} \leq r$ can be appended, restricting the domain to a closed and bounded set but not changing the minimum value. The expenditure function satisfies the following properties:

Proposition 4.5. *The expenditure function $e(\mathbf{p}, u)$ is*

(a) *Homogeneous of degree 1 in $\mathbf{p}$.*

(b) *Nondecreasing in $\mathbf{p}$ and in u separately.*

(c) *Concave with respect to $\mathbf{p}$.*

Proof: Parts (a) and (b) follow easily from the definition. To prove part (c), let $\mathbf{p} = \alpha\mathbf{p}_1 + (1 - \alpha)\mathbf{p}_2$ for some α, $0 < \alpha < 1$. Then

---

[2]The minimum will exist if $\mathbf{p} > \mathbf{0}$. Otherwise, it can be replaced by the infimum, or *inf*. See Appendix A.

$$e(\mathbf{p}, u) = \min \ \alpha\mathbf{p}_1 \cdot \mathbf{x} + (1 - \alpha)\mathbf{p}_2 \cdot \mathbf{x}$$
$$\text{sub to } \ u(\mathbf{x}) \geq u$$
$$\mathbf{x} \in X.$$

Since the minimum of a sum is greater than or equal to the corresponding sum of the minima, we have $e(\mathbf{p}, u) \geq \alpha e(\mathbf{p}_1, u) + (1 - \alpha)e(\mathbf{p}_2, u)$. ∎

The first property, that $e(\mathbf{p}, u)$ is homogeneous of degree 1, means that if all prices are scaled by a certain factor, the required income must scale by the same factor.

The second property, that $e(\mathbf{p}, u)$ is nondecreasing, is also economically clear. If prices increase, the required income will certainly not decrease. Likewise, if one is to obtain increased utility, the required income cannot decrease.

The third property is again a convexity property, which at this stage we know is likely to be associated with a function defined through optimization.

The expenditure function is similar to the cost function of a firm. This is seen by considering the utility function as a kind of consumer production function: $\mathbf{x}$ goes in and "utility" comes out. For this reason the expenditure function is often called the *consumer's cost function*. Proposition 4.5 can therefore be regarded as a special case of the properties of cost functions.

Example 4.11 (Leontief utility).   Let us find the expenditure function of the Leontief utility function

$$u(\mathbf{x}) = \min\left\{\frac{x_1}{a_1}, \frac{x_2}{a_2}, \ldots, \frac{x_m}{a_m}\right\}.$$

Definition (4.9) is identical with the definition of the cost function for a Leontief technology with $u = u(\mathbf{x})$ denoting the production function. Hence, we have from Example 14 in Section 2.13

$$e(\mathbf{p}, u) = u\mathbf{p} \cdot \mathbf{a}.$$

As said earlier, the problems used to define the indirect utility function and the expenditure function are closely related, one being obtained by reversing the objective and constraint of the other. Indeed, under appropriate assumptions, they both yield the same solution point $\mathbf{x}$ if the constraints are consistent. This reciprocal relation is spelled out in the proposition below.

Proposition 4.6 (Equivalence).   *Assume that the utility function is continuous. Let* $\mathbf{x}^* \in X = \mathcal{R}_+^m$. *Define the two problems (and corresponding values)*

$$v(\mathbf{p}, r) = \max_{\mathbf{x}} \ u(\mathbf{x})$$
$$\text{sub to } \mathbf{p} \cdot \mathbf{x} \leq r \tag{4.10}$$
$$\mathbf{x} \in X$$

$$e(\mathbf{p}, u) = \min_{\mathbf{x}} \ \mathbf{p} \cdot \mathbf{x}$$

$$\text{sub to} \ \ u(\mathbf{x}) \geq u \qquad\qquad (4.11)$$

$$\mathbf{x} \in X.$$

Then

(a) *Assume that the preference satisfies local nonsatiation. If* $\mathbf{x}^*$ *solves problem (4.10), then* $\mathbf{x}^*$ *also solves problem (4.11) with* $u = v(\mathbf{p}, r)$.

(b) *Assume that* $\mathbf{p} \cdot \mathbf{x}^* > 0$. *If* $\mathbf{x}^*$ *solves problem (4.11), then* $\mathbf{x}^*$ *also solves problem (4.10) with* $r = e(\mathbf{p}, u)$.

Proof

(a) Suppose $\mathbf{x}^*$ solves (4.10) but not (4.11). Then there is an $\mathbf{x}$ with $\mathbf{p} \cdot \mathbf{x} < \mathbf{p} \cdot \mathbf{x}^*$ and $u(\mathbf{x}) \geq u$. By local nonsatiation there is an $\mathbf{x}_1$, near $\mathbf{x}$, with $\mathbf{p} \cdot \mathbf{x}_1 \leq \mathbf{p} \cdot \mathbf{x}^* \leq r$ and $u(\mathbf{x}_1) > u(\mathbf{x}) \geq u$. This $\mathbf{x}_1$ is feasible for (4.10) and yields $u(\mathbf{x}_1) > v(\mathbf{p}, r)$, which is a contradiction.

(b) Assume that $\mathbf{x}^*$ solves (4.11). Let $r = \mathbf{p} \cdot \mathbf{x}^* > 0$. We must show that if $\mathbf{x} \in X$ satisfies $\mathbf{p} \cdot \mathbf{x} \leq r$, then $u(\mathbf{x}) \leq u(\mathbf{x}^*)$. For this, consider such an $\mathbf{x}$ and let $\mathbf{x}' = \alpha \mathbf{x}$ for some $0 < \alpha < 1$. Clearly $\mathbf{p} \cdot \mathbf{x}' < r$. Therefore $\mathbf{x}'$ must be infeasible for (4.11), which means $u(\mathbf{x}') < u(\mathbf{x}^*)$. By continuity it follows that $u(\mathbf{x}) \leq u(\mathbf{x}^*)$. (See Fig. 4.10 for a case that does not work because $r = 0$. Expenditure is minimized at $\mathbf{x}^*$ but utility is not maximized using the vertical $\mathbf{p}$ shown.) ∎

There is a simple algebraic way to express the relations of the above proposition. Namely,

$$\text{(a)} \quad e(\mathbf{p}, v(\mathbf{p}, r)) = r \qquad\qquad (4.12)$$

$$\text{(b)} \quad v(\mathbf{p}, e(\mathbf{p}, u)) = u . \qquad\qquad (4.13)$$

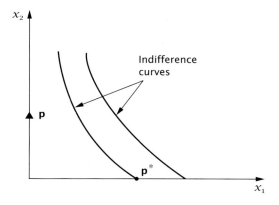

FIGURE 4.10   A case for which the reciprocal relation fails.

Part (*a*) above holds if there is local nonsatiation, and (*b*) holds if $e(\mathbf{p}, u) > 0$. These identities have clear intuitive meaning and show the interrelations between the various constructs based on utility.

Example 4.12 (Cobb-Douglas).   Let us determine the expenditure function for the Cobb-Douglas utility function

$$u(\mathbf{x}) = \prod_{i=1}^{m} x_i^{\alpha_i}.$$

We define $\alpha = \sum_{i=1}^{m} \alpha_i$. We do not need to carry out the details of minimization implied by the definition of the expenditure function. Instead, using the equivalence of the above proposition, we can use the known indirect utility function and simply solve the equation $v(\mathbf{p}, e) = u$ for e in terms of $\mathbf{p}$ and u. Hence we solve

$$\left(\frac{e}{\alpha}\right)^{\alpha} \prod_{i=1}^{m} \left(\frac{\alpha_i}{p_i}\right)^{\alpha_i} = u.$$

This gives

$$e(\mathbf{p}, u) = u^{1/\alpha} \alpha \prod_{i=1}^{m} \left(\frac{p_i}{\alpha_i}\right)^{\alpha_i/\alpha}.$$

Relation between Expenditure and Benefit Functions

The expenditure function can be expressed in terms of the benefit function in a very simple way. In fact, benefit and expenditure are naturally complementary (or dual) concepts. Each is expressed in meaningful units—money units for the expenditure function and units of **g** for the benefit function—whereas the units of utility and indirect utility are arbitrary. This duality between benefit and expenditure is used frequently in later chapters.

The following proposition is a direct analog of Proposition 3.2, which relates the profit function to the shortage function. We shall, however, give the simple proof.

Proposition 4.7.   *Suppose* $\mathbf{p} \in \mathcal{R}^m$ *with* $\mathbf{p} \cdot \mathbf{g} = 1$. *Then*[3]

$$e(\mathbf{p}, u) = \min_{\mathbf{x} \in X} \{\mathbf{p} \cdot \mathbf{x} - b(\mathbf{x}, u)\}.$$

---

[3]The min operation can be replaced by inf.

Proof: We shall prove the relation under the assumption that $e(\mathbf{p}, u)$ is finite and that $\mathbf{p} \cdot \mathbf{x}$ achieves $e(\mathbf{p}, u)$ for some $\mathbf{x}^*$ with $u(\mathbf{x}^*) \geq u$. It follows that $b(\mathbf{x}^*, u) \geq 0$. Hence

$$e(\mathbf{p}, u) \geq \mathbf{p} \cdot \mathbf{x}^* - b(\mathbf{x}^*, u).$$

On the other hand, for any $\mathbf{x} \in X$ we have $u(\mathbf{x} - b(\mathbf{x}, u)\mathbf{g}, u) \geq u$. Therefore

$$e(\mathbf{p}, u) \leq \mathbf{p} \cdot (\mathbf{x} - b(\mathbf{x}, u)\mathbf{g}) = \mathbf{p} \cdot \mathbf{x} - b(\mathbf{x}, u).$$

Combining the two inequalities we find,

$$e(\mathbf{p}, u) = \min_{\mathbf{x} \in X}\{\mathbf{p} \cdot \mathbf{x} - b(\mathbf{x}, u)\}. \quad \blacksquare$$

The relation of Proposition 4.7 can also be illustrated in a simple way graphically through the idea that was used in Section 3.11 to illustrate the relation between the profit function and the shortage function. For a two-dimensional situation, let us select $\mathbf{g} = (1, 0)$. Thus, benefit is measured in the direction of the horizontal axis. We then normalize price vectors $\mathbf{p}$ so that $\mathbf{p} \cdot \mathbf{g} = 1$, meaning that $p_1 = 1$. Now suppose we are given such a $\mathbf{p}$ and an arbitrary $\mathbf{x}$ in the two-dimensional space. We wish to calculate $\mathbf{p} \cdot \mathbf{x}$. We first construct the line perpendicular to $\mathbf{p}$ that passes through the point $\mathbf{x}$. This line is described by the equation $\mathbf{p} \cdot \mathbf{x}' = c$, for some c. The value of c is in fact equal to the x_1 coordinate of the point where the line crosses the horizontal axis because at that point $\mathbf{x}'$ we have $\mathbf{p} \cdot \mathbf{x}' = (1, p_2) \cdot (x_1, 0) = x_1$.

The relation of Proposition 4.7 is shown in Fig. 4.11. Consider the point $\mathbf{x}$ shown in the figure. The value $\mathbf{p} \cdot \mathbf{x}$ is measured on the horizontal axis as indicated. Likewise $e(\mathbf{p}, u)$ can be measured on that axis. The benefit value $b(\mathbf{x}, u)$ is the horizontal distance from $\mathbf{x}$ to the indifference curve u; this distance is indicated by the dashed line in the figure. It should be clear that

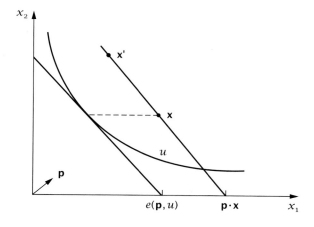

FIGURE 4.11 Relation between the expenditure and benefit functions.

$e(\mathbf{p}, u) = \mathbf{p} \cdot \mathbf{x} - b(\mathbf{x}, u)$ for the $\mathbf{x}$ shown. If, on the other hand, $\mathbf{x}'$ were used, it is clear that $e(\mathbf{p}, u) < \mathbf{p} \cdot \mathbf{x}' - b(\mathbf{x}', u)$. Thus $e(\mathbf{p}, u)$ is found by the minimization operation.

4.4   More Duality

Duality is an important aspect of microeconomics and arises in many different ways and in many different topics. For example, we shall see that duality concepts arise in the theory of the firm, the theory of the consumer, general equilibrium theory, and welfare analysis. Duality is hard to define concisely, for it takes many forms, but basically it expresses the natural relation between commodities on the one hand and prices on the other. Frequently a relation or concept dealing with one of these has a corresponding dual relation dealing with the other.

In this section we further study the duality between some familiar concepts related to preferences. Specifically, we shall first explore the duality between a utility function and its corresponding indirect utility function, and then we shall further explore the duality between the expenditure function and the benefit function.

A utility function expresses preferences over bundles of goods. Because it deals with goods (that is, variables $\mathbf{x}$) it is a *primal* concept (working in the primary space of variables). Indirect utility, on the other hand, measures the utility implied by a price-income combination. Hence, indirect utility is a *dual* concept (working in the space of dual variables $\mathbf{p}$ and r). We know how to construct the function v from u. It turns out that under certain assumptions, the function u can be likewise constructed from v by a process that is symmetric to the way that v was constructed from u. This establishes the duality between u and v. We can start with either one and obtain the other.

The construction of v from u is shown in Fig. 4.12. (We normalize $\mathbf{p}$ so that $r = 1$.) Note that if the function u is not convex, there are certain points

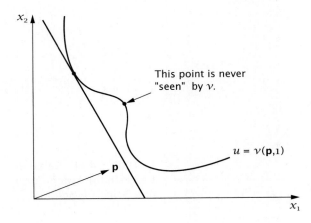

This point is never "seen" by v.

$u = v(\mathbf{p}, 1)$

FIGURE   4.12   Construction of $v(\mathbf{p}, 1)$.

x that will not be optimal for any **p**. Hence, v can only contain information concerning a "quasi-convexified" version of u. Also, if we restrict **p** so that $\mathbf{p} > \mathbf{0}$ then v can only contain information about a strongly monotonic version of u.

Perfect duality between u and v *does* hold if u is quasi-concave and strongly monotonic. This duality is stated in the following proposition. The proof of this theorem uses the supporting hyperplane theorem (see Appendix B). The reader may find it more instructive on first reading to skip the proof and go to the next duality relation which is actually simpler to visualize.

Duality of u and v. *Assume that u is continuous, quasi-concave, and strongly monotonic. Let $X = \mathcal{R}_+^m$.*

(*a*) *For* $\mathbf{p} > \mathbf{0}$

$$v(\mathbf{p}, 1) = \max_{\mathbf{x}} \ u(\mathbf{x})$$

$$\text{sub to } \mathbf{p}\cdot\mathbf{x} \le 1 \tag{4.14a}$$

$$\mathbf{x} \in X.$$

(*b*) *For* $\mathbf{x} > \mathbf{0}$

$$u(\mathbf{x}) = \min_{\mathbf{p}} \ v(\mathbf{p}, 1)$$

$$\text{sub to } \mathbf{p}\cdot\mathbf{x} \le 1 \tag{4.14b}$$

$$\mathbf{p} \ge \mathbf{0}.$$

Proof: Equation (4.14*a*) is a definition and need not be proved. However, it shows immediately that for any $\mathbf{x} > \mathbf{0}$ and $\mathbf{p} > \mathbf{0}$ with $\mathbf{p}\cdot\mathbf{x} \le 1$ there holds $v(\mathbf{p}, 1) \ge u(\mathbf{x})$. Minimizing with respect to $\mathbf{p} \ge \mathbf{0}$ (and by continuity if $\mathbf{p} \not> \mathbf{0}$) leads to

$$u(\mathbf{x}) \le \min_{\mathbf{p}} \ v(\mathbf{p}, 1)$$

$$\text{sub to } \mathbf{p}\cdot\mathbf{x} \le 1 \tag{4.15}$$

$$\mathbf{p} \ge \mathbf{0}.$$

Therefore (4.14*b*) will be established if, for given $\mathbf{x} > \mathbf{0}$, we can find a $\mathbf{p} \ge \mathbf{0}$ with $\mathbf{p}\cdot\mathbf{x} \le 1$ and $u(\mathbf{x}) = v(\mathbf{p}, 1)$.

Let C be the set $C = \{\mathbf{x}' : u(\mathbf{x}') \ge u(\mathbf{x}), \ \mathbf{x}' \in X\}$. C is closed and convex, since u is continuous and quasi-concave. Also $C + \mathcal{R}_+^m = C$ because u is strongly monotonic (hence adding any positive vector to a point in C yields a point that is also in C). Clearly $\mathbf{x}$ is a boundary point of C. By the supporting hyperplane theorem (Appendix B), there is a nonzero $\mathbf{p} \ge \mathbf{0}$ such that $\mathbf{p}\cdot\mathbf{x} \le \mathbf{p}\cdot\mathbf{x}'$ for all $\mathbf{x}' \in C$. Since $\mathbf{x} > \mathbf{0}$, we may scale $\mathbf{p}$ suitably so that $\mathbf{p}\cdot\mathbf{x} = 1$.

The above shows that there is $\mathbf{p} \ge \mathbf{0}$ such that $\mathbf{x}$ solves (4.11). We want to show that $\mathbf{x}$ solves (4.10), and hence we use part (b) of Proposition 4.6. This yields $v(\mathbf{p}, 1) = u(\mathbf{x})$. ∎

Now let us consider the duality between the benefit function b and the expenditure function e. This duality is given in the following theorem.

Duality of b and e.   *Assume that the utility function u is continuous, quasi-concave, and strongly monotonic. Let $X = \mathcal{R}_+^m$, and select $\mathbf{g} \in X$, $\mathbf{g} > 0$.*

(a) *For $\mathbf{p} > 0$ with $\mathbf{p} \cdot \mathbf{g} = 1$*

$$e(\mathbf{p}, u) = \min_{\mathbf{x} \in X}\{\mathbf{p} \cdot \mathbf{x} - b(\mathbf{x}, u)\}.$$

(b) *For $\mathbf{x} > 0$*

$$b(\mathbf{x}, u) = \min_{\mathbf{p} \geq 0}\{\mathbf{p} \cdot \mathbf{x} - e(\mathbf{p}, u)\}$$

sub to $\mathbf{p} \cdot \mathbf{g} = 1$.

Proof: Part (a) is contained in Proposition 4.7. We prove (b) under the assumption that $b(\mathbf{x}, u)$ is finite. Let $S = \{\mathbf{x} : u(\mathbf{x}) \geq u, \ \mathbf{x} \in X\}$. S is closed and convex. Also $S + \mathcal{R}_+^m = S$ because $u(\mathbf{x}) \geq u$ implies $u(\mathbf{x} + \mathbf{n}) \geq u$ for all $\mathbf{n} \geq 0$. Given $\mathbf{x} \in X$ let $b = b(\mathbf{x}, u)$. Then $u(\mathbf{x} - b\mathbf{g}) \geq u$. In fact, by strong monotonicity $\mathbf{x} - b\mathbf{g}$ is on the boundary of S. Hence by the supporting hyperplane theorem (Appendix B) there is a $\mathbf{p} \in \mathcal{R}_+^m$, $\mathbf{p} \neq 0$, such that $\mathbf{p} \cdot \mathbf{x}' \geq \mathbf{p} \cdot (\mathbf{x} - b\mathbf{g})$ for all $\mathbf{x}' \in S$. We can normalize so that $\mathbf{p} \cdot \mathbf{g} = 1$.

It is clear that $e(\mathbf{p}, u) = \mathbf{p} \cdot (\mathbf{x} - b\mathbf{g}) = \mathbf{p} \cdot \mathbf{x} - b$ since the hyperplane defined by $\mathbf{p}$ supports S at $\mathbf{x} - b\mathbf{g}$. Hence $b(\mathbf{x}, u) = \mathbf{p} \cdot \mathbf{x} - e(\mathbf{p}, u)$.

For any $\mathbf{p}' \geq 0$, $\mathbf{p}' \cdot \mathbf{g} = 1$ we have $e(\mathbf{p}', u) \leq \mathbf{p}' \cdot (\mathbf{x} - b\mathbf{g}) = \mathbf{p}' \cdot \mathbf{x} - b$, since $u(\mathbf{x} - b\mathbf{g}) \geq u$. Thus $b(\mathbf{x}, u) \geq \mathbf{p}' \cdot \mathbf{x} - e(\mathbf{p}', u)$. Combined with the above we find

$$b(\mathbf{x}, u) = \min\{\mathbf{p} \cdot \mathbf{x} - e(\mathbf{p}, u) : \mathbf{p} \geq 0 : \mathbf{p} \cdot \mathbf{g} = 1\}. \quad \blacksquare$$

There is a simple economic interpretation of this theorem. Given a specific bundle $\mathbf{x}$ and a price vector $\mathbf{p}$, we compare the cost of the bundle to the expenditure required to attain utility level u. The difference is $\mathbf{p} \cdot \mathbf{x} - e(\mathbf{p}, u)$. However, even if this difference is positive, $\mathbf{x}$ is not necessarily preferred to u. But, if prices are chosen just right, the bundle $\mathbf{x}$ will be optimal for its cost, and then the quantity $\mathbf{p} \cdot \mathbf{x} - e(\mathbf{p}, u)$ will exactly measure the benefit $b(\mathbf{x}, u)$.

Part II
ADDITIONAL CONCEPTS

4.5   Money as a Commodity

In common day-to-day discussions we often refer to money as just another commodity—a special one, but still just a commodity. We rarely make explicit reference to a budget constraint, but instead think in terms of trading off money for various (other) commodities or activities. Our general framework can accommodate this idea, and it provides a useful way to analyze certain situations.

Suppose commodities are partitioned into two groups as $(\mathbf{x}, \mathbf{z})$. Values of the corresponding utility function can be written $u(\mathbf{x}, \mathbf{z})$. We suppose that the $\mathbf{x}$ commodities are being given special attention, while the $\mathbf{z}$ commodities represent everything else. Suppose there are prices $\mathbf{p}$ for the $\mathbf{z}$ commodities and suppose a budget r is allocated to these commodities. We then define

$$\overline{u}(\mathbf{x}, \mathbf{p}, r) = \max_{\mathbf{z}} \ u(\mathbf{x}, \mathbf{z})$$

$$\text{sub to } \mathbf{p} \cdot \mathbf{z} \leq r \qquad (4.16)$$

$$\mathbf{z} \geq \mathbf{0}.$$

We refer to $\overline{u}$ as a *partial indirect utility function*. It is the indirect utility function of $u(\mathbf{x}, \mathbf{z})$ with $\mathbf{x}$ held fixed as a vector of parameters.

If we consider $\mathbf{p}$ fixed, the function $\overline{u}(\mathbf{x}, r) \equiv \overline{u}(\mathbf{x}, \mathbf{p}, r)$ is a utility function with respect to the commodities $\mathbf{x}$ and the budget r. It is clear from (4.16) that $\overline{u}(\mathbf{x}, r)$ is nondecreasing with respect to r.

We can think of the budget r as an additional commodity. The function $\overline{u}(\mathbf{x}, r)$ gives the utility of having $\mathbf{x}$ and a budget r that can be allocated to the $\mathbf{z}$ commodities. The value of $\overline{u}(\mathbf{x}, r)$ assumes that the budget will be allocated optimally among the $\mathbf{z}$ commodities.

Willingness to Pay

The above construction provides the basis for another important concept. Suppose again that commodities are partitioned as $(\mathbf{x}, \mathbf{z})$. We assume that initially an individual has $\mathbf{x}_0$ and has allocated r_0 to the $\mathbf{z}$ commodities. We describe this initial point by $(\mathbf{x}_0, r_0)$. We now consider changing to a new value $\mathbf{x}_1$. We ask how much the individual is willing to pay, in terms of r for the new $\mathbf{x}_1$. That is, we determine w such that $\overline{u}(\mathbf{x}_1, r_0 - w) = \overline{u}(\mathbf{x}_0, r_0)$. The value w is the *willingness to pay*.

In general the willingness to pay depends on the baseline situation $(\mathbf{x}_0, r_0)$. However, it is a convenient measure since it dispenses with explicit consideration of all commodities except $\mathbf{x}$ and has cardinal value. The concept is used frequently to focus quickly on the utility of a change in a specific commodity level without specifying an entire utility function. For example, it is a useful description of preferences when a commodity is not divisible (a house, for instance) and one considers having either zero or one unit of the commodity. The willingness to pay is literally equal to the amount of money allocated to other goods that the consumer would give up to have one unit of this special commodity.

The willingness-to-pay measure is clearly a special case of the benefit function. Once the function $\overline{u}(\mathbf{x}, r)$ is defined, with r acting as a commodity,

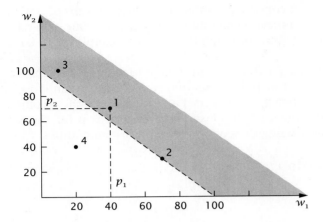

FIGURE 4.13   Bundling.

we just take money to be the reference for the benefit function. That is, we set $\mathbf{g} = (\mathbf{0}, 1)$. Then $b((\mathbf{x}_1, r_0), \overline{u}(\mathbf{x}_0, r_0)) = w$, where w is the willingness to pay to move from $(\mathbf{x}_0, r_0)$ to $\mathbf{x}_1$.

Example 4.13 (Bundling).   A common selling technique designed to enhance profit is bundling, where several goods are sold together as a unit. Examples are packaging of nuts and bolts into packs, and offering of complete meals rather than à la carte. A larger-scale example is an early policy of IBM requiring that companies leasing IBM machines also purchase punch cards from IBM. The effectiveness of bundling can be analyzed in terms of the willingness to pay of potential customers.

As a specific example consider a company that sells two items, with the marginal costs of both items being zero. Consumers purchase at most one of each item, and the willingness to pay for one item is independent of the willingness to pay for the other. Specifically, there are four consumers with willingness-to-pay pairs $(40, 70)$, $(70, 30)$, $(10, 100)$, and $(20, 40)$. These points are shown in Fig. 4.13.

If the firm sets separate prices for the two commodities, the best (that is, maximum profit) choice is $p_1 = 40$, $p_2 = 70$. At these prices consumers 1 and 2 will purchase commodity 1, and consumers 1 and 3 will purchase commodity 2. The corresponding profit is 220. On the other hand, if the two items are bundled and priced at $p = 100$, everyone in the shaded area will purchase the bundle and profit will be 300.

*4.6   Special Preference Structures

When considering a broad assortment of commodities, it is natural to partition them into separate groups. For example, items of food might be grouped separately from those of housing. The preference relation may have a structure that reflects this natural grouping.

Suppose the commodities are partitioned into two groups, with a typical vector written as $\mathbf{x} = (\mathbf{y}, \mathbf{z})$. We write $X = Y \times Z$. For fixed $\mathbf{z}$, we define the *conditional ordering* $\succsim_{\mathbf{z}}$ on Y by the relation $\mathbf{y} \succsim_{\mathbf{z}} \mathbf{y}'$ if and only if $(\mathbf{y}, \mathbf{z}) \succsim (\mathbf{y}', \mathbf{z})$. That is, $\succsim_{\mathbf{z}}$ is a restriction of the original ordering, defined by fixing $\mathbf{z}$. It is easy to check that for any $\mathbf{z}$, the relation $\succsim_{\mathbf{z}}$ is in fact a preference ordering on Y. This ordering will in general depend on the conditioning element $\mathbf{z}$.

Consider listing foods in order of preference, assuming you remain in your current housing situation. Then imagine whether the food ordering would change if your housing changed. Most likely, the food ordering will not change very much (although you can probably imagine some housing circumstances that would influence your food preferences). In general, for the partition $\mathbf{x} = (\mathbf{y}, \mathbf{z})$, if the conditional preference ordering on Y is independent of $\mathbf{z}$, we say that the variable $\mathbf{y}$ is *independent* of $\mathbf{z}$. In this case the utility function takes a special form. For instance, in the example of food and housing, suppose the food items $\mathbf{y}$ are independent of housing $\mathbf{z}$. Then your preferences for food items can be represented by a separate utility function—say $v(\mathbf{y})$. Your overall utility for food and housing then is of the form $U(v(\mathbf{y}), \mathbf{z})$. That is, food items just collapse to a single food variable in the utility.

Independence theorem.   *Suppose a preference ordering is represented by a utility function $u(\mathbf{y}, \mathbf{z})$. Then if $\mathbf{y}$ is independent of $\mathbf{z}$, u can be written as*

$$u(\mathbf{y}, \mathbf{z}) = U(v(\mathbf{y}), \mathbf{z})$$

where $U(v, \mathbf{z})$ is strictly increasing in v. Furthermore, if u is continuous and strongly monotonic, then v and U are continuous and v is strongly monotonic. Conversely, if a preference ordering is represented in the form above, then $\mathbf{y}$ is independent of $\mathbf{z}$.

Proof: Suppose $\mathbf{y}$ is independent of $\mathbf{z}$. Select $\bar{\mathbf{z}}$ and let $v(\mathbf{y}) = u(\mathbf{y}, \bar{\mathbf{z}})$. Then $v(\mathbf{y})$ is a utility function for the preferences conditioned on $\bar{\mathbf{z}}$. Next define U by $U(v(\mathbf{y}), \mathbf{z}) = u(\mathbf{y}, \mathbf{z})$. This is well defined since by independence $v(\mathbf{y}_1) = v(\mathbf{y}_2)$ implies that $u(\mathbf{y}_1, \mathbf{z}) = u(\mathbf{y}_2, \mathbf{z})$ for any $\mathbf{z}$. To show that U is increasing, note that $v(\mathbf{y}_1) > v(\mathbf{y}_2)$ implies that $u(\mathbf{y}_1, \bar{\mathbf{z}}) > u(\mathbf{y}_2, \bar{\mathbf{z}})$, and therefore, by independence, $u(\mathbf{y}_1, \mathbf{z}) > u(\mathbf{y}_2, \mathbf{z})$ for any $\mathbf{z}$. Hence $U(v(\mathbf{y}_1), \mathbf{z}) > U(v(\mathbf{y}_2), \mathbf{z})$.

Now suppose u is continuous and strongly monotonic. Then $v(\mathbf{y}) = u(\mathbf{y}, \bar{\mathbf{z}})$ is clearly continuous and strongly monotonic. U is also continuous.[4]

To prove the converse statement, suppose $\mathbf{y}_1 \succsim_{\bar{\mathbf{z}}} \mathbf{y}_2$ for some $\bar{\mathbf{z}}$. Then $u(\mathbf{y}_1, \bar{\mathbf{z}}) \geq u(\mathbf{y}_2, \bar{\mathbf{z}})$ and hence $v(\mathbf{y}_1) \geq v(\mathbf{y}_2)$. This in turn means $U(v(\mathbf{y}_1), \mathbf{z}) \geq U(v(\mathbf{y}_2), \mathbf{z})$ for any $\mathbf{z}$. Hence $\mathbf{y}_1 \succsim_{\mathbf{z}} \mathbf{y}_2$.   ∎

---

[4]For interested readers: Let Ω be any open set in R. By the continuity of u, the inverse image of Ω is open in $Y \times Z$. Since v is strongly monotonic, the transformation of this into $R \times Z$ by $(v(\mathbf{y}), \mathbf{z})$ is also open. Hence, the inverse image of Ω by U is open, and U is continuous.

The above theorem is very useful since it shows that if **y** is independent of **z** there is a special utility function for the **y** commodities. Its value, together with **z**, is all that matters in the determination of the overall utility.

Stronger structural forms are obtained by introducing additional independence relations. The most important are the weak and strong versions of independence relative to a partition. Suppose there are a total of m commodities partitioned into P groups. Formally, we let N_i denote the subset of the number set $N = \{1, 2, \ldots, m\}$ that corresponds to the indices of the ith group. A partition is therefore defined by $\{N_1, N_2', \ldots, N_P\}$, with $N_i \cap N_j$ empty for $i \neq j$, and $\bigcup_{i=1}^{P} N_i = N$. An arbitrary commodity bundle $\mathbf{x} \in R_+^m$ is partitioned correspondingly as $\mathbf{x} = (\mathbf{x}_1, \mathbf{x}_2, \ldots, \mathbf{x}_P)$. Given any i, $i = 1, 2, \ldots, P$, we let $\mathbf{x}_{-i}$ denote the vector of commodities in the complement to N_i. That is, $\mathbf{x}_{-i} = (\mathbf{x}_1, \mathbf{x}_2, \ldots, \mathbf{x}_{i-1}, \mathbf{x}_{i+1}, \ldots, \mathbf{x}_P)$.

Independence of preferences.   A preference ordering is

(a) *Weakly independent* with respect to the partition $\{N_1, N_2, \ldots, N_P\}$ if for every $i = 1, 2, \ldots, P$ the vector $\mathbf{x}_i$ is independent of its complement $\mathbf{x}_{-i}$;

(b) *Strongly independent* with respect to $\{N_1, N_2, \ldots, N_P\}$ if it is weakly independent with respect to $\{N_1, N_2, \ldots, N_P\}$ and with respect to the partitions consisting of all unions of $N_1, \ldots, N_P$ that are proper subsets of N.

As an example of the difference between these two types, consider the case in which $m = 3$, the preference ordering is defined by $u(x_1, x_2, x_3) = \ln(1 + x_1) + x_2 \ln(1 + x_3)$, and the partition is $N_1 = \{1\}$, $N_2 = \{2\}$, $N_3 = \{3\}$. This ordering is weakly independent with respect to the partition (since u is increasing with respect to each x_i). However, it is not strongly independent with respect to this partition because (x_1, x_3) is not independent of x_2.

Parallel with the above definitions for preference orderings, there are similar definitions for utility functions.

Separability of utility.   A continuous utility function u is

(a) *Weakly separable* with respect to the partition $\{N_1, N_2, \ldots, N_P\}$ if there are continuous functions U and $u_1, u_2, \ldots, u_P$ such that for all $\mathbf{x} \in X$
$$u(\mathbf{x}) = U(u_1(\mathbf{x}_1), u_2(\mathbf{x}_2), \ldots, u_P(\mathbf{x}_P));$$

(b) *Strongly separable* with respect to $\{N_1, N_2, \ldots, N_P\}$ if there exist continuous functions U and $u_1, u_2, \ldots, u_P$ such that for all $\mathbf{x} \in X$
$$u(\mathbf{x}) = U\left(\sum_{i=1}^{P} u_i(\mathbf{x}_i)\right).$$

The weak form of independence with respect to a partition is simply a symmetric form of the independence assumption discussed earlier. It is not surprising, then, that it is equivalent to weak separability of utility functions.

Proposition 4.8. *Suppose a preference ordering $\succsim$ is continuous and strongly monotonic. Suppose the variables are partitioned into P groups. Then $\succsim$ is weakly independent with respect to this partition if and only if every continuous utility function that represents it is weakly separable.*

Proof: Suppose $\succsim$ is weakly independent with respect to the partition. Then the conditional ordering $\succsim_{\mathbf{x}_{-i}}$ is a continuous, strongly monotonic ordering that does not depend on $\mathbf{x}_{-i}$. Hence by the independence theorem earlier in this section, there is a continuous utility function u_i representing this ordering. Let u be any continuous representation of $\succsim$. We then define U by

$$u(\mathbf{x}) = U\left(u_1(\mathbf{x}_1), u_2(\mathbf{x}_2), \ldots, u_n(\mathbf{x}_n)\right).$$

This is well defined since $u_i(\mathbf{x}_i) = u_i(\mathbf{x}_i')$, $i = 1, 2 \ldots, P$, implies $u(\mathbf{x}) = u(\mathbf{x}')$. The remainder of the proof is similar to that of the independence theorem. ∎

This result has great intuitive appeal. It says that under weak independence each commodity group can be assigned its own utility function. As an extension of this idea, we note that there is no reason why the utility functions of the individual groups might not themselves be weakly separable. This leads to the concept of a *utility tree*, with deeper and deeper layers of partitions, perhaps down to the level of a single commodity. An example is shown in Fig. 4.14.

When a utility has a tree structure, budgeting can be treated in stages. A budget can be allocated to a group (corresponding to a node of the tree) and this budget allocated among all lower nodes. The allocation process will not be influenced by the corresponding process in disjoint branches (although

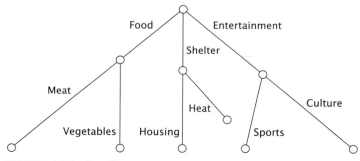

FIGURE 4.14   A utility tree.

determination of the individual budgets does require consideration of the entire utility function).

There is also equivalence between strong independence and strong separability. We state but do not prove the following theorem, originally due (in slightly different form) to Debreu.

Strong independence theorem.   *Suppose a preference ordering $\gtrsim$ is continuous and strongly monotonic. Suppose the variables are partitioned into P groups with $P > 2$. Then $\gtrsim$ is strongly independent with respect to this partition if and only if every continuous utility function which represents it is also strongly separable.*

Note that this theorem requires that $P > 2$. In the case $P = 2$, weak and strong separability of preferences coincide. The special additive form for $P = 2$ requires additional assumptions. (See Exercise 15.)

A very special case of strong separability of utility functions occurs when the partition consists of the element-by-element partition $\{\{1\}, \{2\}, \ldots, \{m\}\}$. In this case the utility function is equivalent to an *additive utility function*

$$u(\mathbf{x}) = \sum_{i=1}^{m} u_i(x_i)$$

where the u_i depend only on individual components x_i.

Example 4.14.   The Cobb-Douglas utility function $u(\mathbf{x}) = \prod_{i=1}^{m} x_i^{\alpha_i}$ with $\alpha_i > 0$ for $i = 1, 2, \ldots, m$ represents a preference ordering that is strongly independent with respect to the components. It is also strongly monotonic in the interior of $X = \mathcal{R}_+^m$. Hence, in that interior, the strong independence theorem applies. Utility can be expressed in additive form by applying a logarithmic transformation

$$\overline{u}(\mathbf{x}) = \sum_{i=1}^{m} \alpha_i \ln x_i .$$

In general, as we know, a utility function is only defined to within a strictly increasing transformation. However, if a continuous utility function is written in strongly separable form $u(\mathbf{x}) = u_1(\mathbf{x}_1) + u_2(\mathbf{x}_2) + \cdots + u_P(\mathbf{x}_P)$, the component utility functions $u_i(\mathbf{x}_i)$ do not have as much flexibility. In fact, these component utility functions are unique to within an arbitrary *positive affine transformation*. That is, u_i can only be changed to $v_i(\mathbf{x}) = au_i(x_i) + b_i$ where $a > 0$ if we wish to keep the strongly separable form. This is stated in the following proposition.

Proposition 4.9.   *Suppose the continuous utility functions*

$$(a) \qquad u(\mathbf{x}) = \sum_{i=1}^{P} u_i(\mathbf{x}_i)$$

$$(b) \qquad v(\mathbf{x}) = \sum_{i=1}^{P} v_i(\mathbf{x}_i)$$

are equivalent, with $v(\mathbf{x}) = f(u(\mathbf{x}))$ where f is continuous and strictly increasing. Suppose at least two u_i's are not identically constant. Then there is an $a > 0$ and b_i's, $i = 1, 2, \ldots, P$, such that

$$(c) \qquad v_i(\mathbf{x}_i) = a u_i(\mathbf{x}_i) + b_i$$

for each i. Conversely, if u and v have the forms (a) and (b), respectively, and v_i, $i = 1, 2, \ldots, P$, satisfies (c), then u and v are equivalent.

Intertemporal Preferences

The concept of independence is useful for describing intertemporal preferences for bundles of dated commodities of the form $\mathbf{x} = (\mathbf{x}_1, \mathbf{x}_2, \ldots, \mathbf{x}_T)$ where $\mathbf{x}_t$ represents a bundle consumed in period t, $t = 1, 2 \ldots, T$. In principle, preferences for dated commodity bundles can be treated in the standard utility framework. We simply assume that the consumer has an overall utility function $u(\mathbf{x}) = u(\mathbf{x}_1, \mathbf{x}_2, \ldots, \mathbf{x}_T)$. But the intertemporal nature of these commodities leads naturally to a special structural assumption for the utility function.

Let us assume that preferences for current and future consumption are independent of past consumption. Applying this at the second period and using the independence theorem implies that u must have the form

$$u(\mathbf{x}_1, \mathbf{x}_2, \ldots, \mathbf{x}_T) = U_1(\mathbf{x}_1, u_2(\mathbf{x}_2, \mathbf{x}_3, \ldots, \mathbf{x}_T)).$$

If this is true at every period, then u has the *strongly recursive* form

$$u(\mathbf{x}) = U_1\{\mathbf{x}_1, U_2[\mathbf{x}_2, U_3(\cdots)]\}.$$

Example 4.15 (Additive discounted form).   In many analytic or empirical studies, an intertemporal utility of the special form

$$u(\mathbf{x}) = \sum_{t=1}^{T} \alpha_t U(\mathbf{x}_t)$$

is used. This function is clearly strongly recursive; in fact, it is strongly separable. Note that the same underlying utility U for single-period consumption is used in each period. The factors α_t are *discount factors*, which show how much future consumption is discounted relative to current consumption (usually $\alpha_t \leq 1$).

*4.7   Revealed Preference

The basic preference axioms are sometimes criticized as being too strong, on the grounds that individuals are unlikely to make choices through conscious use of a preference relation. One response to this criticism is to develop an alternative theory on the basis of a weaker set of hypotheses. One of the most interesting alternative theories is that of *revealed preference*, which is discussed below.

The basic tenet of revealed preference theory is that preference statements should be constructed only from observable decisions, that is, from actual choices made by a consumer. An individual preference relation, even if it exists, can never be directly observed in the market. Thus, revealed preference theory focuses on the choices made by a consumer, not on a hidden preference relation.

A price vector $\mathbf{p} \geq \mathbf{0}$ and income level $r > 0$ define a budget constraint $\mathbf{p} \cdot \mathbf{x} \leq r$, $\mathbf{x} \in X$. We assume that corresponding to any such budget constraint the consumer selects some feasible bundle $\mathbf{x}$. Since $\mathbf{x}$ depends on $\mathbf{p}$ and r, we write $\mathbf{x}(\mathbf{p}, r)$ to represent this choice. We can allow for the fact that $\mathbf{x}$ might not be unique (that is, the consumer cannot decide between a group of $\mathbf{x}$'s). In this case $\mathbf{x}(\mathbf{p}, r)$ denotes a set, and a particular selection is a point $\mathbf{x} \in \mathbf{x}(\mathbf{p}, r)$. Note also that since we assume that the choice is determined relative to the feasible set, the choice function $\mathbf{x}(\mathbf{p}, r)$ must be homogeneous of degree zero with respect to $(\mathbf{p}, r)$.

We now introduce the idea that the choice made reveals something about preferences (in the broad sense).

Direct revealed preference.   Suppose there is a price vector $\mathbf{p}$ and income level r such that $\mathbf{x} \in \mathbf{x}(\mathbf{p}, r)$ and $\mathbf{p} \cdot \mathbf{x}' \leq r$ for some $\mathbf{x}' \in X$. Then $\mathbf{x}$ is said to be *directly revealed preferred* to $\mathbf{x}'$. In this case we write $\mathbf{x}D\mathbf{x}'$.

The relation D is a kind of partial preference relation over X that we might use in building a description of how choices are made. As it stands, however, this relation has very few useful properties. We do have $\mathbf{x}D\mathbf{x}$ if $\mathbf{x}$ is chosen. But despite this, D is not always reflexive because we do not have $\mathbf{x}D\mathbf{x}$ if $\mathbf{x}$ is never chosen. Indeed the relation D is not complete, since it is not defined for every pair $\mathbf{x}, \mathbf{y}$ in X. Furthermore (and most importantly), D is not transitive. It can happen that $\mathbf{x}D\mathbf{x}'$ and $\mathbf{x}'D\mathbf{x}''$ but not $\mathbf{x}D\mathbf{x}''$. Even if the individual does use a preference relation to make choices, D may be nontransitive. To get anywhere theoretically, we must alter D somewhat to obtain some of the standard properties.

Revealed preference.   A point $\mathbf{x}$ is said to be *revealed preferred* to $\mathbf{x}'$ if either $\mathbf{x}D\mathbf{x}'$ or there is a finite number of points $\mathbf{x}_1, \mathbf{x}_2, \ldots, \mathbf{x}_m$ in X such that $\mathbf{x}D\mathbf{x}_1, \mathbf{x}_1D\mathbf{x}_2, \ldots, \mathbf{x}_mD\mathbf{x}'$. In this case we write $\mathbf{x}R\mathbf{x}'$.

The relation R constructed above by considering chains of D relations is called the *transitive closure* of D. We have $\mathbf{x}R\mathbf{x}'$ if $\mathbf{x}$ is chosen over $\mathbf{x}_1$, $\mathbf{x}_1$ over $\mathbf{x}_2, \ldots$, and finally $\mathbf{x}_m$ over $\mathbf{x}'$ for some intermediate points. This widens the scope of the relation since the comparison need not be direct. Moreover, it is

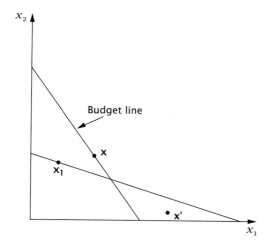

FIGURE 4.15 Revealed preference.

easy to see that R is in fact transitive: If in addition to $\mathbf{x}R\mathbf{x}'$ as above, we also have $\mathbf{x}'R\mathbf{x}''$, then $\mathbf{x}'D\mathbf{x}'_1, \mathbf{x}'_1D\mathbf{x}'_2, \ldots, \mathbf{x}'_nD\mathbf{x}''$ for some $\mathbf{x}'_i$'s. Therefore we have the long chain $\mathbf{x}D\mathbf{x}_1, \mathbf{x}_1D\mathbf{x}_2, \ldots, \mathbf{x}_mD\mathbf{x}', \mathbf{x}'D\mathbf{x}'_1, \ldots, \mathbf{x}'_nD\mathbf{x}''$, which shows that $\mathbf{x}R\mathbf{x}''$. Hence, R is transitive.

An example of revealed preference is shown in Fig. 4.15. In the figure $\mathbf{x}$ is directly revealed preferred to $\mathbf{x}_1$ since it was chosen over $\mathbf{x}_1$ for one budget constraint, and $\mathbf{x}_1$ is directly revealed preferred to $\mathbf{x}'$. Hence $\mathbf{x}R\mathbf{x}'$.

Still, no assumptions have been introduced concerning how an individual actually makes choices. The relations D and R are constructed solely from the choice pattern and hence reflect only observable behavior. Hence, it is not possible to say much, since choices might conceivably be quite bizarre. It is therefore necessary to introduce some hypothesis (in the form of an axiom) about the regularity or consistency of a consumer's choices. We introduce three alternative axioms. The first two have always been closely associated with revealed preference theory, and the third is a more recent alternative.

Weak axiom of revealed preference (WARP). If $\mathbf{x}_1D\mathbf{x}_2$ and $\mathbf{x}_1 \neq \mathbf{x}_2$, then it is not true that $\mathbf{x}_2D\mathbf{x}_1$.

Strong axiom of revealed preference (SARP). If $\mathbf{x}_1R\mathbf{x}_2$ and $\mathbf{x}_1 \neq \mathbf{x}_2$, then it is not true that $\mathbf{x}_2R\mathbf{x}_1$.

The weak and strong axioms state that consumers act in such a way that the relations D and R, respectively, are *antisymmetric*. Two distinct bundles cannot each be revealed preferred to each other (directly in the case of WARP). Note that if an individual actually made choices according to a preference ordering that gave a unique optimal bundle for every budget constraint, the observed choices would satisfy both of the above axioms. Hence, these axioms are consistent with preference maximization when choice is unique. But these axioms are apparently weaker than the assumption that there is an underlying preference ordering.

The next axiom is the newer alternative. In this version, it is not necessary that there be a unique choice bundle for every budget set.

Congruence axiom.   Suppose $\mathbf{x} \in \mathbf{x}(\mathbf{p}, r)$ and $\mathbf{p} \cdot \mathbf{x}' \leq r$, $\mathbf{x}' \in X$. Then $\mathbf{x}' R \mathbf{x}$ implies $\mathbf{x}' \in \mathbf{x}(\mathbf{p}, r)$.

In other words, a feasible bundle not in $\mathbf{x}(\mathbf{p}, r)$ cannot be revealed preferred to a bundle in $\mathbf{x}(\mathbf{p}, r)$. This seems quite reasonable. It says that $\mathbf{x}'$ can never be revealed preferred to $\mathbf{x}$ if, in a situation where both are feasible, $\mathbf{x}$ is chosen strictly over $\mathbf{x}'$. Clearly, the congruence axiom, too, is satisfied by an individual who makes choices using a preference ordering, and unlike WARP and SARP, this will hold even if the preference ordering leads to nonunique choices.

What is the strongest statement that can be made about the process of choice selection when the relation R satisfies the congruence axiom? Certainly R does define a kind of ordering, since it is transitive; but it is neither complete nor symmetric. Many $\mathbf{x}$'s may never be chosen, and hence never observed. It seems unlikely that we could relate R to a legitimate preference ordering.

If we can find a preference ordering that is consistent with R, producing exactly the same choices as those implied by R, we say that that preference ordering *rationalizes* the individual's choice behavior. The individual need not have a preference ordering, or might have one different from the one we find, but that does not matter as long as the choices are identical. If we can produce one that leads to the same choices, it rationalizes the choice behavior.

Perhaps surprisingly, under the congruence axiom there is always a preference ordering that rationalizes the choice behavior. The following theorem is not constructive in nature, so we shall not give the proof.

Rationalized choice theorem.   *Choice behavior can be rationalized if and only if it satisfies the congruence axiom.*

We began without an assumption of an underlying preference ordering. Instead the only assumption introduced was the (seemingly mild) congruence axiom, to add a degree of regularity to revealed preference. We found, however, that this leads back to the existence of a preference ordering that rationalizes choice behavior. This development therefore adds credibility to the assumption that individuals make choices as if they had preference orderings.

4.8 Exercises

1. Let $u(x, y) = x^\alpha y^\beta$ with $0 < \alpha < 1$ and $\beta = 1 - \alpha$.

   (a) By carrying out the indicated minimization, find

   $$e(p, q, u) = \min \ px + qy$$
   $$\text{sub to } u(x, y) \geq u.$$

   (b) Define $g = (0, 1)$, and find $b(x, y, u)$. Normalize prices in the form $(p, 1)$, and find $e(p, u) = \min \ px + y - b(x, y, u)$. Compare with (a).

2. A preference ordering $\succsim$ on $\mathcal{R}_+^m$ is *homothetic* if $\mathbf{x} \sim \mathbf{x}'$ implies $t\mathbf{x} \sim t\mathbf{x}'$ for all $t > 0$. Assume that $\succsim$ is homothetic and represented by the utility function u. Show that u is an increasing transformation of a function that is homogeneous of degree one.

3. (Transitivity) Assume that the preference relation $\succsim$ is complete, reflexive, and transitive on a set X. Show:

   (a) If $x \sim y$ and $y \sim z$, then $x \sim z$.

   (b) If $x \succ y$ and $y \succ z$, then $x \succ z$.

   (c) If $x \succsim y$ and $y \succ z$, then $x \succ z$.

4. Assume that there is a preference ordering on $X = \mathcal{R}_+^m$ that is represented by a continuous utility function u. In each of the following statements, what weakest further assumption on preferences is needed to make the statement true? In each case, choose *one* from the following list: (*i*) none needed, (*ii*) local nonsatiation, (*iii*) strong monotonicity, (*iv*) convexity, (*v*) strict convexity, and (*vi*) not possible (even with one of the additional assumptions).

   (a) If $\mathbf{x}$ is chosen given prices $\mathbf{p}$ and income r, then $\mathbf{p} \cdot \mathbf{x} = r$.

   (b) If $\mathbf{x} \geq \mathbf{x}'$ and $\mathbf{x} \neq \mathbf{x}'$, then $u(\mathbf{x}) > u(\mathbf{x}')$.

   (c) If $\mathbf{x} > \mathbf{x}'$, then $u(\mathbf{x}) > u(\mathbf{x}')$.

   (d) If $\mathbf{x}$ is chosen given $\mathbf{p}$ and r, then for any $\mathbf{x}'$ satisfying $\mathbf{p} \cdot \mathbf{x}' \leq r$ and $\mathbf{x}' \neq \mathbf{x}$, there holds $u(\mathbf{x}') \leq u(\mathbf{x})$.

   (e) u is a quasi-concave function.

5. It is often assumed that consumption of a good falls if the price is raised. In fact, all that can be inferred from economic theory is that the compensated own-price effect is nonpositive. Let $\mathbf{x}$ be the bundle of goods chosen when prices equal $\mathbf{p}$. Suppose prices change to $\mathbf{p}'$ and the consumer's income is compensated so that the original bundle is just affordable at the new prices. That is, if r' is the new income, then $\mathbf{p}' \cdot \mathbf{x} = r'$. Let $\mathbf{x}'$ be the bundle chosen at prices $\mathbf{p}'$ and income r'. Show that

   $$(\mathbf{p}' - \mathbf{p}) \cdot (\mathbf{x}' - \mathbf{x}) \leq 0.$$

6. (Workaholic preferences) Ordinarily labor is viewed as a "bad" rather than a "good," yet some people are observed to work beyond the time for which they are paid a wage.

(a) On a diagram with axes labeled *Work* and *All Other Goods*, draw the budget set of an individual who is paid an hourly wage for up to eight hours per day and zero for overtime.

(b) Draw indifference contours assuming that utility of work is decreasing everywhere.

(c) If an individual chooses to work more than eight hours, can that individual have preferences as drawn in part (b)? If not, sketch indifference contours that would be consistent with this individual's behavior.

*7. (Nested subsets)   Let $\mathbb{P}$ be a family of subsets of a set X with the property that for every $P \in \mathbb{P}$ and $Q \in \mathbb{P}$ either $P \subset Q$ or $Q \subset P$. We then call $\mathbb{P}$ a family of *nested* subsets. Given such a $\mathbb{P}$, we define a relation $\prec$ on X by $x \prec y$ if there is a $P \in \mathbb{P}$ with $y \in P$, $x \notin P$. We write $x \succsim y$ if not $x \prec y$.

(a) Show that $\succsim$ so defined is an ordering of X.

(b) For any ordering of X show that there is a corresponding family $\mathbb{P}$ that defines the ordering.

8. Let

$$u(\mathbf{x}) = \min\left\{ \frac{x_1}{a_1}, \frac{x_2}{a_2}, \ldots, \frac{x_m}{a_m} \right\}, \quad a_i > 0, \quad i = 1, 2, \ldots, m$$

be a Leontief utility function, and let $\mathbf{g} = (1, 1, \ldots, 1)$. Find the corresponding benefit function $b(\mathbf{x}, u)$.

9. Find the indirect utility function and expenditure function corresponding to the utility function

$$u(x_1, x_2) = -\frac{1}{x_1} - \frac{1}{x_2}.$$

10. For the indirect utility function found in Exercise 9, verify the duality relation. That is, find u from v.

11. Suppose commodities are partitioned as $\mathbf{x} = (\mathbf{x}_1, \mathbf{x}_2)$ and suppose utility has the weakly separable form $u(\mathbf{x}) = u_1(\mathbf{x}_1, u_2(\mathbf{x}_2))$ where $u_1(\mathbf{x}_1, u_2)$ is strictly increasing with respect to u_2. Select $\mathbf{g}$ of the form $\mathbf{g} = (\mathbf{g}_1, \mathbf{0})$. Show that the benefit function can be written in the form

$$b(\mathbf{x}, u) = b_1(\mathbf{x}_1, u_2(\mathbf{x}_2), u).$$

12. (Marketing models)   Marketing studies attempt to determine the potential demand for a product. One approach is based on the willingness-to-pay concept. Suppose that a single product is being considered, and individuals will buy a quantity of either one or none. Through survey methods, the willingness to pay for one unit can be determined for a representative sample of individuals, assuming that all other prices remain unchanged. The resulting values can be arranged as a distribution showing the fraction $W(\xi)$ of individuals having willingness to pay greater than an arbitrary level ξ, as shown in Fig. 4.16.

If the product is offered at a price p, all individuals with willingness to pay greater than p will purchase the item. The number of sales is $n =$

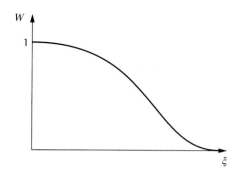

FIGURE 4.16   Marketing data.

$N \cdot W(p)$ where N is the total number of people in the market. (Hence, the curve in Fig. 4.16 is just a normalized demand function, but in this case we have related it to a more basic concept.)

Since W is normalized, the quantity $W(p)$ can be thought of as a probability. To use it this way, we imagine that individuals make purchase decisions probabilistically. The probability that any individual will purchase the product if the price is p is $W(p)$.

An added feature of this approach is that the probabilistic interpretation can directly incorporate probabilistic responses to marketing surveys. Suppose that in response to a questionnaire, individual i, $i = 1, 2, \ldots, N$, states that the probability that he or she would purchase the item at price p is $\pi_i(p)$. Show that a good estimate of $W(p)$ is $(1/N)\sum_{i=1}^{N} \pi_i(p)$.

13. A consumer has the utility function $u(x_1, x_2) = \frac{1}{3}x_1 + \frac{2}{3}x_2 - (x_1 - x_2)^2$, defined on all of $\mathcal{R}^2$ (not just $\mathcal{R}^2_+$).

   (a) Using the reference bundle $\mathbf{g} = (1, 1)$, find the benefit function. Show that it can be written as $b(\mathbf{x}, u) = u(\mathbf{x}) - u$.

   (b) The prices of the two goods p_1 and p_2 satisfy $\mathbf{p}\cdot\mathbf{g} = 1$. Solve the problem of maximizing the net of benefit minus cost. Adjoin the budget constraint and determine the consumer's demand as a function of prices and income.

*14. Suppose $\succsim$ is continuous, convex, and strongly monotonic. Show that there is a representation that is additive and homothetic (see Exercise 2) if and only if there exists a real number $b \leq 1$ and a u such that

$$
u(\mathbf{x}) = \begin{cases}
\sum_{i=1}^{n} \alpha_i x_i^b + y_i & \text{if } b \neq 0 \\
\sum_{i=1}^{n} \alpha_i (\log x_i) + y_i & \text{if } b = 0
\end{cases}
$$

where α_i and y_i are constants, $b\alpha_i > 0$ if $b \neq 0$, and $\alpha_i > 0$ if $b = 0$. Hint: Assume that the function u is twice differentiable.

15. Suppose a utility function has the additive form

$$u(x, y) = v(x) + w(y).$$

Let the marginal rate of substitution between x and y be

$$M(x, y) = \frac{\partial u(x, y)}{\partial x} \bigg/ \frac{\partial u(x, y)}{\partial y}.$$

For the four values x_1, x_2, y_1, and y_2, let M_{ij} correspond to M evaluated at $x = x_i$, $y = y_j$; i.e., $M_{ij} = M(x_i, y_j)$. Find the value of

$$\frac{M_{11}M_{22}}{M_{12}M_{21}}.$$

(It can be shown that the condition you deduce is sufficient, as well as necessary, for the additive form.)

16. (The distance function)   A vector $\mathbf{x}$ can be scaled by a constant $d(u, \mathbf{x})$ so that it just touches the indifference curve $u(\mathbf{x}') = u$. Mathematically we may define the *distance function d* implicitly by

$$u\big(\mathbf{x}/d(u, \mathbf{x})\big) = u$$

(and for simplicity we assume that such a d always exists).

(a) Show that

$$e(\mathbf{p}, u) = \min_{\mathbf{x}} \ \mathbf{p} \cdot \mathbf{x}$$

$$\text{sub to } \ d(u, \mathbf{x}) = 1.$$

(b) Assuming $u(\mathbf{x})$ is quasi-concave, show (by a graphical argument) the dual result

$$d(u, \mathbf{x}) = \min_{\mathbf{p}} \ \mathbf{p} \cdot \mathbf{x}$$

$$\text{sub to } \ e(\mathbf{p}, u) = 1.$$

17. In this exercise we derive conditions on a function that are sufficient for it to be a benefit function. Let $\mathcal{U}$ be a closed interval on the real line and let b be a function on $\mathcal{R}_+^m \times \mathcal{U}$ satisfying the following:

(a) $b(\mathbf{x}, u)$ is continuous on $\mathcal{R}_+^m \times \mathcal{U}$.

(b) For every $\mathbf{x} \in \mathcal{R}_+^m$ there is a $u \in \mathcal{U}$ such that $b(\mathbf{x}, u) \geq 0$.

(c) $b(\mathbf{x}, u)$ is nonincreasing with respect to u.

(d) There is a $\mathbf{g} \in \mathcal{R}_+^m, \mathbf{g} \neq 0$, such that for all $\alpha > 0$, $\mathbf{x} \in \mathcal{R}_+^m$, $u \in \mathcal{U}$, there holds $b(\mathbf{x} + \alpha\mathbf{g}, u) = b(\mathbf{x}, u) + \alpha$.

Show that there is a utility function on $\mathcal{R}_+^m$ with range $\mathcal{U}$ with $b(\mathbf{x}, u)$ as its benefit function (with reference $\mathbf{g}$). Hint: Let $u(\mathbf{x}) = \max \ \{v : b(\mathbf{x}, v) \geq 0\}$.

4.9   References

4.1–4.3   For general material on preference relations see Fishburn (1970), Sen (1970), and Arrow (1951, 1963). For the general proof of the existence of a utility function, see Debreu (1959).

The idea of measuring the benefit of a new bundle as the amount of a single specified good that could be subtracted from that bundle to maintain the original utility level was first introduced by Dupuit (1844), who termed this quantity *relative utility*. Pareto (1906) introduced a related concept, which he termed *equivalent surplus*. The original concept of Dupuit was later developed more fully by Allais (1943), who used the term *distributable surplus*. The *benefit function*, defined using an arbitrary reference **g**, and the related duality result was introduced in Luenberger (1992a).

The indirect utility function was introduced by Roy (1942). The expenditure function was introduced by Hicks (1946). The proof of the theorem on the duality of u and v is in Debreu (1959).

4.4 For duality results in economics see Roy (1942), Diewert (1982), and Blackorby, Primont, and Russell (1978). For general duality concepts see Luenberger (1969) and Luenberger (1984).

4.5 An excellent text on bundling and other nonlinear pricing methods is Wilson (1993).

4.6 For more material on independence and separability, see Krantz, Luce, Suppes, and Tversky (1971), Keeney and Raiffa (1976), Fishburn (1970), and Katzner (1970). For applications to consumption theory, see Phlips (1983a). The original proof of the equivalence of strong independence and strong separability is due to Debreu (1960). The theorem here follows Katzner (1970).

4.7 Revealed preference theory was initiated by Samuelson (1938, 1947). The transitive relation R was introduced by Houthakker (1950). The theorem on the congruence axiom is due to Richter (1976).

4.8 For Exercise 14, see Katzner (1970). For Exercise 16, see Deaton (1979) and Deaton and Muellbauer (1980).

Chapter 5
CONSUMER DEMAND

Demand is recognized as a fundamental economic concept, but it is a relation, or function, rather than a single number. Demand expresses the amount that a consumer will purchase as a function of prices and available income.

Demand functions can, at least to a limited extent, be observed in the market, so they are in some sense real. This contrasts with preference relations, which are abstractions that cannot really be measured, but only inferred from market choices. However, as might be expected, preference theory implies that individual demand functions have certain structural properties, and it is these general properties that we develop in this chapter.

5.1 Demand Functions

We recall the basic choice problem of a consumer selecting a most preferred bundle of commodities from those that satisfy the budget constraint $\mathbf{p} \cdot \mathbf{x} \leq r$. If preferences can be represented by a continuous utility function, this problem can be expressed as

$$\begin{aligned} \max \ & u(\mathbf{x}) \\ \text{sub to } & \mathbf{p} \cdot \mathbf{x} \leq r \\ & \mathbf{x} \in X, \end{aligned} \tag{5.1}$$

where $X = \mathcal{R}_+^m$. A solution to this problem is a point $\mathbf{x} \in X$ representing an optimal commodity bundle. The solution clearly depends on $\mathbf{p}$ and r, and the family of solutions showing this dependency is written $\mathbf{x}(\mathbf{p}, r)$. If the solution is always unique, $\mathbf{x}(\mathbf{p}, r)$ is a function and is called the *demand function* of the consumer. It is also referred to as the *Marshallian demand function*, after Alfred Marshall. (It is also sometimes called the *money income demand*.)

As stated above, a major portion of this chapter is devoted to the study of properties of the demand function that are implied by the preference structure of the previous chapter and by various other economic assumptions. Two important properties of the demand function, however, can be deduced immediately.

Proposition 5.1. *The demand function* $\mathbf{x}(\mathbf{p}, r)$

(a) *Is homogeneous of degree zero: for any* $t > 0$, $\mathbf{x}(t\mathbf{p}, tr) = \mathbf{x}(\mathbf{p}, r)$.

(b) *Satisfies the budget constraint* $\mathbf{p} \cdot \mathbf{x}(\mathbf{p}, r) \leq r$.

The first property, of homogeneity, we have seen before. The constraint set is not changed if both $\mathbf{p}$ and r are scaled by the same factor. Such a scale factor change is equivalent to a change in units. The second property follows by definition of the demand function as being feasible.

5.2 Optimality Conditions

We now determine the optimality conditions associated with the basic consumer choice problem.

First-Order Conditions

We begin by deriving the first-order necessary conditions associated with the consumer choice problem. For this purpose, and throughout much of this chapter, we assume that preferences can be represented by a continuously differentiable utility function. Also, we assume local nonsatiation of preferences, so that the budget constraint is met with equality.

For simplicity we first consider the case of two commodities. In this case the consumer choice problem is

$$\max\; u(x_1, x_2)$$
$$\text{sub to}\; p_1 x_1 + p_2 x_2 = r \tag{5.2}$$
$$x_1 \geq 0, \quad x_2 \geq 0.$$

To find the first-order necessary conditions, we introduce the Lagrangian

$$L = u(x_1, x_2) - \lambda[p_1 x_1 + p_2 x_2 - r]$$

where λ is the Lagrange multiplier associated with the budget constraint. Assuming an interior solution, we set the partial derivatives of the Lagrangian with respect to x_1 and x_2 equal to zero, obtaining

$$\frac{\partial u(x_1, x_2)}{\partial x_1} = \lambda p_1 \tag{5.3a}$$

$$\frac{\partial u(x_1, x_2)}{\partial x_2} = \lambda p_2. \tag{5.3b}$$

In addition, the budget constraint must be satisfied:

$$p_1 x_1 + p_2 x_2 = r. \tag{5.4}$$

Together equations (5.3a), (5.3b), and (5.4) constitute the first-order necessary conditions. The three equations can be used to solve for the three unknowns x_1, x_2, and λ.

Example 5.1 (Cobb-Douglas). Consider again the m-dimensional Cobb-Douglas utility function

$$u(\mathbf{x}) = \prod_{i=1}^{m} x_i^{\alpha_i}, \qquad \alpha \geq 0, \quad i = 1, 2, \ldots, m.$$

Let $\alpha = \sum_{i=1}^{m} \alpha_i$. When computing the corresponding indirect utility in Example 4.9, Section 4.3, we found

$$x_i(p, r) = \frac{\alpha_i r}{\alpha p_i}, \qquad i = 1, 2, \ldots, m.$$

Hence, this is the demand function.

Marginal Rate of Substitution

There is an important economic interpretation of the first-order necessary conditions. Consider the indifference curve $u(x_1, x_2) = u$ for a fixed value of u. This curve can be thought of as defining a function $x_2(x_1)$. We define the *marginal rate of substitution* of good 2 for good 1 as $\mathrm{MRS}_{21} = -dx_2/dx_1$. Thus MRS_{21} is the negative of the slope of the indifference curve. Usually the marginal rate of substitution MRS_{21} decreases as x_1 increases.

Differentiating the relation $u(x_1, x_2) = u$ with respect to x_1 we find

$$\frac{\partial u(x_1, x_2)}{\partial x_1} + \frac{\partial u(x_1, x_2)}{\partial x_2}\frac{dx_2}{dx_1} = 0.$$

Hence

$$\mathrm{MRS}_{21} = \frac{\partial u(x_1, x_2)}{\partial x_1} \bigg/ \frac{\partial u(x_1, x_2)}{\partial x_2}.$$

Now let us return to the first-order conditions. If (5.3a) is divided by (5.3b), we obtain

$$\frac{\partial u(x_1, x_2)/\partial x_1}{\partial u(x_1, x_2)/\partial x_2} = \frac{p_1}{p_2}, \tag{5.5}$$

which does not contain λ. This can be written as

$$\mathrm{MRS}_{21} = \frac{p_1}{p_2}. \tag{5.6}$$

The ratio on the right-hand side of (5.6) is called the *rate of economic substitution* of commodity 2 for commodity 1. It is the negative of the slope of the budget constraint line.

The optimality condition states that the marginal rate of substitution must equal the economic rate of substitution at an optimal consumption

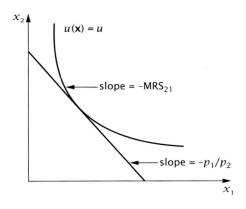

FIGURE 5.1   The optimality condition.

bundle. This is equivalent to the statement that the slope of the indifference curve must equal the slope of the budget line, as shown in Fig. 5.1.

Notice that this condition of equality of the rates of substitution (or equivalently, the slopes) is true for any consumer. In an equilibrium, where every consumer is at a point of maximum feasible utility, every consumer will have the *same* marginal rate of substitution, since they all face the same prices, even though solution points may be quite different for different consumers.

The m-dimensional case is similar. The consumer's problem can be expressed as

$$\max \ u(\mathbf{x})$$
$$\text{sub to } \mathbf{p} \cdot \mathbf{x} = r$$
$$\mathbf{x} \in X,$$

where $X = \mathcal{R}_+^m$. The Lagrangian is $L = u(\mathbf{x}) - \lambda(\mathbf{p} \cdot \mathbf{x} - r)$. At an interior point, the first-order necessary conditions are

$$\frac{\partial u(\mathbf{x})}{\partial x_j} = \lambda p_j, \qquad j = 1, 2, \ldots, m.$$

Dividing the jth equation by the kth leads to

$$\text{MRS}_{kj} = \frac{\partial u(\mathbf{x})/\partial x_j}{\partial u(\mathbf{x})/\partial x_k} = \frac{p_j}{p_k}, \qquad j \neq k,$$

which is a direct generalization of the two-commodity case.

We assumed above that the solution occurred at a point $\mathbf{x}$ with $\mathbf{x} > \mathbf{0}$. It is possible, however, for one or more components of $\mathbf{x}$ to be zero. Such a solution is called a *corner solution*. A two-dimensional case is illustrated in Fig. 5.2. If the solution occurs at a point with $x_1 > 0$ and $x_2 = 0$, the first-order condition is that $\text{MRS}_{21} > p_1/p_2$. This result extends to higher dimensions.

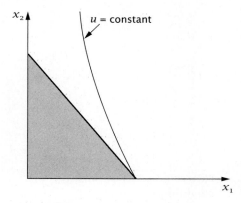

FIGURE 5.2   Corner solution.

Benefit Maximization

The consumer's problem of maximizing utility subject to a budget constraint can be converted to one of maximizing the net of benefits minus cost. This interpretation provides additional insight and leads quickly to some alternative characterizations of the necessary conditions.

Suppose that the solution to the original consumer problem occurs at $\mathbf{x}^*$ and has utility value $u^* = u(\mathbf{x}^*)$. Given a reference bundle $\mathbf{g} \geq 0$, $\mathbf{g} \neq 0$, define the benefit function $b(\mathbf{x}, u)$ as usual. Then consider the function $b(\mathbf{x}, u^*) - \mathbf{p} \cdot \mathbf{x}$. This is the *net* of benefit minus cost for the bundle $\mathbf{x}$. This net benefit will be maximized at $\mathbf{x}^*$, the bundle that is optimal for the first problem. The exact conditions for this equivalence are spelled out in the following proposition.

Proposition 5.2.   *Assume that the utility function u is continuous and $\mathbf{g} \geq 0$, $\mathbf{g} \neq 0$. Let $\mathbf{p} \geq 0$ be given with $\mathbf{p} \cdot \mathbf{g} = 1$. Suppose $\mathbf{x}^* \in X = \mathcal{R}_+^m$ and let $u^* = u(\mathbf{x}^*)$. Define the two problems*

$$\max_{\mathbf{x} \in X} u(\mathbf{x})$$
$$\text{sub to } \mathbf{p} \cdot \mathbf{x} \leq r \tag{5.7a}$$

$$\max_{\mathbf{x} \in X} b(\mathbf{x}, u^*) - \mathbf{p} \cdot \mathbf{x}. \tag{5.7b}$$

Then

    (a) *Assume that the utility function satisfies local nonsatiation. If $\mathbf{x}^*$ solves problem (5.7a), then $\mathbf{x}^*$ also solves problem (5.7b).*

    (b) *Assume that $\mathbf{p} \cdot \mathbf{x}^* > 0$ and that $b(\mathbf{x}^*, u^*) = 0$. If $\mathbf{x}^*$ solves problem (5.7b), then $\mathbf{x}^*$ also solves problem (5.7a) with $r = \mathbf{p} \cdot \mathbf{x}^*$.*

Proof: This is really a restatement of Proposition 4.6, Section 4.3, but we shall sketch a direct proof.

(a) Let $\mathbf{x}^*$ solve (5.7a). Suppose there is $\mathbf{x} \in X$ with

$$b(\mathbf{x}, u^*) - \mathbf{p} \cdot \mathbf{x} > b(\mathbf{x}^*, u^*) - \mathbf{p} \cdot \mathbf{x}^*.$$

Then

$$\mathbf{p} \cdot (\mathbf{x} - b(\mathbf{x}, u^*)\mathbf{g}) < \mathbf{p} \cdot \mathbf{x}^* - b(\mathbf{x}^*, u^*) \le \mathbf{p} \cdot \mathbf{x}^*.$$

By definition of $b(\mathbf{x}, u^*)$, we have

$$u(\mathbf{x} - b(\mathbf{x}, u^*)\mathbf{g}) \ge u^*.$$

By local nonsatiation there is an $\mathbf{x}'$ near $\mathbf{x} - b(\mathbf{x}, u^*)\mathbf{g}$ with $\mathbf{p} \cdot \mathbf{x}' \le \mathbf{p} \cdot \mathbf{x}^*$ and $u(\mathbf{x}') > u(\mathbf{x}^*)$, which is a contradiction.

(b) Let $\mathbf{x}^*$ solve (5.7b). Suppose there is $\mathbf{x} \in X$ with $u(\mathbf{x}) > u^*$, $\mathbf{p} \cdot \mathbf{x} \le \mathbf{p} \cdot \mathbf{x}^*$. Then if $\mathbf{p} \cdot \mathbf{x}^* > 0$, we can move from $\mathbf{x}$ to a nearby interior point. Specifically, there is $\mathbf{x}'$ near $\mathbf{x}$ with $\mathbf{p} \cdot \mathbf{x}' \le \mathbf{p} \cdot \mathbf{x}^*$ and $b(\mathbf{x}', u^*) > 0$. Hence $b(\mathbf{x}', u^*) - \mathbf{p} \cdot \mathbf{x}' > -\mathbf{p} \cdot \mathbf{x}^*$. Using $b(\mathbf{x}^*, u^*) = 0$ we obtain

$$b(\mathbf{x}', u^*) - \mathbf{p} \cdot \mathbf{x}' > b(\mathbf{x}^*, u^*) - \mathbf{p} \cdot \mathbf{x}^*,$$

which is a contradiction. ∎

This result has great intuitive appeal. It says that a consumer acts so as to maximize the difference between benefit and cost—just like a firm maximizing revenue minus cost. The difference, of course, is that the reference utility level u^*, which is part of the benefit function itself, depends on the optimal solution.

In algebraic or numerical calculation, the benefit approach is just as easy to apply as the standard approach. When formulating necessary conditions, one must not use the functional form for u until after differention of the Lagrangian; u is treated as a constant during the differentiation. An advantage, however, is that the benefit problem is unconstrained. The following example illustrates how a problem can be solved with either method.

Example 5.2 (Two methods). A consumer has utility function $u(x, y) = xy^2$ and faces the budget constraint $x + y = 3$. Here are two solution methods.

1. *Utility-based approach.* The problem is

$$\max\ xy^2$$
$$\text{sub to } x + y = 3.$$

Form the Lagrangian $L = xy^2 - \lambda(x + y - 3)$. Differentiation with respect to x and y and use of the budget constraint give the three equations

$$y^2 - \lambda = 0$$
$$2xy - \lambda = 0$$
$$x + y = 3.$$

These are easily solved, giving $x = 1$ and $y = 2$.

2. *Benefit approach.* The benefit function corresponding to the utility function xy^2 is $x - u/y^2$. Therefore the consumer's problem is

$$\max \; x - \frac{u}{y^2} - x - y.$$

The variable x cancels, so upon differentiating, the only equation (aside from the constraint) is $2u/y^3 - 1 = 0$. Now (after differenting) we substitute $u = xy^2$ to get

$$\frac{2x}{y} - 1 = 0$$

$$x + y = 3.$$

These two equations again give $x = 1$ and $y = 2$.

Marginal Benefits

The benefit maximization formulation of the consumer's problem leads to a simple interpretation of prices. From the above discussion we see that if prices are normalized by $\mathbf{p \cdot g} = 1$, the consumer's problem can be expressed as

$$\max_{\mathbf{x} \in X} \; b(\mathbf{x}, u^*) - \mathbf{p \cdot x}.$$

This is an unconstrained problem, and the first-order necessary conditions (assuming an interior point solution) are

$$p_j = \frac{\partial b(\mathbf{x}, u^*)}{\partial x_j}, \qquad j = 1, 2, \ldots, m.$$

Hence, prices are equal to *marginal benefits*. It is not necessary to form ratios, as with marginal rates of substitution. The normalization $\mathbf{p \cdot g} = 1$ means that both benefit and cost are expressed in units of $\mathbf{g}$. Likewise prices and marginal benefits are measured relative to the price of $\mathbf{g}$.

As another interpretation, suppose a consumer has selected $\mathbf{x}^*$ at prices $\mathbf{p}$, and then the consumer is offered a small incremental bundle $\Delta\mathbf{x}$ for no charge. The market value of this increment is $\mathbf{p \cdot \Delta x}$. This is, to a first-order approximation, also equal to the benefit of the increment since

$$\Delta b \simeq \sum_{j=1}^{m} \frac{\partial b_j}{\partial x_j} \Delta x_j = \sum_{j=1}^{m} p_j \Delta x_j = \mathbf{p \cdot \Delta x}.$$

Hence, marginal benefit equals marginal value.

Uniqueness and Continuity

In general, as illustrated in Fig. 5.3, the demand corresponding to a given $\mathbf{p}$ and r may not be unique. In the figure, there are two solutions $\mathbf{x}_A$ and $\mathbf{x}_B$ corresponding to the indicated budget.

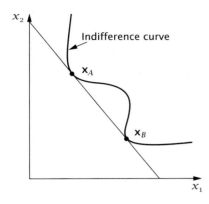

FIGURE 5.3   Nonunique solution.

The following proposition is quite important, at least from a technical viewpoint, since it gives conditions that guarantee that demand is unique and the resulting demand function is continuous.

Proposition 5.3.   *If a preference ordering is continuous, satisfies local non-satiation, and is strictly convex, then for all $\mathbf{p} > 0$, $r > 0$, the demand $\mathbf{x}(\mathbf{p}, r)$ is unique and defines a single-valued, continuous function of $(\mathbf{p}, r)$.*

Proof: The proof follows easily from Proposition C.3 in Appendix C and from the stated properties of the preference ordering. ▋

5.3   Qualitative Characterization of Demand

In addition to the formal mathematical definition of demand, it is helpful to develop certain qualitative concepts that broadly distinguish classes of preference orderings and demand functions.

Substitutes and Complements

Although the preference orderings of different individuals may in general vary widely, the functional relation between certain commodities may lead to similarities in individual demand relations for the commodities. These similarities provide a means for classifying commodities themselves.

A commodity is a *substitute* for another if it provides a similar service or other satisfaction. Examples of substitute pairs are tea and coffee, pie and cake, and TV and movies. Indifference curves for close substitutes look like those shown in Fig. 5.4a. *Perfect substitutes* have indifference curves that are straight lines.

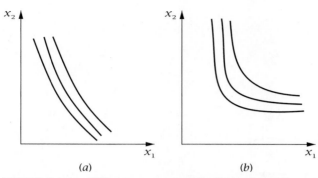

FIGURE 5.4   Indifference curves: (*a*) substitutes; (*b*) complements.

The relative prices of close substitutes are critical. A small change in relative prices can lead to a large change in relative demands. In the extreme case of perfect substitutes, the demand will be a corner solution, unless the price ratio is exactly equal to the MRS.

Commodities are *complements* if they tend to be used together. Examples include bread and jam, automobiles and gasoline, and diapers and baby food. Indifference curves for close complements look like those shown in Fig. 5.4*b*. Two commodities are *perfect complements* if they are always consumed in fixed proportions—like left and right shoes—and an excess of one does not increase utility. Relative prices are not very important for complements. What is important is the total price, which is a weighted sum of the two.

Expansion Paths

It is useful to carry out a form of comparative statics for demand functions, seeing how they might change in response to a change in income or prices. The results can be characterized broadly, considering a range of variations, rather than merely looking at differential effects. Later, in Section 5.6, we present an analysis based on derivatives.

Suppose prices are held fixed, but the income of a consumer is slowly increased. The collection of corresponding demand points will trace out a path in the nonnegative orthant called the *income expansion path*. The path can be projected onto the plane defined by any two commodities, to show the income expansion path relative to these two commodities.

Typical income expansion paths are shown in Fig. 5.5. In Fig. 5.5(*a*) consumption of both goods x_1 and x_2 increases as income increases. In Fig. 5.5(*b*) x_2 is an *inferior good* since its consumption drops as income increases. (An example might be cheap wine—as income increases individuals tend to switch to more expensive brands.)

If the demand of just a single commodity is graphed as a function of income, the result is known as the *Engle curve* for that commodity. An

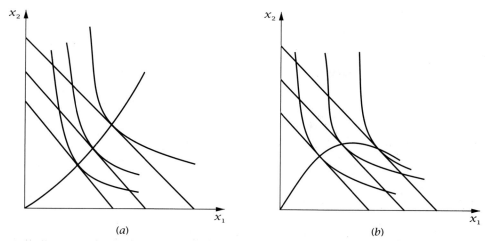

FIGURE 5.5 Income expansion paths: (*a*) normal goods; (*b*) inferior goods.

example is shown in Fig. 5.6. As a special case, suppose preferences are homothetic (see Exercise 2, Chapter 4), that is, utility can be expressed by a function $u(\mathbf{x})$ such that $u(t\mathbf{x}) = tu(\mathbf{x})$ for all $t > 0$. Then the expansion paths and Engle curves are straight lines.

Example 5.3 (City and suburb).   Many urban areas consist of a central city, where most of the business and cultural activities are located, and suburbs, where many people live who work in the city. Usually the very poor and the very rich live in the city itself, while most of the middle class live in the sub-urbs (see Fig. 5.7). Why is that? One possible answer is based on the pattern of income expansion curves that follows from some simple assumptions about preferences.

Assume that the utility function of a typical individual (no matter of what economic class) can be written in the additive form

$$u(h, t, z) = U(h) + V(t) + W(z)$$

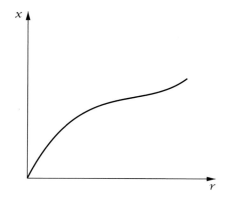

FIGURE 5.6 Engle curve.

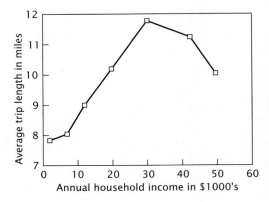

FIGURE 5.7 Commute length versus annual household income, excluding home workers (source: 1977 Nationwide Personal Transportation Study, U.S. Department of Transportation, Federal Highway Administration, Office of Highway Planning).

where h represents housing quantity, t represents commuting distance to the city, and z represents expenditures on all other goods and activities. Here U and W are increasing and concave, and we assume that the marginal utilities of housing and of goods z go to zero as $z \to \infty$. $V(t)$ decreases with respect to t, representing the fact that commuting distance is considered something bad rather than a good. Housing prices decrease with t according to a function $p(t) \geq p_\infty > 0$. We also assume that commuting cost is proportional to t. According to this framework, the individual selects h, t, and z as a solution to

$$\max\ U(h) + V(t) + W(z)$$
$$\text{sub to}\ \ p(t)h + ct + z \leq r$$
$$h \geq 0, \quad t \geq 0, \quad z \geq 0.$$

It can be shown (see Exercise 8) that, under certain technical assumptions, $t = 0$ for r small. Then, as r increases to infinity, t first increases and then decreases toward zero. Hence, according to this model, the poor and the rich live in the central city, while the middle class lives in the suburbs. This result is true even though everyone has the same utility function.

There is a simple explanation of this result. For small h, a move out of the city will increase commuting costs more than can be saved in housing costs (since the savings are only a percentage of housing costs, and commuting costs are in absolute terms). For larger values of h, it does pay to move out. For larger values yet, marginal utility of housing is small and it pays to move back toward the city to cut down on the disutility of commuting.

Offer Curves

We can also plot the demand of a commodity as a function of price while income and all other prices remain fixed. The resulting family of solutions traces out a path in the nonnegative orthant called the *price expansion path*

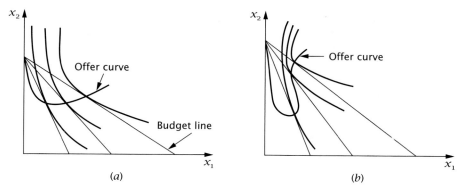

FIGURE 5.8   Offer curves (p_1 is changing): (*a*) normal good; (*b*) Giffen good.

or *offer curve*. Again the results can be projected onto the plane corresponding to any two commodities. Examples are shown in Fig. 5.8.

Fig. 5.8*a* shows a *normal* good, for which the demand increases as the price is decreased. Fig. 5.8*b* shows the special situation of a *Giffen* good, for which, in some region of the curve, demand actually decreases as the price is decreased. The economist Robert Giffen is said to have observed this phenomenon in nineteenth-century Ireland for potatoes. As the price increased, consumers suffered an effective loss of income, forcing them to give up other goods and buy more potatoes. Later analyses cast doubt on whether a Giffen good has actually ever been observed; in any event, such goods are extremely rare.

Elasticity

When discussing the sensitivity of a consumer's demand to changes in economic variables such as price or income level, one might measure this sensitivity directly—say $\Delta x/\Delta r$ or dx/dr in the case of sensitivity to income. As discussed in Section 2.5, a disadvantage of this type of measure is that it depends on the units used. It is therefore traditional to use elasticities for demand sensitivities. For example, the *income elasticity of demand* is

$$\varepsilon_j = \frac{dx_j}{x_j} \bigg/ \frac{dr}{r} = \frac{d \ln x_j}{d \ln r}.$$

It is the ratio of the percentage change in demand to a percentage change in income. Demand elasticities are defined with respect to price changes as well.

There is a simple relation among income elasticities.

Proposition 5.4.   *The average income elasticity is unity. That is, $k_1\varepsilon_1 + k_2\varepsilon_2 + \cdots + k_m\varepsilon_m = 1$ where $k_j = p_j x_j/r$ is the proportion of income spent on commodity j.*

Proof: We have

$$\sum_{j=1}^{m} p_j x_j(\mathbf{p}, r) = r .$$

Hence,

$$\sum_{j=1}^{m} p_j \frac{\partial x_j(\mathbf{p}, r)}{\partial r} = 1 ,$$

and

$$\sum_{j=1}^{m} \frac{p_j x_j}{r} \varepsilon_j = 1 . \quad \blacksquare$$

5.4   Duality and Demand Functions

The indirect utility function is the dual of the original utility function, since it expresses preferences with respect to prices and income rather than quantities. It should not be surprising that the demand function can be recovered from the indirect utility function since, in fact, the value of the indirect utility function is determined by the bundle that maximizes utility subject to the budget constraint defined by given prices and income. The formula for this recovery is known as *Roy's identity.* It is similar to Shephard's lemma and Hotelling's lemma, which give expressions for a firm's demand functions.

Roy's identity.   *Assume that the utility function u satisfies local nonsatiation and that the utility function u and the demand function are continuously differentiable at a point* $(\mathbf{p}, r) > 0$, $\mathbf{x}(\mathbf{p}, r) > 0$. *Then at such a point*

$$x_j(\mathbf{p}, r) = -\frac{\partial v(\mathbf{p}, r)/\partial p_j}{\partial v(\mathbf{p}, r)/\partial r} , \qquad j = 1, 2, \ldots, m ,$$

or in vector form

$$\mathbf{x}(\mathbf{p}, r) = -\frac{\nabla_{\mathbf{p}} v(\mathbf{p}, r)}{\partial v(\mathbf{p}, r)/\partial r} . \tag{5.8}$$

Proof: According to the envelope theorem (Appendix C) we have

$$\frac{\partial v(\mathbf{p}, r)}{\partial p_r} = -\lambda x_j(\mathbf{p}, r), \qquad j = 1, 2, \ldots, m$$

$$\frac{\partial v(\mathbf{p}, r)}{\partial r} = \lambda .$$

Division gives the result. $\blacksquare$

Example 5.4 (General Cobb-Douglas utility). Consider the indirect Cobb-Douglas utility function

$$v(\mathbf{p}, r) = \prod_{j=1}^{m} \left(\frac{\alpha_j r}{\alpha p_j} \right)^{\alpha_j}$$

where $\alpha = \sum_{j=1}^{m} \alpha_j$. We easily calculate

$$\frac{\partial v(\mathbf{p}, r)}{\partial p_j} = - \frac{\alpha_j}{p_j} v(\mathbf{p}, r)$$

$$\frac{\partial v(\mathbf{p}, r)}{\partial r} = \frac{\alpha}{r} v(\mathbf{p}, r).$$

Thus, Roy's identity gives the demand functions as

$$x_j(\mathbf{p}, r) = \frac{\alpha_j r}{\alpha p_j}.$$

This agrees with our earlier derivation.

Example 5.5 (Leontief utility). The Leontief utility function

$$u(\mathbf{x}) = \min \left\{ \frac{x_1}{a_1}, \frac{x_2}{a_2}, \ldots, \frac{x_m}{a_m} \right\}$$

is not itself differentiable, but the indirect utility function

$$v(\mathbf{p}, r) = \frac{r}{\mathbf{p} \cdot \mathbf{a}},$$

where $\mathbf{a} = (a_1, a_2, \ldots, a_m)$, is differentiable. Applying Roy's identity, we obtain

$$\mathbf{x}(\mathbf{p}, r) = - \frac{\nabla_{\mathbf{p}} v(\mathbf{p}, r)}{\partial v(\mathbf{p}, r)/\partial r} = \frac{r\mathbf{a}}{(\mathbf{p} \cdot \mathbf{a})^2} \Big/ \frac{1}{\mathbf{p} \cdot \mathbf{a}} = \frac{r\mathbf{a}}{\mathbf{p} \cdot \mathbf{a}},$$

which is the correct formula. Hence Roy's identity often works even if all the differentiability properties of the statement do not hold.

Inverse Demand Functions

The inverse demand function gives the price vector as a function of demand. However, to define the inverse demand function, income must be normalized, for to invert the demand function, there can be only as many price variables as demand variables. Hence we arbitrarily set $r = 1$. Prices at a different value of income r can be obtained simply by multiplying by r, since the demand function itself is homogeneous of degree zero. The inverse demand function $\mathbf{p}(\mathbf{x})$ is therefore defined by the equation

$$\mathbf{x}(\mathbf{p}(\mathbf{x}), 1) = \mathbf{x}. \tag{5.9}$$

Note that this function is normalized in such a way that for any $\mathbf{x}$ there holds $\mathbf{p}(\mathbf{x}) \cdot \mathbf{x} = 1$. In general the inverse may not exist. If the utility function

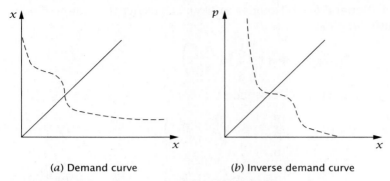

(a) Demand curve   (b) Inverse demand curve

FIGURE 5.9   Demand and inverse demand curves.

is not quasi-concave, for example, there will be **x**'s that are never chosen for any **p**, and **p(x)** is not defined for such **x**'s. However, the inverse will exist under the conditions of Proposition 5.3. In the one-dimensional case the inverse demand curve is found from the ordinary Marshallian demand curve by mere reversal of the two axes. The graph can just be rotated around the line $x = p$ as shown in Fig. 5.9.

5.5   Compensated Demand

The analysis of demand functions is complicated by the fact that as **p** varies, $\mathbf{x}(\mathbf{p}, r)$ moves from one indifference set to another. This observation motivates a new demand function defined relative to a fixed utility level. This new demand function has a meaningful economic interpretation and forms the basis for a deeper analysis of consumer demand.

Hicksian demand.   The *Hicksian demand* is the solution **x** of the problem

$$\min_{\mathbf{x}} \; \mathbf{p}\cdot\mathbf{x}$$

$$\text{sub to } u(\mathbf{x}) \geq u$$

$$\mathbf{x} \in X.$$

The solution **x** (which may be set-valued) is denoted $\mathbf{h}(\mathbf{p}, u)$.

If there is a unique solution for each **p** and u, the solution $\mathbf{h}(\mathbf{p}, u)$ is a well-defined, single-valued function termed the *Hicksian demand* function.

The Hicksian demand function is also called the *compensated demand function* because, as discussed later, it can be viewed as demand after an appropriate income change that compensates for a potential change in utility. Hicksian demand is defined relative to constant utility.

We recall that the expenditure function is defined as

$$e(\mathbf{p}, u) = \min_{\mathbf{x}} \ \mathbf{p} \cdot \mathbf{x}$$

$$\text{sub to } u(\mathbf{x}) \geq u$$

$$\mathbf{x} \in X.$$

Therefore, the Hicksian demand function gives the points that define values of the expenditure function. Specifically $e(\mathbf{p}, u) = \mathbf{p} \cdot \mathbf{h}(\mathbf{p}, u)$. The usual demand function, or Marshallian demand, on the other hand, is the solution point defining the value of the indirect utility function $v(\mathbf{p}, r)$. That is, $v(\mathbf{p}, r) = u(\mathbf{x}(\mathbf{p}, r))$.

The definition of the Hicksian demand and evaluation of the expenditure function are illustrated in Fig. 5.10. The point $\mathbf{x}_1$ corresponds to prices $\mathbf{p}_1$ and utility u. If prices are changed to $\mathbf{p}_2$ and income is held fixed, the new budget line will be the other solid line shown. If income is then changed to $e(\mathbf{p}_2, u)$, the new budget line will be the dashed line shown, and this will give $\mathbf{x}_2$.

The definition of $e(\mathbf{p}, u)$ is analogous to the definition of the cost function $c(\mathbf{w}, \mathbf{q})$ for production, with the set $\{\mathbf{x} : u(\mathbf{x}) \geq u\}$ playing the role of the input requirement set $V(\mathbf{q})$. (As said earlier, the expenditure function is often called the consumer's cost function.) Likewise, the Hicksian demand for a consumer is analogous to the conditional factor demand for a firm. It is the demand of a consumer conditional on obtaining a fixed utility level. Accordingly, there is a simple formula for the Hicksian demand function in terms of the expenditure function.

Shephard's lemma for consumers. *If the expenditure function is differentiable at* $(\mathbf{p}, u)$, *then*

$$h_j(\mathbf{p}, u) = \frac{\partial e(\mathbf{p}, u)}{\partial p_j}, \qquad j = 1, 2, \ldots, m,$$

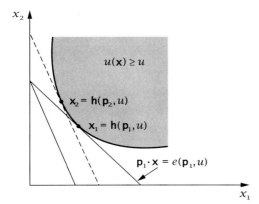

FIGURE 5.10 **Hicksian demand.**

or in vector form

$$\mathbf{h}(\mathbf{p}, u) = \nabla_{\mathbf{p}} e(\mathbf{p}, u).$$

Proof: The proof is identical to that of Shephard's lemma in Section 2.14. ∎

Inverse Compensated Demand and the Benefit Function

It is a bit tricky to define the inverse of the compensated demand function $\mathbf{h}(\mathbf{p}, u)$. Note first that $\mathbf{h}(\mathbf{p}, u)$ is homogeneous of degree zero with respect to **p**. This means that if **p** is multiplied by a positive constant, the demand does not change, because demand must always lie on the same indifference curve. This shows that without some form of normalization the inverse demand (a price vector) will not be unique. Second, note that if an **x** is selected that is not on the proper indifference curve, it is impossible to find **p** such that $\mathbf{h}(\mathbf{p}, u) = \mathbf{x}$. The true inverse is defined only for **x**'s on the indifference curve. Third, some **x**'s on the indifference curve will possibly not be selected for any **p**, and hence no inverse applies to them.

The first two of these problems are handled easily by using the benefit function. We handle the normalization problem by always using $\mathbf{p} \cdot \mathbf{g} = 1$. We handle **x**'s that are off the indifference curve by moving from **x** in the direction **g** until we reach the indifference curve, and then we find the inverse of that point. This is illustrated in Fig. 5.11. The third problem, that some **x**'s on the indifference curve might not be invertible, is solved by assuming that the utility function is quasi-concave.

We construct the appropriate inverse by using the duality between the expenditure function and the benefit function as given in Section 4.4,

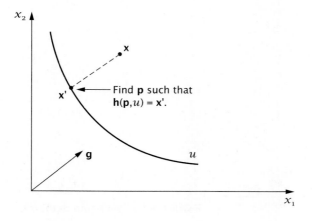

FIGURE 5.11   Finding the inverse.

which is valid if the utility function is strongly monotonic and quasi-concave. Namely,

$$b(\mathbf{x}, u) = \min_{\mathbf{p}}\{\mathbf{p}\cdot\mathbf{x} - e(\mathbf{p}, u) : \mathbf{p}\cdot\mathbf{g} = 1, \ \mathbf{p} \geq \mathbf{0}\}.$$

This leads to the following definition:

Adjusted price function. The *adjusted price function* is the solution of the problem

$$\min_{\mathbf{p}}\ \{\mathbf{p}\cdot\mathbf{x} - e(\mathbf{p}, u)\}$$

$$\text{sub to } \mathbf{p}\cdot\mathbf{g} = 1$$

$$\mathbf{p} \geq \mathbf{0}.$$

This solution is denoted $\mathbf{p}(\mathbf{x}, u)$.

We can express the adjusted price function $\mathbf{p}(\mathbf{x}, u)$ in terms of derivatives of the benefit function.

Proposition 5.5 (Adjusted price expression). *If utility is quasi-concave and the benefit function is differentiable at* $(\mathbf{x}, u)$, *then*

$$p_j(\mathbf{x}, u) = \frac{\partial b(\mathbf{x}, u)}{\partial x_j},$$

or in vector form,

$$\mathbf{p}(\mathbf{x}, u) = \nabla_{\mathbf{x}} b(\mathbf{x}, u).$$

Proof: The proof follows from part (*b*) of the theorem on the duality of *b* and *e* in Section 4.4 and the envelope theorem (Appendix C). ∎

This result can be regarded as the dual of Shephard's lemma for consumers, given above. Indeed, much of the standard material about demand functions that is presented in the next section can be expressed in dual (or inverse) form using the relation between the adjusted price function and the benefit function. The most significant application of this result, however, is presented in Chapter 10, where we wish to quantify the total benefits due to a proposed economic project.

5.6 The Slutsky Equation and Its Consequences

Proposition 4.6, Section 4.3, shows that the demand points used to calculate the indirect utility and the expenditure function are identical if certain technical assumptions are satisfied. The results of the proposition can be expressed in compact form as

$$\mathbf{x}(\mathbf{p}, r) = \mathbf{h}(\mathbf{p}, v(\mathbf{p}, r)) \tag{5.10a}$$

$$\mathbf{h}(\mathbf{p}, u) = \mathbf{x}(\mathbf{p}, e(\mathbf{p}, u)) . \tag{5.10b}$$

These are identities that hold for all values of $\mathbf{p}$, r, and u.

Equation (5.10b) shows directly that the demand $\mathbf{h}(\mathbf{p}, u)$ is a Marshallian demand for some income level. This is the rationale for the term *compensated demand function*. When prices are changed, income is changed also— just enough that the optimizing consumer is perfectly compensated for the price change and ends up at the same utility level.

The identity $\mathbf{h}(\mathbf{p}, u) = \mathbf{x}(\mathbf{p}, e(\mathbf{p}, u))$ given above leads to a classic differential relation between Hicksian and Marshallian demand, known as the Slutsky equation.

Slutsky equation proposition.   *If the Marshallian and Hicksian demand functions are well defined and continuously differentiable, then for $\mathbf{p} > 0$, $\mathbf{x} > 0$,*

$$\frac{\partial x_i(\mathbf{p}, r)}{\partial p_j} = \frac{\partial h_i(\mathbf{p}, u)}{\partial p_j} - \frac{\partial x_i(\mathbf{p}, r)}{\partial r} \cdot x_j(\mathbf{p}, r), \tag{5.11}$$

where $u = v(\mathbf{p}, r)$.

Proof: The equation is obtained through differentiation of identity (5.10b), which leads directly to

$$\frac{\partial h_i(\mathbf{p}, u)}{\partial p_j} = \frac{\partial x_i(\mathbf{p}, r)}{\partial p_j} + \frac{\partial x_i(\mathbf{p}, r)}{\partial r} \cdot \frac{\partial e(\mathbf{p}, u)}{\partial p_j} .$$

Then by use of Shephard's lemma from the previous section, the term $\partial e(\mathbf{p}, u)/\partial p_j$ is just x_j. This yields the Slutsky equation.   ∎

Substitution and Income Effects

The Slutsky equation decomposes the change in demand caused by a price change into two effects: a *substitution effect* and an *income effect*. The substitution effect is the change in compensated demand due to the change in relative prices. The substitution (per unit change in p_i) is represented by the first term on the right side of the equation. The income effect is the change in demand due to the effective change in income caused by the price change. A change Δp_i induces an effective income change of $x_i \Delta p_i$; hence x_i is the rate of income change. That is why x_i appears in the second term of the right side of the equation, representing the income effect. The decomposition is illustrated in Fig. 5.12.

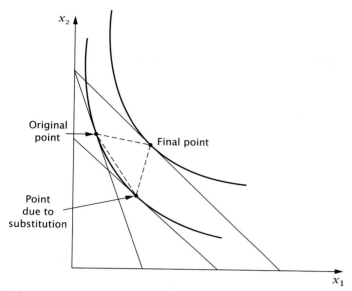

FIGURE 5.12 Decomposition of demand change.

Substitution Terms and the Slutsky Matrix

The substitution effect is measured by the partial derivatives

$$s_{ij} = \frac{\partial h_i(\mathbf{p}, u)}{\partial p_j},$$

and these are referred to as *substitution terms*. The $m \times m$ matrix of substitution terms is

$$\mathbf{S} = \left[\frac{\partial h_i(\mathbf{p}, u)}{\partial p_j} \right]$$

and is called the *substitution matrix* or *Slutsky matrix*. Its principal properties are stated below.

Proposition 5.6 (Substitution properties). *Assume that the substitution terms exist and are continuous. Then the matrix of substitution terms is symmetric and negative semidefinite.*

Proof: By definition,

$$e(\mathbf{p}, u) = \mathbf{p} \cdot \mathbf{h}(\mathbf{p}, u).$$

Since $\mathbf{h}$ is continuously differentiable, we may write

$$\frac{\partial e(\mathbf{p}, u)}{\partial p_i} = h_i(\mathbf{p}, u) + \sum_{j=1}^{m} p_j \frac{\partial h_j(\mathbf{p}, u)}{\partial p_i}.$$

This shows that the expenditure function is continuously differentiable, and hence by Shephard's lemma

$$h_i(\mathbf{p}, u) = \frac{\partial e(\mathbf{p}, u)}{\partial p_i}.$$

We then obtain

$$\frac{\partial h_i(\mathbf{p}, u)}{\partial p_j} = \frac{\partial^2 e(\mathbf{p}, u)}{\partial p_i \partial p_j}.$$

It follows immediately that the matrix of substitution terms is symmetric. Because the expenditure function is concave in $\mathbf{p}$, it also follows that the matrix of substitution terms is negative semidefinite. (See Proposition B.3, Appendix B.) ∎

Comparative Statics of Compensated Demand

The expression for compensated demand through Shephard's lemma leads directly to some important qualitative conclusions. (Also see Appendix D.)

1. *The compensated own price effect is nonpositive.* That is,

$$\frac{\partial h_i(\mathbf{p}, u)}{\partial p_i} \leq 0.$$

This follows directly from the fact that the Slutsky matrix is negative semidefinite, and hence its diagonal terms must be nonpositive.

2. *The compensated cross price effects are symmetric.* That is,

$$\frac{\partial h_i(\mathbf{p}, u)}{\partial p_j} = \frac{\partial h_j(\mathbf{p}, u)}{\partial p_i}.$$

This is a direct result of the symmetry of the Slutsky matrix.

3. *The average compensated price effect is nonpositive.* That is,

$$\mathbf{dp} \cdot \mathbf{dh} \leq 0.$$

This follows from the calculation

$$dh_i = \sum_{j=1}^{m} s_{ij} \, dp_j$$

and hence

$$\mathbf{dp} \cdot \mathbf{dh} = \sum_{i,j=1}^{m} s_{ij} \, dp_i \, dp_j = \mathbf{dp} \cdot \mathbf{S} \, \mathbf{dp}.$$

This is nonpositive since the Slutsky matrix $\mathbf{S}$ is negative semidefinite.

These properties have important intuitive interpretations. The first property is associated with what one commonly thinks about demand, namely, that demand for a good decreases if its price increases. Actually, however, the above result shows that it is the own compensated demand that will decrease. The effect on ordinary Marshallian demand is found through the Slutsky equation to be

$$\frac{\partial x_i(\mathbf{p}, r)}{\partial p_i} = \frac{\partial h_i(\mathbf{p}, u)}{\partial p_i} - \frac{\partial x_i(\mathbf{p}, r)}{\partial r} \cdot x_i(\mathbf{p}, r).$$

The first term on the right is the substitution effect, which, according to the above property, will always be nonpositive. The second term is the income effect. Usually this term will also be negative (accounting for the minus sign), but for an inferior good it may change sign, and conceivably it could be large enough to dominate, leading to a Giffen good.

The second property of symmetric cross-effects is interesting. It is a result of the maximization operations, or in other words, a consequence of our assumption of utility maximization.

The third property is a kind of overall average property similar to the first one. It can be deduced quite directly even for finite-size (rather than differential) changes in price. (See Exercise 5, Chapter 4.) The first property can also be easily deduced from this one.

Finally, before leaving this topic, note that the Slutsky equations relate changes in Hicksian demand, which are nonobservable, to changes in Marshallian demand, which are observable. In particular we can write the substitution matrix, or Slutsky matrix, in terms of the Marshallian demand just by reordering the terms in the Slutsky equation. Thus the substitution terms are

$$s_{ij} = \frac{\partial h_i(\mathbf{p}, u)}{\partial p_j}$$

or

$$s_{ij} = \frac{\partial x_i(\mathbf{p}, r)}{\partial p_j} + \frac{\partial x_i(\mathbf{p}, r)}{\partial r} x_j(\mathbf{p}, r). \tag{5.12}$$

5.7 Consumer's Surplus and Willingness to Pay

A very useful concept for determining (at least approximately) the value to consumers of various changes in the economy (such as the imposition of taxes) is consumer's surplus. Suppose a monopolist is selling a product to a consumer with a known (inverse) demand curve. Such a curve is shown in Fig. 5.13. Suppose that q^* units are to be sold. If these were sold competitively (at a single price), all units would be sold at a price p^*. Suppose, instead, that in an effort to extract as much profit as possible the monopolist negotiates the sale of each unit separately. Following the inverse demand curve, the monopolist would charge p_1 for the first unit, p_2 for the second,

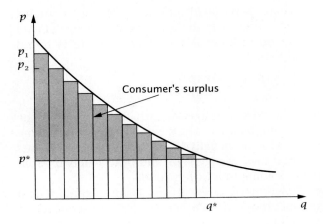

FIGURE 5.13   Consumer's surplus diagram.

and so forth, down to p^* for the last unit. In this case the monopolist would receive revenue equal to the area of the thin rectangles. In the limit where the width of the rectangles is made zero, the total revenue is the area under the demand curve.

In the case of single-price sales, the total revenue associated with the sale of q^* units would be equal to the bottom rectangular area, p^*q^*. This means that the consumer would pay less than otherwise, by an amount equal to the area under the demand curve and above the price p^*. This area is termed the *consumer's surplus* and expresses in monetary terms the surplus that the consumer obtains due to the single-price system.

Actually there is a slight flaw in the above argument, and that is why consumer's surplus is only an approximate measure. If the consumer were forced to buy the individual units at the price on the demand curve, he or she would use more income than if all units were purchased at p^*. This reduction in income would usually mean that fewer units would be purchased. Think of it this way: if the consumer first paid the consumer's surplus to the seller and the seller then offered to sell all units at p^*, the consumer would not purchase q^*. Hence, the process of stepping down the demand curve is not quite what would happen. The consumer would step down a different curve, as discussed in the next subsection. However, if the income effect is small, the simplified argument is approximately correct, and consumer's surplus is a meaningful and convenient measure.

Although we constructed the consumer's surplus on the diagram by summing vertical slivers under the demand curve, the end result can actually be best described as the sum of horizontal slivers from the top down to p^*. Indeed, as a slight generalization, when the price is changed from p^0 to p^1, the associated consumer's surplus is

$$CS = \int_{p^1}^{p^0} x(p)\, dp,$$

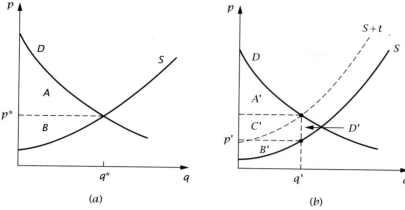

FIGURE 5.14 Analysis of a tax.

where $x(p)$ is the Marshallian demand curve. Consumer surplus is best regarded as a function of price.

The above discussion pertained to a single consumer. However, it is standard practice to apply the final result to a group as well by using the area defined by the aggregate demand curve. Consumer's surplus is extended to consumers' surplus (note the change in the placement of the apostrophe); the resulting concept can be used to analyze the proposed projects or policies. Two examples are offered below.

Example 5.6.   Suppose a good is currently sold competitively, with price p^* and quantity q^* being determined by the intersection of supply and demand curves, as shown in Fig. 5.14. The government plans to add a tax t to the price of the commodity. Let us determine the total value of this change in the economy.

In the original situation the consumers' surplus is the area A, as discussed above. The profit can also be found from the diagram. Since under perfect competition the inverse supply curve is equal to the marginal cost curve, the area under the supply curve is the total variable cost. Hence, the area B is revenue minus variable cost, or profit plus fixed cost.

The situation with the tax is shown in Fig. 5.14b. The tax t shifts the supply curve upward by t units. Consumers will pay $p' + t$ per unit, and producers will receive p' per unit. We have the following associations for areas in the figure:

$$A' = \text{consumers' surplus}$$
$$B' = \text{profit} + \text{fixed cost}$$
$$C' = \text{government revenue}$$
$$D' = \text{loss}.$$

Clearly $A' + B' + C' + D' = A + B$. The area D' is called loss (or *deadweight loss*) because D' is the net decrease in total benefits to all parties (including the government) as a result of the imposed tax.

Willingness to Pay

Suppose a consumer has an opportunity to purchase a quantity q of a commodity. We wish to determine how much this opportunity is worth to the consumer, measured in units of expenditure on other items. To determine this value we again refer to Fig. 5.13, but now the curve shown is the consumer's compensated inverse demand curve. This curve is found by fixing utility u^0 at the original value (at $q = 0$), finding the compensated demand curve with this value of utility, and then drawing it in inverse form. We can then imagine stepping down the curve one unit at a time, buying each unit at the price indicated. The value of the successive units are the areas of the thin vertical slices under the curve. The consumer is willing to pay this much for each unit, and utility remains constant during this process. The total area under the curve is the total willingness to pay. That is, the total willingness to pay is

$$W(q) = \int_0^q p_c(\xi, u^0)\, d\xi,$$

where $p_c(\xi, u^0)$ is the compensated inverse demand (or the adjusted price with the price of all other commodities fixed). Hence,

$$p_c(q, u^0) = W'(q).$$

(See Exercise 3 for an alternative derivation of this result.)

If the consumer purchases q units at price p, the area below the compensated demand curve but above the price p is the *net* willingness to pay. In general, of course, this will be somewhat different from the consumer's surplus, which is computed in a similar way using the Marshallian inverse demand curve. If there is no income effect—that is, if $\partial x(p, r)/\partial r = 0$— the two demand curves are equal, and the net willingness to pay is equal to the consumer's surplus.

These measures of the value of an opportunity are treated in more detail in Chapter 10.

*5.8   The Integrability Problem

Given a demand function $\mathbf{x}(\mathbf{p}, r)$, how can we recover the underlying utility function? This is the integrability problem. We shall show how to solve this problem by solving a differential equation and integrating back, ultimately, to the utility function. The Slutsky matrix plays a key role in this process.

Suppose we have a continuously differentiable (single-valued) demand function $x(\mathbf{p}, r)$. If this function is well behaved, and the budget constraint is always satisfied by equality, then our previous analysis has shown that $x(\mathbf{p}, r)$ satisfies the following conditions:

1. *Nonnegativity:* $x(\mathbf{p}, r) \geq 0$ for all $\mathbf{p}$ and r.
2. *Homogeneity:* $x(t\mathbf{p}, tr) = x(\mathbf{p}, r)$ for all $t > 0$.
3. *Feasibility:* $\mathbf{p} \cdot x(\mathbf{p}, r) = r$.
4. *Symmetry:* The Slutsky matrix S is symmetric.
5. *Negative semidefinite:* The matrix S is negative semidefinite.

The main result of the integrability problem is that these conditions, together with some technical assumptions, are in fact *sufficient* as well as necessary for the integration process.

To solve the integrability problem, we must find an equation to integrate. We recall that Shephard's lemma for consumers provides a link between compensated demand and the expenditure function. Using Shephard's lemma, Section 5.5, and identity (5.10b) at the beginning of Section 5.6, we have

$$\frac{\partial e(\mathbf{p}, u)}{\partial p_i} = x_i(\mathbf{p}, e(\mathbf{p}, u)), \qquad i = 1, 2, \ldots, m. \tag{5.13}$$

The constant u occurs only as a parameter. We also specify a boundary condition of the form $e(\mathbf{p}^*, u) = c$ where $\mathbf{p}^*$ and c are given. We will later show how to recover the utility function from the function e.

Systems of differential equations of the general form (5.13), with a boundary condition $e(\mathbf{p}^*, u) = c$, occur frequently in applied mathematics. It is well known that such a system possesses a solution if the partial derivatives of the x_i's are suitably bounded and symmetric, that is, if $\partial x_i / \partial p_j = \partial x_j / \partial p_i$. The resulting solution of the system is unique and continuous and depends continuously on c.

In our case the matrix of partial derivatives is

$$S = \left[\frac{\partial x_i(\mathbf{p}, r)}{\partial p_j} + \frac{\partial x_i(\mathbf{p}, r)}{\partial r} x_j(\mathbf{p}, r) \right].$$

But S is just the Slutsky matrix. Hence symmetry of the Slutsky matrix together with the other technical assumptions implies that the system (5.13) can be solved.

Under the assumption that all five of the properties listed at the beginning of this section hold, the solution function e will be an expenditure function. Once the function e has been found, we may determine the indirect utility function through the equation

$$e(\mathbf{p}, v) = r.$$

Since e is strictly increasing, this equation can be uniquely inverted to find $v(\mathbf{p}, r)$. The properties possessed by e imply that v has the properties of an indirect utility function spelled out in Proposition 4.4, Section 4.3. This indirect utility function determines an appropriate utility function through the duality relation (4.14b).

A more direct procedure for recovering the utility function is based on a duality relation between the expenditure function and the utility function (see Exercise 14).

Example 5.7 (Cobb-Douglas).   Consider the demand functions

$$x_i(\mathbf{p}, r) = \frac{\alpha_i r}{\alpha p_i}, \quad i = 1, 2, \ldots, m$$

where $\alpha = \sum_{i=1}^{m} \alpha_i$. The system (5.13) becomes

$$\frac{\partial e(\mathbf{p}, u)}{\partial p_i} = \frac{\alpha_i e(\mathbf{p}, u)}{\alpha p_i}, \quad i = 1, 2, \ldots, m.$$

The ith equation can be integrated with respect to p_i to obtain

$$\ln e(\mathbf{p}, u) = \frac{\alpha_i}{\alpha} \ln p_i + c_i$$

where c_i does not depend on p_i (but may depend on p_j for $j \neq i$). Thus, combining these equations we find

$$\ln e(\mathbf{p}, u) = \sum_{i=1}^{m} \frac{\alpha_i}{\alpha} \ln p_i + c$$

where now c is independent of all p_i's. The constant c represents the freedom that we have in setting the boundary condition. For each u, let us take $\mathbf{p}^* = (1, 1, \ldots, 1)$ and use the boundary condition $e(\mathbf{p}^*, u) = u$. Then it follows that

$$\ln e(\mathbf{p}, u) = \sum_{i=1}^{m} \frac{\alpha_i}{\alpha} \ln p_i + \ln u.$$

This is easy to invert, leading to

$$\ln v(\mathbf{p}, r) = - \sum_{i=1}^{m} \frac{\alpha_i}{\alpha} \ln p_i + \ln r$$

which is a monotone transformation of the indirect utility function for a Cobb-Douglas utility found in Section 4.3.

*5.9   Multiple Constraints

Consumer choice is sometimes restricted by constraints beyond the standard nonnegativity and budget constraints. Analysis of such situations can usually be treated by minor extensions of the general theory, but there is an interesting result that relates such problems to the standard problem with a single constraint.

Example 5.8 (Rationing). Rationing usually imposes additional consumption constraints. The simplest rationing procedure restricts the level of consumption of a commodity to be no greater than a fixed amount. This restriction is enforced by issuing ration coupons that must be submitted together with the usual cash payment for each unit of purchase. If, for example, x_1 denotes coffee consumption and an individual has c_1 coffee ration tickets, the constraint is of the form $x_1 \leq c_1$ where c_1 is fixed.

Rationing also can be applied to a group of commodities. For example, a ration ticket might be issued that is valid for purchase of either tea or coffee. The constraint would be of the form $x_1 + x_2 \leq c_1$.

Point rationing assigns points to various critical commodities. Individuals are issued a number of ration points that may be used, along with cash, to purchase the rationed commodities. The point values of the various commodities act like a second set of prices, and the rationing constraint takes the form
$$v_1 x_1 + v_2 x_2 + \cdots + v_m x_m \leq c$$
where v_i is the point value assigned to the ith commodity.

Example 5.9 (Time as a constraint). Enjoyment of some commodities (or activities) requires time, and hence consumption of such items is limited by an implicit total time constraint. To formalize this, we suppose that consumption of a unit of commodity i requires time t_i, $i = 1, 2, \ldots, m$. Other levels of consumption require proportionate amounts of time. Many sporting, leisure, and educational activities have this property. The consumer's choice problem is then

$$\max \ u(x_1, x_2, \ldots, x_m)$$
$$\text{sub to } \ p_1 x_1 + p_2 x_2 + \cdots + p_m x_m \leq r \tag{5.14}$$
$$t_1 x_1 + t_2 x_2 + \cdots + t_m x_m \leq T$$

where T is the total time available.

The following theorem shows that a choice problem with multiple constraints is in some sense equivalent to a problem with a single constraint that is a suitable nonnegative combination of the original constraints. The theorem itself is of general interest, and we shall refer to it later. A reader may wish to pass over the proof, which is based on the separating hyperplane theorem.

Multiple constraints theorem. *Consider the problem*

$$\max \ u(\mathbf{x})$$
$$\text{sub to } \ g_1(\mathbf{x}) \leq 0$$
$$g_2(\mathbf{x}) \leq 0$$
$$\vdots$$
$$g_s(\mathbf{x}) \leq 0$$
$$\mathbf{x} \in \mathcal{X}. \tag{5.15}$$

Suppose u is continuous and quasi-concave, each g_i is convex, and X is a convex set. Suppose also there is an $x_1 \in X$ with $g_i(x_1) < 0$ for all $i = 1, 2, \ldots, s$. Then if x^* is a solution to this problem, there are $\lambda_1, \lambda_2, \ldots, \lambda_s$, all nonnegative but not all zero, such that x^* is also a solution to the problem

$$\max \ u(x)$$

$$\text{sub to } \sum_{i=1}^{s} \lambda_i g_i(x) \le 0 \tag{5.16}$$

$$x \in X.$$

Proof: Let $g = (g_1, g_2, \ldots, g_s)$ be the s-dimensional function consisting of the constraint functions. Let $\mu_0 = u(x^*)$. Define the sets $C, D \subset \mathcal{R}^s$ by

$$C = \{z : g(x) \le z, \quad \text{for some } x \in X\}$$

$$D = \{z : g(x) \le z, \text{and } u(x) > \mu_0, \text{ for some } x \in X\}.$$

It follows that C and D are convex monotonic sets. (See Appendix B.) The set C is nonempty by assumption. We can assume that D is nonempty, for otherwise the theorem is true for any positive λ_i's. By definition of μ_0, it follows that $0 \notin D$. Hence, by the monotonic separation theorems (Appendix B), there is a $v \in \mathcal{R}^s$, $v \ne 0$, $v \ge 0$, such that $v \cdot z \ge 0$ for all $z \in D$.

Suppose there is a $z_0 \in C$ with $v \cdot z_0 = 0$. Let x_0 be such that $g(x_0) \le z_0$. Define $z_1 = g(x_1)$ where x_1 is as given in the theorem statement. We have $z_1 < 0$ by assumption. Since $z_0, z_1 \in C$, and C is convex, then $z_\alpha = \alpha z_1 + (1 - \alpha)z_0 \in C$ for any α, $0 \le \alpha \le 1$. It is clear that $v \cdot z_\alpha < 0$ for $0 < \alpha \le 1$, and hence $z_\alpha \notin D$. Since g is convex, $g(\alpha x_1 + (1 - \alpha)x_0) \le z_\alpha$, and it follows that $u(\alpha x_1 + (1 - \alpha)x_0) \le \mu_0$ for $0 < \alpha \le 1$. By continuity, $u(x_0) \le \mu_0$. Since x_0 is an arbitrary point satisfying $g(x_0) \le z_0$, it follows that $z_0 \notin D$.

By definition of v, we have $z \in D$ implies $v \cdot z \ge 0$, and we have just shown that $v \cdot z = 0$ implies $z \notin D$. Therefore, $v \cdot z \le 0$ implies $z \notin D$. This means that $x \in X$ with $v \cdot g(x) \le 0$ implies $u(x) \le \mu_0$. Now set $(\lambda_1, \lambda_2, \ldots, \lambda_s) = v$. Since x^* is feasible for (5.16), it follows that x^* solves (5.16). ∎

The λ_i's in the theorem can be interpreted as *relative* prices. They can be scaled together, arbitrarily, by a positive scale factor.

An example of this result is shown in Fig. 5.15 for two linear constraints: $p_1 \cdot x \le y_1$ and $p_2 \cdot x \le y_2$. A combination of these two of the form $(\lambda_1 p_1 + \lambda_2 p_2) \cdot x \le \lambda_1 y_1 + \lambda_2 y_2$ yields the constraint with the dashed boundary. That constraint alone is sufficient to lead to the correct solution.

Example 5.10 (Time as a constraint).   Consider again the problem with a time constraint (5.14). The two linear constraints are clearly convex, and if $r > 0$ and $T > 0$, the point $x = 0$ will satisfy the interior point requirement. Hence there are λ_1 and λ_2 such that the problem is equivalent to

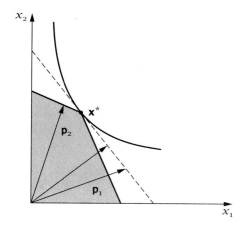

FIGURE 5.15 Replacing two constraints by one.

$$\max\ u(\mathbf{x})$$

$$\text{sub to } (\lambda_1 p_1 + \lambda_2 t_1)x_1 + (\lambda_1 p_2 + \lambda_2 t_2)x_2 + \cdots$$

$$+ (\lambda_1 p_m + \lambda_2 t_m)x_m \le \lambda_1 r + \lambda_2 T .$$

If the budget constraint is binding with λ_1 strictly positive, we can scale the λ's so that $\lambda_1 = 1$. The aggregate constraint then has the form

$$(p_1 + \lambda_2 t_1)x_1 + (p_2 + \lambda_2 t_2)x_2 + \cdots + (p_m + \lambda_2 t_m)x_m \le r + \lambda_2 T .$$

In this case λ_2 has an obvious interpretation as the value of time. It is the factor by which a unit of time, say an hour, can be converted to monetary units. The single constraint, equivalent to the two original constraints, is an overall budget constraint with time converted to money.

Multiperiod Budget Constraints

Consider a consumer in a two-period world. The consumer has a utility function of the form $u(\mathbf{x}_1, \mathbf{x}_2)$ where $\mathbf{x}_1$ and $\mathbf{x}_2$ are consumption bundles in period 1 and period 2, respectively. Likewise, $\mathbf{p}_1$ and $\mathbf{p}_2$ are prices and r_1 and r_2 are incomes for the two periods. Commodities are perishable (that is, they cannot be stored from one period to the next). However, income can be saved and carried from the first period to the second, earning an interest rate s. We assume that no borrowing is allowed. Under these assumptions, the consumer's problem is

$$\max_{\mathbf{x}_1, \mathbf{x}_2, z}\ u(\mathbf{x}_1, \mathbf{x}_2)$$

$$\text{sub to } \mathbf{p}_1 \cdot \mathbf{x}_1 + z \le r_1$$

$$\mathbf{p}_2 \cdot \mathbf{x}_2 \qquad \le r_2 + (1 + s)z$$

$$\mathbf{x}_1 \ge \mathbf{0}, \quad \mathbf{x}_2 \ge \mathbf{0}, \quad z \ge 0,$$

where z is the amount of income carried over (that is, invested) in the first period. By the multiple constraints theorem, this problem is equivalent (with $\lambda_2 = 1$) to

$$\max_{\mathbf{x}_1,\mathbf{x}_2,z} u(\mathbf{x}_1,\mathbf{x}_2)$$

$$\text{sub to } \lambda_1 \mathbf{p}_1 \cdot \mathbf{x}_1 + \mathbf{p}_2 \cdot \mathbf{x}_2 \leq \lambda_1 r_1 + r_2 + [(1+s) - \lambda_1]z$$

$$\mathbf{x}_1 \geq \mathbf{0}, \quad \mathbf{x}_2 \geq \mathbf{0}, \quad z \geq 0$$

for an appropriate value of λ_1. Assuming local nonsatiation, any solution can be improved by increasing the right-hand side of the (combined) budget constraint. Since this cannot be possible by increasing z, we must have $(1 + s) \leq \lambda_1$. The factor $\lambda_1 - 1$ can be considered the consumer's personal interest rate. The consumer will save (that is, lend) in the first period only if the market interest rate is equal to the consumer's interest rate.

Now suppose the consumer can borrow or lend at the rate s. Then z can be of any value. It follows in that case $1 + s = \lambda_1$. The budget constraint reduces to

$$\mathbf{p}_1 \cdot \mathbf{x}_1 + \left(\frac{1}{1+s}\right) \mathbf{p}_2 \cdot \mathbf{x}_2 \leq r_1 + \frac{r_2}{1+s},$$

which is exactly what we would write directly using present-value evaluations of expenditures and income.

*5.10   Aggregate Demand and the Gorman Form

In many economic models, consumers are aggregated to form a single representative consumer. The rigorous justification of such aggregation requires special assumptions about preferences, and we shall investigate those here.

Suppose an economy consists of n individuals, each with a demand function $\mathbf{x}_i(\mathbf{p}, r_i)$, where the subscript i denotes the ith individual. The aggregate, or total, demand is then $\mathbf{x}(\mathbf{p}, \mathbf{r}) = \sum_{i=1}^{n} \mathbf{x}_i(\mathbf{p}, r_i)$, which depends on all income levels r_i as well as the price vector $\mathbf{p}$. One must keep track of the separate income levels to evaluate this function. It is not possible, in general, to express this function equivalently in terms of total income. This is true even if all individuals have the same utility function—aggregate income does not provide enough information to determine demand.

Aggregation of income is appropriate if preferences have a certain relation to each other. Specifically, suppose each indirect utility has the form

$$v_i(\mathbf{p}, r) = a_i(\mathbf{p}) + b(\mathbf{p})r.$$

This is termed the *Gorman form*. Within one family of these indirect utilities, the $a_i(\mathbf{p})$ terms can differ among consumers, but the $b(\mathbf{p})$ term is the same for each consumer.

By Roy's identity we can calculate the corresponding demand functions as

$$\mathbf{x}_i(\mathbf{p}, r_i) = \mathbf{A}_i(\mathbf{p}) + \mathbf{B}(\mathbf{p}) r_i$$

where

$$\mathbf{A}_i = \nabla a_i(\mathbf{p})$$
$$\mathbf{B} = \nabla b(\mathbf{p}).$$

The aggregate demand over all consumers is therefore

$$\mathbf{x}(\mathbf{p}, r_1, r_2, \ldots, r_n) = \sum_{i=1}^{n} \{\mathbf{A}_i(\mathbf{p}) + \mathbf{B}(\mathbf{p}) r_i\}.$$

This demand depends on the income levels only through the sum $r = \sum_{i=1}^{n} r_i$. Hence aggregation of income is appropriate.

In fact, the aggregate demand behaves as if it were determined by a single consumer with indirect utility

$$v(\mathbf{p}, r) = \left\{ \sum_{i=1}^{n} a_i(\mathbf{p}) \right\} + b(\mathbf{p}) r,$$

where again $r = \sum_{i=1}^{n} r_i$. This is seen by merely applying Roy's identity to this $v(\mathbf{p}, r)$ and seeing that it gives the same aggregate demand.

Let us examine a special case of the Gorman form. Note that if $X = \mathcal{R}_+^m$, demand must be zero if $r_i = 0$. This means that $a_i(\mathbf{p}) = 0$ for each i, and hence that $v_i(\mathbf{p}, r_i) = b(\mathbf{p}) r_i$. This will hold if the utility functions are identical and homogeneous of degree 1 (implying that they are homothetic). Of course, if an increasing transformation is applied to the utility functions, the same result will hold. Hence, we conclude that if all utility functions are equivalent to the same homothetic utility function, aggregate income determines demand. For example, if (for the two-commodity case) everyone had utility $u(x_1, x_2) = x_1 x_2$, they would act in aggregate as a single consumer with this same utility function.

5.11 Exercises

1. (Labor supply) Suppose individuals can freely choose the length of their work day and the wage rate is fixed at w. Assume also that other goods can be represented by an aggregate commodity with price 1. Finally, assume that a consumer's sole income is that derived from his or her own labor.

    (a) Draw a two-dimensional diagram with the two axes (1) daily leisure hours and (2) consumption of the aggregate commodity. Indicate the feasible set, and show how a consumer will select a point in this diagram.

    (b) Suppose the government establishes a guaranteed annual income I. Draw the new feasible set. Will the incomes of some individuals decrease under this plan?

2. Suppose an individual consumes three goods, food, clothing, and automobiles, denoted x_1, x_2, and x_3, respectively. The individual's utility function is $u(\mathbf{x}) = x_1^5 x_2^4 (1 + x_3)$. The prices of the goods are $p_1 = 1$, $p_2 = 2$, and $p_3 = 2000$, and the individual's total income is \$9,000. Automobiles must be bought in integral units. How will an individual allocate his or her income so as to maximize utility?

3. Let $\bar{u}(x, r)$ denote the partial indirect utility for having an amount x of one commodity and spending r on all others. The willingness to pay $w(x)$ for x satisfies $\bar{u}(x, r - w(x)) = \bar{u}(0, r)$. Differentiate this with respect to x to show that $w'(x) = p_c(x)$ where $p_c(x)$ is the compensated inverse demand for x (with price $r = 1$). (This is also the adjusted price function.)

4. Consider a utility function of the form

$$u(\mathbf{x}) = \frac{B_1 x_1}{A + x_1} + \frac{B_2 x_2}{A_2 + x_2} + \cdots + \frac{B_n x_n}{A_n + x_n}.$$

Note that u saturates (asymptotically). Show that the income expansion curves are straight lines (except when $x_i = 0$ for some i).

5. (Housing subsidies)   The government has considered various subsidy and incentive programs to induce low-income families to live in better-quality housing than they would otherwise live in. Three plans are

   (*i*) Income subsidy: provide additional income I to a family that can be spent in any way.

   (*ii*) Price subsidy: pay a fixed percentage p of a family's rent.

   (*iii*) Voucher: pay an amount s toward a family's rent, provided the normal rent is at least R.

   Suppose commodities can be separated into housing (in amount x) and a general commodity representing all other goods (in amount z). Suppose a family has utility function

   $$u(x, z) = z^{4/5} x^{1/5}$$

   and a monthly income of \$500. The government wishes this family to live in a house that rents for at least \$150. Suppose the prices are each \$1.00 per unit.

   (*a*) Without any subsidy, how much will the family spend on rent?

   (*b*) Under each of the plans above, how much subsidy would be required to induce the family to live in a \$150 house?

6. A consumer's preference for $x_1 = $ apples and $x_2 = $ oranges is represented by the utility function $U(x_1, x_2) = x_1 x_2 + 10 x_2$. Prices are $p_1 = 1$ and $p_2 = 2$. The consumer's budget is $r = 60$. Apples and oranges are rationed, however. Along with the money payment, the purchase of each apple costs 2 ration tickets, while each orange costs 1 ration ticket. The consumer is allocated 30 ration tickets.

   (*a*) Find the commodity bundle of apples and oranges that the consumer will choose. Sketch the attainable set in this case.

(b) Suppose the consumer can buy or sell ration tickets at one monetary unit each. Find the commodity bundle that the consumer will choose. Sketch the attainable set and compare it to the attainable set in part (a).

(c) Suppose the black market has transactions costs, so that ration tickets may be bought for one monetary unit but sold for only 3/4 of a monetary unit. Sketch the attainable set and find the consumer's choice.

7. Prove the following alternate form of Roy's identity:

$$\mathbf{x}(\mathbf{p}, 1) = \frac{\nabla_{\mathbf{p}} \nu(\mathbf{p}, 1)}{\mathbf{p} \cdot \nabla \nu(\mathbf{p}, 1)}.$$

8. For the city and suburb example of Section 5.3 assume the following:

(1) If for fixed $p > 0$, $h(z)$ is defined by $U'(h) = pW'(z)$, then $hU'(h) \to 0$ as $z \to \infty$.

(2) $V(t)$ is concave with $V'(0) < 0$.

(3) $p'(t) < 0$.

(4) All functions are differentiable.

(a) Derive the necessary conditions

(i) $U'(h) - \lambda p(t) \le 0$

(ii) $V'(t) - \lambda[p'(t)h + c] \le 0$

(iii) $W'(z) - \lambda \le 0$

where each of these is satisfied by equality if $h > 0$, $t > 0$, or $z > 0$, respectively.

(b) Show that if r is small, the budget constraint and (ii) imply that $t = 0$.

(c) Assume that $h \to 0$ as $r \to \infty$. Show that $t = 0$ for r's sufficiently large.

9. (Separable preferences)   Assume that the utility function for three goods can be written in the form

$$u(\mathbf{x}) = U(w(x_1, x_2), x_3).$$

(a) Show that demands for goods 1 and 2 can be written as functions of only p_1, p_2, and the total amount spent on x_1 and x_2.

(b) Consider the two utility functions

$$u_1(\mathbf{x}) = [\alpha x_1^\rho + (1 - \alpha)x_2^\rho]^{a/\rho} x_3^{1-a}$$
$$u_2(\mathbf{x}) = \left\{a[\alpha x_1^\rho + (1 - \alpha)x_2^\rho]^{r/\rho} + (1 - a)x_3^r\right\}^{1/r}.$$

Show that although the demand for x_1 and x_2 is totally independent of p_3 for u_1, it depends implicitly on p_3 for u_2 through the expenditures devoted to x_1 and x_2.

10. (Trial demand functions)   Determine whether the following are demand functions in the region where they are positive.

(a) $$x_1 = -p_1 + 2p_2 + r \qquad x_2 = 2p_1 - 2p_2 + r$$

(b) $$x_1 = \frac{1}{4}\left(\frac{r + p_2}{p_1}\right) \qquad x_2 = \frac{3}{4}\left(\frac{r + 2p_1}{p_2}\right)$$

(c) $$x_1 = \frac{1}{2}\left(\frac{p_2 + r}{p_1}\right) \qquad x_2 = \frac{1}{2}\left(\frac{-p_2 + r}{p_2}\right).$$

11. Find the expenditure function, the Hicksian demand functions, and the Marshallian demand functions corresponding to the indirect utility function

$$v(\mathbf{p}, r) = \left(\frac{a_1}{p_1} + \frac{a_2}{p_2}\right) r.$$

12. Let $S = [s_{ij}]$ be the substitution matrix of a consumer. Commodities i and j are Hicksian substitutes if $s_{ij} > 0$; they are Hicksian complements if $s_{ij} < 0$. Prove that at least two of the n commodities are Hicksian substitutes. Hint: Use Euler's theorem (Appendix A).

13. Show that $\mathbf{Sp} = \mathbf{0}$, where S is the Slutsky matrix at $\mathbf{x}(\mathbf{p}, r)$.

14. Suppose that $e(\mathbf{p}, u)$ has the properties of an expenditure function as stated in Proposition 4.5, Section 4.3, and let

$$u(\mathbf{x}) = \max_{u}\{u : e(\mathbf{p}, u) \le \mathbf{p} \cdot \mathbf{x} \text{ for all } \mathbf{p} \in R^m_+, \mathbf{p} \neq \mathbf{0}\}.$$

Show that u is a utility function having e as its expenditure function.

15. An individual has demand functions

$$x = \frac{r}{\sqrt{p}\,(\sqrt{p} + \sqrt{q})}, \qquad z = \frac{r}{\sqrt{p}(\sqrt{p} + \sqrt{q})}$$

where r is income, p is the price of x, and q is the price of z. Find a utility function that rationalizes these demands by the following steps:

(a) Find the expenditure function $e(p, q, u)$. Let $u = e(\frac{1}{4}, \frac{1}{4}, u)$. Hint:

$$\frac{d}{dp}[2\log(\sqrt{p} + \sqrt{q})] = \frac{1}{\sqrt{p}\,(\sqrt{p} + \sqrt{q})}.$$

(b) Find $u(x, z)$ from $e(p, q, u)$ using Exercise 14.

16. (Benefit maximization)   Assume that the utility function is continuous and $\mathbf{g} \ge 0, \mathbf{g} \neq \mathbf{0}$. Let $\mathbf{p} \ge 0$. Suppose $\mathbf{x}^* \in X = R^m_+$ and let $u^* = u(\mathbf{x}^*)$. Consider the two problems

(A) $$\max_{\mathbf{x} \in X} u(\mathbf{x})$$
       sub to $\mathbf{p} \cdot \mathbf{x} \le \mathbf{p} \cdot \mathbf{x}^*$

(B) $$\max_{\mathbf{x} \in X} b(\mathbf{x}, u^*)$$
       sub to $\mathbf{p} \cdot \mathbf{x} \le \mathbf{p} \cdot \mathbf{x}^*.$

Show that if $\mathbf{g}$ is good, then if $\mathbf{x}^*$ solves (A) it also solves (B). Also show that if $\mathbf{p} \cdot \mathbf{x}^* > 0$ and $b(\mathbf{x}^*, u^*) = 0$, then if $\mathbf{x}^*$ solves (B), it also solves (A).

17. (Allocation of time and money)   Suppose that associated with consumption of every commodity there is an activity that requires time. Suppose also that

one activity, labor, generates income. The consumer's problem can then be formulated as in Section 5.9 as

$$\max\ u(\mathbf{x})$$
$$\text{sub to } \sum_{i=1}^{m} p_i x_i - w x_{n+1} = I$$
$$\sum_{i=1}^{m+1} t_i x_i = H$$

where I is nonwage income, H is the total number of hours available in the period, and x_{m+1} is number of hours worked. The consumer's utility function u is strictly concave. The constraints can be combined to the form

$$\sum_{i=1}^{m}(p_i + v t_i)x_i + (v t_{m+1} - w)x_{m+1} = I + vH.$$

Assume that $u(\mathbf{x}) = u(x_1, x_2, \ldots, x_m)$; that is, utility does not depend on hours worked. Find an explicit expression for v in terms of the given parameters of the original problem.

18. (Consumption over time) A consumer receives income and purchases an aggregate good in each of two periods. The consumer's utility function is $u(x_1, x_2) = x_1 x_2 + 5x_2$ where x_1 and x_2 denote consumption in periods 1 and 2, respectively. Income in the two periods is $r_1 = 10$ and $r_2 = 20$, and prices are $p_1 = p_2 = 1$. The consumer may save income not used in period 1 for use in period 2 (at zero interest) but cannot borrow.

    (a) Formulate the problem as one with two linear constraints in nonnegative variables. What x_1 and x_2 will be chosen?

    (b) Assume now that the consumer may borrow or lend at an interest rate s. At what rate would the consumer's consumption pattern be identical to that of part (a)?

19. (A diet problem) A certain consumer has preferences for just two characteristics of foods: protein and vitamins. However, there are only two types of food available at the market: meat and potatoes. Attributes (in appropriate units) and prices per kilogram of the two foods are given in the following table:

	Meat	Potatoes
Protein	20	0.5
Vitamins	5	2.0
Price	10	1

Suppose the consumer has utility function $u(q, s) = qs$, where q denotes units of protein and s denotes units of vitamins, and suppose the consumer's food budget is limited to $100.

    (a) How much of each food will the consumer select?

    (b) Peanuts, which were previously unavailable, arrive at the market. A kilogram of peanuts provides 3 units of protein and 3 units of vitamins and costs $2.00. Now how much of each food will the consumer select?

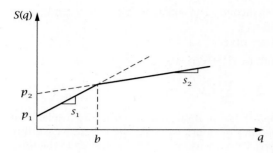

FIGURE 5.16 Price schedule for Exercise 20.

20. (Nonlinear pricing)   A monopolist can generally increase profits by charging different prices to different consumers. It may be impossible to implement this procedure if consumers of different types cannot be distinguished by any physical characteristic. However, for some products or services—such as long distance telephone calls, which can be metered and cannot be resold—it is possible to offer a menu of prices for various quantities rather than a uniform price per unit. By proper design of the price schedule, consumers may be induced to separate into groups according to type, and the firm may be able to achieve significant discrimination benefits.

We will analyze a simple situation in which there are two consumer types. Assume income effects are negligible for the good in question. Let $W(q; i)$ be type i's willingness to pay for a quantity q of the good. Then $w(q; i) = \partial W(q; i)/\partial q$ is the inverse demand function for consumer type i. Assume that $\partial w/\partial q \leq 0$ for all q and i, and that $w(q; 1) < w(q; 2)$ for all q. (Hence $W(q; 1) < W(q; 2)$ for all $q > 0$.)

The firm will design a price schedule denoted by $S(q)$ giving the total purchase price for q units of the form shown in Figure 5.16. There is a fixed charge of p_1, a per-unit charge of s_1 for the first b units, and a charge of s_2 per unit above b. If $s_2 < s_1$, this schedule exhibits volume discounts. The problem is how to choose the parameters p_1, s_1, p_2, and s_2. The firm is assumed to have variable costs that are additively separable among buyers. Hence, $C(q)$ is the cost of supplying any buyer with a purchase of size q.

(a) First suppose two quantities $q_1 < q_2$ are fixed. The prices $S_1 \equiv S(q_1)$ and $S_2 \equiv S(q_2)$ are to be set to induce consumers to separate according to type: type i consumers would rather purchase q_i than q_j if $j \neq i$. We assume that consumers maximize their consumer's surplus, which is the difference between their willingness to pay and their purchase price. The firm's problem is therefore to solve the following linear programming problem (assuming equal numbers of consumers of each type):

$$\max_{S_1, S_2} S_1 - C(q_1) + S_2 - C(q_2)$$
$$\text{sub to } W(q_1; 1) - S_1 \geq 0$$
$$W(q_2; 2) - S_2 \geq 0$$
$$W(q_2; 2) - S_2 \geq W(q_1; 2) - S_1.$$

The last constraint is the self-selection constraint: it ensures that consumer 2 will choose q_2 rather than q_1. Solve this problem for S_1 and S_2. Which constraints are binding? Show that consumer surplus is greater for consumers of type 2 than for those of type 1.

(b) Now let q_2 vary. Show that q_2 must satisfy

$$\frac{\partial W(q_2; 2)}{\partial q} = C'(q_2).$$

(c) Next, let q_1 vary. Give an expression that can be solved for q_1.

(d) Show how to find p_1 and s_1 so as to induce type 1 consumers to choose quantity q_1. (Give two equations for the two unknowns.) Similarly, show how to find p_2 and s_2 so that type 2 consumers will choose quantity q_2.

5.12 References

5.1–5.3 For general discussions of consumer demand see the texts by Nicholson (1985), Quirk (1982), and Hirshleifer (1984). Also see Hicks (1956) for a discussion of substitutes and complements and other important developments. An advanced treatment of demand is Katzner (1970). See also Samuelson (1947). For the benefit function relations see Luenberger (1992a).

5.4 For a general discussion of duality concepts see Blackorby, Primont, and Russell (1978), as well as Varian (1992), Diewert (1982), and Roy (1942).

5.5 Compensated demand was introduced in Hicks (1946) and Hicks (1956), and he also developed the substitution–income decomposition. The adjusted price function was introduced in Luenberger (1994b).

5.6 For the original derivation of the Slutsky equation, see Slutsky (1952). The short proof given here is due to Cook (1972). For a study of the approximation made by using the income and substitution effects, see de La Grandville (1989).

5.7 Consumer's surplus has long been used as a method for evaluating public projects. It was first introduced by Dupuit (1844). For an introductory treatment of its use, see Gramlich (1981). Also see the discussion and references in Chapter 10 of this text.

5.8 This short resolution of the integrability problem was adapted from Hurwicz and Uzawa (1971) and Varian (1992). For the relation to revealed preference theory see Samuelson (1947). A development of differential revealed preference theory was done by Ville (1951–52). Also see Hurwicz and Richter (1979) and Khilstrom, Mas-Colell, and Sonnenschein (1976).

5.9 For the multiple constraints theorem, see Luenberger (1968).

5.10 See Gorman (1953) for the original theory of this type of aggregation. Also see Varian (1992) for a simple discussion similar to that given here.

Chapter **6**
ECONOMIC EFFICIENCY

The previous chapters presented the theories of production and of individual choice. They showed in some detail how firms select production plans and how individuals select consumption bundles. This chapter takes a broader and more integrative viewpoint by considering the workings of the whole economy consisting of many firms and many consumers. Our attention focuses on certain general properties of the final allocation of goods to individuals—judging whether the allocation is desirable and hence whether the mechanisms discussed in the earlier chapters produce desirable results.

It is natural to judge an economy by examining its final allocation to individuals, but it is difficult to define a coherent basis for such judgment. To illustrate this judgment difficulty, suppose that in one possible allocation most individuals receive high material wealth but poor health services, while in another alternative, the reverse is true. Can we judge which allocation is best without relying on purely subjective assessments? The answer is that subjective assessments do seem to be required for the complete resolution of such questions, but significant progress can, in fact, be made using the fairly objective criterion of *economic efficiency*, which is discussed in this chapter. Economic efficiency provides a preliminary, but not complete, judgment criterion; it eliminates many possibilities but does not pinpoint just one. It is attractive because it provides a more or less judgment-free first step towards evaluation, a step that is likely to be noncontroversial.

6.1   Efficient Allocations

An economy can be a very complex entity. A complete description of the outcome of an economy might list all production levels, individual consumption levels, and prices. However, it makes sense to judge the effectiveness of an outcome solely in terms of the commodity bundles obtained by the individuals in the economy. Production levels, prices, and other variables are secondary in that they only indirectly influence the set of consumption bundles received by individuals. Therefore, for purposes of assessment, all that we need to know about an economy is what it is capable of delivering.

Formally, suppose there are n individuals and m commodities. An *allocation* is a vector $\mathbf{X} = (\mathbf{x}_1, \mathbf{x}_2, \ldots, \mathbf{x}_n) \in \mathcal{R}^{nm}$. (Note[1] the use of the capital letter $\mathbf{X}$.) This vector represents a set of commodity bundles, with $\mathbf{x}_i$ being the m-dimensional bundle for individual i. If we focus on allocations, then all that is relevant about an economy is the set of allocations it can generate. This leads to the following very general definition.

Economy.   An *economy* of n individuals and m commodities is a set $F \subset \mathcal{R}^{nm}$ defining the set of feasible allocations.

An economy is therefore a collection of possible allocations. The means by which an allocation is achieved, through a transformation of resources into goods and then distribution of these goods, is purposely not incorporated into the general definition. However, there are instances where the feasible allocations are restricted by specific allocation mechanisms (such as competition); then the definition of the economy is restricted accordingly. The examples we consider in the next two chapters should make this clear.

Although it is natural to think of an allocation as a physical division of goods, the definition is actually much broader. Some goods have the property that consumption by one individual does not preclude consumption by others. Radio broadcasts are an example. Such goods are called *public goods*, and they are discussed extensively in Chapter 9. This current chapter is devoted to *private goods*, such as food, of which joint consumption is precluded. However, it is important to realize that the fundamental definitions have wider scope.

Efficiency of Allocations

We now consider how to evaluate the relative merits of two alternative feasible allocations. A fundamental premise for this evaluation is that the judgment of the welfare of any individual should be left entirely to that individual. That is, if two allocations yield two different bundles to a certain individual, that individual's preference ordering, not some other criterion, evaluates the relative merits of the two bundles. After all, we have spent a good deal of effort describing the nature of individual preferences, and it would be foolish at this point to abandon it. Of course, conflict arises if we attempt to compare one individual's gains with another's losses. We avoid this (temporarily) by considering only changes that are unanimously preferred. This limitation motivates the concept of Pareto efficiency.

---

[1]In general we use bold capital letters for vectors of n objects when n is the number of individuals. Hence, if each individual i has income r_i and commodity bundle $\mathbf{x}_i$, we write $\mathbf{R} = (r_1, r_2, \ldots, r_n)$ and $\mathbf{X} = (\mathbf{x}_1, \mathbf{x}_2, \ldots, \mathbf{x}_n)$. This capital letter convention *only* applies when n is the number of individuals.

Pareto efficiency. A feasible allocation $\mathbf{X}$ is *Pareto efficient* (or *Pareto optimal*) if there is no other feasible allocation $\mathbf{X'}$ such that all individuals (weakly) prefer $\mathbf{X'}$ to $\mathbf{X}$ and at least one individual strictly prefers $\mathbf{X'}$ to $\mathbf{X}$. Specifically, $\mathbf{X} = (\mathbf{x}_1, \mathbf{x}_2, \dots, \mathbf{x}_n)$ is Pareto efficient if there is no $\mathbf{X'} = (\mathbf{x}_1', \mathbf{x}_2', \dots, \mathbf{x}_n')$ such that $\mathbf{x}_i' \succsim \mathbf{x}_i$ for all $i = 1, 2, \dots, n$ and $\mathbf{x}_j' \succ \mathbf{x}_j$ for some j.

In other words, an allocation is Pareto efficient if there is no way to change it to make one individual better off without making someone else worse off. Pareto efficiency is a fairly weak concept, since there may be a large collection of Pareto efficient allocations. For example, if a pie is to be divided between two people who like pie, *any* division is Pareto efficient; for it is impossible to give one person more without giving the other less. If, on the other hand, two commodities are to be divided, such as a pie and a pitcher of milk, arbitrary divisions will generally not be Pareto efficient because there may be mutually beneficial trades that improve the utility of both individuals—but still there may be a large family of Pareto-efficient allocations. Really, the technical weakness of the Pareto efficiency concept underlies its theoretical attractiveness. There is likely to be wide agreement that Pareto efficiency is desirable.

If individual preferences can be represented by utility functions u_i, $i = 1, 2, \dots, n$, then associated with a feasible allocation $\mathbf{X} = (\mathbf{x}_1, \mathbf{x}_2, \dots, \mathbf{x}_n)$ is a set of corresponding utility values $u_1(\mathbf{x}_1), u_2(\mathbf{x}_2), \dots, u_n(\mathbf{x}_n)$. Ideally we would make each of these values as large as possible. A feasible allocation is Pareto efficient if it is not possible to strictly increase one of the utility values without decreasing any of the others.

The fact that Pareto efficiency usually does not isolate a single feasible allocation is illustrated in terms of utility values in Fig. 6.1 for the case of two individuals. Every feasible allocation $\mathbf{X} = (\mathbf{x}_1, \mathbf{x}_2)$ yields a pair of utility values $u_1(\mathbf{x}_1), u_2(\mathbf{x}_2)$. The entire set of possible utility pairs, corresponding

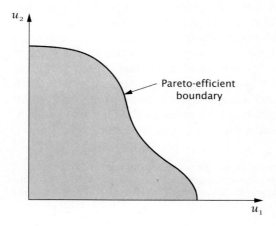

FIGURE 6.1 Feasible utility pairs.

to feasible allocations for a certain economy, is shown as the shaded region
of the figure. The Pareto-efficient points correspond to the points on the
outer boundary of this region, for at such points no single utility can be
increased without decreasing another. Points that are interior to the region
are not Pareto efficient because a movement diagonally upward and to the
right would increase both utility values.

In many cases the following property holds for an economy, greatly sim-
plifying analysis.

Free distribution.   An economy $F \subset \mathcal{R}_+^{mn}$ is said to satisfy *free distribution*
if $\mathbf{X} = (\mathbf{x}_1, \mathbf{x}_2, \ldots, \mathbf{x}_n) \in F$ implies that $\mathbf{X}' = (\mathbf{x}_1', \mathbf{x}_2', \ldots, \mathbf{x}_n') \in F$ for all $\mathbf{X}' \in$
$\mathcal{R}_+^{mn}$ with $\sum_{i=1}^n \mathbf{x}_i' = \sum_{i=1}^n \mathbf{x}_i$.

If an economy satisfies free distribution, an aggregate bundle of commodities can be distributed arbitrarily among the individuals. In other
words, there are no constraints on how goods can be allocated.

The following proposition provides an alternative characterization of
Pareto efficiency that holds in an economy satisfying free distribution.

Proposition 6.1.   *Suppose an economy satisfies free distribution. Suppose
also that preferences are continuous and strongly monotonic. Then a feasible allocation* $\mathbf{X}$ *is Pareto efficient if and only if there is no other feasible
allocation* $\mathbf{X}'$ *that is strictly preferred by all individuals.*

Proof: The *only if* portion is immediate.

To prove the *if* portion, suppose the feasible allocation $\mathbf{X}$ is not Pareto
efficient. Then there is a feasible allocation $\mathbf{X}''$ that is preferred (weakly)
by all individuals and strictly preferred by some individual i. At least one
component of $\mathbf{x}_i''$ (corresponding to an amount of a commodity k) must be
strictly greater than the corresponding component of $\mathbf{x}_i$. Hence, by conti-
nuity, we can find $\varepsilon > 0$ such that if component k of $\mathbf{x}_i''$ is reduced by ε and
distributed equally among the $n - 1$ other individuals, individual i will still
prefer the resulting allocation $\mathbf{X}'$ to the original allocation $\mathbf{X}$. Furthermore,
by strong monotonicity, the other individuals will strictly prefer $\mathbf{X}'$ to $\mathbf{X}$.   ∎

Transformation Economies

Although a general economy is defined by an arbitrary set $F \subset \mathcal{R}^{mn}$ of feasible allocations, the set F usually has special structure. Typically the economy is described by two separate types of restrictions. First, for each i, there
is a set $\mathcal{X}_i$ termed the *consumption set* of consumer i. If $\mathbf{x}_i$ is part of a feasible allocation, then $\mathbf{x}_i \in \mathcal{X}_i$. Almost always, unless stated to the contrary,
we take $\mathcal{X}_i = \mathcal{R}_+^m$; but occasionally it is useful to consider other possibilities. Second, there is a set $\mathcal{T} \subset \mathcal{R}^m$ termed the *transformation set*. The trans-

formation set is the set of all aggregate bundles that are available, either from initial endowment of resources or from transformation of those resources into other commodities through production. This structure is very important, and hence we formally define a special version of an economy.

Transformation economy.   A *transformation economy* is an economy in which the set F of feasible allocations is defined by

(a) $\mathbf{x}_i \in X_i$ for each $i = 1, 2, \ldots, n$.

(b) $\sum_{i=1}^{n} \mathbf{x}_i \in \mathcal{T}$.

where both $X_i \subset \mathcal{R}^m$, $i = 1, 2, \ldots, n$, and $\mathcal{T} \subset \mathcal{R}^m$ are fixed sets.

A simple case is the one in which $X_i = \mathcal{R}_+^m$ for $i = 1, 2, \ldots, n$ and $\mathcal{T}$ consists of a single element $\mathbf{w}$ (that is, $\mathcal{T} = \{\mathbf{w}\}$). Physically this means that a single bundle $\mathbf{w}$ defines all feasible allocations by the requirement $\sum_{i=1}^{n} \mathbf{x}_i = \mathbf{w}$. In this case, an allocation represents a distribution of $\mathbf{w}$ among the n consumers. This special case of a transformation economy is called a *distribution economy*.

In general, of course, $\mathcal{T}$ will contain more than a single point. Physically, this is usually because production capability can transform an original bundle into a range of possible alternative bundles, which can then be distributed. We later discuss in detail how production affects the structure of $\mathcal{T}$, but it is simpler at present to work with $\mathcal{T}$ directly.

6.2   Necessary Conditions for Consumers

We now assume that we have an economy described by a transformation set $\mathcal{T}$ and $\mathbf{x}_i$'s restricted by $\mathbf{x}_i \in X_i = \mathcal{R}_+^m$, $i = 1, 2, \ldots, n$. We shall develop first-order necessary conditions that apply to Pareto efficient allocations. In this section we concentrate on the consumer aspect of the problem, and then in Section 6.4 we shall consider the role of production as it enters through the transformation set.

We can consider the consumer portion by itself because of the following observation: Suppose the allocation $\mathbf{X}^*$ is Pareto efficient for the economy with transformation set $\mathcal{T}$. Let $\mathbf{t}^* = \sum_{i=1}^{n} \mathbf{x}_i^*$. Then $\mathbf{X}^*$ is Pareto efficient with respect to all allocations that have $\sum \mathbf{x}_i = \mathbf{t}^*$. That is, $\mathbf{X}^*$ is Pareto efficient with respect to the distribution economy having $\mathbf{w} = \mathbf{t}^*$, for clearly if an improved allocation can be found with this $\mathbf{t}^*$, the original allocation cannot be Pareto efficient.

Let us assume that preferences are described by utility functions. We may then use the above idea to transform Pareto efficiency into a set of optimization problems. We simply maximize one individual's utility while holding the others above a fixed level. This transformation is used tradition-ally to convert Pareto efficiency to a tractable form. (In Section 6.7 another method for converting to an optimization problem using benefit functions is discussed.)

Proposition 6.2. *Suppose the feasible allocation* $\mathbf{X}^* = (\mathbf{x}_1^*, \mathbf{x}_2^*, \ldots, \mathbf{x}_n^*)$ *is Pareto efficient with* $\sum_{i=1}^{n} \mathbf{x}_i^* = \mathbf{t}^*$. *Then* $\mathbf{X}^*$ *solves the following problem for each* $i = 1, 2, \ldots, n$:

$$\max\ u_i(\mathbf{x}_i)$$

$$\text{sub to } \sum_{j=1}^{n} \mathbf{x}_j = \mathbf{t}^* \tag{6.1}$$

$$u_j(\mathbf{x}_j) \ge u_j(\mathbf{x}_j^*), \quad j \ne i, \quad j = 1, 2, \ldots, n$$

$$\mathbf{x}_j \ge \mathbf{0}, \quad j = 1, 2, \ldots, n.$$

Proof: Suppose $\mathbf{X}^*$ does not solve problem i, for some particular $i = 1, 2, \ldots, n$. Then there is a feasible allocation $\mathbf{X} = (\mathbf{x}_1, \mathbf{x}_2, \ldots, \mathbf{x}_n)$ with $u_i(\mathbf{x}_i) > u_i(\mathbf{x}_i^*)$ and $u_j(\mathbf{x}_j) \ge u_j(\mathbf{x}_j^*)$ for all $j \ne i$. Hence $\mathbf{X}^*$ is not Pareto efficient.   ∎

We can use the above maximization formulation to derive necessary con-ditions for Pareto efficiency by applying the first-order necessary conditions for constrained optimization.

We assume here that the utility functions are differentiable. For any allo-cation $\mathbf{X} = (\mathbf{x}_1, \mathbf{x}_2, \ldots, \mathbf{x}_n)$ we let x_{ik} denote the allocation to individual i of commodity k. Now suppose $\mathbf{X}^*$ is a Pareto-efficient allocation, and assume that $x_{ik}^* > 0$ for all $i = 1, 2, \ldots, n, k = 1, 2, \ldots, m$. In this case the solution to any of the problems defined by (6.1) must satisfy the first-order necessary conditions. Select any i. For the ith problem we have the Lagrangian

$$L = u_i(\mathbf{x}_i) - \sum_{k=1}^{m} q_k \left[\sum_{j=1}^{n} x_{jk} - t_k \right] \tag{6.2}$$

$$- \sum_{j \ne i} s_j [u_j(\mathbf{x}_j^*) - u_j(\mathbf{x}_j)],$$

where the q_k, $k = 1, 2, \ldots, m$, and the s_j, $j \ne i$, are Lagrange multipliers. Differentiating with respect to each x_{jk} variable, we obtain

$$\frac{\partial u_i(\mathbf{x}_i^*)}{\partial x_{ik}} - q_k = 0, \quad k = 1, 2, \ldots, m$$

$$-s_j \frac{\partial u_j(\mathbf{x}_j^*)}{\partial x_{jk}} - q_k = 0, \quad j = 1, 2, \ldots, n, \quad j \ne i \tag{6.3}$$

$$k = 1, 2, \ldots, m.$$

Note that the first set of these equations (those for i) is identical in form to the second set (for arbitrary j) if we define $s_i = -1$ and multiply the first term in the top equation by $-s_i$. We can in every case eliminate s_j by dividing two equations with the same j (but with different k's—say k and l). Thus we easily find

$$\frac{\partial u_j(\mathbf{x}_j^*)/\partial x_{jk}}{\partial u_j(\mathbf{x}_j^*)/\partial x_{jl}} = \frac{q_k}{q_l} \tag{6.4}$$

for all $j = 1, 2, \ldots, n$ and all $k, l = 1, 2, \ldots, m$. The left side of this equation is recognized as MRS_{lk}^j, the marginal rate of substitution of commodity l for k for individual j. This leads to the following classic result.

Pareto-efficient conditions.   *A necessary condition for a feasible allocation* $\mathbf{X}^* > \mathbf{0}$ *to be Pareto efficient is that*

$$\frac{\partial u_i(\mathbf{x}_i^*)/\partial x_{ik}}{\partial u_i(\mathbf{x}_i^*)/\partial x_{il}} = \frac{\partial u_j(\mathbf{x}_j^*)/\partial x_{jk}}{\partial u_j(\mathbf{x}_j^*)/\partial x_{jl}}.$$

for all i, j, k, l. *That is, the marginal rates of substitution between any two commodities must be the same for all individuals.*

The condition above can be interpreted economically in terms of potential trades. If two individuals had different marginal rates of substitution, they could devise a trade that would be preferred by both. They would arrange this trade by exchanging at a rate that was intermediate between the two marginal rates of substitution, and in such a direction that both benefit. This is illustrated graphically in the next section. As a simple example, suppose that at a given allocation, individual A could exchange three apples for one orange (in either direction) without changing utility (that is, the marginal rate of substitution of apples for oranges is three). Suppose that for B the neutral exchange ratio is one for one. Then if B would give A one orange in exchange for two apples, both would be better off than before (by one apple).

In Chapter 5 it was found that under perfect competition the marginal rate of substitution between two commodities is the same for all consumers, the common rate being the ratio of the two commodity prices. This is an indication of the strong connection between Pareto efficiency and the market mechanism, and this connection is further explored in the following few sections.

Example 6.1 (Coffee and doughnuts).   Suppose we must divide supplies C of coffee and D of doughnuts among n people, each of whom has a (Cobb-Douglas) utility function $u(c, d) = cd$. We let c_i and d_i be the amounts allocated to i. This is a distribution economy with a fixed total allocation. The Pareto efficient conditions are that each MRS_{cd}^i is a constant and therefore that each c_i/d_i is a constant. Hence, for Pareto efficiency, everyone receives coffee and doughnuts in identical ratios. However, the magnitudes are otherwise unspecified; some individuals may receive large quantities and some small. Hence, there are α_i's, $\sum_{i=1}^{n} \alpha_i = 1$, such that $c_i = \alpha_i C$ and $d_i = \alpha_i D$ for all i.

6.3 The Edgeworth Box

The consumer conditions for Pareto efficiency for the problem of distributing two commodities to two consumers can be illustrated very nicely through a construction devised by F. Edgeworth and termed the *Edgeworth box*, shown in Fig. 6.2. Suppose the economy contains two commodities in amounts w^1 and w^2, respectively. There are two individuals, labeled A and B. The width of the box is equal to w^1, and the height is equal to w^2. A point in the box represents a distribution of the two commodities in the following manner. The allocation to the first individual is determined by the standard Cartesian convention using the lower left-hand corner as the zero point. Thus, the amount of commodity 1 allocated to A is the horizontal distance from this corner, and the amount of commodity 2 is the vertical distance. The allocation to individual B is determined in a complementary way, by measuring from the upper right-hand corner. Thus, the amount of commodity 1 allocated to B is the horizontal distance from that corner, and the amount of commodity 2 is the vertical distance. Because the dimensions of the box are chosen equal to the total amounts of the commodities available, this complementarity exactly balances. The total width and the total height of the box are allocated to the two individuals. A point in the box uniquely specifies the allocation.

The indifference curves of the two individuals can also be drawn in the box. Those of individual A are drawn in the familiar way with the lower

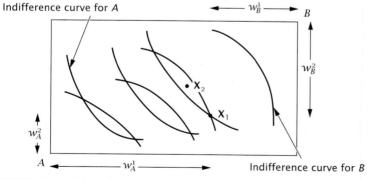

FIGURE 6.2 The Edgeworth box.

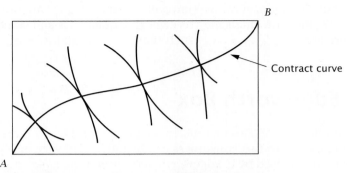

FIGURE 6.3   Locus of Pareto-efficient points.

left-hand corner as the zero point. Those of individual B are drawn with the upper right-hand corner as reference, and hence they appear to curve in the opposite direction.

A point in the box is Pareto efficient if there is no other point that improves one individual (in the sense of preference) while not hurting the other. The point X_1 shown in Fig. 6.2 is not Pareto efficient, since X_2 represents an improvement for both individuals. According to the conditions derived in the previous section, in order for a point in the interior of the Edgeworth box to be Pareto efficient, the marginal rates of substitution between the two commodities must be the same for both individuals. We know that the marginal rate of substitution for A at a point X is the negative of the slope of A's indifference curve there. Likewise, it is easy to see that the marginal rate of substitution for B is the negative of the slope of B's indifference curve. (The fact that B is represented upside down and backward yields cancelling sign changes.) Hence at a Pareto efficient point the slopes of the two indifference curves must be equal—or, equivalently, the two indifference curves must be tangent at that point. If this condition does not hold at a point (such as at X_1 in Fig. 6.2), a direction of movement can be found that cuts inside the upper preference contours defined by both indifference curves, indicating a trade that would be an improvement for both A and B.

The tangency condition itself defines a collection of points in the box, and if preferences are convex, these points will be Pareto efficient. A locus of such points, shown in Fig. 6.3, is called the *contract curve*.

6.4   Production Efficiency

A firm is represented in an economy by its production possibility set in $\mathcal{R}^m$. The firm's productive capability changes the transformation set since it adds options to the aggregate bundle that can be distributed.

Suppose there are K firms with corresponding production possibility sets $\mathcal{Y}_1, \mathcal{Y}_2, \ldots, \mathcal{Y}_K$. Each firm k can select any netput vector $\mathbf{y}_k \in \mathcal{Y}_k$, independent of what other firms do. After each firm selects a netput vector, the overall netput vector for the economy is $\mathbf{y} = \mathbf{y}_1 + \mathbf{y}_2 + \cdots + \mathbf{y}_K$; that is, the economy's netput vector is the sum of netput vectors of the individual firms. We may express this by stating that the overall production possibility set for the economy is

$$\mathcal{Y} = \mathcal{Y}_1 + \mathcal{Y}_2 + \cdots + \mathcal{Y}_K$$
$$= \{\mathbf{y} : \mathbf{y} = \mathbf{y}_1 + \mathbf{y}_2 + \cdots + \mathbf{y}_K, \, \mathbf{y}_k \in \mathcal{Y}_k\}.$$

A list of specific netput vectors $(\mathbf{y}_1, \mathbf{y}_2, \ldots, \mathbf{y}_K)$ with $\mathbf{y}_k \in \mathcal{Y}_k$, $k = 1, 2, \ldots, K$, is sometimes referred to as a *production plan*, although it may not be literally planned by anyone. Such a plan leads to an aggregate netput $\mathbf{y} = \sum_{k=1}^K \mathbf{y}_k$ in $\mathcal{Y}$.

The transformation set for the economy is determined by two components: the aggregate production possibility set and the initial aggregate endowment of the economy. The endowment $\mathbf{w}$ is the set of resources available. These resources can either be distributed directly to consumers or employed as inputs to production, which converts them to other goods that are then distributed. The complete transformation set is therefore

$$\mathcal{T} = \mathbf{w} + \mathcal{Y}.$$

An important special case, of course, is where $\mathcal{Y} = \{\mathbf{0}\}$ in which case $\mathcal{T} = \{\mathbf{w}\}$ corresponds to a distribution economy.

In the previous section we showed that Pareto efficiency implied certain conditions for consumers. Here we show that Pareto efficiency imposes certain conditions on the production choices of firms. However, in order that production efficiency and consumption efficiency together imply overall efficiency, we need to assume strong monotonicity of individual preferences. It then follows that firms should always select netput vectors that are efficient in the usual sense of productive efficiency. That is, they should never select a netput vector that can be dominated by one with larger components. We summarize this with the following simple proposition, which the reader can prove.

Proposition 6.3. *Assume all preferences are strongly monotonic. Suppose $\mathbf{X}^* = (\mathbf{x}_1^*, \mathbf{x}_2^*, \ldots, \mathbf{x}_n^*)$ is a Pareto-efficient allocation with $\sum_{i=1}^n \mathbf{x}_i^* = \mathbf{w} + \mathbf{y}^*$. Then $\mathbf{y}^* \in \mathcal{Y}$ is efficient in the sense that there is no other $\mathbf{y}' \in \mathcal{Y}$ such that $\mathbf{y}' \geq \mathbf{y}^*$.*

The main question concerning production efficiency is how to characterize efficient points of $\mathcal{Y}$ in terms the individual plans $\mathbf{y}_k$ in the sets $\mathcal{Y}_k$. In particular, it should be noted that even if each firm k selects a $\mathbf{y}_k$ that is efficient in $\mathcal{Y}_k$, the resulting aggregate $\mathbf{y}$ may not be efficient in $\mathcal{Y}$. Differential conditions can be derived that are analogous to those for consumption efficiency. See Exercise 1. We shall find a better characterization of production efficiency at the end of the next section.

When the production possibilities are described by a transformation function T, it is easy to augment the necessary conditions for Pareto efficiency found in Section 6.2. Pareto efficiency is equivalent to the following modification of (6.1):

$$\max\ u_i(\mathbf{x}_i)$$

$$\text{sub to}\ T\left(\sum_{j=1}^{n}\mathbf{x}_j\right)\le 0$$

$$u_j(\mathbf{x}_j)\ge u_j(\mathbf{x}_j^*),\qquad j\ne,\quad j=1,2,\dots,n$$

$$\mathbf{x}_j\ge \mathbf{0},\qquad j=1,2,\dots,n.$$

Forming the Lagrangian as before and eliminating the Lagrange multipliers, we obtain for all i, k, and l

$$\frac{\partial u_i(\mathbf{x}_i^*)/\partial x_{ik}}{\partial u_i(\mathbf{x}_i^*)/\partial x_{il}}=\frac{\partial T(\mathbf{x}^*)/\partial x_k}{\partial T(\mathbf{x}^*)/\partial x_l}$$

where $x^*=\sum_{j=1}^{n}\mathbf{x}_j^*$. The right-hand side of this equation is termed the *marginal rate of transformation of good l for good k*, which is abbreviated MRT$_{lk}$. Hence for Pareto efficiency it must be true that, for each consumer, the marginal rate of substitution between any two goods is equal to the marginal rate of transformation between those goods.

6.5   Competitive Equilibria

We now study the relation between allocations that are Pareto efficient and allocations that are part of a competitive equilibrium. The First and Second Theorems of Welfare Economics give conditions under which the two are equivalent. As implied by their names, the First and Second Theorems are fundamental to the whole theory of microeconomics. They provide a strong connection between the two most important economic concepts.

The basic idea of a competitive equilibrium is that it reflects the outcome of perfect competition. Each agent, whether a firm or a consumer, acts on the basis of fixed prices when making production or consumption decisions. The agents therefore act as if they have no influence on the prices (as opposed, for example, to a monopoly). The prices are fixed; the agents are *price takers.* The lack of influence is assumed even if there are only a few agents, each of whose actions do influence prices, so that the agents could act differently to exploit this influence. Such alternative behavior can also be analyzed, but it leads to a different concept than competitive equilibrium.

Competitive equilibrium is therefore an idealization. It is formulated to capture the idea that in a real market economy there are thousands of agents and the action of any one has an imperceptible influence on the market. When models are made with just a few agents, there is an implication that these are merely representative of a much larger number of agents or it is understood that a competitive equilibrium is just one possible outcome worthy of study.

We consider a transformation economy with a transformation set $\mathcal{T}$ and the consumption sets $\mathcal{X}_i$, $i = 1, 2, \ldots, n$. A competitive equilibrium in such an economy consists of a feasible allocation $\mathbf{X}^* = (\mathbf{x}_1^*, \mathbf{x}_2^*, \ldots, \mathbf{x}_n^*)$ and a set of commodity prices $\mathbf{p}^*$. The pair $(\mathbf{X}^*, \mathbf{p}^*)$ forms a competitive equilibrium if no individual i can select another bundle $\mathbf{x}_i$ that is preferred to $\mathbf{x}_i^*$ and costs no more than $\mathbf{x}_i^*$, where the cost is determined by the prices $\mathbf{p}^*$. This is formalized by the following definition.

Equilibrium. A pair $(\mathbf{X}^*, \mathbf{p}^*)$ where $\mathbf{X}^* = (\mathbf{x}_1^*, \mathbf{x}_2^*, \ldots, \mathbf{x}_n^*) \in \mathcal{R}_+^{nm}$ and $\mathbf{p}^* \in \mathcal{R}_+^m$ is a *competitive equilibrium for a transformation economy*[2] if

1. For each i, $\mathbf{x}_i^* \in \mathcal{X}_i$.

2. $\sum_{i=1}^n \mathbf{x}_i^* = \mathbf{t}^* \in \mathcal{T}$.

3. For each $i = 1, 2, \ldots, n$, if $\mathbf{p}^* \cdot \mathbf{x}_i \le \mathbf{p}^* \cdot \mathbf{x}_i^*$ then $\mathbf{x}_i \precsim \mathbf{x}_i^*$.

4. For all $\mathbf{t} \in \mathcal{T}$ there holds $\mathbf{p}^* \cdot \mathbf{t}^* \ge \mathbf{p}^* \cdot \mathbf{t}$.

The first two conditions in this definition state that the allocation $\mathbf{X}^*$ is feasible. The third condition shows that individual consumers are each in equilibrium. Specifically, if the prices $\mathbf{p}^*$ are used to evaluate goods, and hence used as a basis for any possible trade between consumers, no one has any incentive to trade away from the allocation $\mathbf{X}^*$. As an example, imagine a situation where a bundle of apples and oranges is distributed to a group, with different amounts going to different people. Unit prices are also announced for the apples and oranges. Individuals are then free to exchange their assigned bundles as long as the total value, measured by these prices, is not increased. If no one can improve his or her combination, the allocation and prices form an equilibrium, even though there may be great disparities among the group in terms of what they receive.

The fourth condition states that the aggregate bundle of goods chosen must have maximum value with respect to all possibilities. In the case of a distribution economy, where $\mathcal{T} = \{\mathbf{w}\}$ consists of a single point, this condition disappears because there are no alternatives to consider. When $\mathcal{T}$ is derived from productive capability, with $\mathcal{T} = \mathbf{w} + \mathcal{Y}$, this condition implies that $\mathbf{p}^* \cdot \mathbf{y}^* \ge \mathbf{p}^* \cdot \mathbf{y}$ for all $\mathbf{y} \in \mathcal{Y}$. That is, $\mathbf{y}^*$ is the netput vector in $\mathcal{Y}$ that corresponds to maximum profit using the prices $\mathbf{p}^*$. Hence, the aggregate firm maximizes profit in equilibrium.

---

[2]In the literature, this concept is variously referred to as a valuation equilibrium, a competitive equilibrium, an equilibrium relative to prices $\mathbf{p}^*$, or simply as an equilibrium. We emphasize here that it applies to a transformation economy. Later, the definition will be modified to include economies in which consumers own resources.

If there are K firms, the aggregate production possibility set is constructed from the individual production possibility sets as $\mathcal{Y} = \mathcal{Y}_1 + \mathcal{Y}_2 + \cdots + \mathcal{Y}_K$. We have $\mathbf{y}^* = \mathbf{y}_1^* + \mathbf{y}_2^* + \cdots + \mathbf{y}_K^*$ for some $\mathbf{y}_k^*$'s with $\mathbf{y}_k^* \in \mathcal{Y}_k$. Hence $\mathbf{p}^* \cdot \mathbf{y}^* = \sum_{k=1}^{K} \mathbf{p}^* \cdot \mathbf{y}_k^*$, and from this it is clear that each $\mathbf{y}_k^*$ must maximize profit with $\mathcal{Y}_k$—otherwise, the sum could be increased. Hence, all firms maximize profit using prices $\mathbf{p}^*$.

We now come to the First Theorem.

First Theorem of Welfare Economics.   *Suppose preferences are defined on $\mathcal{R}_+^m$ and are continuous and satisfy local nonsatiation. If $(\mathbf{X}^*, \mathbf{p}^*)$ is a competitive equilibrium, then $\mathbf{X}^*$ is Pareto efficient.*

Proof: Suppose $(\mathbf{X}^*, \mathbf{p}^*)$ is a competitive equilibrium and suppose $\mathbf{X}^*$ is not Pareto efficient. There is another feasible allocation $\mathbf{X} = (\mathbf{x}_1, \mathbf{x}_2, \ldots, \mathbf{x}_n)$ that is weakly preferred by all individuals and strictly preferred by one, say j. We have $\mathbf{p}^* \cdot \mathbf{x}_i \geq \mathbf{p}^* \cdot \mathbf{x}_i^*$ for $i = 1, 2, \ldots, n$. (To see this, suppose $\mathbf{p}^* \cdot \mathbf{x}_i < \mathbf{p}^* \cdot \mathbf{x}_i^*$. Then by local nonsatiation, for any $\varepsilon > 0$ there is an $\mathbf{x}_i'$ with $||\mathbf{x}_i' - \mathbf{x}_i|| < \varepsilon$ and $\mathbf{x}_i' \succ \mathbf{x}_i \succsim \mathbf{x}_i^*$. Thus $\mathbf{p}^* \cdot \mathbf{x}_i' < \mathbf{p}^* \cdot \mathbf{x}_i + ||\mathbf{p}^*||\varepsilon$. Hence for ε sufficiently small, $\mathbf{p} \cdot \mathbf{x}_i' \leq \mathbf{p}^* \cdot \mathbf{x}_i^*$ and, by continuity, $\mathbf{x}_i' \succ \mathbf{x}_i^*$, contradicting the equilibrium conditions. Hence it cannot be true that $\mathbf{p}^* \cdot \mathbf{x}_i < \mathbf{p}^* \cdot \mathbf{x}_i^*$.)

By the definition of a competitive equilibrium, we also have $\mathbf{p}^* \cdot \mathbf{x}_j > \mathbf{p}^* \cdot \mathbf{x}_j^*$. Summing the above inequalities over i, we find

$$\sum_{i=1}^{n} \mathbf{p}^* \cdot \mathbf{x}_i > \sum_{i=1}^{n} \mathbf{p}^* \cdot \mathbf{x}_i^* .$$

This can be written as

$$\mathbf{p}^* \cdot \sum_{i=1}^{n} \mathbf{x}_i > \mathbf{p}^* \cdot \sum_{i=1}^{n} \mathbf{x}_i^* .$$

Hence for $\mathbf{t} = \sum_{i=1}^{n} \mathbf{x}_i$ and $\mathbf{t}^* = \sum_{i=1}^{n} \mathbf{x}_i^*$ we have $\mathbf{p}^* \cdot \mathbf{t} > \mathbf{p}^* \cdot \mathbf{t}^*$, contradicting the fourth condition of an equilibrium. ∎

The above theorem lends support to the use of free markets to allocate commodities, since the theorem guarantees that a competitive equilibrium is Pareto efficient. (However, the question of determining *which* of the many possible equilibria of the transformation economy is most appropriate still remains.)

Local nonsatiation is important in the First Theorem of Welfare Economics for it ensures that equilibrium solutions must meet the budget constraint with equality. Suppose it did not hold for, say, individual i. Then if $\mathbf{x}_i^*$ were the corresponding equilibrium bundle, it might be possible to find an equally preferred bundle $\mathbf{x}_i'$ that did not require the full budget. This implies a waste of resources that could be exploited by giving the extra budget to someone else and obtaining a Pareto improvement.

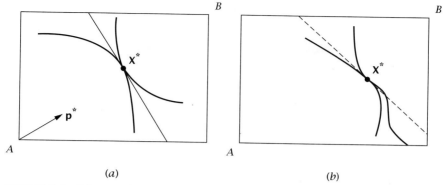

FIGURE 6.4 Edgeworth box.

The relation of Pareto efficiency and equilibria can be illustrated quite effectively for a two-consumer, two-commodity distribution economy with an Edgeworth box, as shown in Fig. 6.4. In Fig. 6.4a a competitive equilibrium is defined by $\mathbf{X}^*$ and $\mathbf{p}^*$. The point and the price vector define budget constraints for individuals A and B, as indicated by the line shown. Individual A must select points on or below this line, and B must select points on or above the line. Under these conditions, neither is motivated to change. The theorem above says that such a point is always Pareto efficient, as is also clear from the figure.

Fig. 6.4b shows that the converse is not always true. The point $\mathbf{X}^*$ is Pareto efficient (and the first-order conditions of Section 6.2 are satisfied). However, this point cannot be part of an equilibrium. The price vector defining the budget constraint shown as a dashed line in the figure, for instance, does not serve as an equilibrium price because the dashed line does not lie on one side of A's upper contour set. To guarantee that a Pareto-efficient point can be supported by an equilibrium, convexity of the upper contour sets is required. Indeed, this condition, together with some additional technical assumptions, is sufficient to establish a converse to the First Theorem.

Second Theorem of Welfare Economics. *Suppose preferences for all individuals are defined on $\mathcal{R}_+^m$ and are continuous, convex, and strongly monotonic and that $\mathcal{T}$ is convex. Suppose $\mathbf{X}^*$ is a Pareto-efficient feasible allocation with $\sum_{i=1}^n \mathbf{x}_i^* > 0$. Then there is a $\mathbf{p}^* > 0$ such that $(\mathbf{X}^*, \mathbf{p}^*)$ is a competitive equilibrium.*

Proof: For each i, let $S_i = \{\mathbf{x}_i \in \mathcal{R}_+^m : \mathbf{x}_i \succsim_i \mathbf{x}_i^*\}$. Each S_i is closed, convex, and nonempty since it contains $\mathbf{x}_i^*$. Let $S = \sum_{i=1}^n S_i = \{\mathbf{z} : \mathbf{z} = \sum_{i=1}^n \mathbf{x}_i, \ \mathbf{x}_i \in S_i\}$. Then S is also closed,[3] convex, and nonempty. S consists of all aggregate

---

[3] S is closed because each $S_i \subset \mathcal{R}_+^m$ and is closed. Hence if $\sum_{i=1}^n \mathbf{z}_i^k \to \mathbf{z}$, with $\mathbf{z}_i^k \in S_i$, each sequence $\{\mathbf{z}_i^k\}$ is bounded, implying that a subsequence converges to some $\bar{\mathbf{z}}_i \in S_i$ and therefore that $\sum_{i=1}^n \bar{\mathbf{z}}_i = \mathbf{z}$.

bundles that have allocations that are preferred by all individuals to the allocation $\mathbf{X}^*$.

Let $\mathbf{t}^* = \sum_{i=1}^{n} \mathbf{x}_i^*$. By definition $\mathbf{t}^* \in S$, and by Pareto efficiency, $\mathbf{t}^*$ is a boundary point of S. To prove this, suppose there were $\mathbf{t}' < \mathbf{t}^*, \mathbf{t}' \in S$. Then there would be $\mathbf{X}' = (\mathbf{x}_1', \mathbf{x}_2', \ldots, \mathbf{x}_n')$ with $\sum_{i=1}^{n} \mathbf{x}_i' = \mathbf{t}'$ and $\mathbf{x}_i' \succsim \mathbf{x}_i^*$ for all i. The allocation defined by $\mathbf{x}_i'' = \mathbf{x}_i' + (\mathbf{t}^* - \mathbf{t}')/n$ would, by strong monotonicity, satisfy $\mathbf{x}_i'' \succ \mathbf{x}_i' \succsim \mathbf{x}_i^*$ and $\sum_{i=1}^{n} \mathbf{x}_i'' = \mathbf{t}^*$, contradicting the Pareto efficiency of $\mathbf{X}^*$. Since $\mathbf{t} < \mathbf{t}^*$ implies $\mathbf{t} \notin S$, it follows that $\mathbf{t}^*$ is a boundary point.

By the separating hyperplane theorem (Appendix B), there is a hyperplane through $\mathbf{t}^*$ with S contained in one half space and $\mathcal{T}$ in the other. That is, there is a $\mathbf{p}^* \in \mathcal{R}^m$, $\mathbf{p}^* \neq \mathbf{0}$, such that $\mathbf{p}^* \cdot \mathbf{z} \geq \mathbf{p}^* \cdot \mathbf{t}^*$ for all $\mathbf{z} \in S$ and $\mathbf{p}^* \cdot \mathbf{t} \leq \mathbf{p}^* \cdot \mathbf{t}^*$ for all $\mathbf{t} \in \mathcal{T}$. (See Fig. 6.5.) We shall show that $\mathbf{p}^*$ has the required properties.

Let $\mathbf{e}_k$ be the kth unit vector in $\mathcal{R}^m$ and let $\mathbf{1}$ be the vector of all ones. By strong monotonicity, the aggregate bundle $\mathbf{t}^* + \mathbf{e}_k \in S$ since the additional amount of the kth commodity can be distributed among the n individuals, making them all better off. Hence, $\mathbf{p}^* \cdot (\mathbf{t}^* + \mathbf{e}_k) \geq \mathbf{p}^* \cdot \mathbf{t}^*$, or equivalently, $\mathbf{p}^* \cdot \mathbf{e}_k \geq 0$ for any k. Thus $\mathbf{p}^* \geq \mathbf{0}$. The above argument can be extended, by continuity (and because $\mathbf{t}^* > \mathbf{0}$), to infer that $\mathbf{t}^* + \mathbf{e}_k - \varepsilon \mathbf{1} \in S$ for small $\varepsilon > 0$. Hence $\mathbf{p}^* \cdot (\mathbf{t}^* + \mathbf{e}_k - \varepsilon \mathbf{1}) \geq \mathbf{p}^* \cdot \mathbf{t}^*$, or equivalently, $\mathbf{p}^* \cdot \mathbf{e}_k \geq \varepsilon \mathbf{p}^* \cdot \mathbf{1} > 0$. Thus $\mathbf{p}^* > \mathbf{0}$.

Next suppose $\mathbf{x}_i \succ_i \mathbf{x}_i^*$ for some i. Then clearly $\mathbf{x}_i \neq \mathbf{0}$. Consider the allocation $\mathbf{X}' = (\mathbf{x}_1', \mathbf{x}_2', \ldots, \mathbf{x}_n')$ where

$$\mathbf{x}_i' = (1 - \varepsilon)\mathbf{x}_i$$
$$\mathbf{x}_j' = \mathbf{x}_j^* + \frac{\varepsilon}{n-1}\mathbf{x}_i, \qquad j \neq i,$$

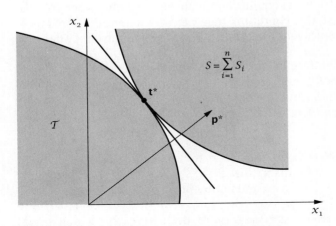

FIGURE 6.5 Pareto efficiency and competitive equilibrium.

obtained by distributing part of $\mathbf{x}_i$ among the other individuals. By continuity and strong monotonicity, there is an $\varepsilon > 0$ such that this allocation is preferred to X^* by all individuals. The associated aggregate is $\sum_{j=1}^n \mathbf{x}'_j = \mathbf{x}_i + \sum_{j \neq i} \mathbf{x}^*_j = \mathbf{x}_i + (\mathbf{t}^* - \mathbf{x}^*_i)$, and this must be in S. Therefore,

$$\mathbf{p}^* \cdot (\mathbf{x}_i + \mathbf{t}^* - \mathbf{x}^*_i) \geq \mathbf{p}^* \cdot \mathbf{t}^* ,$$

or, equivalently, $\mathbf{p}^* \cdot \mathbf{x}_i \geq \mathbf{p}^* \cdot \mathbf{x}^*_i$. However, given $\mathbf{x}_i \succ_i \mathbf{x}^*_i$, there is $\alpha, 0 < \alpha < 1$, such that $\alpha \mathbf{x}_i \succ_i \mathbf{x}^*_i$. The above argument shows that $\alpha \mathbf{p}^* \cdot \mathbf{x}_i \geq \mathbf{p}^* \cdot \mathbf{x}^*_i$. But since $\mathbf{p}^* \cdot \mathbf{x}_i > 0$, it follows that $\mathbf{p}^* \cdot \mathbf{x}_i > \mathbf{p}^* \cdot \mathbf{x}^*_i$. Thus $u_i(\mathbf{x}_i) > u_i(\mathbf{x}^*_i)$ implies $\mathbf{p}^* \cdot \mathbf{x}_i > \mathbf{p}^* \cdot \mathbf{x}^*_i$, which is the equilibrium condition for consumers.

The condition $\mathbf{p}^* \cdot \mathbf{t} \leq \mathbf{p}^* \cdot \mathbf{t}^*$ for all $\mathbf{t} \in \mathcal{T}$ is satisfied because of the original definition of $\mathbf{p}^*$ as separating S and $\mathcal{T}$. $\blacksquare$

The two key assumptions in this theorem are, first, convexity, so that a separating hyperplane can be found, as emphasized earlier; and second, that $\sum_{i=1}^n \mathbf{x}^*_i > 0$. This latter assumption is important because it enables variations around the given allocation to be considered. However, it is only the total of all bundles that must be strictly positive, not each one individually.

There are other versions of the Second Theorem of Welfare Economics, based on different assumptions. For example, the condition of strong monotonicity can be relaxed, although then prices are not guaranteed to be positive. In all versions, however, some form of convexity and some kind of positivity are required.

Since the version of the theorem stated above does not require preferences to be described by a differentiable utility function or that $X^* > 0$, it is technically stronger than the equality of marginal rates of substitution obtained in Section 6.2. However, there is actually a close connection between this theorem and the earlier development. The price vector $\mathbf{p}^*$ of this theorem is (to within a constant multiple) equal to the vector $\mathbf{q}$ of Lagrange multipliers associated with the constraint $\sum_{i=1}^n \mathbf{x}_i = \mathbf{t}^*$. The scale factor is unimportant, since prices may be scaled arbitrarily in the Second Theorem.

Example 6.2 (Coffee and doughnuts).   Consider again the example of distributing coffee and doughnuts considered in Section 6.2. Suppose there were exactly as many cups of coffee as doughnuts. Then we know from the earlier example that in a Pareto efficient distribution everyone will get one doughnut for every cup of coffee (but some may have many of both).

We now introduce a price system. In this case we know by symmetry that the two prices must be equal, so set both prices equal to 1. An individual with $c^*_i = d^*_i$ will have budget $c^*_i + d^*_i = 2c^*_i$. That individual may then consider other bundles c_i, d_i satisfying $c_i + d_i \leq c^*_i + d^*_i = 2c^*_i$. However, the bundle maximizing $u(c_i, d_i) = c_i d_i$ and satisfying this constraint is again $c_i = d_i = c^*_i$. Hence, the individual will find that the current bundle is optimal.

Example 6.3.   Consider an economy that produces q using z according to $q = z^{1/2}$. There are w units of z available. There is a single consumer with utility function $u(q, z) = qz$. We want to find the Pareto efficient and competitive equilibrium allocations.

First, let us approach this by seeking a Pareto efficient allocation. Since there is only one consumer we just maximize utility. The problem is

$$\max \ qz$$
$$\text{sub to } \ q = (w - z)^{1/2},$$

where we used the fact that the amount of z going to production is what is left from the endowment after consumption. We can now substitute q from the production equation. Thus we want to solve

$$\max \ (w - z)^{1/2}z.$$

Differentiation with respect to z gives

$$-\tfrac{1}{2}(w - z)^{-1/2}z + (w - z)^{1/2} = 0$$

or $z^* = \tfrac{2}{3}w$.

Let us now start over using a competitive equilibrium viewpoint. Let p and s be the prices for the variables q and z, respectively. The consumer solves

$$\max \ qz$$
$$\text{sub to } \ pq + sz = pq^* + sz^*$$

which yields the necessary condition

$$\frac{z}{q} = \frac{p}{s}.$$

The firm maximizes profit, which is $p(w - z)^{1/2} - sz$. This yields

$$\tfrac{1}{2}p(w - z)^{-1/2} = s.$$

So, from the consumer's problem we have

$$\frac{p}{s} = \frac{z}{(w - z)^{1/2}}$$

and from the firm's problem we have

$$\frac{p}{s} = 2(w - z)^{1/2}.$$

Equating these we obtain $z = 2(w - z)$ or, finally $z^* = \tfrac{2}{3}w$, which is the same as before.

An important interpretation of the Second Theorem of Welfare Economics is that various Pareto efficient allocations can be achieved by transfers of *income* between individuals. First we note that if $\mathbf{X}^* = (\mathbf{x}_1^*, \mathbf{x}_2^*, \ldots, \mathbf{x}_n^*)$ is Pareto efficient, we can obtain the required aggregate bundle from $\mathcal{T}$ and then allocate the $\mathbf{x}_i^*$'s and simultaneously announce the corresponding equilibrium price vector, which will support this allocation in the sense that no one will be motivated to change. Second, we notice that really all that matters to consumers, once the price vector is established, is the market value of the allocated bundles. If consumer i is allocated the budget $r_i = \mathbf{p}^* \cdot \mathbf{x}_i^*$ and allowed to select any bundle costing no more than r_i, the bundle $\mathbf{x}_i^*$ will be among those of maximal preference. Maximization of $\mathbf{p}^* \cdot \mathbf{t}$ will likewise lead to generation of the required aggregate. Hence, any Pareto efficient allocation can be achieved indirectly by suitable assignment of prices and incomes. This argument is frequently carried further to suggest that in a real economy with a given current allocation, an alternative Pareto efficient allocation can be achieved by imposed transfers of income (through confiscations and grants, for example). This is technically achievable according to the Second Theorem, although it is usually impractical to carry out such lump-sum transfers.

*A Geometric Principle

A simple geometric principle underlies the relation between efficiency and equilibria. The Edgeworth box is one way to illustrate this principle, but another way is more general. This principle is the basis of the proof of the Second Theorem of Welfare Economics given above, but it is useful to focus on it explicitly.

Suppose $\mathbf{X}^* = (\mathbf{x}_1^*, \mathbf{x}_2^*, \ldots, \mathbf{x}_n^*)$ is an allocation (not necessarily a Pareto-efficient allocation) and assume that all preferences are continuous and strongly monotonic. Define the upper contour sets $S_i = \{\mathbf{x}_i : \mathbf{x}_i \succsim \mathbf{x}_i^*\}$. Then under the above assumptions, each $\mathbf{x}_i^*$ is a boundary point of the corresponding S_i.

Now let $S = \sum_{i=1}^n S_i$. This set addition is illustrated schematically in the top part of Fig. 6.6, which shows the upper contour sets of two individuals in two different copies of $\mathcal{R}^2$; the result of the addition is shown in a third copy. Really, of course, all sets are in the same space $\mathcal{R}^2$ and addition is carried out by the usual operation of set addition.

The point $\mathbf{t}^* = \sum_{i=1}^n \mathbf{x}_i^*$ belongs to S. However, it will usually *not* be a boundary point of S. That is, the sum of points may not be a boundary point of S even though each of the points in the sum is a boundary point of its corresponding S_i. (Try it!) For the vectors shown in the figure, the resulting $\mathbf{t}^* = \mathbf{x}_1^* + \mathbf{x}_2^*$ *is* a boundary point of S, representing a special situation. The reason that it works for the vectors in the figure is that they are not arbitrary, but are *coordinated* by a price vector. In general, if each $\mathbf{x}_i^*$ is a boundary point of S_i where a hyperplane of the form $\mathbf{p} \cdot \mathbf{x} = c$ supports S_i *with the same* $\mathbf{p}$ *for all* i, the resulting sum will be a boundary point of S with a similar supporting hyperplane. The price vector $\mathbf{p}$ *coordinates* all the points so that they all fall on boundaries.

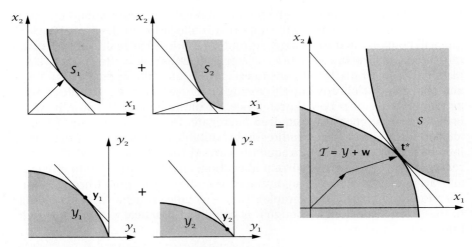

FIGURE 6.6   The geometry of equilibria.

Suppose also that there are K firms, with production possibility sets $\mathcal{Y}_k$, $k = 1, 2, \ldots, K$. Assume that each firm selects $\mathbf{y}_k^*$ as a boundary point of $\mathcal{Y}_k$. The resulting $\mathbf{y}^* = \sum_{k=1}^{K} \mathbf{y}_k^*$ may *not* be a boundary point of $\mathcal{Y} = \sum_{k=1}^{K} \mathcal{Y}_k$. Hence $\mathbf{t}^* = \mathbf{w} + \sum_{k=1}^{K} \mathbf{y}_k^*$ may not be a boundary point of $\mathcal{T}$. However, the bottom part of Fig. 6.6 shows a case where $\mathbf{t}^*$ *is* a boundary point of $\mathcal{T}$. The reason is that the $\mathbf{y}_k^*$'s are all coordinated by the price vector $\mathbf{p}$. Each $\mathbf{y}_k^*$ was chosen to maximize profit with respect to this price vector. For overall production efficiency, it is not enough for each firm to be operating at an efficient (boundary) point. They must be coordinated by a common price vector. This is a general characterization of production efficiency.

Figure 6.6 shows a complete picture of a competitive equilibrium. On the top left are the figures for individual consumers, each optimizing with respect to given prices. On the bottom left are the individual firms, each maximizing profit. On the right is the aggregate picture, showing how aggregate consumption is likewise a kind of optimal aggregate with respect to the prices, and showing how this aggregate simultaneously maximizes profit over $\mathcal{T}$. Or viewed the other way, the right-hand part of the figure shows the basic Pareto efficient relation and the left shows an exploded view of this for individuals and firms.

*6.6   Social Welfare and Economic Efficiency

As emphasized before, Pareto efficiency is actually a fairly weak concept. It defines only a partial ordering among the possible allocations, leaving a wide spectrum of choice remaining. In any particular case, some selection among the Pareto-efficient states must be made—either explicitly or implicitly—and it can be argued that this choice should be accomplished rationally by society as a whole, in much the same way that individuals make their own choices. One way to do this is through the introduction of a *social welfare function*. Such a function depends on the allocation to all individuals in the society and assigns a value measuring the collective welfare of this allocation. One particular type of social welfare function, for n individuals, is the *Bergson-Samuelson* form,

$$S(u_1(\mathbf{x}_1), u_2(\mathbf{x}_2), \ldots, u_n(\mathbf{x}_n))$$

where $\mathbf{x}_i$, $i = 1, 2, \ldots, n$, is the commodity allocation to individual i and u_i is the utility function of individual i. It is assumed that S is a strictly increasing function of each of its arguments; that is, it increases as each individual's utility increases. This form of function respects individuals' assessments of their own welfare, through their utility functions, and merely combines them to obtain an overall welfare measure. Such a social welfare function can be thought of as a kind of utility function for society.

Recall that an economy can be characterized as consisting of a set F of feasible allocations. An allocation $\mathbf{X} = (\mathbf{x}_1, \mathbf{x}_2, \ldots, \mathbf{x}_n)$ maximizes a social welfare function if it is a solution to the following optimization problem

$$\max \ S(u_1(\mathbf{x}_1), u_2(\mathbf{x}_2), \ldots, u_n(\mathbf{x}_n)) \tag{6.5}$$

$$\text{sub to } (\mathbf{x}_1, \mathbf{x}_2, \ldots, \mathbf{x}_n) \in F.$$

A fundamental property of a Bergson-Samuelson social welfare function is that its use as a basis of societal choice implies Pareto efficiency.

Welfare efficiency theorem.   *If a feasible allocation* $\mathbf{X}$ *maximizes a Bergson-Samuelson social welfare function, it is Pareto efficient.*

Proof: This theorem follows immediately from the strict monotonicity of the social welfare function. ∎

An interesting converse to the welfare efficiency theorem states that for every Pareto-efficient allocation there is a linear social welfare function that is maximized by that allocation. Note, however, that this theorem requires that individual utility functions be concave rather than merely quasi-concave.

Negishi theorem.   *Suppose the utility functions* u_i, $i = 1, 2, \ldots, n$, *are concave, continuous, and strongly monotonic on* $\mathcal{R}_+^m$. *Suppose the allocation* $\mathbf{X}^* = (\mathbf{x}_1^*, \mathbf{x}_2^*, \ldots, \mathbf{x}_n^*)$ *is Pareto efficient and the set* F *is closed and convex. Then there are weights* c_i, $c_i \geq 0$, $i = 1, 2, \ldots, n$, *not all of which are zero, such that* $\mathbf{X}^*$ *maximizes the linear social welfare function*

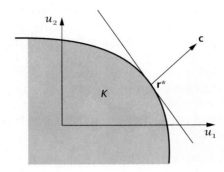

FIGURE 6.7   Definition of linear social welfare function.

$$S = \sum_{i=1}^{n} c_i u_i(\mathbf{x}_i)$$

subject to $\mathbf{X} = (\mathbf{x}_1, \mathbf{x}_2, \ldots, \mathbf{x}_n) \in F$.

Proof: Define the set $K \subset \mathcal{R}^n$ by $K = \{\mathbf{r} : r_i \le u_i(\mathbf{x}_i),\ i = 1, 2, \ldots, n,\ \mathbf{X} \in F\}$. Thus K is the set of all vectors of utility values that are at most equal to those that are feasible. (See Fig. 6.7.) We shall show that K is convex. Let $\mathbf{r}, \mathbf{s} \in K$ with $r_i \le u_i(\mathbf{x}_i)$ and $s_i \le u_i(\mathbf{x}_i')$ where $\mathbf{X}$ and $\mathbf{X}'$ are in F. Then for $0 \le \alpha \le 1$,

$$\alpha r_i + (1 - \alpha)s_i \le \alpha u_i(\mathbf{x}_i) + (1 - \alpha)u_i(\mathbf{x}_i') \le u_i(\alpha \mathbf{x}_i + (1 - \alpha)\mathbf{x}_i')$$

by the concavity of u_i. Since F is convex, $\alpha \mathbf{X} + (1 - \alpha)\mathbf{X}'$ is feasible, and $\alpha \mathbf{r} + (1 - \alpha)\mathbf{s} \in K$. By continuity K is closed.

Now let $\mathbf{X}^*$ be a Pareto-efficient allocation, and define $\mathbf{r}^*$ by $r_i^* = u_i(\mathbf{x}_i^*)$, $i = 1, 2, \ldots, n$. Then by strong monotonicity and continuity, $\mathbf{r}^*$ is on the boundary of K. Thus by the supporting hyperplane theorem (Appendix B), there is a vector $\mathbf{c} \ne \mathbf{0}$ such that

$$\mathbf{c} \cdot \mathbf{r} \le \mathbf{c} \cdot \mathbf{r}^*$$

for all $\mathbf{r} \in K$. Since $\mathbf{r}^* - \mathbf{e}_i \in K$ for all unit coordinate vectors, it follows immediately that $\mathbf{c} \ge \mathbf{0}$. It also follows that $\mathbf{r}^*$ maximizes $\mathbf{c} \cdot \mathbf{r}$ over $\mathbf{r} \in K$ and hence $\mathbf{X}^*$ solves the social welfare maximization problem. ∎

This theorem gives an (implicit) way of parameterizing the Pareto-efficient allocations. By varying the c_i's we can get all such allocations, so if we were able to plan the allocation for society, it would be reasonable to solve this problem for various c_i's and select the one we liked best.

6.7   Benefits and the Zero-Maximum Principle

Pareto efficiency is closely related to optimization, since it implies that one individual's utility is maximized with the constraint that the utility of all others does not decrease. Indeed, the optimization flavor of Pareto efficiency is often explicitly acknowledged in terminology by referring to it alternatively as *Pareto optimality.*

Pareto efficiency was shown to be related to optimality in another way in the previous section, which discussed social welfare functions. However, since a social welfare function is quite arbitrary and has no established units, this relation is not entirely natural.

The optimal character of Pareto efficiency can be made explicit in still another way by consideration of total benefits, defined as the sum of individual benefits. Basically, Pareto efficiency corresponds to maximization of total benefits. This correspondence provides a link between Pareto efficiency and optimality, which has a strong economic interpretation.

Consider an economy consisting of n consumers. Consumer i, $i = 1, 2, \ldots, n$, has a preference relation on $X_i = \mathcal{R}_+^m$ that is represented by a continuous utility function u_i. The set of attainable values for $u_i(\mathbf{x}_i)$ as $\mathbf{x}_i$ ranges over $\mathcal{R}_+^m$ is denoted $\mathcal{U}_i$. An allocation $\mathbf{X} = (\mathbf{x}_1, \mathbf{x}_2, \ldots, \mathbf{x}_n)$ is feasible in the economy if $\mathbf{x}_i \geq \mathbf{0}$ for each i and $\sum_{i=1}^{n} \mathbf{x}_i \in \mathcal{T}$ where $\mathcal{T}$ is a given transformation set. We select a vector $\mathbf{g} \geq \mathbf{0}$, $\mathbf{g} \neq \mathbf{0}$, to be a reference vector for measuring benefits. Hence, each consumer i has a benefit function $b_i(\mathbf{x}, u)$.

Now let $\mathbf{U} = (u_1, u_2, \ldots, u_n)$ where each u_i is a value in $\mathcal{U}_i$. Let $\mathbf{X} = (\mathbf{x}_1, \mathbf{x}_2, \ldots, \mathbf{x}_n)$. We define the *total benefit function* as

$$B(\mathbf{X}, \mathbf{U}) = \sum_{i=1}^{n} b_i(\mathbf{x}_i, u_i).$$

Thus B measures the total benefit occurring to all individuals associated with $\mathbf{X}$ and relative to $\mathbf{U}$.

We now introduce a bit of useful terminology.

Zero-maximality. A feasible allocation $\mathbf{X}^0$ is said to be *zero-maximal* for $B(\mathbf{X}, \mathbf{U})$ if $\mathbf{X}^0$ maximizes $B(\mathbf{X}, \mathbf{U})$ with respect to all feasible allocations and if $B(\mathbf{X}^0, \mathbf{U}) = 0$.

In other words, the term *zero-maximal* means both maximal (with respect to the implied constraints) and zero-valued. It is just a composition of the two properties.

Now suppose a particular allocation $\mathbf{X}^*$ is given. There will be associated utility values $u_i^* = u_i(\mathbf{x}_i^*)$. We accordingly define $\mathbf{U}^* = (u_1^*, u_2^*, \ldots, u_n^*)$. The total benefit of an allocation $\mathbf{X}$ relative to the utility levels associated with $\mathbf{X}^*$ is thus $B(\mathbf{X}, \mathbf{U}^*)$.

We now state the first result relating Pareto efficiency to total benefits.

First zero-maximum theorem. *Suppose $\mathbf{g}$ is good for at least one individual. Suppose $\mathbf{X}^* = (\mathbf{x}_1^*, \mathbf{x}_2^*, \ldots, \mathbf{x}_n^*)$ is a Pareto-efficient allocation of a transformation economy. Then $\mathbf{X}^*$ is zero-maximal for*

$$B(\mathbf{X}, \mathbf{U}^*) = \sum_{i=1}^{n} b_i(\mathbf{x}_i, u_i^*)$$

$$\text{sub to } \sum_{i=1}^{n} \mathbf{x}_i \in \mathcal{T}.$$

Proof: It is clear that $b_i(\mathbf{x}_i^*, u_i^*) \geq 0$ for each i. Suppose there were some j with $b_j^* = b_j(\mathbf{x}_j^*, u_j^*) > 0$. Then $\mathbf{g}$ cannot be good for j since $u_j(\mathbf{x}_j^* - b_j^* \mathbf{g}) \geq u_j^*$ would imply that $u_j(\mathbf{x}_j^*) > u_j^*$, contradicting the definition of u_j^*. Therefore there must be another individual k for which $\mathbf{g}$ is good.

We then define the allocation $\mathbf{X} = (\mathbf{x}_1, \mathbf{x}_2, \ldots, \mathbf{x}_n)$ with $\mathbf{x}_i = \mathbf{x}_i^*$ for $i \neq j$ and $i \neq k$; $\mathbf{x}_j = \mathbf{x}_j^* - b_j^* \mathbf{g}$; and $\mathbf{x}_k = \mathbf{x}_k^* + b_j^* \mathbf{g}$. We have $u_i(\mathbf{x}_i) \geq u_i^*$ for all $i \neq k$ (including $i = j$) and $u_k(\mathbf{x}_k) > u_k^*$. This contradicts the Pareto efficiency of $\mathbf{X}^*$. Thus, $b_i(\mathbf{x}_i^*, u_i^*) = 0$ for all i. Hence $B(\mathbf{X}^*, \mathbf{U}^*) = 0$.

To prove maximality, suppose there were a feasible allocation $\mathbf{X}$ with $B(\mathbf{X}, \mathbf{U}^*) = B > 0$. Clearly, each $b_i(\mathbf{x}_i, u_i^*)$ is finite since on $\mathcal{R}_+^m$ all benefits are less than $+\infty$. For each i, let $b_i = b_i(\mathbf{x}_i, u_i^*)$. Without loss of generality, we can assume that $\mathbf{g}$ is good for consumer n. Consider the allocation $\mathbf{X}'$ defined by $\mathbf{x}_i' = \mathbf{x}_i - b_i \mathbf{g}$ for $i = 1, 2, \ldots, n-1, \mathbf{x}_n' = \mathbf{x}_n - b_n \mathbf{g} + B\mathbf{g}$. This allocation is feasible because in fact $\sum_{i=1}^{n} \mathbf{x}_i' = \sum_{i=1}^{n} \mathbf{x}_i - \sum_{i=1}^{n} b_i \mathbf{g} + B\mathbf{g} = \sum_{i=1}^{n} \mathbf{x}_i$. Also, by definition of the benefit function, $u_i(\mathbf{x}_i') \geq u_i^*$ for all $i = 1, 2, \ldots, n-1$. Finally, $u_n(\mathbf{x}_n') > u_n^*$ since $B > 0$ and $\mathbf{g}$ is good for n. Thus $\mathbf{X}'$ is a Pareto improvement over $\mathbf{X}^*$, which is a contradiction. ∎

This theorem has a very nice interpretation relating Pareto efficiency to an intuitive notion of overall welfare. It says that if $\mathbf{X}^*$ is Pareto efficient, then first, $\mathbf{X}^*$ maximizes the total benefit of the economy, and second, this benefit is zero. The maximization means that there is no way to decrease the benefit of some individuals and obtain a greater increase for others. The net benefit must always be less than at the current allocation $\mathbf{X}^*$. The reason the benefit is zero is that benefits are measured relative to the utility levels at $\mathbf{X}^*$.

It is therefore quite appropriate to speak about Pareto-efficient allocations as those that provide the greatest benefit to consumers. The units of this benefit are well defined to be units of the reference bundle $\mathbf{g}$. The only point that must be emphasized is that benefits are measured relative to a set of utility levels, which are taken to be those of the Pareto-efficient allocation $\mathbf{X}^*$ itself.

Example 6.4 (Coffee and doughnuts). Let us again consider the coffee and doughnuts example, Example 6.1 at the end of Section 6.2. We have $u_i(c, d) = cd$ for $i = 1, 2, \ldots, n$. Let us use coffee as reference. Then $b_i(c, d, u_i) = c - u_i/d$. The total benefit function is therefore

$$B = \sum_{i=1}^{n} \left\{ c_i - \frac{u_i}{d_i} \right\}.$$

This must be maximized subject to the constraints $\sum_{i=1}^{n} c_i = C$ and $\sum_{i=1}^{n} d_i = D$. The maximization with respect to the c_i's is degenerate, since only their sum, which is fixed, appears in the total benefit. All sets of c_i's that produce that sum give the same value. For the d_i's we obtain $u_i/d_i^2 = \lambda$, where λ is the Lagrange multiplier. Using $u_i = c_i d_i$, this yields $c_i/d_i = \lambda$; that is, c_i/d_i is constant with respect to i. This agrees with our earlier conclusion.

Note also that at the solution, $B = \sum_{i=1}^{n} c_i - u_i/d_i = \sum_{i=1}^{n} c_i - c_i d_i/d_i = 0$. Thus total benefit is zero as well as maximal.

A converse of the above zero-maximum theorem is also true, as shown below.

Second zero-maximum theorem. *Suppose that each utility function is continuous, strongly monotonic, and quasi-concave on $\mathcal{R}_+^m$ and that $\mathcal{T}$ is convex. Assume that $\mathbf{X}^*$ is zero-maximal for*

$$B(\mathbf{X}, \mathbf{U}^*) = \sum_{i=1}^{n} b_i(\mathbf{x}_i, u_i^*)$$

$$\text{sub to } \sum_{i=1}^{n} \mathbf{x}_i \in \mathcal{T}$$

and that $\sum_{i=1}^{n} \mathbf{x}_i^* > \mathbf{0}$. Then $\mathbf{X}^*$ is Pareto efficient.

Proof: Clearly $b_i(\mathbf{x}_i^*, u_i^*) = 0$ for all i. Assume that $\mathbf{X}^*$ is not Pareto efficient. Then there is a feasible allocation $\mathbf{X}$ such that $u_i(\mathbf{x}_i) \geq u_i^*$, $i = 1, 2, \ldots, n$, with $u_j(\mathbf{x}_j) > u_j^*$ for some j.

Without loss of generality we may assume that $\sum_{i=1}^{n} \mathbf{x}_i > \mathbf{0}$. If not, we could construct the allocation $\mathbf{X}' = \alpha \mathbf{X} + (1 - \alpha)\mathbf{X}^*$. For $0 < \alpha \leq 1$ we have $u_i(\mathbf{x}_i') \geq u_i(\mathbf{x}_i^*)$ for $i = 1, 2, \ldots, n$ by the quasi-concavity of the u_i's. $\mathbf{X}'$ is feasible since $\mathcal{T}$ is convex. Also, for some $\alpha > 0$ we must have $u_j(\mathbf{x}_j') > u_j(\mathbf{x}_j^*)$ by continuity. The resulting $\mathbf{X}'$ is a Pareto improvement of $\mathbf{X}^*$ that does satisfy $\sum_{i=1}^{n} \mathbf{x}_i' > \mathbf{0}$. Hence we assume this is true for $\mathbf{X}$.

All $b_i(\mathbf{x}_i, u_i^*) \geq 0$. If $\mathbf{x}_j > \mathbf{0}$, we have $b_j(\mathbf{x}_j, u_j^*) > 0$, contradicting the zero-maximality of $\mathbf{X}^*$. Hence $(\mathbf{x}_j)_k = 0$ for some component k. By strong monotonicity $\mathbf{x}_j \neq \mathbf{0}$, and hence $(\mathbf{x}_j)_{k'} > 0$ for some other k'. By continuity there is an $\varepsilon > 0$ such that if we take ε units of commodity k' from consumer j, he or her will still be better off than at $\mathbf{x}_j^*$. We then give $\varepsilon/(n-1)$ units of commodity k' to each of the other $n-1$ consumers. By strong monotonicity they will all be better off than at $\mathbf{X}^*$. This new allocation, which we call $\mathbf{X}'$, is feasible and has $u_i(\mathbf{x}_i') > u_i^*$ for each i.

Since $\sum_{i=1}^{n} \mathbf{x}_i > \mathbf{0}$, there is, in aggregate, a positive amount of every commodity. We modify $\mathbf{X}'$ to make sure that everyone has a positive amount of commodity 1. This is done by subtracting a small amount from someone who has it and distributing that amount among those who do not. By continuity, this can be done in such a way so as to keep everyone strictly better off than at $\mathbf{X}^*$. By repeating this process for each commodity, we obtain a final allocation $\mathbf{X}''$ where $\mathbf{x}_i'' > \mathbf{0}$ and $u_i(\mathbf{x}_i'') > u_i^*$ for each i. This implies that $b_i(\mathbf{x}_i'', u_i^*) > 0$ for each i, contradicting the zero-maximality of $\mathbf{X}^*$. ∎

It is possible to dispense with the assumption of strong monotonicity and the assumption that $\sum_{i=1}^{n} \mathbf{x}_i^* > \mathbf{0}$. However, other assumptions are necessary to prevent problems at boundary points. An alternative is to assume that all utility functions are strongly quasi-concave.[4] Then the conclusion of the second zero-maximum theorem is valid if $\mathbf{X}^*$ is an interior point (of $\mathcal{R}_+^{mn}$).

The two zero-maximum theorems can be considered to compose a general principle termed the *zero-maximum principle*. This principle states that, under suitable technical assumptions, the Pareto efficiency of an allocation corresponds to zero-maximization of total benefits. In view of the First and Second Theorems of Welfare Economics, the zero-maximum principle also states that the allocation of a competitive equilibrium corresponds to zero-maximization of benefits. We shall use the principle both ways.

The Edgeworth Box and Necessary Conditions

The zero-maximum principle can be well illustrated in an Edgeworth box. Figure 6.8 represents the standard situation of distributing two commodities among two consumers. We have taken $\mathbf{g} = \frac{1}{2}\sqrt{2}(1, 1)$ (which is normalized so that $||\mathbf{g}|| = 1$). The point $\mathbf{X}^*$ is clearly a Pareto-efficient allocation.

Now consider the allocation $\mathbf{X}$ in the figure. The benefit to A of this point is positive and equal to the distance in the $\mathbf{g}$ direction from $\mathbf{X}$ to A's indifference curve. This distance is the dashed line in the figure. The benefit to B of $\mathbf{X}$ is negative and equal in magnitude to the distance in the $\mathbf{g}$ direction from $\mathbf{X}$ to B's indifference curve. The total benefit is the sum of these, which is negative and equal in magnitude to the length of the solid line between the two indifference curves.

The total benefit at $\mathbf{X}^*$ is clearly zero, which is the maximum of any point in the box. The zero-maximality condition corresponds to the condi-

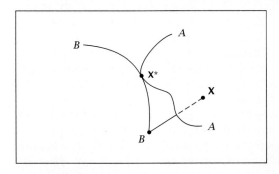

FIGURE   6.8   Zero-maximum condition.

---

[4]The function u is strongly quasi-concave if for all $\mathbf{x}_1, \mathbf{x}_2 \in \mathcal{R}^n$ with $u(\mathbf{x}_1) > u(\mathbf{x}_2)$ there holds $u(\alpha \mathbf{x}_1 + (1 - \alpha)\mathbf{x}_2) > u(\mathbf{x}_2)$ for all α, $0 < \alpha \le 1$.

tion that the two indifference curves touch at $\mathbf{X}^*$ and do not overlap at any other point. No convexity is required for this to work (except at the edges). Conceptually, this diagrammatic property is in fact simpler than the earlier interpretation of Pareto efficiency in terms of tangency conditions: curves touching but not crossing is a simpler concept than tangency.

Differential conditions can also be derived easily from the zero-maximality condition. For a distribution economy with total endowment $\mathbf{w}$, the zero-maximum condition is that $\mathbf{X}^*$ solves

$$\max \sum_{i=1}^{n} b_i(\mathbf{x}_i, u_i^*)$$

$$\text{sub to } \sum_{i=1}^{n} \mathbf{x}_i = \mathbf{w}$$

$$\mathbf{x}_i \geq \mathbf{0}.$$

It is easy to show that

$$\frac{\partial b_i(\mathbf{x}_i, u_i^*)}{\partial x_{ik}} = p_k,$$

where p_k is the Lagrange multiplier of the constraint on commodity k. Thus, as shown in Section 5.2, price is equal to marginal benefit. From this it follows immediately that

$$\frac{\partial b_i(\mathbf{x}_i, u_i^*)}{\partial x_{ik}} = \frac{\partial b_j(\mathbf{x}_j, u_j^*)}{\partial x_{jk}},$$

which says that the marginal benefit of commodity k is the same for all consumers. This is analogous to (in fact equivalent to) the statement of Section 6.2 that the marginal rates of substitution are the same for all consumers.

Of course, the p_k's are also equilibrium prices (but normalized with $\mathbf{p} \cdot \mathbf{g} = 1$). So we see also that equilibrium prices are equal to marginal benefits.

*The Shortage Function

The shortage function can provide an alternative formulation of the zero-maximization principle. This formulation takes the transformation set out of the constraints and includes its influence in the definition of the objective function.

Corresponding to the transformation set $\mathcal{T}$ define the *shortage function* $\overline{\sigma}$ by

$$\overline{\sigma}(\mathbf{t}) = \begin{cases} \min\{s : \mathbf{t} - s\mathbf{g} \in \mathcal{T}\} \\ \qquad \text{if there is } s \text{ such that } \mathbf{t} - s\mathbf{g} \in \mathcal{T} \\ +\infty \quad \text{otherwise.} \end{cases}$$

We use the overbar, $\overline{\sigma}$, to distinguish the shortage function of $\mathcal{T}$ from that of $\mathcal{Y}$, which would normally be denoted σ. If $\mathcal{T}$ is closed and satisfies other standard conditions, then $\mathcal{T} = \{\mathbf{y} : \overline{\sigma}(\mathbf{y}) \leq 0\}$.

Instead of formulating the zero-maximum theorems using $\mathbf{y} \in \mathcal{T}$ as a constraint, we can instead consider the problem

$$\max_{\mathbf{x},\mathbf{y}} \sum_{i=1}^{n} b_i(\mathbf{x}_i, u_i^*) - \overline{\sigma}(\mathbf{y})$$

$$\text{sub to } \sum_{i=1}^{n} \mathbf{x}_i = \mathbf{y}$$

$$\mathbf{x}_i \geq \mathbf{0}.$$

We maximize the net of benefits minus shortage. This automatically accounts for $\mathbf{y} \in \mathcal{T}$. It is easy to extend the previous zero-maximum theorems to show that a Pareto-efficient allocation corresponds to a zero-maximum of the above problem.

Example 6.5.   Let us solve the production problem of Example 6.3 of Section 6.5 using the approach above. We select the reference commodity to be q. Then

$$b(q, z, u) = q - \frac{u}{z}$$

$$\overline{\sigma}(q, z) = q - (w - z)^{1/2}.$$

Therefore we maximize $q - u/z - q + (w - z)^{1/2}$. The q's cancel, and hence we obtain $u/z^2 = \frac{1}{2}(w - z)^{-1/2}$. We can solve this explicitly by using $u = (w - z)^{1/2}z$. This gives

$$\frac{(w - z)^{1/2}}{z} = \frac{1}{2}(w - z)^{-1/2}.$$

Hence, $z = \frac{2}{3}w$ as before.

6.8   Surplus and the Zero-Minimum Principle

A dual concept that is very powerful and hence very important is the concept of a *surplus function*, which is essentially the dual of the total benefit function minus the shortage function. Correspondingly, there is a zero-minimum principle, expressed in terms of surplus, that is dual to the zero-maximum principle. The zero-minimum principle forms the foundation for both the proof of existence of competitive equilibria, as presented in the next chapter, and for computation of such equilibria.

We introduce the notation $\overline{\pi}(\mathbf{p}) = \sup\{\mathbf{p} \cdot \mathbf{t} : \mathbf{t} \in \mathcal{T}\}$. Thus $\overline{\pi}(\mathbf{p})$ is the profit function of the transformation set $\mathcal{T}$. If $\mathcal{T} = \mathbf{w} + \mathcal{Y}$, then $\overline{\pi}(\mathbf{p}) = \mathbf{p} \cdot \mathbf{w} + \pi(\mathbf{p})$ where $\pi(\mathbf{p})$ is the profit function of the production possibility set $\mathcal{Y}$. The function $\overline{\pi}$ includes the value of the endowment as well.

The surplus function is defined as follows:

Surplus function.   Let $\mathbf{U} = (u_1, u_2, \ldots, u_n)$ with $u_i \in \mathcal{U}_i$ for each i and let $\mathbf{p} \in \mathcal{R}_+^m$. The *surplus function* is defined as

$$S(\mathbf{p}, \mathbf{U}) = \overline{\pi}(\mathbf{p}) - \sum_{i=1}^{n} e_i(\mathbf{p}, u_i),$$

where e_i is the expenditure function associated with the ith utility function.

There are many concepts of surplus in economic theory, so to distinguish this one, we can refer to it as the *income surplus function*. However, in our discussions such a distinction is rarely required.

The surplus function has a simple interpretation. Suppose prices $\mathbf{p}$ and utility levels $\mathbf{U}$ are specified. Then the total amount of income generated by the transformation set is $\overline{\pi}(\mathbf{p})$. If we simultaneously require that consumers achieve the utility levels indicated in $\mathbf{U}$, then consumer i must spend at least $e_i(\mathbf{p}, u_i)$. The total amount spent in order to achieve the specified utility levels is therefore $\sum_{i=1}^{n} e_i(\mathbf{p}, u_i)$. The surplus is the difference of the two, that is, the difference between the income generated and the income spent.

In equilibrium the surplus is zero. In fact, equilibrium is characterized by the condition that surplus is zero and cannot be decreased below zero by changing prices. This statement is the essence of the zero-minimum principle, which is formalized by the two theorems below. We prove only the first of these (the easy one). For the proof of the second one, see Exercise 16.

First zero-minimum theorem. *Suppose all utility functions are continuous and satisfy local nonsatiation on $\mathcal{R}_{+}^{m}$. Suppose $(\mathbf{X}^*, \mathbf{p}^*)$ is a competitive equilibrium for a transformation economy. Then $\mathbf{p}^*$ is zero-minimal for*

$$S(\mathbf{p}, \mathbf{U}^*) = \overline{\pi}(\mathbf{p}) - \sum_{i=1}^{n} e_i(\mathbf{p}, u_i^*)$$

over $\mathbf{p} \cdot \mathbf{g} = 1$.

Proof: For any $\mathbf{p}$ we have $\overline{\pi}(\mathbf{p}) \geq \mathbf{p} \cdot \sum_{i=1}^{n} \mathbf{x}_i^*$ because $\sum_{i=1}^{n} \mathbf{x}_i^* \in \mathcal{T}$. Also $\mathbf{p} \cdot \mathbf{x}_i^* \geq e_i(\mathbf{p}, u_i^*)$ for all $i = 1, 2, \ldots, n$. Combining these inequalities we have

$$\overline{\pi}(\mathbf{p}) \geq \sum_{i=1}^{n} e_i(\mathbf{p}, u_i^*),$$

or equivalently, $S(\mathbf{p}, \mathbf{U}^*) \geq 0$.

On the other hand, for $\mathbf{p}^*$ we have (under local nonsatiation) equalities instead of inequalities in all the above relations. Thus $\mathbf{p}^*$ is zero-minimal. ∎

Second zero-minimum theorem. *Suppose all utility functions are quasi-concave on $\mathbf{R}_{+}^{m}$. Suppose that $\mathcal{T}$ is closed and convex, satisfies free disposal, and is such that $\mathcal{T} \cap \mathcal{R}_{+}^{m}$ is nonempty and bounded. Assume that $\mathbf{g} > \mathbf{0}$ and let $u_i^* \in \mathcal{U}_i$, $i = 1, 2, \ldots, n$, be given. Finally, suppose $\mathbf{p}^* \geq \mathbf{0}$ is zero-minimal for*

$$S(\mathbf{p}, \mathbf{U}^*) = \overline{\pi}(\mathbf{p}) - \sum_{i=1}^{n} e_i(\mathbf{p}, u_i^*)$$

over $\mathbf{p} \cdot \mathbf{g} = 1$, $\mathbf{p} \geq \mathbf{0}$; *and suppose* $e_i(\mathbf{p}^*, u_i^*) > 0$ *for* $i = 1, 2, \ldots, n$. *Then there is a feasible allocation* $\mathbf{X}^*$ *such that* $u_i^* = u_i(\mathbf{x}_i^*)$, $i = 1, 2, \ldots, n$, *and such that* $(\mathbf{p}^*, \mathbf{X}^*)$ *is a competitive equilibrium.*

There is an interesting economic interpretation of the zero-minimality condition. Imagine a "market maker" who is responsible for trading commodities to firms and consumers at a fixed price, which the market maker can determine. Consumers are required to achieve utility levels u_i^*. If the market maker announces prices $\mathbf{p}$, the aggregate firm (defined by the transformation set) will seek to maximize profit. Therefore the firm will trade and produce items in such a way as to make a profit of $\overline{\pi}(\mathbf{p})$. This profit is obtained from trades with the market maker, so the market maker loses an amount $\overline{\pi}(\mathbf{p})$. Consumers will obtain the required utility at minimum cost. They will therefore pay the market maker $\sum_{i=1}^{n} e_i(\mathbf{p}, u_i^*)$. Overall, the market maker loses $\overline{\pi}(\mathbf{p}) - \sum_{i=1}^{n} e_i(\mathbf{p}, u_i^*) = S(\mathbf{p}, \mathbf{U}^*)$. Hence, the market maker will select $\mathbf{p}$ to minimize this quantity. That is, the market maker finds $\mathbf{p}^*$ to minimize $S(\mathbf{p}, \mathbf{U}^*)$. In equilibrium, everything will balance, and the market maker will have no net profit or loss. Thus $S(\mathbf{p}^*, \mathbf{U}^*) = 0$.

Example 6.6 (Coffee and doughnuts). Let us consider the coffee and doughnuts example from the viewpoint of the zero-minimality of surplus. The expenditure function corresponding to the utility function $u(c, d) = cd$ is $e(p_c, p_d, u) = 2(p_c p_d u)^{\frac{1}{2}}$. If we normalize prices with $p_c = 1$, we may drop the subscript on p_d and consider price vectors of the form $(1, p)$. Hence the surplus function is

$$S(p, \mathbf{U}) = C + Dp - \sum_{i=1}^{n} 2\sqrt{p u_i},$$

where C and D are the aggregate endowments of coffee and doughnuts. We write the necessary condition for minimization of $S(p, \mathbf{U})$ with respect to p. This condition is

$$D - \sum_{i=1}^{n} \sqrt{\frac{u_i}{p}} = 0.$$

This gives $p = [\sum_{i=1}^{n} \sqrt{u_i}]^2 / D^2$. We can substitute this value into the surplus function and use the fact that the surplus must be zero. This gives

$$S = C + \frac{1}{D}\left[\sum_{i=1}^{n} \sqrt{u_i}\right]^2 - \frac{2}{D}\left[\sum_{i=1}^{n} \sqrt{u_i}\right]\left[\sum_{i=1}^{n} \sqrt{u_i}\right] = 0,$$

or upon reduction,

$$CD = \left[\sum_{i=1}^{n} \sqrt{u_i}\right]^2.$$

Substitution of this into the formula for p found above yields $p = C/D$. This is the (unique in this case) Pareto-efficient price of doughnuts.

*6.9 Dual Pareto Efficiency

Pareto efficiency is a primal concept, since it is a property of allocations of goods. However, in an economy where goods can be freely traded, it is natural to introduce prices for the commodities and incomes for consumers. These price-income combinations are ordered by consumers by their indirect utility functions. Using the collection of n indirect utility functions, it is possible to express a notion of dual Pareto efficiency, defined in terms of prices and incomes.

The concept of dual Pareto efficiency leads to duals of the First and Second Theorems of Welfare Economics. These dual theorems provide additional economic insight for the fundamental concept of equilibria, and provide alternative characterizations of equilibria that can be used in calculations.

Dual Pareto efficiency is defined with respect to prices and income levels, and there is a notion of feasibility for such price-income combinations. Again, we use the notation $\bar{\pi}(\mathbf{p}) = \sup\{\mathbf{p} \cdot \mathbf{t} : \mathbf{t} \in \mathcal{T}\}$, which, when $\mathcal{T} = \mathcal{Y} + \mathbf{w}$, is $\mathbf{p} \cdot \mathbf{w} + \pi(\mathbf{p})$.

Assignment. An *assignment* is a pair $(\mathbf{p}, \mathbf{R})$ where $\mathbf{p} \in \mathcal{R}_+^m$ is a price vector and $\mathbf{R} = (r_1, r_2, \ldots, r_n)$ is a set of income levels with $r_i \geq 0$ for all i. An assignment $(\mathbf{p}, \mathbf{R})$ is feasible if $\sum_{i=1}^n r_i = \bar{\pi}(\mathbf{p})$.

This says that an assignment $(\mathbf{p}, \mathbf{R})$ is feasible if the total amount of income assigned to consumers is equal to the total income generated by the transformation set when the prices equal $\mathbf{p}$. That is, an assignment is a price vector and a distribution, among all consumers, of the income produced from it.

We now define dual Pareto efficiency, which is a property of certain assignments.[5]

Dual Pareto efficiency. A feasible assignment $(\mathbf{p}^*, \mathbf{R}^*)$ is *dual Pareto efficient* if there is no other feasible assignment $(\mathbf{p}, \mathbf{R})$ such that $v_i(\mathbf{p}, r_i) \leq v_i(\mathbf{p}^*, r_i^*)$ for each $i = 1, 2, \ldots, n$ with $v_j(\mathbf{p}, r_j) < v_j(\mathbf{p}^*, r_j^*)$ for some j.

Therefore an assignment is dual Pareto efficient if there is no other feasible assignment that makes someone *worse off* without making someone else *better off*. Note that this is the reverse of the kind of wording used to describe Pareto efficiency. The dual turns things around. Dual Pareto efficiency corresponds, in some sense, to the worst possible assignments.

---

[5]Recall that $v(\mathbf{p}, r) = \max\{u(\mathbf{x}) : \mathbf{p} \cdot \mathbf{x} \leq r, \mathbf{x} \in X\}$. In general, to ensure that $v(\mathbf{p}, r)$ is defined for all pairs $(\mathbf{p}, r)$, the max operation is replaced by sup.

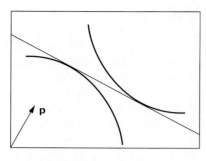
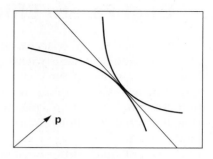

(a) Not dual Pareto efficient   (b) Dual Pareto efficient

FIGURE 6.9   (a) Not dual Pareto efficient. (b) Dual Pareto efficient.

The definition of dual Pareto efficiency has a simple interpretation in an Edgeworth box for the case of distributing two commodities among two consumers. Such a box is shown in Fig. 6.9. An assignment in this case corresponds to a line drawn through the box. The line is perpendicular to the assigned price vector. This line defines budget sets for the two consumers: A's set is to the left, and B's is to the right. The total income available, $\mathbf{p} \cdot \mathbf{w}$, is divided in two by the line. (Note, for example, that if all income went to A, the budget line would go through the upper right-hand corner of the box. If it were all given to B, the line would go through the lower left-hand corner. In general, it will be in between.)

The line shown in Fig. 6.10a is *not* dual Pareto efficient. If the line is tipped slightly more toward the vertical, each consumer will, when maximizing utility subject to the new budget constraint, obtain a lower value of utility than before. Thus both consumers have been made worse off with the new assignment. Figure 6.10b shows a situation that is dual Pareto efficient. Any change in the line will make someone better off.

The reason that dual Pareto efficiency looks for the worst assignment is that, generally, the points selected by the two consumers do not form a feasible allocation. This shows up in the Edgeworth box by the fact that the two selected points do not correspond to the same point in the box. If primal feasibility is not required, it is not surprising that consumers obtain higher indirect utility than they should. Dual-Pareto-efficient prices force feasibility of the selected points and accordingly lower the utility levels.

It should be clear that dual-Pareto-efficient assignments lead to $\mathbf{X}$'s that are themselves part of a competitive equilibrium. In the Edgeworth box, a dual-Pareto-efficient assignment will yield indirect utilities that correspond to indifference curves that touch each other and are supported by the price vector.

This relation between dual Pareto efficiency and competitive equilibrium is true in general (under certain assumptions) and gives the duals of the First and Second Theorems of Welfare Economics. These two dual theorems are given below, but we omit the proof of the second one since it is quite long.

Dual of the First Theorem of Welfare Economics. *Suppose* $(\mathbf{X}^*, \mathbf{p}^*)$ *is a competitive equilibrium for a transformation economy, and let* $\mathbf{R}^* = (r_1^*, r_2^*, \ldots, r_n^*)$ *with* $r_i^* = \mathbf{p}^* \cdot \mathbf{x}_i^*$ *for* $i = 1, 2, \ldots, n$. *Assume that all utility functions satisfy local nonsatiation on* $\mathcal{R}_+^m$. *Then* $(\mathbf{p}^*, \mathbf{R}^*)$ *is dual Pareto efficient.*

Proof: First we note that $(\mathbf{p}^*, \mathbf{R}^*)$ is feasible, because $\sum_{i=1}^n r_i^* = \mathbf{p}^* \cdot \sum_{i=1}^n \mathbf{x}_i^* = \overline{\pi}(\mathbf{p}^*)$, where the last equality follows from the equilibrium condition.

Define $v_i^* = v_i(\mathbf{p}^*, r_i^*)$, $i = 1, 2, \ldots, n$. We have $u_i(\mathbf{x}_i^*) = v_i^*$ for all i by the equilibrium property.

Suppose $(\mathbf{p}^*, \mathbf{R}^*)$ is not dual Pareto efficient. Then there is a feasible assignment $(\mathbf{p}, \mathbf{R})$ such that $v_i(\mathbf{p}, r_i) \leq v_i^*$ for all $i = 1, 2, \ldots, n$, with $v_j(\mathbf{p}, r_j) < v_j^*$ for some j.

Suppose $\mathbf{p} \cdot \mathbf{x}_i^* = r_i' < r_i$. Then $v_i(\mathbf{p}, r_i') \geq v_i^*$, since $\mathbf{x}_i^*$ is feasible for the combination $(\mathbf{p}, r_i')$. By local nonsatiation it follows that there is an $\mathbf{x}_i \geq \mathbf{0}$ with $\mathbf{p} \cdot \mathbf{x}_i \leq r_i$ and $u_i(\mathbf{x}_i) > v_i^*$. Hence $v_i(\mathbf{p}, r_i) > v_i^*$. This contradicts the previous paragraph, and thus $\mathbf{p} \cdot \mathbf{x}_i^* \geq r_i$ for all i.

Likewise, suppose $\mathbf{p} \cdot \mathbf{x}_j^* = r_j$. Then $v_j(\mathbf{p}, r_j) \geq v_j^*$, which is again a contradiction. Thus $\mathbf{p} \cdot \mathbf{x}_j^* > r_j$.

Summing the inequalities found above, we obtain

$$\mathbf{p} \cdot \sum_{i=1}^n \mathbf{x}_i^* > \sum_{i=1}^n r_i = \overline{\pi}(\mathbf{p}).$$

But since $\sum_{i=1}^n \mathbf{x}_i^* \in \mathcal{T}$ this contradicts the definition of $\overline{\pi}(\mathbf{p})$. ∎

Dual of the Second Theorem of Welfare Economics. *Assume that all utility functions are continuous, strongly monotonic, and quasi-concave on* $\mathcal{R}_+^m$. *Assume that* $\mathcal{T}$ *is closed and convex. Suppose* $(\mathbf{p}^*, \mathbf{R}^*)$ *is dual Pareto efficient with* $\mathbf{p}^* > \mathbf{0}$ *and* $\mathbf{R}^* > \mathbf{0}$. *Then there is an allocation* $\mathbf{X}^*$ *such that* $(\mathbf{X}^*, \mathbf{p}^*)$ *is a competitive equilibrium for the transformation economy with* $\mathbf{p}^* \cdot \mathbf{x}_i^* = r_i^*$ *for all* i.

Example 6.7 (Quick calculation). Here is a quick way to find dual Pareto efficient prices. Consider an economy with two consumers and two commodities. Both consumers have utility function $u(x, y) = (xy)^{1/2}$. The total amount of the two commodities is $x = 1$ and $y = 2$.

The indirect utility function is

$$v(p_1, p_2, r) = \frac{r}{2\sqrt{p_1 p_2}}.$$

We can find a set of dual Pareto efficient prices by minimizing the sum of the indirect utilities. We note that the sum of the incomes is $p_1 + 2p_2$. Hence we solve

$$\min \frac{p_1 + 2p_2}{\sqrt{p_1 p_2}}.$$

After a bit of algebra, this leads to $p_1 = 2p_2$.

6.10 Exercises

1. Suppose there are K firms. The efficient surface of the production possibility set of each firm k can be described by the transformation function $T_k(\mathbf{y}_k) = 0$. Assuming interior solutions, show that a necessary condition for efficient production is equality of marginal rates of transformation. Specifically,

$$\frac{\partial T_k(\mathbf{y}_k)/\partial y_{ki}}{\partial T_k(\mathbf{y}_k)/\partial y_{kj}} = \frac{\partial T_l(\mathbf{y}_l)/\partial y_{li}}{\partial T(\mathbf{y}_l)/\partial y_{lj}},$$

for all i, j, k, l.

2. (Cake and milk) Joe and Mary must divide a 12-ounce cake and a 16-ounce pitcher of milk between them. Joe always consumes these in a ratio of one to one on a weight basis, while Mary always consumes two ounces of milk for every ounce of cake; they each have Leontief utility functions. They both would prefer as much of their ideal combination as possible.

   (a) Draw an Edgeworth box for this situation and indicate the Pareto-efficient divisions of cake and milk.

   (b) What is the one point where equilibrium prices for cake and milk exist that are both positive? Is the ratio of these prices unique? If so, what is it?

   (c) What are the equilibrium prices at other Pareto-efficient points?

3. An economy is described by two individuals who have linear utility functions for consumption of two goods. Individual A's utility is $U_A(x_1, x_2) = x_1 + 2x_2$. Individual B's utility function is $U_B(x_1, x_2) = x_1 + x_2$. Neither individual consumes negative amounts. Aggregate supply of the first good equals 2 while aggregate supply of the second good is 1.

   (a) Construct the Edgeworth box for this economy and draw two sample indifference curves for each individual. Label the origins and axes clearly.

   (b) Determine the set of Pareto-efficient points.

   (c) Suppose that at a Pareto-efficient point the equilibrium price for the first good is $p_1 = 1$. What are the upper and lower bounds for the price p_2 of the second good at this allocation?

4. (Cobb-Douglas and efficiency) Suppose two individuals have identical Cobb-Douglas utility functions for m commodities: $u(\mathbf{x}) = \prod_{j=1}^{m}(x_j)^{\alpha_j}$, with $0 < \alpha_j < 1$. Let $\alpha = \sum \alpha_j$. Let the available aggregate commodity bundle be $\mathbf{w}$. Show that all Pareto-efficient allocations can be parameterized by β, $0 < \beta < 1$, with β corresponding to the fraction of the total market value of $\mathbf{w}$ allocated to individual 1. Find the Pareto-efficient allocations and the prices that support them.

5. Suppose n individuals all have identical homothetic, strictly quasi-concave utility functions. Let $\mathbf{X} = (\mathbf{x}_1, \ldots, \mathbf{x}_n)$ be a Pareto-efficient allocation of a commodity bundle $\mathbf{w}$. Show that each $\mathbf{x}_i$ is a fraction of $\mathbf{w}$. That is, $\mathbf{x}_i = \alpha_i \mathbf{w}$ for some $\alpha_i \geq 0$.

6. Consider an economy with two firms and three commodities. The first firm produces commodity 1 using commodities 2 and 3 as inputs. Production must satisfy

$$y_1 \le (-y_2)^{1/2}(-y_3)^{1/2},$$

which defines y_1. The second firm produces the first two commodities from the third. Production must satisfy

$$y_1 + y_2 \le (-y_3)^{1/3},$$

which defines y_2. Consider the production plan

$$\begin{aligned}
\text{Firm 1:} \quad & \mathbf{y}_1 = (1, \quad -1, \quad -1) \\
\text{Firm 2:} \quad & \mathbf{y}_2 = (1, \quad 1, \quad -8) \\
\text{Total:} \quad & \mathbf{y} = (2, \quad 0, \quad -9)
\end{aligned}$$

The plans selected by each firm are clearly efficient, but it does not necessarily follow that the total plan is efficient. Find an alternate plan with aggregate identical to that of the first plan in the first two components and strictly greater in the third component.

7. Ciz, a small isolated country, can produce a level x of agricultural commodities and a level y of electronic products. Its production facilities and labor and land resources are such that the production must satisfy

$$x^2 + y^2 \le 1000.$$

Every individual in Ciz has preferences for the two products, represented by the utility function $u(x, y) = xy$. (Hence the society of Ciz will want to maximize $u = xy$.) In the following analysis include drawings in each part.

(a) How much of each commodity should Ciz produce?

(b) Suppose now that Ciz breaks its isolation and trades with other countries at fixed prices of 1 (for agriculture) and 3 (for electronics). What should be the new production levels and the new consumption levels? Does utility in Ciz always increase with trade (at any prices) over the no-trade situation of part (a)?

(c) Ciz notices that it can earn more in the international market producing electronics than it can producing agriculture, so it expands capacity so that its new production possibilities are

$$x^2 + \tfrac{4}{5}y^2 \le 1000.$$

Suppose all individuals in all the trading countries have utility $u(x, y) = xy$. Is the utility of all trading countries increased by Ciz's expansion? What do you expect to happen to the price of electronics (relative to agriculture) as a result of the expansion?

(d) Suppose the new equilibrium price of electronics drops to $p = 2$ after Ciz expands its capacity. Does the utility in Ciz increase over that in part (b)?

8. A power plant charges different prices for peak periods and nonpeak periods. The peak period is a fraction θ_1 of each day, and the nonpeak

period is θ_2; $\theta_1 + \theta_2 = 1$. The inverse demand curves for these periods are $p_1 = \alpha_1 - \beta_1 q_1$ and $p_2 = \alpha_2 - \beta_2 q_2$, respectively, where q_1 and q_2 denote kilowatts. (We assume that the loads are constant during each of the two periods.) There is an operating cost c per kilowatt per day in both periods (i.e., the total operating cost for period i is $\theta_i c q_i$). There is a cost of K per day for each kilowatt of installed capacity (installed capacity = q_1). Find the socially optimal quantities and corresponding prices during peak and nonpeak periods.

9. An economy has a technology containing just two production processes, each of which produces wheat and milk from labor and capital according to Leontief technologies as specified in the table below. (All quantities are measured in appropriate units.)

Process	Output		Input	
	Wheat	Milk	Labor	Capital
I	3	1	2	1
II	2	1	1	2

Each individual in the economy has a utility function $u(w, m) = wm$ where w is consumption of wheat and m is consumption of milk. The economy has a total of 300 units of labor and 300 units of capital.

(a) Find the relative prices of capital, labor, wheat, and milk in equilibrium.

(b) Describe the effect on the distribution of income by factor shares of each of the following types of tax (assume that the government spends the tax revenue just like a consumer):

  (i) An excise tax e (as a fraction of selling price) on wheat,

  (ii) A payroll tax t on the use of labor.

10. (Storage) In each of two periods a certain economy can produce gasoline from oil according to the production function $g = g(r)$ where g = gasoline and r = oil. There is a fixed level R of oil reserves. Gasoline not used in the first period may be stored for use in the second period. Characterize the efficient production plans for this economy.

11. (Aggregation) An economy consists of n individuals, all having a common homothetic quasi-concave utility function. The economy also has a convex production possibility set $\mathcal{Y}$ and a bundle of resources $\mathbf{w}$.

(a) Show that the aggregate consumption bundles corresponding to Pareto-efficient points are those solving a certain optimization problem.

(b) Show how to determine the price vector corresponding to Pareto efficiency.

(c) Assuming that the solutions to parts (a) and (b) are unique (prices to within a scale factor), show how all Pareto-efficient allocations can be determined.

12. Set up the first-order necessary conditions for an interior Pareto-efficient point of an economy with production. Show that $\text{MRS}^i_{sr} = \text{MRT}^k_{sr}$ for all commodity pairs r, s, all individuals i, and all firms k.

13. Two firms produce food using labor, one with production function $q = \sqrt{l}$ and one with production function $q = \beta\sqrt{l}$.

    (a) Find each firm's supply function, $q(w, p)$.

    (b) Find the social production function (i.e., for each level of labor input $\bar{l}$, find the maximum production possible, splitting the input between the firms) and the corresponding supply function.

    (c) Compare the social supply function to the sum of the individual supply functions.

14. (Second Theorem of Welfare Economics—Alternate Version) Prove the following: Suppose preferences for all individuals are continuous, strictly convex, and have no bliss point. Suppose also that $\mathbf{X}^*$ is a Pareto-efficient allocation of $\mathbf{w}$. Then there is a $\mathbf{p} \neq \mathbf{0}$ such that $(\mathbf{X}^*, \mathbf{p}^*)$ is a distribution equilibrium for $\mathbf{w}$.

15. (Class demonstration) Obtain several decks of cards with three different back designs: types A, B, and C. Make up packets of cards having the compositions given in the columns of the table below. Each column shows the number of each of the three types of cards in that packet.

A	5	4	9	6	0	12	2	3	13	10	7	1
B	5	1	3	0	6	3	5	3	1	1	4	4
C	1	4	1	4	2	0	2	3	1	2	1	3

When making the packets, cycle through the list repeatedly until there is one packet for each class member.

In class give each student one packet. Each student has the utility function $U = ABC$, where A, B, and C denote the number of cards of the respective types that they have. The class trades cards among themselves in order to maximize individual utility. (Pooling of resources is not allowed.) When trading dies down, find who has the highest utility. Determine the final relative "market" prices for the different types of cards. Discuss the following:

    (a) Is the final allocation Pareto efficient?

    (b) What are the theoretical equilibrium price ratios for this economy?

    (c) What is the theoretical market value of each of the original packets?

    (d) What utility level would be attainable by each packet if trading were allowed at the theoretical prices?

16. (Zero-minimum proof) Fill in the details of the following proof of the second zero-minimum theorem.

    (a) Let $S = \{\mathbf{z} : \mathbf{z} = \sum_{i=1}^{n} \mathbf{x}_i, u_i(\mathbf{x}_i) \geq u_i^*\}$. Show that S is nonempty, closed, and convex.

    (b) Show that S and $\mathcal{T}$ are separated (weakly) by the hyperplane $H = \{\mathbf{y} : \mathbf{p}^* \cdot \mathbf{y} = \bar{\pi}(\mathbf{p}^*)\}$.

(c) It follows from the assumption that $\mathcal{T} \cap \mathcal{R}_+^m$ is nonempty and bounded that the minimum distance between S and $\mathcal{T}$ is achieved. (You need not prove this.) Let this minimum distance be δ. Suppose $\delta > 0$. Let $\mathbf{z}_0 \in S$ and $\mathbf{t}_0 \in \mathcal{T}$ be such that $\|\mathbf{z}_0 - \mathbf{t}_0\| = \delta$, and put $\mathbf{p}_0 = \mathbf{z}_0 - \mathbf{t}_0$. Show that $\mathbf{p}_0 \geq \mathbf{0}$ and that $\mathbf{p}_0$ defines a hyperplane strictly separating S and $\mathcal{T}$. Show that this contradicts the zero-minimality of $\mathbf{p}^*$ and hence $\delta = 0$.

(d) Let $\mathbf{X}^* = (\mathbf{x}_1^*, \mathbf{x}_2^*, ..., \mathbf{x}_n^*)$ be such that $\mathbf{z}_0 = \sum_{i=1}^{n} \mathbf{x}_i^*$ with $u_i(\mathbf{x}_i^*) \geq u_i^*$ for $i = 1, 2, ..., n$. Now prove that $(\mathbf{X}^*, \mathbf{p}^*)$ is an equilibrium. (Use Proposition 4.6.)

17. Suppose $\mathbf{p}^* > \mathbf{0}$ is zero-minimal for the problem

$$\min\ S(\mathbf{p}, \mathbf{U}^*)$$
$$\text{sub to}\ \mathbf{p} \cdot \mathbf{g} = 1$$
$$\mathbf{p} \geq \mathbf{0}.$$

(a) Write the first-order necessary conditions and express them in terms of demand and supply.

(b) Show that the Lagrange multiplier associated with the constraint $\mathbf{p} \cdot \mathbf{g} = 1$ is zero. Hence, conclude that total demand is equal to total supply. Hint: Multiply by $\mathbf{p}$.

18. Consumers A and B both have indirect utility

$$v(p_1, p_2, r) = r \left(\frac{\alpha}{p_1}\right)^{\alpha} \left(\frac{1 - \alpha}{p_2}\right)^{1-\alpha}.$$

There is a fixed aggregate bundle $\mathbf{w} = (w_1, w_2)$ to be distributed between them. Find the set of a dual-Pareto-efficient assignments.

19. Suppose n consumers each have utilities oriented by $\mathbf{g}$. That is, $u_i(\mathbf{x}_i + \alpha\mathbf{g}) = u_i(\mathbf{x}_i) + \alpha$ for all i. Using the zero-maximum property, characterize all Pareto-efficient distributions of an aggregate bundle $\mathbf{w}$.

20. (Negishi's method)   This problem shows (formally) that Negishi's result (Section 6.6) can be derived from the zero-maximum principle. Suppose that for $i = 1, 2, ..., n$ the utility function f_i on $\mathcal{R}_+^m$ is *concave* and negative. (If the f_i's are bounded above, we can always assume they are negative.) Let E be the corresponding distribution economy, with aggregate endowment $\mathbf{w}$. Define an expanded economy $\overline{E}$ by introducing an additional commodity, labeled z, in aggregate amount 1. Define new utility functions on $\mathcal{R}_+^{m+1}$ by $u_i(\mathbf{x}_i, z_i) = -z_i / f_i(\mathbf{x}_i)$. The functions u_i are then quasi-concave on $\mathcal{R}_+^{m+1}$.

(a) In the expanded economy $\overline{E}$, let z be the reference commodity. Show that $b_i(\mathbf{x}_i, z_i, u_i) = u_i f(\mathbf{x}_i) + z_i$ for $u_i \geq 0$.

(b) Show that $(\mathbf{X}^*, \mathbf{Z}^*)$ is Pareto efficient for $\overline{E}$ if and only if $\mathbf{X}^*$ solves

$$\max_{\mathbf{X}} \sum_{i=1}^{n} u_i^* f_i(\mathbf{x}_i)$$
$$\text{sub to} \sum_{i=1}^{n} \mathbf{x}_i = \mathbf{w},$$

where $u_i^* = -z_i^* / f_i(\mathbf{x}_i^*)$ and $\mathbf{Z}^* = (z_1^*, z_2^*, ..., z_n^*)$.

(c) Show that $\mathbf{X}^*$ is Pareto efficient for E if and only if there is $\mathbf{Z}^* = (z_1^*, z_2^*, \ldots, z_n^*)$ such that $(\mathbf{X}^*, \mathbf{Z}^*)$ is Pareto efficient for $\overline{E}$. Hint: For "only if" let $z_i^* = c_i f(\mathbf{x}_i^*) / \sum_{j=1}^n c_j f_j(\mathbf{x}_j^*)$, where the c_i's are those of the Negishi theorem.

6.11 References

6.1 Welfare issues have a long history in economics, and Pareto efficiency has traditionally been a focal point. For good general discussions see Quirk and Saposnik (1968), Feldman (1980), Graaff (1967), and Varian (1992).

6.2 For derivation and application of first-order conditions, see Samuelson (1947).

6.3 See Edgeworth (1881, 1932).

6.4 For a good treatment of production efficiency, see Feldman (1980).

6.5 For an early version of the First Theorem of Welfare Economics, see Pigou (1920). The treatment here follows Koopmans (1957). The formulation of the modern version of the Second Theorem using convexity is due to Arrow (1951).

6.6 The central ideas for this section are in Negishi (1960).

6.7 The zero-maximum principle has its roots in the classic treatise of Allais (1943), who formulated the idea in terms of distributable surplus for the case where $X_i = \mathcal{R}^m$. Dierker and Lenninghaus (1986) have a similar result. The formulation as a zero-maximum principle and with X_i having boundaries is in Luenberger (1992b).

6.8 There are many concepts of surplus in economics (see Chapter 10), several of which can be related to the surplus function of this section. The surplus function and the zero-minimum results are in Luenberger (1992b) and Luenberger (1994b).

6.9 Dual Pareto efficiency was implicitly recognized by Milleron (1968) and Weddepohl (1972). Balasko (1988) showed the equivalence of equilibria and what we call dual Pareto efficiency in the differentiable case. Formulation of a dual concept with theorems dual to the first and second theorems of welfare economics is in Luenberger (1994a).

Chapter 7
GENERAL COMPETITIVE EQUILIBRIUM

The term *equilibrium* commonly connnotes a condition of *balance* in a system: all forces balance, and hence there is no tendency for the system to move. In an economy, the term *equilibrium* also refers to a condition of perfect balance—in this case a balance between economic incentives—there are no economic incentives for consumers or firms to move from the equilibrium situation.

The basic idea of an equilibrium was used in Chapter 3, when prices were determined by the intersection of a supply curve and a demand curve. This kind of analysis is a *partial equilibrium* analysis, since it assumes that all prices and quantities except those being considered are fixed. In reality, all prices and quantity levels interact, and a complete analysis must account for this interaction. An analysis in which all commodities and prices are considered simultaneously is a *general equilibrium* analysis.

A competitive equilibrium is based on the hypothesis that all agents assume that prices are fixed, independent of their own actions. For example, a competitive firm assumes that the demand curve for its product is perfectly flat, constant for all levels of price. This hypothesis that prices are not influenced by individual action approximates an idealized economy in which each agent's influence is imperceptibly small and is therefore swamped by aggregate effects. That agents do not individually move prices is the essence of perfect competition.

If these two ideas of generality and perfect competition are combined, we obtain the definition of a general competitive equilibrium. All economic activity is considered simultaneously, and all such activity is carried out on a competitive basis, the end result being a competitive equilibrium.

The notion of a competitive equilibrium was used in Chapter 6 in the study of economic efficiency, specifically in the First and Second Theorems of Welfare Economics. However, attention was focused on a transformation economy, where resources are not owned before they are allocated. In such a framework, many different equilibria are possible. By contrast, in this chapter resources are owned by various consumers, and this prior ownership determines a specific resulting equilibrium after these resources are traded competitively or deployed for production.

General competitive equilibrium theory is one of the major components of modern economic theory. It establishes the mutual consistency of the underlying theories of production and consumer demand as presented in earlier chapters, it highlights the role of prices in a competitive economy, and as we know from Chapter 6, it is an important component of the theory of economic efficiency and welfare theory. The first part of Chapter 7 presents the main elements of this general theory. We shall find in later chapters that the theory can be partially extended to situations that are not perfectly competitive, but the case of perfect competition retains special importance.

The theory can also be used as a basis for actual computation, to solve important economic planning and policy problems for industry and government. However, formulation and computation in a completely general structure is often impractical. Therefore the study of special model structures and various partial equilibrium models is essential for the effective practical use of the theory. These matters are considered in the second part of this chapter.

Part I
BASIC THEORY

7.1 Exchange Economies

Consider an economy consisting of n individuals and m commodity types. Suppose each individual i, $i = 1, 2, \ldots, n$, possesses an initial endowment $\mathbf{w}_i$ of the commodities, that is, a bundle of commodities. We write $\mathbf{W} = (\mathbf{w}_1, \mathbf{w}_2, \ldots, \mathbf{w}_n)$ to denote the collection of these endowments. Assuming that there is no other source of commodities, the aggregate level of commodities in the economy is simply the sum $\mathbf{w} = \sum_{i=1}^{n} \mathbf{w}_i$ of the individual endowments. In an *exchange economy* individuals may exchange these commodities among themselves to reach a new, potentially more desirable, allocation.

The mechanism of perfect competition is one method for accomplishing such an exchange. It is based on a special set of prices, which establish a budget constraint for each individual. If individual i considers buying the bundle $\mathbf{x}_i = (x_{i1}, x_{i2}, \ldots, x_{im})$ when the prices are $\mathbf{p}$, the budget constraint is

$$\mathbf{p} \cdot \mathbf{x}_i \leq \mathbf{p} \cdot \mathbf{w}_i .$$

The left-hand side of the inequality represents the total cost of that individual's final allocation assuming fixed prices $\mathbf{p} = (p_1, p_2, \ldots, p_m)$. The right-hand side of the inequality represents the total value of the individual's endowment evaluated at the same prices.

At first it may seem strange to include all the endowment of the right-hand side of the budget constraint, since an individual may be content with much of that endowment and not care to place it in the market. However, since the endowment is priced the same way as purchases, an individual may purchase commodities from the endowment; this purchase will have exactly the same effect as leaving the corresponding term out of both the right-hand and the left-hand sides of the budget constraint.

We now introduce a special form of equilibrium that is applicable to an exchange economy. It is termed a *Walrasian equilibrium,* after the French economist Leon Walras. As the reader can see, this concept is closely related to a competitive equilibrium, considered in Chapter 6. Throughout this discussion, the consumption sets are $X_i = R_+^m$ as usual.

Walrasian equilibrium.   A *Walrasian equilibrium* for the set of initial endowments $\mathbf{w}_i$, $i = 1, 2, \ldots, n$, is a pair $(\mathbf{X}^*, \mathbf{p}^*)$ where $\mathbf{X}^* = (\mathbf{x}_1^*, \mathbf{x}_2^*, \ldots, \mathbf{x}_n^*)$ is an allocation and $\mathbf{p}^* \geq \mathbf{0}$ is an m-dimensional price vector. The pair satisfies

1. $\mathbf{x}_i^* \geq \mathbf{0}$ for $i = 1, 2, \ldots, n$.

2. $\mathbf{p}^* \cdot \mathbf{x}_i^* \leq \mathbf{p}^* \cdot \mathbf{w}_i$, for $i = 1, 2, \ldots, n$ ($\mathbf{x}_i$ satisfies the budget constraint of individual i).

3. If $\mathbf{x}_i \geq \mathbf{0}$ and $\mathbf{p}^* \cdot \mathbf{x}_i \leq \mathbf{p}^* \cdot \mathbf{w}_i$, then $\mathbf{x}_i \precsim_i \mathbf{x}_i^*$. ($\mathbf{x}_i^*$ is weakly preferred to any other $\mathbf{x}_i$ that satisfies the budget constraint.)

4. $\sum_{i=1}^{n} \mathbf{x}_i^* \leq \mathbf{w} \equiv \sum_{i=1}^{n} \mathbf{w}_i$. (The allocation is feasible.)

Note that requirement 4 above is $\sum_{i=1}^{n} \mathbf{x}_i^* \leq \mathbf{w}$ rather than $\sum_{i=1}^{n} \mathbf{x}_i^* = \mathbf{w}$. The less than or equal constraint allows free disposal; that is, not everything available must be consumed. It is important to allow for this if we require $\mathbf{p}^* \geq \mathbf{0}$, because there may be (undesirable) commodities that no one would want to pay for.

If a Walrasian equilibrium exists, it defines a consistent market. Once the prices $\mathbf{p}^*$ are established, each individual will independently select the appropriate equilibrium allocation by maximizing relative to preferences subject to the budget constraint.

We can state the concept alternatively in terms of individual demand. For prices $\mathbf{p}$, individual i will have income $r_i = \mathbf{p} \cdot \mathbf{w}_i$ and will therefore demand $\mathbf{x}_i = \mathbf{x}_i(\mathbf{p}, r_i) = \mathbf{x}_i(\mathbf{p}, \mathbf{p} \cdot \mathbf{w}_i)$. As discussed in Chapter 5, if preferences are continuous and strictly convex, $\mathbf{x}_i(\mathbf{p}, \mathbf{p} \cdot \mathbf{w}_i)$ is a well-defined, single-valued demand function. This will lead to an aggregate demand vector $\mathbf{x} = \sum_{i=1}^{n} \mathbf{x}_i(\mathbf{p}, \mathbf{p} \cdot \mathbf{w}_i)$. For arbitrary prices, the aggregate demand will generally *not* be feasible. However, if a Walrasian equilibrium exists, there *is* a price vector $\mathbf{p}^*$ such that the aggregate demand *is* feasible, that is, such that

$\mathbf{x} \leq \mathbf{w}$. In this sense a Walrasian equilibrium can be thought of as the condition that total demand satisfies the supply constraint.

It should be noted that we have said nothing to this point about how the equilibrium prices might be determined in a real economy. In the above development, it is implied that the prices are simply announced so that individuals can use them to determine their optimal bundles. Some type of iterative process, involving perhaps a sequence of trades, might take place to lead to the final prices, but this is not clear. This topic will be discussed later. At this point we are considering an idealization that ignores this question.

7.2   The Edgeworth Box and Equilibrium

The concept of a Walrasian equilibrium can be illustrated quite nicely by the Edgeworth box, introduced in Chapter 6 and shown again in Fig. 7.1. As before, there are two consumers and two commodities. Consumer A has the lower left-hand corner as a reference point, and B has the upper right-hand corner. The width and height of the box are proportional to the two components of the total endowment. The original allocation defined by the individual endowments corresponds to a point in the box, as shown.

A set of prices together with the original individual endowments determines specific budget constraints. Consumer A's budget set is the portion of the box below and to the left of the line with slope $-p_1/p_2$ passing through the endowment point. Consumer B's budget set is the region above and to the right of this line. If preferences are locally nonsatiated, both consumers will select a point on the line. An equilibrium consists of a set of prices (defining a line through the original endowment point) and an allocation (which is a single point on the line if $\mathbf{w}$ is fully allocated). The indifference curves of both consumers touch the line at that point and do not cross the line.

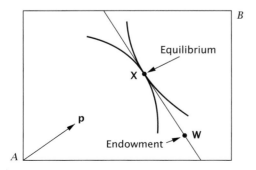

FIGURE 7.1   Edgeworth box.

7.3   Existence of Walrasian Equilibria

A central issue of general competitive equilibrium theory is that of existence. We have defined an equilibrium, but we have not yet established that an equilibrium exists. The proof of existence is one of the major achievements of modern economic theory, and the methods used for this proof draw on some powerful mathematics. This section presents a relatively simple existence theorem, which will later be generalized.

Assume that each individual i has a demand function $x_i(\mathbf{p}, \mathbf{p} \cdot \mathbf{w}_i)$ that for any $\mathbf{p} \geq \mathbf{0}$ is single-valued (that is, demand is unique). This demand function might be derived from individual preference maximization, but that is not really necessary for this discussion. All that is required is that the demand function satisfy the following conditions:

1. It is homogeneous of degree zero in $\mathbf{p}$; that is, $x_i(t\mathbf{p}, t\mathbf{p} \cdot \mathbf{w}_i) = x_i(\mathbf{p}, \mathbf{p} \cdot \mathbf{w}_i)$ for $t > 0$.

2. It satisfies the budget constraint; that is, $\mathbf{p} \cdot x_i(\mathbf{p}, \mathbf{p} \cdot \mathbf{w}_i) = \mathbf{p} \cdot \mathbf{w}_i$.

Note that in condition 1 the budget constraint is assumed to be satisfied by equality. This would be the case if the demand functions were derived from preference maximization and preferences satisfied local nonsatiation. This assumption is relaxed in a later section.

We introduce the function

$$\mathbf{z}(\mathbf{p}) = \sum_{i=1}^{n} x_i(\mathbf{p}, \mathbf{p} \cdot \mathbf{w}_i) - \sum_{i=1}^{n} \mathbf{w}_i,$$

called the *excess demand function.* For any price vector $\mathbf{p}$, the excess demand function measures how much the aggregate demand exceeds available supply, as determined by the total endowment.

We can readily establish the following basic fact associated with the excess demand function.

Walras' law (strong form).   For any $\mathbf{p} \in \mathcal{R}_+^m$ there holds

$$\mathbf{p} \cdot \mathbf{z}(\mathbf{p}) = 0.$$

Proof: Each individual demand function x_i satisfies the budget constraint

$$\mathbf{p} \cdot x_i(\mathbf{p}, \mathbf{p} \cdot \mathbf{w}_i) = \mathbf{p} \cdot \mathbf{w}_i.$$

Summing these over i leads immediately to the result.   ∎

It should be clear that Walras' law is a direct consequence of the fact that individual demands satisfy the budget constraint as in condition 2 above. Likewise condition 1 above directly implies that $\mathbf{z}(\mathbf{p})$ is homogeneous of degree zero. The weak form of Walras' law is that $\mathbf{p} \cdot \mathbf{z}(\mathbf{p}) \le 0$. This form holds if the budget constraints are $\mathbf{p} \cdot \mathbf{x}_i \le \mathbf{p} \cdot \mathbf{w}_i$, and it cannot be guaranteed that they hold with equality. We assume the strong form, with equality, here.

Under our assumption that demand functions are single-valued, the excess demand function is also a single-valued function of prices. Therefore, only the equilibrium price need be determined—the corresponding allocation can subsequently be determined by the demand functions. Hence, the definition of an equilibrium can be abbreviated to the specification of a price $\mathbf{p}^*$ only.

Walrasian equilibrium price.   The price $\mathbf{p}^* \ge \mathbf{0}$ is a *Walrasian equilibrium price* if $\mathbf{z}(\mathbf{p}^*) \le \mathbf{0}$.

As pointed out before, the definition of a Walrasian equilibrium requires nonnegative prices, but allows free disposal. That is, $\mathbf{p}^* \ge \mathbf{0}$ and $\mathbf{z}(\mathbf{p}^*) \le \mathbf{0}$. Although we also allow arbitrary demand functions, which may not correspond to an underlying utility function, it seems intuitively clear that if a commodity j has negative excess demand in equilibrium (that is, $z_j(\mathbf{p}^*) < 0$), people do not like it very much. Even if it is given away (at $p_j^* = 0$), they will not purchase all of it. This intuition is verified in the following proposition.

Proposition 7.1.   *If $\mathbf{p}^*$ is a Walrasian equilibrium, then $z_j(\mathbf{p}^*) < 0$ implies that $p_j^* = 0$; conversely, $p_j^* > 0$ implies that $z_j(\mathbf{p}^*) = 0$.*

Proof: By definition $z_j(\mathbf{p}^*) \le 0$ and $p_j^* \ge 0$ for each $j = 1, 2, \ldots, m$. Hence $p_j^* z_j(\mathbf{p}^*) \le 0$ for each j. However, by Walras' law the sum of these terms must be zero; hence $p_j^* z_j(\mathbf{p}^*) = 0$ for each j.   ∎

Walras' law and the equilibrium problem can be illustrated quite clearly in an Edgeworth box, as shown in Fig. 7.2. The dimensions of the box are determined by the total endowment $\mathbf{w}$. This total is comprised of endowments $\mathbf{w}_A$ and $\mathbf{w}_B$ of the two individuals A and B; hence $\mathbf{w} = \mathbf{w}_A + \mathbf{w}_B$. The

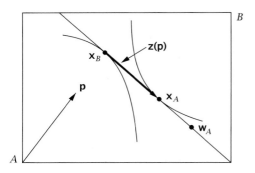

FIGURE 7.2   **Walras' law.**

point $\mathbf{w}_A$ is shown relative to A's coordinate system. This point also represents B's endowment in B's coordinate system. The diagonal line shown is the budget line determined by a price vector $\mathbf{p}$ and the endowment $\mathbf{W}$. Normally we consider single points in the box, since they represent feasible allocations of the aggregate endowment $\mathbf{w}$ through the measurement system of the box construction. In this case, however, A and B have selected separate points, and hence this is not a distribution of $\mathbf{w}$. The difference vector $\mathbf{z}(\mathbf{p})$ (shown as measured in A's coordinate system) is the excess demand vector. (To see this, note that in A's coordinate system, B's point is $\mathbf{w} - \mathbf{x}_B$; hence, the difference is $\mathbf{z} = \mathbf{x}_A - (\mathbf{w} - \mathbf{x}_B) = \mathbf{x}_A + \mathbf{x}_B - \mathbf{w}$.) This difference lies on the budget line and is therefore orthogonal to $\mathbf{p}$. Hence $\mathbf{p} \cdot \mathbf{z}(\mathbf{p}) = 0$. The figure therefore illustrates the problem of determining $\mathbf{p}$ to cause $\mathbf{z}(\mathbf{p}) \leq \mathbf{0}$. (The case with $z_j(\mathbf{p}) < 0$ for some j implies unusual indifference curves, which the reader may wish to explore.)

If $\mathbf{p}^* > \mathbf{0}$, then from Proposition 7.1 it is clear that $\mathbf{z}(\mathbf{p}^*) = \mathbf{0}$ in a Walrasian equilibrium; every commodity has demand exactly equal to supply, and the equilibrium condition becomes a system of equations. To consider the possibility of solving this system of equations, one might first count the number of unknowns and equations. There are m unknowns, corresponding to the m prices. There are also m equations in the vector equation $\mathbf{z}(\mathbf{p}^*) = \mathbf{0}$; however, these equations are *not* independent. Walras' law, $\mathbf{p} \cdot \mathbf{z}(\mathbf{p}) = 0$, shows explicitly that (in the range where $\mathbf{p} > \mathbf{0}$) any one of these equations can be expressed in terms of the others. Hence there are at most only $m - 1$ independent equations. On the other hand, $\mathbf{z}(\mathbf{p})$ is homogeneous of degree zero, and this means that prices are meaningful only to within a scalar multiple. Therefore the system can be regarded as having $m - 1$ independent equations and $m - 1$ unknowns.

To cut the number of degrees of freedom in $\mathbf{p}$ down to $m - 1$, we scale $\mathbf{p}$ by requiring $\mathbf{p} \cdot \mathbf{g} = 1$ for some $\mathbf{g} > 0$. Usually we take $\mathbf{g} = (1, 1, \ldots, 1)$. Thus the set of allowable $\mathbf{p} = (p_1, p_2, \ldots, p_m)$ comprises those $\mathbf{p}$'s with $p_i \geq 0$, $i = 1, 2, \ldots, m$, and $\sum_{i=1}^{m} p_i = 1$. This set is termed the *unit simplex* in $\mathcal{R}^m$ and is denoted S^{m-1}. See Fig. 7.3. Thus the problem of determining a Walrasian equilibrium can be cast as that of finding a $\mathbf{p}^*$ in S^{m-1} such that $\mathbf{z}(\mathbf{p}^*) \leq \mathbf{0}$. The proof that such a $\mathbf{p}^*$ exists is based on Brouwer's fixed point theorem, one of the most important theorems in mathematics.

Brouwer's fixed point theorem states that if the unit simplex is continuously transformed into itself, at least one point must be left unchanged. For example, if a two-dimensional simplex (a triangle) is rotated one-third of a revolution, it is transformed to itself but the center remains fixed. If the simplex is squeezed down, a point also remains fixed. Any continuous transformation leaves a point fixed. The general theorem is stated below.

Brouwer's fixed point theorem.   *Let $\mathbf{f}$ be a continuous mapping from the unit simplex S^{m-1} into S^{m-1}. Then $\mathbf{f}$ has a fixed point. That is, there is an $\mathbf{x}^* \in S^{m-1}$ such that $\mathbf{f}(\mathbf{x}^*) = \mathbf{x}^*$.*

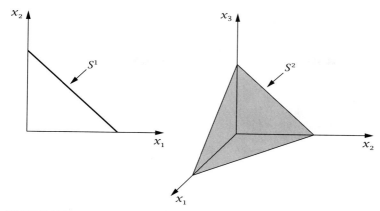

FIGURE 7.3 Unit simplices.

Proof: We shall only prove the theorem in one dimension here. In this case we can use the interval $[0, 1]$ of the real line rather than the simplex S^1. Hence, suppose f is a continuous function $f : [0, 1] \rightarrow [0, 1]$. This is represented by the graph shown in Fig. 7.4. The diagonal line in the figure represents the special function $y(x) = x$. Define the function $g(x) = f(x) - x$. Clearly, $g(0) \geq 0$, and $g(1) \leq 0$; hence, by the intermediate value theorem of elementary calculus, there is x, $0 \leq x \leq 1$, with $g(x) = 0$. This point represents a fixed point of f. This proves the theorem for the one-dimensional case. (The proof for higher dimensions is much more difficult.) ∎

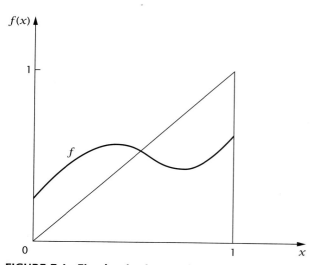

FIGURE 7.4 Fixed point in one dimension.

We may now directly apply the fixed point theorem to prove the existence of a Walrasian equilibrium.

Existence of Walrasian equilibrium. Suppose $\mathbf{z} : S^{m-1} \rightarrow \mathcal{R}^m$ is continuous and satisfies $\mathbf{p} \cdot \mathbf{z}(\mathbf{p}) \equiv 0$. There is a $\mathbf{p}^* \in S^{m-1}$ such that $\mathbf{z}(\mathbf{p}^*) \leq \mathbf{0}$.

Proof: Let us introduce the notation $z_i^+(\mathbf{p}) = \max(0, z_i(\mathbf{p}))$. Thus $z_i^+(\mathbf{p})$ is equal to $z_i(\mathbf{p})$ if $z_i(\mathbf{p}) > 0$; otherwise, it is zero. Now define the mapping $\mathbf{h}$ on S^{m-1} by

$$h_i(\mathbf{p}) = \frac{p_i + z_i^+(\mathbf{p})}{1 + \sum_{j=1}^m z_j^+(\mathbf{p})}, \qquad i = 1, 2, \ldots, m.$$

We note that $h_i(\mathbf{p}) \geq 0$ for each i and $\sum_{i=1}^m h_i(\mathbf{p}) = 1$. Thus $\mathbf{h} : S^{m-1} \rightarrow S^{m-1}$.

It is clear that $\mathbf{h}$ is continuous. It therefore follows from Brouwer's fixed point theorem that $\mathbf{h}$ has a fixed point $\mathbf{p}^*$. For this point

$$p_i^* = \frac{p_i^* + z_i^+(\mathbf{p}^*)}{1 + \sum_{j=1}^m z_j^+(\mathbf{p}^*)}, \qquad i = 1, 2, \ldots, m.$$

Multiplication by the denominator and cancellation of p_i^* yields

$$p_i^* \sum_{j=1}^m z_j^+(\mathbf{p}^*) = z_i^+(\mathbf{p}), \qquad i = 1, 2, \ldots, m.$$

Multiplying the ith equation by $z_i(\mathbf{p}^*)$ and summing the resulting m equations, we obtain

$$\sum_{i=1}^m p_i^* z_i(\mathbf{p}^*) \sum_{j=1}^m z_j^+(\mathbf{p}^*) = \sum_{i=1}^m z_i(\mathbf{p}^*) z_i^+(\mathbf{p}^*).$$

By Walras' law $\sum_{i=1}^m p_i^* z_i(\mathbf{p}^*) = 0$; hence we have

$$\sum_{i=1}^m z_i(\mathbf{p}^*) z_i^+(\mathbf{p}^*) = 0.$$

Now, the only way the ith term in this sum can be nonzero is for $z_i(\mathbf{p}^*) > 0$. Hence if any term were nonzero, the sum would be positive. It follows that $z_i(\mathbf{p}^*) \leq 0$ for $i = 1, 2, \ldots, m$. ∎

The above theorem is illustrated geometrically in Fig. 7.5. The vector $\mathbf{z}(\mathbf{p})$ is always perpendicular to $\mathbf{p}$. In the situation shown, as $\mathbf{p}$ slides up the simplex S^1, $\mathbf{z}(\mathbf{p})$ must either shrink to zero at some point or, when $\mathbf{p}$ is vertical, be horizontal pointing to the left, meaning that $\mathbf{z}(\mathbf{p}) \leq \mathbf{0}$ there. Either way, there is a $\mathbf{p}$ with $\mathbf{z}(\mathbf{p}) \leq \mathbf{0}$.

An important assumption of the theorem is that the excess demand function $\mathbf{z}(\mathbf{p})$ is continuous on the unit simplex S^{m-1}. As discussed in Chapter 5 (Proposition 5.3), if consumers' preferences are continuous, satisfy local nonsatiation, and are strictly convex, the demand functions will indeed

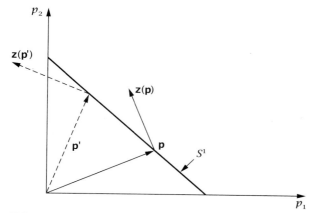

FIGURE 7.5   Geometry of equilibrium proof.

be continuous for $\mathbf{p} > 0$. The demand functions may, however, be discontinuous on the boundary, where one or more of the prices is zero. In fact, if preferences are strongly monotonic, demand for a good may be infinite if its price is zero. This situation can be easily accounted for in the existence theorem by noting that only continuity of the function $\mathbf{h}$ is required in the proof. An excess demand function that is infinite at the boundary will (usually) lead to an $\mathbf{h}$ that is continuous. This argument applies in all the examples we present in the text and in the exercises. However, this observation points out a technical limitation of the general demand function approach. Ultimately we must go back to the preference framework to justify the required assumptions.

7.4   Examples of Equilibria

We present two rather comprehensive examples in this section. The second is a general structure that can be solved explicitly in closed form.

Example 7.1 (Symmetric fixed-proportions utilities).   Consider an exchange economy consisting of three individuals and three commodities. The individuals have the utility functions

$$u_1(x_1, x_2, x_3) = \min\{x_1, x_2\}$$
$$u_2(x_1, x_2, x_3) = \min\{x_2, x_3\}$$
$$u_3(x_1, x_2, x_3) = \min\{x_1, x_3\}.$$

The original endowments are (1,0,0), (0,1,0), and (0,0,1).

Individual 1 will solve the problem

$$\max \ \min\{x_1, x_2\}$$
$$\text{sub to} \ \ p_1 x_1 + p_2 x_2 = p_1$$

leading to the demand function

$$\mathbf{x}_1 = \left(\frac{p_1}{p_1 + p_2}, \frac{p_1}{p_1 + p_2}, 0 \right).$$

The demand functions for the other two individuals have a similar form, and the overall excess demand is easily seen to have the components

$$z_1(\mathbf{p}) = \frac{p_1}{p_1 + p_2} + \frac{p_3}{p_1 + p_3} - 1$$

$$z_2(\mathbf{p}) = \frac{p_1}{p_1 + p_2} + \frac{p_2}{p_2 + p_3} - 1$$

$$z_3(\mathbf{p}) = \frac{p_2}{p_2 + p_3} + \frac{p_3}{p_1 + p_3} - 1.$$

The excess demand function is clearly continuous for $\mathbf{p} > 0$. By construction we know it satisfies Walras' law (but it is instructive for the reader to check it explicitly).

The equilibrium prices can be deduced by symmetry to be $\mathbf{p} = \left(\frac{1}{3}, \frac{1}{3}, \frac{1}{3} \right)$ with a corresponding allocation of $\mathbf{x}_1 = \left(\frac{1}{2}, \frac{1}{2}, 0 \right)$, $\mathbf{x}_2 = \left(0, \frac{1}{2}, \frac{1}{2} \right)$, and $\mathbf{x}_3 = \left(\frac{1}{2}, 0, \frac{1}{2} \right)$. If the prices are scaled by any positive constant, they will still serve as equilibrium prices for this allocation.

Example 7.2 (Cobb-Douglas world).   We have patiently marched through several Cobb-Douglas examples to illustrate various concepts. Now, we reach the logical culmination: a world where equilibrium is determined among n Cobb-Douglas consumers. But the result is remarkably elegant— unexpectedly so, considering the usual messy formulas associated with Cobb-Douglas forms. Equilibrium is defined by a system of *linear* equations.

Suppose there are n individuals and m commodities. Individual i has utility function

$$u_i(\mathbf{x}_i) = \prod_{j=1}^{m} (x_{ij})^{a_{ij}}.$$

The exponents a_{ij} define an $n \times m$ matrix $\mathbf{A}$. The ith row of this matrix contains the Cobb-Douglas exponents for individual i. We assume, without loss of generality, that the sum of any row of $\mathbf{A}$ is 1; hence $\sum_{j=1}^{m} a_{ij} = 1$, or in matrix form, $\mathbf{A1} = \mathbf{1}$.

Each individual i has an endowment of the m commodities. We normalize the commodity units so that the total endowment of each commodity is 1. Individual i has an endowment s_{ij} of the jth commodity. The coefficients s_{ij} form an $n \times m$ matrix $\mathbf{S}$. The ith row of $\mathbf{S}$ gives the endowments of individual i. Each column of $\mathbf{S}$ sums to 1; hence $\sum_{i=1}^{n} s_{ij} = 1$, or in matrix form, $\mathbf{S}^{\mathsf{T}} \mathbf{1} = \mathbf{1}$.

Now let prices $\mathbf{p} = (p_1, p_2, \ldots, p_m)$ be introduced. Individual i then has income $r_i = \sum_{k=1}^{m} s_{ik} p_k$. From our knowledge of Cobb-Douglas demand functions, we know that the associated demands are

$$x_{ij} = \frac{a_{ij} r_i}{p_j}.$$

In equilibrium, the sum over i of the left side must be 1; hence we have

$$p_j = \sum_{i=1}^{n} a_{ij} r_i.$$

Using the expression for r_i, we obtain

$$p_j = \sum_{i=1}^{n} a_{ij} \sum_{k=1}^{m} s_{ik} p_k,$$

or in matrix form

$$\mathbf{p} = \mathbf{A}^{\mathsf{T}} \mathbf{S} \mathbf{p}.$$

Therefore an equilibrium price vector $\mathbf{p}$ is an eigenvector of the matrix $\mathbf{E} = \mathbf{A}^{\mathsf{T}} \mathbf{S}$ corresponding to an eigenvalue of 1. To find the Cobb-Douglas world equilibrium, therefore, it is only necessary to find this eigenvector of $\mathbf{E}$. See Exercise 11 for an example.

*7.5   Fixed Point Methods

Fixed points of mappings (or Walrasian equilibrium points of exchange economies) can in practice be computed numerically through use of special fixed point methods. These methods (or algorithms) also provide constructive proofs of the basic Brouwer fixed point theorem. We shall briefly describe one simple algorithm to show the basic concept.

Sperner's Lemma

We begin by proving one version of a classic combinatorial result, known as Sperner's lemma. Consider the two-dimensional simplex shown in Fig. 7.6. It is divided into subsimplices. We have divided each edge of the original simplex into five segments, but this number is arbitrary. Each vertex of the resulting triangular mesh is labeled either 1, 2, or 3. The labels on the edge of the original simplex must be as indicated. Specifically, the three edges are designated 1, 2, and 3 and labeled accordingly; the corner points, where two edges meet, can take the label of either edge. The labels at interior vertices are arbitrary (as long as they are 1, 2, or 3).

Sperner's lemma states that no matter how the interior labels are assigned, there will be at least one subsimplex with a complete set of three distinct labels (in which case we say the subsimplex is *completely labeled*).

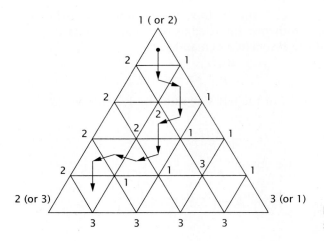

FIGURE 7.6   Path in a simplex.

The proof we give is just as important as the lemma itself, for it shows how to find the completely labeled subsimplex.

Sperner's lemma.   *If labels are assigned as stated above, and if the subdivision is not trivial (edges are divided at least once), there is a completely labeled subsimplex in the division.*

Proof: We prove this lemma by finding a completely labeled simplex using an algorithm due to Lemke and Howson. This algorithm steps from one small simplex to a neighboring one according to a simple rule: We start in a subsimplex that is in a corner of the original large simplex. The interior edge of this corner triangle has two distinct labels, and we move through this edge to the neighboring triangle. Now this new triangle is either completely labeled, in which case we can terminate the search, or the new label duplicates one of those on the edge we just crossed. In the latter case, there is still one other edge with two distinct labels, and we cross this to a new neighbor. This stepping procedure is repeated, as shown in Fig. 7.6.

We shall show that this procedure must find a completely labeled simplex. First, we note that edges that are crossed always have the same two labels (1 and 2 in the figure) because the third could enter only if a completely labeled simplex were found. From this we conclude that the path of the algorithm will never enter another corner triangle, since their interior edges are labeled differently than the original one.

Second, the path will never go through an edge on the exterior, since those edges do not have distinct labels.

Finally, the algorithm cannot reenter a triangle that it visited before. To prove this, suppose $S_1, S_2, \ldots$ is an ordered list of the triangles visited. Suppose S_i were the first one revisited. Only two edges of this triangle are distinctly labeled, so we must reenter through one of them. However, both of these were crossed before (one going in and the other going out), so we must have been in both of the corresponding neighbor triangles. This means that we must first reenter S_{i-1} or S_{i+1}, contradicting the assumption that S_i was revisited first.

Because the algorithm can always move one more step unless a completely labeled subsimplex is encountered, because it never repeats, and because there is a finite number of subsimplicies, a completely labeled simplex must be found at some stage. ∎

The lemma and its proof can be easily extended to a simplex S^{m-1} for any m. The actual definition and bookkeeping associated with the subdivision process are accomplished by a special systematic process, which we shall not discuss here. However, it is reasonably straightforward. Labels can be assigned arbitrarily in the interior of S^{m-1}, but they are assigned on the boundary in a special way analogous to that shown in Fig. 7.6. The algorithm again starts at a corner subsimplex and moves through a distinctly labeled $(m-2)$-dimensional face into a new subsimplex. Eventually a completely labeled subsimplex will be attained.

Application to a Walrasian Equilibrium

We now illustrate how the above result and method can be applied to the problem of determining a Walrasian equilibrium in three dimensions. Suppose $z(\mathbf{p})$ is a continuous excess demand function satisfying homogeneity $z(t\mathbf{p}) = z(\mathbf{p})$ for $t > 0$ and satisfying Walras' law, $\mathbf{p} \cdot z(\mathbf{p}) = 0$. We form the unit simplex $S^2 = \{\mathbf{p} : \sum_{i=1}^{3} p_i = 1\}$. This is subdivided as shown in Fig. 7.7.

We assign labels to the vertices of the subdivision in the following way. Along an edge of the original simplex, we assign label i such that $p_i = 0$. (At the corners, where two such i's are possible, we select either one.) At a vertex $\mathbf{p}$ of the subdivision interior to S^2, we assign the label i corresponding to a maximal component $z_i(\mathbf{p})$. All the conditions of Sperner's lemma are satisfied, so there must be a completely labeled subsimplex.

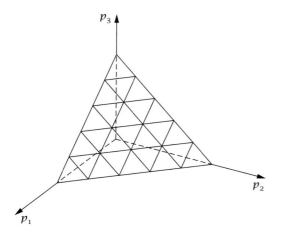

FIGURE 7.7 Simplex for Walras' law.

Consider the price vector $\mathbf{p}^*$ at the center of the completely labeled subsimplex. Each component is the maximum component of the function $\mathbf{z}(\mathbf{p})$ at some nearby point, and hence all components are approximately equal to some constant c at $\mathbf{p}^*$. Since $\mathbf{p}^* \cdot \mathbf{z}(\mathbf{p}^*) = 0$, it follows that $c \approx 0$. Hence $\mathbf{z}(\mathbf{p}^*) \approx \mathbf{0}$, and we say that $\mathbf{p}^*$ is an approximate equilibrium point. (See Exercise 13.)

The labeling technique forms the basis of the following computational method. One selects a subdivision that is considered fine enough for required accuracy and labels it as above. Note that not all labels need to be calculated before the search is begun. Instead, labels can be calculated as they are needed. When a new subsimplex is entered, $\mathbf{z}(\mathbf{p})$ is evaluated for the new vertex and the label of that vertex is calculated by determining the maximum component of $\mathbf{z}(\mathbf{p})$. When a completely labeled simplex is found, its center point is taken to be an approximate equilibrium price vector.

7.6   Equilibria in a Productive Economy

A full theory of general equilibrium must certainly account for production as well as distribution of goods. This is done by building on the earlier framework for describing firms in terms of production possibility sets.

Suppose there are K firms, each firm k being characterized by the production possibility set $\mathcal{Y}_k$, $k = 1, 2, \ldots, K$. The aggregate production possibility set is therefore $\mathcal{Y} = \mathcal{Y}_1 + \mathcal{Y}_2 + \cdots + \mathcal{Y}_K$. If there is a price vector $\mathbf{p}$, firm k will select $\mathbf{y}_k \in \mathcal{Y}_k$ to maximize profit. That is, firm k will select $\mathbf{y}_k$ to maximize $\mathbf{p} \cdot \mathbf{y}_k$, yielding profit π_k. The total profit of all firms will be $\pi = \pi_1 + \pi_2 + \cdots + \pi_K$, and this is equal to the total profit associated with the aggregate production possibility set. Hence, we can write $\pi = \max \{\mathbf{p} \cdot \mathbf{y} : \mathbf{y} \in \mathcal{Y}\}$. The question that arises in an economy with production is, Where does this profit go? The economy must be a closed system, so any profit generated must somehow be accounted for; in particular, it must be returned to consumers for expenditure on commodity bundles.

Private Ownership Economy

A natural way to distribute profit is through the rules of a *private ownership economy*, also referred to as an Arrow-Debreu economy. In such an economy individuals own shares of the firms. We denote by θ_{ik} the fraction of firm k owned by individual i, and we require $\theta_{ik} \geq 0$ for all $i = 1, 2, \ldots, n$, $k = 1, 2, \ldots, K$. Also for each k, $\sum_{i=1}^{n} \theta_{ik} = 1$, so that ownership of the entire firm is distributed among the individuals. If a firm makes positive profit, that profit is distributed to the owners in proportion to their ownership. Thus individual i receives $\sum_{k=1}^{K} \theta_{ik} \pi_k$ as income derived from the firm profits $\pi_1, \pi_2, \ldots, \pi_K$.

The ownership fractions θ_{ik} are assumed to be given as part of the description of the economy. In other models, considered in Chapter 11, individuals are allowed to trade firm ownership as well as commodities.

The profit distributed to an individual augments that individual's total income. Individual i's final budget constraint, accounting for both original endowment $\mathbf{w}_i$ and share of profits, is therefore

$$\mathbf{p} \cdot \mathbf{x}_i \leq \mathbf{p} \cdot \mathbf{w}_i + \sum_{k=1}^{K} \theta_{ik} \pi_k. \tag{7.1}$$

This set of budget constraints closes the system, since all income generated through endowment ownership and firm ownership is returned to consumers who, in turn, return it to the system by purchasing commodities. There is therefore no generation or loss of "money." The definition of equilibrium for a private ownership economy follows quite naturally from the structure described above.

In the definition below we slightly generalize our usual description by considering arbitrary individual consumption sets $X_i \subset \mathcal{R}^m$. Usually we take $X_i = \mathcal{R}_+^m$, but the more general framework is useful. For example, if one good is leisure time (which can be sold to a firm as labor), it is natural to assume that at most 24 hours per day of that good can be selected. This is accounted for by an X_i that is bounded in that component.

In the following definition, everything else besides the additions discussed above is the same as before. That is, the n consumers have preference relations $\succsim_i$ and (private) endowments $\mathbf{w}_i$.

Equilibrium. A *competitive equilibrium* in a private ownership economy is a triple $(\mathbf{X}^*, \mathbf{Y}^*, \mathbf{p}^*)$ consisting of an allocation $\mathbf{X}^* = (\mathbf{x}_1^*, \mathbf{x}_2^*, \ldots, \mathbf{x}_n^*)$, a production plan $\mathbf{Y}^* = (\mathbf{y}_1^*, \mathbf{y}_2^*, \ldots, \mathbf{y}_K^*)$, and a price vector $\mathbf{p}^*$, such that for $\pi_k^* = \mathbf{p}^* \cdot \mathbf{y}_k^*$ the following hold:

For each $i = 1, 2, \ldots, n$:

1. $\mathbf{x}_i^* \in X_i$.

2. $\mathbf{p}^* \cdot \mathbf{x}_i^* \leq \mathbf{p}^* \cdot \mathbf{w}_i + \sum_{k=1}^{K} \theta_{ik} \pi_k^*$ ($\mathbf{x}_i^*$ satisfies the ith budget constraint).

3. If $\mathbf{x}_i \in X_i$ and $\mathbf{p}^* \cdot \mathbf{x}_i \leq \mathbf{p}^* \cdot \mathbf{w}_i + \sum_{k=1}^{K} \theta_{ik} \pi_k^*$, then $\mathbf{x}_i \precsim_i \mathbf{x}_i^*$ (no other bundle satisfying the budget constraint is strictly preferred by any individual).

For each $k = 1, 2, \ldots, K$:

4. $\mathbf{y}_k^* \in \mathcal{Y}_k$.

5. $\pi_k^* \geq \mathbf{p}^* \cdot \mathbf{y}_k$ for all $\mathbf{y}_k \in \mathcal{Y}_k$ for $k = 1, 2, \ldots, K$ (each firm's plan maximizes profit).

6. $\sum_{i=1}^{n} \mathbf{x}_i^* = \mathbf{w} + \sum_{k=1}^{K} \mathbf{y}_k^*$ (market clearing—or feasibility).

The interpretation of the conditions in this definition should be fairly clear. The first two are feasibility conditions for consumers, restricting $\mathbf{x}_i^*$ first to the consumption set and second to satisfy the budget constraint having income equal to the sum of endowment value and share of profits. The third condition is the standard condition that $\mathbf{x}_i^*$ is chosen to maximize preference with respect to the budget constraint.

The fourth condition is a feasibility constraint for each firm, and the fifth condition states that each $\mathbf{y}_k^*$ maximizes profit with respect to all feasible choices for firm k. The final condition is the overall feasibility constraint, stating that the total amount consumed must equal the sum of the total endowment and the total (net) production. Note that in this case the condition is expressed with an equality constraint, rather than an inequality constraint as used in the earlier definition of a Walrasian equilibrium. This is because we can assume that the aggregate production possibility set $\mathcal{Y}$ satisfies free disposal, so inequality is then implicitly allowed.

A Classic Example

Example 7.3 (Robinson Crusoe economy).   The Robinson Crusoe economy is frequently used to illustrate a competitive equilibrium. We assume that Robinson Crusoe lives alone on an island and has a fixed supply L of time per day that can be allocated between leisure l and labor $z = L - l$. Labor produces food c according to a production function $c = f(L - l)$. Robinson has a utility function $u(l, c)$ defined over quantities of leisure time and food.

Robinson Crusoe will maximize utility subject to the technological constraints of production. This problem can be expressed as

$$\max\ u(l, c)$$
$$\text{sub to}\ \ c \le f(L - l) \tag{7.2}$$
$$l \le L.$$

If we let $\mathcal{Y}$ denote the production possibility set corresponding to $c \le f(z)$ and let $\mathbf{w} = (L, 0)$ denote Robinson's endowment, the problem can be written as

$$\max\ u(l, c)$$
$$\text{sub to}\ \ (l, c) \in \mathcal{Y} + \mathbf{w}$$
$$l \ge 0,\ \ c \ge 0.$$

The solution to 7.2 can be found directly.

Alternatively, by introducing equilibrium prices, Robinson Crusoe can operate with a split personality in an imaginary market. Given the equilibrium prices $(1, p)$ for leisure and food, on the one hand, he assumes the role of a consumer, and maximizes utility subject to a budget constraint. On the

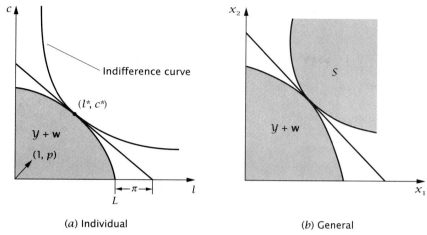

(a) Individual   (b) General

FIGURE 7.8   Robinson Crusoe economy.

other hand, he assumes the role of a producer and maximizes profit subject to the technical constraints, purchasing his own labor. The situation is illustrated in Fig. 7.8a.

Let us first consider Robinson's production activity. Given the prices $(1, p)$, he maximizes $\pi = pc - (L - l)$ over $\mathcal{Y} + \mathbf{w}$. This is equivalent to maximizing $pc + l$ over $\mathcal{Y} + \mathbf{w}$ and leads to the point (l^*, c^*), shown in the figure where the line orthogonal to $(1, p)$ is tangent to the boundary of $\mathcal{Y} + \mathbf{w}$. The profit is $\pi = pc^* - (L - l^*) = pc^* + l^* - L$. Since $pc + l$ is constant on the diagonal budget line, we see that π is equal to the horizontal segment shown in the figure.

The profit is given to Robinson, who then acts like a preference-maximizing consumer. The budget constraint is $pc + l \leq L + \pi$, which is bounded by exactly the same line used to define the tangency condition for profit maximization. In his role as consumer, Robinson also selects the point (l^*, c^*).

The Robinson Crusoe diagram can be extended to many individuals and many firms, as shown in Fig. 7.8b. We define S (as in Chapter 6, section 6.5) by

$$S = \{\mathbf{z} : \mathbf{z} = \sum_{i=1}^{n} \mathbf{x}_i, \ \mathbf{x}_i \succsim \mathbf{x}_i^*, \ i = 1, 2, \ldots, n\},$$

so that S is the set of Pareto-preferred aggregate bundles. This diagram can be exploded as in Chapter 6 to show that each individual's upper contour set defined by $\mathbf{x}_i$ just touches that individual's budget set, and that each firm's netput $\mathbf{y}_k$ maximizes profit.

7.7   Fundamental Existence Theorem

We are now able to state the fundamental existence theorem for a private ownership economy. This theorem represents one of the greatest achievements of modern microeconomic theory. It ties together the theories of competitive action for consumers and for firms within the structure of a closed economy—guaranteeing that under appropriate assumptions the concept of a competitive equilibrium is not only mathematically meaningful but economically useful as well.

The conditions required in the theorem are stated directly in terms of preferences and production possibility sets, the economic structure of the economy, rather than indirectly through properties of the excess demand function, as in the proof of existence of a Walrasian equilibrium. This more firmly ties the result to the underlying economics.

There are various versions of the fundamental existence theorem. We give below what is perhaps the most standard version, as first proved by Debreu.

Fundamental existence theorem.   *A private ownership economy has a competitive equilibrium if the following conditions are satisfied:*

1. *Each individual's consumption set X_i is closed, convex, and bounded below.*

2. *There is no satiation bundle in any consumer's consumption set.*

3. *For each consumer i, the sets $\{\mathbf{x}_i : \mathbf{x}_i \succsim_i \mathbf{x}_i'\}$ and $\{\mathbf{x}_i : \mathbf{x}_i' \succsim_i \mathbf{x}_i\}$ are closed for each $\mathbf{x}_i' \in X_i$.*

4. *Each individual's initial endowment vector is in the interior of the consumption set X_i.*

5. *For each individual i, if $\mathbf{x}_i$ and $\mathbf{x}_i'$ are two consumption bundles in X_i such that $\mathbf{x}_i \succ_i \mathbf{x}_i'$, then $t\mathbf{x}_i + (1 - t)\mathbf{x}_i' \succ_i \mathbf{x}_i'$ for all $t \in (0, 1)$.*

6. $\mathbf{0} \in \mathcal{Y}_k$ *for every k.*

7. $\mathcal{Y}$ *is closed and convex.*

8. $\mathcal{Y} \cap (-\mathcal{Y}) = \{\mathbf{0}\}$.

9. $\mathcal{R}_-^m \subset \mathcal{Y}$.

Let us review the economic interpretation of these assumptions. Conditions 1 through 5 are technical assumptions about the individual's preference relations, endowment, and consumption set. Most of these we have used often before. The requirement in 1 that X_i is bounded below means that there is an $\underline{\mathbf{x}}$ such that $\mathbf{x} \geq \underline{\mathbf{x}}$ for all $\mathbf{x} \in X_i$. Note also that condition 2 only rules out a satiation (or bliss) point; it does not (by itself) imply local nonsatiation. Condition 4 is fairly strong, for it requires that everyone owns a bit of every commodity. This assumption can be weakened by introducing strong monotonicity. Condition 5 is a convexity assumption on preferences, referred to as *strong convexity*. In this form it, together with condition 2, implies local nonsatiation, for it says that if $\mathbf{x}_i$ is a better point than $\mathbf{x}_i'$ (and by condition 2 there is always a better point), then any point on the line between them is better than $\mathbf{x}_i'$.

Condition 6 states that a firm can choose the zero plan, ensuring that the maximum equilibrium profits are nonnegative. Conditions 7 through 9 are stated in terms of the aggregate production possibility set. Condition 7 is the technical assumption of closedness and the requirement of convexity, which is equivalent to nonincreasing returns to scale. Note especially that there is no boundedness assumption, and hence constant-returns-to-scale technologies are allowed. Condition 8 is known as an *irreversibility* assumption, for it states that if a nonzero plan $\mathbf{y}$ is possible, the plan $-\mathbf{y}$, with all the outputs now used as inputs and the inputs becoming outputs, is not possible. This assumption serves to bound the possible production plans given a fixed set of endowments. Condition 9 is a free disposal assumption, stating that unneeded goods can always be absorbed by the technology.

We shall not give a complete proof of this theorem, but the next three sections discuss alternative approaches to the proof, based on alternative economic viewpoints.

Example 7.4 (Two-period consumption).   Consider a two-period economy with two individuals A and B. There is a single commodity type (say food) that can be consumed in either of the two periods. The individuals have endowments of the commodity in the two periods separately, perhaps representing crop harvests. The individual endowment vectors are $\mathbf{w}^A = (w_1^A, w_2^A) > \mathbf{0}$ and $\mathbf{w}^B = (w_1^B, w_2^B) > \mathbf{0}$, respectively. The commodity can be stored from the first period to the second.

We assume that the consumers have continuous, convex, locally nonsatiated utility functions $u_A(x_1^A, x_2^A)$ and $u_B(x_1^B, x_2^B)$ where $\mathbf{x}^A = (x_1^A, x_2^A)$ and $\mathbf{x}^B = (x_1^B, x_2^B)$ are the consumption patterns for the two individuals. We let p_1 and p_2 denote the prices of the commodity in periods 1 and 2, respectively.

We treat the possibility of storage by defining constant-returns-to-scale production technology that has as input the commodity in period 1 and yields output of equal magnitude in period 2. We then may fully distinguish the commodity consumed (or employed as input) in period 1 from the commodity consumed in period 2. Because the technology satisfies constant returns to scale, profit in the storage industry is zero.

The conditions for an equilibrium are

1. $\mathbf{x}^A$ and $\mathbf{x}^B$ are solutions to

$$\max \ u_A(\mathbf{x}^A)$$
$$\text{sub to } \mathbf{p}\cdot\mathbf{x}^A \le \mathbf{p}\cdot\mathbf{w}^A$$
$$\mathbf{x}^A \ge \mathbf{0}$$

and

$$\max \ u_B(\mathbf{x}^B)$$
$$\text{sub to} \ \mathbf{p} \cdot \mathbf{x}^B \leq \mathbf{p} \cdot \mathbf{w}^B$$
$$\mathbf{x}^B \geq \mathbf{0}.$$

2. The following relations hold:

$$x_1^A + x_1^B \leq w_1^A + w_1^B - z$$
$$x_2^A + x_2^B \leq w_2^A + w_2^B + z$$
$$z \geq 0.$$

3. $p_2 \leq p_1$. Further, $p_2 < p_1$ implies $z = 0$.

The first two conditions correspond to individual optimality and feasibility, respectively. The second condition is the market clearing condition. The variable z represents the level of storage from period 1 to period 2. The third condition is the zero profit condition. If $p_2 > p_1$, positive profits could be made by storage, so $p_2 \leq p_1$. If $p_2 < p_1$, there must be no storage, for otherwise profit would be negative.

If appropriate assumptions on u_A and u_B are satisfied and if $\mathbf{w}_A > \mathbf{0}$ and $\mathbf{w}_B > \mathbf{0}$, then all conditions of the fundamental existence theorem are satisfied and an equilibrium exists satisfying the conditions above.

7.8   Excess Demand

One method of proof of the fundamental existence theorem is outlined in this section: the excess demand method. The method of proof is an extension of the method of proof used in Section 7.3 to establish the existence of a Walrasian equilibrium. However, a number of important modifications of the earlier proof are required in order to accommodate the generality inherent in the fundamental existence theorem.

Suppose a vector of prices $\mathbf{p}$ is given. This price vector determines a net-put vector $\mathbf{y}_k(\mathbf{p})$ for each firm $k = 1, 2, \ldots, K$. For the moment we assume, for simplicity, that these are single-valued functions of $\mathbf{p}$. These functions determine the profits $\pi_k(\mathbf{p}) = \mathbf{p} \cdot \mathbf{y}_k(\mathbf{p})$ and the aggregate supply function $\mathbf{y}(\mathbf{p}) = \sum_{k=1}^{K} \mathbf{y}_k(\mathbf{p})$. The price vector $\mathbf{p}$ and the profits $\pi_k(\mathbf{p})$ then determine the budget constraints for the consumers. Specifically, consumer i faces the budget constraint $\mathbf{p} \cdot \mathbf{x}_i \leq \mathbf{p} \cdot \mathbf{w}_i + \sum_{k=1}^{K} \theta_{ik} \pi_k(\mathbf{p})$. The consumer maximizes preference with respect to this constraint, obtaining the demand $\mathbf{x}_i(\mathbf{p})$. Again, for simplicity we assume that each $\mathbf{x}_i(\mathbf{p})$ is a single-valued function of $\mathbf{p}$. These functions are combined to yield the aggregate demand function $\mathbf{x}(\mathbf{p}) = \sum_{i=1}^{n} \mathbf{x}_i(\mathbf{p})$. Then the aggregate demand and aggregate supply functions are combined to define the excess demand function

$$\mathbf{z}(\mathbf{p}) = \mathbf{x}(\mathbf{p}) - \mathbf{y}(\mathbf{p}) - \mathbf{w},$$

where **w** is the total endowment $\sum_{i=1}^{n} \mathbf{w}_i$. This function has an interpretation similar to that for a pure exchange economy. Each component of $\mathbf{z}(\mathbf{p})$ represents the difference, in the amount of some good, between what is demanded at prices **p** and what is available at prices **p**. In this case production is included, for it contributes to demand (for inputs) and augments endowment (for outputs).

The excess demand function defined this way satisfies Walras' law.

Walras' law (private ownership economy). *For any* $\mathbf{p} \geq \mathbf{0}$ *there holds* $\mathbf{p} \cdot \mathbf{z}(\mathbf{p}) \leq 0$.

Proof: By definition

$$
\mathbf{p} \cdot \mathbf{z}(\mathbf{p}) = \mathbf{p} \cdot \left[\sum_{i=1}^{n} \mathbf{x}_i(\mathbf{p}) - \sum_{k=1}^{K} \mathbf{y}_k(\mathbf{p}) - \sum_{i=1}^{n} \mathbf{w}_i \right]
$$

$$
= \sum_{i=1}^{n} \left[\mathbf{p} \cdot \mathbf{x}_i(\mathbf{p}) - \mathbf{p} \cdot \mathbf{w}_i \right] - \sum_{k=1}^{K} \mathbf{p} \cdot \mathbf{y}_k(\mathbf{p}).
$$

With the budget constraint this becomes

$$
\mathbf{p} \cdot \mathbf{z}(\mathbf{p}) \leq \sum_{i=1}^{n} \sum_{k=1}^{K} \theta_{ik} \mathbf{p} \cdot \mathbf{y}_k(\mathbf{p}) - \sum_{k=1}^{K} \mathbf{p} \cdot \mathbf{y}_k(\mathbf{p}).
$$

Interchanging the order of summation in the first term and using the fact that $\sum_{i=1}^{n} \theta_{ik} = 1$, we obtain

$$
\mathbf{p} \cdot \mathbf{z}(\mathbf{p}) \leq \sum_{k=1}^{K} \mathbf{p} \cdot \mathbf{y}_k(\mathbf{p}) - \sum_{k=1}^{K} \mathbf{p} \cdot \mathbf{y}_k(\mathbf{p}) = 0. \quad \blacksquare
$$

Because Walras' law holds, we can use the existence result of Section 7.3 to prove the existence of a price vector $\mathbf{p} \geq \mathbf{0}$ such that $\mathbf{z}(\mathbf{p}) \leq \mathbf{0}$. This can be directly translated into an equilibrium existence result for a private ownership economy. (The vector **p** is the appropriate price vector, and we find the allocation by using each consumer's demand function.) Likewise the algorithmic methods for determining an equilibrium using (modified) fixed point methods can be employed here as well to solve the equation $\mathbf{z}(\mathbf{p}) \leq \mathbf{0}$. However, this method must be modified in several ways to obtain the full generality expressed by the fundamental existence theorem in Section 7.7. First, note that if the production possibility sets are not strictly convex—and they are *not* in the important case of constant returns to scale—the supply functions are not single-valued, but set-valued. In fact, the sets $\mathbf{y}_k(\mathbf{p})$ are unbounded. Similarly, if preferences are not strictly convex, demand functions are also set-valued. Furthermore, these set-valued functions are not continuous in the usual sense. Much deeper methods must therefore be used, and it is quite a challenge to find a suitable combination of technical assumptions that are both mathematically adequate and economically acceptable. The version stated in Section 7.7 is such a combination.

The original proof of the fundamental existence theorem by Debreu is indeed based on a generalized excess demand viewpoint. It employs the Kakutani fixed point theorem, which establishes fixed points for point-to-set mappings, not just for single-valued functions. This theorem, described in Appendix E, is now used in many areas of microeconomics (for example, it is used in Chapter 8). However, the underlying concept of the excess demand approach, whether the simple version using the Brouwer theorem or the more advanced version using the Kakutani theorem, is the same. The idea is that demands and supplies can be considered as functions of $\mathbf{p}$. We search around on the unit simplex S^{m-1} for a $\mathbf{p}$ that makes total demand and supply balance.

7.9   The Zero-Minimum Principle

There are other viewpoints of competitive equilibrium that lead to alternative methods of the proof of existence. In this section we present an alternative based on the zero-minimum principle.

We use the same framework as in the previous two sections, except that we suppose that preferences are described by a continuous utility function u_i on $\mathcal{R}_+^m$ with range $\mathcal{U}_i \subset \mathcal{R}$. We define $\mathcal{U} = \mathcal{U}_1 \times \mathcal{U}_2 \times \cdots \times \mathcal{U}_n$.

The basic idea is simple. We start with a price vector $\mathbf{p} \geq \mathbf{0}$. Given this price vector, we can calculate the utility values that the various consumers would achieve. These values are given by the indirect utility functions $V_i(\mathbf{p}, \mathbf{p} \cdot \mathbf{w}_i)$ for $i = 1, 2, \ldots, n$. Then given these utility values we squeeze as much surplus as possible out of the system by minimizing the surplus function. This will produce a new price vector $\mathbf{p}'$. If $\mathbf{p}' = \mathbf{p}$, then $\mathbf{p}$ is an equilibrium price vector. If $\mathbf{p}' \neq \mathbf{p}$, we must adjust $\mathbf{p}$.

Two Basic Mappings

We formalize the above idea by introducing two mappings, corresponding to two processes: first, finding the indirect utilities, and second, minimizing surplus. These two mappings are later combined, in either of two ways, to obtain a single mapping that is used in a fixed-point method.

The Mapping V. This mapping just transforms a price vector $\mathbf{p}$ into a corresponding set of utility values. Let Λ be the unit simplex defined by $\mathbf{p} \cdot \mathbf{g} = 1$, $\mathbf{p} \geq \mathbf{0}$ (with $\mathbf{g} = \mathbf{1}$). Specifically,

$$\Lambda = \left\{ \mathbf{p} : \sum_{i=1}^{m} p_i = 1, p_i \geq 0, i = 1, 2, \ldots, m \right\}.$$

The mapping $\mathbf{V}$ goes from Λ into $\mathcal{U}$. That is, $\mathbf{V} : \Lambda \to \mathcal{U}$. It is defined as follows: Given $\mathbf{p} \in \Lambda$, let

$$\nu_i(\mathbf{p}) = \max \; u_i(\mathbf{x}_i)$$

$$\text{sub to } \mathbf{p} \cdot \mathbf{x}_i \le \mathbf{p} \cdot \mathbf{w}_i + \sum_{k=1}^{K} \theta_{ik} \pi_k(\mathbf{p})$$

$$\mathbf{x}_i \ge \mathbf{0}.$$

Thus $\nu_i(\mathbf{p})$ is the indirect utility defined by $\mathbf{p}$ and the budget constraint.
    Next define

$$\mathbf{V}(\mathbf{p}) = (\nu_1(\mathbf{p}), \nu_2(\mathbf{p}), \ldots, \nu_n(\mathbf{p})).$$

Thus $\mathbf{V}(\mathbf{p})$ is a composite of the individual $\nu_i(\mathbf{p})$'s. Clearly $\mathbf{V} : \Lambda \to \mathcal{U}$.

The Mapping P. The mapping $\mathbf{P}$ transforms a set of utilities into a price
vector. That is, $\mathbf{P} : \mathcal{U} \to \Lambda$. It is defined by minimization of surplus. Thus
given $\mathbf{U} = (u_1, u_2, \ldots, u_n) \in \mathcal{U}$, define $\mathbf{p}$ as the price vector that minimizes

$$S(\mathbf{p}, \mathbf{U}) = \mathbf{p} \cdot \mathbf{w} + \pi(\mathbf{p}) - \sum_{i=1}^{n} e_i(\mathbf{p}, u_i)$$

over $\mathbf{p} \in \Lambda$. Recall that $\pi(\mathbf{p})$ is convex with respect to $\mathbf{p}$ and $e_i(\mathbf{p}, u_i)$ is concave. Hence, $S(\mathbf{p}, \mathbf{U})$ is a convex function of $\mathbf{p}$. The minimum price corresponding to $\mathbf{U}$ is $\mathbf{p} = \mathbf{P}(\mathbf{U})$.

Composite Mappings

Now define the composite mapping $\mathbf{F}(\mathbf{p}) = \mathbf{P}(\mathbf{V}(\mathbf{p}))$. Thus $\mathbf{F} : \Lambda \to \Lambda$. $\mathbf{F}$ starts
with a $\mathbf{p} \in \Lambda$, finds the corresponding utility values by solving the consumer
problems, and then finds a new $\mathbf{p}$ by minimizing the surplus associated with
those utility values. Overall, $\mathbf{F}$ transforms one price vector into another.
    If we make strong assumptions, $\mathbf{F}$ will be single-valued and continuous
on Λ. Hence the Brouwer theorem guarantees the existence of a fixed point
$\mathbf{p}^* \in \Lambda$ with $\mathbf{p}^* = \mathbf{F}(\mathbf{p}^*)$. There will be an associated vector of utilities $\mathbf{U}^* =
\mathbf{V}(\mathbf{p}^*)$.
    The price vector $\mathbf{p}^*$ will define a competitive equilibrium for the private
ownership economy. The full equilibrium is constructed by finding the $\mathbf{Y}^*$
that maximizes profit and the $\mathbf{X}^*$ that corresponds to the maximization of
utility by every consumer subject to the budget constraint. (We are assuming
here that all solutions are unique.) Since $\mathbf{p}^*$ and $\mathbf{U}^*$ yield budget matching
for individuals, the total surplus is zero. Since $\mathbf{p}^*$ minimizes the surplus as
well, it follows that $\mathbf{p}^*$ is zero-minimal. The combination $(\mathbf{X}^*, \mathbf{Y}^*, \mathbf{p}^*)$ is a
competitive equilibrium.
    The above argument can be refined so that it becomes a proof of the
fully general fundamental existence theorem. In this case the Kakutani fixed
point theorem is applied to $\mathbf{F}$.

We can also work in a complementary fashion by first selecting a set of utility values **U**. We then, first, find a price vector **p** by minimizing surplus, and second, find a new set of utility values **U**′ by computing indirect utilities for the given price vector. If **U**′ = **U**, we have found equilibrium values. If **U**′ ≠ **U**, we must adjust **U**. This complementary method is formalized by the complementary composite mapping **G** that takes utility vectors **U** into other utility vectors **U**. Specifically, $\mathbf{G} : \mathcal{U} \to \mathcal{U}$ is defined as $\mathbf{G}(\mathbf{U}) = \mathbf{V}(\mathbf{P}(\mathbf{U}))$. This mapping will have a fixed point **U***. Once **U*** is known, we can find the equilibrium price vector as $\mathbf{p}^* = \mathbf{P}(\mathbf{U}^*)$.

We can solve an equilibrium problem computationally by finding a fixed point of either **F** or of **G**. The advantage of using **G** instead of **F** is that the dimension of **G** may be smaller. Typical equilibrium models have many, often thousands, of commodities (perhaps due to time indexing), but they have few, often no more than 10, consumers (because it is usually only practical to model a few representatives). Therefore by using **G** it is only necessary to apply a fixed point algorithm in a space of utility values rather than a space of prices. Indeed, this method has been implemented and has been found to be both reliable and extremely efficient.

7.10   The Zero-Maximum Principle

An equilibrium for a private ownership economy can also be found by using the zero-maximum principle. This is the dual of the method based on the zero-minimum principle, so we shall only sketch the idea. Set $\mathbf{g} = (1, 1, \ldots, 1)$. Consider the problem

$$\max \sum_{i=1}^{n} b_i(\mathbf{x}_i, u_i)$$

$$\text{sub to} \sum_{i=1}^{n} \mathbf{x}_i = \mathbf{w} + \sum_{k=1}^{K} \mathbf{y}_k \qquad (7.3)$$

$$\mathbf{x}_i \geq \mathbf{0}, \qquad i = 1, 2, \ldots, n,$$

$$\mathbf{y}_k \in \mathcal{Y}_k, \qquad k = 1, 2, \ldots, K.$$

The Lagrange multiplier vector **p** of the equality constraint will satisfy $\mathbf{p} \cdot \mathbf{g} = 1$. This vector depends on the assumed utility values and hence defines a mapping $\mathbf{P} : \mathcal{U} \to \Lambda$. This is the same function **P** as used with the zero-minimum principle, and therefore we have an alternative way to evaluate **P**.

The Shortage Form

The zero-maximum principle can be expressed in an alternative form that is sometimes useful. Let σ_k be the shortage function of $\mathcal{Y}_k$ defined by using the same reference vector $\mathbf{g}$ as used in the benefit functions. Then problem (7.3) is equivalent to

$$\max \sum_{i=1}^{n} b_i(\mathbf{x}_i, u_i) - \sum_{k=1}^{K} \sigma_k(\mathbf{y}_k)$$

$$\text{sub to} \sum_{i=1}^{n} \mathbf{x}_i = \mathbf{w} + \sum_{k=1}^{K} \mathbf{y}_k$$

$$\mathbf{x}_i \geq \mathbf{0}, \qquad i = 1, 2, \ldots, n.$$

This is the shortage form of the zero-maximum principle. It states that an equilibrium allocation maximizes the net difference between total benefit (for consumers) and total shortage (for firms), subject only to the conditions that total consumption is equal to endowment plus production and that consumption be feasible. There is no explicit requirement that production be feasible (although it is).

7.11 Simple Equilibrium Principles

The simplest statement of equilibrium is that supply equals demand, and this statement is frequently illustrated by drawing a downward-sloping inverse demand curve and an upward sloping supply curve and pointing to their intersection as the equilibrium point. This is, of course, only a partial equilibrium view, but it is powerful and descriptive. Moreover, it is possible to devise some intriguing optimization principles on the basis of this diagram.

An equilibrium situation is shown in Fig. 7.9a, with the equilibrium quantity and price being q^* and p^*. The area bounding the inverse supply and demand curves from zero to the equilibrium point can be divided into two

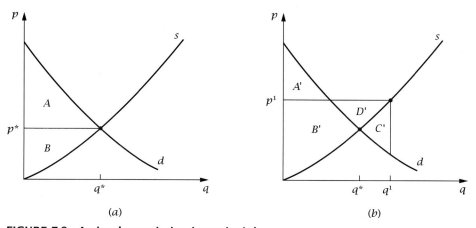

(a)   (b)

FIGURE 7.9 A simple maximization principle.

parts. Part A is the consumer area (which is calculated by evaluating the consumer surplus), and part B is the producer area (which is the profit plus the fixed cost—see Example 5.6). Suppose now that we change the quantity of the good, say to q^1. Then the corresponding sum of consumer area and producer area will decrease. To see this, we select a price between the two curves and evaluate each area relative to that price. The case of the increase to q^1 is shown in Fig. 7.9b. We chose p^1 to be the highest price on the segment between the inverse supply and demand curves, but any other choice would lead to the same conclusion. The consumer area is now $A' - C' - D'$, and the producer area is $B' + D'$. The net is therefore $A' + B' - C'$, which represents a decrease over the equilibrium situation. If q is decreased, the overall area also decreases, as is easily seen. Hence we may state the following intriguing principle:[1] *the sum of the consumer area and the producer area is maximized at the equilibrium value of q.*

The above argument is really only a geometric trick that works in one dimension. To give it economic content that can be generalized to higher dimensions, we must make a few adjustments. As we know, consumer area calculated from an inverse demand curve is only an approximation of a real consumer welfare measure. A better measure is obtained by using a compensated inverse demand curve. However, to use such a curve, utility levels must be specified, and it is natural to use the utility values corresponding to the equilibrium. Furthermore, it is more appropriate to measure areas relative to the equilibrium point rather than the arbitrary point of zero price and quantity. The same geometric principle will apply, for by moving the reference we are merely subtracting a constant area, but the new area has real meaning. With these two changes, the sum of the consumer welfare area and the producer area is again maximized at the equilibrium quantity, and this maximum value is zero. In this form the principle corresponds to a more general one. Indeed, in this revised form, this geometric principle exactly corresponds to the shortage version of the zero-maximum principle. In this case the reference bundle **g** is made up of other commodities, not the one shown in the diagram. The two areas are the total benefit and the negative of the shortage measured relative to the reference **g**. (The proofs of these statements are not difficult but require some of the constructions presented in Chapter 10.) The zero-maximum principle is therefore a proper generalization to general equilibria of the simple geometric maximization principle that holds for a one-dimensional partial equilibrium.

There is another simple geometric principle based on what happens to the total welfare area as price, rather than quantity, is varied. This principle

---

[1]This principle is often summarized by stating that the sum of the consumer surplus and the profit is maximized at the equilibrium point. In our formalism this is misleading. Both consumer surplus and profit, when defined as functions, are functions of price, but in this principle it is quantity that is varied. It is true that the areas are calculated using consumer surplus and profit arguments, but the single price used to define areas is not on both the inverse demand and the inverse supply curves.

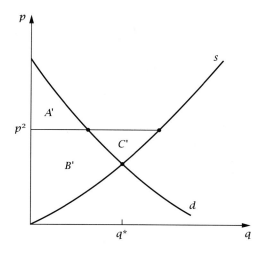

**FIGURE 7.10   A simple minimiza-
tion principle.**

is dual to the first one. At a given price, we use different quantities for the
consumers and the producers, corresponding to the points on the demand
and supply curves. Fig. 7.10 shows how to evaluate a change to a price p^2.
The consumer area is defined to be the consumer surplus corresponding
to this price, which is area A'. The producer area is profit plus fixed cost,
which is $B' + C'$. The sum is $A' + B' + C'$, which is always larger than the
area obtained when the price is the equilibrium price. Hence we may state
the following alternative principle: *the sum of the consumer area and the
producer area is minimized at the equilibrium value of p.*

Again, to transform this geometric principle into one with real economic
content requires that the initial reference point be taken as the equilibrium
point itself, and the inverse demand curve be the compensated inverse demand curve defined by the equilibrium utility values. When this is done, the
principle exactly corresponds to the zero-minimum principle, which says
that the surplus is minimized at the equilibrium point and that this surplus
is zero. The prices are normalized by $\mathbf{p} \cdot \mathbf{g} = 1$ where $\mathbf{g}$ is the reference bundle (which is made up of other commodities than the one being considered
as variable in the diagram).

*7.12   Uniqueness of Equilibria

A very important question concerning an equilibrium is whether it is unique.
If there were more than one equilibrium, the theory could not make strong
predictive statements about a real economy. Unfortunately, the uniqueness
question is troublesome because well-structured models of economies often
do have more than a single equilibrium. What we can hope for in these cases
is that there is only a finite number of equilibria, in which case each one is
at least locally unique. It is then possible to focus on a particular one of the
finite equilibria for study.

The most direct approach to the study of the uniqueness question is to use the excess demand formation of equilibria. This means that equilibria are characterized by solutions to

$$\mathbf{z}(\mathbf{p}) \leq \mathbf{0}$$
$$\mathbf{p} \geq \mathbf{0}.$$

Gross Substitutes

We present here a standard result, which, although restrictive in its assumptions, is simple.

Gross substitutes.   Goods i and j are *gross substitutes* at prices $\mathbf{p}$ if

$$\frac{\partial z_i(\mathbf{p})}{\partial p_j} \geq 0.$$

The economic interpretation is clear. Increasing the price of one of the two goods results in an increase in the excess demand for the other: there is a substitution effect on an aggregate basis.

Proposition 7.2.   *Suppose all pairs of goods are gross substitutes at all prices. If an equilibrium price vector $\mathbf{p}^* > \mathbf{0}$ exists, it is unique.*

Proof: Let $\mathbf{p}'$ be another equilibrium. We define the scalar $\lambda = \max_i p_i'/p_i^*$. Clearly $\lambda > 0$, for otherwise $\mathbf{p}' = \mathbf{0}$. Let j be the index for which the maximum ratio is achieved; that is, $p_j' = \lambda p_j^*$.

Since $\mathbf{p}^* > \mathbf{0}$, we have $\mathbf{z}(\mathbf{p}^*) = \mathbf{0}$, and by homogeneity $\mathbf{z}(\lambda \mathbf{p}^*) = \mathbf{0}$. We can obtain the vector $\mathbf{p}'$ from $\lambda \mathbf{p}^*$ by reducing the components appropriately, except that the jth component need not be reduced since it is already equal to p_j'. As a result, the prices of all goods other than j have been reduced, and hence the excess demand of good j must decrease. Thus $z_j(\mathbf{p}') < 0$. ∎

Local Uniqueness

Another way to attack the question of uniqueness is to look for conditions that ensure that the equilibrium is unique in a small region around a known equilibrium. This amounts, essentially, to ensuring that the linearized version of the equilibrium equations is nonsingular.

Let us consider a strictly positive equilibrium defined by $\mathbf{p}^* > \mathbf{0}$. In that case the equilibrium satisfies $\mathbf{z}(\mathbf{p}^*) = \mathbf{0}$. The linearized version is obtained by taking the differential, resulting in

$$\nabla \mathbf{z}(\mathbf{p}^*)\, d\mathbf{p} = \mathbf{0}. \qquad (7.4)$$

In the above, $\nabla \mathbf{z}(\mathbf{p}^*)$ is the matrix $[\partial z_i / \partial p_j]$.

Note, however, that this system is *always* singular. This fact follows immediately from Walras' law, $\mathbf{p} \cdot \mathbf{z}(\mathbf{p}) = \mathbf{0}$, which when differentiated yields $\nabla \mathbf{z}(\mathbf{p})\,\mathbf{p} + \mathbf{z}(\mathbf{p}) = \mathbf{0}$. At the equilibrium this gives $\nabla \mathbf{z}(\mathbf{p}^*)\,\mathbf{p}^* = \mathbf{0}$, which shows that the system (7.4) is singular. We need to know that there is no other solution to (7.4) independent of $d\mathbf{p} = \mathbf{p}^*$.

We can get some help in studying this from the Slutsky equation. For an exchange economy we have

$$\mathbf{z}(\mathbf{p}) = \sum_{i=1}^{n} \{\mathbf{x}_i(\mathbf{p}, \mathbf{p} \cdot \mathbf{w}_i) - \mathbf{w}_i\}.$$

Hence,

$$\nabla \mathbf{z}(\mathbf{p}) = \sum_{i=1}^{n} \left\{ \nabla_{\mathbf{p}} \mathbf{x}_i(\mathbf{p}, \mathbf{p} \cdot \mathbf{w}_i) + \frac{\partial \mathbf{x}_i(\mathbf{p}, \mathbf{p} \cdot \mathbf{w}_i)}{\partial r} \mathbf{w}_i \right\}.$$

We now apply the Slutsky equation to the first term. Hence, overall, we find

$$\nabla \mathbf{z}(\mathbf{p}) = \sum_{i=1}^{n} \left\{ \mathbf{S}_i + \frac{\partial \mathbf{x}_i(\mathbf{p}, \mathbf{p} \cdot \mathbf{w}_i)}{\partial r} (\mathbf{w}_i - \mathbf{x}_i) \right\}$$

where $\mathbf{S}_i$ is the Slutsky matrix for consumer i. The sufficient conditions for the consumer's problem of maximizing utility guarantee that each $\mathbf{S}_i$ is positive semidefinite with rank equal to $m - 1$. Therefore if these were the only terms, we would have the required property. Unfortunately, there is also the income effect term. We cannot say much in general about this term. However, if it is small—either because the marginal rates of consumption due to increased income are small or because the final consumptions are close to initial endowments—then the other terms dominate and the uniqueness condition holds.

*7.13 Dynamics

A competitive equilibrium identifies a certain combination of consumer allocation, production plan, and price system resulting from a given set of consumer endowments and ownership shares. However, although there is a proof of the existence of an equilibrium, we have no assurance that such an equilibrium would actually be achieved in an economy. Of course, it could simply be dictated and all agents forced to move to it, but this would contradict the whole idea of an equilibrium, which is, after all, an attempt to reflect the characteristics of a free market economy.

The question that arises, therefore, is how an equilibrium might be achieved in an actual economy. To address this question analytically, it is necessary to impose some sort of dynamic process on top of the purely static model of equilibrium theory. We may then analyze the convergence of this dynamic process.

Tâtonnement

Walras introduced a very simple price adjustment mechanism called *tâtonnement*. This process is based on a hypothetical referee who initiates the process by announcing a set of prices for the m commodities. Following this announcement, members of the economy determine demands and supplies based on perfect price-taking behavior and submit their requirements to the referee. If the net excess demand is zero, the announced prices are taken as final, and trading and production take place at those prices. If, on the other hand, excess demand is nonzero for some commodities, no trading is allowed. Instead, the prices are adjusted by increasing those corresponding to commodities with positive excess demand and decreasing those corresponding to commodities with negative excess demand. After the price adjustments, the members of the economy submit new lists to the referee and the process is continued until equilibrium is achieved.

The idea of the iterative process described above can be captured mathematically by posing a system of differential equations governing prices. The price vector is initiated at some vector $\mathbf{p}(0)$, and then it follows a path $\mathbf{p}(t)$, $t > 0$, governed by the system of differential equations. The system corresponding to tâtonnement is

$$\dot{p}_1(t) = z_1(\mathbf{p}(t))$$
$$\dot{p}_2(t) = z_2(\mathbf{p}(t))$$
$$\vdots$$
$$\dot{p}_m(t) = z_m(\mathbf{p}(t)),$$

or in vector form

$$\frac{d\mathbf{p}(t)}{dt} \equiv \dot{\mathbf{p}}(t) = \mathbf{z}(\mathbf{p}(t)), \tag{7.5}$$

where $\mathbf{p}$ is the price vector and $\mathbf{z}(\mathbf{p})$ is the excess demand associated with $\mathbf{p}$. We assume here that $\mathbf{z}(\mathbf{p})$ is single-valued. If a component $z_i(\mathbf{p})$ is positive, $\dot{p}_i$ is also positive, leading to an increase in p_i. The reverse is true when $z_i(\mathbf{p})$ is negative. Hence this process captures the essence of the tâtonnement argument.

If the excess demand function satisfies Walras' law (in the strong, equality form), the norm $\|\mathbf{p}(t)\|^2 \equiv \sum_{i=1}^m p_i(t)^2$ is constant on a solution path as stated below.

Lemma 7.1. *If* $\mathbf{z}(\mathbf{p})$ *satisfies* $\mathbf{p} \cdot \mathbf{z}(\mathbf{p}) \equiv 0$, *then* $\|\mathbf{p}(t)\|^2$ *is constant with respect to* t *in any solution to* (7.5).

Proof: We have $(d/dt)\|\mathbf{p}(t)\|^2 = 2\mathbf{p}(t) \cdot \dot{\mathbf{p}}(t) = 2\mathbf{p}(t) \cdot \mathbf{z}(\mathbf{p}(t)) = 0$. ∎

From the above we see that a solution of the system (7.5) travels on the surface of a sphere in m-dimensional space. The particular sphere is determined by the initial point.

In general very little more can be said about the convergence of the dynamic process (7.5). It is entirely possible that the solution will cycle around indefinitely, never approaching an equilibrium, even if a unique equilibrium exists. To ensure that the process does converge to the equilibrium, additional assumptions must be introduced.

Various assumptions have been found that guarantee convergence, but all of them are quite restrictive—amounting almost to the assumption that the economy has only a single consumer. By making this assumption directly, we can obtain a very simple proof of convergence.

Tâtonnement convergence theorem. *Suppose the economy has a single consumer. Suppose that the corresponding indirect utility function v has continuous partial derivatives and is bounded below and that there is a unique equilibrium price $\mathbf{p}^*$ with $\mathbf{z}(\mathbf{p}^*) = \mathbf{0}$. Then the tâtonnement process (7.5) converges to $\mathbf{p}^*$.*

Proof: For simplicity we assume that there is no production. Let

$$V(t) = v(\mathbf{p}(t), \mathbf{p}(t) \cdot \mathbf{w}).$$

We compute

$$\dot{V}(t) = \nabla_{\mathbf{p}} v(\mathbf{p}, \mathbf{p} \cdot \mathbf{w}) \cdot \dot{\mathbf{p}} + \frac{\partial v(\mathbf{p}, \mathbf{p} \cdot \mathbf{w})}{\partial r} \dot{\mathbf{p}} \cdot \mathbf{w}.$$

By Roy's identity this can be written

$$\dot{V}(t) = [-\mathbf{x}(\mathbf{p}, \mathbf{p} \cdot \mathbf{w}) + \mathbf{w}] \cdot \dot{\mathbf{p}} \frac{\partial v(\mathbf{p}, \mathbf{p} \cdot \mathbf{w})}{\partial r} = -\|\mathbf{z}(\mathbf{p})\|^2 \frac{\partial v(\mathbf{p}, \mathbf{p} \cdot \mathbf{w})}{\partial r}.$$

Since $\partial v / \partial r > 0$, it follows that $\dot{V}(t) < 0$ unless $\mathbf{z}(\mathbf{p}) = \mathbf{0}$. Hence $V(t)$ is monotonically decreasing. Since $V(t)$ is bounded below, it must converge to a limit $\underline{V}$. By continuity of $\dot{V}$, it follows that $\dot{V} = 0$ at $V = \underline{V}$. Therefore, $\mathbf{z}(\mathbf{p}(t)) \rightarrow \mathbf{0}$, implying that $\mathbf{p}(t) \rightarrow \mathbf{p}^*$. ∎

Other Processes

The tâtonnement process is rather artificial, and it is generally regarded only as a simple mechanism illustrating how dynamics can be incorporated into equilibrium theory. There are many generalizations of the idea, some of which allow trading along the path to equilibrium. In most models, however, as in a real economy, the actual equilibrium is itself affected by the process, since trades out of equilibrium tend to change the effective individual endowments.

Consider an exchange economy. A simple process for achieving *an* equilibrium is just to let individuals trade among themselves. An individual engages in a trade only if that trade will increase utility. Hence, the trading process monotonically increases all utility levels until no further increase can be made. The resulting point is by definition Pareto efficient, and hence, under appropriate assumptions (especially convexity), the final allocation will define an equilibrium. It will be found that at the end of the process, trades at the margin will occur at the equilibrium prices.

This simple process does lead to *an* equilibrium, but not necessarily to the Walras equilibrium specified by the original endowments. It is likely that during the process trades will be made with terms that are not in accord with the Walras equilibrium prices, and therefore one party, although achieving a utility increase, will lose relative to what could be achieved using these prices. For this reason the final equilibrium may differ from the Walras equilibrium.

Part II
SPECIAL MODELS

7.14   Quasi-Linear Models

General equilibrium theory provides a good foundation for analysis of perfectly competitive economies, but to apply the theory in real situations it is valuable to develop specific model structures. The remainder of this chapter presents a few of these important structures.

A Basic Quasi-Linear Model

Suppose there are $m + 1$ commodities, with a typical bundle written as $(\mathbf{x}, z)$ with[2] $\mathbf{x} \geq \mathbf{0}$. Suppose a utility function defined over such bundles is of the form $v(\mathbf{x}) + z$. This is termed a *quasi-linear* form.

Let us take z as the reference commodity; that is, we take $\mathbf{g} = (\mathbf{0}, 1)$. Then the benefit function is

$$b(\mathbf{x}, z, u) = \max\{\beta : v(\mathbf{x}) + z - \beta \geq u\}.$$

Hence

$$b(\mathbf{x}, z, u) = v(\mathbf{x}) + z - u.$$

We also normalize prices so that they have the form $(\mathbf{p}, 1)$. Then z has the same price as income itself. Therefore $v(\mathbf{x})$ can be regarded as the *willingness to pay* for $\mathbf{x}$ measured in income terms—that is, the consumer is indifferent between $\mathbf{x}$ and an increment of z equal to $v(\mathbf{x})$.

---

[2]Note that we do not require $z \geq 0$. This greatly simplifies use of the quasi-linear utility function.

Now suppose there are n consumers with utility functions $v_i(\mathbf{x}_i) + z_i$ for $i = 1, 2, \ldots, n$. Consider an exchange economy with these individuals. According to the zero-maximum principle, the equilibrium will solve

$$\max_{\mathbf{x}_i, z_i} \sum_{i=1}^{n} v_i(\mathbf{x}_i) + z_i - u_i^*$$

$$\text{sub to } \sum_{i=1}^{n} \mathbf{x}_i \leq \mathbf{w}$$

$$\sum_{i=1}^{n} z_i \leq z^0,$$

where $(\mathbf{w}, z^0)$ comprises the aggregate endowments. We see that the equilibrium $\mathbf{x}_i^*$'s solve the problem

$$\max \sum_{i=1}^{n} v_i(\mathbf{x}_i)$$

$$\text{sub to } \sum_{i=1}^{n} \mathbf{x}_i \leq \mathbf{w}.$$

This single optimization problem characterizes any equilibrium. Hence, an equilibrium maximizes the total willingness to pay.

Oriented Quadratic Model

Consider a utility function of the form

$$u(\mathbf{x}) = \overline{\mathbf{d}} \cdot \mathbf{x} - \tfrac{1}{2} \mathbf{x} \cdot \overline{\mathbf{Q}} \mathbf{x}$$

where the matrix $\overline{\mathbf{Q}}$ is positive semidefinite but possesses one degree of singularity. The vector $\mathbf{g} \neq \mathbf{0}$ satisfies $\overline{\mathbf{Q}} \mathbf{g} = \mathbf{0}$. The utility function is said to be *oriented* in the direction $\mathbf{g}$. An example is the utility function $u(x_1, x_2) = 2x_1 + 3x_3 - (x_1 - x_2)^2$, which is oriented in the direction $(1, 1)$. Such a utility function has a curved shape that can serve as a local approximation to any smoothly shaped set of indifference curves. It behaves like a quasi-linear utility except that the role of the linear commodity z in the basic quasi-linear model is now played by the combination of commodities making up $\mathbf{g}$. Increments of $\mathbf{g}$ are reflected linearly in u. (Try it for the two-dimensional example.)

If we assume that the vector $\mathbf{x}$ is not constrained by $\mathbf{x} \geq \mathbf{0}$, we can analyze this model by the same techniques as in the quasi-linear model and get more explicit results. To carry out the analysis we simply change coordinates so that $\mathbf{g}$ becomes one of the new coordinate directions—the last one. (The mechanics of this transformation are linear, but we omit the details here.) We denote this last coordinate by z and the utility function takes the form $u(\mathbf{x}) = \mathbf{d} \cdot \mathbf{x} - \tfrac{1}{2} \mathbf{x} \cdot \mathbf{Q} \mathbf{x} + z$, where the dimensions of the new vector $\mathbf{x}$ and the new $\mathbf{Q}$ and $\mathbf{d}$ are all one less than above. This is now a special case of the quasi-linear form.

The benefit maximization problem becomes

$$\max \sum_{i=1}^{n} \mathbf{d}_i \cdot \mathbf{x}_i - \frac{1}{2}\mathbf{x}_i \cdot \mathbf{Q}_i \mathbf{x}_i$$

$$\text{sub to } \sum_{i=1}^{n} \mathbf{x}_i = \mathbf{w}.$$

With $\mathbf{p}$ as the Lagrange multiplier, this has solution $\mathbf{x}_i = -\mathbf{Q}_i^{-1}\mathbf{p} - \mathbf{d}_i$. We can find $\mathbf{p}$ from the constraint equation, which yields $\mathbf{p} = -\mathbf{Q}\mathbf{d} + \mathbf{w}$, where $\mathbf{Q} = \left[\sum_{i=1}^{n} \mathbf{Q}_i^{-1}\right]^{-1}$ and $\mathbf{d} = \sum_{i=1}^{n} \mathbf{d}_i$. Thus we have an explicit solution to this interesting model.

The Assignment Model

A useful structure is an *assignment economy*. Consider a market for an indivisible product, such as housing. Suppose there are n sellers, each of whom has exactly one such item for sale, and m buyers, each of whom wishes to buy at most one item. The value to the ith seller of that seller's item is c_i dollars. The jth buyer values the same item at h_{ij} dollars. These are actual willingness-to-pay values. The problem of the assignment economy is for buyers to be assigned to sellers and for items and money to be correspondingly exchanged.

The willingness-to-pay terms will always come in pairs, corresponding to a buyer and a seller. Suppose seller i is assigned to buyer j. The net willingness to pay for that pair is $a_{ij} = \max\{0, h_{ij} - c_i\}$, since by exchange the buyer gains h_{ij} and the seller loses c_i. Any associated monetary exchange cancels out. They can choose not to exchange at all, yielding 0.

From the basic quasi-linear model, we know that the equilibrium will maximize the total net willingness to pay, summed over all assigned pairs of sellers and buyers. To formulate this problem, we introduce the variables x_{ij} for $i = 1, 2, \ldots, n$ and $j = 1, 2, \ldots, m$. We put $x_{ij} = 1$ if seller i is assigned to buyer j, and we put $x_{ij} = 0$ otherwise. The problem of maximizing the total willingness to pay is then

$$\max \sum_{i,j} a_{ij} x_{ij}$$

$$\text{sub to } \sum_{j=1}^{m} x_{ij} \le 1 \quad \text{for all } i = 1, 2, \ldots, n$$

$$\sum_{i=1}^{n} x_{ij} \le 1 \quad \text{for all } j = 1, 2, \ldots, m$$

$$x_{ij} = 0 \quad \text{or} \quad x_{ij} = 1 \quad \text{for all } i, j.$$

The first constraint says that at most one buyer can be assigned to any seller, and the second says that at most one seller can be assigned to any buyer.

It can be shown that the optimal value of this problem is unchanged if the constraint that $x_{ij} = 0$ or $x_{ij} = 1$ is relaxed to simply $x_{ij} \geq 0$. This considerably simplifies the problem, for it then becomes a linear programming problem. The solution of that linear program therefore provides a solution to the assignment economy.

The Lagrange multiplier of the constraint $\sum_{j=1}^{m} x_{ij} \leq 1$ is the price of the commodity owned by the ith seller. This price can be found by solving the dual of the linear program.

7.15 Leontief Systems

In a *Leontief system* there are m produced commodities and m industries. Each industry produces exactly one of the commodities as output. The inputs required by an industry are those produced by the other industries plus an additional *primary* input, usually thought of as labor. The Leontief model is a description of the *input-output* relations holding between industries and is often alternatively referred to as an input-output model.

Example 7.5.   An economy has just two industries, wheat and iron. Production of each unit of wheat requires 0.1 units of wheat (for seed and animal feed), 0.2 units of iron (for tools), and 1.0 unit of labor. Production of each unit of iron requires 0.3 units of iron and 0.5 units of labor. (See Table 7.1, where the columns represent the production "recipes.")

If q_1 and q_2 represent the amounts of production of wheat and iron, respectively, and d_1 and d_2 represent the surplus after use in production of these commodities, then the following must hold:

$$q_1 = 0.1q_1 + 0.0q_2 + d_1$$
$$q_2 = 0.2q_1 + 0.3q_2 + d_2$$
$$L = \quad q_1 + 0.5q_2 .$$

The first equation is the wheat balance equation. Total production is equal to that required by each of the industries plus the wheat surplus. The second

TABLE 7.1   A simple economy

Input	Output	
	Wheat	Iron
Wheat	0.1	0.0
Iron	0.2	0.3
Labor	1.0	0.5

equation is the iron balance equation, and the third equation gives the total labor requirement.

In general, a Leontief system is defined by an $m \times m$ matrix **A** of *input-output coefficients* a_{ij} and a vector **b** of primary input coefficients. The coefficient a_{ij} is the amount of commodity i required to produce one unit of commodity j, and the coefficient b_j is the amount of labor required to produce one unit of commodity j. The coefficients a_{ij} and b_j are all non-negative. The diagonal terms a_{ii}, $i = 1, 2, \ldots, m$, are frequently assumed to be zero, but we allow them to be positive as well. The input-output relations are linear (or exhibit constant returns to scale) in the sense that an increase in production by a factor $\alpha > 0$ of the output of an industry requires that each input be increased by α.

If an aggregate bundle of commodities is to be produced for final consumption—say d_i of commodity i, for $i = 1, 2, \ldots, m$—each industry i must produce d_i plus what is used as input in other industries. This yields the equations

$$q_i = \sum_{i=1}^{m} a_{ij}q_i + d_i, \qquad i = 1, 2, \ldots, m,$$

or in vector-matrix form

$$\mathbf{q} = \mathbf{Aq} + \mathbf{d}. \tag{7.6}$$

In addition there is the labor equation

$$L = \mathbf{b} \cdot \mathbf{q}.$$

Leontief Production Functions

The above description of a Leontief system does not explicitly refer to the production functions of the industries. It should be no surprise, however, that the Leontief model is based on Leontief production functions.

As before, suppose the production of one unit of commodity j requires a_{ij} units of commodity i and b_j units of labor. Additional amounts of *some* of the inputs will not yield additional output; *all* inputs must be increased in order to increase output. If the level of commodity inputs to industry j are $z_{1j}, z_{2j}, \ldots, z_{mj}$ and labor is l_j, then the output is

$$q_j = \min\left\{ \frac{z_{1j}}{a_{1j}}, \frac{z_{2j}}{a_{2j}}, \ldots, \frac{z_{mj}}{a_{mj}}, \frac{l_j}{b_j} \right\}, \tag{7.7}$$

which is the Leontief, or fixed-proportions, technology introduced in Chapter 2.

Prices in a Leontief System

Suppose now that prices are assigned to the m commodities and represented by the positive vector $\mathbf{p}$, and as a reference suppose the price of labor is 1. The cost to produce a unit of commodity i is then $\sum_{j=1}^{m} a_{ji} p_j + b_i$, since a_{ji} units of commodity j, $j = 1, 2, \ldots, m$, are required. The profit associated with a unit of production in industry i is therefore $p_i - \sum_{j=1}^{m} a_{ji} p_j - b_i$. Since each industry has a constant-returns-to-scale technology, the profit should be zero in each industry under perfect competition. Assuming the industries produce at positive levels, this means that the unit profits must all be zero. This condition is

$$\mathbf{p} = \mathbf{A}^{\mathrm{T}} \mathbf{p} + \mathbf{b}. \tag{7.8}$$

If the Leontief system is "productive,"[3] this system of equations has a nonnegative solution $\mathbf{p}$ for every $\mathbf{b} \geq \mathbf{0}$, and the original system (7.6) has a nonnegative solution $\mathbf{q}$ for every $\mathbf{d} \geq \mathbf{0}$.

Example 7.6. For the wheat and iron economy the prices must satisfy

$$0 = p_1 - 0.1 p_1 - 0.2 p_2 - 1.0$$
$$0 = p_2 - \qquad 0.3 p_2 - 0.5.$$

Indeed $p_1 = 80/63$, and $p_2 = 5/7$.

In a productive Leontief model under perfect competition and with a single primary factor such as labor, prices are uniquely determined by the production structure. Demand does not enter the system of equations (7.8) that determine $\mathbf{p}$. Therefore the price of a given manufactured good can be determined from the cost of the inputs that enter its production. It is not necessary to know anything about demand; the production process and the prices of the input factors are all that must be known to determine the equilibrium price of the given good.

Matrix Inversion in Practice

Most firms are naturally very concerned about possible changes in industry output levels or prices. Therefore, in the light of the previous discussion, we might expect a concerned firm to construct a (large) table of input-output coefficients representing the entire economy. Then, if the firm had a forecast of consumption $\mathbf{d}$, it could determine required industry output as $\mathbf{q} = (\mathbf{I} - \mathbf{A})^{-1} \mathbf{d}$. Or if the firm anticipated a technological innovation, which

---

[3]For it to be productive, $\mathbf{A}$ must have small component values. In particular, the eigenvalues of $\mathbf{A}$ must be less than 1 in magnitude.

would change the values of some of the coefficients a_{ij}, it could predict the new prices from $\mathbf{p} = (\mathbf{I} - \mathbf{A}^T)^{-1}\mathbf{b}$. However, real firms do not often build such models. Why is that?

To be reliable, the input-output matrix for a real economy must be very large, and obtaining the data for such a matrix is extremely costly. Furthermore, the final result is not likely to be very accurate in the sectors of interest to a given firm. However, for the sake of argument, suppose that such a matrix were available. Although it would be large, it would also be sparse; that is, there would be relatively few nonzero terms. In fact, in the row of the matrix corresponding to a given industry i, there would generally be only a few significant terms, corresponding to the industries that use the output of industry i as direct input. This fact can be exploited in the computation of output requirements.

We may write

$$(\mathbf{I} - \mathbf{A})^{-1} = \mathbf{I} + \mathbf{A} + \mathbf{A}^2 + \mathbf{A}^3 + \cdots.$$

This series will converge if the economy is productive, and it will converge rapidly if the economy is highly productive. In order to evaluate q_i, it is only necessary to know the ith row of $(\mathbf{I} - \mathbf{A})^{-1}$, not the entire matrix. Firm i can perform this evaluation by using the series above and the sparsity of the matrix. The terms in the ith row of $\mathbf{A}$ correspond to direct supplies from firm i to other industries. The terms in the ith row of $\mathbf{A}^2$ are supplies from i required to (indirectly) supply the second-tier firms that those first firms supply, and so forth. The firm can combine this information with the consumption forecasts to obtain an overall forecast that approximates q_i. This procedure is likely to be satisfactory in many cases, and it certainly resembles common practice, where firms keep careful track of conditions in their major market industries and in associated indirect markets. For more refined analyses an explicit analytic model may be valuable, but as evidenced from this discussion, this model should be tailored to the industry being considered.

*7.16   General Production Analysis

In many economic models, the production sector is much more elaborate than the consumer sector. One reason for this is that the structure of the production sector is based on clearly defined technological relations, and hence this sector can be defined somewhat more objectively than the consumer sector. In other words, the production sector lends itself naturally to detailed sophisticated modeling.

Another, perhaps better, reason that more attention is often devoted to modeling the production sector is that the structure of the production sector often by itself determines important price relations. The extreme example of this is a Leontief model, where the production sector completely determines prices, independent of demand. In more general models, prices are not completely independent of demand, but the production sector alone may determine several important price relations. Hence it is often actually quite appropriate to develop a detailed production sector model and a simple demand model. This structure implies that solution methods will also focus primarily on the production sector. This section outlines some methods that result from this viewpoint.

Cost Minimization

Suppose a sector of an economy consists of K firms. The activity of the sector as a whole is described by a netput vector of the form $(-\mathbf{z}, \mathbf{q})$. The vector $\mathbf{q}$ represents output from the sector, which may go to consumption or other sectors; and the vector $\mathbf{z}$ represents inputs to the sector, which may come from other sectors. Each firm k in the sector has a convex production possibility set Y_k. The aggregate production possibility set of the sector is $Y = \sum_{k=1}^{K} Y_k$.

The sector is coupled to the rest of the economy by specifying input prices $\mathbf{w}$ and an aggregate output[4] $\mathbf{q}^*$. In some cases these values can be assumed to be determined by the rest of the economy. In other cases they must simply be regarded as parameters or assumptions that might be varied later in order to meet overall equilibrium conditions. Given $\mathbf{w}$ and $\mathbf{q}^*$, we wish to determine the input vector $\mathbf{z}$, the commodity flows, and the prices of outputs. See Fig. 7.11. In perfect competition all firms maximize profit with respect to a common set of prices, or they simply minimize cost if there are output requirements. In our situation the aggregate production sector will act as a single firm, minimizing cost to meet the aggregate output requirement. (This follows from the basic efficiency principles of Chapter 6.) Therefore the appropriate $\mathbf{z}$ can be

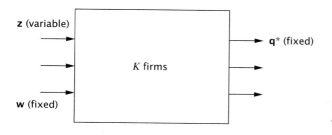

z (variable)

q* (fixed)

K firms

w (fixed)

FIGURE 7.11 Production sector.

---

[4]There may be intermediate goods as well, that is, goods that are only produced and used within the sector. These can be treated as sector outputs whose levels are all zero (or greater).

found by treating the sector as a single firm. Hence, we may determine $\mathbf{z}$ by solving

$$\min \ \mathbf{w} \cdot \mathbf{z} \tag{7.9}$$
$$\text{sub to } (-\mathbf{z}, \mathbf{q}^*) \in \mathcal{Y}.$$

Although this is a simple principle, it forms a very effective basis for actual computations. It reduces the problem of solving the production sector to a single optimization problem. We duplicate the result of perfect competition by solving this centralized cost minimization problem.

Example 7.7 (An electric power sector). Suppose electric power is required at two locations in fixed quantities q_1 and q_2. Power is generated from coal, which has price w_1 and w_2 at the two locations, respectively, and there are power plants at both locations. Power can be transmitted from one location to the other, although there will be losses so that only a fraction α of what is sent is received at the destination. See Fig. 7.12. Power is generated from coal according to production function f. This sector problem can be formulated as follows:

$$
\begin{aligned}
\min \quad & w_1 x_1 + w_2 x_2 \\
\text{sub to} \quad & x_3 + x_4 && \leq f(x_1) \\
& \qquad\qquad x_5 + x_6 \leq f(x_2) \\
& x_3 \qquad + \alpha x_5 \qquad \geq q_1 \\
& \qquad \alpha x_4 \qquad + x_6 \geq q_2 \\
& x_i \geq 0, \quad i = 1, 2, 3, 4, 5, 6.
\end{aligned}
$$

The solution to this problem yields the required coal inputs x_1 and x_2 as well as the value of intermediate production variables. The Lagrange mul-

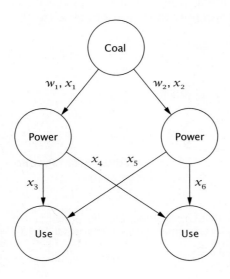

FIGURE 7.12   Power production example.

tipliers of the last two constraints are the competitive prices for power at the two locations. (Models of this type with hundreds of variables accounting for different energy types, transportation, conversion, different time periods, etc. have been used for both private investment analysis and public policy analysis.)

Duality

The above approach is direct, but it requires that the sector's production be computed in a centralized manner. An alternative approach, based on duality, decentralizes the production decisions, with each firm responding individually to prices. In the dual formulation of the sector's problem, prices rather than individual production plans are the unknowns. In this dual formulation, it turns out that the equilibrium solution *maximizes* an expression like cost.

The basis for the dual approach is the zero-minimum principle. Consider again the sector problem discussed above. We can treat the requirement $\mathbf{q} = \mathbf{q}^*$ as if there is an aggregate endowment of $-\mathbf{q}^*$. We assume also that intermediate goods are not consumed (by consumers). Hence, the expenditure functions depend only on the input price vector $\mathbf{w}$ (which is fixed). Therefore we can neglect the expenditure function and minimize surplus as

$$\min_{\mathbf{p}} \ -\mathbf{p}\cdot\mathbf{q}^* + \pi(\mathbf{w},\mathbf{p}),$$

or equivalently,

$$\max_{\mathbf{p}} \ \mathbf{p}\cdot\mathbf{q}^* - \pi(\mathbf{w},\mathbf{p}).$$

The profit function $\pi(\mathbf{w},\mathbf{p})$ is found from

$$\pi(\mathbf{w},\mathbf{p}) = \sum_{k=1}^{K} \pi_k(\mathbf{w},\mathbf{p}),$$

where π_k is the profit function of the kth firm.

Note that the expression $\mathbf{p}\cdot\mathbf{q}^* - \sum_{k=1}^{K} \pi_k(\mathbf{w},\mathbf{p})$ itself can be interpreted as a cost associated with prices $(\mathbf{w},\mathbf{p})$ and aggregate production $\mathbf{q}^*$. The first term is the total revenue associated with $\mathbf{q}^*$, and the summation is the profit associated with the prices. Revenue minus profit is cost (although this is not a true cost because revenue assumes that $\mathbf{q} = \mathbf{q}^*$, but profit does not). Hence we select $\mathbf{p}$ to maximize this dual cost function.

The procedure implied by the above duality theorem is decentralized, since to determine the prices it is only necessary to know the profit function of each industry. It is not necessary to consider every possible production plan, as in the previous minimum-cost procedure. This is very useful if the production model contains detailed submodels of individual industries, such that once prices are given (say over several years), detailed capital expansion and production plans can be deduced to evaluate profit.

Example 7.8.   Consider the electric power sector example treated above. Suppose the sector consists of two separate firms—the two power plants. Suppose the production function is $f(x) = \sqrt{x}$, and let p_1 and p_2 denote the price of power at the two locations. For the first plant

$$\pi_1(w_1, p_1, p_2) = \max \ p_1 x_3 + \alpha p_2 x_4 - w_1 x_1$$
$$\text{sub to } x_3 + x_4 \le \sqrt{x_1} .$$

This results in

$$\pi_1(w_1, p_1, p_2) = \frac{1}{4w_1} \max\{p_1^2, (\alpha p_2)^2\} ,$$

and a similar expression for $\pi_2(w_2, p_1, p_2)$. The prices can then be found as the solution to

$$\max_{p_1, \ p_2} \left\{ p_1 y_1 + p_2 y_2 - \frac{1}{4w_1} \max\{p_1^2, (\alpha p_2)^2\} - \frac{1}{4w_2} \max\{p_2^2, (\alpha p_1)^2\} \right\} .$$

(We cannot give a simple closed-form solution, but the solution can be found by treating separately the four cases implied by the two max operators, or it may be found numerically.)

7.17   Exercises

1. Consider a two-person, two-commodity, pure-exchange, competitive economy. The consumer's utility functions are

$$u_A(x_1, x_2) = x_1 x_2 + 12x_1 + 3x_2$$
$$u_B(x_1, x_2) = x_1 x_2 + 8x_1 + 9x_2 .$$

   Consumer A has initial endowments of 8 and 30 units of x_1 and x_2, respectively; consumer B has endowments of 10 units of each commodity. Determine the excess demand functions for the two consumers, and find an equilibrium price ratio for this economy. Sketch the situation in an Edgeworth box.

2. Consider the following two-person, two-period economy. Individual A earns income W_0 in period 0 and nothing in period 1. Individual B earns W_1 in period one and nothing in period 0. Individual B will borrow from individual A. Let r be the equilibrium interest rate. Also assume both A and B have utility functions of the following form: $U(c_0, c_1) = \ln c_0 + \beta \ln c_1, 0 < \beta < 1$, where c_0 and c_1 are consumption in periods 0 and 1, respectively. Determine the equilibrium interest rate in this economy. Is it always greater than 0?

3. (Interest rate with production)   Suppose n individuals have identical preferences for present consumption c_0 and future consumption c_1 given by

$$u(c_0, c_1) = \log c_0 + \alpha \log c_1$$

   and each has endowments $w_0 = 1$ and $w_1 = 0$. Each individual has an equal share in the economy's sole firm, which has a production function $q_1 = \beta(x_0)^{1/2}$, where q_1 denotes the funds produced in period 1 and x_0 denotes funds invested in period 0.

(a) Let $p = 1/(1+r)$ be the price of period 1 funds relative to period 0 funds. Set up and solve the firm's net present value maximization problem taking the interest rate r as given.

(b) Find the individuals' demands for present consumption, taking the interest rate as given.

(c) Solve for the interest rate in this economy.

(d) Suppose a technological improvement makes the economy more productive so that β increases. Will the interest rate increase or decrease?

4. (General equilibrium for infinitely many commodities) Suppose there are two consumers in an exchange economy that exists over an infinite number of time periods. Let x_i be consumption at time i, and suppose consumers 1 and 2 have the following intertemporal utility functions:

$$u_1(x_0, x_1, \ldots) = \sum_{i=0}^{\infty} \alpha^i \ln x_i$$

$$u_2(x_0, x_1, \ldots) = \sum_{i=0}^{\infty} \beta^i \ln x_i.$$

Suppose the endowment vectors for both consumers are $\mathbf{w} = (1, 1, \ldots)$. Solve for the equilibrium prices $p_1, p_2, \ldots$, taking $p_0 = 1$, and determine the demand functions for the first consumer at these prices. Interpret the prices by comparing the prices of commodities at adjacent time periods (such as x_i and x_{i+1}).

5. (Class demonstration—triangle game) This is a game for two players. Construct a triangle as shown in Fig. 7.13. Player A begins by putting a dot in one of the smaller corner triangles and draws a line across the boundary into the adjacent triangle. This triangle has only two labeled corners, so on the corner with no label player A puts a label (1, 2, or 3), but the new label

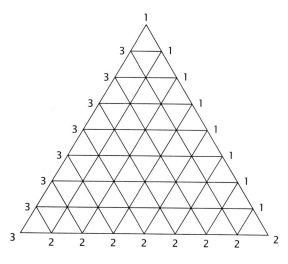

FIGURE 7.13 Triangle game.

must duplicate one of the other two. Player B continues from this new triangle. In general, a player moves across a boundary with two different labels
into an adjacent triangle. If all three corners of this triangle are labeled,
the player moves again through another boundary with two different labels. When the player finally enters a triangle with an unlabeled corner,
that player assigns a label, duplicating one of the two existing labels, and
the next player takes over from there.

A player loses if he or she enters a triangle that has three distinct labels
(1, 2, and 3). Play this game, and show that it always must end.

6. Construct a large triangle and divide it as in Fig. 7.6, with each side divided
   into eight segments. Find an approximate equilibrium point for Example
   7.1 by applying the algorithm at the end of Section 7.5 on the triangular
   structure.

7. The nonretraction theorem states that there is no continuous mapping from
   the unit ball $B = \{\mathbf{x} : \|\mathbf{x}\| \le 1\}$ in $\mathcal{R}^n$ onto its surface $S = \{\mathbf{x} : \|\mathbf{x}\| = 1\}$. Use
   this to prove the Brouwer fixed point theorem. Hint: This requires a very
   short one-line proof.

8. Prove the Brouwer fixed point theorem for the two-dimensional simplex
   $S^2 = \{\mathbf{x} : \sum_{i=1}^{3} x_i = 1, \ x_i \ge 0, \ i = 1, 2, 3\}$ using Sperner's lemma. Hint: Assign labels l to vertices as follows. On an edge vertex $\mathbf{x}$, assign $l(\mathbf{x}) = i$ where
   i is the first zero component; on an interior vertex $\mathbf{x}$, assign $l(\mathbf{x}) = i$ where
   i is such that $x_i \le f_i(\mathbf{x})$. Find an approximate fixed point.

9. Consider a two-commodity, productive economy of N individuals, each with
   the same utility $u(x, y) = xy$. They are co-owners of one firm whose production function is given by $y = x^\alpha$, $0 < \alpha < 1$. In addition to an initial
   endowment of one unit of x, individual i receives a fraction $\theta_i \ge 0$ of the
   firm's profit π. All profit is distributed. Determine the equilibrium price p
   of y in terms of N and α. Set the price of x to 1.

10. On an island economy the only basic resources available are labor time $T = 12$ and land $L = 24$. With these factors strawberries s and wheat w can be
    grown according to the production functions

    $$s = \min\{\tfrac{1}{2}t_1, l_1\}$$

    $$w = \min\{t_2, l_2\}.$$

    All individuals have utility function $u = sw/(t_1 + t_2)$.

    (a) Formulate a problem that when solved will yield the competitive values
        of s, w, l, and t.

    (b) Find the competitive solution and prices expressed relative to the price
        of time.

11. (a) The equilibrium price $\mathbf{p}^*$ of the Cobb–Douglas world satisfies $\mathbf{p}^* = A^T S \mathbf{p}^*$, which is an mth-order system. Show that $\mathbf{p}^*$ can alternatively
        be found by solving the nth-order system

        $$\mathbf{q}^* = SA^T \mathbf{q}^* .$$

(b) Consider an exchange economy with two consumers and three commodities. The two utility functions and endowment vectors are

$$u_A = xyz^2, \qquad u_B = xy^2z$$
$$\mathbf{w}_B = (2,1,3), \qquad \mathbf{w}_B = (2,3,1).$$

Formulate this economy as a Cobb-Douglas world, and find the equilibrium prices $\mathbf{p}$.

12. Consider the constant-returns-to-scale Cobb-Douglas production function

$$q = z_1^{\beta_1} z_2^{\beta_2} \cdots z_m^{\beta_m},$$

where $\beta_j > 0$ and $\sum_{j=1}^m \beta_j = 1$. Let the output price be p and the input prices be w_j, $j = 1, 2, \ldots, m$. Show that for positive production to occur under perfect competition, the prices must satisfy

$$p = \left(\frac{w_1}{\beta_1}\right)^{\beta_1} \left(\frac{w_2}{\beta_2}\right)^{\beta_2} \cdots \left(\frac{w_m}{\beta_m}\right)^{\beta_m}.$$

13. (Walras computation) Consider the algorithm for finding a Walras equilibrium presented at the end of Section 7.5. Let C be the completely labeled simplex. Suppose δ is the width of an edge, and let $\varepsilon > 0$ be such that no component of $\mathbf{z}(\mathbf{p})$ varies by more than ε over C. Index the vertices of C by their labels and denote the price at i by $\mathbf{p}^i$. Let $I \subset \{1, 2, 3\}$ be the set of vertices of C internal to S^2 (as opposed to on the boundary). Let M be the maximum component value of $\mathbf{z}$ at an internal vertex, and let m be the minimum at a boundary vertex. Show that

(a) $z_i(\mathbf{p}^i) \le M + \varepsilon$ for all i.

(b) $z_i(\mathbf{p}^i) \ge M - \varepsilon$ for $i \in I$.

(c) $z_i(\mathbf{p}^i) \ge m$ for $i \notin I$.

Use Walras' law to show

$$0 = \sum_{i \in I} p_i^* z_i(\mathbf{p}^*) + \sum_{i \notin I} p_i^* z_i(\mathbf{p}^*) \ge M - 2\varepsilon - \delta |m|,$$

and hence $M \le 2\varepsilon + \delta |m|$. Thus from (a) we know that $\mathbf{z}(\mathbf{p})$ is an approximate equilibrium.

14. Suppose there are n consumers and two commodities. The ith consumer has utility function

$$u_i(x_1, x_2) = d_1^i x_1 + d_2^i x_2 + \tfrac{1}{2}(x_1 - x_2)^2,$$

where $d_1^i + d_2^i = 1$. Consumer i also has endowments w_1^i and w_2^i of the two commodities. Find the Walras equilibrium. Hint: Normalize prices so that $p_1 + p_2 = 1$, and work directly without using the general formula.

15. Individuals A and B are farmers, and each will grow an amount w_1 of corn in period 1 and an amount w_2 of corn in period 2. However, A and B have different preferences for corn in the two periods, represented by utility functions of the form $u_A(c_1^A, c_2^A) = \ln c_1^A + \alpha \ln c_2^A$, $0 < \alpha < 1$, and $u_B(c_1^B, c_2^B) = \ln c_1^B + \beta \ln c_2^B$, $0 < \beta < 1$, respectively.

TABLE 7.2 Units of corn received per contract.

	Contract a	Type b
Period 1	-1	-1
Period 2	2	1

Instead of borrowing and lending corn directly, individuals exchange *contracts* having the terms shown in Table 7.2.

For example, a *buyer* of one contract of type a agrees to deliver one unit of corn in period 1 and is entitled to receive two units of corn in period 2. An individual's endowments of corn may be regarded as initial endowments of contract through the relation

$$\mathbf{A}\begin{bmatrix} y_a \\ y_b \end{bmatrix} = \begin{bmatrix} w_1 \\ w_2 \end{bmatrix}$$

where y_a and y_b are endowments of type a and b contracts, respectively, and $\mathbf{A}$ is the payoff matrix (Table 7.2).

(a) Let p_a and p_b be the prices of the two contracts. Formulate individual A's problem as one of choosing x_a and x_b contracts of types a and b so as to maximize utility of consumption.

(b) Eliminate x_a and x_b from the problem by expressing them in terms of c_1 and c_2. Recast individual A's problem as one of choosing c_1 and c_2 directly. Give an expression for the "real prices" ϕ_1 and ϕ_2 of consumption in terms of the contract prices p_a and p_b.

(c) Derive A's demand function for c_1^A in terms of the real prices ϕ_1 and ϕ_2.

(d) Find the equilibrium real price ratio ϕ_2/ϕ_1 in terms of α, β, w_1, and w_2.

(e) Suppose a new contract is introduced, requiring the holder to deliver one unit of corn in period 1 and entitling the holder to receive three units of corn in period 2. What is the price of this new contract?

16. A country has a large number of competitive firms and produces only two commodities: watches and cheese. Watches are sold at the world price of $40 each, and cheese is sold at a world price of $16 per round. Both products require inputs of capital and labor and are produced at constant returns to scale according to the table below:

	Capital	Labor
1 watch	0.2	1.0
1 round of cheese	0.1	0.1

The country has a yearly supply of 2,000 units of capital and 6,000 units of labor. The residents of the country consume many goods, including the two that they produce; the other goods consumed are purchased on the world market. Revenues obtained through the sale of watches and cheese support these purchases. Find the amounts of watches and cheese produced and the equilibrium prices of capital and labor. How do these answers depend on the country's consumption preferences?

17. Use the zero-minimum principle to find the equilibrium price vector for the Cobb-Douglas world.

18. Consumers A and B each have utility $u(x_1, x_2) = x_1^\alpha x^{1-\alpha}$, $\alpha > 0$. A fixed bundle $\mathbf{w} = (w_1, w_2)$ is to be distributed between them. Assume that in the final distribution they obtain utility values u_A and u_B, respectively. Let $\mathbf{g} = (1, 0)$, and formulate the corresponding benefit maximization problem. Show that if the distribution is Pareto efficient, then

$$\frac{x_1^B}{x_1^A} = \frac{x_2^A}{x_2^B} = \frac{u_A}{u_B}.$$

19. We say that the excess demand function satisfies the weak axiom of revealed preference if the following is true: if $\mathbf{z(p)} \neq \mathbf{z(p')}$, then $\mathbf{p \cdot z(p')} \leq \mathbf{p \cdot z(p)}$ implies that $\mathbf{p' \cdot z(p)} > \mathbf{p' \cdot z(p')}$. Show that if $\mathbf{z(p)}$ is continuous, satisfies Walras' law, is homogeneous of degree zero, and satisfies the weak axiom of revealed preference, and if there is a unique $\mathbf{p^*}$ with $\mathbf{z(p^*)} = \mathbf{0}$, then the tâtonnement process converges to $\mathbf{p^*}$. Hint: Show that the function $f(t) = \frac{1}{2}\|\mathbf{p}(t) - \mathbf{p^*}\|^2$ is monotonically decreasing.

20. (Stability of price adjustment) Given the following excess demand functions for three commodities $z_1 = 1 - p_1^2$, $z_2 = -p_1 p_2$, and $z_3 = -p_1 p_3$ on the unit sphere $p_1^2 + p_2^2 + p_3^2 = 1$, determine whether the price adjustment mechanism

$$\frac{dp_i}{dt} = z_i(\mathbf{p})$$

converges to the equilibrium price vector $\mathbf{p^*}$.

21. Given the excess demand functions for two commodities

$$z_1(\mathbf{p}) = \frac{1}{2p_1}(p_1 + 2p_2) - 1$$

$$z_2(\mathbf{p}) = \frac{1}{2p_2}(p_1 + 2p_2) - 2,$$

(a) Is Walras' law satisfied?

(b) Find the equilibrium price vector $\mathbf{p^*}$ (normalize with $p_2^* = 1$).

(c) Show that the tâtonnement process will converge to the equilibrium. Hint: Show that $\frac{1}{2}\|\mathbf{p}-\mathbf{p^*}\|^2$ decreases monotonically. Note that $x+1/x > 2$ for any $x > 0$, $x \neq 1$.

22. A five-sector Leontief system $\mathbf{q} = \mathbf{Aq} + \mathbf{d}$ has

$$\mathbf{A} = \begin{bmatrix} 0.1 & 0.5 & 0.0 & 0.1 & 0.0 \\ 0.0 & 0.0 & 0.2 & 0.0 & 0.0 \\ 0.0 & 0.0 & 0.2 & 0.0 & 0.2 \\ 0.0 & 0.2 & 0.0 & 0.1 & 0.0 \\ 0.1 & 0.0 & 0.1 & 0.0 & 0.0 \end{bmatrix}.$$

The units have been chosen so that the entries are in monetary units. Suppose the demand for sector 2 goods is increased by 1 unit. How much will total output in the first sector increase? (Find the result to two places beyond the decimal point.)

23. (Nonsubstitution theorem) Suppose there are n industries and n produced goods, with each industry producing a single good with a constant-returns-to-scale technology that uses as inputs the n produced goods plus labor. Let $c_i(\mathbf{p}, t)$ be the cost per unit function for the ith industry where $\mathbf{p}$ is the n-dimensional vector of prices for the produced goods and t is the price of labor.

    (a) If $t = 1$, show that if all industries produce positive output under perfect competition, then the prices must satisfy the system of equations

$$p_i = c_i(\mathbf{p}, 1) \qquad i = 1, 2, \ldots, n.$$

    (b) Suppose labor is essential to production in each industry in the sense that

$$c_i(\mathbf{p}, t) < c_i(\mathbf{p}, 1)$$

    for $0 \le t < 1$ and for each i. Show that in this case the solution to the system in part (a) is unique. Conclude that as the output varies, prices do not vary, and the *means* of production do not vary—that is, industries vary output by just scaling a given production process. No new processes are substituted as output varies.

7.18   References

7.1–7.4   The concept of a competitive equilibrium is due to Walras (1874,1877). The first rigorous analysis was carried out by Wald (1936,1951). The modern treatment was developed principally by Arrow and Debreu. See Arrow and Hahn (1971), Debreu (1952), Debreu (1959), and McKenzie (1959). Good textbooks in this area are Lancaster (1968), Takayama (1974), and Quirk and Saposnik (1968). The structure of the Cobb-Douglas world when the E matrix is not strictly positive is discussed in Afriat (1987) and Eaves (1985).

7.5   A fixed point algorithm first appeared in Lemke and Howson (1964) and Lemke (1965). These methods have been greatly improved by the incorporation of vector labeling methods. See Scarf (1982) for a good overview on the application of these methods to general equilibrium problems.

7.9–7.10   The zero-minimum method of proof is presented in Luenberger (1994b). For computational results using this method see Luenberger and Maxfield (1995).

7.12   See Arrow and Hahn (1971) for the gross substitutes proposition.

7.13   The tâtonnement concept was formulated mathematically as a system of differential equations by Samuelson (1947). For additional results on the behavior of such systems see Arrow and Hahn (1971).

7.14   For a good discussion of quasi linear utility functions see Varian (1992).

7.15   The Leontief system has been used extensively to represent real economies. See Leontief (1941) and Leontief (1966). For a textbook exposition of these systems see Dorfman, Samuelson, and Solow (1958). For practical methodology, see Miller and Blaire (1985) and Brucker and Hastings (1984).

Chapter **8**
GAME THEORY

Game theory is the study of interactive situations in which various "players" take actions that together determine a set of individual rewards or penalties. One application of game theory—brought to mind by the very name of the subject—is to actual games: board games, card games, and gambling games. Indeed, this is an area to which game theory was originally applied, and the special topic of two-person game theory was the initial foundation of the subject. But even from the beginnings of the subject, game theory was aimed at a broader spectrum of activities involving conflict and interaction, including warfare, negotiation, and economics. In recent years, game theory has been increasingly applied to economic issues, enriching both fields. Today game theory is considered essential background for intermediate and advanced study of microeconomics.

We have already considered some game-theoretic concepts in previous chapters. The study of the strategic aspects of the behavior of a firm, including oligopolistic and monopolistic competition are important examples. In fact, the Cournot equilibrium concept for oligopoly leads directly to the general Nash equilibrium solution of noncooperative games, which is discussed in the early portion of this chapter. The reexamination of these topics in the more general context provides additional insight.

The subject of general equilibrium theory is also closely related to the Nash equilibrium concept of game theory. Indeed, historically, the Nash theorem was used in an early proof of the existence of a general competitive economic equilibrium. The concepts of game theory continue to provide a foundation for more general notions of equilibrium theory.

Game theory provides an important basis for the study of the public goods and welfare issues of the next chapters. These topics can be developed by themselves, but game theory provides a sound basis and is essential for understanding modern developments in these areas. This chapter is an introduction to this important unifying subject.

8.1 Description of Games

When describing the general character of games, one thinks naturally of the *moves* taken by individual players. In expert play, however, the moves are really part of an overall *strategy*, which bases each move on the previous moves of all players. Some games are also characterized by the formation of *coalitions* and agreements between players. Each of these features forms the basis for a different description of a game: (1) the *extensive form*, based on a full description of the moves available to the players, (2) the *strategic form*, which amalgamates individual moves to form a description of strategies, and (3) the *characteristic function form*, which describes the rewards that can be attained through formation of coalitions. The first two of these descriptions are outlined in this section, and the third is introduced in Section 8.6 in the study of cooperative games.

Game Trees and Extensive Form

Consider a game with n players. At any point in the game, some player must select a move from a set of possible moves available at that point. When the set of possible moves is finite at every point, a *game tree* provides a simple representation of the game.

A *node* in a game tree corresponds to a point in the game when a move must be made. The label of the player who must make the next move is indicated at the node. From each node are *branches* corresponding to the moves available to the player. The bottom, or *root*, of the tree corresponds to the beginning of the game. The top of the tree, formed of the ends of branches having no further moves, is a list of rewards for each player and corresponds to the final position of the game.

As an example, consider an abbreviated game of nim played by two people. Originally there are five matchsticks on a table. Each player in turn picks up either one or two matchsticks from those remaining. The player taking the last matchstick loses the game. The game tree for this game is shown in Fig. 8.1, with the root (or starting point) at the bottom. In this case the two players are labeled A and B, and the label at each node indicates the

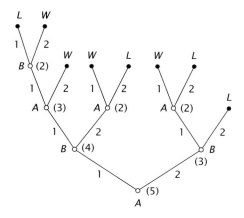

FIGURE 8.1 Game tree for nim.

player who must move at that node. Each node has two branches leaving it, labeled 1 and 2, corresponding to the possible moves of taking one or two matchsticks, respectively. The number in parentheses at each node indicates how many matchsticks remain at that point. This information is not strictly necessary and is included in this example only for clarification. The endpoints correspond to either zero or one matchstick remaining, for if only one matchstick remains, the next player is forced to take it. At each endpoint, the letter W or L is shown indicating whether player A wins or loses. In a general game tree, numerical values of reward for each player might be indicated. In this game, player A can be sure of a win by playing appropriately. The reader might wish to determine A's winning strategy.

The representation for other games is similar to that of the above example, but clearly the game tree can be very large for even simple games. For example, the game tree for tick-tack-toe has several thousand nodes.

Randomness

Many games are characterized by chance, or random, elements, derived from the shuffling of cards, the roll of dice, or, in an economic setting, the weather or other external influences on supply and demand. Randomness can be introduced in the description of a game by introduction of a special player, known as *nature*, that makes an arbitrary move when the player's turn occurs. We shall not consider randomness in this chapter.

Information Patterns

The *extensive form* of a game includes not only a description of the moves of the game, as represented by the game tree, but also the structure of information available to the players. Much of this information can be included in the game tree diagram. We shall assume that all players have *complete information* concerning the description of the game. That is, every player knows who the other players are, all actions available to the players, and all potential rewards to all the players. In other words, all players know the complete structure of the game tree, and they all know that the other players have this information. We also assume that all players have *perfect recall* in that they remember all past information.

A most important piece of information is knowledge of the position in the game tree. In some games, players do not always know exactly where they are in the game tree when it is their turn. This uncertainty occurs when the moves of other players, including those of nature, are not immediately revealed. In such cases a player cannot know exactly which node was attained, but only that it is one of a set of possible nodes in the game tree.

The set of possible game tree nodes known to a player at his turn is called an *information set*. It is depicted on the game tree by encircling the

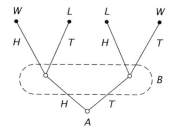

FIGURE 8.2 Game tree for penny matching.

nodes of the set with a dashed line. If an information set consists of a single node, the player has perfect information at that point, and for simplicity no dashed line is drawn around that single node. Note that the set of moves available to a player must be the same for all nodes in an information set; otherwise the nodes would be distinguishable.

As an example of how information sets arise, consider the classic game of matching pennies. In this game each of two players places a penny under cover with either the head or the tail upward. The coins are then simultaneously revealed. If they match (that is, if both are heads or both are tails), player A wins; otherwise player B wins. Although both players move simultaneously in this game, we arbitrarily select one player to move first in the extensive form description of the game, but we must hide the first player's choice from the second by use of an information set. The extensive form representation, assuming player A moves first, is shown in Fig. 8.2. The information set for player B consists of the two nodes shown in the dashed enclosure. Again, the rewards are shown for player A only.

If all information sets consist of a single node, the game is said to be one of *perfect information*. This chapter is restricted to such games or to games where the lack of perfect information is due to the simultaneous revelation of moves by different players, as discussed in the example of matching pennies, in which case the information set is really an artifice to account for this simultaneity within the extensive form framework. More complex issues of imperfect information are treated in Chapter 12.

It should be clear that the concepts discussed above can be extended to games in which players have an infinity (possibly a continuum) of available actions at each move. Such a game usually cannot be described by a finite game tree, but the term extensive form still refers to a complete, move-by-move description of the possibilities and the information available to the players.

Strategic Form

A *pure strategy* for a player is a set of rules that uniquely determines the player's moves at all information sets where that player could move. Once a pure strategy is specified, the play of the game is automatic, and its

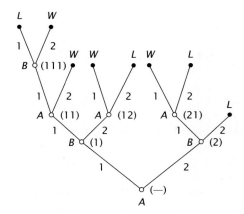

FIGURE 8.3   Tree with new labels.

execution could be turned over to an agent. When an information set is reached where a move is possible, the agent makes the move specified by the strategy. A pure strategy for the game of nim, for example, would give a definite rule for picking up either one or two matchsticks in every possible situation.

It is clear that if all players select a pure strategy, the outcome of the game is completely determined. If every player would submit a pure strategy to us, we could work out the associated outcomes and rewards. The game can therefore be considered as a mapping from pure strategies (for all players) to rewards. A description of this mapping is the *strategic* (or *normal*) form of a game.

Example 8.1.   Consider the game of nim discussed earlier. To describe a strategy for a player, we must specify a move (a 1 or 2 in this case) at each node where that player must move. To do this systematically we note that each node has a unique representation as a sequence of 1s and 2s corresponding to the sequence of decisions by all players to that point. This is shown in Fig. 8.3. The initial node is the blank sequence, the two nodes above that are 1 and 2, and the highest node on the left is 1111.

We can list all possible strategies for players A and B, as shown in Fig. 8.4, in a *strategy table* that lists horizontally a decision for every node that might be encountered. The first strategy listed for player A, for example, is that of taking 1 matchstick in every situation.

Some of the strategies listed are operationally equivalent to each other, in that they lead to identical sequences of moves. For example, strategies 1 and 2 for player A are operationally equivalent because use of their first three elements means that node 21 could never be reached. In fact in this example, player A actually has only six operationally distinct strategies, and player B also has six. For convenience, however, and for important technical reasons, it is standard practice to define strategies in the complete form as shown in Fig. 8.4.

Player A strategy

Node	1	2	3	4	5	6	7	8	9	10	11	12	13	14	15	16
	1	1	1	1	1	1	1	1	2	2	2	2	2	2	2	2
11	1	1	1	1	2	2	2	2	1	1	1	1	2	2	2	2
12	1	1	2	2	1	1	2	2	1	1	2	2	1	1	2	2
21	1	2	1	2	1	2	1	2	1	2	1	2	1	2	1	2

Player B strategy

Node	1	2	3	4	5	6	7	8
1	1	1	1	1	2	2	2	2
2	1	1	2	2	1	1	2	2
111	1	2	1	2	1	2	1	2

FIGURE 8.4 Strategy tables for nim.

Given a strategy from each player, we can determine the outcome for each strategy, leading to a matrix of outcomes. Part of this matrix for nim is shown in Fig. 8.5. The reader should verify one or two of its entries. Note that A can guarantee a win by using strategy 5 or its operational equivalent, 6. (If the rewards were reversed so that the player taking the last matchstick wins rather than loses, player A could still guarantee a win. Can you find the strategy?)

				A		
B	*1*	*2*	*3*	*4*	*5*	⋯
1	L	L	L	L	W	
2	W	W	W	W	W	
3	L	L	L	L	W	
4	W	W	W	W	W	
5	W	W	L	L	W	
6	W	W	L	L	W	
7	W	W	L	L	W	
8	W	W	L	L	W	

FIGURE 8.5 Outcome matrix for nim.

The strategic form representation of the game is simple in structure but not necessarily compact—for the number of strategies grows rapidly with the number of nodes in the game tree. In addition, the strategic form may suppress the essential character of the game, which is often better preserved in the extensive form. Nevertheless, because its structure is simple, the strategic form provides a good foundation for a fairly comprehensive theory of noncooperative games, as discussed in the next section.

8.2   Noncooperative Games

Noncooperative games are games where binding agreements between players are not possible. The impossibility of agreements may arise from pure practicality, as in a large competitive market where coordination is very difficult, or by law, as in the illegality of collusion among firms.

We formalize the definition of a noncooperative game in strategic form as follows.

Noncooperative game.   A *noncooperative game in strategic form* consists of

(a) A set of *players* indexed by a set $N = \{1, 2, \ldots, n\}$.

(b) A collection of *strategy sets* S_i, $i = 1, 2, \ldots, n$, with S_i being the strategy set for player i. The set $S = S_1 \times S_2 \cdots \times S_n$ is the corresponding *strategy set* of the game. A point $\mathbf{s}_i \in S_i$ is a strategy for player i, and a point $\mathbf{s} = (\mathbf{s}_1, \mathbf{s}_2, \ldots, \mathbf{s}_n) \in S$ is a (complete) strategy.

(c) A set of *reward* (or payoff) *functions* P_i, $i = 1, 2, \ldots, n$, defined on S. For $\mathbf{s} = (\mathbf{s}_1, \mathbf{s}_2, \ldots, \mathbf{s}_n) \in S$, the value $P_i(\mathbf{s})$ is the reward for the i-th player. The vector-valued function $\mathbf{P} = (P_1, P_2, \ldots, P_n)$ is the game *reward function*.

For notational convenience, the game is denoted $\{S_i, P_i\}_{i \in N}$.

The strategy sets S_i are usually represented by subsets of a finite-dimensional space, but in some cases more general sets are used. In the simplest games, such as the game of nim discussed in the last section, the strategy sets consist of a finite number of elements. However, as we shall see, in many applications the strategy sets have an infinite number of elements. We often require that these sets be convex subsets of a finite-dimensional space.

Example 8.2 (Oligopoly).   Recall that an oligopoly consists of n firms producing identical common products. Firm i has a cost function $c_i(q_i)$, and the industry inverse demand is $p(q)$ where $q = q_1 + q_2 + \cdots + q_n$. In the framework of a noncooperative game, the players are the n firms. A strategy for firm i

is a choice of a production level q_i that can lie within the interval $[0, M_i]$ of the real line, where M_i is the capacity of the firm. The reward function for the firm is its profit, which is

$$\pi_i = p(q_1 + q_2 + \cdots + q_n)q_i - c_i(q_i).$$

Clearly the profit of firm i depends on the strategies selected by all firms.

Example 8.3 (Monopolistic competition). As discussed in Section 3.8, monopolistic competition among firms producing similar products is a generalization of oligopoly. In this case there is an inverse demand function for each firm i, $i = 1, 2, \ldots, n$, which is $p_i(q_1, q_2, \ldots, q_n)$. The set of players and the strategy sets are defined as in the oligopoly model, but the reward (profit) function for the ith firm now has the form

$$\pi_i = p_i(q_1, q_2, \ldots, q_n)q_i - c_i(q_i).$$

Example 8.4 (Bimatrix games). Consider a two-person game where each player has available a finite number of strategies, say k and l in number, respectively. It is not too important to define specific strategy-set representations, since we can easily keep track of the possible strategies by just numbering them (in which case the strategy sets are sets of integers). The reward function for a player can be represented by a $k \times l$ matrix, with the (ij)th entry being the reward if player 1 uses strategy i and player 2 uses strategy j. Two reward matrices, one for each player, define the game; games of this type are referred to as *bimatrix games*.

It is actually simpler to represent the two payoff matrices together in a single matrix whose entries are ordered pairs, with the first element being player 1's reward and the second being player 2's reward.

A simple example of a bimatrix game is provided by the penny-matching game. Each player has two strategies: selecting heads or tails. Suppose that if the pennies match, player 1 receives one unit from player 2, and the reverse payment is made if they do not match. The corresponding payoff matrix is shown in Fig. 8.6.

Example 8.5 (Mixed strategies). Consider a bimatrix game. Each player has a finite number of strategies, which we refer to as *pure strategies*. Now suppose that, rather than selecting one of these pure strategies, a player makes the choice of strategy depend on a random event. In the game of

Player 2

	H	T
Player 1 H	$(1, -1)$	$(-1, 1)$
T	$(-1, 1)$	$(1, -1)$

FIGURE 8.6 Payoff matrix for penny matching.

penny matching, for example, a player might just flip the coin to determine whether to play heads or tails. In fact, this is a good strategy to use. In general, suppose player 1 assigns (nonnegative) probabilities $p_1, p_2, \ldots, p_k$ with $p_1 + p_2 + \cdots + p_k = 1$ to the k available pure strategies. During actual play of the game, a specific pure strategy is chosen randomly according to these probabilities. Player 1's strategy set now can be considered to be the simplex

$$S_1 = \left\{ \mathbf{p} : \mathbf{p} = (p_1, p_2, \ldots, p_k), \ \sum_{i=1}^{k} p_i = 1, \ p_i \geq 0, \ i = 1, 2, \ldots, k \right\}$$

in $\mathcal{R}^k$. The ith pure strategy corresponds to the corner point having $p_i = 1$, and $p_j = 0$ for $j \neq i$. Player 2 could use mixed strategies as well, by assigning probabilities $q_1, q_2, \ldots, q_l$ to the l available pure strategies. Then player 2's set could be represented by the unit simplex in R^l. In this example, strategies therefore consist of probability vectors $\mathbf{p}$ and $\mathbf{q}$.

The reward functions defined for pure strategies can be extended to larger mixed-strategy sets. For the mixed strategies using probabilities $p_1, p_2, \ldots, p_k$ and $q_1, q_2, \ldots, q_l$, we define the reward $P_1(\mathbf{p}, \mathbf{q}) = \sum_{i=1, j=1}^{k, l} p_i q_j P_1(i, j)$ and define P_2 similarly. This new reward is the expected value (in a probabilistic sense) of the reward as originally defined. It is the average reward that would be obtained in a long sequence of plays of the game using the mixed strategies.

Mixed strategies are useful because they transform discrete-valued strategy sets into convex sets, ensuring, as shown in the next section, the existence of special equilibrium points.

In certain cases a strategy can be eliminated from consideration without regard for how other players will play because there is another strategy that is always better. In order to explain this concept, it is useful to introduce some special notation. We let $S_{-i} = S_1 \times S_2 \times \cdots \times S_{i-1} \times S_{i+1} \times \cdots \times S_n$, which is the space of strategies for all players except player i. Given a strategy vector $\mathbf{s} = (\mathbf{s}_1, \mathbf{s}_2, \ldots, \mathbf{s}_n) \in S$, we define $\mathbf{s}_{-i} \in S_{-i}$ by $\mathbf{s}_{-i} = (\mathbf{s}_1, \mathbf{s}_2, \ldots, \mathbf{s}_{i-1}, \mathbf{s}_{i+1}, \ldots, \mathbf{s}_n)$, so $\mathbf{s}_{-i}$ is the original vector with the ith strategy vector removed. We may insert a new value for the missing component through the notation $\mathbf{s}_{-i} \backslash \mathbf{t} = (\mathbf{s}_1, \mathbf{s}_2, \ldots, \mathbf{s}_{i-1}, \mathbf{t}, \mathbf{s}_{i+1}, \ldots, \mathbf{s}_n)$.

Domination.   In a noncooperative game $\{S_i, P_i\}_{i \in N}$ a strategy $\mathbf{s}_i \in S_i$ is said to *dominate* $\mathbf{s}'_i \in S_i$ if $P_i(\mathbf{s}_{-i} \backslash \mathbf{s}_i) \geq P_i(\mathbf{s}_{-i} \backslash \mathbf{s}'_i)$ for all $\mathbf{s}_{-i} \in S_{-i}$. The strategy $\mathbf{s}_i \in S_i$ is *dominant* if it dominates all other strategies in S_i.

As an example, in the simple version of nim we found (in Fig. 8.5) that strategy 5 or 6 for player A always wins—no matter what strategy is used by player B. Hence strategy 5 is a dominant strategy for player A. Also, in the same example it can be noted that strategy 1, although not itself fully dominant, does dominate strategy 3.

If a dominant strategy exists, it would certainly be used. However, most games are not that simple. Indeed, the interesting feature of most games is just the fact that there is no dominant strategy for either player. An alternative solution concept is therefore required.

8.3 Nash Equilibrium Points

In the general framework of noncooperative games, the principal solution concept is that of a Nash equilibrium point.

Nash equilibrium.   Let $\{S_i, P_i\}_{i \in N}$ be a noncooperative game in strategic form. A point $\mathbf{s}^* \in S$ is a *Nash equilibrium point* (or simply an *equilibrium point*) for this game if for every $i \in N$

$$P_i(\mathbf{s}^*_{-i} \backslash \mathbf{s}_i) \le P_i(\mathbf{s}^*), \qquad \text{for all } \mathbf{s}_i \in S_i.$$

Thus a strategy vector (consisting of a strategy choice for each player) is a Nash equilibrium if no player's own reward can be increased by a unilateral strategy change. That is, if all other players' strategies are fixed, it does not pay to change one's own strategy. It should be clear that this is merely a generalization of the definition of equilibrium introduced in the context of oligopoly by Cournot, presented in Section 3.8.

As an example, consider again the game of nim with payoff matrix shown in Fig. 8.5. The strategy combination of the form $(5, 3)$ is an equilibrium point, since no player's reward can be improved by a change in that player's strategy. As another example, note that the bimatrix game corresponding to penny matching, shown in Fig. 8.6, has no equilibrium point in pure strategies. This can be checked by trying any pair of strategies—for instance (H, T)—and noting that at least one player (player 1 in the instance mentioned) will have an incentive to change strategy. This example shows that Nash equilibria need not exist, and therefore we wish to find conditions that do guarantee their existence.

It should be clear, however, that even if an equilibrium exists there is no simple way to ensure that it will be obtained. In this regard the Nash equilibrium is plagued by all the difficulties of competitive equilibria. Nevertheless, it is a useful idealization.

*Existence

Nash equilibria exist under very general conditions. Essentially all that is required is that the individual strategy sets be convex and compact and that the reward functions be continuous and satisfy a concavity assumption. We shall outline the proof of the existence of Nash equilibria and then study the relation of a Nash equilibrium to Pareto efficiency.

The existence of Nash equilibria is established, under certain conditions, through use of the Kakutani fixed point theorem (see Appendix E). In order to apply this theorem, we define a mapping associated with a noncooperative game.

Reaction function.   The *reaction function* for player i is the point-to-set mapping $\mathbf{r}_i$ from S_{-i} to S_i defined by

$$\mathbf{r}_i(\mathbf{s}_{-i}) = \{\mathbf{s}_i : P_i(\mathbf{s}_{-i}\backslash\mathbf{s}_i) = \max_{\mathbf{t}\in S_i} P_i(\mathbf{s}_{-i}\backslash\mathbf{t})\}\,.$$

In words, the reaction function is player i's best reply (or set of best replies) to a given choice of strategies by the other players. If the maximum of $P_i(\mathbf{s}_{-i}\backslash\mathbf{t})$ with respect to $\mathbf{t}$ is achieved at a unique point $\mathbf{t}$ (depending on $\mathbf{s}_{-i}$), we obtain a standard single-valued function $\mathbf{t}(\mathbf{s}_{-i})$. In general, however, the maximizing point will not be unique and we include all maximizing points in the mapping. Hence for every $\mathbf{s}_{-i}$ the reaction $\mathbf{r_i}(\mathbf{s}_{-i})$ may be a set. Thus $\mathbf{r}_i$ maps points into sets.

For notational convenience we sometimes consider the reaction function to be defined on S rather than S_{-i} by putting $\mathbf{r}_i(\mathbf{s}) = \mathbf{r}_i(\mathbf{s}_{-i})$, ignoring the ith component. The reaction function is well defined only if the maximization operation in the definition is well defined. This will be true if player i's strategy set consists of a finite number of points or if it is compact (closed and bounded) in a finite-dimensional space and P_i is continuous. The individual reaction functions are combined to define an overall reaction function for the game.

Specifically, the *reaction function* for a noncooperative game is the point-to-set mapping $\mathbf{R} : S \to S$ defined by

$$\mathbf{R}(\mathbf{s}) = (\mathbf{r}_1(\mathbf{s}_{-1}), \mathbf{r}_2(\mathbf{s}_{-2}), \dots, \mathbf{r}_n(\mathbf{s}_{-n}))\,.$$

Thus, given a strategy choice for each player, everyone computes his or her best response, and the resulting new strategy choices define the overall reaction.

Reaction functions can be depicted in strategy space, as illustrated for the case of two players in Fig. 8.7. (In this case, $s_{-1} \equiv s_2$, and $s_{-2} \equiv s_1$.) For every value of $s_1 \in S_1$, there is a nonempty set $r_2(s_1)$. We show this as a graph depicting the set $r_2(s_1)$ above the point $s_1 \in S_1$. A similar graph is constructed for r_1, although it is oriented sideways.

Nash equilibrium points correspond to points that are common to the graphs of the individual reaction functions. This should be clear from the figure. At such a point (s_1, s_2), player 1 cannot improve for the given s_2, since $s_1 \in r_1(s_2)$; similarly player 2 cannot improve for the given s_1. The existence of such points should be clear: the graph r_1 must go from the bottom to the top, and the graph of r_2 must go from the left to the right. Hence if both are connected (as they will be under suitable continuity and convexity

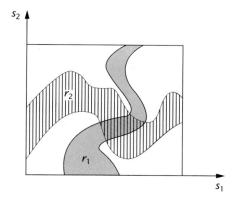

FIGURE 8.7 Reaction functions and Nash points.

assumptions), they must intersect. The existence of equilibrium points is rigorously established by the Kakutani fixed point theorem.

The following definition introduces a property that is important for guaranteeing the existence of a Nash equilibrium.

Individual quasi-concavity. The functions P_i, $i = 1, 2, \ldots, n$, are *individually quasi-concave* if each $P_i(\mathbf{s}_{-i}\backslash\mathbf{t})$ is quasi-concave with respect to $\mathbf{t}$ in S_i for every value of $\mathbf{s}_{-i}$.

If the P_i's are individually quasi-concave, the set of points $\mathbf{t}$ that maximizes $P_i(\mathbf{s}_{-i}\backslash\mathbf{t})$ will be convex (see Appendix B). Hence, the point-to-set mapping defined by the reaction function $\mathbf{r}_i(\mathbf{s}_{-i})$ always has a convex set as its image point.

We can now outline the proof of the main existence theorem.

Nash theorem. *Let $\{S_i, P_i\}_{i\in N}$ be a noncooperative game. Suppose the strategy sets are convex compact subsets of a finite-dimensional space and the reward functions are continuous and individually quasi-concave. Then a Nash equilibrium exists.*

Proof: We first note that the reaction function $\mathbf{R}$ is well defined on S since S is compact and the P_i's are continuous. $\mathbf{R}(\mathbf{s})$ is nonempty for every $\mathbf{s} \in S$. Next we note that if $\mathbf{s}^* \in S$ is a fixed point of the game reaction function $\mathbf{R}$ (that is, $\mathbf{s}^* \in \mathbf{R}(\mathbf{s}^*)$), then $\mathbf{s}^*$ is a Nash equilibrium point. This is true because if $\mathbf{s}^*$ is a fixed point, then for all $i \in N$, $\mathbf{s}_i^* \in r_i(\mathbf{s}_{-i}^*)$ and hence there is no $\mathbf{t} \in S_i$ with $P_i(\mathbf{s}_{-i}^*\backslash\mathbf{t}) > P_i(\mathbf{s}_{-i}^*\backslash\mathbf{s}_i^*) \equiv P_i(\mathbf{s}^*)$.

We shall now show that for any $\mathbf{s} \in S$ the image set $\mathbf{R}(\mathbf{s})$ is convex and compact. For any $i \in N$, the set of points $\mathbf{t}_i$ maximizing $P_i(\mathbf{s}_{-i}\backslash\mathbf{t}_i)$ is convex by the individual quasi-concavity of P_i. This set is compact (and nonempty) because P_i is continuous and S_i is compact. Since $\mathbf{R}(\mathbf{s})$ is the Cartesian product of these sets, it is also convex and compact.

It can be shown (but we omit the details here) that the reaction function $\mathbf{R}$ is upper semicontinuous since the reward functions are continuous. Hence, all the assumptions of the Kakutani theorem are satisfied. S is convex, and compact, $\mathbf{R}(\mathbf{s})$ is nonempty, convex, and compact for each $\mathbf{s}$, and $\mathbf{R}$ is upper semicontinuous. Thus, there is a fixed point, and hence a Nash equilibrium.

∎

The reader may find it instructive to draw some diagrams analogous to Fig. 8.7 but with one or more of the key assumptions of the above theorem violated and with no equilibrium point.

Example 8.6 (Mixed strategies).   The simple penny-matching game shows that not every bimatrix game has a Nash equilibrium in terms of pure strategies. However, for any bimatrix game consider the corresponding induced game with mixed strategies defined as in Example 8.5. In this new game each player's strategy is a vector of probabilities, and the strategy set can be taken to be the unit simplex in the space $\mathcal{R}^{m_i}$ where m_i is the number of pure strategies of player i. This strategy set is clearly compact and convex. Furthermore, the induced reward function is continuous. In fact, it is linear in each strategy vector, and hence it is also individually quasi-concave. Therefore, the Nash existence theorem applies. The same argument applies to any noncooperative game of n players (not just two players) in which each player has a finite number of pure strategies. We can extend the argument to convex strategy sets by using mixed strategies. Hence, we can state that *any game with finite strategy sets has a Nash equilibrium in mixed strategies.* In fact, the same argument even applies to any noncooperative game with closed and bounded strategy sets. Mixed strategies convexify these sets so that the Nash existence theorem applies.

Example 8.7 (Penny matching).   As a specific example of the above, consider the game of penny matching, which does not have a Nash equilibrium in pure strategies. Player 1 plays the mixed strategy (p_1, p_2) and player 2 plays (q_1, q_2). The payoff function for player 1 (who gets 1 unit if the coins match and loses 1 unit if they do not) is

$$P_1(\mathbf{p}, \mathbf{q}) = p_1 q_1 - p_1 q_2 - p_2 q_1 + p_2 q_2 .$$

We also have $P_2(\mathbf{p}, \mathbf{q}) = -P_1(\mathbf{p}, \mathbf{q})$. Substituting $p_2 = 1 - p_1$ and $q_2 = 1 - q_1$, we can set the derivative of P_1 with respect to p_1 to zero, and likewise for the derivative of P_2 with respect to q_1, to obtain the conditions for a Nash equilibrium

$$q_1 - q_2 + q_1 - q_2 = 0$$
$$-p_1 - p_1 + p_2 + p_2 = 0,$$

respectively. Hence, $p_1 = p_2 = \frac{1}{2}$ and $q_1 = q_2 = \frac{1}{2}$ form a equilibrium. That is, the mixed strategy of each player selecting heads or tails each with probability $\frac{1}{2}$ is a Nash equilibrium.

Example 8.8 (Oligopoly). In Section 3.8 we stated the necessary conditions for a Cournot equilibrium point in an oligopoly, but we had no guarantee that such a solution exists. We can now state conditions sufficient for existence. As before, we assume that there are n firms producing an identical product. We also assume the following:

(a) The inverse demand function $p(q)$ is defined for all $q > 0$, is finite-valued, continuous, nonnegative, decreasing, and has $p(0) > 0$.

(b) For each $i = 1, 2, \ldots, n$ the cost function c_i is nonnegative and is convex on $[0, \infty)$. Furthermore, there is an $\varepsilon > 0$ such that for all $i = 1, 2, \ldots, n$, $c_i(q) \geq c_i(0) + \varepsilon q$ for all $q > 0$.

(c) The product $qp(q)$ is uniformly bounded and concave for all q in the interval where $p(q) > 0$.

The reader can easily relate the first two conditions to standard economic assumptions. Note that we allow for the possibility that the inverse demand function may be identically zero for q larger than some q_0.

In order to apply the existence theorem, we first show that the strategy space for each player i can be restricted to a finite interval $[0, \overline{q}]$ without loss of generality. Using (c), let $\overline{r}$ be such that $qp(q) < \overline{r}$ for all $q \geq 0$. Let $\overline{q} = \overline{r}/\varepsilon$. Then for $q > \overline{q}$,

$$\pi_i = qp(q) - c_i(q) \leq qp(q) - c_i(0) - \varepsilon q < \overline{r} - c_i(0) - \varepsilon q < \overline{r} - c_i(0) - \overline{r}.$$

Hence, revenue does not cover variable costs, and $q = 0$ is superior, so, no firm will ever choose $q > \overline{q}$. The effective strategy sets $S_i = [0, \overline{q}]$ are convex and compact. The reward function $\pi_i = q_i p(q_1 + \cdots + q_n) - c_i(q_i)$ is continuous and is concave with respect to q_i (and hence quasi-concave). All the conditions of the existence theorem are satisfied, so a Cournot (Nash) equilibrium exists for this model.

Relation to Pareto Efficiency

A Nash equilibrium point is not necessarily Pareto efficient. Thus, even though a Nash equilibrium point is defined so that each individual's reward cannot be unilaterally improved, it might be possible to improve everyone's reward by a coordinated change of all strategies. Basically, it is the noncooperative nature of the game that keeps the players from attaining as much as they could through cooperation. A classic example of a noncooperative game that illustrates this fact is the *prisoner's dilemma.*

Example 8.9 (Prisoner's dilemma). Two thieves with stolen goods in their possession have been captured and are being questioned by the police in two separate rooms. Each has the option to confess or not to confess. If

	Player 2	
Player 1	Confess	Not confess
Confess	(–8,–8)	(0,–10)
Not confess	(–10,0)	(–1,–1)

FIGURE 8.8   The prisoner's dilemma.

both confess, they will receive severe penalties. If neither confesses, there is no solid evidence of theft, and they will receive only light penalties for possession of stolen goods. However, if one confesses and provides state's evidence against the other, the one that confesses will be set free and the other will receive a very severe penalty.

This situation can be represented by the 2×2 bimatrix game shown in Fig. 8.8, where the entries in the matrix represent the (negative) rewards, representing, perhaps, years in jail. It is easily verified that the only Nash equilibrium point corresponds to the case in which both prisoners confess; however, a superior point for both would be achieved if neither confesses. Hence the Nash equilibrium (confess, confess) is *not* Pareto efficient. This shows rather dramatically that although a Nash equilibrium is a natural solution concept, players may have strong incentives to achieve cooperation in inherently noncooperative situations.[1]

Example 8.10 (Duopoly). Suppose two identical firms make the same product. The industry inverse demand function is $p = 14 - q_1 - q_2$ where q_1 and q_2 are the outputs of the two firms. Each firm has a constant marginal production cost of 2.

The profit of a firm (say firm 1) is

$$\pi_1 = [14 - q_1 - q_2]q_1 - 2q_1 .$$

The Cournot-Nash equilibrium is the solution to the simultaneous equations

$$14 - 2q_1 - q_2 - 2 = 0$$
$$14 - 2q_2 - q_1 - 2 = 0,$$

which is $q_1 = q_2 = 4$, yielding $\pi_1 = \pi_2 = 16$.

This point is not efficient. Greater profit can be achieved by collusion. In particular, if q is chosen to maximize

$$(14 - q)q - 2q ,$$

the result is $q = 6$. If this is divided equally with $q_1 = q_2 = 3$, the resulting profit is $\pi_1 = \pi_2 = 18$. This is a joint-profit-maximizing point.

---

[1]Note that in this example the Nash solution happens to be a dominant solution for both players.

On the other hand, since the collusive solution is not a Nash equilibrium, it is difficult to achieve. Each firm has an incentive to increase production unilaterally to obtain even greater profit at the expense of the other firm.

8.4 Subgames

The concept of a subgame of a game is important for general noncooperative game theory, and it is especially important for the study of multistage games, discussed in the following section. The concept of a subgame also leads naturally to a definition of equilibrium that is stronger than the Nash definition.

Subgame. Let G be a game represented in extensive form. Let n be a node of perfect information of G and let T be the portion of the game tree emanating from n. Assume that all information sets involving nodes in T are completely contained in T. Then the tree T together with its information sets is a *subgame* G' of G.

This definition is illustrated in Fig. 8.9. (The definition applies to games with either a finite or an infinite number of nodes, although a tree cannot be drawn in an infinite case.) A subgame is a *proper subgame* if it is not equal to the game itself.

Many games have proper subgames, and it is often natural to think of such a game as progressing in stages—a new stage being initiated when a node is reached that is the root of a new subgame. Conversely, games composed of a succession of simpler games have natural subgames starting at the beginning of each simple game if there is perfect information at that point.

We now strengthen the Nash equilibrium concept. Suppose G is a noncooperative game and G' is a subgame of G. A strategy for G assigns a move for the appropriate player at every information set in the game. By restricting

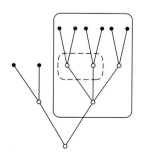

Subgame

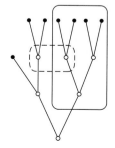

Not a subgame

FIGURE 8.9 Illustration of subgames.

this assignment to information sets in G', we obtain a strategy for the subgame G'. This is said to be the strategy for G' *induced* by the strategy for G. The induced strategy is the same as the original—merely, it is used only in the subgame.

Subgame perfection.   A strategy $\mathbf{s}^*$ is a *subgame perfect equilibrium* for a game G if it and its induced strategies are Nash equilibria for G and every subgame of G.

Example 8.11 (Stackelberg equilibrium).   In the Stackelberg approach to duopoly, there is a leader firm, which selects its output level first, and a follower firm, which, knowing what level the first firm chose, then selects its level. This can be regarded as a game with a simple two-stage tree (although with a continuum of branches) as shown in Fig 8.10. At the initial node, firm 1 selects a branch (which is an output level), and then firm 2 moves from there. In the Stackelberg solution to this game, player 2 is assumed to maximize profit given knowledge of the first firm's output. The first firm, realizing how the second player will react, selects a level that will yield maximum profit based on the reaction that its choice will produce.

This solution is a subgame perfect equilibrium—almost by definition. The proper subgames are those that continue after firm 1 makes its selection. Clearly, since firm 2 maximizes profit accounting for firm 1's choice, firm 2 cannot find an improved strategy and hence its choice is a Nash equilibrium for the subgame. Similarly, the overall equilibrium is a Nash equilibrium for the whole game.

The main motivation for subgame perfect equilibria is that such equilibria retain the force of the equilibrium logic even after the game has progressed to a new point. This is particularly important in cases in which equilibrium strategies contain implied or explicit threats, which may lose credibility if they are not subgame perfect. This is illustrated in the following section.

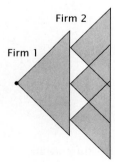

FIGURE 8.10   The Stackelberg game.

8.5 Multistage Games

Although some games are *single-stage*, in the sense that each player makes a single move, many others are *multistage*, with players repeatedly making moves in response to previous actions. The examples of the oligopoly model, the prisoner's dilemma, and penny matching were all formulated in previous sections as single-stage games. The game of nim is a multistage game.

Many single-stage games have natural extensions as multistage games. Firms competing in an oligopolistic market, for example, must each choose a time sequence of production levels, and the choice at any one time will most likely be influenced by the previous choices of all firms in the market. These larger games, built up from a series of single-stage games, are often referred to as *supergames*. Supergames are games in their own right and can be treated by the concepts we have developed. Such treatment is consistent with the general view, emphasized in previous chapters as well, that economic action over time sequences should be viewed as an integrated whole rather than as isolated actions.

Some features of multistage games can be deduced by explicit recognition of the stage structure. Hence, rather than considering the game abstractly in strategic form, it is advantageous to consider a semiextensive form that recognizes the separate stages. Strategies can then be constructed naturally from the structure of the game, rather than being abstract points in a strategy space.

Suppose that $\{S_i, P_i\}_{i \in N}$ is a noncooperative game. We imagine that the players play this game repeatedly a total of T times. At stage t player i receives the reward $P_i(\mathbf{s}^t)$ where $\mathbf{s}^t$ is the aggregate strategy used by the players during that stage. To determine the overall reward for the sequence of T games, player i discounts the stream of rewards. Hence the overall reward is

$$\overline{P}_i = \sum_{t=1}^{T} (\delta_i)^t P_i(\mathbf{s}^t),$$

where δ_i is a discount factor, usually such that $0 < \delta_i \le 1$.

We assume that all players have complete information concerning the structure of the game. We also assume that each player has perfect information at the end of each play. That is, before committing to a strategy $\mathbf{s}_i^t$ for the tth play, player i knows the complete history $(\mathbf{s}^1, \mathbf{s}^2, \ldots, \mathbf{s}^{t-1}) \in S^{t-1}$. A game of this structure is called a *repeated game*. If $\delta_i < 1$, the game is said to be a repeated game with discounting. We also allow the possibility that $T = \infty$.

A *supergame* is somewhat more general in that the games at different stages need not be identical and the discount factors need not be constant. The treatment of supergames is nearly identical to that of repeated games, except that the notation may become more complicated.

In repeated games, the overall strategy space is much larger than just T copies of the single-stage game. For example, as shown below, a 2×2 matrix game played two times is an 8×8 matrix game. In general, the choice of strategy played in the tth repetition can be a function of all plays up to that stage.

We illustrate the theory of multistage games and its potential application to economic problems through the following two examples.

Example 8.12 (Two-stage game). Consider the 2×2 matrix game shown below.

		Player 2	
		1	2
	1	(10,10)	(15,5)
Player 1			
	2	(5,1)	(0,0)

Note that from among the four possible pure strategies, exactly one is a Nash equilibrium, namely, the strategy $(1, 1)$. Now suppose the game is played twice without discounting. A typical strategy for either player can be represented by a triple $(p; q, r)$ of numbers that are all either 1 or 2. The number p is the move made on play 1, q is what is played second if the other player played 1 in the first game, and r is what is played second if the other player played 2 in the first game. There will be a total of eight strategies for each player, resulting in an 8×8 matrix game with 64 aggregate strategies. It should be noted, however, that these are not 64 different outcomes, or even 64 different play sequences. There are, however, 64 different ways to define strategies as above.

It is natural to conjecture that the Nash equilibrium of the single-stage game can be played twice in the two-period game to yield an equilibrium for that game. Indeed it is true in general that a Nash equilibrium of a single-stage game can be played repeatedly in a finitely repeated version of the game to yield an equilibrium for the repeated game. For our example, this repetition of the single-stage equilibrium actually translates into four different equilibrium strategies in the two-period game. Both players can use either of the strategies $(1; 1, 1)$ or $(1; 1, 2)$. All four combinations of these two strategies played together lead to the moves $(1, 1)$ and $(1, 1)$ and hence to a total payoff of $(20, 20)$.

There are, however, two additional Nash equilibria. The first of these is for player 1 to use $(1; 2, 1)$ and player 2 to use $(2; 1, 1)$, and the second is for player 1 again to use $(1; 2, 1)$ and player 2 to use $(2; 1, 2)$. In either case the resulting moves are $(1, 2)$ and $(1, 1)$ with a total payoff of $(25, 25)$. This set of equilibria result from a *threat strategy* by player 1. Basically, player 1 says that player 2 better use move 2 on the first play, or else player 1 will invoke a penalty by playing move 2 at the second stage. This set of equilibria corresponds to a higher payoff for player 1 than the equilibria derived from the single-stage Nash equilibrium. (The reader should verify that these additional strategies are indeed Nash equilibria.)

The second set of equilibria are not subgame perfect, because all sub-games resulting after the first play are identical with the original single-stage game, which has a unique Nash equilibrium (1,1). Therefore, *if* player 2 chose to make move 1 in the first play, player 1 would be violating the condition of a subgame perfect equilibrium by carrying out the threat in the second move. The threat by player 1 implicit in these additional Nash equilibrium strategies is not really credible, since it is not in player 1's best interest to carry it out.

Example 8.13 (Duopoly).   Consider the duopoly model of Example 8.10. The industry inverse demand function is

$$p = 14 - (q_1 + q_2)$$

where q_1 and q_2 are the quantities produced by the two firms. Each firm has a (constant) marginal production cost $c = 2$ and, in this example, a capacity limit of $Q = 6$ per year. From Example 8.10 the single-year Cournot (Nash) equilibrium is $q_1 = q_2 = 4$, with $\pi_1 = \pi_2 = 16$. We also found that the co-operative maximum profit level is $q = 6$, which we assume is shared with $q_1 = q_2 = 3$ and $\pi_1 = \pi_2 = 18$. We can also consider the maximum level of 6 to be a penalty level, since production at that level lowers the price. We shall show that in the noncooperative framework the threat of penalties can induce cooperation over time, when cooperation would not exist in the single-stage game.

If we label the three production levels for firms by C (cooperative, $q_i = 3$), N (Nash, $q_i = 4$), and P (penalty, $q_i = 6$), and assume that each firm will select one of these levels,[2] the 3×3 matrix game shown below results.

	C	N	P
C	(18,18)	(15,20)	(9,18)
N	(20,15)	(16,16)	(8,12)
P	(18,9)	(12,8)	(0,0)

---

[2]This is reasonable because the best response (over the continuum of production levels) to $q_1 = 6$ is $q_2 = 3$, the cooperative level. So if you know you will be penalized, you can do no better than play C.

Note that the upper 2×2 matrix has the structure of a prisoner's dilemma game. The only equilibrium point for the game is (N, N), with payoff $(16, 16)$.

Now suppose that the duopoly exists over several years and that the game is to be played repeatedly. For simplicity we assume that the game is to be played a total of T times and that there is no discounting. We define a special strategy made up of a sequence of T moves. This sequence is $U = (C, C, \ldots, C, N)$. Both players use the following individual strategy: play the move indicated by the U sequence unless during the previous stage the other player did not play C, in which case play P.

If both players follow this strategy, both will actually play the sequence U and cooperation will be achieved during the first $T - 1$ stages. We can show that this strategy is in fact a Nash equilibrium for the repeated game. If a player disobeys U at any of the first $T - 1$ stages, that player can gain at most \$2.00 relative to the play of C during that stage[3] but will lose at least \$9.00 during the next stage (or \$7.00 if the deviation is at $T - 1$). Hence it does not pay to deviate at any of the first $T - 1$ stages. It does not pay to deviate during the last stage, since that is the single-stage Nash equilibrium point.

This equilibrium strategy is not subgame perfect. If the other player deviates at some stage, it is not optimal, from a subgame perspective, to carry out the threat and use P in the next stage.

8.6   Cooperative Games

Some games are not strictly competitive, for there are aspects that make cooperation both beneficial and feasible. Such games are called *cooperative games*. Cooperative games are defined explicitly as having the feature that players can make agreements regarding the strategies they will play. Such agreements can drastically affect the outcome of the game, and the formulation of beneficial agreements is therefore an important part of players' overall strategies.

Economic situations that have the characteristic of cooperative games are quite common. For example, when two parties design and sign a contract, it is presumably beneficial to both and partially cooperative. Likewise, if individuals in a group donate money for a common project, their actions can be analyzed as a cooperative game.

In a cooperative game an agreement is made by a *coalition*, which is a nonempty subset of the players. A coalition may consist of a single player, the entire group of n players, or something between these extremes. In actual play, several different coalitions may form, each agreeing on the strategies to be played by its members.

---

[3]Actually the best deviation from C is $q_i = 4\frac{1}{2}$ rather than $q_i = 4$, corresponding to N. The gain in profit is then \$2.25.

Example 8.14 (Dividing a Pie). Suppose three women may divide a pie among themselves. They use majority voting to determine the division. (Specifically, each woman in turn puts forward a proposal, which is voted upon. The first proposal that receives at least two votes is accepted.) Here, it is clear that any coalition of two women can enforce any division it wishes.

Example 8.15 (Trade barriers). Consider a number of countries that engage in mutual trade. Any group of these countries may decide to form a trade coalition and impose import taxes on goods from other countries.

Solution Concepts

Let us consider a game in strategic form. There is a set $N = \{1, 2, \ldots, n\}$ of players. Each player has a strategy set S_i and a payoff function P_i defined over $S = S_1 \times S_2 \times \cdots \times S_n$. A coalition K is a subset of N. If a coalition K is formed, it has available to it the strategies of its individual members; that is, the coalition can control the components of $\mathbf{s} \in S$ corresponding to the members of K.

With these ideas we can define some basic notions of how coalitions can influence strategies, and then we can define some solution concepts.

Upsetting. A strategy $\mathbf{s} \in S$ can be *upset* by coalition K if there is a strategy $\mathbf{s}' \in S$ with $\mathbf{s}_i = \mathbf{s}'_i$ for all $i \notin K$ and $P_i(\mathbf{s}') \geq P_i(\mathbf{s})$ for all $i \in K$ with the inequality being strict for at least one $i \in K$.

Basically, a coalition can upset a strategy if it can enforce an alternative that it prefers, assuming that no one outside the coalition changes strategy. Applied to different coalitions, this leads to alternative equilibrium (or solution) concepts:

(a) If $\mathbf{s} \in S$ cannot be upset by the grand coalition of all players, then $\mathbf{s}$ is *Pareto efficient*.

(b) If $\mathbf{s} \in S$ cannot be upset by any coalition consisting of a single player, then $\mathbf{s}$ is a *Nash equilibrium*.

(c) If $\mathbf{s} \in S$ cannot be upset by any coalition, then $\mathbf{s}$ is said to be a *strong equilibrium*.

The first two of these definitions are quite familiar. The last, that of a strong equilibrium, is clearly a natural extension of these familiar concepts to the case where cooperation is allowed. As the name implies, it is a strong requirement, and very few cooperative games actually have strong equilibria. It is actually more common, in the context of cooperative games, to use the alternative concept defined below.

Blocking. A strategy $\mathbf{s} \in S$ is *blocked* by coalition K if there is a set of individual strategies $\mathbf{s}'_i$, $i \in K$, such that for all feasible strategies $\bar{\mathbf{s}} \in S$ with $\bar{\mathbf{s}}_i = \mathbf{s}'_i$ for $i \in K$ there holds $P_i(\bar{\mathbf{s}}) \geq P_i(\mathbf{s})$ for all $i \in K$ with the inequality being strict for at least one $i \in K$.

Basically, a coalition can block a strategy if it can find a strategy for the coalition that yields a result superior to the given strategy no matter what the other players choose. Clearly, it is harder for a coalition to block a strategy than to upset it.

The concept of blocking leads to three natural solution concepts:

(a) If $\mathbf{s} \in S$ cannot be blocked by the grand coalition of all players, then $\mathbf{s}$ is *Pareto efficient*.

(b) If $\mathbf{s} \in S$ cannot be blocked by any coalition consisting of a single player, then $\mathbf{s}$ is *individually rational*.

(c) If $\mathbf{s} \in S$ cannot be blocked by any coalition K, then $\mathbf{s}$ belongs to the *core* of the game.

Because blocking is more difficult than upsetting, these concepts based on blocking are weaker than those based on upsetting. (This is because the equilibrium definitions are based on the impossibility of upsetting or blocking, respectively.) Hence, any Nash equilibrium is individually rational, and any strong equilibrium is in the core. (The reader should verify this.)

In cooperative game theory, the most popular solution concept is that of the core. However, the core may be empty!

Example 8.16 (Pie division).   The core of the pie division game is empty. Whenever a division is proposed, the two players with the smallest portions can together improve these portions.

However, there are many examples in which the core is nonempty. One simple example is given in the next section. And the most important example for the study of microeconomics is the core of an exchange economy, discussed in Section 8.8.

8.7   Characteristic Functions and Benefits

A complete study of a cooperative game can be exceedingly complex. Note in particular that the number of possible coalitions in an n-person game is $2^n - 1$. A complete analysis of the game would require consideration of all these possible coalitions and the multitude of strategies available to them. The description of a cooperative game is greatly simplified by the use of *characteristic functions*, which are defined by considering the rewards that each coalition can guarantee itself.

We assume here that players receive rewards that can be transferred among themselves directly. This is true, for example, when rewards are measured in monetary units and individuals have utility that is linear in money and are free to make side payments by transferring the reward.

If reward is transferable, a coalition only need consider the total reward that it can obtain. Then later it can worry about how to divide that aggregate reward among its members. Accordingly, in this case we define $V(K)$ to be the maximum total reward that coalition K can guarantee itself by acting alone. The mapping V from coalitions to values is the characteristic function of the game.

The solution concepts discussed in the previous section can all be related to the characteristic function, and indeed use of the characteristic function often simplifies the analysis. (When the characteristic function is used, the core, for example, is usually reported in terms of the reward values to coalitions rather than in terms of the strategies that yield those rewards.)

Example 8.17 (Three-cornered market). A farmer owns a piece of land that can earn him $100,000 in agricultural use. This same land is worth $200,000 as a plant site to a manufacturer and $300,000 to a residential developer. Let us regard the possible sale of the land as a game among the three players F (farmer), M (manufacturer), and D (developer). We assume that the reward (dollars) is transferable. We easily determine the characteristic function (which is scalar-valued in this case).

$$V(F) = 100,000 \qquad V(M) = 0 \qquad V(D) = 0$$
$$V(FM) = 200,000 \qquad V(FD) = 300,000 \qquad V(MD) = 0$$
$$V(FMD) = 300,000 \,.$$

Now let us determine the core. Let x_F, x_M, and x_D be the rewards to the three players. The value of the characteristic function for each coalition translates into an inequality for the rewards:

$$x_F \geq 100,000 \qquad x_M \geq 0 \qquad x_D \geq 0$$
$$x_F + x_M \geq 200,000 \qquad x_F + x_D \geq 300,000 \qquad x_M + x_D \geq 0$$
$$x_F + x_M + x_D = 300,000 \,,$$

where the final equality follows from feasibility and Pareto efficiency.

These inequalities are easily reduced to

$$x_F + x_D = 300,000$$
$$x_F \geq 200,000 \,.$$

Hence in the core, the farmer will sell to the developer for a price between $200,000 and $300,000.

Suppose now that utility is not transferable but some commodity (or bundle) $\mathbf{g}$ is transferable. We can define the benefit functions $b_i(\mathbf{x}_i, u_i)$ as usual where $\mathbf{x}_i$ is the total bundle assigned to individual i as a result of the game. (Some components of x_i may not even be affected by the game.) We let

$$V(K, \mathbf{U}_K) = \max \sum_{k \in K} b_k(\mathbf{x}_k, u_k),$$

where the maximum is the maximum amount that coalition K can guarantee. Then a feasible $\mathbf{U}^*$ is a utility vector in the core if and only if

$$V(K, \mathbf{U}_K^*) \leq 0$$

for all coalitions K.

*8.8   The Core of an Exchange Economy

The concept of the core grew out of Edgeworth's investigation of an exchange economy. We study that special application of the now general core concept in this section.

Suppose n individuals have initial endowments $\mathbf{w}_i$, $i = 1, 2, \ldots, n$. They wish to exchange these, and they are not required to use a price system. Free disposal applies. They may exchange in any way that recognizes the individual ownership of initial endowments. This exchange economy can be considered to be a cooperative game. The outcome of the game is an allocation of the aggregate endowment. We wish to determine what final allocations are in the core, taking account of the ownership condition.

In general, an allocation $\mathbf{X} = (\mathbf{x}_1, \mathbf{x}_2, \ldots, \mathbf{x}_n)$ is in the core if it satisfies the following requirements:

(a) $\sum_{i=1}^{n} \mathbf{x}_i \leq \sum_{i=1}^{n} \mathbf{w}_i$ (feasibility).

(b) No coalition can block $\mathbf{X}$ (no domination).

In this case, blocking takes a very explicit form. The coalition K can block $\mathbf{X}$ if there is an allocation $\mathbf{X}' = (\mathbf{x}_1', \mathbf{x}_2', \ldots, \mathbf{x}_n')$ such that

(a) $\mathbf{x}_i' \succsim_i \mathbf{x}_i$ for all $i \in K$, with $\mathbf{x}_j' \succ_j \mathbf{x}_j$ for some $j \in K$.

(b) $\sum_{i \in K} \mathbf{x}_i' \leq \sum_{i \in K} \mathbf{w}_i$.

These conditions are that (a) members of K prefer $\mathbf{X}'$ to $\mathbf{X}$, with strict preference for at least one member, and (b) the members of coalition K can achieve their $\mathbf{x}_i'$'s.

The core can be nicely illustrated for the two-person, two-commodity economy in an Edgeworth box, as shown in Fig. 8.11. The core is the set of points that are Pareto efficient and are preferred by both individuals to the original endowment. In the Edgeworth box the core is the segment of the Pareto efficient curve (the contract curve) lying between the indifference curves through the endowment.

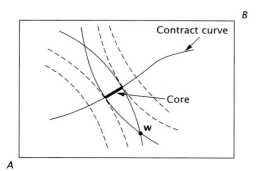

FIGURE 8.11   The core of an exchange economy.

We now state a fundamental result relating the core and a Walrasian equilibrium of an exchange economy.

Proposition 8.1.   *Consider an exchange economy with initial endowments* $W = (w_1, \ldots, w_n)$. *Assume that individual preferences satisfy local nonsatiation. If* (X^*, p^*) *is a Walrasian equilibrium for the endowments, then* X^* *is in the core.*

Proof: The proof follows the same pattern as that of the First Theorem of Welfare Economics, just applied to K rather than N. Assume that X^* is not in the core. Then there is a feasible allocation X' and a coalition K such that all individuals in K prefer X' to X^* (with at least one strict preference) and such that

$$\sum_{i \in K} x'_i \le \sum_{i \in K} w_i .$$

Since all individuals in K prefer X' to X^*, it follows from local nonsatiation that

$$p^* \cdot x'_i \ge p^* \cdot w_i$$

for all $i \in K$ with $p^* \cdot x'_j > p^* \cdot w_j$ for some $j \in K$. Then, summing these inequalities, we obtain

$$p^* \cdot \sum_{i \in K} x'_i > p^* \cdot \sum_{i \in K} w_i,$$

which contradicts the earlier inequality.   ∎

The above proposition shows, incidentally, that if a Walrasian equilibrium exists, the core of the exchange economy is nonempty. We recall, however, that a fixed point theorem is used to establish the existence of a Walrasian equilibrium, so it is really a fairly deep result that the core of an exchange economy is nonempty.

From the Edgeworth box diagram, it is clear that the core contains points in addition to the Walrasian equilibrium point. A little reflection might suggest that these are due to there being only two individuals in the economy. If there were several individuals, many additional coalitions could be formed, imposing additional constraints on core vectors, and it seems reasonable that the relative size of the core might shrink—maybe even to the single point represented by the Walrasian equilibrium. Indeed, we can prove a result of this type.

If we were to add individuals successively to the economy, the dimension of an allocation would increase accordingly, and hence the successive cores would be defined in spaces of different dimensions. In order to avoid this difficulty, we consider individuals of only two types, A and B. Individuals of the same type have identical preferences and identical endowments. We then define an r-replication of the basic two-person, two-good economy to be the economy with r individuals of each type. The core of an r-replication is termed the r-core. The following lemma establishes that all individuals of the same type have identical allocations in the r-core, and this is what keeps the effective dimension of the problem equal to 2.

Lemma 8.1 (Equal treatment in the core).   *Suppose all individuals' preferences are continuous, strictly convex, and strongly monotonic. Then if* X *is an allocation in the r-core, all individuals of the same type receive the same commodity bundle.*

Proof: Let X be a feasible allocation in the r-replication, and denote by

$$\mathbf{x}_{A1}, \mathbf{x}_{A2}, \ldots, \mathbf{x}_{Ar} \quad \text{and} \quad \mathbf{x}_{B1}, \mathbf{x}_{B2}, \ldots, \mathbf{x}_{Br}$$

the $2r$ individual bundles. We form the two *average bundles*

$$\overline{\mathbf{x}}_A = \frac{1}{r} \sum_{i=1}^{r} \mathbf{x}_{Ai} \qquad \overline{\mathbf{x}}_B = \frac{1}{r} \sum_{i=1}^{r} \mathbf{x}_{Bi}.$$

Suppose not all of the individuals of the same type receive the average. In particular suppose not all A individuals receive $\overline{\mathbf{x}}_A$. By strict convexity and strong monotonicity of preferences, the average of two distinct bundles is always strictly preferred to the less preferred of the two. Hence $\overline{\mathbf{x}}_A$ is strictly preferred to the bundle that at least one A individual receives.

Now consider a coalition K consisting of such an A individual and a B individual who receives a bundle no better than $\overline{\mathbf{x}}_B$. We have

$$\overline{\mathbf{x}}_A + \overline{\mathbf{x}}_B = \frac{1}{r} \sum_{i=1}^{r} (\mathbf{x}_{Ai} + \mathbf{x}_{Bi}) \leq \mathbf{w}_A + \mathbf{w}_B.$$

Hence, since the coalition K owns $\mathbf{w}_A + \mathbf{w}_B$, it can obtain the allocation $(\overline{\mathbf{x}}_A, \overline{\mathbf{x}}_B)$ for its two members. Furthermore, the type A individual in K strictly prefers $\overline{\mathbf{x}}_A$ to the original bundle. Hence, this new allocation dominates X through K. Therefore X is not in the r-core. ∎

The above lemma shows that all individuals of a given type receive the same commodity bundle in any allocation that is in the r-core. It is therefore possible to use the Edgeworth box to represent the r-replication. Positions in the box now correspond to the typical bundle for individuals of type A and type B. The following theorem shows that as r increases, the r-core shrinks to a single point, corresponding to the Walrasian equilibrium.

Walras core theorem.   *Assume that individual preferences are continuous, strictly convex, and strongly monotonic. Suppose* $\mathbf{X}$ *is an allocation, but not a Walrasian equilibrium allocation. Then there is an r such that* $\mathbf{X}$ *is not a (typical) allocation in the r-core.*

Proof: Consider the Edgeworth box shown in Fig. 8.12a. Two points, 1 and 2, are on a common line through the original endowment, point 0. We show that a coalition can be formed such that all its A players get the allocation corresponding to point 1 while all its B players get the allocation corresponding to point 2. The only requirement is that the ratio of line segment lengths from 0 be a rational number.

To see how this is possible, let μ be the length of the segment $(2,0)$ divided by the length of $(1,0)$, and assume that this is rational with $\mu \leq 1$. Let $\mathbf{x}_A^i$ and $\mathbf{x}_B^i$ be the allocations to A and B represented by the point $i, i = 1,2$. Then

$$\mu \mathbf{x}_A^1 + (1 - \mu)\mathbf{w}_A = \mathbf{x}_A^2,$$

or using $\mathbf{w}_A + \mathbf{w}_B - \mathbf{x}_A^2 = \mathbf{x}_B^2$,

$$\mu \mathbf{x}_A^1 + \mathbf{x}_B^2 = \mu \mathbf{w}_A + \mathbf{w}_B.$$

Hence a coalition in which the number of members of type A is μ times the number of members for type B has the endowment required to give the required allocation to its members. Such a coalition can be formed if μ is rational, with $\mu = s/r$, say, by selecting s of type A and r of type B. Clearly,

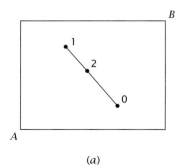

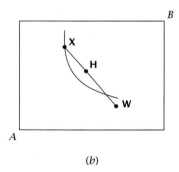

(a)   (b)

FIGURE 8.12   Edgeworth boxes for proof.

the argument is symmetric, so we could reverse the allocations to types A and B.

Now, to turn to the proof of the main theorem, let X be a point in the Edgeworth box that is not a Walrasian equilibrium allocation. See Fig. 8.12b. Then the line from W through X must cut one individual's indifference curve through X. Hence there is a point H on this line that one individual, say A, strictly prefers to X. (The point H may lie between W and X, as shown, or beyond X.) By continuity of preferences, we can assume that the ratio of the distances from W to X and W to H is rational.

From the earlier construction, there is an integer r and a coalition in the r-replication such that the type A members in this coalition can obtain the allocation at H and the type B members can obtain the allocation at X. Since the type A members in this coalition are better off than at X, the A portion of X cannot be a (typical) allocation to type A members in the r-core. ∎

The above theorem can be easily generalized to accommodate any finite number of types. The theorem is important theoretically for it makes a strong statement linking the game theory concept of the core and the notion of economic equilibrium.

8.9 Exercises

1. (Battle of the sexes)   A married couple is trying to decide what to do for an evening out. The woman would like to go to the theater, and the man would like to go to a football game. Because they enjoy each other's company, they will enjoy the outing only if they go together. Letting the first option be football and the second be theater, the payoff matrix is

Woman

(4,1)		(0,0)
(0,0)		(1,4)

Man

Accounting for mixed strategies, find the *three* equilibrium solutions.

2. (Dominant strategies)   Consider the 3×5 bimatrix game shown below.

$$\begin{bmatrix} (1,3) & (1,5) & (3,5) & (3,2) & (2,4) \\ (2,4) & (1,4) & (0,4) & (4,5) & (2,4) \\ (1,5) & (2,4) & (1,3) & (3,4) & (0,3) \end{bmatrix}$$

Find a strategy for player B that is dominated by another, and eliminate the dominated strategy. Repeat this in the reduced game, alternatively considering both players, until a 1×1 game is all that remains. In what sense does this represent a solution to the original game?

3. How many strategies are there if nim is played with six matchsticks?

4. (Entry prevention) A product is currently supplied by a monopolist (firm 0), but n other firms might enter the market. The monopolist has cost function $c_0(q) = S + mq$ where S is a sunk cost. Each potential entrant has cost function $c_i(q) = F + mq$ where F is a fixed cost that accrues only if the firm enters. The inverse demand curve for the product is downward sloping. The area under the inverse demand curve and above $p = m$ is less than nF.

Suppose the parameters are such that if the monopolist chose the normal monopoly output level Q_0, a new firm could enter and make positive profit. There is a $Q^* > Q_0$ for the monopolist such that if a new firm entered, it would make zero net profit.

Now consider the game in which the monopolist first selects an output level q_0 and then the entrants, one by one, decide whether to enter and how much to produce. Show that a Nash subgame perfect strategy for the monopolist is $q_0 \geq Q^*$. (It is assumed that a firm enters only if it can attain positive profit.)

Hint: If $q_0 < Q^*$ and $q_0 + q_1 > Q^*$, then firm 0 is worse off than at $q_0 = Q^*$. Hence $q_0 < Q^* \Rightarrow q_0 + q_1 \leq Q^*$. Use this to infer that further entry will take place.

5. (Tripoly) Suppose three firms compete in a market for a single product with industry inverse demand curve $p = A - q$. All three firms have constant marginal cost m. Firm 1 is a leader and selects output level q_1. Firms 2 and 3 are followers and select q_2 and q_3 after q_1. Total output is $q = q_1 + q_2 + q_3$. Find a Nash subgame perfect equilibrium solution.

6. (Hotelling's problem) Along a highway of length l two stores are located at points A and B as shown in Fig 8.13. They carry exactly the same good. Consumers are uniformly distributed along the highway, and each will purchase 1 unit of the commodity (demand is perfectly inelastic). Consumers bear a cost c for each mile traveled to a store to purchase the good. The effective price for a consumer located at a point E is therefore $p = P_A + cx$ or $p = P_B + cy$ where x and y are the distances to stores A and B, respectively, and P_A and P_B are the prices at the stores.

(a) Given P_A and P_B, find the equilibrium point E that splits the market, with all to the left buying from A and to the right buying from B.

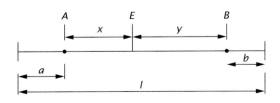

FIGURE 8.13 Diagram for Exercise 6.

(b) Find the profit function of each store and find the Nash equilibrium prices for both stores. What are the demands under these prices? (Assume that the sellers' cost is zero.)

(c) If the stores are free to move along the highway without cost and then set prices, what is the Nash equilibrium value for a and b? Hint: Do not try to differentiate. Find the solution by inspection.

7. (Infinite horizon trigger strategy)   Suppose $(S_i, P_i)_{i \in N}$ is a single-period non-cooperative game. Suppose $\mathbf{s}^c$ is a Nash equilibrium for the game, and suppose $\mathbf{s}^*$ is a strategy that has higher payoff for every player but is not a Nash equilibrium. Now suppose the game is infinitely repeated, with overall payoff to individual i, $i \in N$, being

$$\sum_{t=1}^{\infty} (\delta_i)^t P_i(\mathbf{s}_t)$$

where $\mathbf{s}_t$ is the strategy used in period t and δ_i, $0 < \delta_i < 1$, is a discount factor. To enforce the outcome associated with $\mathbf{s}^*$, all players adopt the *trigger strategy* $(\mathbf{s}^*, \mathbf{s}^c)$: play $\mathbf{s}^*$ in the first move and in all subsequent moves as long as all other players have played $\mathbf{s}^*$; otherwise play $\mathbf{s}^c$ in *all* future moves. Show that the trigger strategy is a subgame perfect equilibrium if

$$\delta_i > \frac{\phi_i(\mathbf{s}^*) - P_i(\mathbf{s}^*)}{\phi_i(\mathbf{s}^*) - P_i(\mathbf{s}^c)}, \quad i \in N,$$

where $\phi_i(\mathbf{s})$ is the maximum single-period payoff that can be obtained by i if other players play $\mathbf{s}$.

8. Find the dimensions of the bimatrix game that represents a 2×2 bimatrix game repeated T times. In particular, show that for $T = 4$ each player has 32,768 strategies.

9. Consider an economy composed of $2N + 1$ individuals. N own one right shoe and $N + 1$ own one left shoe. Shoes are divisible (by sharing over time). Everyone has the same utility function, which is

$$u = \min(R, L),$$

where R and L are the quantities of right and left shoes consumed, respectively.

(a) Show that any allocation of shoes such that all N possible pairs are matched is a Pareto optimum.

(b) Define the core of an exchange economy. Which Pareto optima are in the core of this economy?

(c) Let p_R and p_L be the prices of the two kinds of shoes. What is the competitive equilibrium of this economy?

10. (A cheese co-op)   A consumer cooperative of n consumers is formed to take advantage of quantity discounts on cheese offered by a local dairy. Consumer i has a fixed requirement x_i for cheese, so the co-op purchases an amount $\sum_{i=1}^{n} x_i$ for its members. The dairy charges $C(x)$ for an amount x of cheese, where C is a concave function with $C(0) = 0$. The co-op allocates the total cost $C(\sum_{i=1}^{n} x_i)$ among its members so that consumer i pays c_i.

(a) State the conditions under which a cost allocation $(c_1, \ldots, c_n)$ is in the core of the game defined by the characteristic function

$$V(S) = -C\left(\sum_{i \in S} x_i\right), \quad S \subset \{1, \ldots, n\}.$$

(b) Let p denote the average cost of cheese purchased by the coop; that is,

$$p = \frac{C\left(\sum_{i=1}^{n} x_i\right)}{\sum_{i=1}^{n} x_i}.$$

If consumer i pays an amount $c_i = px_i$, is $(c_1, \ldots, c_n)$ in the core? Hint: If C is concave and $C(0) = 0$, then $C(\alpha x) \geq \alpha C(x)$ for all $0 \leq \alpha \leq 1$ and $x \geq 0$.

11. (Garbage game) Each of n people has a bag of garbage that he or she must dump on someone's yard. The utility of having b bags of garbage dumped on one's yard is $-\alpha b$, where $\alpha > 0$. Assume that utility is transferable among members of any coalition. Find the characteristic function and core of this game.

12. (a) Find the core for the exchange economy with two consumers below:

$$U_A = \ln x_A^1 + \ln x_A^2 \qquad W_A = (1, 4)$$
$$U_B = \ln x_B^1 + \ln x_B^2 \qquad W_B = (4, 1)$$

(b) Replicate the economy above so there are four consumers, two As and two Bs. Find the new core.

13. (The core of a productive economy) Consider an economy in which consumers have initial endowments and every coalition of consumers has access to the same production possibilities, defined by the subset $\mathcal{Y}$ of the commodity space. The set $\mathcal{Y}$ is assumed to be a convex cone with vertex at the origin (i.e., if $\mathbf{y} \in \mathcal{Y}$ then $\alpha \mathbf{y} \in \mathcal{Y}$ for any $\alpha > 0$). An allocation $\mathbf{X} = (\mathbf{x}_1, \mathbf{x}_2, \ldots, \mathbf{x}_n)$ is feasible if

$$\sum_{i=1}^{n} \mathbf{x}_i = \mathbf{y} + \sum_{i=1}^{n} \mathbf{w}_i$$

for some $\mathbf{y} \in Y$. A feasible allocation $\mathbf{X}$ is dominated by $\mathbf{X}'$ through coalition S if $\mathbf{X}'$ is feasible and

(a) $\sum_{i \in S} \mathbf{x}_i' = \mathbf{y} + \sum_{i \in S} \mathbf{w}_i$.

(b) $\mathbf{x}_i' \succ \mathbf{x}_i$ for all $i \in S$.

The core of this economy is the set of all undominated feasible allocations.

An allocation is competitive if there exists a price vector $\mathbf{p}$ such that profit is maximized over $\mathcal{Y}$ and $\mathbf{x}_i$ maximizes the preferences for consumer i over the constraint $\mathbf{p} \cdot \mathbf{x}_i \leq \mathbf{p} \cdot \mathbf{w}_i$. Note that the maximum profit is zero, since $\mathcal{Y}$ is a cone with vertex at the origin. Prove that a competitive allocation is in the core.

8.10   References

8.1   The foundation of game theory was laid by von Neumann and Morgenstern (1944). It was developed quite fully in Luce and Raiffa (1957), which lays out the various types of game forms. Good general texts on game theory include Owen (1982), Shubik (1982), Thomas (1984), and Friedman (1986). See Fisher (1989) for an interesting viewpoint of the role of game theory in the study of oligopoly. A general microeconomics textbook emphasizing game theory is Kreps (1990).

8.2–8.3   The equilibrium concept for noncooperative games can be traced back to Cournot (1897), and a general existence theorem was first given by Nash (1951). This result was extended to pseudogames by Debreu (1952) and used in an early existence proof of economic equilibria.

8.4   The concept of subgame perfection is due to Selten (1975).

8.5   Good general discussions of multistage games and their associated subgame perfect equilibria are contained in Shubik (1982) and Friedman (1986).

8.6   The general approach of this section is adopted from Dasgupta and Heal (1979) and Aumann (1967).

8.7   The three-cornered market example is adopted from Shubik (1982).

8.8   The concept of the core originated from Edgeworth (1881), who initiated the idea that it shrinks to a single point as the number of players is increased. The modern version of the proof is due to Debreu and Scarf (1963).

8.9   The battle of the sexes game is from Luce and Raiffa (1957). For a theory encompassing Exercise 6, see Hotelling (1929). For theory related to Exercise 7, see Friedman (1986). The garbage game (Exercise 11) is adopted from Shubik (1982). Exercise 13 is based on Debreu and Scarf (1963).

Chapter 9
PUBLIC GOODS AND EXTERNALITIES

Previous chapters emphasized that competitive markets generate Pareto efficient allocations if all the required assumptions are satisfied. In reality, however, the required assumptions are frequently *not* all satisfied, possibly causing substantial departures from efficiency or the breakdown of markets. For instance, Pareto efficiency may not be obtained if (1) markets are not perfectly competitive, in the sense that some individuals or firms have market power (as in the case of monopolies), (2) a complete set of markets does not exist, (3) there are nonconvexities, or (4) commodities are nondivisible. Each of these clearly violates the assumptions used to establish the First and Second Theorems of Welfare Economics. Another, perhaps less obvious but extremely important violation of the underlying assumptions occurs if there are *externalities*.

An externality is a nonmarket link between the decision structures of two or more agents. Perhaps the simplest type is that of a *consumption externality*, present when the consumption of one individual directly affects the preferences of another (as in "keeping up with the Joneses"). Another type is that of a *production externality*, which is present when the action of one firm affects the production possibility set of another (as when the pollution of a river by one factory affects the production possibility set of another firm downstream). *Mixed externalities* are links between preferences and production. Externalities are assumed away in the First and Second Theorems of Welfare Economics, since in those theorems the utility of an individual depends only on his or her own consumption, and the production possibility set of each firm is defined only with respect to its own netput vectors. This chapter explores the impact of externalities and, most importantly, examines mechanisms, alternative to competitive markets, that can achieve Pareto efficient allocations even in the presence of externalities.

We consider first the case of public goods, which is an extreme version of a consumption externality and one that deserves special treatment.

Part I
PUBLIC GOODS

9.1 Public Goods and Pareto Efficiency

Most commodities discussed in earlier chapters are *private goods*, in that they are purchased and consumed individually. Whatever one individual consumes is lost to other consumers. Public goods have two properties that distinguish them from private goods. First, consumption by one individual does not preclude consumption by others. The good is not really *consumed;* it is just used. The classic example of a good of this kind is the light beacon produced by a lighthouse. The use of this beacon as a guide by one ship does not preclude its use by other ships. Often the term *nonrivalness of consumption* is used to describe this property. Other examples of goods with this property are television broadcasts, beautification projects, and national defense.

A second property of public goods is that of nonexclusive use. If the good is available, it is available equally to everyone, independently of whether they pay for it or not. If the use of the good can be restricted to those who pay for it, it is not a public good. Some goods satisfying the first criterion of not being used up by individual consumption fail this second criterion. For example, a bridge supplies a service that is not depleted when used (ignoring congestion), but it can be made exclusive by installation of a toll booth, so it is not a public good. Likewise, television signals can be scrambled so that a decoder is required for program reception, and the light from a lighthouse could, in principle, be beamed directly to a specific ship in response to a radio request. But in many cases the effort required to ensure exclusivity is extremely costly and hence impractical, and the good is accordingly deemed to be a public good.

A *pure public good* is a public good that must be consumed in identical amounts by everyone. Examples include (when idealized) national defense, police protection, and clean air. This section deals with pure public goods defined this way.

Public goods fall outside the assumptions surrounding the theory of perfect competition and economic efficiency discussed in earlier chapters. Therefore it is not surprising to find that normal market mechanisms do not guarantee the Pareto efficient[1] allocation of such goods. This is essentially the issue that is discussed in this and the next few sections. We shall first formulate the conditions that are necessary for the Pareto efficient

---

[1]Throughout this chapter we use the obvious extension of Pareto efficiency, originally stated in Chapter 6 for a private goods economy, to mean that there is no way to improve all individuals with at least one improvement being strict.

allocation of pure public goods, and then investigate possible mechanisms for achieving such allocations.

For simplicity, consider an economy consisting of two individuals. Suppose there is a single pure public good, to be supplied in amount x, and a single private good, supplied in aggregate at level y. Individual i, $i = 1, 2$, receives y_i units of the private good and x units of the public good. We assume that the set of efficient production possibilities is the set of solutions to

$$T(x, y - Y_0) = 0,$$

where T is a transformation function and Y_0 is the aggregate endowment of the private good. (Hence, $Y_0 - y$ is used to produce x.)

We assume that both individuals have continuous, strongly monotonic utility functions with respect to consumption (or use) of the public and private goods. An allocation has the form (x, y_1, y_2). If an allocation is Pareto efficient, it will maximize the utility of any one individual, given that the utility of the other individual does not decrease. Hence if the allocation (x^*, y_1^*, y_2^*) is Pareto efficient, it is a solution to

$$\max_{x, y_1, y_2} u_1(x, y_1)$$

$$\text{sub to } u_2(x, y_2) \geq u_2(x^*, y_2^*)$$
$$T(x, y_1 + y_2 - Y_0) = 0$$
$$x \geq 0, \quad y_1 \geq 0, \quad y_2 \geq 0.$$

Introducing Lagrange multipliers λ and μ, and assuming an interior solution, the associated first-order necessary conditions are

$$\frac{\partial u_1(x^*, y_1^*)}{\partial x} + \lambda \frac{\partial u_2(x^*, y_2^*)}{\partial x} + \mu \frac{\partial T(x^*, y^* - Y_0)}{\partial x} = 0$$

$$\frac{\partial u_1(x^*, y_1^*)}{\partial y_1} + \phantom{\lambda \frac{\partial u_2(x^*, y_2^*)}{\partial x}} + \mu \frac{\partial T(x^*, y^* - Y_0)}{\partial y} = 0$$

$$\lambda \frac{\partial u_2(x^*, y_2^*)}{\partial y_2} + \mu \frac{\partial T(x^*, y^* - Y_0)}{\partial y} = 0$$

where $y^* = y_1^* + y_2^*$. The last two equations can be written

$$\frac{\partial u_1(x^*, y_1^*)}{\partial y_1} = \lambda \frac{\partial u_2(x^*, y_2^*)}{\partial y_2} = -\mu \frac{\partial T(x^*, y^* - Y_0)}{\partial y}.$$

We may then divide the three terms of the first equation by the first, second, or third term, respectively, in the above to obtain

$$\frac{\partial u_1(x^*, y_1^*)/\partial x}{\partial u_1(x^*, y_1^*)/\partial y_1} + \frac{\partial u_2(x^*, y_2^*)/\partial x}{\partial u_2(x^*, y_2^*)/\partial y_2} = \frac{\partial T(x^*, y^* - Y_0)/\partial x}{\partial T(x^*, y^* - Y_0)/\partial y}.$$

The first two terms are marginal rates of substitution, and the term on the right is the marginal rate of transformation of the private good for the public good. We can write the equation in the short hand form $\text{MRS}_1 + \text{MRS}_2 = \text{MRT}$.

For an economy with n individuals, a similar argument shows that a necessary condition for Pareto efficient allocation of a pure public good is that the marginal rates of substitution of this good for any private good summed over all consumers is equal to the marginal rate of transformation. That is,

$$MRS_1 + MRS_2 + \cdots + MRS_n = MRT. \tag{9.1}$$

This is the fundamental necessary condition in the case of pure public goods and is referred to as the *Samuelson condition.*

Recall that for private goods a necessary condition for Pareto efficiency is that for each individual the marginal rate of substitution between every pair of private goods is equal to the marginal rate of transformation between these goods. That is, $MRS_i = MRT$ for each $i = 1, 2, \ldots, n$. (See Section 6.4.) In the case of a pure public good, it is the sum of the marginal rates of substitution, summed over all consumers, that must be equal to the marginal rate of transformation.

This condition for Pareto efficiency can be understood intuitively. Suppose that in a city of 10,000 people, each person would be willing to give up one pair of shoes for an additional city park. Everyone then has an MRS of shoes for the park equal to 1. If the park could be constructed for the same effort as 10,000 pairs of shoes or less, it is Pareto efficient to build the park. Since the park is a public good, everyone can contribute to it, and all will enjoy the benefit.

The Pareto efficiency condition can also be illustrated graphically. Suppose production of one unit of the public good requires one unit of the private good. That is, x and y are related by $x = Y_0 - y$ where Y_0 is the total endowment of the private good. Fig. 9.1 shows the consumption spaces for two individuals, together with their indifference curves through the Pareto efficient allocations. To increase x from this point, to say $x + \Delta$, requires that, in sum, the two individuals give up exactly Δ units of y. Moving up the tangents to the respective indifference curves will do this provided the sum of the MRS's is 1.

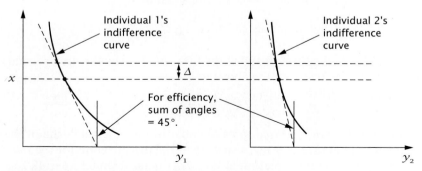

FIGURE 9.1   Pareto efficiency for a public good.

Inefficiency of a Private Market

In a private-goods market, the equilibrium price ratio between two goods is equal to the MRS for every consumer simultaneously and also equal to the MRT. The price system thereby guarantees Pareto efficiency because it ensures that the MRS of every individual is equal to MRT. A competitive price system does not yield Pareto efficiency for public good allocations, since the necessary conditions are different.

Typically, the MRS of a private good for a public good is relatively large for small values of the public good (since a unit increment in the public good is then highly valued) and decreases for larger values (since the marginal benefit decreases). It is useful to think of MRS as the degree of desirability for incremental amounts. It tends to be high if we do not have any of the good. At a Pareto efficient allocation satisfying (9.1), it is clear that the MRS for each individual is lower than it would be if MRS = MRT. Thus, the private market mechanism leads to higher MRSs than is Pareto efficient, meaning that too little of the good is produced.

To illustrate the inefficiency of a private market more dramatically, suppose for simplicity that MRT $\equiv 1$; that is, a unit of public good can always be produced from a unit of the private good according to the relation $x = Y_0 - y$. Suppose there is initially no public good available. Then individuals, in turn, purchase increments of the public good as if it were a private good. Individual 1 would purchase an amount x that would lower MRS_1 to 1, and this level of x would be enjoyed by all individuals. If $MRS_2 > 1$ at this level, individual 2 would purchase an incremental level so as to lower MRS_2 to 1; however, if $MRS_2 \leq 1$ already, individual 2 would not purchase an additional amount. As the process continues, the higher-indexed individuals would be progressively less likely to purchase increments of the public good, since they would already enjoy the aggregate level resulting from the earlier purchases. These later individuals would get a *free ride.* They have little motivation to purchase the public good, when an adequate amount is supplied by others. Of course, the order of individuals is arbitrary, so really each individual will prefer to wait for others to purchase the public good. Each individual is tempted to be a free rider, obtaining the benefits of the public good that others supply. The result is that the MRSs are not low enough and too little of the public good is supplied.

As a concrete example, imagine a small group of houses located at the end of a road in an area that gets heavy snow. A snowplow can be called for a fixed price at any time. Because every resident can enjoy the benefits of a plowed road, each hopes to become a free rider, with someone else paying for the plow. With a strict private market where a single individual must call for the plow, the amount of plowing will certainly be less than is efficient.

One good way to analyze the private market structure is to formalize it as a noncooperative game and find the Nash equilibrium points. Accordingly we consider a game with n players: player i has utility $u_i(x, y_i)$ and endowment $\overline{y}_i$. We assume again that $x = Y_0 - y$, so production of one unit of the public good entails a loss of one unit of the private good. Let x_i be the amount of the public good that individual i would incrementally add to that supplied by everyone else. If $\mathbf{x}^* = (x_1^*, x_2^*, \ldots, x_n^*)$ is a Nash equilibrium, then x_i^* must be the solution to

$$\max_{x_i \geq 0} u_i(x_1^* + x_2^* + \cdots + x_i + \cdots + x_n^*, \ \overline{y}_i - x_i).$$

Setting $x^* = \sum_{i=1}^{n} x_i^*$ and $y_i^* = \overline{y}_i - x_i^*$, we find the first-order condition for this problem to be

$$\frac{\partial u_i(x^*, y_i^*)}{\partial x_i} - \frac{\partial u_i(x^*, y_i^*)}{\partial y} \leq 0,$$

or equivalently, $\mathrm{MRS}_i \leq 1$, with equality if $x_i^* > 0$. Hence, any individual who finds $\mathrm{MRS}_i < 1$, based on the contributions by others, will set $x_i^* = 0$ (obtaining a free ride). This will mean that the person who most wants the public good will have to pay for it all, and hence little will be provided. (See Exercise 2.)

*9.2   Majority Voting

The previous section showed that if public goods are allocated by a private-goods market, the result may be far from efficient. Hence, in practice, public goods are allocated and paid for by different mechanisms—a common method being voting and taxation. We examine that mechanism briefly here.

As before, suppose there are only two goods: a pure public good and a private good. Also assume that $x = Y_0 - y$, so that $\mathrm{MRT} = 1$ and one unit of public good production requires one unit of the private good. Payment for the public good is made through taxation. Each individual i pays a fixed proportion t_i of the total cost, measured in terms of the private good. The t_i's satisfy $t_i \geq 0$ and $\sum_{i=1}^{n} t_i = 1$. The simplest case is $t_i = 1/n$, but other proportions may be used.

Given the tax proportion t_i, the most favored level x of the public good for individual i can be found by solving

$$\max u_i(x, y_i)$$
$$\text{sub to } t_i x + y_i = \overline{y}_i,$$

where $\overline{y}_i$ is i's initial endowment of the private good. Equivalently, we solve $\max u_i(x, \overline{y}_i - t_i x)$, obtaining

$$\frac{\partial u_i}{\partial x} - t_i \frac{\partial u_i}{\partial y} = 0,$$

which is

$$\mathrm{MRS}_i = t_i. \tag{9.2}$$

The level of the public good desired by i is greater here than with the private-goods market mechanism because $\text{MRS}_i = t_i < 1$, (lower MRS means higher x).

Any level $x \geq 0$ defines an allocation $(x, y_1, y_2, \ldots, y_n)$ through the relation $y_i = \overline{y}_i - t_i x$. We can describe a special equilibrium concept for such allocations based on majority voting.

Majority equilibrium. A level $x \geq 0$ with associated allocation $(x, y_1, y_2, \ldots, y_n)$ is a *majority equilibrium* if for any other level x' and associated $(x', y_1', y_2', \ldots, y_n')$ there holds $u_i(x, y_i) \geq u_i(x', y_i')$ for at least $n/2$ i's in $N = \{1, 2, \ldots, n\}$. (That is, no x' could win in a vote between it and x.)

We can show that under fairly mild assumptions a majority equilibrium level exists for the case of a single public good. For each i we suppose that the function

$$\text{MRS}_i(x) = \frac{\partial u_i(x, \overline{y}_i - t_i x)}{\partial x} \Big/ \frac{\partial u_i(x, \overline{y}_i - t_i x)}{\partial y}$$

is continuous and that $u_i(x, \overline{y}_i - t_i x)$ is concave with respect to x. We also assume that there is a level $X > 0$ such that for each $i \in N$, $\text{MRS}_i(0) > t_i$ and $\text{MRS}_i(X) < t_i$.

At $x = 0$ we have $\text{MRS}_i(x) > t_i$ for all $i \in N$, and at $x = X$ we have $\text{MRS}_i(x) > t_i$ for no $i \in N$. Hence, by continuity, there is an intermediate value $\overline{x}$ such that $\text{MRS}_i(\overline{x}) > t_i$ for $i \in N_1$, $\text{MRS}_i(\overline{x}) = t_i$ for $i \in N_2$, and $\text{MRS}_i(\overline{x}) < t_i$ for $i \in N_3$ where N_1 and N_3 each have no more than $n/2$ members.

We can see that this $\overline{x}$ is a majority equilibrium. By the concavity assumption, for any $x < \overline{x}$ the members in $N_1 \cup N_2$ will prefer $\overline{x}$, and hence $\overline{x}$ will win in a vote between x and $\overline{x}$. Likewise, for any $x > \overline{x}$, $N_2 \cup N_3$ will prefer $\overline{x}$. Thus a majority equilibrium exists.

This idea is illustrated in Fig. 9.2 for five individuals with $t_i = \frac{1}{5}$ for each i. MRS curves are shown. At small values of x all five individuals have MRS $> \frac{1}{5}$ and hence all want a higher x. At $\overline{x}$ two individuals (numbers 1 and 2) want a higher x, one individual (number 3) is perfectly satisfied, and two others (numbers 4 and 5) want a lower x. No proposal can win a majority over $\overline{x}$.

We argue that a majority equilibrium has a chance of being Pareto efficient. For example, if everyone's most desired level (where $\text{MRS}_i = t_i$) happened to be identical, that level would be a majority equilibrium. That level also would be Pareto efficient because in that case $\sum_{i=1}^{n} \text{MRS}_i = \sum_{i=1}^{n} t_i = 1$. In other cases the majority elected level will normally have $\text{MRS}_i > t_i$ for about half of the individuals and $\text{MRS}_i < t_i$ for the other half. Hence it is conceivable that $\sum_{i=1}^{n} \text{MRS}_i$ will be close to 1. Of course, closeness to 1 is not always assured. In cases where relatively few individuals benefit greatly from the public good and others do not, the distortion from

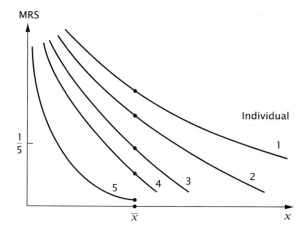

FIGURE 9.2 A majority equilibrium for five individuals.

Pareto efficiency resulting from the majority voting mechanism can be quite large. (A more complete discussion of voting mechanisms is contained in Chapter 10.)

9.3   Lindahl Equilibria

A private-goods market does not allocate public goods efficiently—but this does not rule out the possibility that there is a different form of market that does. Indeed, there is a market structure and an associated equilibrium concept that, except for one (rather important) weakness related to incentives, does provide an elegant solution to the problem of allocating public goods. The concept is that of Lindahl equilibria.

To explain the essence of the idea, let us, as in the previous section, consider an economy consisting of n individuals and two goods: a pure public good and a private good with MRT $\equiv 1$. Suppose a set of individual tax rates (or prices) t_i, $i = 1, 2, \ldots, n$, $t_i \geq 0$, $\sum_{i=1}^{n} t_i = 1$, are established for payment of the public good, measured in terms of the private good. Faced with the tax rate t_i, individual i can determine (by maximizing utility subject to the induced budget constraint) an associated optimal personal level of the good, say $x_i(t_i)$. By varying t_i we can consider the function $x_i(t_i)$. In general, as t_i decreases, $x_i(t_i)$ will increase.

It certainly seems plausible that we could select the n separate tax rates t_i, $i = 1, 2, \ldots, n$, just right, so that all desired levels are equal, that is, so that there is an x such that $x_i(t_i) = x$ for all i. If so, these tax rates and the resulting common desired level x of the public good is a Lindahl equilibrium.

The Lindahl equilibrium concept can be illustrated graphically for the case of two individuals, as shown in Fig. 9.3. The figure shows the graphs of the two demand functions $x_1(t_1)$ and $x_2(t_2)$. For individual 1 the curve is

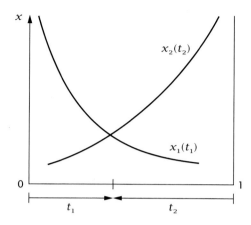

FIGURE 9.3 Lindahl equilibrium from demand curves.

drawn in the conventional way. For individual 2 we reverse the direction of the t axis. A point where these curves cross defines a Lindahl equilibrium.

A Lindahl equilibrium is Pareto efficient since $MRS_i = t_i$ for each i and for $\sum_{i=1}^{n} t_i = 1$. Furthermore, at the equilibrium values of the t_i's, everyone prefers the associated x over any other value. This, then, seems to be a very desirable solution to the public goods problem. So what is wrong with Lindahl equilibria?

The major problem is that a Lindahl equilibrium is hard to achieve. Individual incentives work against it. To establish the Lindahl equilibrium, the Lindahl taxes (or, more generally, Lindahl prices) must be determined, and traditional market mechanisms, which work for quantities, cannot allocate prices. Some other means must be used to find these prices.

The simplest method for trying to find the right prices would be to just ask individuals to report their Lindahl functions $x_i(t_i)$ for all t_i. We could then compute the Lindahl solution. However, if individuals know that they will be charged according to the rates they report, they have strong incentives to skew their curves to emphasize low tax rates, so as to obtain a relatively free ride. For the process to work, individuals must report truthfully, and there is no incentive to do so. Think of the snowplow situation, and imagine the success, or lack of success, a neighborhood agent might have going through the neighborhood asking individuals how much snowplowing was worth to them—given that they will be charged whatever they report.

Incentive problems occur in private-goods markets as well. For instance, if there are relatively few consumers, they may each realize they are not really price takers, and they may "game" the allocation process. In the case of public goods, however, the problem appears to be more acute, and it does not decrease as the number of individuals increases. Hence, although the concept of a Lindahl equilibrium has some attractive properties, it suffers from the fatal flaw of being inconsistent with individual incentives.

9.4   Incentive-Compatible Revelation Procedures

The previous section has raised the basic problem of how to elicit true statements of preference from individuals. Truthfulness is important not merely
for its own sake, but because it provides a means for achieving Pareto efficiency. However, people have an astonishing capability to discern the impact
on their own welfare of procedures that link information they supply with
rewards they receive. They are remarkably good game players, especially
when *real* money is involved. It is therefore not surprising that it is difficult
to get people to report truthfully if it is not in their own best interest to do
so. This is all the more true if the information required is not a verifiable
fact but merely vague information about personal preference.

Since true information appears to be necessary to make socially efficient
decisions about public goods, we are motivated to launch a deeper investigation of how to construct allocation mechanisms that have two roles: they
elicit truthful reports from self-interested individuals, and they produce
allocations that are good for everyone (that is, they are Pareto efficient). A
mechanism with the first property, in which truthfulness is compatible with
self-interest, is termed an *incentive-compatible revelation procedure.*

The Vickrey Auction

We begin by considering incentives for truthful revelation of preferences
in a simple private-goods market. Suppose a single (nondivisible) item is to
be sold. There are n potential buyers and a single seller. A familiar selling
procedure for this situation is the highest-bid auction. Each potential buyer
submits a sealed bid, and the item is sold to the highest bidder at a price
equal to that bid. This procedure is straightforward and often works well in
practice, but it is *not* incentive compatible and hence leads to gaming and
second-guessing.

Imagine that you are one of a number of potential bidders for a major
item, such as a house. You might begin the process of formulating your bid
by assessing the maximum amount that you would pay for the item (your
willingness to pay). Suppose it is v. However, if you are wise, you would also
estimate the corresponding values for the other bidders. Then you might
submit a bid somewhat lower than v in the hope that you will obtain the
object at this lower bid and thereby obtain a measure of consumer surplus.
(Indeed, assuming a probability distribution for the other bids, you could
work out your optimal bid.) You would rarely bid your *true* willingness to
pay v. Hence the auction is not incentive compatible.

As a simple example, suppose there were only one other bidder and you
know that his or her bid was going to be either v_H or v_L with $v_H > v > v_L$,
where v is your willingness to pay. In this case you should bid $b = v_L + \varepsilon$ for

some small $\varepsilon > 0$ so that you will obtain a surplus of $v - b$ in your willingness to pay if the opponent bids low. If the opponent bids high, you will lose the auction anyway, and you want to lose in this event.

A *Vickrey auction* is similar to the highest-bid auction, but with a slight twist. Again each potential buyer submits a sealed bid, and the object is awarded to the highest bidder, *but at the price of the second-highest bid.*

What would you bid if you were participating in such an auction? Clearly you would not bid above v, since you might win the object and have to pay a price higher than v. Also, there is no advantage to bidding lower than v, for if your bid is highest, a small change in your bid makes no difference in the actual price you will pay. If you lower your bid, you risk losing the object. Hence a bid equal to v, your true willingness to pay, is optimal.[2]

The Groves Mechanism

We now consider a method for eliciting truthful preference statements in connection with public goods. Suppose the level of a single public good, denoted x, is to be selected and there is a single private good. A central authority asks individuals to state their willingness to pay (in terms of the private good) for various values of x. Then, assuming this information to be true, the central authority computes the socially best value of x, and this value is in fact supplied. Individuals are also taxed on the basis of the information they supply.

To more fully describe the process, we assume, as in earlier sections, that MRT $\equiv 1$ (that is, production of one unit of x requires one unit of y). We *must* also assume here that the utility function of the ith individual has the *quasi-linear* form $v_i(x) + y$ where y is the level of the private good (thought of as money). In this case $v_i(x)$ is the willingness to pay since $v_i(x)$ and y trade off directly. (Note also that $v_i(x) + y - u$ in this case equals the benefit function, measured with respect to y as the reference commodity.)

Each individual submits a reported willingness to pay function $w_i(x)$, for all values of x, which may or may not agree with the true willingness to pay function $v_i(x)$. The central authority receives the reported functions and selects the level $\overline{x}$ as the solution to the problem

$$\max_{x} \sum_{i=1}^{n} w_i(x) - x. \qquad (9.3)$$

That is, the central authority maximizes the total consumer surplus (or net willingness to pay or net benefit) based on the reported functions. Notice

---

[2]Note that a calling-out auction, in which increasing bids are successively called out, approximates the results of a Vickrey auction, since the second highest bidder should stop at his willingness to pay. The highest bidder gets the object at a cost somewhat higher than this, but perhaps considerably below his or her own willingness to pay.

that if the reported functions are the true willingness-to-pay functions (that is, $w_i(x) = v_i(x)$), then in the differentiable case, the public goods level $\overline{x}$ maximizing (9.3) satisfies the first-order necessary condition of the above problem $\sum_{i=1}^{n} v_i'(\overline{x}) = 1$, which is also the first-order necessary condition for Pareto efficiency—the Samuelson condition. So the level $\overline{x}$ will be Pareto efficient *if* all reports are truthful and *if* the total payments (in terms of y) are equal to $\overline{x}$.

Now consider how to pay for $\overline{x}$. We need a tax scheme, preferably one that provides incentives for consumers to report $w_i = v_i$. Individual $i, i = 1, 2, \ldots, n$, is taxed the amount

$$T_i = t_i\overline{x} - \sum_{j \neq i} \left[w_j(\overline{x}) - t_j\overline{x} \right], \tag{9.4}$$

where the $t_i > 0$ satisfy $\sum_{i=1}^{n} t_i = 1$. The proportions t_i are fixed beforehand and are therefore not influenced by the reports. The first term of the tax is individual i's proportional cost share. The term $w_j(\overline{x}) - t_j\overline{x}$ is individual j's reported net willingness to pay. The second term in (9.4) is therefore the total reported net willingness to pay, exclusive of that of individual i.

In the reporting process it is assumed that each individual takes the reports of others as given. However, each person i accounts for the influence of his report on the bundle of public goods supplied and on the tax T_i.

Now let us consider whether individual i will choose to report truthfully. Individual i seeks to maximize $v_i(x) - T_i$. We have

$$v_i(x) - T_i = v_i(x) - x + \sum_{j \neq i} w_j(x). \tag{9.5}$$

Now the reported function w_i has no *direct* effect on $v_i(x) - T_i$, but it does affect the ultimate value through the choice of x. Hence individual i wants x to be selected so as to maximize (9.5). However, it is clear that if individual i reports truthfully (that is, puts $w_i(x) = v_i(x)$ for all x), the central authority's objective will be identical to that of individual i, and the value that individual i desires will in fact be selected.

The strategy of reporting truthfully is therefore an optimal strategy for individual i, whether or not the reports by others are true. That is, truthful reporting is a dominant strategy for individual i (see Section 8.2).

The above procedure for selecting $\overline{x}$ by maximizing total net reported willingness-to-pay functions and taxing according to (9.4) is the Groves procedure, or Groves mechanism. The following example illustrates how the mechanism works for a project of fixed size and also shows that the Groves mechanism is closely related to the Vickrey auction.

Example 9.1 (A single project).   A small rural community is considering paving its residential streets. If the project is accepted, all streets will be paved. The project will be paid for by assessing each landowner an amount proportional to the length of his or her property frontage. There is some doubt as to whether the project is desirable, so it is useful to obtain truthful statements of the preferences from the landowners.

In this case, since there are only two levels being considered—no project or full project—each landowner's preference can be characterized by a single number, the net willingness to pay for the full project. The net willingness to pay for no project is assumed to be zero. The Groves mechanism can be instituted in this case by asking each landowner to submit such a number w_i, which of course may or may not be equal to the corresponding true value v_i. (In this case, the v_i's and w_i's are net quantities, after the assessments; they may very well be negative for some individuals.)

The community government will accept the project if $\sum_{j=1}^{n} w_j \geq 0$; otherwise it will reject the project. This rule maximizes the total reported net willingness to pay. Further, in addition to the proportional costs, each landowner i must pay an amount

$$-\sum_{j \neq i} w_j \qquad \text{if the project is accepted}$$

$$0 \qquad \text{if the project is rejected.}$$

We can directly see how the incentive mechanism works in this example. The total payoff to individual i is

$$v_i + \sum_{j \neq i} w_j \qquad \text{if the project is accepted}$$

$$0 \qquad \text{if the project is rejected.}$$

Individual i wants the project to be accepted only if the first payoff is greater than or equal to zero. That result can be guaranteed by setting $w_i = v_i$.

Here we can see the analogy with a Vickrey auction. Consider the value $s = -\sum_{j \neq i} w_j$, the negative of the sum of the willingness-to-pay figures reported by everyone but individual i. If the number is positive, others do not want the project. Then s can be thought of as a joint bid by everyone else for the right to kill the project. To win the project, individual i must outbid these others by reporting a value higher than s. Hence, s acts like a second-highest bid for individual i. If i's bid w_i exceeds s, he or she will win the project and be required to pay an amount s. Our previous analysis of the Vickrey auction shows that i's best bid is $w_i = v_i$.

Critique

A major problem with the Groves mechanism is that the budget is not balanced; that is, the sum of the taxes paid may not equal the total project cost. The tax formula may actually require that individuals *receive* significant sums of the private good. This would happen in the above example if everyone had a positive net willingness to pay for the project. The incentive mechanism requires that each person receive a payment equal to the total net surplus of everyone else. This budget imbalance means that the solution found by the Groves mechanism is actually not a feasible allocation. The Samuelson necessary conditions for Pareto efficiency do hold for the chosen $\bar{x}$, but this in itself is not enough. The aggregate payment must equal $\bar{x}$.

To implement the Groves mechanism, additional funds are required, but the source of these funds is not clear. If these funds are derived even partially from the individuals themselves, these individuals would account for this fact when formulating their own optimization problems, and a different result would be obtained. If, on the other hand, the funds are derived from another group, that group's welfare should also be considered in the derivation of the Pareto efficiency conditions.

The unbalanced budget condition can be ameliorated (sometimes significantly) by slightly changing the formula for individual taxes. We note that the incentive for truthful revelation of preferences is not destroyed if a term A_i, independent of i's report, is added to individual i's tax. This term can depend on the reports of others, but as long as it does not depend directly on the function w_i or on x (which depends indirectly on w_i), the incentive structure is not changed. With this modification, the tax has the form

$$T_i = t_i x - \sum_{j \neq i} \left[w_j(x) - t_j x \right] + A_i. \tag{9.6}$$

Proper selection of the A_i's can help close the budget gap. One useful choice for A_i is

$$A_i = \max_x \sum_{j \neq i} \left[w_j(x) - t_j x \right]. \tag{9.7}$$

Note that although A_i depends on the w_j functions for $j \neq i$, it does not depend on w_i, so it meets the required criterion.

The x that achieves the maximum in (9.7) is the one that would be computed if individual i submitted the completely neutral report $w_i(x) = t_i x$, stating no net willingness to pay. A_i is therefore the total net willingness to pay that would be received by others under this neutral report. If the final level of the public good is $\bar{x}$, the term $A_i - \sum_{j \neq i}[w_j(\bar{x}) - t_j \bar{x}]$ is the amount that the net surplus decreases as a result of i's participation. This term is always nonnegative. It follows that $\sum_{i=1}^n T_i \geq \sum_{i=1}^n t_i \bar{x} = \bar{x}$. Hence there is always enough tax collected by this mechanism to finance the public good.

The above choice of the A_i's is good for the central authority, but it may not be very good for the individuals. In fact, with this choice of the A_i's, some individuals may end up at negative willingness to pay points. In other words, some individuals may be worse off than at $x = 0$. So in this sense the procedure is not individually rational. (See Section 8.6.)

Unfortunately, the budget imbalance associated with the Groves mechanism is a fundamental limitation. It can be shown that there is no choice of A_i, $i = 1, 2, \ldots, n$, depending only on the w_j's, $j \neq i$, such that a balanced budget is assured. Therefore, the Groves mechanism cannot be regarded as a complete solution to the problem of allocating public goods.

*Other Mechanisms

The problem of determining a suitable mechanism for allocating public goods can be cast in a game theoretic framework. The n individuals in the economy are players of the game. The strategies for player i consist of the choice of a message m_i, within a class of allowable messages, to be sent to a coordinating center. The messages received by the center from the n players are then combined by an outcome function to determine the allocations, including the level of public goods and the individual costs. We may consider the design of such a game as the specification of allowable messages and specification of the outcome function. We then ask whether games can be designed whose Nash equilibria have suitable properties.

The private market for public goods was treated as a game of this type in Section 9.1, where the messages were incremental amounts to be purchased. However, the Nash solutions to this game were far from Pareto efficient. The Groves mechanism corresponds to a game in which the messages are reported willingness-to-pay functions. We have seen that truthful reporting is a dominant strategy for every player in this game. However, the solution is not balanced—that is, the budget is not balanced—and hence it is not feasible.

An alternative approach is to weaken the solution concept of the game by considering strategies that constitute a Nash equilibrium, rather than dominant strategies. This approach was followed by Groves and Ledyard, and it has a number of very attractive features.

Rather than present the Groves-Ledyard mechanism directly, let us follow this general idea and see where it leads. We assume as before that there is only one public good and one private good, with MRT $\equiv 1$. There are n individuals, and individual i has utility function $u_i(x, y_i)$.

For our design we specify the individual messages m_i to be single (scalar) numbers. For convenience, we define these as desired increments of the public good, as in the private market game, but we keep the specification of cost assignment quite arbitrary. We let $\mathbf{m} = (m_1, m_2, \ldots, m_n)$ be the vector of messages. After receiving $\mathbf{m}$, we set

$$x = \sum_{i=1}^{n} m_i$$

$$T_i = F_i(\mathbf{m}), \qquad i = 1, 2, \ldots, n,$$

where the functions F_i are yet to be chosen. A choice of F_i's is a design of the game. Suppose $\mathbf{m}^*$ is a Nash equilibrium of our general game. Then m_i^* is a solution to the problem

$$\max_{m_i} \ u(m_1^* + \cdots + m_i + \cdots + m_n^*, \overline{y}_i - T_i)$$

where $\overline{y}_i$ is i's original endowment of the private good. Assuming an interior point solution, we may write the first-order condition

$$\frac{\partial u(x, \overline{y}_i - T_i)}{\partial x} - \frac{\partial u(x, \overline{y}_i - T_i)}{\partial y} \frac{\partial F_i(\mathbf{m}^*)}{m_i} = 0.$$

Or equivalently,

$$\text{MRS}_i = \frac{\partial F_i(\mathbf{m}^*)}{\partial m_i}.$$

We would like the Nash solution to correspond to a Pareto efficient allocation. For this to be the case we require that the Samuelson condition $\sum_{i=1}^{n} \text{MRS}_i = 1$ be satisfied and that $\sum_{i=1}^{n} T_i = x$ so that the budget is balanced. These translate into the two requirements on the F_i's, namely,

$$\sum_{i=1}^{n} \frac{\partial F_i(\mathbf{m})}{\partial m_i} = 1 \qquad (9.8)$$

$$\sum_{i=1}^{n} F_i(\mathbf{m}) = \sum_{i=1}^{n} m_i \qquad (9.9)$$

at $\mathbf{m}^*$. To design a game that is sure to work, we must select F_i's for which the above equations hold identically for all $\mathbf{m}$.

There is one obvious design satisfying (9.8) and (9.9), which we denote by $\overline{F}_i$. It is

$$\overline{F}_i(\mathbf{m}) = t_i \sum_{j=1}^{n} m_j,$$

where $\sum_{i=1}^{n} t_i = 1$. This is the game in which each person submits a desired increment knowing that he or she will be required to pay a fixed share of the total—quite a simple game.

Unfortunately the above simple solution is so degenerate that it is not workable. Suppose, for example, that the u_i's were of the quasi-linear form $u_i(x, y_i) = v_i(x) + y_i$ and that $t_i = 1/n$. Then an interior point equilibrium would require $v_i'(x^*) = 1/n$ for all i. But this could never hold unless the v_i's just happened to share a point where the derivatives were all equal to $1/n$.

We can modify the design by appending some nonlinear terms to the proposed F_i's, which will eliminate the degeneracy. If we let $F_i(\mathbf{m}) = \overline{F}_i(\mathbf{m}) + G_i(\mathbf{m})$, the G_i's must satisfy equations similar to (9.8) and (9.9) but with zero on their right-hand sides. One solution (for $n \geq 3$) is

$$G_i(\mathbf{m}) = y \left[(m_i - m_{i+1})^2 - (m_{i+1} - m_{i+2})^2 \right],$$

where $y > 0$ and where $i = n + 1$ and $i = n + 2$ are interpreted as $i = 1$ and as $i = 2$, respectively. The two required conditions can be checked by inspection. So we have designed a game whose Nash solution yields a Pareto efficient allocation. This mechanism is not degenerate because $\partial G_i/\partial m_i$ is not constant. Note that this mechanism charges individual i a larger tax if m_i deviates from m_{i+1}, but this penalty is reduced if m_{i+1} deviates from m_{i+2}. Hence, it induces people to tend toward a common level. The Groves–Ledyard mechanism uses a similar, but more complex, form for the G_i's. See Exercise 7.

Although the above mechanism is an interesting approach to the incentive-compatibility problem, it has some serious shortcomings. First, it too fails to be individually rational. Because of the tax, some individuals end up at points that are worse than their original endowments. Second, it is not clear how the Nash equilibrium would be achieved. An iterative process may not be stable and would itself be subject to gaming.

From the above examples we have learned a bit about incentives and the difficulty of designing incentive-compatible mechanisms. However, we have not found a fail-proof mechanism. Indeed, it has been shown, by Hurwicz, under quite general conditions, that if we want Pareto efficiency and individual rationality to be realized as a Nash solution to a game, that solution must be a Lindahl equilibrium. This is perhaps disheartening, for we know that a Lindahl solution is not incentive compatible, and the Groves mechanism, while incentive compatible, is not individually rational. Life is more complicated than we might hope. But we can now address incentive issues from an informed perspective and devise mechanisms that, although not perfect, are useful for the situation at hand.

Part II
EXTERNALITIES

9.5 Benefits and Externalities

We now turn attention to more general externalities, seeking to characterize Pareto efficiency and see how it might be achieved. We shall find that although the presence of externalities invalidates the relation between Pareto efficiency and equilibria, it does not invalidate the general principle that Pareto efficiency is related to benefit maximization.

We focus first on consumption externalities in order to keep the notation as simple as possible. Production externalities are easily added to the discussion; they are in fact easier to treat because profits or costs can be aggregated, while utilities cannot.

As usual we consider a set of n individuals and m commodities. An allocation is a vector $\mathbf{X} = (\mathbf{x}_1, \mathbf{x}_2, \ldots, \mathbf{x}_n)$ where each $\mathbf{x}_i \in X_i = \mathcal{R}_+^m$. The bundle $\mathbf{x}_i$ is thought of as the consumption bundle for individual i, but in the case of externalities, the association between particular bundles and particular individuals is not quite strict.

Each individual i has a continuous utility function u_i defined over allocations in $\mathcal{R}^{mn}$. That is, individual i's utility has the form $u_i(\mathbf{x}_1, \mathbf{x}_2, \ldots \mathbf{x}_n)$, which we can write as $u_i(\mathbf{X})$. The fact that the function u_i depends on all $\mathbf{x}_j$'s reflects the consumption externalities. Without externalities, u_i depends only on $\mathbf{x}_i$. (Of course, in a given situation u_i may depend only on a few components of other consumption bundles, but for generality we include them all.) The n individual utility functions can be combined into a single vector valued function $\mathbf{U}$ having as components the u_i's. Thus $\mathbf{U}(\mathbf{X})$ is a vector giving the n utility levels associated with the allocation $\mathbf{X}$. We let $\mathcal{U}$ denote the range of the function $\mathbf{U}$ in $\mathcal{R}^n$.

Consumption externalities are usually subjective. Just like normal utility functions, a utility function with externalities reflects preferences, and these are often difficult to measure precisely. However, if one accepts the preference framework for analysis of economic choice behavior, it is apparent that externalities must be accommodated. As an example, suppose you live near the ocean, but your neighbor buys a large van and parks it in his driveway, blocking your view of the ocean. You may find that your utility has fallen as a result of your neighbor's van purchase. If you were to write out your utility function it may well have a term (with a negative coefficient) that represented your neighbor's van acquisition.

Pareto efficiency is usually not achieved by a private market when consumption externalities are present. In the case of the van blocking the view, for example, in a purely private market, your neighbor has no incentive for not parking the van in his driveway. However, a Pareto improvement could possibly be arranged if the van's presence there is more detrimental to you than it is advantageous to him. For example, you might let the neighbor use your swimming pool if he parks his van somewhere else. Of course this kind of trade-off argument cannot be made on the basis of utility values (since utility units are essentially meaningless), but the idea is more or less sound. The trade-offs can be evaluated through a generalized benefit concept. In the case of externalities the benefit function is properly defined for the economy as a whole.

The benefit function of the economy is derived from the vector function $\mathbf{U}$. As in the case of individual utility functions, we measure benefits with respect to a given reference commodity bundle $\mathbf{g} \geq \mathbf{0}$, $\mathbf{g} \neq \mathbf{0}$. The definition of total benefit is given below.

Social benefit function.   The *social benefit function* (relative to $\mathbf{g}$) corresponding to the vector utility function $\mathbf{U}$ is

$$b(\mathbf{X}, \mathbf{U}) \;=\; \max \sum_{i=1}^{n} \beta_i$$

$$\text{sub to } u_1(\mathbf{x}_1 - \beta_1\mathbf{g}, \mathbf{x}_2 - \beta_2\mathbf{g}, \ldots, \mathbf{x}_n - \beta_n\mathbf{g}) \geq u_1$$
$$u_2(\mathbf{x}_1 - \beta_1\mathbf{g}, \mathbf{x}_2 - \beta_2\mathbf{g}, \ldots, \mathbf{x}_n - \beta_n\mathbf{g}) \geq u_2$$
$$\vdots$$
$$u_n(\mathbf{x}_1 - \beta_1\mathbf{g}, \mathbf{x}_2 - \beta_2\mathbf{g}, \ldots, \mathbf{x}_n - \beta_n\mathbf{g}) \geq u_n$$

and

$$\mathbf{x}_i - \beta_i\mathbf{g} \in \mathcal{X}_i = \mathcal{R}_+^m \qquad \text{for all } i.$$

If the constraints above are not feasible, then $b(\mathbf{X}, \mathbf{U}) = -\infty$.

This definition of the social benefit function is exactly analogous to that of a single individual, but in this case it is defined for the entire group. It measures how much of the commodity $\mathbf{g}$ the group would be willing to trade for the opportunity to move from a given utility vector $\mathbf{U}$ to the allocation $\mathbf{X}$. In the new definition of the benefit function, the group optimizes the trade by taking amounts of $\mathbf{g}$ away from individuals in various portions so as to maximize the total. Hence the social benefit function measures the maximum amount that the group would give up to move to $\mathbf{X}$.

Note that this definition is completely consistent with our earlier definition in the case where there are no externalities. In that case, we find

$$b(\mathbf{X}, \mathbf{U}) = \sum_{i=1}^{n} b_i(\mathbf{x}_i, u_i),$$

where the b_i's are the individual benefit functions. Hence, the social benefit function defined in the general sense of this section is just equal to the sum of the individual benefit functions.

It is useful to have a concept of $\mathbf{g}$ being good for an economy with externalities. We present a general definition below.

Good bundle.   A bundle $\mathbf{g} \in \mathcal{R}_+^m$ is *good* for an economy if for any $\mathbf{X} \subset \mathcal{R}_+^{mn}$ and any $\alpha > 0$ there is a way to add $\alpha \mathbf{g}$ to the aggregate of $\mathbf{X}$ in such a way as to obtain a Pareto improvement. Specifically, $\mathbf{g}$ is good if for any $\mathbf{X}$ and any $\alpha > 0$ there are $\alpha_1, \alpha_2, \ldots, \alpha_n$ with $\alpha = \sum_{i=1}^{n} \alpha_i$ such that for $\mathbf{X}' = (\mathbf{x}_1 + \alpha_1\mathbf{g}, \mathbf{x}_2 + \alpha_2\mathbf{g}, \ldots, \mathbf{x}_n + \alpha_n\mathbf{g})$ there holds $\mathbf{U}(\mathbf{X}') \geq \mathbf{U}(\mathbf{X})$, with strict inequality in at least one component.

As a special case, note that if there are no externalities, then if $\mathbf{g}$ is good for at least one individual in the sense of Section 4.2, $\mathbf{g}$ is good for the group.

We now present the theorem that relates Pareto efficiency to zero-maximality of the social benefit function. It is a direct generalization of the first zero-maximum theorem of Section 6.7. As before, an economy consists of the m commodities and n consumers as described above. The feasible allocations are of the form $\mathbf{X} = (\mathbf{x}_1, \mathbf{x}_2 \ldots \mathbf{x}_n)$ where $\mathbf{x}_i \in X_i = \mathcal{R}_+^m$ for each i, and $\sum_{i=1}^{n} \mathbf{x}_i \in \mathcal{T}$ where $\mathcal{T}$ is a given transformation set.

Zero-maximum principle for externalities.   *Suppose $\mathbf{g}$ is good. Let $\mathbf{X}^*$ be a feasible allocation and set $\mathbf{U}^* = \mathbf{U}(\mathbf{X}^*)$. If $\mathbf{X}^*$ is Pareto efficient, then $\mathbf{X}^*$ is zero-maximal for $b(\mathbf{X}, \mathbf{U}^*)$ with respect to all feasible allocations.*

Proof: The proof is a direct generalization of that of the first zero-maximum theorem of Section 6.7. Assume that $b(\mathbf{X}^*, \mathbf{U}^*) = b > 0$. Then there is an allocation $\mathbf{X}'$ defined by $\mathbf{x}_i' = \mathbf{x}_i^* - \beta_i\mathbf{g}$, $i = 1, 2, \ldots, n$, with $\sum_{i=1}^{n} \beta_i = b$ such that $\mathbf{U}(\mathbf{X}') \geq \mathbf{U}^*$. Since $\mathbf{g}$ is good, there is a way to distribute $b\mathbf{g}$ so as to improve $\mathbf{X}'$. That is, there is $\mathbf{X}''$ defined by $\mathbf{x}_1'' = \mathbf{x}_i' + \alpha_i\mathbf{g}$, $i = 1, 2, \ldots, n$, with $\sum_{i=1}^{n} \alpha_i = b$, such that $\mathbf{U}(\mathbf{X}'') \geq \mathbf{U}^*$ with strict inequality in at least one component. Since $\sum_{i=1}^{n} \mathbf{x}_i'' = \sum_{i=1}^{n} \mathbf{x}_i^*$, the allocation $\mathbf{X}''$ is feasible. Hence $\mathbf{X}^*$ is not Pareto efficient. Therefore, the original assumption is not valid, and $b(\mathbf{X}^*, \mathbf{U}^*) = 0$.

To prove the maximal nature of $\mathbf{X}^*$, suppose there were a feasible allocation $\mathbf{X}$ with $b(\mathbf{X}, \mathbf{U}^*) = b > 0$. Then, correspondingly, let $\mathbf{X}'$ be the allocation of the form $\mathbf{x}_i' = \mathbf{x}_i - \beta_i \mathbf{g}$, $i = 1, 2, \ldots, n$, with $\sum_{i=1}^n \beta_i = b$, such that $\mathbf{U}(\mathbf{X}') \geq \mathbf{U}^*$. Then since $\mathbf{g}$ is good, we can distribute $b\mathbf{g}$ back to $\mathbf{X}'$ to get an improvement. The resulting $\mathbf{X}''$ represents a Pareto efficient improvement over $\mathbf{X}^*$. Hence, if $\mathbf{X}^*$ is Pareto efficient, there can be no such $\mathbf{X}$.   ∎

Under appropriate additional assumptions (such as a quasi-concavity assumption on the utility function $\mathbf{U}$), the converse of the above theorem can be established. Hence, under suitable assumptions, Pareto efficiency is exactly equivalent to zero-maximality of benefits even in the presence of externalities. This equivalence enables us to approach externalities with familiar methods.

Internal Commodities

Externalities are usually associated with only certain commodities, so there are other commodities that are ordinary. Formally, we say that a bundle $\mathbf{g}$ is *internal* if

$$u_i(\mathbf{x}_1, \mathbf{x}_2, \ldots, \mathbf{x}_j + \alpha \mathbf{g}, \ \mathbf{x}_{j+1}, \ldots, \mathbf{x}_n) = u_i(\mathbf{X})$$

for all i, all $j \neq i$, and all $\alpha \geq 0$. In words, $\mathbf{g}$ is internal if increments of $\mathbf{g}$ added to someone else's consumption bundle do not affect utility. For example, although you might care whether the family next door gets a fancy new car (so cars are externalities), you may not care whether they eat steak (so steak is internal). Internal goods are just the kind we always considered before discussing externalities. In earlier chapters all goods were internal. It is natural to use an internal variable as a reference by which to measure benefits. As an example, suppose one is studying the value of a public park. It is natural to measure benefits relative to some private good or bundle, rather than in terms of the park. In fact, using an internal commodity as reference simplifies the calculation of the social benefit function, breaking it into n separate evaluations.

Suppose $\mathbf{g}$ is internal. Then in the general definition of the social benefit function, a constraint of the form $u_i(\mathbf{x}_1 - \beta_1 \mathbf{g}, \mathbf{x}_2 - \beta_2 \mathbf{g}, \ldots, \mathbf{x}_n - \beta_n \mathbf{g}) \geq u_i$ becomes simply $u_i(\mathbf{x}_1, \mathbf{x}_2, \ldots, \mathbf{x}_i - \beta_i \mathbf{g}, \ldots, \mathbf{x}_n) \geq u_i$. Hence the social benefit function is

$$b(\mathbf{X}, \mathbf{U}^*) \ = \ \max \sum_{i=1}^n \beta_i$$
$$\text{sub to } \ u_i(\mathbf{x}_1, \mathbf{x}_2, \ldots, \mathbf{x}_i - \beta_i \mathbf{g}, \ldots, \mathbf{x}_n) \geq u_i^*$$
$$\mathbf{x}_i - \beta_i \mathbf{g} \in \mathcal{X}_i, \quad \text{for } i = 1, 2, \ldots, n.$$

In this case β_i appears only in the constraints on u_i and $\mathbf{x}_i - \beta_i \mathbf{g}$. Accordingly, we define

$$b_i(\mathbf{X}, u_i^*) \;=\; \max \; \beta_i$$
$$\text{sub to } \; u_i(\mathbf{x}_1, \mathbf{x}_2, \ldots, \mathbf{x}_i - \beta_i \mathbf{g}, \ldots, \mathbf{x}_n) \geq u_i^*$$
$$\mathbf{x}_i - \beta_i \mathbf{g} \in X_i$$

as the *personal social benefit functions*. The personal social benefit function measures the benefit received by an individual due to the change in everyone's allocation. It is a simple generalization of the standard individual benefit function when there are no externalities. It follows that

$$b(\mathbf{X}, \mathbf{U}^*) = \sum_{i=1}^{n} b_i(\mathbf{X}, u_i^*).$$

When $\mathbf{g}$ is internal, we do not need to worry about the cross effects on one individual due to subtracting $\mathbf{g}$ from another, and hence the maximum amount that can be subtracted is additive across individuals.

Example 9.2 (Public goods).   As an example of the results of this section, we shall find the necessary conditions satisfied by a Pareto efficient allocation that includes a public good. These conditions are equivalent to the Samuelson conditions.

As in Section 9.1, we consider an economy with a single pure public good and a single private good. There are n consumers, each having a utility function of the form $u_i(x, y_i)$ where x is the level of the public good and y_i is consumer i's level of the private good. We can assume that each consumer i selects an increment x_i and $x = \sum_{i=1}^{n} x_i$. Other individuals then share the benefits of x through the consumption externality inherent in their utility functions.

The public good is generated from the private good from the relation

$$h(x) + \sum_{i=1}^{n} y_i = Y_0,$$

where the function h represents an inverse production function and Y_0 is the aggregate endowment of the private good.

The private good is an internal good. Hence we let $\mathbf{g} = (0, 1)$, corresponding to one unit of the private good. Let $\mathbf{X} = (x, y_1, y_2, \ldots, y_n)$. The social benefit function is

$$b(\mathbf{X}, \mathbf{U}^*) = \sum_{i=1}^{n} b_i(x, y_i, u_i^*),$$

where b_i is the ith personal social benefit function.

According to the zero-maximum principle for externalities, if the allocation $\mathbf{X}^*$ is Pareto efficient, it is zero-maximal for the problem

$$\max \; b(\mathbf{X}, \mathbf{U}^*)$$
$$\text{sub to } \; h(x) + \sum_{i=1}^{n} y_i = Y_0.$$

The first-order necessary conditions are found by introducing a Lagrange multiplier. Assuming an interior solution, this Lagrange multiplier must equal 1. (Why? Because the partial derivative of the Lagrangian with respect to y_i is $1 - \lambda$, and this must be 0.) Setting the derivative of the Lagrangian with respect to x equal to 0, we find

$$\sum_{i=1}^{n} \frac{\partial b_i(x, y_i)}{\partial x} = \frac{\partial h(x)}{\partial x}.$$

This is the required necessary condition. It is equivalent to the Samuelson condition that says that the sum of the MRS_i's is equal to the MRT. In this case, it says that the marginal social benefit (of extra x) must equal the marginal cost—both measured relative to the private good. Note that the summation condition arises naturally from the sum of personal social benefits. Hence, we have a unified theory for deriving necessary conditions that applies to public goods and private goods equally. We simply set the derivative of the social benefit function equal to the derivative of the cost.

Example 9.3 (Altruism).   Consider a distribution economy of two goods and two individuals A and B. The total amounts available of the goods are x and y, respectively. The two utility functions are

$$u_A = x_A y_A + x_B \qquad u_B = x_B y_B.$$

Hence, individual A is altruistic, since A's utility is increased if B's consumption of x is increased.

Good y is an internal good, so we use it as a reference. The personal social benefit functions are

$$b_A = y_A - \frac{(u_A - x_B)}{x_A} \qquad b_B = y_B - \frac{u_B}{x_B}.$$

The necessary conditions for Pareto efficiency are that the solution should be zero-maximal for

$$\max \ b_A + b_B$$

$$\text{sub to } x_A + x_B = x$$

$$y_A + y_B = y.$$

The Lagrange multiplier for the second constraint will be 1 because y is the reference commodity. Hence the conditions at an interior solution are found by differentiating

$$b_A + b_B - \lambda(x_A + x_B) - (y_A + y_B)$$

with respect to x_A and x_B (but treating u_A and u_B as constants). This yields

$$\frac{u_A - x_B}{x_A^2} = \lambda \qquad \frac{1}{x_A} + \frac{u_B}{x_B^2} = \lambda.$$

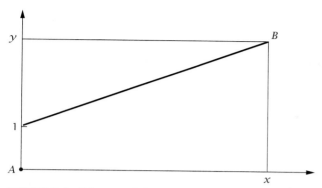

FIGURE 9.4   Edgeworth box for altruism example.

Now, substituting for u_A and u_B, we find

$$\frac{y_A}{x_A} = \lambda = \frac{1}{x_A} + \frac{y_B}{x_B}.$$

Hence,

$$\frac{y_A - 1}{x_A} = \frac{y_B}{x_B}$$

is satisfied at interior solutions. The set of Pareto efficient solutions is shown in an Edgeworth box in Fig. 9.4. Note that if the externality term x_B were not present in u_A, the corresponding set of Pareto efficient solutions would be the diagonal line in the box. Hence the externality shifts the Pareto points leftward—meaning that A gives up some x so that B can have more.

Social Prices

Suppose $\mathbf{X}^*$ is a Pareto efficient allocation. It follows from the zero-maximum principle that $\mathbf{X}^*$ is zero-maximal for

$$\max\ b(\mathbf{X}, \mathbf{U}^*)$$
$$\text{sub to}\ \sum_{i=1}^{n} \mathbf{x}_i = \sum_{i=1}^{n} \mathbf{x}_i^*$$
$$\mathbf{x}_i \in X_i, \qquad i = 1, 2, \ldots, n.$$

We now let $\mathbf{p}^*$ be the vector of Lagrange multipliers of the constraints. Assuming that $\mathbf{X}^*$ is interior (that is, $\mathbf{X}^* > \mathbf{0}$) the Lagrange multipliers will be normalized with $\mathbf{p}^* \cdot \mathbf{g} = 1$. The vector $\mathbf{p}^*$ can be considered to be *shadow prices, social prices,* or *Pareto prices* of the commodities. It follows that $\mathbf{X}^*$ also solves

$$\max\ b(\mathbf{X}^*, \mathbf{U}^*) - \mathbf{p}^* \cdot \mathbf{x}^*$$
$$\text{sub to}\ \mathbf{x}_i \in X_i, \qquad i = 1, 2, \ldots, n.$$

The first-order conditions then lead directly to the equation

$$\frac{\partial b(\mathbf{X}^*, \mathbf{U}^*)}{\partial x_{ik}} = p_k^*$$

for each k and each i. The marginal social benefit of any good is equal to that good's price, and this is true no matter who obtains the increment of the good. This generalizes the equation that holds without externalities. It also contains the Samuelson condition as a special case.

9.6 Competitive Equilibria and Externalities

It is quite straightforward to define competitive equilibria in the presence of externalities by relying, once again, on the concept of a Nash equilibrium.

Competitive equilibrium. A pair $(\mathbf{X}^*, \mathbf{p}^*)$ consisting of an allocation and a price vector is a *competitive equilibrium* for the transformation economy if

(*a*) $\sum_{i=1}^{n} \mathbf{x}_i^* \in \mathcal{T}$ (feasibility).

(*b*) For each[3] i, $\mathbf{p}^* \cdot \mathbf{x}_i \leq \mathbf{p}^* \cdot \mathbf{x}_i^*$ implies that $u_i(\mathbf{X}_{-i}^*, \mathbf{x}_i) \leq u_i(\mathbf{X}^*)$ (individual utility maximization).

(*c*) $\mathbf{p}^* \cdot \sum_{i=1}^{n} \mathbf{x}_i^* \geq \mathbf{p}^* \cdot \mathbf{y}$ for all $\mathbf{y} \in \mathcal{T}$ (profit maximization).

Although the concept of a competitive equilibrium generalizes quite easily to economies with externalities, we know from our study of public goods that competitive equilibria may yield highly degenerate solutions that are far from being Pareto efficient. There is no direct link between competitive equilibria and Pareto efficiency when there are externalities, and hence it is difficult to compare the two. However, there is a link between competitive equilibria and zero-maximization of benefits even when there are externalities. This again provides a way to apply familiar concepts to our analysis.

The key idea that relates competitive equilibria to zero-maximality of benefits is the concept of a private benefit function—which is different from the social benefit function introduced in the previous section. The private benefit function measures the benefit accruing only to a single individual, and it purposefully ignores the benefits accruing to others. When individuals act competitively, they maximize their own private benefit functions, and this leads to equilibrium. When society acts for the collective interest,

---

[3] Recall that $(\mathbf{X}_{-i}^*, \mathbf{x}_i) = (\mathbf{x}_1^*, \mathbf{x}_2^*, \ldots, \mathbf{x}_{i-1}^*, \mathbf{x}_i, \mathbf{x}_{i+1}^*, \ldots, \mathbf{x}_n^*)$.

individuals collectively maximize the total social benefit function, and this leads to Pareto efficiency. Therefore, the difference between Pareto efficiency and equilibrium solutions can be traced to the difference between the benefit functions that are used.

Private benefit. The *private benefit function* for individual i corresponding to the allocation $\mathbf{X}^*$ is

$$\beta_i(\mathbf{x}_i, \mathbf{X}^*) = \begin{cases} \max\{b : u_i(\mathbf{X}^*_{-i}, \mathbf{x}_i - b\mathbf{g}) \geq u_i^*\} \\ \quad \text{if } \mathbf{x}_i - b\mathbf{g} \in X_i \text{ and } u_i(\mathbf{X}^*_{-i}, \mathbf{x}_i - b\mathbf{g}) \geq u_i^* \text{ for some } b \\ -\infty \text{ otherwise}. \end{cases}$$

The private benefit function measures how much of commodity $\mathbf{g}$ consumer i is willing to trade for the opportunity to change $\mathbf{x}_i^*$ within the allocation $\mathbf{X}^*$ to the bundle $\mathbf{x}_i$ assuming that the consumption bundles of all other consumers remain unchanged. It is a natural extension of the standard benefit function in the absence of externalities, based on the Nash concept of considering one's own actions under the assumption that others do not change. Clearly, the private benefit function reduces to the standard one when there are no externalities.

We now show that equilibrium points yield zero-maximality of the total private benefits. In the theorem below the concept of local nonsatiation refers to the function $u_i(\mathbf{X}^*_{-i}, \mathbf{x}_i)$ as a function of $\mathbf{x}_i$ only, but valid for all $\mathbf{X}^*_{-i}$.

Zero-maximum principle for equilibria. *Suppose $(\mathbf{X}^*, \mathbf{p}^*)$ is a competitive equilibrium for the transformation economy and $\mathbf{p}^* \cdot \mathbf{g} > 0$. Suppose each u_i satisfies local nonsatiation. Then $\mathbf{X}^*$ is zero-maximal for*

$$\beta(\mathbf{X}, \mathbf{X}^*) = \sum_{i=1}^{n} \beta_i(\mathbf{x}_i, \mathbf{X}^*)$$

$$\text{sub to } \sum_{i=1}^{n} \mathbf{x}_i \in \mathcal{T}.$$

Proof: Suppose there were $\mathbf{X}$ satisfying $\sum_{i=1}^{n} \mathbf{x}_i \in \mathcal{T}$ and such that $\beta(\mathbf{X}, \mathbf{X}^*) = \beta > 0$. Let $\beta_i = \beta_i(\mathbf{x}_i, \mathbf{X}^*)$ for $i = 1, 2, \ldots, n$. For each i consider the bundle $\mathbf{x}'_i = \mathbf{x}_i - \beta_i \mathbf{g}$. We have $u_i(\mathbf{X}^*_{-i}, \mathbf{x}'_i) \geq u_i^*$. Thus by local nonsatiation and the equilibrium conditions, $\mathbf{p}^* \cdot \mathbf{x}'_i \geq \mathbf{p}^* \cdot \mathbf{x}_i^*$ for all i. Therefore

$$\mathbf{p}^* \cdot \sum_{i=1}^{n} \mathbf{x}_i^* \leq \mathbf{p}^* \cdot \sum_{i=1}^{n} \mathbf{x}'_i = \sum_{i=1}^{n} \mathbf{p}^* \cdot (\mathbf{x}_i - \beta_i \mathbf{g}) = \mathbf{p}^* \cdot \sum_{i=1}^{n} \mathbf{x}_i - \beta \mathbf{p}^* \cdot \mathbf{g}.$$

Hence $\mathbf{p}^* \cdot \sum_{i=1}^{n} \mathbf{x}_i > \mathbf{p}^* \cdot \sum_{i=1}^{n} \mathbf{x}_i^*$, contradicting the maximum profit condition of $\mathbf{X}^*$. Hence, no such $\mathbf{X}$ can exist. ∎

Again, a converse of the above theorem holds under appropriate as-sumptions (including a quasi-concavity assumption on the utility functions, and a convexity assumption on $\mathcal{T}$). Therefore, under these assumptions, allocations that form equilibria are equivalent to allocations that are zero-maximal for the sum of the private benefit functions. Hence, the benefit theory of competition carries over almost exactly to economies with exter-nalities.

Relation between Private and Social Benefits

Assume that $\mathbf{g}$ is an internal good. This means that the social benefit func-tion can be written in the form

$$b(\mathbf{X}, \mathbf{U}^*) = \sum_{i=1}^{n} b_i(\mathbf{X}, u_i^*),\qquad(9.10)$$

where the $b_i(\mathbf{X}, u_i^*)$'s are the personal social benefit functions. Note that if $\mathbf{x}_i$ is changed, each $b_j(\mathbf{X}, u_j^*)$ may change, because $\mathbf{x}_i$ may influence the benefit received by everyone. We can formalize this by fixing all components of $\mathbf{X}^*$ except $\mathbf{x}_i$ and seeing the impact on all individuals. We find that this *total impact* is

$$b(\mathbf{X}_{-i}^*, \mathbf{x}_i, \mathbf{U}^*) = \sum_{j=1}^{n} b_j(\mathbf{X}_{-i}^*, \mathbf{x}_i, u_j^*).$$

For convenience, we let

$$t_{ij}(\mathbf{x}_i, \mathbf{X}^*) = b_j(\mathbf{X}_{-i}^*, \mathbf{x}_i, u_j^*),$$

and we call $t_{ij}(\mathbf{x}_i, \mathbf{X}^*)$ the *impact function* of i on j. It measures the benefit to j of changes in $\mathbf{x}_i$ assuming that all other components $\mathbf{X}_{-i}^*$ are held fixed. The total impact to the group due to $\mathbf{x}_i$ is

$$T_i(\mathbf{x}_i, \mathbf{X}^*) = \sum_{j=1}^{n} t_{ij}(\mathbf{x}_i, \mathbf{X}^*) = b(\mathbf{X}_{-i}^*, \mathbf{x}_i, \mathbf{U}^*).$$

Using the ideas of the previous section, we can state that a Pareto effi-cient allocation is zero-maximal for

$$\max\ b(\mathbf{X}, \mathbf{U}^*)$$
$$\text{sub to } \mathbf{p}^* \cdot \sum_{i=1}^{n} \mathbf{x}_i = \mathbf{p}^* \cdot \sum_{i=1}^{n} \mathbf{x}_i^*$$
$$\mathbf{x}_i \in X_i, \qquad i = 1, 2, \ldots, n.$$

where $\mathbf{p}^*$ is the vector of Pareto (social) prices. If only $\mathbf{x}_i$ is variable, this means that $\mathbf{x}_i^*$ is zero-maximal for

$$\max\ T_i(\mathbf{x}_i, \mathbf{X}^*)$$
$$\text{sub to } \mathbf{p}^* \cdot \mathbf{x}_i = \mathbf{p}^* \cdot \mathbf{x}_i^*$$
$$\mathbf{x}_i \in X_i, \qquad i = 1, 2, \ldots, n.$$

Therefore, consumer i acts in the best interests of *society* by maximizing the total impact with respect to $\mathbf{x}_i$ subject to i's budget constraint. If $\mathbf{X}^*$ is Pareto efficient and if the prices are the Pareto (or social) prices, each $\mathbf{x}_i^*$ will zero-maximize the total impact. Hence, Pareto efficiency can be achieved by individual maximization, just as equilibrium can. The only difference is that each individual must maximize the total social impact of his or her commodity bundle choice.

Now let us consider the competitive situation. Here we know that individuals maximize their *private* benefit functions $\beta_i(\mathbf{x}_i, \mathbf{X}^*)$. It is natural to ask how this relates to total impact.

It is easy to see that, in fact,

$$\beta_i(\mathbf{x}_i, \mathbf{X}^*) = t_{ii}(\mathbf{x}_i, \mathbf{X}^*).$$

That is, the private benefit function is identical to the impact of i on i. If an individual acts competitively, he or she maximizes this single impact term, rather than the sum of all impacts. Acting competitively, a consumer neglects the impact of his or her actions on others.

Based on the above, it is clear how the incentives of individuals should be modified in order that their competitive action will lead to Pareto efficiency. We must simply augment their private benefit functions to include the impacts on others. Specifically, we must convert their perceived benefit to

$$\beta_i(\mathbf{x}_i, \mathbf{X}^*) + \sum_{j \neq i} t_{ij}(\mathbf{x}_i, \mathbf{X}^*),$$

where the first term is the private benefit function and the remaining terms are the impacts of i on j for all $j \neq i$. Midway through the next section, we shall show how this can be accomplished through government action.

Example 9.4 (Altruism). We consider again the altruism situation of Example 9.3. There are two goods, x and y, and two individuals, A and B. We have $u_A = x_A y_A + x_B$ and $u_B = x_B y_B$. Let us compute the impacts associated with a particular point indicated by $*$. As before, we use y as the reference commodity for computing benefits. First, $t_{AB}(x_A, y_A, x_B^*, y_B^*) = 0$ because A's choices do not affect B's utility. However, $t_{BA}(x_A^*, y_A^*, x_B, y_B)$ is not zero. We have $t_{AB} = \max \{\beta : x_A^* y_A^* + (x_B - \beta) \geq u_A^*\}$. Thus $t_{AB} = x_A^* y_A^* - u_A^* + x_B = x_B - x_B^*$.

Now assume that A has an endowment of 2 units of commodity x and B has 2 units of commodity y. Assume that the price of x is p and the price of y is 1. We shall consider competitive action by the two individuals, and modify the solution by use of the impact function.

Consumer A: This consumer maximizes a Cobb-Douglas utility function subject to the budget constraint $px_A + y_A = 2p$. The solution is

$$x_A^* = 1 \qquad y_A^* = p.$$

Consumer B: If this consumer acts competitively the solution is $x_B = 1/p$, $y_B = 1$. However, let us suppose that this individual maximizes the total impact of B, but does so in a competitive manner. The total impact is the sum of the private benefit function and the impact t_{BA}. The problem of this consumer is therefore

$$\max \ y_B - \frac{u_B^*}{x_B} + x_B - x_B^*$$

$$\text{sub to } px_B + y_B = 2.$$

This has solution

$$x_B^* = \frac{2}{2p-1} \qquad y_B^* = \frac{p-1}{2p-1}.$$

Market clearing: To clear the market we find p such that the sum of the demands equals the total endowment. This gives $p = \frac{3}{2}$.

Hence the final solution is

$$x_A^* = 1 \quad y_A^* = \frac{3}{2} \quad x_B^* = 1 \quad y_B^* = \frac{1}{2}.$$

How do we know whether this is Pareto efficient? We can test it against the conditions found in the earlier example, namely,

$$\frac{y_A - 1}{x_A} = \frac{y_B}{x_B}.$$

Both sides are equal to $\frac{1}{2}$ for the above solution, so it is indeed Pareto efficient.

We have shown that competitive behavior leads to Pareto efficiency if individuals consider total impact rather than their own private benefits. Later we shall show how we might get people to do this.

9.7   Correction Methods

We have seen that the presence of externalities in an economy generally causes the private market mechanism to produce equilibria that are not Pareto efficient. One purpose of public policy is to attempt to alter the market mechanism, typically by changing the incentives and constraints on individuals and firms, so that the new corrected private markets will in fact produce Pareto efficiency. We consider some of the possible methods for doing this in this section.

From our study in the first half of this chapter, we expect that there is no perfect correction procedure, since every correction method will raise additional incentive issues. However, it is useful to consider the possibilities for correction without delving too deeply into the incentive questions. Later we can decide whether in a given situation the incentive issues are so strong that they invalidate the method.

Internalization

The simplest way to eliminate externalities is through internalization. As an example, consider the situation of an apple orchard and an adjacent bee-keeping activity. There are mutually beneficial production externalities. The beekeeping activity is enhanced by the orchard, since the apple blossoms supply nectar to the bees, and apple production is enhanced by the polli-nation caused by the bees' activity. If these two businesses were combined into one single business that produced both apples and honey, the exter-nality would disappear: it would be absorbed into the new larger firm. The combined business could operate to maximize profit, and this would lead to efficient production decisions regarding operation of both the orchard and the beekeeping. Or, consider the situation of a smoky factory and nearby residents. If the residents owned and operated the factory, they could de-termine, and enforce, a Pareto efficient operating (and cleanup) policy. The internalization process absorbs the externality.

Internalization can also be applied to consumption externalities. For ex-ample, many household goods generate externalities among various family members. The numerous externalities present in a household are frequently internalized by arriving at joint consumption decisions, rather than simply dividing the family budget and allowing each family member to make indi-vidual purchases. Likewise, purchases by churches, clubs, and other organi-zations often represent internalization of the (typically positive) externali-ties among members.

Internalization is useful in certain limited situations, but it certainly can-not be used to resolve all externality problems. For example, numerous small externalities can exist between many firms, especially those in the same business. Yet we would not recommend that they all be combined into a single large firm just to eliminate the externalities. The resulting large or-ganization would represent a monopoly, characterized as we know by other incentive problems.

Similarly, it would be impractical to internalize consumption externali-ties on a large scale, for that would entail the assignment of our consump-tion decisions to a central authority, defeating the advantages of markets. In practice, a balance is sought in which some consumption decisions are relegated to the government if there are strong externalities (as in welfare for the poor or in basic education) but other decisions are maintained at the individual level even if some externalities remain.

Complete Markets

One explanation of the inefficiency of private markets in the presence of externalities is that the ordinary system of markets is incomplete. By pro-viding a truly complete market, efficiency will be restored.

The reason that ordinary markets are incomplete is that an individual is not able freely to select all the commodities that influence his or her utility. If, for example, my food consumption affects your utility (through altruism), you should be able to purchase an item for your consumption that represents food for me. Of course, I shall also purchase food for myself. If markets clear, we shall both select the same amount. Generally, in this kind of expanded market, everyone has a chance to purchase everything that influences his or her utility, and hence by the ordinary welfare theorems, the resulting equilibrium will be efficient.

There is another way to view the complete markets approach. Externalities represent links between the decision problems of different agents. We break those links by introducing markets. In the case of the apple orchard and beekeeping activity, for example, we break the decision link between pollination and apple production by charging a fee for pollination by the bees and for nectar. The physical link still exists, but each party acts as if it can control its magnitude, and the market guides both parties to the proper level. A difficulty of this approach is that these linking markets are "thin," with few participants, and hence not perfectly competitive.

Benefit and Cost Restructuring

We saw in the previous section that the lack of Pareto efficiency in private markets can be traced to the fact that the private benefit function is different from the social benefit function. If the private benefit function were augmented so that each individual accounted for the impact of his or her decision on everyone, the result would be Pareto efficient. We now show how this insight can be used to develop other correction methods.

Suppose $\mathbf{X}^*$ is Pareto efficient and $\mathbf{p}^*$ is a corresponding (social) price vector. We let $r_i^* = \mathbf{p}^* \cdot \mathbf{x}_i^*$, $i = 1, 2, \ldots, n$. Let us consider the problem faced by a single consumer. If we attempt to maintain this allocation by perfect competition, the consumer will solve the problem

$$\max_{\mathbf{x}_i} \ u_i(\mathbf{X}_{-i}^*, \mathbf{x}_i)$$
$$\text{sub to } \mathbf{p}^* \cdot \mathbf{x}_i \le r_i^* . \tag{9.11}$$

However, the result would generally not be $\mathbf{x}_i^*$.

Suppose instead that the government gives a subsidy to i equal to $\sum_{j \ne i} t_{ij}(\mathbf{x}_i, \mathbf{X}^*)$, which depends on $\mathbf{x}_i$ and which is the total cross-impact due to $\mathbf{x}_i$. Consumer i then will solve

$$\max \ u_i(\mathbf{X}_{-i}^*, \mathbf{x}_i)$$
$$\text{sub to } \mathbf{p}^* \cdot \mathbf{x}_i - \sum_{j \ne i} t_{ij}(\mathbf{x}_i, \mathbf{X}^*) \le r_i^* . \tag{9.12}$$

This problem is equivalent to one of the same form but with the objective function changed to the private benefit function $\beta_i(\mathbf{x}_i, \mathbf{X}^*)$. (See Exercise 16, Chapter 5.) Further, if $\mathbf{p}^*$ is normalized so that $\mathbf{p}^* \cdot \mathbf{g} = 1$ and if $\mathbf{g}$ is an internal bundle, the Lagrange multiplier for the constraint will be $+1$ and the consumer's problem can be expressed in the alternative form (assuming concavity)

$$\max_{\mathbf{x}_i}\left\{\beta_i(\mathbf{x}_i,\mathbf{X}^*) + \sum_{j\neq i} t_{ij}(\mathbf{x}_i,\mathbf{X}^*) - \mathbf{p}^*\cdot\mathbf{x}_i + r_i^*\right\}. \qquad (9.13)$$

The use of a Lagrange multiplier has moved the constraint up to the objective function and hence the cross-impact terms combine with the private benefit function. Therefore (9.13) corresponds to maximization of the total impact T_i minus the standard cost $\mathbf{p}^*\cdot\mathbf{x}_i$.

We can make a further transformation of this problem. The cross-impact terms in (9.13) can be left in the objective function, and the cost terms can be pushed back down as a constraint. Hence (9.13) can be reexpressed as

$$\max_{\mathbf{x}_i}\left\{\beta_i(\mathbf{x}_i,\mathbf{X}^*) + \sum_{j\neq i} t_{ij}(\mathbf{x}_i,\mathbf{X}^*)\right\} \qquad (9.14)$$

$$\text{sub to } \mathbf{p}^*\cdot\mathbf{x}_i \leq r_i^*.$$

This problem is entirely equivalent to (9.12). The objective is now equivalent to the total impact $T_i(\mathbf{x}_i,\mathbf{X}^*)$, which is i's portion of the total benefit $b(\mathbf{X}_{-i}^*,\mathbf{x}_i,\mathbf{U}^*)$. Hence this problem is exactly the right problem for consumer i to solve in order to achieve Pareto efficiency.

In summary, starting with the basic competitive problem (9.11), modification of the budget constraint to that of (9.12) is equivalent to changing the consumer's problem to (9.14), which is the basic problem for Pareto efficiency. The objective function is $T_i(\mathbf{x}_i,\mathbf{X}^*)$, which is the total impact function. If $\mathbf{X}^*$ is selected to be Pareto efficient and $\mathbf{p}^*$ is the corresponding vector of social prices, then when all consumers solve (9.12), they will equivalently solve (9.14), and the result will be $\mathbf{X}^*$. Therefore, adding the subsidy automatically transforms the individual's problem into one that is compatible with Pareto efficiency. The reason that the constraint can be combined with the objective is that both are measured in the same units, namely, $\mathbf{g}$.

The method above can be simplified by using linearized versions of the impact functions instead of the functions themselves. The linearized versions can be implemented by imposing proportional taxes or subsidies. In particular, let

$$\mathbf{s}_i = \sum_{j\neq i} \nabla_{\mathbf{x}_i} t_{ij}(\mathbf{x}_i^*,\mathbf{X}^*),$$

and note that $t_{ij}(\mathbf{x}_i^*,\mathbf{X}^*) = 0$. Then we can change consumer i's budget constraint to

$$\mathbf{p}^*\cdot\mathbf{x}_i - \mathbf{s}_i\cdot(\mathbf{x}_i - \mathbf{x}_i^*) \leq r_i^*$$

through subsidies (or taxes if some components of $\mathbf{s}_i$ are negative). This will not change the first-order necessary conditions, so the result is the same as before. (Exercise 11 provides a simple example of how this all works.) This method is a classic correction method, and the taxes (or subsidies) are called Pigouvian taxes after the economist who first proposed them.

The tax and subsidy approach has several advantages over the complete markets approach. First, the number of special prices is reduced in the most general case from mn^2 to mn, and the method does not rely on thin markets. For this reason the tax method is actually practical and is in fact used in some situations. Second, the new method does not rely as much on convexity as the complete markets approach. Since there are fewer prices, and decisions are made over fewer variables, suitable prices and subsidies can exist even when, because of nonconvexities, complete market prices do not.

The disadvantage of the tax and subsidy method is that the appropriate taxes are hard to determine. The required information must usually be obtained from the participants, and they have incentives to distort that information. In addition, the method has the disadvantage that it may be difficult to monitor the externality and collect the proper tax.

Example 9.5 (River pollution). We can illustrate all of the methods discussed in this section with a classic example of a production externality. Suppose a factory is located upstream from a large laundry facility. Operation of the factory yields, as a by-product, pollutants that enter the river. This pollution is an externality for the laundry, since as pollution increases, additional steps of purification are required.

Let us denote factory and laundry outputs by q_f and q_l, respectively, and the market prices of these outputs by p_f and p_l. (These are determined exogenously.) The cost functions of the two facilities are $c_f(q_f)$ and $c_l(q_f, q_l)$, where we have indicated that q_f affects the cost function of the laundry.

Under perfect competition, the two firms would determine outputs satisfying

$$p_f = c_f'(q_f)$$
$$p_l = \frac{\partial c_l(q_f, q_l)}{\partial q_l}.$$

These outputs are not efficient because of the externality.

Efficiency can be achieved by internalization—that is, by maximizing the total profit of the two firms

$$\pi = p_f q_f + p_l q_l - c_f(q_f) - c_l(q_f, q_l).$$

This yields the conditions

$$p_f = c_f'(q_f) + \frac{\partial c_l(q_f, q_l)}{\partial q_f}$$
$$p_l = \frac{\partial c_l(q_f, q_l)}{\partial q_l}.$$

If we assume that $\partial c_l / \partial q_f$ is positive (corresponding to a negative externality) and that $c_f'(q_f)$ is increasing (corresponding to decreasing returns to scale), then we can deduce that the new (efficient) level of q_f is lower than that of perfect competition.

Under perfect competition, the factory accounts only for its private cost of production, not the full social cost, which includes the cost of pollution borne by the laundry. In the internalized solution, marginal revenue (equal to p_f) is set equal to the marginal social cost. This produces efficiency.

Let us see how the complete markets approach works in this example. The output q_f is the only externality, so we introduce a market for it between the two facilities. This can be thought of as a market for the pollutant, since there is a direct translation between q_f and the pollutant level. Let the price of this externality in this market be r. The factory will pay rq_f to the laundry. The factory will select q_f to satisfy

$$p_f - r = c'_f(q_f),$$

and the laundry will select q_f and q_l to satisfy

$$p_l = \frac{\partial c_l(q_f, q_l)}{\partial q_l}$$

$$r = \frac{\partial c_l(q_f, q_l)}{\partial q_f}.$$

If r is chosen so that the two solutions are consistent, then r is the marginal cost to the laundry for q_f; therefore, in this method the factory must again include this term in its own cost calculation. This gives the same solution as that determined by internalization.

Finally, we can consider imposing a tax on the factory to induce the efficient output level. In this case, we set the tax rate equal to

$$r = \frac{\partial c_l(q_f, q_l)}{\partial q_f}$$

evaluated at the optimal solution. This will cause the factory to produce at the same q_f as under internalization—the socially efficient level. The only difference with the complete markets solution is that we have not specified that the laundry gets the tax revenue.

Property Rights

Another way to correct the influence of externalities is by a clear definition of property rights and an effective legal system for collection of damages. The approach was delineated by Coase. The *Coase theorem* states that under such a system of property rights, individual parties negotiate to a Pareto efficient point.

Let us illustrate this viewpoint with the factory and laundry example, which in this case boils down to the issue of pollution rights. Either the factory has the right to pollute, or the laundry has the right to a pollution-free river.

Suppose first that the laundry has the right to a pollution-free river. It can then obtain damages from the factory equal to the loss in profit incurred because of the factory's operation. Let $\pi_l(q_f)$ denote the maximum profit of the laundry when the factory operates at level q_f. Under the given property rights, the factory will operate so as to maximize its net profit after damages; namely, it will maximize

$$\pi_f(q_f) - [\pi_l(0) - \pi_l(q_f)].$$

We may ignore the constant $\pi_l(0)$, and hence the factory operates so as to maximize the total profit of the two firms: the factory and the laundry. The externality has been effectively internalized, and the Pareto efficient solution is obtained.

Now let us consider the opposite situation, the one in which the factory has an unlimited right to pollute the river. In this case, the laundry will pay the factory to reduce its production. If $\pi_f(q_f)$ denotes the profit of the factory at level q_f, the laundry must pay the factory $\pi_f(q_f^*) - \pi_f(q_f)$ to reduce output from q_f^* to q_f. Hence the laundry will maximize $\pi_l(q_f) - [\pi_f(q_f^*) - \pi_f(q_f)]$, and again the externality has been effectively internalized.

There are a few difficulties with this approach, too. Although negotiation may work for some types of property, there are difficulties in assigning rights to others (such as a river). Furthermore, when several firms interact with the same externality, the determination of appropriate damages can be quite complex. Or, if the externality affects individuals, as in the case of smoke from a factory, it is difficult to determine the true willingness-to-pay values.

Other Methods

We have shown how inefficiencies due to externalities can be corrected through internalization, the addition of markets, restructuring of perceived benefits through taxes and subsidies, and a system of property rights. These methods all work indirectly and rely on proper responses to economic incentives. But there are two other obvious and much more direct approaches: regulation and direct control. In these methods, the government or another central authority simply regulates the externalities or supplies them in proper amounts. These methods have many operational advantages, but (not surprisingly) they are also subject to the estimation problems associated with most externality situations.

Examples of direct action designed to ameliorate the effects of externalities are abundant. The number of campers permitted in a national park is frequently limited, in part because campers impose a crowding externality on each other. Most residential neighborhoods have antinoise laws that limit the negative externalities of, say, loud radio music forced on those who do not want to hear it. Such laws are simpler to implement than, for example, taxing loud noise in some proportional manner.

Regulation is more robust, even in theory, than market approaches because it does not rely on convexity assumptions. Regulation also does not rely on the (doubtfully) smooth operation of thin markets or on successful negotiation between parties. Therefore, it is not surprising that regulation is in fact frequently employed to improve efficiency.

Another direct approach for obtaining efficiency in the presence of externalities is for the government or central authority directly to produce the service associated with the externality. This is frequently done for public goods such as national defense, public health programs, and education, as discussed earlier in the chapter. This approach may also be used within organizations, as in the provision of a central computing facility within a business.

Although the methods of regulation and direct control are conceptually simple, their efficiency relies completely on the judgments of policy makers. Greater efficiency is likely to be achieved if market forces can be employed, but in a manner that recognizes the shortcomings associated with them. An example of a useful blend of techniques is the establishment of a fixed number of air pollution rights in a region and the formation of a market for these rights. In such a system, judgment is applied at the highest level (to set the number of rights) and market forces sort out the details.

9.8 Exercises

1. (Splitting the bill) A group of people go out to dinner together, deciding beforehand that they will divide the final bill equally among them. Assuming that each person's utility of a meal increases with its menu price, does that procedure lead to a Pareto efficient outcome?

2. Suppose $u_i(x, y_i) = v_i(x) + y_i$ for $i = 1, 2, \ldots, n$. Assume that each v_i is an increasing concave function with $v_i(0) = 0$. Suppose also that the v_i's are different from each other in the sense that for any $x \geq 0$, $v_i'(x) \neq v_j'(x)$ for $i \neq j$. Characterize the Nash equilibria of the market mechanism noncooperative game in Section 9.1.

3. Consider an economy with two consumers and two goods. One of these goods, x, is public, and the other good, y, is private. The consumers' preferences can be represented by $u_1(x, y) = xy$ and $u_2(x, y) = yx^2$. The public good can be produced, by either consumer, with the production function $x = \frac{1}{2}y$. Consumer 1 has 20 units of y, and consumer 2 has 10 units of y. Let x_i be the production of x by consumer i.

    (a) Find the conditions for Pareto efficiency in this economy. (These will be equations in y_1, y_2, x_1, and x_2 and the original endowments.)

    (b) Assume that each consumer takes the other's production of x as given and then maximizes personal utility. What is the Nash equilibrium? Is it Pareto efficient?

    (c) Now assume that there is a leader-follower situation. Find the Stackelberg equilibrium with 2 acting as follower and 1 as leader. Is it Pareto efficient?

4. (The Lindahl mechanism)

   (a) Using the Lindahl distributive mechanism, find the amounts of x_1 and x_2 produced by the economy in the previous exercise and the amounts y_1 and y_2.

   (b) Show that this production and allocation for the economy is Pareto efficient.

   (c) Suppose consumer 2 is allowed to lie about the amount of public good he prefers, but consumer 1 is not. Find the new y_1, y_2, and x using Lindahl distribution for this asymmetric situation.

   (d) Is this new production and distribution Pareto efficient?

5. (Donation matching) Two individuals have identical willingness-to-pay functions $v(x) = x^{1/2}$ for a public good. These two individuals must share the cost of the public good, and hence each will try to maximize $\pi_i = v(x) - x_i$ where x_i is the amount i pays and $x = x_1 + x_2$.

   They decide to use a two-stage process. In the first stage each selects a matching coefficient b_i, $i = 1, 2$, and in the second stage they select a flat contribution a_i, $i = 1, 2$. The total payment by i is then $x_i = a_i + b_i a_j$, $j \neq i$.

   (a) Suppose $b_1 > b_2$ are given. Show that then $a_1 = 0$, and find the resulting π_1 and π_2.

   (b) Find the Nash equilibrium values of b_1 and b_2 and show that the resulting allocation is Pareto efficient.

6. Show that for $n = 2$, the only mechanism of the type satisfying both (9.8) and (9.9) is $T_1 = F(x)$ and $T_2 = x - F(x)$.

7. The Groves-Ledyard mechanism sets (for $n \geq 3$)

$$T_i = t_i x + \frac{y}{2} \left[\frac{n-1}{n} \left(m_i - A_i \right)^2 - \sum_{j \neq i} \frac{1}{n-2} \left(m_j - A_i \right)^2 \right],$$

where

$$x = \sum_{i=1}^{n} m_i \qquad A_i = \frac{1}{n-1} \sum_{j \neq i} m_j,$$

and the t_i's and y are fixed constants with $\sum_{i=1}^{n} t_i = 1$. Show that these functions satisfy (9.8) and (9.9).

8. (Hurwicz mechanism) Suppose there are $n \geq 3$ individuals each with utility defined over a public good and a private good. The MRT between these two goods is MRT $\equiv 1$. Consider a game mechanism whereby each individual i submits a message $(p_i, x_i) \geq 0$. Given all messages, the total level of public good supplied is

$$x = \frac{1}{n} \sum_{i=1}^{n} x_i.$$

Individual i's private good contribution is

$$T_i = R_i x + p_i (x_i - x_{i+1})^2 - p_{i+1}(x_{i+1} - x_{i+2})^2,$$

(with $n + 1 \equiv 1$ and $n + 2 \equiv 2$), where

$$R_i = \frac{1}{n} + p_{i+1} - p_{i+2}.$$

(a) Show that this mechanism is balanced.

(b) Show that at a Nash equilibrium $p_i(x_i - x_{i+1}) = 0$ for all i.

(c) Show that a Nash equilibrium yields a Lindahl allocation, with the R_i's equal to the Lindahl prices.

(d) Is this procedure likely to have good dynamic properties?

9. (Class demonstration)   *Preparation*: Select a positive number X. Prepare five slips of paper, each with a payoff function written on it of the form $f_i(x) = c_i x^{\alpha_i}$, $i = 1, 2, \ldots, 5$. The five α_i's are $\alpha_i = 0.5, 0.6, 0.6, 0.75, 0.8$. The c_i's are given numerically (so that X is not revealed) as $c_i = X^{(1-\alpha_i)}/[M \cdot (1 - \alpha_i)]$ where $M = 11$.

In class: Divide the class into five groups and distribute one of the five slips of paper to each group. The groups may *not* show their slips to others. The five groups now each contribute money to a central pool. The total amount contributed is denoted x. Groups are then paid according to their $f_i(x)$'s. It will be challenging for the groups to decide how much to contribute, since x is a public good. The class may try some mechanism, such as repeatedly submitting proposals to determine the contributions, and see whether a Lindahl solution is attained.

Note that this demonstration loses about $5X/11$ dollars. (In the Lindahl solution $x = X$ and each group gets $X/11$ dollars profit.) For variety select arbitrary α_i's and let $M = \sum_{i=1}^{n} \alpha_i/(1 - \alpha_i)$.

10. Consider a two-person, two-commodity economy with a consumption externality:

$$u_A = x_A y_A x_B \qquad u_B = x_B y_B \qquad \mathbf{w}_A = (1, 0) \qquad \mathbf{w}_B = (0, 1).$$

Consumer A controls x_A and y_A, but not x_B. Find the symmetric competitive equilibrium for this economy and all Pareto efficient allocations. Is the equilibrium Pareto efficient?

11. (Benefit theory of externalities)   Consider an economy of two individuals, A and B, and two commodities, x and y, with utility functions

$$u_A = x_A y_A x_B \qquad u_B = x_B y_B x_A.$$

(Note that there are positive externalities in both directions through x.) Commodity x is produced from y on a one-to-one basis. In particular,

$$x_A + x_B + y_A + y_B = 1.$$

(a) Find the Pareto efficient allocations using a direct approach. Let the price of y be 1. Argue that the social price of x is 1. In the symmetric Pareto efficient solution, what are the values of x_A, y_A, u_A, x_B, y_B, and u_B?

(b) Assume that A and B each own $\frac{1}{2}$ unit of y and no unit of x. Thus, together they own the 1 unit represented on the right-hand side of the production equation. Find the competitive equilibrium. Note that the price of x is the same as in part (a). What are x_A, x_B, u_A, x_B, y_B, and u_B? Note that x_A and x_B are smaller than in part (a) because the positive externality has not been properly accounted for.

(c) Find the general expression for the private benefit function β_A using y as the reference commodity. Specialize to find the functions of x_A and y_A denoted $\beta_A(x_A, y_A, P)$ and $\beta_A(x_A, y_A, E)$, where the argument P or E denotes the symmetric Pareto efficient or equilibrium solution, respectively, taken as the reference point.

(d) Solve the problem

$$\max \; \beta_A(x_A, y_A, E)$$
$$\text{sub to } \; x_A + y_A = \tfrac{1}{2}.$$

This is the problem of maximizing private benefits. Show that the equilibrium solution is obtained.

(e) Find the impact function of A on B. That is, find $t_{AB}(x_A, y_A, P)$. Also find the total impact function through

$$T_A(x_A, y_A, P) = \beta_A(x_A, y_A, P) + t_{AB}(x_A, y_A, P).$$

(f) Solve the problem

$$\max \; T_A(x_A, y_A, P)$$
$$\text{sub to } \; x_A + y_A = \tfrac{1}{2}.$$

Show that the Pareto efficient solution is obtained. Note that the Lagrange multiplier is 1 (or -1, depending on how it is entered).

(g) Solve the problem

$$\max \; \beta_A(x_A, y_A, P)$$
$$\text{sub to } \; x_A + y_A - t_{AB}(x_A, y_A, P) = \tfrac{1}{2}.$$

Here private benefits are being maximized, but the cross-impact is put into the constraint. Show that the same solution is obtained. Note that again $\lambda = 1$.

(h) Solve the problem

$$\max \; u_A(x_A, y_A, \tfrac{1}{3})$$
$$\text{sub to } \; x_A + y_A - t_{AB}(x_A, y_A, P) = \tfrac{1}{2}.$$

This is the problem obtained by putting the cross-impacts in the budget constraint, which could be done by a subsidy, and using the utility function as objective. Show that the same solution is obtained.

(i) Let

$$s_A = \left. \frac{\partial t_{AB}(x_A, y_A, P)}{\partial x_A} \right|_{x_A = 1/3}.$$

Solve the proportional subsidy problem

$$\max \; u_A(x_A, y_A, \tfrac{1}{3})$$
$$\text{sub to } \; x_A + y_A - s_A(x_A - \tfrac{1}{3}) = \tfrac{1}{2},$$

and show that the same solution is obtained.

12. Consider an economy with two firms, one consumer, and three goods: labor l and two produced goods q_1 and q_2. Firm 1's production function is $q_1 = l_1$. Firm 2's production function is $q_2 = q_1 l_2$, and it therefore has an externality with q_1. The consumer's utility is $u = q_1 q_2$, and the endowment of labor is 1. Let the price of labor be 1.

   (a) Find the competitive equilibrium for the economy.

   (b) Find the unique Pareto efficient allocation for the economy.

   (c) The government wishes to obtain Pareto efficiency by putting an excise tax t on good 2 and giving the money collected back to the consumer as a lump-sum subsidy S. What t and S should be used?

13. (Waste treatment plant)   Several firms have agreed to build a waste treatment plant jointly in order to meet federal regulations on industrial wastes. Each firm, however, can reduce the amount of waste that it generates, but at some cost. The firms would like to minimize the total costs of reaching the federal standards, including the cost of building and running the treatment plant and the abatement costs accruing to all firms that reduce their waste generation.

   Let R_i represent the rate of waste generation of the ith firm, and let $R = \sum_i R_i$ represent the total rate of waste generation by all firms. Let the cost per year of building and running the waste treatment plant be $C(R)$, where $C(R) > 0$, $C'(R) > 0$, and $C''(R) > 0$.

   The cost per year of abatement by the ith firm is determined by $C_i(R_i)$, where $C_i(R) > 0$, $C_i'(R) \le 0$, and $C_i''(R) \ge 0$. Above some level $\bar{R}_i$ the value of C_i is zero.

   (a) Calculate the necessary conditions for total cost minimization in terms of marginal costs. At optimality, how are the marginal abatement costs of the various firms related?

   (b) Suppose $C(R) = aR$ and $C_i(R_i) = b_i(\bar{R}_i - R_i)^2$ for $0 \le R_i \le \bar{R}_i$. Use the results of part (a) to solve for the optimal R_i's and for all relevant costs.

   (c) Assume that each firm pays a fixed fraction of the central treatment plant costs, and all of its own abatement costs. Find the Nash equilibrium set of R_i's assuming that each firm selects its own R_i. First write necessary optimal conditions in general. Then, solve these conditions for the functional forms assumed in part (b). How do your results compare with the results in part (b)?

   (d) Assume now that each firm is assessed a service charge PR_i. Calculate the necessary conditions for an optimal R_i for each firm (using P as a parameter). Show that each R_i is a nonincreasing function of P.

   (e) Under the conditions of part (d), find the price P^* that causes firms to meet the optimality conditions derived in part (a). Argue that if P^* is charged, the decentralized system will operate so as to minimize total costs. How is P^* related to the various marginal costs?

   (f) If P^* is assessed as above, show that the total service charges collected will be at least as large as the cost of the waste treatment plant. That is, if the optimal service charges are imposed, no additional assessments will be required to run the system.

14. (Fishing boats) If x boats fish in a certain common area, the total catch is $x^{1/2}$. The cost for sending a boat is c, and the price of fish is 1.

   (a) What is the optimal number of boats?

   (b) Suppose two fishing companies send out boats and the total catch is divided in proportion to the number of boats from each company. If each company takes the number of boats of the other company as fixed, how many total boats will be sent?

   (c) What license fee f on boats would cause the total number of boats, when there are two companies, to be optimal? (Leave in equation form.)

15. (Park use) There are n individuals who enjoy visiting a national park, but their enjoyment decreases as the park becomes more crowded. Each individual i has utility function

$$u_i(x_1, x_2, \ldots, x_n, y_i) = x_i^\alpha \left(\sum_{j \neq i} x_j \right)^{-\beta} y_i^{1-\alpha}$$

where x_i is the total number of days spent by i in the park during a year and y_i is the days spent on other activities. We have $0 < \beta < \alpha < 1$. Each individual i may allocate a total of T days between x_i and y_i.

   (a) If all individuals act independently, how many days will they each spend in the park? (That is, what is the Nash equilibrium?)

   (b) The government has decided to regulate visits by issuing a limited number of permits, thereby restricting the total number of visitor-days to a fixed constant. What would be the Pareto efficient number of permits, assuming they are distributed equally among individuals? For $\alpha = \frac{1}{2}$, and $\beta = \frac{1}{4}$, by what percentage is use changed from part (a)?

16. Consider a firm that is a monopolist in the output market for its product and a monopsonist (the only purchaser) in the market for its single input. The firm's production function is $q(x) = \frac{1}{2}x$. The inverse demand function for output is $p(q) = 210 - 3q$, and the inverse supply function for its input is $r(x) = 10 + 4x$ where r is the per unit input price.

   (a) Find the value of q that maximizes the firm's profit, and find the resulting x, p, and r.

   (b) Find the values corresponding to perfect competition in both markets.

   (c) Find subsidy rate s on the use of x and a lump-sum tax S on the firm so that the profit maximizing output level is Pareto efficient and the firm's profits are those of part (a).

   (d) Find a subsidy rate t on output and a lump-sum tax T that will have the same effect as (c).

17. (Club goods) Consider a club (such as a swimming and tennis club) that is formed to supply a good jointly to its members. The club good supplied has

the properties of a public good for members. Such a club must determine the optimal level of the club good and the optimal membership size.

(*a*) Suppose every potential member of a certain club has income Y and utility function $u(x, y, s)$ where x is the level of the club good, y is the expenditure on other goods, and s is the membership size. Assume that the cost for the club to supply x is $c(x, s)$ and that this cost is apportioned equally among the s members. Write three equations that are necessary for maximization of the utility of club members in terms of the three unknowns x, y, and s. Hint: Remember the budget constraint.

(*b*) Suppose a group of families is going to build a swimming pool. Each has utility

$$u(x, y, s) = \frac{x y^{1000}}{(s + 10)^3},$$

where x is the size of the pool (in square yards), s is the number of families, and y is the expenditure on other commodities. The annual cost of the pool is $200 x^{1/2}$. Each family has an income of $\$100,000$. How many members should be in the club, how large a pool should be constructed, and how much does each family pay?

9.9 References

9.1 The basic theory of public goods is due to Samuelson (1954). For a good textbook discussion, see Feldman (1980). For a nice survey of the role of game theory in problems of public goods, externalities, and welfare, see Schotter and Schwödiauer (1980).

9.2 There are generalizations of the majority equilibrium concept to account for additional goods and weaker technical assumptions. See Slutsky (1977), Denzau and Parks (1983), and Greenberg and Shitovitz (1988).

9.3 The Lindahl solution was put forward in Lindahl (1919) but it had roots in Wicksell (1896). For modern proofs of existence, see Roberts (1974) and Foley (1970), which also discuss the relation of Lindahl allocations to the core.

9.4 The Vickrey auction is presented in Vickrey (1961), which considers several other allocation situations as well. The Groves mechanism was first presented in Groves (1973). Also see Clarke (1971) and Groves and Loeb (1975). The idea of using Nash equilibria instead of dominant solutions was put forth by Groves and Ledyard (1977). Such mechanisms were studied in depth in Hurwicz (1979a) and Hurwicz (1979b), which showed that (under appropriate assumptions) the only Pareto efficient, individually rational allocations that can be attained as Nash equilibrium points of a mechanism are Lindahl equilibria. For some alternative mechanisms, see Kalai, Postlewaite, and Roberts (1979) and Nakayama (1980).

9.5-9.6 For a good review article of the problems caused by externalities, see Bator (1958) and Buchanan and Stubblebine (1962). The benefit approach to externalities is presented in Luenberger (1994c). The altruism example is adapted from Feldman (1980).

9.7   The complete markets approach was developed by Arrow (1969). The idea of using taxes and subsidies to correct externalities goes back to Pigou (1920). It was more fully analyzed by Meade (1952). For a modern approach see Starrett (1972). The impact method is apparently new. The role of property rights in correcting externality problems was elucidated by Coase (1960). Also see Cooter (1980).

9.9   Exercise 5 is based on an idea of Guttman (1978). Exercise 8 is based on Hurwicz (1979b). Exercise 17 is an example of the theory of club goods originated by Buchanan (1965); for an overview of the theory, see Cornes and Sandler (1986).

Chapter 10
WELFARE AND SOCIAL CHOICE

A most important set of economic issues are those involving choices that society makes collectively, as a governed body. These include choices about particular public projects (such as whether to build a dam) and the formulation of general policy (such as tax policy), but they also include fundamental questions such as whether markets should be used to distribute goods and what type of voting procedure should be used for making societal decisions. Because these choices have such manifest impact, it is important to devote considerable effort toward understanding the possible objectives, limitations, and general methods for analyzing such choices. This chapter outlines many of the principles that can form a basis for this understanding.

Societal decisions can be analyzed in the light of two principal objectives: efficiency and equity. We have discussed efficiency a great deal in previous chapters (based on the Pareto concept). We have seen that government action may improve efficiency by regulating natural monopolies, providing public goods, and correcting production externalities by taxation or regulation. Efficiency is clearly an element that guides public decisions.

Equity is concerned with fairness—fairness of the distribution of economic goods and fairness with respect to how choices are made. For example, how much should individuals be rewarded for their natural talents as opposed to their efforts or their needs? As another example, should highly successful people have greater influence on public decisions than less-successful people? In general, equity issues appear to be more complex than efficiency issues, primarily because equity is hard to define precisely—it is the reflection of a kind of collective conscience, and this is hard to capture by simple quantitative measures. Yet it is clear that equity, like efficiency, should be a fundamental guiding principle of public decisions.

Equity can be absorbed into efficiency, at least formally, by treating equity as a consumption externality, with each person's utility function becoming a complicated function of all decisions. This trick of formalism, however, shows us little more than that equity is subject to all the difficulties of measurement and incentive incompatibility that are associated with externalities in general. Hence it is more practical to do our analysis with standard individualized utility functions—with equity concerns stripped out of them—as we have throughout the earlier chapters. Equity issues are then formally distinct from efficiency issues, although we recognize that they both are ultimately traceable to individual desires.

A fundamental tension between efficiency and equity manifests itself in different ways throughout this chapter. Pareto efficiency purposefully (and ingeniously) avoids interpersonal comparisons. Equity, on the other hand, is fundamentally concerned with interpersonal comparisons. The two concepts, therefore, seem to provide a neat partition of social questions, one avoiding interpersonal comparisons and the other focusing on them. However, as we explore welfare issues further, we find that the two concepts become surprisingly intertwined. This chapter investigates these issues, attempting to develop practical approaches to analysis of policy and attempting to explore the fundamental issues of the subject.

Part I
WELFARE MEASURES

10.1 Income Distributions and Welfare

A very simple (and common) way to assess equity is to look at the distribution of individual income in the economy. It seems clear (at least at first) that an economy with widely divergent individual incomes is qualitatively different in terms of equity than a similar economy in which individual incomes are more homogeneous.

The idea of using income distributions for welfare judgments can be formalized by our standard concepts. Let us postulate that social welfare is determined by the value of a Bergson-Samuelson social welfare function

$$S(u_1(\mathbf{x}_1), u_2(\mathbf{x}_2), \ldots, u_n(\mathbf{x}_n)),$$

defined over the utilities of the n individuals in the economy. This can be regarded as a kind of aggregate utility function. If the economy is perfectly competitive with market prices $\mathbf{p}$ and individual incomes $r_1, r_2, \ldots, r_n$, this welfare function can be written

$$S(v_1(\mathbf{p}, r_1), v_2(\mathbf{p}, r_2), \ldots, v_n(\mathbf{p}, r_n)),$$

where v_i is the indirect utility function of individual i. If we suppress $\mathbf{p}$, because it is considered fixed, the welfare function further reduces to the form

$$F(r_1, r_2, \ldots, r_n).$$

Hence, if prices are fixed and allocations are made through competitive markets, welfare is completely determined by incomes.

In any given economy, we might specify a particular form for F, reflecting our concept of equity. A popular class of such choices is

$$F(r_1, r_2, \ldots, r_n) = \left[\sum_{i=1}^{n} r_i^{\beta} \right]^{1/\beta}.$$

The choice $\beta = 1$ reflects a concern for efficiency only, since in this case only total income matters. This case is frequently referred to as a *utilitarian* social welfare function. Another extreme is $\beta = -\infty$, which reflects overriding concern for equality, since $\lim_{\beta \to -\infty} F(r_1, r_2, \ldots, r_n) = \min\{r_i, \ i = 1, 2, \ldots, n\}$, which shows that welfare is measured by the income of the poorest individual. This case is often associated with Rawls, who advocated it.

This simple approach to welfare evaluation does reflect many common concerns, but it does not provide a basis for full analysis. First of all, the method implicitly assumes that prices are fixed. But if we plan to impose changes in the economy, prices will generally vary. Second, it is not clear how the welfare function should be determined. However, this simple approach does set the stage for what follows.

10.2 Individual Benefits

As a starting point for quantifying welfare, it is natural to consider the impact on a single individual of a change in his or her consumption bundle. Study of this simple problem will help us develop the machinery necessary to consider more complex questions.

Suppose an individual initially has an allocation $\mathbf{x}^0$ with corresponding utility u^0, and then the allocation is changed to $\mathbf{x}^1$ with corresponding utility u^1. The change is either beneficial or not, depending, of course, on whether or not $u^1 > u^0$. Although the difference $u^1 - u^0$ is an ordinal measure of the value of the change, as determined by the sign, the magnitude of $u^1 - u^0$ has no real meaning. One natural way to assign a cardinal measure to the change is to use the benefit function. To do this we must decide on a standard bundle $\mathbf{g}$ that will be used as a basis for measuring benefits. This might be a standard bundle of consumer goods, although the choice is not very critical.

Once $\mathbf{g}$ is selected, there are two ways to define the benefit of the change, corresponding to using either the initial utility level u^0 or the final level u^1 as reference. Hence, we introduce the two-part definition below.

Compensating benefit and equivalent benefit. Suppose a consumer's bundle is changed from $\mathbf{x}^0$ with utility u^0 to $\mathbf{x}^1$ with utility u^1. Then the *compensating benefit*, CB, and the *equivalent benefit*, EB, are defined by

$$\text{CB} = b(\mathbf{x}^1, u^0)$$

and

$$\text{EB} = -b(\mathbf{x}^0, u^1).$$

The compensating benefit CB is the maximum amount of **g** that the consumer would be willing to give up to ensure that the change takes place. It is called the *compensating* benefit because we can compensate for the change by taking that much **g** from the individual, returning him or her to utility level u^0.

The equivalent benefit EB is the minimum amount of **g** needed to move the consumer to utility level u^1 if the change were not made. It is called the *equivalent* benefit because it is the amount of **g** that is equivalent to the change.

Use of these definitions to assign a benefit to a change tacitly assumes that all values of the benefit function are finite. Note also that if **g** is good, then $b(\mathbf{x}^0, u^0) = b(\mathbf{x}^1, u^1) = 0$. Hence, in that case we can use the more symmetric forms

$$CB = b(\mathbf{x}^1, u^0) - b(\mathbf{x}^0, u^0)$$
$$EB = b(\mathbf{x}^1, u^1) - b(\mathbf{x}^0, u^1).$$

CB and EB are illustrated in Fig. 10.1. In the figure we have used $\mathbf{g} = (1, 0)$, and we are considering the change from $\mathbf{x}^0$ to $\mathbf{x}^1$ shown by the dashed line. Note that CB and EB are usually different, but they must always have the same sign. Either one can be larger than the other. This is illustrated in Fig. 10.1 by starting at $^0\mathbf{x}$ and ending at $^1\mathbf{x}$. CB and EB are then interchanged from before.

Example 10.1 (Cobb-Douglas).   Consider the utility function $u(x, y) = xy$, and let $\mathbf{x}^0 = (1, 1)$ and $\mathbf{x}^1 = (2, 2)$. We have $u^0 = 1$, and $u^1 = 4$. Using $\mathbf{g} = (0, 1)$, the benefit function is $b(x, y, u) = y - u/x$. Hence

$$CB = 2 - \tfrac{1}{2} = \tfrac{3}{2}$$
$$EB = -1 + \tfrac{4}{1} = 3.$$

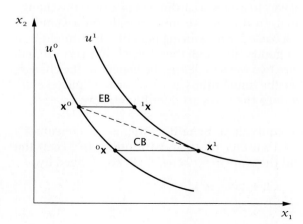

FIGURE 10.1   Illustration of CB and EB.

Adjusted Price Functions

The evaluation of CB and EB in terms of the benefit function as discussed and illustrated above is quite straightforward. However, the benefit function, like the utility function, is not generally observable. To use CB and EB, it is desirable to relate them to market (observable) quantities. As a step in this direction we show how CB and EB can be expressed in terms of the adjusted price function (defined in Section 5.5).

Recall that the adjusted price function is defined as

$$\mathbf{p}(\mathbf{x}, u) = \underset{\mathbf{p}}{\mathrm{argmin}} \{\mathbf{p}\cdot\mathbf{x} - e(\mathbf{p}, u) : \mathbf{p}\cdot\mathbf{g} = 1, \ \mathbf{p} \geq 0\}.$$

(See Appendix A for "argmin.") We are tacitly assuming that the indicated minimum is achieved by some $\mathbf{p}$ (and that the utility function is strongly monotonic). In general, of course, if this minimum is achieved, it may not be unique; in which case the adjusted price function is a set-valued correspondence. However, in this section we assume that $\mathbf{p}(\mathbf{x}, u)$ exists and is unique. Uniqueness is guaranteed if the underlying utility function is free of kinks, that is, points that allow more than one supporting hyperplane.

If the utility function is quasi-concave, we have, by Proposition 5.5, Section 5.5,

$$\mathbf{p}(\mathbf{x}, u) = \nabla_\mathbf{x} b(\mathbf{x}, u),$$

at points where b is differentiable.

The adjusted price function can be used to measure the CB and EB. If the utility function is quasi-concave and satisfies local nonsatiation so that $b(\mathbf{x}^0, u^0) = 0$, then from the above we can immediately write

$$\mathrm{CB} = b(\mathbf{x}^1, u^0) - b(\mathbf{x}^0, u^0) = \int_{\mathbf{x}^0}^{\mathbf{x}^1} \nabla b(\mathbf{x}, u^0)\cdot\mathbf{dx} = \int_{\mathbf{x}^0}^{\mathbf{x}^1} \mathbf{p}(\mathbf{x}, u^0)\cdot\mathbf{dx}$$

and

$$\mathrm{EB} = b(\mathbf{x}^1, u^1) - b(\mathbf{x}^0, u^1) = \int_{\mathbf{x}^0}^{\mathbf{x}^1} \nabla b(\mathbf{x}, u^1)\cdot\mathbf{dx} = \int_{\mathbf{x}^0}^{\mathbf{x}^1} \mathbf{p}(\mathbf{x}, u^1)\cdot\mathbf{dx},$$

where in either case the indicated integral is along *any* path[1] between $\mathbf{x}^0$ and $\mathbf{x}^1$. The value of the integral is independent of the path because the integrand is a gradient function.

There is a particular path that makes the integral formula obvious. It is illustrated in Fig. 10.2. From the point $\mathbf{x}^0$, we move along the indifference curve until we reach the point $\bar{\mathbf{x}}$ shown. The integral of $\mathbf{p}(\mathbf{x}, u^0)$ along this

---

[1] In particular, let $\mathbf{x}(t)$, $0 \leq t \leq 1$, be a smooth path with $\mathbf{x}(0) = \mathbf{x}^0$ and $\mathbf{x}(1) = \mathbf{x}^1$. At any point t, $0 \leq t \leq 1$, let $\dot{\mathbf{x}}(t) = d\mathbf{x}(t)/dt$. Then the integral of $\mathbf{p}(\mathbf{x}, u^0)$ along this path is $\int_0^1 \mathbf{p}(\mathbf{x}(t), u^0)\cdot\dot{\mathbf{x}}(t)\, dt$, which is an integral along one dimension. Such an integral generally depends on the particular path connecting the endpoints, but it is independent of the path if $\mathbf{p}(\mathbf{x}, u^0)$ can be expressed as the gradient of another function, as in this case.

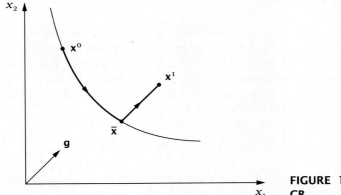

FIGURE 10.2 Evaluation of CB.

portion of the path is zero, since $\mathbf{p}(\mathbf{x}, u^0)$ is orthogonal to the indifference curve. We then move from $\bar{\mathbf{x}}$ to $\mathbf{x}^1$ in the $\mathbf{g}$ direction. Since $\mathbf{p}(\mathbf{x}, u^0) \cdot \mathbf{g} = 1$, the integral along this portion of the path equals the length in units of $\mathbf{g}$, which is equal to the benefit.

Example 10.2 (Cobb-Douglas again). Consider again the situation of Example 10.1 with $u(x, y) = xy$, $\mathbf{x}^0 = (1, 1)$, and $\mathbf{x}^1 = (2, 2)$. Let us compute CB and EB using the adjusted price function. As before we take $\mathbf{g} = (0, 1)$. First we must find the adjusted price function.

Given a point $\mathbf{x} = (x, y)$ and a reference value u, we adjust $\mathbf{x}$ to the form $(x, y - \beta)$ so that $x(y - \beta) = u$. This gives $\beta = y - u/x$. Hence the adjusted point is $(x, u/x)$, which is on the reference indifference curve.

The gradient of the utility function $u(x, y) = xy$ is (y, x) so at the adjusted point it is $(u/x, x)$. We must normalize this so that the second component is 1. Thus

$$\mathbf{p}(\mathbf{x}, u) = \left(\frac{u}{x^2}, 1 \right) .$$

Now that the adjusted price function is known, we can evaluate CB and EB. First,

$$\mathrm{CB} = \int_{(1,1)}^{(2,2)} \mathbf{p}(\mathbf{x}, 1) \cdot d\mathbf{x}$$

$$= \int_1^2 \frac{1}{x^2}\, dx + \int_1^2 dy = \left. -\frac{1}{x} \right|_1^2 + 1 = \frac{3}{2} .$$

Second,

$$\mathrm{EB} = \int_{(1,1)}^{(2,2)} \mathbf{p}(\mathbf{x}, 4) \cdot d\mathbf{x}$$

$$= \int_1^2 \frac{4}{x^2}\, dx + \int_1^2 dy = \left. -\frac{4}{x} \right|_1^2 + 1 = 3 .$$

These agree with the direct evaluations found in Example 10.1.

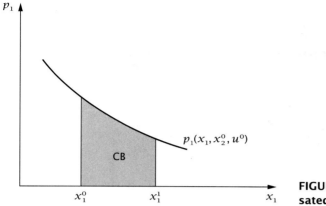

FIGURE 10.3 Compensated benefit.

The integral formula for CB can be illustrated in terms of an inverse compensated demand curve as shown in Fig. 10.3. We consider a two-commodity situation. Starting at some initial point (x_1^0, x_2^0) the consumer moves to a new point (x_1^1, x_2^0) with a different amount of the first commodity and the same amount of the second commodity. We set $\mathbf{g} = (0, 1)$ and hence measure benefits in units of the second commodity. The curve shown in the figure is $p_1(x_1, x_2^0, u^0)$, which is the first component of the adjusted price vector. The second component is identically equal to 1. The area under the curve is the compensated benefit.

The formulas for CB and EB expressed in terms of the adjusted price function relate the benefit of a move to an inverse demand function. This function itself is not directly observable, but it can be related to the ordinary inverse demand function; see Exercise 2. Therefore the benefits can be derived from observable quantities. Furthermore, the expression in terms of the adjusted price function is valuable in its own right, and it will be used again in Section 10.5.

10.3 Individual Variations

Government programs and projects can affect individuals indirectly as well as directly. Indirect impacts arise from price and income changes that are induced by the government action. These changes might be caused by the imposition of taxes or by grants and aid, for example. Public works projects also have indirect as well as direct effects, since a completed project will most likely affect the prices of other related commodities. For example, construction of a highway may influence property values and the travel time on other roads, thus affecting even those who do not use the highway.

Indirect effects can be measured in terms of indirect utility. If a price change causes indirect utility to increase, the change is beneficial for that individual. However, the units of indirect utility are arbitrary, since they mirror the units of utility. It is desirable to find a way to measure the indirect effect in units that have some general meaning. A convenient choice is to use units of income, and this leads to the concepts of compensating variation and equivalent variation.

Compensating and Equivalent Variations

Suppose there are m private goods. (For simplicity, we ignore public goods, since their level is assumed fixed here.)

Imagine an individual who originally faces prices $\mathbf{p}^0$, receives income r^0, and enjoys utility level u^0, and suppose prices and income are changed to $\mathbf{p}^1$ and r^1. We measure the magnitude of this change in income terms in two alternative ways, depending on whether u^0 or u^1 is used as reference.

Compensating variation and equivalent variation.   Suppose a consumer's situation is changed from $\mathbf{p}^0$, r^0, and u^0 to $\mathbf{p}^1$, r^1, and u^1. Then the *compensating variation,* CV, and the *equivalent variation,* EV, are defined by

$$\text{CV} = e(\mathbf{p}^0, u^0) - e(\mathbf{p}^1, u^0) - r^0 + r^1$$
$$\text{EV} = e(\mathbf{p}^0, u^1) - e(\mathbf{p}^1, u^1) - r^0 + r^1 .$$

Let us first interpret CV. Note that by definition $r^0 = e(\mathbf{p}^0, u^0)$, so CV $= r^1 - e(\mathbf{p}^1, u^0)$. Hence $r^1 - \text{CV} = e(\mathbf{p}^1, u^0)$. This shows that CV is the amount that must be subtracted from the individual's income in the second situation to return him or her to the original utility level u^0. That is, CV is the amount of income that, if subtracted, would compensate for the change.

We write CV $= e(\mathbf{p}^0, u^0) - e(\mathbf{p}^1, u^0) - r^0 + r^1$ rather than the simpler CV $= r^1 - e(\mathbf{p}^1, u^0)$ for the sake of symmetry and because we usually assume that $r^1 = r^0$.

The value EV $= e(\mathbf{p}^0, u^1) - r^0$ can likewise be interpreted as the amount of income that must be given to the individual that would be equivalent to the change, assuming that the change does not take place.

Note that if a change is beneficial, both CV and EV are positive. Hence, CV and EV are alternative quantitative measures of the consumer's welfare change due to a price change.

It is clear that CV and EV are, respectively, duals to CB and EB, just as the expenditure function is dual to the benefit function. CB and EB are direct measures, and CV and EV are indirect measures.

Actually, CV and EV are *surplus* quantities for a single individual in the sense of our earlier general definition of surplus as used in the zero-minimum principle (Section 6.8). For example, we can write CV $= r^1 - e(\mathbf{p}^1, u^0) = \mathbf{p}^1 \cdot \mathbf{x}^1 - e(\mathbf{p}^1, u^0)$, which is the surplus when the endowment is

x^1, prices are $\mathbf{p}^1$, and the reference utility is u^0. Similarly, EV is the negative surplus when endowment is x^0, prices are $\mathbf{p}^0$, and the reference utility is u^1. This highlights the duality of the benefit and variation quantities.

Example 10.3 (Cobb-Douglas). Suppose a consumer has the Cobb-Douglas utility function $u(x, y) = xy$. The corresponding expenditure function is $e(p_x, p_y, u) = 2(p_x p_y u)^{1/2}$. If the consumer moves from an initial point (x^0, y^0) with utility u^0 and prices p_x^0 to p_y^0 to a new point (x, y) and prices p_x and p_y, then EV is

$$EV = p_x x + p_y y - 2\sqrt{p_x p_y u^0}.$$

Calculation of CV and EV

From the direct formula

$$CV = e(\mathbf{p}^0, u^0) - e(\mathbf{p}^1, u^0) - r^0 + r^1$$

we can write

$$CV = \int_{\mathbf{p}^1}^{\mathbf{p}^0} \nabla_\mathbf{p} e(\mathbf{p}, u^0) \cdot \mathbf{dp} - r^0 + r^1 .$$

This integral is over any path from $\mathbf{p}^1$ to $\mathbf{p}^0$. (The value of the integral is independent of which path is used, since the integrand is a gradient function.) Using Shephard's lemma for consumers (Section 5.5), we can write this as

$$CV = \int_{\mathbf{p}^1}^{\mathbf{p}^0} \mathbf{h}(\mathbf{p}, u^0) \cdot \mathbf{dp} - r^0 + r^1 ,$$

where $\mathbf{h}$ is the Hicksian (compensated) demand function.

The above general formula for CV is expressed in terms of the compensated demand function, which is not directly observable. However, this formula can be converted into a procedure for evaluation that only requires the Marshallian demand. See Exercise 2.

The integral formula for CV and EV can be related to the area under a demand curve, as shown in Fig. 10.4. As in the previous section we consider a two-commodity situation. We normalize the prices so that the price of the second commodity is 1. We also assume that income remains fixed. The consumer initially sees p_1^0 and has utility u^0. The new situation has p_1^1 and u^1. The Hicksian demand for commodity 1 is $h_1(p_1, u)$. This function is the inverse of the adjusted price function $p_1(x_1, u)$. The value of CV is the area under the Hicksian demand curve between the two prices or, equivalently, the area of the horizontal wedge shown in the figure. (Note that this is a different change from that of Fig. 10.3. Here income is held fixed; earlier, the amount of commodity 2 was held fixed.)

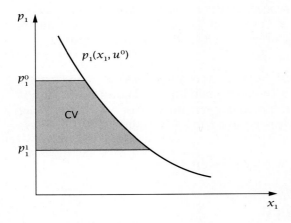

FIGURE 10.4 CV as area bounded by compensated demand curve.

It should also be clear that all of the above can be duplicated for EV as well. That is, EV can also be expressed as an integral of the compensated demand function.

Relation to Consumer's Surplus

Again suppose prices change from $\mathbf{p}^0$ to $\mathbf{p}^1$, and let $\mathbf{p}(t)$ be a smooth curve with $\mathbf{p}(0) = \mathbf{p}^0$ and $\mathbf{p}(1) = \mathbf{p}^1$. The change in consumer's surplus associated with this price change *and this path* is defined to be

$$\text{CS} = \int_0^1 \mathbf{x}(\mathbf{p}(t), r) \cdot \dot{\mathbf{p}} \, dt \, .$$

This integral is not path independent, since the integrand is not a gradient function.

If only one price varies, the integration path is taken to be the direct one, all other prices being held constant. Accordingly, the change in consumer's surplus is the area to the left of the corresponding inverse (Marshallian) demand curve.

The change in consumer's surplus is frequently used in place of either the compensating variation or the equivalent variation to convert a price change to monetary terms. Its use is justified mainly by its simplicity, for it does not have the theoretical justification of CV or EV, and when several prices change, it is not even well defined because it depends on the path between the two prices.

A simple relation holds between a change in consumer's surplus and the values CV and EV that sometimes justifies using the change in consumer's surplus as an approximation to CV or EV. We assume that the price of only one good changes, and that that good is a noninferior good (that is, $\partial x / \partial r > 0$). We denote the change in consumer's surplus associated with this change by CS. Recall the Slutsky equation,

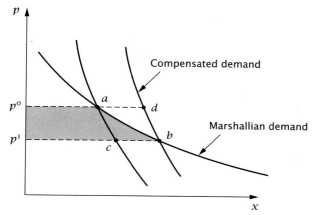

FIGURE 10.5 Demand curves and relations between CV, CE, and CS.

$$\frac{\partial x_j}{\partial p_i} = \frac{\partial h_j}{\partial p_i} - \frac{\partial x_j}{\partial r} x_i.$$

For a noninferior good, it follows that

$$\frac{\partial h}{\partial p} > \frac{\partial x}{\partial p}.$$

This means that the demand curves used to calculate the three quantities CV, EV, and CS have the relation shown in Fig. 10.5. The original price is p^0, and hence the original position of the consumer is the point a on the ordinary demand curve. Likewise, the final point is the point b on the demand curve. The compensating variation is computed using the original utility level and is the area to the left of the compensated demand curve passing through the point a. The equivalent variation, on the other hand, is computed from the compensated demand curve that passes through the point b. The three quantities are defined by the three areas

$$\text{CV} = \text{Area of } p^0 a c p^1$$
$$\text{CS} = \text{Area of } p^0 a b p^1$$
$$\text{EV} = \text{Area of } p^0 d b p^1.$$

Clearly, we have

$$\text{CV} \le \text{CS} \le \text{EV}.$$

Furthermore, if there were no income effect (that is, if $\partial x / \partial r = 0$), all three quantities would be equal. For small income effects, the consumer's surplus is a good approximation to CV or EV; however, small changes in consumer's surplus might *not* closely approximate small *changes* in CV and EV.

Evaluating Other Changes

Many public projects change the structure of the economy; for example, by the production of public goods. These projects affect an individual's utility both directly, through the project itself, and indirectly, through the price and income changes it may induce. It is easy to account for such projects explicitly in the formulation of CV and EV.

Let $\mathbf{z}$ and $\mathbf{x}$ represent bundles of public (or publicly supplied) goods and private (tradable) goods, respectively. Assume that an individual has utility function $u(\mathbf{z}, \mathbf{x})$. We define the corresponding expenditure function

$$e(\mathbf{z}, \mathbf{p}, u) = \min_{\mathbf{x}} \ \mathbf{p} \cdot \mathbf{x}$$

$$\text{sub to} \ \ u(\mathbf{z}, \mathbf{x}) \geq u$$

$$\mathbf{x} \geq \mathbf{0}.$$

Consider now a change from an initial point $(\mathbf{p}^0, \mathbf{z}^0, r^0)$ to a new point $(\mathbf{p}^1, \mathbf{z}^1, r^1)$. The compensating variation of this change is

$$\text{CV} = e(\mathbf{z}^0, \mathbf{p}^0, u^0) - e(\mathbf{z}^1, \mathbf{p}^1, u^0) - r^0 + r^1.$$

The equivalent variation is

$$\text{EV} = e(\mathbf{z}^0, \mathbf{p}^0, u^1) - e(\mathbf{z}^1, \mathbf{p}^1, u^1) - r^0 + r^1.$$

10.4   Compensation Criteria

It is quite easy to determine whether a change in the economy makes a single individual better off. We simply check the utility function or the indirect utility function. Alternatively, we can check CB, EB, CV, or EV. What is not easy is determining whether a change is good for the economy as a whole. However, there is one case where we would agree that a change is beneficial, and that is when the change leads to a Pareto improvement, that is, when everyone is at least as well off as before and at least one individual is better off. Unfortunately, most changes resulting from government action leave some consumers better off and others worse off, so the Pareto test cannot be applied.

The compensation criterion discussed in this section is based on an intriguing modification of the Pareto concept. *Potential* Pareto improvement is used as a criterion rather than *actual* Pareto improvement. The basic idea of the compensation criterion (due originally to Hicks and Kaldor) is to imagine that after a change is made, the winners attempt to compensate the losers. This compensation might be in terms of income, as originally proposed by Hicks and Kaldor, or more directly by transferring goods. If this compensation can be accomplished in such a way that the end result is a Pareto improvement over the original situation, then the first change (before the compensation) is said to be an improvement. We formalize this idea of using tradable goods for compensation as follows:

Tradable preferred. A new situation is said to be *tradable preferred* to an original one if there is a way to reallocate tradable goods in the new situation so that everyone is at least as well off as in the original situation. If, in addition, at least one individual can be made strictly better off, the new situation is *strictly tradable preferred* to the original situation.

There are two important things to notice about this definition. First, the compensation is only *potential* compensation—it is not actually carried out. The new situation is considered to be an improvement if it is *possible* to compensate the losers; the compensation need not take place.

The second thing to notice is that the compensation is restricted to tradable goods. This usually means private goods. The original change itself may consist of the addition of a public good, or perhaps even a structural change in the economy (such as the opening of new markets). We do not allow the compensation to reverse those same nontradable changes, restoring the status quo, for then every new situation would be (weakly) preferred to every other. A simple example is a highway built near some residences. Many people benefit from the highway, but the nearby residents may lose. The highway project is considered to be an improvement if, after paying for the project, the net winners could compensate the net losers so that everyone is better off than before the highway project.

The compensation criterion (but originally in income terms) was originally proposed as a kind of social ordering—a method for ordering the possible configurations of the economy. However, this ordering does not possess the properties required of a true ordering. Unfortunately, it is possible for two different configurations each to be tradable preferred to the other. This phenomenon is illustrated in Fig. 10.6. The two curves

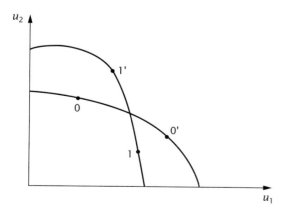

FIGURE 10.6 **Tradable preference is not a true ordering.**

represent the feasible levels of utility combinations for the two consumers in the economy under two alternative situations. First, we note that point 1 is tradable preferred to 0 because 1 can, by reallocation, be transformed to $1'$. Likewise, point 0 is preferred to 1 because 0 can be transformed to $0'$. Despite this "minor" difficulty, the compensation criterion forms the basis for many project evaluation procedures. We explore its use in the next few sections.

The Compensation Criterion and CB

Consider an economy with n individuals. In an initial configuration the level of public goods is z^0 and individual i has bundle x_i^0 of private goods. In the next configuration these levels are z^1 and x_i^1. We denote the corresponding allocations as (z^0, X^0) and (z^1, X^1).

We write the utility of consumer i as $u_i(z, x_i)$, partitioning the public and private goods. We take g to be a bundle of private goods to use as reference. Then we define $b_i(z, x_i, u)$ in the usual manner

$$b_i(z, x_i, u) = \max\{\beta : u_i(z, x_i - \beta g) \geq u\}$$

(with the usual constraints). And, using (z^0, x_i^0) as base point, we define the compensating benefit for each i by

$$CB_i(z, x_i) = b_i(z, x_i, u_i^0),$$

which is a function of the new point.

We now completely characterize tradable preference in terms of a maximum principle stated in terms of the total CB. This result generalizes the zero-maximum principle for Pareto efficiency.

Tradable preference maximum theorem.   *Suppose g is weakly good for at least one individual. The allocation (z^1, X^1) is (weakly) tradable preferred to (z^0, X^0) if and only if*

$$B = \max_{X} \sum_{i=1}^{n} CB_i(z^1, x_i)$$

$$\text{sub to } \sum_{i=1}^{n} x_i = \sum_{i=1}^{n} x_i^1$$

$$x_i \geq 0, \qquad i = 1, 2, \ldots, n$$

satisfies $B \geq 0$.

Proof: Suppose that (z^1, X^1) is (weakly) tradable preferred to (z^0, X^0). Then there is $\overline{X}$ with $\sum_{i=1}^{n} \overline{x}_i = \sum_{i=1}^{n} x_i^1$ such that $u_i(z^1, \overline{x}_i) \geq u_i(z^0, x_i^0) = u_i^0$ for each i. This means that $b_i(z^1, \overline{x}_i, u_i^0) \geq 0$ for all i. Hence $B \geq 0$.

Now suppose $B \geq 0$. Then there is $\overline{X}$ such that $\sum_{i=1}^{n} b_i(z^1, \overline{x}_i, u_i^0) \geq 0$ and $\sum_{i=1}^{n} \overline{x}_i = \sum_{i=1}^{n} x_i^1$. Let $b_i = b_i(z^1, \overline{x}_i, u_i^0)$ for all i. (Without loss of generality, assume that g is (weakly) good for n.) Define the new allocation X^* by

$$
x_i^* = \begin{cases} \overline{x}_i - b_i g, & i < n \\[2ex] \overline{x}_n - b_n g + \sum_{j=1}^{n} b_j g. \end{cases}
$$

For each $i < n$, $x_i^* \geq 0$, by definition of b_i. Also, $x_n^* \geq 0$ and $u_n(x_n^*) \geq u_n^0$, since g is weakly good for n. We have $u_i(z^1, x_i^*) \geq u_i^0$ for all i. Thus (z^1, X^*) is (weakly) Pareto preferred to (z^0, X^0). This means (z^1, X^1) is (weakly) tradable preferred to (z^0, X^0). ∎

Example 10.4 (Cotton and dairy). Suppose there are two agricultural regions, C and D, that produce cotton and dairy products, respectively. Inhabitants of both regions all have the utility function $u(c, d) = cd$ where c and d are the consumption of cotton and dairy products. The production in each region can be considered as a (say yearly) endowment. The inhabitants of C accordingly have an endowment of $(2, 0)$, and those of region D have $(0, 2)$. The government is planning to divert a river that currently flows primarily in region D into region C in order to stimulate the production of cotton. The diversion will change the endowments to $(3.5, 0)$ and $(0, 1)$ for regions C and D, respectively. Is this a beneficial change in the compensation sense?

By symmetry it is clear that the equilibrium allocation in the original situation is $c = d = 1$ in both regions. Hence the utility values are $u_C^0 = u_D^0 = 1$. We take cotton to be the reference commodity for measuring benefits. The benefit function for both regions is therefore $b(c, d, u) = c - u/d$. To evaluate the change, we solve for the maximum benefit

$$
B = \max \; c_C + c_D - \frac{1}{d_C} - \frac{1}{d_D}
$$

$$
\text{sub to } \; c_C + d_D = 3.5
$$

$$
d_C + d_D = 1.
$$

This gives $B = 3.5 - 2/(1/2) = -0.5$. Hence the change is not beneficial.

The above theorem also leads to a simple test, which if passed ensures that the compensation criterion is satisfied by an allocation (z^1, X^1). We just check whether $\sum_{i=1}^{n} CB_i(z^1, x_i^1) \geq 0$. If so, the new situation is preferred to the original one, since X^1 is feasible for the maximization. Therefore evaluation of $\sum_{i=1}^{n} CB_i(z^1, x_i^1)$ provides a quick sufficiency test for preference in this sense.

Example 10.5 (Cotton and dairy). Consider again the cotton and dairy example. The final allocation is easily found from Cobb-Douglas formulas to be $c_C = \frac{7}{4}$, $d_C = \frac{1}{2}$, $c_D = \frac{7}{4}$, and $d_D = \frac{1}{2}$. We can apply the simple test to know that

$$B \geq c_C + c_D - \frac{1}{d_C} - \frac{1}{c_D}$$

$$= 3.5 - 4.0$$

$$= -.5$$

Hence the simple test is indecisive in this case.

The Compensation Criterion and CV

The criterion used above can also be related to the sum of individual CVs. In fact, the relation is just the dual of that for the CBs.

Again consider the economy discussed above. However, now we characterize situations by the triples (z, p, R) where z denotes the level of the public goods (or parameters), p is the price vector for the private goods, and $R = (r_1, r_2, \ldots, r_n)$ is the vector of individual incomes. Again, we consider an initial situation (z^0, p^0, R^0) and a new situation (z^1, p^1, R^1).

Relative to the base point (z^0, p^0, r_i^0) we define the compensating variation for each i by

$$CV_i(z, p, r_i) = e(z^0, p^0, u_i^0) - e(z, p, u_i^0) - r_i^0 + r_i,$$

which is a function of the new situation.

We then have the following characterization.

Tradable preference minimum theorem.   *Assume that all utility functions are quasi-concave and strongly monotonic. The situation (z^1, p^1, R^1) with allocation X^1 and $r_i = p \cdot x_i^1$, $i = 1, 2, \ldots, n$, is tradable preferred to (z^0, p^0, R^0) if and only if*

$$V = \min_{p \cdot g = 1} \sum_{i=1}^{n} CV_i(z^1, p, p \cdot x_i^1)$$

satisfies $V \geq 0$.

Proof: Define B as in the tradable preference maximum theorem. We use the basic duality relation $b(z, x, u) = \min_{p \cdot g = 1} \{ p \cdot x - e(z, p, u) \}$ (which holds under the quasi-concavity and strong monotonicity assumptions) to write

$$B = \max_{X} \left\{ \min_{p \cdot g = 1} \sum_{i=1}^{n} \left[p \cdot x_i - e_i(z^1, p, u_i^0) \right] \right\}$$

$$\text{sub to } \sum x_i = \sum x_i^1.$$

Since $\sum_{i=1}^{n} x_i$ is fixed, the maximization over X is redundant. Hence

$$B = \min_{p \cdot g = 1} \sum_{i=1}^{n} \left[p \cdot x_i^1 - e_i(z^1, p, u_i^0) \right]$$

$$= \min_{p \cdot g = 1} \sum_{i=1}^{n} CV_i \left(z^1, p \cdot x_i^1 \right).$$

Hence, $V = B$, and the result follows from the tradable preference maximum theorem. ∎

The normalization $\mathbf{p}\cdot\mathbf{g} = 1$ in the theorem is really not necessary. This normalization renders $V = B$. If another normalization is used, V will simply be multiplied by a positive constant, and hence the test, which just involves the sign of V, will be unchanged.

We can use half the above theorem to estimate whether a change is an improvement. We may set $\mathbf{p} = \mathbf{p}^1$ in the objective function defining V. Then we obtain $V \leq \sum_{i=1}^n CV_i(\mathbf{z}^1, \mathbf{p}^1, r^1)$. Therefore, the condition $\sum_{i=1}^n CV_i(\mathbf{z}^1, \mathbf{p}^1) \geq 0$ is necessary for the new situation to be preferred to the original one. That is, if the project is tradable preferred, then $\sum_{i=1}^n CV_i(\mathbf{z}^1, \mathbf{p}^1, r^1) \geq 0$.

Example 10.6 (Cotton and dairy). The expenditure function corresponding to the utility function $u(c, d) = cd$ when the price vector is normalized as $(1, p)$ is $e(p, u) = 2(pu)^{1/2}$. Hence the CVs for the example considered before are $CV_C = 3.5 - 2\sqrt{p}$ and $CV_D = p - 2\sqrt{p}$. We thus evaluate

$$V = \min\{3.5 + p - 4\sqrt{p}\}.$$

The solution has $p = 4$ and $V = -0.5$, agreeing with the value of B found earlier.

We can also apply the simple test by checking the total CV at the final price $p = 3.5$. This gives the bound

$$V \leq 3.5 + 3.5 - 2\sqrt{3.5} > 0.$$

So the test is inconclusive.

Income Compensation

As stated earlier, the compensation criterion was originally formulated in terms of compensation by income. Income compensation is certainly appealing but it is not well defined in all cases, for there is in general no guarantee that such compensation will lead to a feasible allocation of goods. Nevertheless the concept is still a useful one.

The test for improvement based on income compensation is straightforward. Since individual i's compensating variation CV_i is a direct measure of the income compensation required by that individual, a new situation is compensation preferred in terms of income if and only if $\sum_{i=1}^n CV_i \geq 0$.

It should be noted that if income effects can be neglected, then $CV = CB$. (See Exercise 3.)

10.5 Prices and Welfare

Public works projects frequently transform an existing set of private endowments into a different set. For example, sidewalks built in a neighborhood

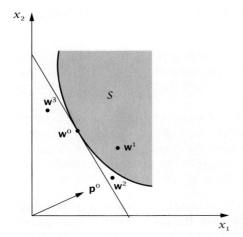

x_1 **FIGURE 10.7 Prices and benefit.**

transform a homeowner's house into a house with sidewalks. In general, suppose a public works project increases the level of endowment of some goods by using others as input. Is there an easy way to determine whether the net change in endowment is beneficial? An almost obvious test is to check whether the change increases the total value of endowment, as determined by existing prices. That is, if the change increases the value of the nation's resources, it must be beneficial. This simple test is, in fact, essentially correct. Prices do provide a means for evaluating welfare changes.

The result can be easily seen by referring to Fig. 10.7. We let

$$S = \left\{ z : z = \sum_{i=1}^{n} x_i, \quad x_i \geq 0, \quad u_i(x_i) \geq u_i^0, \quad i = 1, 2, \ldots, n \right\}.$$

The equilibrium situation at w^0 and p^0 is represented by the fact that p^0 defines a hyperplane tangent to S at w^0.

In the figure the allocation w^1 is an improvement, and hence it lies in S. Accordingly, it must lie on the upper side of the tangent plane—that is, $p^0 \cdot w^1 \geq p^0 \cdot w^0$. Therefore the value of w^1 at the original prices must be no less than the value of w^0 at these prices.

We note, however, that this conclusion is not reversible. The point w^2 in the figure has an increased value, at prices p^0, but is not in S. On the other hand, the criterion is reversible in the sense that if value decreases, as represented by the point w^3, the new point represents an inferior point.

The above implications can be reversed simply by using new prices instead of old prices. For example, $p^0 \cdot w^1 > p^0 \cdot w^0$ does not necessarily imply that w^1 is an improvement over w^0. But if $p^1 \cdot w^1 > p^1 \cdot w^0$, then w^0 is inferior to w^1.

The above criterion is often referred to as an aggregate (or sometimes national) income test, since the quantity $p \cdot w$ is aggregate income. The criterion says roughly that welfare (determined by the compensation test) and aggregate income move together.[2]

As pointed out above, the aggregate income criterion is not definitive, since income can increase while welfare decreases. However, for small changes, the test is fairly accurate. Because the hyperplane determined by **p** is tangent to S, a small change in a direction of increasing income will be contained in S. (In fact, the first-order change in CB is just $\mathbf{p}^0 \cdot (\mathbf{w}^1 - \mathbf{w}^0)$.) For this reason, the income test is frequently used to justify proposed projects that are small relative to national income. But this justification is unsatisfactory. Typically, projects have dramatic effects on some individuals, and hence on some components of **w**. The widening of a highway, for example, may be small compared to national income, but it could cause large changes in local endowments. A fuller analysis would calculate aggregate compensating variation or equivalent variation, as discussed in Section 10.4.

Example 10.7 (Cotton and dairy).   In the cotton and dairy example of the last section, the initial prices are by symmetry $(1,1)$. The change in aggregate endowment is $(3.5 - 2, 1 - 2) = (1.5, -0.5)$. Hence the value of this change, as measured by initial prices, is positive. However, we know from our earlier analysis that this change is in fact not beneficial. The national income test is incorrect because the change is not small.

10.6   Cost-Benefit Analysis

The formal application of the theory of the previous sections to the analysis of particular projects is referred to as *cost-benefit analysis*. The subject was originally founded on the basis of the compensation criterion. The total benefits (positive compensating variations and profit increases) are put on one side of a ledger, and total costs (negative compensating variations and profit reductions) are put on the other. A project is considered worthwhile if the difference is positive (or if the ratio is greater than one). However, a thorough cost-benefit analysis can provide much more information than the simple bottom-line figures. A factoring of benefits and costs across different groups and sectors can be included, as well as an analysis of the efficiency effects of the taxes used to finance the project. Hence, a modern cost-benefit analysis can provide an insightful illumination of the impacts of a project, although other terms are often used for more inclusive studies because the term *cost-benefit analysis* is frequently associated with the simple calculation of net benefit.

---

[2]The quantity $s = \mathbf{p}^0 \cdot \mathbf{w}^1 - \mathbf{p}^0 \cdot \mathbf{w}^0$ is sometimes called the surplus associated with the change from $\mathbf{w}^0$ to $\mathbf{w}^1$. Note that $s = \mathbf{p}^0 \cdot \mathbf{w}^1 - \sum_{i=1}^{n} e_i(\mathbf{p}^0, u_i^0) = S(\mathbf{p}^0, \mathbf{U}^0)$ (with the understanding that $\mathbf{w} = \mathbf{w}^1$). Hence the income test is $S(\mathbf{p}^0, \mathbf{U}^0) \geq 0$.

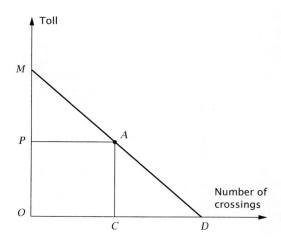

FIGURE 10.8 Demand for a bridge.

We cannot give a comprehensive summary of the subject here, so we shall simply illustrate the possibilities by giving two highly simplified examples.

Example 10.8 (Bridge building). The idea of measuring benefits and costs for projects must trace back to the very first human societies. However, the idea of counting as a benefit the somewhat intangible concept of consumer surplus was apparently first put forward by the French engineer Jules Dupuit in 1844 as part of an argument for the building of bridges even though they were not commercially profitable. He considered the inverse demand function showing the toll of the proposed bridge versus the number of crossings, as depicted in Fig. 10.8. If the bridge were operated at zero toll, the total value to society, using the now familiar consumer surplus argument, would be the complete area under the function. On the other hand, if the bridge were to be built commercially, it would be operated so as to maximize profit, at an operating point such as A in the figure. The total value to society in this case is the sum of the consumer surplus and profit, which is the area $MACO$. However, the profit $PACO$ might easily be less than the cost of the bridge, in which case it would not be built. Yet, the total potential gain to society, being the complete area MDO, will certainly exceed the profit (and in fact is twice as great in the case of a linear inverse demand curve) and might easily exceed the cost of construction.

Example 10.9 (Land use project). Consider a region of farm land located in the flood plain of a river. Suppose periodic flooding of this region causes substantial crop damage. A publicly financed flood control project (such as the building of a dam) is proposed.

A simple economic analysis of such a project would measure the obvious costs and benefits. The obvious costs would include the cost of construction and the decrease in crop production of upstream farms displaced by the dam. Direct environmental costs might also be included. The benefits would be the (time discounted) value of the crops that would otherwise be destroyed. The calculation of the costs and benefits would be based on current market prices. (If there are monopolies, prices used in these calculations might be adjusted.) The compensation criterion would then dictate that the project should be built if the benefits exceed the costs.

An analysis along the above lines is seriously flawed, however, for there are other important benefits and costs that arise indirectly. Indeed, such an analysis may substantially underestimate the benefits.

If the project were built and the land were no longer subject to the risk of flooding, the land would likely then be suitable for alternative, "higher" uses, such as housing, which were economically infeasible before because of the risk of flooding. A careful analysis must account for this potential shift in use and the associated land price changes. Such an analysis requires a forecast of the economic equilibrium that would hold if the project were built.

One way to carry out a suitable equilibrium analysis is to define a *study region* that is somewhat larger than the flood plain itself. We suppose that the study region is a self-contained economic region with no interactions with the outside environment (this assumption can be relaxed—see Exercise 7). We also assume that, within the region, prices other than those of land are not affected by the project. We divide the region into m individual land parcels by imposing a grid structure, as shown in Fig. 10.9. We also identify a set of n ($n \geq m$) activities, each of which may locate on one of the parcels.

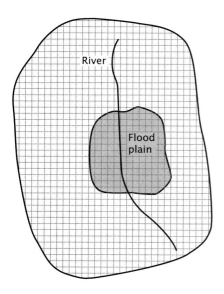

FIGURE 10.9 Study region.

We define a_{ij} to be the value[3] to activity i it locates on parcel j. In the case of a productive activity, a_{ij} is the net income (before the rent of the parcel itself is subtracted) that the activity would derive if located on parcel j. In the case of a household, a_{ij} is the willingness to pay for location j by household i. Both of these are measured in units of a reference commodity whose price is not influenced by conditions in the study region. The project influences the economy by changing the values of some of the a_{ij}'s. (It will presumably increase some a_{ij}'s.)

For a given set of a_{ij}'s the equilibrium pattern of location can be determined by maximizing the total benefit, which is the sum of all willingness-to-pay values plus the sum of all profits. See Section 7.14. The linear program is

$$\max \sum_{ij} a_{ij} x_{ij}$$
$$\text{sub to } \sum_{i=1}^{n} x_{ij} \leq 1 \quad \text{for all } j = 1, 2, \ldots, m$$
$$\sum_{j=1}^{m} x_{ij} \leq 1 \quad \text{for all } i = 1, 2, \ldots, n$$
$$x_{ij} \geq 0 \quad \text{for all } i \text{ and } j.$$

A solution always exists with all x_{ij}'s equal to 0 or 1. If $x_{ij} = 1$, activity i is located on parcel j in the equilibrium solution.

Let a_{ij} and $\bar{a}_{ij}$, $i = 1, 2, \ldots, n$, $j = 1, 2, \ldots, m$, denote the coefficients without and with the project, respectively. Let x_{ij} and $\bar{x}_{ij}$ denote the corresponding solutions. The net benefit of the project is

$$B = \sum_{ij} \bar{a}_{ij} \bar{x}_{ij} - \sum_{ij} a_{ij} x_{ij}.$$

In practice, the existing locations and prices might be used to define the original equilibrium. Techniques for updating this equilibrium to reflect the new $\bar{a}_{ij}$'s, by moving individual activities, can then be employed to determine the new equilibrium and the net benefit.

Once the two equilibria are computed, many summary accounts can be constructed, in addition to the net benefit. Benefits and costs accruing to different groups—landowners, factories, homeowners, etc.—can be computed. The equilibrium model provides an estimation of what will occur if the project is built. Evaluation of that equilibrium can be carried out by cost-benefit analysis or by other means.

10.7   Social Utility Functions

Compensation criteria have the desirable property of being objective, but as we have seen, they suffer two major drawbacks: they do not induce

---

[3]We are assuming that there are no externalities of location; that is, we are assuming that the value to activity i of a given location is not influenced by where other activities locate.

consistent orderings, and they are based only on potential, rather than actual, Pareto improvements. These problems are so severe that we are led back to the idea of using an explicit social utility function or social ordering to evaluate changes. A social utility function measures welfare directly, and therefore, by definition, it induces a consistent ordering. We must recognize, however, that use of such a function implies that we are making interpersonal comparisons of utilities, which we had hoped to avoid, but this path seems to be worth further investigation at this point.

Consider an economy consisting of n individuals. A social utility function is defined over allocations $X = (x_1, x_2, \ldots, x_n)$ where, as usual, x_i denotes the bundle of goods received by individual i. Hence we can write $S(X)$ for such a function. A special case, discussed before, is the Bergson-Samuelson welfare function[4] form $S(X) = S(u_1(x_1), u_2(x_2), \ldots, u_n(x_n))$. But in general, a social utility function may reflect societal interests that differ from strict individual utility. For example, an individual may have high utility for alcohol consumption, but this might be downgraded in the social utility function.

Use of Equivalent Variation

A Bergson-Samuelson social welfare function can be expressed in indirect utility form, and this form is useful for evaluating endowment changes when the corresponding x_i's are determined indirectly by markets. Suppose individuals initially have endowments $W = (w_1, w_2, \ldots, w_n)$ and equilibrium prices are $\mathbf{p}$. Then for the corresponding equilibrium allocation, we have

$$S(u_1(\mathbf{x}_1), u_2(\mathbf{x}_2), \ldots, u_n(\mathbf{x}_n))$$
$$= S(v_1(\mathbf{p}, \mathbf{p} \cdot \mathbf{w}_1), v_2(\mathbf{p}, \mathbf{p} \cdot \mathbf{w}_2), \ldots, v_n(\mathbf{p}, \mathbf{p} \cdot \mathbf{w}_n)).$$

Now suppose a government project changes the endowments to

$$W' = (w'_1, w'_2, \ldots, w'_n).$$

These lead to new equilibrium prices $\mathbf{p}'$ and a new allocation X'. We can then compare the new allocation with the old. We have

$$S(u_1(\mathbf{x}'_1), u_2(\mathbf{x}'_2), \ldots, u_n(\mathbf{x}'_n))$$
$$= S(v_1(\mathbf{p}', \mathbf{p}' \cdot \mathbf{w}'_1), v_2(\mathbf{p}', \mathbf{p}' \cdot \mathbf{w}'_2), \ldots, v_n(\mathbf{p}', \mathbf{p}' \cdot \mathbf{w}'_n))$$
$$= S(v_1(\mathbf{p}, \mathbf{p} \cdot \mathbf{w}_1 + E_1), v_2(\mathbf{p}, \mathbf{p} \cdot \mathbf{w}_2 + E_2), \ldots, v_n(\mathbf{p}, \mathbf{p} \cdot \mathbf{w}_n + E_n)),$$

---

[4]According to our usage, a *social welfare function* transforms individual preferences into social preferences, and a *social utility function* is defined over allocations. Hence a given social welfare function responds to changes in individual preferences, whereas a given social utility function does not.

where the E_i's are the equivalent variations of the change. Hence, using the original point as a base, we see there is a function F such that

$$S = F(E_1, E_2, \ldots, E_n).$$

We therefore see that welfare can be expressed in income terms by using equivalent variations. This takes us back to the simple approach of Section 10.1 of evaluating an economy in terms of its income distribution. Now, however, we have a deeper formulation of that approach.

Part II
SOCIAL CHOICE THEORY

10.8   Social Preference and Majority Voting

Of all the approaches to making social decisions discussed in the previous sections of this chapter, the simple one of using a social utility function, or a social preference ordering, is the most general and most complete. However, we have not really addressed the question of how such a social preference ordering should be selected.

Ideally, this social preference ordering would properly reflect the preferences of all citizens—both their "individualistic" preferences and their "externality" welfare concerns—so that choices determined by the preference ordering would be efficient and fair. Once such a preference ordering were determined, societal choices could be made by straightforward computation. It is the search for such an ordering (including a more precise formulation of just what properties we want it to have) that we pursue in this and the next few sections.

Majority Voting

Majority voting has long been used as a method for making group decisions. We shall examine it as a possible mechanism for defining group (or societal) preferences.

Suppose there is a group of n individuals and a fixed set of alternatives X. Assume also that each individual i has a preference ordering $\succsim_i$ on X (a relation on $X \times X$). We then define a group relation on $X \times X$ through majority voting. Specifically, to determine the relation between two elements x and y in X, a vote between the two is held. Each individual votes for the alternative x or y if he or she prefers it to the other, and abstains if he or she is indifferent between the two. We say that x is *majority preferred* to y if x receives at least as many votes as y. In this case we write xMy. Note that

M is analogous to weak preference. Indeed if there were only a single individual, or if all individuals had identical preferences, the relation M would exactly equal the underlying preference ordering. Hence majority voting is a natural way to extend individual preferences to a relation M among the alternatives X.

Let us determine whether M satisfies the properties required of a preference order. First, we see that the relation M is complete, since for any x and y either xMy or yMx. Second, we see that the relation M is reflexive, since for any x, everyone would abstain in a vote between x and x, yielding xMx. However, the relation M is not transitive. To see this, we consider a classic example due to Condorcet: There are three individuals 1, 2, and 3, and three alternatives x, y, and z. The three individuals rank the alternatives in the following order:

$$
\begin{array}{cccc}
1: & x & y & z \\
2: & y & z & x \\
3: & z & x & y
\end{array}
$$

where the alternatives are listed left to right from highest to lowest preference. Let us determine the majority relation M for these alternatives. In a vote between x and y, individuals 1 and 3 would vote for x and individual 2 would vote for y. Hence xMy. Similarly, we find yMz and zMx. These relations are all strict, in the sense that the reverse relations do not hold. Hence we have xMy and yMz, but not xMz, showing that M is not transitive.

The nontransitivity of M is often described as cyclic behavior. If one conducted actual pairwise votes in the above situation, y would win over z, and x would win over y, but then z would win over x, so that no clear choice is determined.

Single-Peakedness

The above result is a serious blow to the theoretical justification of majority voting. But in practice, majority voting is frequently felt to be a reasonable way to define group preferences. Cyclic behavior is not particularly common, and in fact it seems pretty clear that cyclic behavior occurs only if the pattern of individual preferences is somewhat unusual. Perhaps by restricting the pattern of preferences, we can definitely exclude cycles and cause M to be transitive.

A property of preferences that ensures that M is transitive is single-peakedness. Roughly, a set of preference orders satisfies the single-peakedness property if as one scans across the alternatives, all preferences monotonically increase and then decrease, each preference order tracing out a single peak.

To formulate the concept more rigorously, we must first order the alternatives so that we can meaningfully scan through them sequentially. This notion is captured by the following definition.

Strong order.   A *strong order* of a set X is a binary relation S satisfying the following:

(i) for all $x \in X$, not xSx (irreflexivity).

(ii) for all x and y in X, $x \neq y$, either xSy or ySx (completeness).

(iii) for all x, y, and z in X, xSy and ySz implies xSz (transitivity).

A strong order is analogous to "less than" or "greater than" in the real numbers, as well as to strict preference. Condition (ii) ensures that no two elements are equal according to S. If the elements are strongly ordered, they can be considered to be laid out on an axis, with the order of two elements corresponding to their relative position on that axis (say with the "higher" elements being farthest to the right). We then say an element y is *between* x and z if either (a) xSy and ySz or (b) zSy and ySx. This corresponds to y being between x and z on the axis. We want to strongly order the elements of X just for convenience. The strong order has nothing to do with an individual's actual preferences; it is just a way of listing the elements.

If there are only a finite number of elements, they can be strongly ordered by just assigning them arbitrarily to distinct positions on the axis. Likewise it is easy to strongly order alternatives that depend on a single variable, such as money, by using the numerical order of that variable.

We now define single-peakedness.

Single-peakedness.   A set of preferences $\succsim_i$, $i \in N$ on X satisfies the *single-peakedness property* if there is a strong ordering S of X such that for every $i \in N$, if $x \succsim_i y$ and y is between x and z, then $y \succ_i z$.

The single-peakedness property is best illustrated by representing the preferences by utility functions, as shown in Fig. 10.10. As one scans the

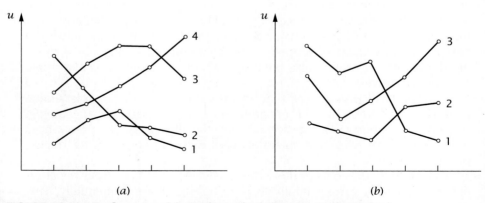

(a)   (b)

FIGURE 10.10   Preferences: (a) single-peaked, (b) not single-peaked.

axis of alternatives, the utility functions must rise and fall at most once, forming a single peak (or short plateau between two elements). It is not the magnitudes of utilities that matter, only the relative values.

We now show that the single-peakedness property is enough to ensure that the majority voting relation M is transitive.

Proposition 10.1. *Suppose that the number of individuals n is odd and that preferences satisfy the single-peakedness property. Then M is transitive and is therefore a preference order on X.*

Proof: Take any three distinct alternatives x, y, and z and suppose xMy and yMz. We must show that xMz. We must consider the various possible orderings of x, y, and z as induced by the strong order S of the single-peakedness property. There are six possible orderings, and hence six cases.
Case 1. (Ordering (x, y, z); that is, xSy and ySz). Let $V \subset N = \{1, 2, \ldots, n\}$ denote the individuals who vote for x or abstain in a vote between x and y. V contains at least $n/2$ members since xMy. For $i \in V$ we have $x \succsim_i y$, and by the single-peakedness assumption, $y \succ_i z$. Hence by transitivity $x \succ_i z$, and therefore all $i \in V$ will vote for x over z. Thus xMz.
Case 2. (Ordering (x, z, y)). Let $V \subset N$ be the set of individuals who vote for y or abstain in a vote between y and z. V contains at least $n/2$ members. For $i \in V$ we have $y \succsim_i z$ since yMz. Thus by the single-peakedness assumption $z \succ_i x$. By transitivity this means $y \succ_i x$, and hence yMx (strictly), which is a contradiction. Hence the ordering (x, z, y) is not consistent with the hypothesis.
Case 3. (Ordering (y, x, z)). We want to show that xMz. Suppose to the contrary that zMx. Let $V \subset N$ be the set of individuals who vote for z or abstain in a vote between z and x. Then V contains at least $n/2$ members. For $i \in V$ we have $z \succsim_i x$, and by single-peakedness $x \succ_i y$. By transitivity $z \succ_i y$, contradicting yMz.
Cases 4, 5, and 6. These cases correspond to orderings (z, y, x), (y, z, x), and (z, x, y), which are mirror images of cases 1, 2, and 3, respectively; hence, corresponding arguments apply. ∎

Example 10.10 (Public good). Suppose n individuals must jointly decide on the level x of a public good that costs \$1.00 per unit. Each individual i has a willingness to pay $v_i(x)$ as a function of the level x and will be taxed $t_i x$ if the project is adopted ($\sum_{i=1}^{n} t_i = 1$). The individuals rank the levels by majority voting. That is, level x is preferred to level x' if in a vote between x and x', x receives at least as many votes as x'.

In this case we can take the set of alternatives to be the set X of levels x. The strong order is just the standard numerical order. We can use the net willingness-to-pay values as the utility of a level x. If the willingness-to-pay functions are increasing and concave, the net willingness to pay, $v_i(x) - t_i x$, will have a single peak. Hence, majority voting will define a preference ordering for the level of the project, and this can be considered to be a group preference ordering.

As discussed in Section 9.2, however, the maximal element of this ordering may not correspond to a Pareto efficient allocation. To achieve Pareto efficiency, it is necessary to adjust the pattern of individual payments as well as the level of the public good.

10.9   The Arrow Possibility Theorem

Our previous attempts to define social preferences have not been very successful. The compensation criterion defines relations that are not antisymmetric (it can happen that an allocation **X** is strictly preferred to **X'** and yet **X'** is preferred to **X**). The relation defined by majority voting is not transitive. It is time now to directly attack the question of whether it is possible to construct a suitable preference order for society based on the preferences of the individuals in that society.

The main result of this investigation is the celebrated *Arrow possibility theorem*. This theorem states that if five certain reasonable requirements are imposed, it is not possible to find a way to combine individual preferences to yield an acceptable social preference. This negative result clears away much conjecture and forces us to think clearly about the requirements that we might reasonably impose.

Social Welfare Functions

Throughout this section we focus on a finite set N of n individuals and a fixed set X of alternatives. Each individual in N has a preference ordering of X. To conform to convention, we represent preference orderings in binary notation rather than with the $\succeq$ symbol. We review that notation below.

Preferences.

(*a*) A preference ordering is a binary relation R on $X \times X$ satisfying

(*i*) For all $x, y \in X$, either xRy or yRx (completeness).

(*ii*) For all $x, y, z \in X$, xRy and yRz implies xRz (transitivity).

(We read xRy as "x is preferred to y.") The associated relations P (strict preference) and I (indifference) are defined as follows:

(*b*) xPy means not yRx.

(*c*) xIy means both xRy and yRx.

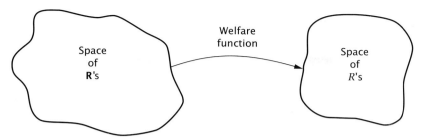

FIGURE 10.11 A social welfare function.

Although we have used this framework before, it is being used more generally here than in much of our earlier work. X might be the space of allocations of commodities, and R a preference over these (which could include externality welfare concerns). But X might also include candidates for national office, possible public-good projects, or proposed laws.

Each individual i has a preference ordering R_i. We let $\mathbf{R} = (R_1, R_2, \ldots, R_n)$ denote the collection of individual preferences. We call $\mathbf{R}$ a *profile* of individual orderings. It is desired to somehow combine these individual orderings to produce an ordering R for the group. The process by which the individual orderings are combined is a social welfare function.

Social welfare function. A *social welfare function* for the set of individuals N and the set of alternatives X is a mapping from the set of possible $\mathbf{R}$'s to an ordering R. The value of this function is denoted $R(\mathbf{R})$.

Note that the social welfare function is not the final ordering itself. It is a process for combining the individual orderings, whatever they happen to be. A social welfare function is a *function*, not a result.[5] This is illustrated in Fig. 10.11.

Consider again the majority rule procedure. It is a mapping from individual orderings (the space of $\mathbf{R}$'s) into the space of binary relations. Every $\mathbf{R}$ leads to a relation M. In general the resulting binary relation is not an ordering, so the majority rule procedure is not a social welfare function. However, if the domain were restricted to $\mathbf{R}$'s that satisfy the single-peakedness property, then, as shown in the previous section, the resulting M's would be transitive. Hence, majority rule is a social welfare function on this restricted domain.

We now lay out a set of requirements that we shall impose on a social welfare function. The first such requirement will rule out the majority voting procedure.

---

[5] An example for allocations is a Bergson–Samuelson welfare function of the form $S(u_1(\mathbf{x}_1), u_2(\mathbf{x}_2), \ldots, u_n(\mathbf{x}_n))$. This is a mapping from individual utilities (measured in some standard way) giving an overall social utility.

A1 (Unrestricted domain).

(*a*) There are at least three alternatives in X.

(*b*) The number of members in N is finite.

(*c*) The welfare function is defined for all possible individual preference orderings. That is, $R(\mathbf{R})$ is defined for all $\mathbf{R}$'s.

A2 (Pareto principle).   If xP_iy for all $i \in N$, then $xP(\mathbf{R})y$. That is, if everyone strictly prefers x to y, then x must be strictly preferred to y in the group ordering.

For the third requirement we need another simple definition. Given x, $y \in X$, two orderings R and R' are said to *agree* on $\{x, y\}$ if xRy implies $xR'y$ and yRx implies $yR'x$. Likewise, two profiles $\mathbf{R} = (R_1, R_2, \ldots, R_n)$ and $\mathbf{R}' = (R'_1, R'_2, \ldots, R'_n)$ are said to agree on $\{x, y\}$ if for each i, R_i and R'_i agree on $\{x, y\}$.

A3 (Independence of irrelevant alternatives).   Let $x, y \in X$ and suppose $\mathbf{R}$ and $\mathbf{R}'$ agree on $\{x, y\}$. Then $R(\mathbf{R})$ and $R(\mathbf{R}')$ agree on $\{x, y\}$.

In words, the above asserts that if we consider two different preference profiles that are the same on x and y, the social order must also be the same on x and y. Or said another way, the ranking between two alternatives is independent of changes in rankings of other alternatives.

A4 (Monotonicity).   Let $\mathbf{R} = (R_1, R_2, \ldots, R_n)$ be a profile and suppose $xP(\mathbf{R})y$. Let $\mathbf{R}' = (R'_1, R'_2, \ldots, R'_n)$ be another profile with the property that for any $i \in N$, xR_iy implies xR'_iy and xP_iy implies xP'_iy. Then $xP(\mathbf{R}')y$.

In words, if x is socially preferred to y, it remains socially preferred for any profile that increases (or does not decrease) the ordering of x over y for each individual. The social welfare function therefore responds nonnegatively to increases in the individual rankings of an alternative.

A5 (No dictator).   There is no individual $j \in N$ such that for all profiles $\mathbf{R}$ and all pairs $x, y \in X$, $xP(\mathbf{R})y$ if and only if xP_jy. In other words, no individual can enforce personal preference.

These five requirements should seem quite reasonable. In fact, one could argue that these properties are not only desirable, but almost essential for any social welfare function that is to truly represent group preferences. Nevertheless, we shall show that there is no social welfare function satisfying all five of these requirements. For this purpose we require a further definition and a lemma.

Decisiveness.

(*a*) Let S be a subset of N and let $x, y \in X$. S is *decisive for x against y* with respect to a given welfare function if xP_iy for all $i \in S$ and yP_ix for all $i \in \overline{S}$ implies $xP(\mathbf{R})y$. (Here $\overline{S}$ denotes the complement of S.)

(*b*) A set $S \subset N$ is said to be *decisive* if there is some pair $x, y \in X$ such that S is decisive for x against y.

(*c*) A set M is a *minimal decisive set* if M is decisive and no proper subset of M is decisive.

In words, a set S is decisive for x against y if whenever everyone in S strictly prefers x to y, *and everyone else has the reverse preference*, then x is socially strictly preferred to y.

Lemma.   *Suppose a social welfare function satisfies A1 and A3. Let $S \subset N$ and let $x, y \in X$. Suppose there is a profile $\mathbf{R}$ such that xP_iy for all $i \in S$, yP_ix for all $i \in \overline{S}$, and $xP(\mathbf{R})y$. Then S is decisive for x against y.*

Proof: Let $\mathbf{R}'$ be any other profile for which $xP_i'y$ for all $i \in S$ and $yP_i'x$ for all $i \in \overline{S}$. Then $\mathbf{R}$ and $\mathbf{R}'$ agree on $\{x, y\}$. Hence by A1, $P(\mathbf{R})$ and $P(\mathbf{R}')$ must be defined, and by A3 they must agree on $\{x, y\}$. By hypothesis $xP(\mathbf{R})y$, so $xP(\mathbf{R}')y$. This means that S is decisive for x against y.   ∎

Arrow possibility theorem.   *There is no social welfare function satisfying conditions A1–A5.*

Proof: We begin with an arbitrary social welfare function. We shall assume that A1–A4 hold and show that A5 is violated, that is, that there is a dictator.

We observe first that by the Pareto principle A2, the entire set N is decisive. If N consists of a single individual, it follows from the decisiveness of N that that individual is a dictator, and the proof is complete. Hence, we may assume that there are at least two individuals.

Let $M \subset N$ be a minimal decisive set. Such a set exists since N itself is decisive. If M were empty, its complement $\overline{M} = N$ would not be decisive for some x against y, violating the Pareto principle. Hence M contains at least one member—say j.

We now partition N into the three sets $\{j\}$, $W = M - \{j\}$, and $\overline{M}$. Since N contains at least two members, W or $\overline{M}$ is nonempty (or both are). Suppose M is decisive for x against y. Let z be any other alternative; such a z exists, because we assumed that X contains at least three elements. We now specify a particular preference profile, constant on each portion of the partition of N.

For each subgroup we list the three alternatives in order of (strict) decreasing preference:

$$
\begin{array}{rccc}
\{j\} & : & x & y & z \\
W & : & z & x & y \\
\overline{M} & : & y & z & x.
\end{array}
$$

(Note that this is the same set of preferences used in the Condorcet voting paradox.) We denote the corresponding social order, determined by the welfare function, by R (and P for strict preference).

For the profile defined above, all individuals in M strictly prefer x to y and all individuals in $\overline{M}$ strictly prefer y to x. Since M is decisive for x against y, it follows that x is preferred to y in the social ordering; that is, xPy.

Now suppose zPy and assume that W is nonempty. By the lemma it follows that W is decisive for z against y, since zP_iy for all $i \in W$ and yP_iz for all $i \in \overline{W}$. But this contradicts the minimal nature of M. Hence, it cannot be true that zPy. If W is empty, then yPz by A2. In either case, we have yRz. Combining this with the fact that xPy, as found in the previous paragraph, we find that xPz.

Now j is the only member that prefers x to z. Hence from the fact that xPz it follows that $\{j\}$ is decisive for x against z. However, $\{j\} \subset M$, and since M is minimal, $\{j\} = M$. Therefore $\{j\}$ is decisive for x against y as well. Since z was arbitrary, we conclude that $\{j\}$ is decisive for x against any z not equal to x. We want to show that $\{j\}$ is also decisive for any $w \neq x$ against any z and against x. Hence, select $w \neq x$ and $z \neq x$ and construct a profile with the following preferences:

$$
\begin{array}{rccc}
M = \{j\} & : & w & x & z \\
\overline{M} & : & z & w & x.
\end{array}
$$

Since wP_ix for all $i \in N$, it follows by the Pareto principle that now wPx. Also since $\{j\}$ is decisive for x against z, it follows that xPz. By transitivity, wPz. However, since $\{j\}$ is the only individual that prefers w over z, it follows from the lemma that $\{j\}$ is decisive for w against z.

Finally, consider a profile such that

$$
\begin{array}{rccc}
M = \{j\} & : & w & z & x \\
\overline{M} & : & z & x & w.
\end{array}
$$

Since we just showed that $\{j\}$ is decisive for w against z, we have wPz for this profile. Also by the Pareto principle zPx. By transitivity, wPx. However, since $\{j\}$ is the only individual that prefers w to x, it follows again by the lemma that $\{j\}$ is decisive for w against x.

We have shown that $\{j\}$ is decisive for any alternative in X against any other. That is, for any $x, y \in X$, if xP_jy and yP_ix for all $i \in N - \{j\}$, then xPy. Now by monotonicity, if xP_jy, then xPy regardless of the ordering of other individuals. Hence, j is a dictator, and A5 is violated. ∎

The above theorem is frequently called the Arrow *impossibility* theorem, because it states that it is impossible to construct a welfare function satisfying A1–A5. There are several variations of the theorem using alternative sets of requirements. Indeed the original version of the theorem has slightly different requirements than those stated here. Those used here are now usually preferred, although it can be shown that A4, monotonicity, is not necessary for the result. See the references at the end of the chapter for alternate versions.

The impact of the Arrow possibility theorem on welfare economics has been quite substantial. The most pessimistic reaction to it is to conclude that there is just no acceptable way to aggregate individual preferences, and hence no theoretical basis for treating welfare issues. A more moderate reaction, however, is to examine each of the assumptions of the theorem to see which might be given up. For example, the universality assumption might be relaxed. Indeed, we found earlier that majority voting provides an aggregation procedure in the case of single-peaked preferences—perhaps less restrictive assumptions will work for other procedures. Another assumption that has been considered to be too strong is that of independence of irrelevant alternatives. This assumption is similar to a strong independence assumption for preferences on commodity bundles. It is technically quite important for the proof, since it enables us to make comparisons between two elements directly, without worrying about their relation to all others. But it has been argued that its elimination might lead to suitable aggregation mechanisms. A considerable body of research has been conducted along these lines.

An assumption that is often suggested to be the best candidate for removal, however, is the implicit one that there is no strength of preferences. Arrow's framework, being based on ordinal preferences, cannot distinguish whether x is slightly preferred to y or x is greatly preferred to y (this is primarily embodied in the assumption about the independence of irrelevant alternatives). Hence, the social welfare function cannot incorporate interpersonal comparisons of preference. A willingness-to-pay criterion, for example, would incorporate this difference in preference strength. One interpretation of the Arrow possibility theorem, therefore, is that we cannot escape from making interpersonal comparisons when defining welfare and designing public policy. There is no satisfactory mechanism that can mechanically aggregate preferences. Judgment is an essential ingredient in the process of defining social welfare.

10.10 Social Choice Functions and Strategy

The important products of the social choice process are the actual social choices made, not a hypothetical underlying social preference. It is true that if a suitable social preference ordering were available, then an obvious and good method of choice would follow—society could select the most preferred alternative (or one from among the set of most preferred alternatives). However, the previous section showed that construction of such a social preference ordering, satisfying all the requirements we would like, is not generally possible. So we cannot use this "ideal" method of choice. However, this does not necessarily foreclose the possibility of devising a good method for making choices that does not first construct a social preference ordering. We examine that possibility in this section.

Suppose as in the previous section that there are a set X of alternatives and a set N of n individuals. In line with the above comments, what is required is a method for passing from a profile $\mathbf{R} = (R_1, R_2, \ldots, R_n)$ of individual preferences to a group or collective choice from the set of alternatives.

Social choice function.   A *social choice function* C is a mapping from the set of individual preference profiles $\mathbf{R} = (R_1, R_2, \ldots, R_n)$ into subsets of X. We write $C(\mathbf{R}) \subset X$. A *single-valued social choice function* is a function from the set of profiles into subsets of X having one element. ($C(\mathbf{R})$ is the set of alternatives chosen by the group of n individuals when C is used.)

We present some examples of social choice functions.

Example 10.11.   Suppose $n = 1$. In this case, it is natural to use the most preferred elements of X. Hence, we define $C(R_1) = \{x : xR_1y \text{ for all } y \in X\}$. We know that $C(R_1)$ is nonempty if X consists of a finite number of elements. It is also nonempty if X is a compact subset of m-dimensional space and the ordering R_1 is continuous. Note that this choice function is not single-valued, for there are preference orderings with more than one most-preferred element. However, the function can usually be modified so that it is single-valued. For example, in the case of a finite number of elements, we may index the elements and select the element of smallest index from among those most preferred.

Example 10.12 (Pareto set).   For $n > 1$, select all members in the Pareto set. That is, for $\mathbf{R} = (R_1, R_2, \ldots, R_n)$, $C(\mathbf{R}) = \{x \in X : \text{there is no } y \in X \text{ such that } yP_ix \text{ for all } i\}$. This is a weak social choice function because it is typically multivalued, and there is no way to reduce the number of alternatives chosen without introducing an additional choice principle.

Example 10.13 (Borda voting method).   Suppose there are a finite number of alternatives. Each individual separates the alternatives into groups of indifferent elements, with the first group being most preferred, and so forth. Numerical points are then assigned to the alternatives in the following manner: One point is given to an alternative every time it appears in someone's first group, two points every time it appears in a second group, and so forth. The final social choice(s) are those alternatives that have the lowest total number of points.

Example 10.14 (Lindahl choice method).   Suppose the level of a public good is to be determined. Select that level that corresponds to a Lindahl equilibrium.

Strategic Behavior

We considered the Lindahl equilibrium earlier (in Chapter 9) and found that, although it has some extremely desirable properties, it is not very practical because of incentive incompatibilities. Such incentive problems characterize many voting procedures as well, as the example below illustrates.

Example 10.15 (Manipulation of the Borda voting method).   Suppose there are two individuals and four alternatives, w, x, y, and z. The preference orders (which are strict) are listed below (from best to worst):

$$1: \quad w \quad x \quad y \quad z$$
$$2: \quad x \quad y \quad w \quad z.$$

If each individual accurately marks a ballot according to the Borda voting scheme, the points received by the various alternatives will be $w = 4, x = 3, y = 5$, and $z = 8$, so x will be chosen. Individual 1 would rather have w chosen. That individual might notice that if his or her preferences were misrepresented during the voting process to be in the order w, z, y, and x, the resulting points would be $w = 4, x = 5, y = 5$, and $z = 6$, and w would be chosen. Misrepresentation leads to a better result for individual 1.

Judging from our earlier examples, manipulation of outcomes by the misrepresentation of individual preferences seems to plague many voting procedures and social choice functions. Hence, we are motivated to address this issue directly. We shall define *strategy-proofness* and then seek strategy-proof choice functions. Again, however, the central result is a negative one. It is impossible to construct a social choice function that satisfies certain desirable properties and cannot be manipulated by some individual to his or her advantage.

We consider a single-valued social choice function C and denote its value on the profile $\mathbf{R} = (R_1, R_2, \ldots, R_n)$ by $C(\mathbf{R})$.

Manipulability.   A single-valued social choice function C is *manipulable* by $i \in N$ at $\mathbf{R} = (R_1, R_2, \ldots, R_n)$ if there is a profile

$$\mathbf{R}' = (R_1, R_2, \ldots, R_{i-1}, R_i', R_{i+1}, \ldots, R_n)$$

such that $C(\mathbf{R}')P_iC(\mathbf{R})$. We say that C is *nonmanipulable* or *strategy-proof* if C is nowhere manipulable by anyone.

In words, a social choice function is manipulable by i at $\mathbf{R}$ if it is to i's advantage to misrepresent the ordering R_i by some other ordering R'_i. The misrepresentation would lead to a social choice that i strictly prefers to the one that would be obtained with true preferences. The preceding example shows that the Borda voting system is manipulable, at least for some sets and at some profiles.

It is important to consider the range of a social choice function, that is, the alternatives that can be chosen. It is conceivable that some alternatives can never be selected, no matter what the profile of individual preferences. For example, suppose that out of a field of three candidates, one is to be selected by a group of 100 people. Each voter must vote for at least two candidates. The candidates are then considered in alphabetical order, and the first to obtain 50 votes wins. It can be seen that the candidate listed last can never win such an election. Hence, this person is not in the range of the process. In general the range of C is the union of all alternatives in $C(\mathbf{R})$ for all possible $\mathbf{R}$'s, and this will be a subset of X. We single out an important special case.

Nonimposition.   A social choice function on X is *nonimposed* if its range is equal to X.

We have one final definition.

Dictator.   An individual $i \in N$ is a *dictator* with respect to the single-valued social choice function C if for every profile $\mathbf{R} = (R_1, R_2, \ldots, R_n)$ and every alternative x in the range of C, there holds $C(\mathbf{R})R_i x$. If a dictator exists, C is said to be *dictatorial*.

This definition probably does not require much explanation. It states that a social choice function is dictatorial if the choice is always taken from the dictator's most preferred subset of the range of C.

We now state the impossibility theorem for social choice functions. The proof is quite complex, and hence is omitted.

Gibbard-Satterthwaite theorem.   *Let C be a social choice function on a finite set of alternatives X satisfying the following:*

 (i) C is single valued.

 (ii) The range of C contains at least three elements.

(iii) C is strategy-proof.

Then C is dictatorial.

The Gibbard-Satterthwaite theorem can be interpreted in game-theoretic terms. Consider a game in which each individual i submits a ballot B_i that is a preference listing. The ballots are used to determine the choice $C(B_1, B_2, \ldots, B_n)$. A Nash equilibrium point is a set of submitted orderings $B_1, B_2, \ldots, B_n$ with the property that no individual i has an incentive to change B_i unilaterally. The Gibbard-Satterthwaite theorem says that no C can be constructed that is single-valued, has a range of at least three elements, is nondictatorial, and has truthful reporting of $R_1, R_2, \ldots, R_n$ as a Nash equilibrium point.

The Gibbard-Satterthwaite theorem clarifies the incentive issues that arose when we considered mechanisms for determining the level of public goods or for obtaining efficiency in the presence of externalities. Like the Arrow possibility theorem, this theorem establishes an important limit on what is possible. In reality, however, social choices are made by some procedure (often by majority voting), and often the results are satisfactory, even though the procedures used are not strictly strategy-proof.

10.11 Exercises

1. Consider the two situations $(\mathbf{x}^0, \mathbf{p}^0, r^0)$ and $(\mathbf{x}^1, \mathbf{p}^1, r^1)$. Assume that prices are normalized with $\mathbf{p} \cdot \mathbf{g} = 1$. Show that

$$CB - EB \leq CV - EV.$$

2. Let $\mathbf{p}(t)$, $0 \leq t \leq 1$, be any smooth path such that $\mathbf{p}(0) = \mathbf{p}^0$ and $\mathbf{p}(1) = \mathbf{p}^1$. Define $e(t) = e(\mathbf{p}(t), u^0)$ and let $\dot{\mathbf{p}}(t) = d\mathbf{p}(t)/dt$. Note that

$$e(t) - e(0) = \int_0^t \nabla e(\mathbf{p}(t), u^0) \cdot \dot{\mathbf{p}} \, dt$$

$$= \int_0^t \mathbf{h}(\mathbf{p}(t), u^0) \cdot \dot{\mathbf{p}} \, dt .$$

Hence

$$\dot{e}(t) = \mathbf{h}(\mathbf{p}(t), u^0) \cdot \dot{\mathbf{p}}^0 .$$

This can be expressed in terms of the Marshallian demand as

$$\dot{e}(t) = \mathbf{x}(\mathbf{p}(t), e(t)) \cdot \dot{\mathbf{p}}(t).$$

Hence, if the Marshallian demand function is known, the above differential equation can be solved for $e(t)$ using the initial condition $e(0) = e(\mathbf{p}^0, u^0) \equiv r^0 = r^1$. Then we can find CV from

$$CV = e(0) - e(1).$$

Show how the CB can likewise be found using only the Marshallian demand function.

3. Suppose a consumer has a utility function of the quasi-linear form $u(x, y) = v(x) + y$. Let y be the reference commodity, and let p denote the price of x.

(a) Show that the adjusted price function is

$$p(x) = v'(x).$$

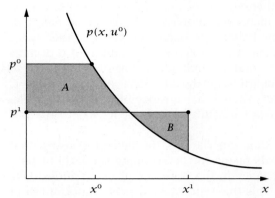

FIGURE 10.12   CB for a change.

(b) Suppose the initial position (x^0, y^0) is changed to (x^1, y^1). Find the corresponding value of CB using the integral formula.

(c) Suppose the initial price is p^0 and the final price is p^1, and suppose income is fixed; that is, $p^0 x^0 + y^0 = p^1 x^1 + y^1$. Show that CB = CV in this case.

4. Suppose an individual has utility function $u(x, y)$ for two goods. Let y be the reference commodity (with price equal to 1) and let p denote the price of the good x. Suppose the initial situation has p^0, x^0, y^0, and u^0. A new situation is obtained by reducing p to p^1, resulting in a new x^1 and y^1. The income is the same in both situations.

   (a) Referring to Fig. 10.12, show that CB is the area A minus the area B.

   (b) What is the CV for this change?

5. Consider the social choice criterion, which is the dual of the tradable criterion: the allocation $(\mathbf{z}^1, \mathbf{X}^1)$ is preferred to $(\mathbf{z}^0, \mathbf{X}^0)$ if there is no reallocation $(\mathbf{z}^0, \overline{\mathbf{X}}^0)$ of $(\mathbf{z}^0, \mathbf{X}^0)$ that is strictly Pareto preferred to $(\mathbf{z}^1, \mathbf{X}^1)$. Said another way, option 1 is preferred to option 0 if the potential losers (for a move from 0 to 1) cannot profitably bribe the potential winners into not changing from 0 to 1. Develop a proposition for this dual criterion that is the analog of the tradable preference maximum theorem.

6. (Marginal cost pricing)   Suppose a product has (inverse) demand function $p(x)$ and cost function $c(x)$. Consider the problem of selecting x to maximize the sum of consumers' surplus and profit. Show that the first-order conditions imply marginal cost pricing.

7. (Land use planning)   Consider the land use planning problem of Example 10.9. The region of influence is divided into two main parts: a study region (near the project) and an outside region. It is assumed that land prices in the outside region are not influenced by the project.

   Suppose a detailed optimal land use plan is available for each case, that without the project and that with the project. (They are optimal in the sense of maximizing total regional economic rent.) The number of activities is equal to the number of land parcels; that is, $m = n$. By definition, the

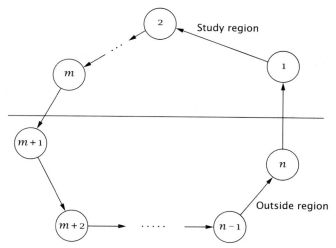

FIGURE 10.13 Cycle of relocation.

locational pattern of the second plan must be just a permutation of the first plan. Any such permutation can be characterized as a set of cycles, in which one activity replaces a second, that one replaces a third, and so forth until a last activity replaces the first. Suppose the indexing is arranged so that, for a certain cycle of length n, in the first plan activity i locates on location i, and in the second plan activity i locates on location $i + 1$ (with n locating on 1). See Fig. 10.13. Let

$$\delta a_i = \begin{cases} \bar{a}_{i,i+1} - a_{ii} & i < n \\ \bar{a}_{n1} - a_{nn} \end{cases}$$

and let p_j be the land price of parcel j if j is in the outside region.

(a) Show that for i and $i + 1$ both in the outside region $\delta a_i = p_{i+1} - p_i$.

(b) Argue that the net benefit associated with a cycle entirely in the outside region is zero.

(c) Show that for a cycle that is partially inside and outside the study region, as in the figure, the net benefit is

$$B = \delta a_n + \sum_{i=1}^{m} \delta a_i + (p_n - p_{m+1}).$$

Hence, it is not necessary to have the details of the plan in the outside region.

8. Express the net benefit of a land use project (formulated as an assignment problem) in terms of the dual to the assignment problem. Relate the resulting minimization problem to the minimization of CV.

9. (Subway project) A city is considering building a subway system that will replace an existing bus line. It is estimated that the inverse demand curve for public transportation along this route is $p = 75 - q/4$ where p is cents and

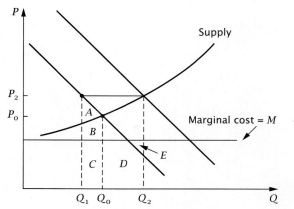

FIGURE 10.14   Subway project.

q is thousands of rides. It is estimated that the marginal cost of a subway ride will be $.25, which will be the fare if the subway is built. By contrast, the marginal cost of a bus ride is $.40, but the current fare is $.50.

(a) Neglecting the construction cost, what is the net social value of the subway project? (Neglect income effects.)

(b) The cost of the subway is due entirely to construction materials. These are produced at constant marginal cost M per unit. But there are monopoly effects in this industry, so the inverse supply curve is upward sloping, as shown in Fig. 10.14. The private demand for materials is governed by a demand curve, and the total demand without the project would be Q_0. The project will shift the demand curve so that the new private demand is Q_1 and the total demand is Q_2. Show that the total social cost (equal to the cost to taxpayers, plus the cost to consumers, minus the gain to producers) is the area $A + B + C + D + E$.

(c) Suppose the project size $\overline{Q} = Q_2 - Q_1$ is small compared with Q_0. Show that the social cost is approximately equal to $\overline{P} = [\alpha P + (1 - \alpha)M]$ per unit, where

$$\alpha = \frac{S'(Q_0)}{S'(Q_0) - D'(Q_0)}$$

and S and D are the inverse supply and demand curves. $\overline{P}$ is called the shadow price, since it is the true social price that should be attributed to the project.

10. Assume a society of three people has a number of alternatives to choose among. The preference rankings are listed in descending order below:

Individual 1	Individual 2	Individual 3
a	b	g
x	d	t
b	e	d
g	g	e
d	t	a
e	a	x
t	x	b

(a) Determine the set of Pareto efficient alternatives and the set of non–Pareto efficient alternatives.

(b) Assume that this society votes on alternatives pairwise and eliminates the loser from successive ballots until the final winner remains. Show that this process can lead to a chosen alternative that is not even Pareto efficient.

11. Consider a social ordering situation with three alternatives and five voters. The alternatives are ranked by a series of ballots (and each voter must vote for one and only one alternative on each ballot). On the first ballot individuals vote for their most preferred alternative, and the alternative receiving the fewest votes is ranked last in the social order. (If there is a tie between two alternatives receiving the fewest votes on this ballot, a second ballot is taken between these two, and the one receiving the fewest votes is ranked last.)

Next, the lowest-ranked alternative as determined above is eliminated, and a new ballot is held between the remaining two alternatives. The one receiving the greatest number of votes is ranked first, and the other is ranked second.

(a) What is the *social* ordering of alternatives x, y, and z for the profile below?

Rankings			Individuals		
	A	B	C	D	E
First	x	x	z	z	y
Second	y	y	y	y	x
Third	z	z	x	x	z

(b) Suppose individual A reverses the ordering of x and y but keeps z in third place. What is the new social ordering?

(c) Which of Arrow's axioms is violated by this procedure?

12. Consider a distribution economy in which an allocation $X = (x_1, x_2, \ldots, x_n)$ is feasible if it satisfies $X \geq 0$ and $\sum_{i=1}^{n} x_i \leq w$, where $w > 0$ is fixed. All individuals have continuous, strongly monotonic preferences. A Bergson-Samuelson welfare function of the form $S = \sum_{i=1}^{n} a_i u_i(x_i)$, where $a_i > 0$ for $i = 1, 2, \ldots, n$, is used to define a social ranking. The Bergson-Samuelson welfare function uniquely transforms individual preferences into social preferences. Aside from A1, are all other conditions of the Arrow possibility theorem satisfied?

13. (Robustness of Arrow's theorem) Let R be a complete binary relation on X. Let xPy mean xRy but not yRx. The relation R is *semitransitive* if xPy and yPz implies that for all other $s \in X$ there holds xPs and sPz.

(a) Show that semitransitivity implies transitivity for strictly ordered triples: that is, xPy and yPz implies xPz.

(b) Show that the Arrow possibility theorem still holds even if the social ordering is allowed to be semitransitive rather than transitive. In particular, show that a decisive set M with more than one member contains a proper subset that is itself decisive. (Assume that there are at least four alternatives in X.)

14. Suppose members of a class each have one of the following three preference orderings of colors (ranked from highest to lowest).

1.	Red	Yellow	Blue	Green
2.	Blue	Red	Green	Yellow
3.	Green	Yellow	Blue	Red

Assume that there are equal numbers of each type in the class. The class attempts to select a "preferred class color" by using the Borda voting method. Discuss what may happen if purposeful misrepresentation occurs.

15. (Dodgson's social choice method) Suppose n people have preference rankings of m alternatives. We define C as the set of alternatives that would require the fewest stepwise changes in individual rankings to defeat every other alternative according to majority voting between those two. Show by an example that this method is not strategy-proof.

10.12   References

10.1   Income distribution has long been used as a basis for welfare analysis. See Sen (1973) for a good overview. For an argument favoring the Rawls welfare measure see Rawls (1971).

10.2   The idea of using the willingness to trade a specific single commodity as a measure of welfare improvement was introduced by Dupuit (1844), who used the term *relative utility*. This idea was developed extensively in Allais (1943) and Allais (1981, 1989) using the term *distributable surplus*. We use the terms *compensating benefit* and *equivalent benefit* with respect to a general bundle **g** to parallel the income-based concepts of compensating and equivalent variation. See Luenberger (1994d).

10.3   For an overview of standard surplus economics, see Hammond (1990). The concepts of compensating and equivalent variations are due to Hicks (1956). The error bound of consumer surplus relative to compensating and equivalent variations is due to Willig (1976). Hausman (1981) points out that evaluation of changes in welfare require more exact formulas. For general discussion of these concepts, see Chipman and Moore (1980).

10.4   The compensation criterion was proposed by Kaldor (1939) and Hicks (1939). Scitovsky (1941) showed that such a criterion was not antisymmetric and proposed an alternative (which is not transitive).

10.5   The income test is due to Barone (1908), who called the income changes to individuals (at original prices) the *surplus*. Also see Radner (1993). The *coefficient of resource utilization* is a quantity introduced by Debreu (1951) that essentially measures benefit in the direction $\mathbf{w}^1$ and converts it to a ratio. He presents a duality result that relates this to income changes.

10.6   For good discussions of modern cost-benefit analysis, see Gramlich (1981) and Pearce and Nash (1981). The flood plain example is based on Arvanitidis et al. (1972).

10.7   The result on single-peaked utilities and majority voting is due to Black (1948). See also Black (1958). For general discussion of this topic see Sen (1970) and Feldman (1980).

10.8   For the original work on the Arrow possibility theorem, see Arrow (1951, 1963). This work spawned hundreds of other papers and books on the subject. As a sampling, see Sen (1970), Kelly (1978), and Kim and Roush (1983). The proof in this section is based on Sen (1970).

10.9   The Gibbard-Satterthwaite theorem was proved independently in Gibbard (1973) and Satterthwaite (1975).

10.10 The first discussion in Exercise 2 is due to Vartia (1983) and McKenzie and Ulph (1986). Exercise 9 is based on an example in Gramlich (1981).

Chapter 11
ECONOMICS OF UNCERTAINTY

Anyone who has wrestled with a complex economic decision has surely been forced to face uncertainty: the monetary value of an investment may increase or decrease, a project may or may not be successful, product sales may fluctuate, and crop production may be low or high depending on future weather. Indeed, in some economic activities, such as gambling and the purchase of insurance, uncertainty is *the* dominant feature of the activity, and while most other economic activities are not as completely dominated by uncertainty, uncertainty is frequently an important aspect. It is therefore essential that economic theory encompass this feature. Fortunately, the theory presented in earlier chapters can rather directly be extended to situations characterized by uncertainty.

The broad outline of this chapter parallels a standard presentation of microeconomic theory for deterministic situations. It first considers the problem of an individual consumer facing an uncertain environment. It shows how preference structures can be extended to uncertain situations and describes the nature of the consumer's choice problem. Many of the standard tools of consumer theory, such as indirect utility and benefit functions, arise naturally in this more general framework. This discussion of individual preferences spans several sections and makes up the first part of the chapter. The second part introduces markets and shows how individuals can exchange goods in an uncertain environment and how prices reflecting uncertainty are formed. A new feature is that consumers must make both consumption decisions and (risky) investment decisions. Finally, firms are introduced into the uncertain economy. The decision problem of the firm is, however, somewhat more complex than in the deterministic setting. This indirectly further complicates the consumer's investment problem since in general consumers are allowed to change their firm ownership shares. All of these developments are natural extensions of the framework presented in earlier chapters for deterministic situations. But uncertainty adds interesting new features that provide new insights and greatly expand the range of applicability of microeconomic theory.

There are several theoretical methods for characterizing uncertainty. The classical method is probability theory, but this has the limitation that probabilities must be assigned to the various possible outcomes. Although such assignment is fairly simple for some objective uncertainties—such as those governed by the roll of a die—it is not so simple for subjective uncertainties—such as whether a new product will be successful. For purposes of decision making, however, it is possible to bypass probability theory. One need only consider the *possibilities* (or states) that can occur and define preferences over them that account for the subjective likelihood of occurrence. This second approach is more general than the one based on probabilities, and it is the one that we develop first. However, probability theory can be incorporated into this approach to obtain important specialized results. It is for this reason that our treatment of the individual facing uncertainty spans several sections of the chapter. Both approaches to treating uncertainty and their relation are developed.

Part I
PREFERENCES UNDER UNCERTAINTY

11.1 States

Suppose we must select an action today that will yield a payoff tomorrow. However, the payoff we receive tomorrow may depend not only on what we do today, but it may also depend on things beyond our control. We define a *state* to be a description of our environment, which, together with the knowledge of our action, completely determines the consequences. Uncertainty is captured by the uncertainty of which state actually occurs. If there are a finite number of possible states, we typically index them as $1, 2, \ldots, S$. However, the theory can allow for states belonging to sets of any size or dimension.

States are typically associated with particular events or values of certain variables. For example, a farmer whose crop production will depend on the weather may include in his list of states the (future) weather states: $1 =$ sunny, $2 =$ cloudy, $3 =$ rainy.

Usually the state is known exactly at a later time. We then say that the uncertainty is *resolved* at that time. For example, the uncertainty associated with tomorrow's weather will be resolved tomorrow. But there are more complex situations where uncertainty is resolved in steps or where it is resolved for some individuals before it is for others. These more complicated situations are discussed in the next chapter. In this chapter, uncertainty is typically resolved all at once, at the second period of a two-period process.

If several variables are needed to define a state, the total number of states grows rapidly. For example, if 10 weather conditions are possible and we must consider the weather at two locations, there would be a total of 100 possible states.

11.2   State-Indexed Commodities and Utility

Suppose you are today considering the purchase of a commodity that you will receive tomorrow. There are S possible states of the world, and you will know the state tomorrow. For instance, suppose you are considering the purchase of an umbrella, and two possible states describe tomorrow's weather: rainy or sunny. Your purchase decision requires some deliberation because the umbrella will have low utility if it is sunny, but high utility if it is rainy. It is clear that the uncertainty will influence your decision.

One way to approach such situations is to introduce the concept of *state-indexed commodities*. In this approach, a commodity available when state s occurs is considered to be different from one that is physically identical but is available when state r occurs. For instance, an umbrella together with rain tomorrow is regarded as different from the same umbrella together with sunshine tomorrow. Indexing of commodities by the states this way is analogous to the indexing of commodities by time (that is, dated commodities), which we use to study economic problems over several time periods. At first such indexing may seem artificial; in fact, it not only makes the theory flow easily, but it also has practical significance.

The distinction between various commodity-state combinations can be formally recognized in economic activity. When deliberating over your possible purchase of an umbrella, you might decide that you would be willing to pay a certain price for an agreement that an umbrella would be delivered to you only if it rains; if it is sunny, you would receive nothing. This agreement might cost less than the outright purchase of an umbrella. In general, agreements that depend on the state that occurs are called *contingent agreements*. In this case you would be purchasing a *contingent claim*, since your claim to an umbrella depends on the state, which will be known tomorrow. You could also consider purchasing a contingent claim that delivers an umbrella only if it is sunny (and this claim might cost less than the other one). The outright purchase of an umbrella, without contingencies, would correspond to the purchase of both contingent claims: one delivering an umbrella if it rains, and the other if it is sunny.

Markets for contingent claims do not exist for all commodities—they do not normally exist for umbrellas—but such markets do exist for some important commodities. An important example is insurance, which is basically a claim contingent on the occurrence of a well-defined event. For example, a fire insurance policy on a house pays a fixed amount x if the house is destroyed by fire; that is, it pays if the state *fire* occurs.

Suppose now that there is a single physical commodity and S possible states. We then consider commodity bundles of the form $\mathbf{x} = (x_1, x_2, \ldots, x_S)$ where x_s corresponds to an amount of the commodity available if state s occurs. We suppose an individual has a preference ordering over such bun-

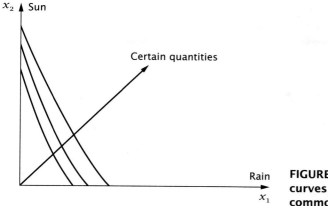

Certain quantities

Rain **FIGURE 11.1 Indifference curves for a state-indexed commodity.**

x_1

dles. This preference ordering describes the individual's preferences before the state is revealed. It is thus a preference ordering for contingent claims to the one physical commodity.

To use our umbrella example here we must modify it somewhat. Umbrellas are discrete, indivisible commodities; so let us allow division by assuming that you may rent an umbrella by the minute. The rental agreement is contingent on the weather, so you can rent a different number of minutes for rain (state 1) or sun (state 2). To avoid degeneracy, we also assume that an umbrella is valuable in either state (as shade if there is sun), although perhaps not equally so. In this situation you would define a preference relation over the variables (x_1, x_2), representing how you value the prospect of facing the uncertainty of tomorrow with guaranteed levels of umbrella coverage x_1 and x_2 for states 1 and 2. This preference relation depends on your desire for the coverage an umbrella can provide in the two states, your general assessment of the relative likelihood of the two states, and your averseness to risk and ambiguity. A typical preference relation is illustrated in Fig. 11.1, which is by now quite familiar. The axis denotes the amount of each of the state-contingent claims. Points along the 45° line represent deterministic (that is, certain) quantities, since the same level is available in each of the states.

Example 11.1. An investor is considering investing in a new venture. From his analysis he decides that there are only two possible states: success and failure. Because the investment only involves cash and will return cash, he considers cash as the only relevant commodity. In order to determine his investment strategy he uses a preference relation defined with respect to two variables, x_1 and x_2: cash if the business is a success, and cash if it is a failure. It is true, of course, that the investor likes cash equally no matter what state occurs, but if presented with the opportunity to obtain different cash amounts in the two states, the investor will have indifference curves.

For example, if the investor feels that there is very little chance that the project will be successful, the investor will prefer a claim that pays $1.00 in the failure state over a claim that pays $1.00 in the success state.

The investor might have a preference relation that is described by a Cobb-Douglas utility function

$$u(x_1, x_2) = x_1^\alpha x_2^{1-\alpha}$$

where $0 < \alpha < 1$. (Although the Cobb-Douglas form seems to be always used for analytic simplicity, it has a special significance for this problem, as will be pointed out in Section 11.6.) This utility function may represent a complex set of factors summarizing the investor's desire for cash and his assessment of the particular venture.

Suppose the venture will double in value if successful and have zero value if it fails. The investor may purchase shares in the venture and must decide what portion of his current wealth X to invest.

If a fraction z is invested, the final value of wealth in the two states is

$$x_1 = X(1 - z + 2z)$$
$$x_2 = X(1 - z).$$

Hence the investor seeks to solve

$$\max_z X(1 + z)^\alpha (1 - z)^{1-\alpha}.$$

The first-order condition (and a bit of algebra) leads to the solution

$$z = 2\alpha - 1,$$

and hence a positive investment should be made if $\alpha > \frac{1}{2}$.

The above framework can be directly extended to the case where there are m, rather than one, physical goods. In this case a state-indexed bundle has the form $\mathbf{x} = (\mathbf{x}_1, \mathbf{x}_2, \dots, \mathbf{x}_S)$ where each $\mathbf{x}_s$ is a bundle of the m physical goods. In other words, indexes can be tagged onto each commodity.

Risk Aversion

Suppose there is a single physical commodity (which can be thought of as money) and S possible states. An individual currently owns a bundle $\mathbf{x} = (x_1, x_2, \dots, x_S)$ of the corresponding contingent claims. Two symmetric propositions are offered to the individual that would modify $\mathbf{x}$ by $\mathbf{z}$. In one proposition the individual is offered $\mathbf{x} + \mathbf{z}$, and in the other the individual is offered $\mathbf{x} - \mathbf{z}$. The vectors $\mathbf{x} + \mathbf{z}$ and $\mathbf{x} - \mathbf{z}$ are both assumed to be feasible (that is, nonnegative). It is quite possible that at least one of these propositions will be strictly preferred to $\mathbf{x}$. For instance, if $\mathbf{z} > \mathbf{0}$ (a trivial case) and preferences are monotonic, then $\mathbf{x} + \mathbf{z}$ will be preferred to $\mathbf{x}$, but $\mathbf{x} - \mathbf{z}$ will not be preferred to $\mathbf{x}$. More typically, $\mathbf{z}$ will have both positive and negative components—in which case the propositions involve some risk, since some of the basic commodity will be given up in some states for gains in other states. The preference relation is said to be *risk averse* at **x** if there is no **z** such that the propositions **x** + **z** and **x** − **z** are both strictly preferred to **x**.

As an example, suppose you have $100 and are offered a wager on the outcome of a football game between teams A and B. There are two states, corresponding to whether team A wins or does not win. Your current bundle is **x** = ($100, $100), corresponding to $100 with certainty. A wager of $10 on team A corresponds to **z** = ($10, −$10) and the proposition **x** + **z** = ($110, $90). You might find this wager attractive (that is, strictly preferred to **x**), but it is then unlikely that you would strictly prefer the opposite wager **x** − **z** as well, betting against team A. You are risk averse at **x** if there are no wagers for which you would desire both sides over the status quo **x**. It is conceivable, however, that someone might be willing to take either side of the bet. (That person might just enjoy betting for its own sake.) Such a person is risk preferring.

To generalize, suppose there are m physical commodities and S states. Let $\Omega = \mathcal{R}_+^{mS}$. That is, Ω is the set of all nonnegative state-contingent bundles. Suppose that, as above, an individual has a preference relation defined on Ω. A general definition of risk aversion is then as follows.

Risk aversion. An individual's preference relation is said to be *risk averse at* **x** $\in \Omega$ if for all **z** such that **x** + **z** and **x** − **z** $\in \Omega$ the bundles **x** + **z** and **x** − **z** are not both strictly preferred to **x**. If the preference relation is risk averse at all **x** $\in \Omega$, then it is said to be *risk averse everywhere*, or simply *risk averse*.

Although risk aversion is stated in terms of the desirability of two symmetric propositions, the definition is really equivalent to the familiar convexity assumption. The definition is illustrated in Fig. 11.2, where its relation to convexity should be clear.

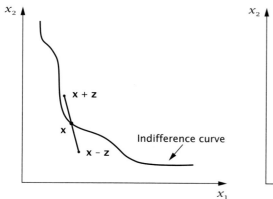

(a) **x** is a risk averse point

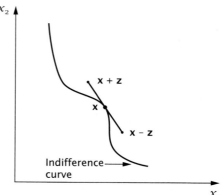

(b) **x** is not a risk averse point

FIGURE 11.2 Risk aversion.

Proposition 11.1. *A preference relation is risk averse everywhere if and only if it is convex.*

Proof: Let $\mathbf{x}$, $\mathbf{x} + \mathbf{z}$, and $\mathbf{x} - \mathbf{z}$ be in Ω. We have $\mathbf{x} = \frac{1}{2}(\mathbf{x} + \mathbf{z}) + \frac{1}{2}(\mathbf{x} - \mathbf{z})$, and hence $\mathbf{x}$ is the midpoint of the two points. This point is always preferred (weakly) to one of the endpoints if and only if the preference relation is convex. ∎

Note that a special case is where the indifference contours are flat, which is referred to as a *risk neutrality*. We can distinguish strict risk aversion as being equivalent to strict convexity of preferences.

The definition of risk aversion given above implies that the individual has convex preferences with respect to ordinary commodities. This becomes clear when the definition is applied to the case of a single state. In that case the definition reduces to convexity with respect to commodities. We could distinguish the two definitions by separating out differences in states from differences in commodities, but that does not seem worth the notational complexity, especially since we generally assume overall convexity.

Certain Equivalents and Certain Benefits

There is a natural way to quantify utility or benefit in uncertain situations: namely, comparing all bundles to a bundle that is obtained with certainty. There are two ways to do this, and they lead to two important measures. In the two definitions that follow, there is a fixed bundle $\mathbf{g} \in \mathcal{R}_+^m$, $\mathbf{g} \neq \mathbf{0}$, that is available in all states. The overall bundle that corresponds to having $\mathbf{g}$ in every state (that is, having $\mathbf{g}$ with certainty) is $\overline{\mathbf{g}} = (\mathbf{g}, \mathbf{g}, \dots, \mathbf{g})$.

Certain equivalent.   Given an initial point $\mathbf{x}^0 = (\mathbf{x}_1^0, \mathbf{x}_2^0, \dots, \mathbf{x}_S^0)$ and an alternative point with utility u^1, the *certain equivalent* of a change from $\mathbf{x}^0$ to the alternative point is

$$\mathrm{CE} = \min\left\{ y : u(\mathbf{x}^0 + y\overline{\mathbf{g}}) \geq u^1, \ \mathbf{x}^0 + y\overline{\mathbf{g}} \in \mathcal{R}_+^{mS} \right\} .$$

In words, CE is the amount of $\mathbf{g}$, given to an individual for certain, that is equivalent to the move to u^1.

In the special case where there is a single physical commodity, such as money, but an individual may get different amounts in different states, the certain equivalent is the amount of money for certain that the individual would accept in lieu of moving to the risky point.

Example 11.2.   Suppose an individual faces a proposition that will be x_1 or x_2 in each of two states. This individual has utility function $u(x_1, x_2) = x_1^\alpha x_2^\beta$. The certain equivalent relative to the initial point of zero is the value x satisfying $x^\alpha x^\beta = x_1^\alpha x_2^\beta$. Hence $\mathrm{CE} = \left(x_1^\alpha x_2^\beta \right)^{1/(\alpha+\beta)}$.

Certain benefit. Given an initial utility level and an alternative point $\mathbf{x}^1 = (\mathbf{x}_1^1, \mathbf{x}_2^1, \ldots, \mathbf{x}_S^1)$, the *certain benefit* of this change is

$$\text{CB} = \min\left\{\beta : u(\mathbf{x}^1 - \beta\overline{\mathbf{g}}) \geq u^0,\ \mathbf{x}^1 - \beta\overline{\mathbf{g}} \in \mathcal{R}_+^{mS}\right\}.$$

In words, CB is the amount of $\mathbf{g}$ that the individual would forgo for certain in order to obtain the new point. It is exactly equal to the benefit function, but with a special reference commodity $\overline{\mathbf{g}}$.

Both certain equivalent and certain benefit are useful. However, for purposes of characterizing Pareto efficiency, equilibria, and consumer action, the certain benefit is the appropriate measure.

Special Forms of Utility

In most situations involving uncertainty, it is reasonable to make an additional assumption about the underlying preference relation.

Weak independence. A preference relation over state-indexed commodities is *weakly independent* with respect to states if the (conditional) preference relation of commodities in any state s is independent of the commodity levels in other states. (That is, the preference relation is weakly independent with respect to the partition corresponding to state indexing—see Section 4.6.)

For instance, in the two-state world of rainy or sunny weather, suppose you must select amounts of the three basic commodities umbrellas, food, and shelter. The weak independence assumption implies that your preference ordering of the three commodities contingent on rain is independent of the level of these commodities that you would obtain if it were sunny.

According to Proposition 4.8, it follows that if preferences are weakly independent with respect to states and if preferences are described by a continuous, strongly monotonic utility function, the utility function can be written in the weakly separable form

$$u(\mathbf{x}_1, \mathbf{x}_2, \ldots, \mathbf{x}_S) = U(u_1(\mathbf{x}_1), u_2(\mathbf{x}_2), \ldots, u_S(\mathbf{x}_S)).$$

This is not helpful in the case of a single physical commodity, since the two forms are identical in that case; but when there is more than one underlying physical commodity, this assumption provides useful structure. In fact, we shall almost always assume that weak separability holds when considering uncertainty. The reason for this is explained in Section 11.8.

We can also adopt the notion of strong independence presented in Section 4.6.

Strong independence. The preference relation over state-indexed commodities is *strongly independent* with respect to states if the preference relation among commodities in any group of states is independent of the commodity levels in the other states.

Under the assumption of strong independence, if preferences are described by a continuous, strongly monotonic utility function (and if $S > 2$), then, according to the strong independence theorem of Section 4.6, the utility function can be written in the strongly separable form

$$u(\mathbf{x}_1, \mathbf{x}_2, \ldots, \mathbf{x}_S) = u_1(\mathbf{x}_1) + u_2(\mathbf{x}_2) + \cdots + u_S(\mathbf{x}_S).$$

This assumption is technically much stronger than weak independence. However, in the context of state preferences it is frequently adopted. It is justified by arguing that when evaluating a set of contingent claims over a subset of states, one may not care about commodity levels in the other states; for unlike ordinary commodities, of which joint use induces substitute and complement effects, joint use is not possible for different contingent commodities. On the other hand, in the presence of risk, especially unclearly specified risk, people often act as though their preferences are not strongly independent. The following famous example, due to Ellsberg, illustrates this and casts doubt on the validity of the strong independence assumption.

Example 11.3 (Ellsberg paradox). Consider an urn containing 90 colored balls. It is known that 30 of the balls are red, and the other 60 are a mixture of black and white. The number of black and the number of white balls are not specified. Four propositions are considered, with payoffs that depend on the color of a single ball that is to be drawn from the urn. The payoffs associated with the four propositions P_1, P_2, P_3, and P_4 and the color of the ball drawn are shown in the table below. The entries can be thought of as money, with a 1 indicating a large amount (say \$10,000). Note that the payoff of P_1 is objectively $\frac{1}{3}$ since it is known that $\frac{1}{3}$ of the balls are red. The payoff of P_2 is not so objective, although it can be argued to be "about" $\frac{1}{3}$ as well.

	Red	Black	White
P_1	1	0	0
P_2	0	1	0
P_3	1	0	1
P_4	0	1	1

We first ask someone to indicate a preference between P_1 and P_2. Most people select P_1, presumably because the uncertainty of the reward is objectively known in P_1 but not in P_2. Next we ask for a choice between P_3 and P_4. Most people select P_4, since, again, the uncertainty is objectively known in P_4.

This can be viewed as a three-state situation. If the preferences were separable, we could write

$$U(x_R, x_B, x_W) = U_R(x_R) + U_B(x_B) + U_W(x_W),$$

where x_R is the payoff if red occurs and similarly for x_B and x_W. Without loss of generality we can assume

$$U_R(0) = U_B(0) = U_W(0) = 0.$$

The fact that $P_1 \succ P_2$ means

$$U_R(1) > U_B(1),$$

and the fact that $P_4 \succ P_3$ means

$$U_B(1) + U_W(1) > U_R(1) + U_W(1).$$

By canceling $U_W(1)$ from both sides of the second inequality, we obtain a contradiction with the first inequality. Hence an individual making the choices stated has preferences that are not strongly independent.

In the next section we consider the case where uncertainty is specified in terms of probabilities. Under some reasonable assumptions, an expected-value utility function is found, representing a very special, strongly separable form.

11.3 Expected Utility

We now explicitly introduce a probabilistic structure to represent uncertainty. This leads to a special and convenient representation of individual preferences, whereby preferences are described by the expected value of a utility function defined over commodities, not state-indexed commodities. The expectation operation automatically accounts for the uncertainty of the state.

The key idea underlying the development of expected utility theory is to expand the domain of objects of choice from commodities to lotteries. This new domain must be constructed so that it is meaningful to combine lotteries to obtain new lotteries.

We begin by defining an elementary lottery. An *elementary lottery* is based on an uncertain situation defined by a set of possible states. Associated with the set of states is a probability distribution for their occurrence and a reward function defined over the states. The rewards are commodity bundles. For example, suppose there are S states. Then associated with each state s is a probability p_s representing the probability that state s will

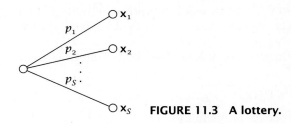

FIGURE 11.3   A lottery.

occur. We have $p_s \geq 0$ for all s and $\sum_{s=1}^{S} p_s = 1$. Also associated with each state s is a commodity bundle $\mathbf{x}_s$ representing the prize or reward that will be won if state s occurs. Symbolically, we can represent such an elementary lottery by the notation

$$p_1 \circ \mathbf{x}_1 \vee p_2 \circ \mathbf{x}_2 \vee \cdots \vee p_S \circ \mathbf{x}_S.$$

Elementary lotteries are often represented graphically by a fan of possibilities as in Fig. 11.3.

Compound lotteries are defined by allowing prizes themselves to be lotteries. Hence if $\mathbf{x}$ and $\mathbf{y}$ are lotteries, previously defined, we can define a new compound lottery $\mathbf{z}$:

$$\mathbf{z} = p \circ \mathbf{x} \vee (1 - p) \circ \mathbf{y} \quad \text{for any } p, \ 0 \leq p \leq 1.$$

A compound lottery is shown in Fig. 11.4a. This lottery is between two prizes: a lottery between $\mathbf{x}$ and $\mathbf{y}$, and a bundle $\mathbf{z}$.

Suppose the set of commodity bundles $\mathcal{X}$ is fixed. We denote the set of all possible lotteries based on these commodities by $\mathcal{L}$. We wish to study preference orderings on $\mathcal{L}$.

A common form of preference ordering for simple lotteries is the *expected value form*. This type of ordering is defined by a utility function u over the space of lotteries. First note that for a certain (or sure) lottery $1 \circ \mathbf{x}$ the utility is $u(1 \circ \mathbf{x})$, which can be abbreviated as $u(\mathbf{x})$. The function u therefore reduces, in this case, to a function on $\mathcal{X}$, the space of commodities. We

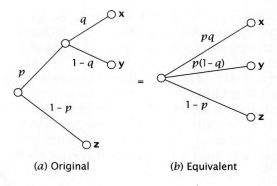

(a) Original   (b) Equivalent

FIGURE 11.4   Compound lottery.

then extend u to any elementary lottery by the equation

$$u(p_1 \circ \mathbf{x}_1 \vee p_2 \circ \mathbf{x}_2 \vee \cdots \vee p_S \circ \mathbf{x}_S) = \sum_{s=1}^{S} p_s u(\mathbf{x}_s).$$

It is important to recognize that it is the same function u on both sides of
the equation, except that for convenience we write $u(\mathbf{x}_s)$ instead of $u(1 \circ \mathbf{x}_s)$
on the right. Clearly, this is strongly separable with respect to the payoffs
in different states.

We can extend this form of utility to compound lotteries by imposing a
compounding rule—namely, we simply use the overall (compound) probabilities of all final bundles, thereby reducing a compound lottery to an elementary lottery. This is shown in Fig. 11.4 for a simple compound lottery.
The compounding formula is, in general,

$$p \circ [q \circ \mathbf{x} \vee (1-q) \circ \mathbf{y}] \vee (1-p) \circ \mathbf{z} \sim pq \circ \mathbf{x} \vee p(1-q) \circ \mathbf{y} \vee (1-p) \circ \mathbf{z}.$$

The equivalent elementary probabilities for complicated compound lotteries can be found by repeated application of this formula. Overall, then, we
see that an expected value utility function is completely defined once $u(\mathbf{x})$ is
defined for all (certain) bundles $\mathbf{x}$. We find the utility of a general lottery by
reducing it to an elementary lottery and using the corresponding additive
formula.

Example 11.4 (Indirect utility). Frequently the prizes in lotteries are income units rather than commodity bundles. The indirect utility function is
then used in place of the utility function. To see how this transformation
works, suppose a consumer is facing a lottery that yields income r_s in state
s. That consumer would evaluate the lottery by the function

$$\sum_{s=1}^{S} p_s v(\mathbf{w}_s, r_s) \equiv \max_{\mathbf{x}} \sum_{s=1}^{S} p_s u(\mathbf{x}_s)$$
$$\text{sub to } \mathbf{w}_s \cdot \mathbf{x}_s \le r_s, \quad s = 1, 2, \ldots, S$$

where $\mathbf{w}_s$ are the commodity prices in state s. If the prices are constant,
independent of the state, we can omit the $\mathbf{w}_s$ dependence from v. Hence
the consumer will use the function

$$V(r_1, r_2, \ldots, r_S) = \sum_{s=1}^{S} p_s v(r_s)$$

to evaluate the lottery. This is again an expected value criterion but one
based on v, which can be thought of as the utility of money.

Note that if commodity prices depend on the state, the expected value
form must be modified to include that effect. Imagine, for example, an investor considering a project that will make a lot of money only if oil prices
should rise. Since prices of many other commodities will also change as a

result of the oil price change, the investor should account for this in an evaluation of the project.

Uniqueness of Expected-Value Utility Functions

If u is an expected-value utility function, then the affine relation

$$u(p \circ \mathbf{x} \vee (1 - p) \circ \mathbf{y}) = pu(\mathbf{x}) + (1 - p)u(\mathbf{y})$$

holds for every p, $0 \le p \le 1$, and for every pair of lotteries $\mathbf{x}$ and $\mathbf{y}$ (not just bundles). This relation is in fact fully equivalent to the expected-value form, since by successive applications of it the utility of a compound lottery can be reduced to the proper weighted sum of utilities of commodity prizes.

In the deterministic case, treated in Chapter 4, we found that a continuous utility function representing a given preference ordering is not unique, but is unique to within a continuous monotonically increasing transformation. Expected-value utility functions are not unique either, but since the affine property must be preserved, the set of allowable transformations is more restrictive. The following result shows that such utility functions are unique to within positive affine transformations.

Proposition 11.2.   *Let u be an expected-value utility function on $\mathcal{L}$ (assume that u takes on at least two values). Then the function*

$$v(\mathbf{x}) = au(\mathbf{x}) + b,$$

where $a > 0$, is also an expected-value utility function representing the same preferences. Conversely, if v is any expected-value utility function equivalent to u, then v must have the above form.

Proof: If v has the given form, it clearly represents the same preferences as u. We merely need to check whether it satisfies the affine property. We have

$$v(p \circ \mathbf{x} \vee (1 - p) \circ \mathbf{y}) = au(p \circ \mathbf{x} \vee (1 - p) \circ \mathbf{y}) + b$$
$$= apu(\mathbf{x}) + a(1 - p)u(\mathbf{y}) + b$$
$$= pv(\mathbf{x}) + (1 - p)v(\mathbf{y}).$$

We now prove the converse. Fix $\mathbf{x}$ and $\mathbf{y}$ with $\mathbf{x} \succ \mathbf{y}$, and let u and v be equivalent expected-value utility functions. Select $\mathbf{z}$ with $\mathbf{x} \succsim \mathbf{z} \succsim \mathbf{y}$. Then there is a β, $0 \le \beta \le 1$, such that $u(\mathbf{z}) = \beta u(\mathbf{x}) + (1 - \beta)u(\mathbf{y}) = u(\beta \circ \mathbf{x} \vee (1 - \beta) \circ \mathbf{y})$. Thus, $\mathbf{z} \sim \beta \circ \mathbf{x} \vee (1 - \beta) \circ \mathbf{y}$, and $\beta = [u(\mathbf{z}) - u(\mathbf{y})]/[u(\mathbf{x}) - u(\mathbf{y})]$. It follows that $v(\mathbf{z}) = \beta v(\mathbf{x}) + (1 - \beta)v(\mathbf{y}) \equiv au(\mathbf{z}) + b$ where the constants $a > 0$ and b are $a = [v(\mathbf{x}) - v(\mathbf{y})]/[u(\mathbf{x}) - u(\mathbf{y})]$, and $b = v(\mathbf{y}) - au(\mathbf{y})$.

For elements $\mathbf{z}$ outside $\mathbf{x} \succsim \mathbf{z} \succsim \mathbf{y}$ we select new reference points $\mathbf{x}'$ and $\mathbf{y}'$ so that $\mathbf{x}' \succsim \mathbf{x}$, $\mathbf{y}' \precsim \mathbf{y}$, and $\mathbf{x}' \succsim \mathbf{z} \succsim \mathbf{y}'$. The same argument shows that $v(\mathbf{z}) = a'u(\mathbf{z}) + b'$ for $\mathbf{z}$ in this expanded range. But clearly $a' = a$ and $b' = b$ since both forms agree on the smaller range.   ∎

11.4 Existence of Expected-Value Utility Functions

A major result of the theory of decision making under uncertainty is that under a set of fairly natural axioms governing preferences on the space of lotteries $\mathcal{L}$, an individual's preferences can be described by an expected-value utility function. This result is extremely attractive, since it justifies the use of the simple expected-value form in analysis of specific problems, where otherwise concrete results would be difficult to obtain.

The required axioms are stated below.

A1 (Certainty). $1 \circ \mathbf{x} \vee (1-1) \circ \mathbf{y} \sim \mathbf{x}$.

A2 (Independence of order). $p \circ \mathbf{x} \vee (1-p) \circ \mathbf{y} \sim (1-p) \circ \mathbf{y} \vee p \circ \mathbf{x}$.

A3 (Compounding). $p \circ \{q \circ \mathbf{x} \vee (1-q)\mathbf{y}\} \vee (1-p) \circ \{r\mathbf{x} \vee (1-r)\mathbf{y}\}$ $= (pq + r - pr) \circ \mathbf{x} + (1 - pq - r + pr) \circ \mathbf{y}$.

A4 (Strong independence). $\mathbf{x} \sim \mathbf{x}'$ implies $p \circ \mathbf{x} \vee (1-p) \circ \mathbf{y} \sim p \circ \mathbf{x}' \vee (1-p) \circ \mathbf{y}$ for all p, $0 \le p \le 1$, and all $\mathbf{y}$.

A5 (Continuity). For any $\mathbf{x}, \mathbf{y}, \mathbf{z} \in \mathcal{L}$, the sets $\{p : p \circ \mathbf{x} \vee (1-p) \circ \mathbf{y} \succsim \mathbf{z}\}$ and $\{p : \mathbf{z} \succsim p \circ \mathbf{x} \vee (1-p) \circ \mathbf{y}\}$ are closed.

A6 (Monotonicity). If $\mathbf{a} > \mathbf{b}$, then $p \circ \mathbf{a} \vee (1-p) \circ \mathbf{b} > q \circ \mathbf{a} \vee (1-q) \circ \mathbf{b}$ if and only if $p > q$.

These axioms have simple intuitive interpretations. Axiom A1 states that a lottery that yields a prize $\mathbf{x}$ with probability 1 is equivalent to that prize. In particular, an elementary lottery that yields a particular commodity bundle with certainty is equivalent to that bundle. A2 says that index ordering does not matter. In particular, for elementary lotteries, the indexing of the states does not matter—only the prizes and the probabilities of winning those prizes matter. This axiom, although usually quite reasonable, can be violated if states have hidden subjective meaning. For example, we may agree that the sunny and rainy states each have probability $\frac{1}{2}$, and hence, objectively, we should be indifferent as to the state in which we receive \$1.00. However, we may also intrinsically prefer to spend money when it is sunny rather than rainy, and hence prefer \$1.00 in the sunny state to \$1.00 in the rainy state. The axiom on independence of order rules this out. Axiom A3 is a fundamental axiom used to reduce compound lotteries—by determining the overall probabilities associated with its components. It essentially states that it is only the net probability of getting a reward that matters. A4 is an independence axiom. It states that if $\mathbf{x}$ is a component of a lottery, then changing things in other components does not change equivalence with respect to the **x** component. Axiom A5 states that preferences are continuous with respect to probabilities. A6 is a monotonicity property that can be derived from the other axioms, but its use considerably shortens the proof of the main theorem below.

We now use these axioms to prove that preferences can be described by an expected-value utility function.

Expected-value utility theorem.   *Let $\succsim$ be a preference ordering on $\mathcal{L}$ satisfying Axioms A1–A6.[1] Then $\succsim$ can be represented by a utility function u satisfying*

$$u\left(p \circ \mathbf{x} \vee (1-p) \circ \mathbf{y}\right) = pu(\mathbf{x}) + (1-p)u(\mathbf{y})$$

for all p, $0 \le p \le 1$, and $\mathbf{x}, \mathbf{y} \in \mathcal{L}$.

Proof: Here is an outline of the proof. We select $\mathbf{a}, \mathbf{b} \in \mathcal{L}$ with $\mathbf{a} \succ \mathbf{b}$. For any **x** between these, that is, for $\mathbf{a} \succsim \mathbf{x} \succsim \mathbf{b}$, we find p such that $p \circ \mathbf{a} \vee (1-p) \circ \mathbf{b} \sim \mathbf{x}$. We then define $u(\mathbf{x}) = p$. In other words, we define u by the relation $u(\mathbf{x}) \circ \mathbf{a} \vee [1-u(\mathbf{x})] \circ \mathbf{b} \sim \mathbf{x}$. This function u is then shown to have the expected-value form.

To extend the definition to include **x**'s outside the region $\mathbf{a} \succsim \mathbf{x} \succsim \mathbf{b}$, we select $\mathbf{c} \succ \mathbf{a}$ and $\mathbf{d} \prec \mathbf{b}$ and use the same method based on **c** and **d**. Then we normalize this new utility by an affine transformation so that it agrees with the original utility at **a** and **b**. Here is the full proof.

Let $\mathbf{a}, \mathbf{b} \in \mathcal{L}$ be selected with $\mathbf{a} \succ \mathbf{b}$. (If no such pair exists, $u \equiv 0$ is a suitable utility function and the proof is complete.) Given **x** with $\mathbf{a} \succsim \mathbf{x} \succsim \mathbf{b}$ consider the subsets of the interval $[0, 1]$

$$T = \{p : p \circ \mathbf{a} \vee (1-p) \circ \mathbf{b} \succsim \mathbf{x}\}$$

and

$$W = \{p : p \circ \mathbf{a} \vee (1-p) \circ \mathbf{b} \precsim \mathbf{x}\}.$$

By Axiom A5 both T and W are closed subsets of $[0, 1]$. By A1, $1 \in T$ and $0 \in W$, so both sets are nonempty. Furthermore, by completeness of $\succsim$, $[0, 1] = T \cup W$.

It follows that T and W must have a point in common, say p. We have $p \circ \mathbf{a} \vee (1-p) \circ \mathbf{b} \sim \mathbf{x}$. Furthermore, by the monotonicity axiom A6 it is clear that this p is unique. Accordingly we set $u(\mathbf{x}) = p$.

For any **x** satisfying $\mathbf{a} \precsim \mathbf{x} \precsim \mathbf{b}$ we define $u(\mathbf{x})$ as the unique value satisfying $u(\mathbf{x}) \circ \mathbf{a} + [1 - u(\mathbf{x})] \circ \mathbf{b} \sim \mathbf{x}$. If **y** has $\mathbf{a} \succsim \mathbf{y} \succsim \mathbf{b}$ with $\mathbf{y} \succ \mathbf{x}$, then from

---

[1]In this theorem, Axiom A3 can be replaced by the weaker A3′:

$$p \circ [q \circ \mathbf{x} \vee (1-q) \circ \mathbf{y} \ ] \vee (1-p) \circ \mathbf{y} \sim pq \circ \mathbf{x} \vee (1-pq) \circ \mathbf{y}.$$

A6 it follows that $u(\mathbf{y}) > u(\mathbf{x})$. Hence the function u is a utility function representing $\succsim$ on $S_{\mathbf{ab}} = \{\mathbf{x} : \mathbf{a} \succsim \mathbf{x} \succsim \mathbf{b}\}$.

We now show that u has the expected-value property. By Axioms A4 and A3 (and A2),

$$p \circ \mathbf{x} \vee (1-p) \circ \mathbf{y} \sim p \circ [u(\mathbf{x}) \circ \mathbf{a} \vee (1-u(\mathbf{x})) \circ \mathbf{b}]$$
$$\vee (1-p) \circ [u(\mathbf{y}) \circ \mathbf{a} \vee (1-u(\mathbf{y})) \circ \mathbf{b}]$$
$$\sim [pu(\mathbf{x}) + (1-p)u(\mathbf{y})] \circ \mathbf{a} \vee [p(1-u(\mathbf{x})) + (1-p)(1-u(\mathbf{y}))] \circ \mathbf{b}.$$

Hence, $u(p \circ \mathbf{x} \vee (1-p) \circ \mathbf{y}) = pu(\mathbf{x}) + (1-p)u(\mathbf{y})$, and u is an expected-value utility function on $S_{\mathbf{ab}}$.

Now we define the utility function everywhere. Given $\mathbf{a}$ and $\mathbf{b}$ with $\mathbf{a} \succ \mathbf{b}$, let $u_{\mathbf{ab}}$ be the utility function on $S_{\mathbf{ab}}$ defined as above. Now fix $\mathbf{a}_0 \succ \mathbf{b}_0$. Then for any $\mathbf{x} \in L$ select $\mathbf{a} \succ \mathbf{b}$ such that $\mathbf{x} \in S_{\mathbf{ab}}$, $\mathbf{a}_0 \in S_{\mathbf{ab}}$, and $\mathbf{b}_0 \in S_{\mathbf{ab}}$. Let

$$M_{\mathbf{ab}}(\mathbf{x}) = \frac{u_{\mathbf{ab}}(\mathbf{x}) - u_{\mathbf{ab}}(\mathbf{b}_0)}{u_{\mathbf{ab}}(\mathbf{a}_0) - u_{\mathbf{ab}}(\mathbf{b}_0)},$$

which is a positive affine transformation of $u_{\mathbf{ab}}$. Note that $M_{\mathbf{ab}}(\mathbf{a}_0) = 1$ and $M_{\mathbf{ab}}(\mathbf{b}_0) = 0$. If $\mathbf{c}$ and $\mathbf{d}$ were selected such that $\mathbf{c} \succ \mathbf{a} \succ \mathbf{b} \succ \mathbf{d}$, it follows from the uniqueness result that $M_{\mathbf{cd}}$ and $M_{\mathbf{ab}}$ would agree on $S_{\mathbf{ab}}$. Hence, the choice of $\mathbf{a}$ and $\mathbf{b}$ to define $M_{\mathbf{ab}}(\mathbf{x})$ does not matter. We may therefore let $u(\mathbf{x}) = M_{\mathbf{ab}}(\mathbf{x})$ with any $\mathbf{a}$ and $\mathbf{b}$ selected as above. It is clear that u has all the required properties. ∎

11.5 Risk Aversion

We now give an independent definition of risk aversion for expected-value utility functions. Later we shall show that this definition does in fact correspond to the definition given earlier for the state-contingent framework.

Risk aversion. An expected-value utility function, defined by $u(\mathbf{x})$ for all $\mathbf{x} \in X = \mathcal{R}_+^m$ is *risk averse* if it is concave on X.

Note that we are again, as in the earlier definition of risk aversion for the state-contingent framework, implicitly assuming that preferences are convex with respect to certain bundles; for u concave implies in particular that u is quasi-concave.

Let us see what this definition says for a simple two-state lottery. Suppose there is probability p that bundle $\mathbf{x}$ will be obtained and probability $1 - p$ that bundle $\mathbf{y}$ will be obtained. The utility of this lottery is $pu(\mathbf{x}) + (1-p)u(\mathbf{y})$. On the other hand, the expected value of the two commodity bundles (the weighted average) is $p\mathbf{x} + (1-p)\mathbf{y}$, and the lottery that yields this value with certainty has utility $u(p\mathbf{x} + (1-p)\mathbf{y})$. If the utility is risk averse (concave) there will hold

$$u(p\mathbf{x} + (1-p)\mathbf{y}) \geq pu(\mathbf{x}) + (1-p)u(\mathbf{y}).$$

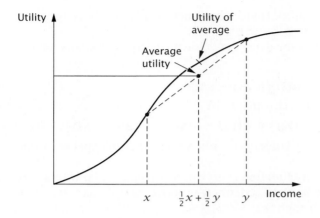

FIGURE 11.5 A utility function.

In other words, under risk aversion the expected value of two bundles is always preferred to the lottery with the bundles as separate prizes. The sure thing is preferred to the risky lottery having the same expected reward. The definition of risk aversion can be applied over a convex subset of X, as well as over all of X. That is, an individual might be risk averse in some regions and not in others. This variation often occurs as a function of total wealth, as discussed below.

Lotteries with income prizes are evaluated by the expected value of indirect utility. The indirect utility function will be concave if the original utility function is concave. For simplicity, we just regard the indirect utility as the utility for income, and it can be graphed as in Fig. 11.5. (The function u is assumed to be increasing in this case.) The figure shows the utility function of an individual who is risk averse in the upper region. Note that the individual prefers the sure amount $\frac{1}{2}x + \frac{1}{2}y$ over the lottery that pays x or y with probability $\frac{1}{2}$.

In tests of various individuals, it has been found that most people possess (indirect) utility functions that look something like that of Fig. 11.5. They are risk averse over a wide range of income levels, but in the low income levels, their utility functions are actually convex rather than concave, indicating that they strictly prefer a fair gamble to its expected value.

It seems clear that the degree of risk aversion is in some sense directly related to the degree of concavity of the utility function, and this observation motivates a quantitative measure of risk aversion. The degree of concavity is related to $u''(x)$; however, to be useful, a measure must be invariant under an affine transformation since the utility function itself is unique only to within such a transformation. This leads to the definition of the *Arrow-Pratt risk aversion coefficient*

$$r(x) = \frac{-u''(x)}{u'(x)}.$$

Example 11.5 (Constant risk aversion). Suppose an individual has a constant risk aversion coefficient r. Then the utility function satisfies

$$u''(x) = -ru'(x).$$

One may easily check that all solutions are

$$u(x) = -ae^{-rx} + b$$

where a and b are arbitrary. For $u(x)$ to be increasing in x, we must take $a > 0$. The constants are otherwise unimportant, so we just take the simplest version, $u(x) = -e^{-rx}$. All others are obtained by application of an affine transformation.

Example 11.6. A woman with current wealth X has the opportunity to bet any amount on the occurrence of an event that she knows will occur with probability p. If she wagers w, she will receive $2w$ if the event occurs and 0 if it does not. She has a constant risk aversion coefficient utility $u(x) = -e^{-rx}$ with $r > 0$. How much should she wager?

Her final wealth will be either $X + w$ or $X - w$. Hence she solves

$$\max_w \{pu(X+w)+(1-p)u(X-w)\} = \max_w \left\{-pe^{-r(X+w)} - (1-p)e^{-r(X-w)}\right\}.$$

Setting the derivative to zero yields

$$(1-p)e^{rw} = pe^{-rw}.$$

Hence,

$$w = \frac{1}{2r} \ln \frac{p}{(1-p)}.$$

Note that a positive wager will be made for $p > \frac{1}{2}$. The wager decreases as the risk coefficient increases. Note also that in this case the result is independent of the initial wealth—a particular feature of this utility function.

Equivalence Result

We conclude this section with a result that relates risk aversion in the general state-contingent model to risk aversion in the expected utility framework. Let there be S states of the world and suppose $U(\mathbf{x}_1, \mathbf{x}_2, \dots, \mathbf{x}_S)$ is a utility function for state-contingent commodities. Suppose U happens to have the expected-value form $U(\mathbf{x}_1, \mathbf{x}_2, \dots, \mathbf{x}_S) = \sum_{i=1}^S p_i f(\mathbf{x}_i)$ with f continuous. Then, according to the theorem below, if U is risk averse according to the general state-contingent definition (that is, U quasi-concave), it follows that f is concave. Hence, the utility function is also risk averse according to the expected-value definition. Note that the converse is trivially true; that is, if f is concave, then U is quasi-concave. Hence, risk aversion in one sense is equivalent to risk aversion in the other when utility has the von Neumann–Morgenstern additive form!

Quasi-concave expected-value theorem.   *Suppose the functions U and f are related by*

$$U(\mathbf{x}_1, \mathbf{x}_2, \ldots, \mathbf{x}_S) \equiv \sum_{i=1}^{S} p_i f(\mathbf{x}_i)$$

identically for all $\mathbf{x}_i \in X$, $i = 1, 2, \ldots S$, where X is a convex set with at least two points and where $\sum_{i=1}^{S} p_i = 1$, $p_i \geq 0$, $i = 1, 2, \ldots, S$. Suppose also that at least two p_i's are nonzero and that U is quasi-concave. Then f is concave. (And hence, U is in fact concave.)

Proof: It is only necessary to prove the theorem for the two-state case, since fixing all $\mathbf{x}_s$'s for all but two states still keeps U quasi-concave with respect to the bundles of those two states (and any constant terms on the right side can be moved to the left side). Further, we can then normalize the two corresponding nonzero probabilities to sum to 1. We shall prove the theorem for the case where these two probabilities are both $\frac{1}{2}$. (The proof of the more general result is substantially more complex.)

Suppose f is not concave. Then there are $\mathbf{x}, \mathbf{w} \in X$ such that $\mathbf{x} + \mathbf{w}$ and $\mathbf{x} - \mathbf{w}$ are in X with

$$\tfrac{1}{2} f(\mathbf{x} + \mathbf{w}) + \tfrac{1}{2} f(\mathbf{x} - \mathbf{w}) > f(\mathbf{x}).$$

This means

$$U(\mathbf{x} + \mathbf{w}, \mathbf{x} - \mathbf{w}) > U(\mathbf{x}, \mathbf{x})$$
$$U(\mathbf{x} - \mathbf{w}, \mathbf{x} + \mathbf{w}) > U(\mathbf{x}, \mathbf{x}).$$

However, in $X \times X$ we have

$$(\mathbf{x}, \mathbf{x}) = \tfrac{1}{2}(\mathbf{x} + \mathbf{w}, \mathbf{x} - \mathbf{w}) + \tfrac{1}{2}(\mathbf{x} - \mathbf{w}, \mathbf{x} + \mathbf{w}).$$

Therefore, the above inequalities mean that $U(\mathbf{x}, \mathbf{x})$ is smaller than U at the endpoints of a line segment on which $(\mathbf{x}, \mathbf{x})$ lies. This contradicts the quasi-concavity of U.   ∎

11.6   Subjective Probability

Sometimes it is appropriate to act on the basis of an expected-value utility function even though there are, in fact, no objective state probabilities. The "probabilities" used in the utility function are termed *subjective probabilities,* for they are derived from the individual's assessment of the likelihood of the various states.

Example 11.7.   Consider the example in Section 11.2 of the investor considering a venture in which he would either double his investment or lose it entirely. That investor used the Cobb-Douglas utility function

$$U(x_1, x_2) = x_1^{\alpha} x_2^{1-\alpha},$$

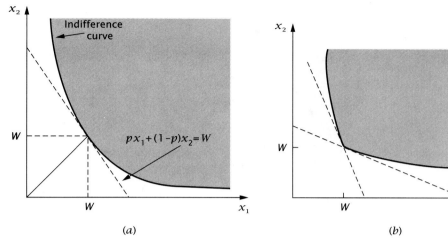

FIGURE 11.6   Contour sets.

where $0 < \alpha < 1$, to evaluate the venture. Taking the logarithm shows this to be equivalent to the utility function

$$\overline{U}(x_1, x_2) = \alpha \ln x_1 + (1 - \alpha) \ln x_2 .$$

Hence we can conclude that the investor behaves *as if* he assigned probabilities α and $1 - \alpha$ to the two states and had $u(x) = \ln x$ as a utility function for wealth. Then α and $(1 - \alpha)$ are subjective probabilities.

Now consider the case where there are two states with known probabilities p and $(1 - p)$ and an expected-value utility function. An upper contour set looks like that of Fig. 11.6a. (We are assuming there is only a single physical commodity.) Consider points (x_1, x_2) close to the certainty point (W, W) that are on the contour. They satisfy $p u(x_1) + (1 - p)u(x_2) = u(W)$. A first-order approximation near W gives $p u'(W)(x_1 - W) + (1 - p)u'(W)(x_2 - W) = 0$, which is $px_1 + (1 - p)x_2 = W$. Therefore, points on the line tangent to the contour at the point of certainty satisfy the equation $px_1 + (1 - p)x_2 = W$ for W equal to current wealth.

Now suppose the probabilities of the two states are not objectively known and the individual does not use an expected-value utility function, but rather a more general, state-indexed utility function. Suppose also that the only difference between the two states is their likelihood of occurrence. (That is, we equally prefer either state if the associated bundles are also equal.) Then the line tangent to the indifference contour at (W, W) can be considered as defining a set of subjective probabilities that are valid at least locally, near (W, W). These probabilities are the p and $(1 - p)$ that define the equation of the tangent line.

It is entirely possible, however, as shown in Fig. 11.6*b*, for the state-indexed utility contour to be kinked at (W, W). In this case a subjective probability concept does not work—at least in simple form. There is essentially a whole set of subjective probabilities, lying between two extreme values. In higher dimensions (that is, more than two states) the situation can become much more complex even in a local analysis.

Risk Aversion Coefficient

We have defined a preference ordering for a single physical commodity to be risk averse if its upper contour set is convex. That is the situation shown in Fig. 11.6*a* and *b*. In the case in which the contour is smooth and subjective probabilities are well defined, a quantitative measure of the degree of risk aversion can be defined. This is most naturally done using the certain benefit as illustrated in Fig. 11.7. Consider the point (x_0, x_0), representing attainment of x_0 with certainty, with corresponding utility u^0. Suppose p and $q = (1 - p)$ are the implied probabilities at that point. Let us select $z_1 = (q/p)^{1/2}$ and $z_2 = -(p/q)^{1/2}$, which satisfy $pz_1 + qz_2 = 0$ (and are conveniently normalized). Points on the tangent line through (x_0, x_0) are of the form $(x_0 + \alpha z_1, x_0 + \alpha z_2)$ for any real value α. We can then consider the certain benefit as a function of α. Specifically, we define

$$b(\alpha) = b(x_0 + \alpha z_1, x_0 + \alpha z_2, u^0).$$

It follows that $b'(\alpha) = 0$ at $\alpha = 0$. The second derivative is a measure of the curvature. We therefore define the risk aversion coefficient

$$r(x_0) = -b''(0).$$

If the preference ordering is of the expected-value form, this value corresponds identically to the Arrow-Pratt risk aversion coefficient. (See Exercise 7.) We now have a natural generalization of this coefficient.

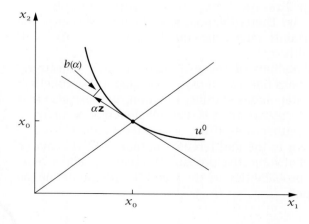

FIGURE 11.7   **General risk aversion coefficient.**

*11.7 Utilities and Subjective Probability

Using subjective probabilities in an expected-value utility function as if they were objective can be formally justified by a system of axioms. An essential feature of the development is that the underlying space of uncertainty is a continuum; that is, there is a continuum of states.[2]

To motivate the various concepts employed, consider the following example. Suppose that in exactly five minutes, timed by a timer set now, you will receive a reward based on the position of the minute hand on your wristwatch at that time. Assume that you have not looked at the actual time recently, say within the last two hours or so, and are not permitted to look until the timer rings. You might have some idea where the minute hand will be then, since you have a rough idea of actual time, but you do not know for sure. Mathematically, we can represent this as uncertainty with respect to a point in the interval (0,60].

We assume also that reward functions are defined on (0,60]. For example, someone might offer to bet you $10 that the minute hand is within the first half-hour rather than the second half-hour. This corresponds to a reward function having values +$10 and −$10 on the two halves of the interval. Someone might present you with another, much more complicated, reward structure. You need a way to evaluate any such proposition.

This example represents the type of problem treated in the general theory, namely, the type having uncertainty involving more than a finite number of possibilities. The nondiscreteness of the underlying space is critical.

To formulate a simple version of a subjective probability theorem, assume that the uncertainty can be regarded as uncertainty with respect to a point in the interval $[0, 1]$ of the real line. Reward functions are defined on this interval and have values equal to bundles of m basic commodities. Hence, a specific reward is $\mathbf{x}(t)$ where $t \in [0, 1]$ is fixed and $\mathbf{x}(t) \in \mathcal{R}^m$. A reward *function* is written $\mathbf{x}(\cdot)$ and defines how reward is a function on $[0, 1]$. We let D be the set of all piecewise continuous reward functions on $[0, 1]$. We suppose that there is a preference ordering $\succsim$ on D (satisfying completeness and transitivity). From several axioms introduced below it follows that this preference ordering can be represented by an expected-value utility function using a subjective probability distribution on $[0, 1]$.

The idea of the theorem and its proof is to approximate the problem with finite-dimensional problems, for which we have a strong theory. This is done by partitioning $[0, 1]$ into subintervals. Suppose $[0, 1]$ is partitioned into m subintervals defined by $0 = t_0 < t_1 \cdots < t_m = 1$. If we restrict attention to reward functions that are constant on each subinterval, we can

---

[2]This section is quite technical in nature and can be safely skipped.

consider a finite-dimensional set of rewards, each of which can be written $\mathbf{x} = (\mathbf{x}_1, \mathbf{x}_2, \ldots, \mathbf{x}_m)$. An ordering on D induces an ordering of these vectors. We now state the axioms.

A1 (Continuous ordering).   Let $\{\mathbf{x}^n(\cdot)\}$ be a sequence in D converging (uniformly over [0,1]) to $\mathbf{x}(\cdot) \in D$. Then $\mathbf{x}^n(\cdot) \succsim \mathbf{y}(\cdot)$ for all n implies $\mathbf{x}(\cdot) \succsim \mathbf{y}(\cdot)$.

This axiom is the basic continuity axiom required for the theorem. It says that if we make finer and finer piecewise-constant approximations to $\mathbf{x}(\cdot)$ and if each of these is preferred to $\mathbf{y}(\cdot)$, then $\mathbf{x}(\cdot)$ itself is preferred to $\mathbf{y}(\cdot)$.

A2 (Strong independence).   The preference ordering induced by any finite partition is strongly independent.

Axiom A2 is the main structural axiom. Together with A1 and A3, it guarantees that the finite-dimensional ordering corresponding to a partition is strongly separable.

A3 (Monotonicity).   The preference ordering induced by any finite partition is strongly monotonic.

To define the next axiom, we require some new notation. Let I^1 and I^2 be subintervals of [0, 1]. Let $\mathbf{x}$ and $\mathbf{y}$ be two reward values, and let $f^i_{\mathbf{x},\mathbf{y}}(t) = \mathbf{x}$ for $t \in I^i$ and $f^i_{\mathbf{x},\mathbf{y}}(t) = \mathbf{y}$ for $t \notin I^i$. (Thus $f^i_{\mathbf{x},\mathbf{y}}(\cdot)$ is the piecewise-constant function that is equal to $\mathbf{x}$ on I^i and equal to $\mathbf{y}$ elsewhere.) Then I^1 is said to be *equivalent* to I^2 if $f^1_{\mathbf{x},\mathbf{y}}(\cdot) \sim f^2_{\mathbf{x},\mathbf{y}}(\cdot)$ for all $\mathbf{x}$ and $\mathbf{y}$. This means that a reward function that gives $\mathbf{x}$ on I^1 and $\mathbf{y}$ otherwise is equally preferred to one that gives $\mathbf{x}$ on I^2 and $\mathbf{y}$ otherwise. In the watch example above, it might be that the five-minute interval (0, 5] is equivalent to the five-minute interval [55, 60) because your uncertainty about the position of the minute hand is symmetric about 0.

A4 (Equal division).   Any interval in [0, 1] can be divided into two equivalent subintervals.

This is the axiom that incorporates the nondiscreteness of the underlying probability. A finite-state model of uncertainty would not satisfy this axiom.

In the above watch example, this axiom implies that you can divide any interval (say the first quarter hour) into two subintervals (say the first 6 minutes and the next 9 minutes) in such a way that you would be indifferent between rewards that paid $10 in one interval or the other and (say) zero elsewhere. Furthermore, no matter how small an interval is given, you could divide it this way.

The final axiom is a special continuity axiom.

A5 (Interval continuity).   There is an $\varepsilon > 0$ with the following property. Let I^1 and I^2 be intervals of lengths L_1 and L_2, respectively. Then $f_{1,0}^1(\cdot) \succ f_{1,0}^2(\cdot)$ if $L_2 < \varepsilon L_1$.

This says that if L_2 is sufficiently small compared with L_1, the two intervals cannot be equivalent. A reward of **1** on the large interval will be strictly preferred to a reward of **1** on the small interval.

We can now state the main theorem. The important aspect of this theorem is that a preference order on D can be represented by an expected-value utility function. In this case, however, rather than a finite sum, the expected value is expressed as an integral (in Stieltjes form). The function P in the integral is a (subjective) cumulative probability distribution function.

Subjective probability.   *Let $\succsim$ on D satisfy Axioms A1–A5. Then $\succsim$ can be represented by a utility function of the form*

$$U(\mathbf{x}(\cdot)) = \int_0^1 u(\mathbf{x}(t))\, dP(t),$$

where u is continuous and P is a continuous (strictly increasing) probability distribution.

Proof: (Sketch). By the equal division axiom divide $[0, 1]$ into two disjoint intervals $[0, a_1)$ and $[a_1, 1]$ that are equivalent. Repeat this process, dividing each of these intervals. After n steps of this kind we have a partition $\mathcal{P}_n$ with 2^n equivalent subintervals defined by the end points $0 = t_0 < t_1 < t_2 \cdots < t_{2^n} = 1$. A utility function for corresponding piecewise continuous functions can, by A1, A2, and A3, be written as $U^n(\mathbf{x}_1, \mathbf{x}_2, \ldots \mathbf{x}_{2^n}) = \sum_{i=1}^{2^n} u_i^n(\mathbf{x}_i)/2^n$ with $u_i^n(\mathbf{0}) = 0$. By the equal division property it can be shown that $u_i^n(\mathbf{x}) = u_j^n(\mathbf{x})$ for all i, j. So we drop the subscript and normalize with $u^n(\mathbf{1}) = 1$.

If a reward function is constant on the subintervals of the partition $\mathcal{P}_{n-1}$ with values $\mathbf{y}_1, \mathbf{y}_2, \ldots, \mathbf{y}_{2^{n-1}}$, it is also in the domain of U^n, and $U^n = \sum_{i=1}^{2^{n-1}} [u^n(\mathbf{y}_i) + u^n(\mathbf{y}_i)]/2^n = \sum_{i=1}^{2^{n-1}} u^n(\mathbf{y}_i)/2^{n-1}$. This function must be equivalent to U^{n-1}. However, since (by Proposition 4.9) strongly separable utility functions are unique to within affine transformations and since $u^n(\mathbf{0}) = u^{n-1}(\mathbf{0}) = 0$ and $u^n(\mathbf{1}) = u^{n-1}(\mathbf{1}) = 1$, it follows that $u^n \equiv u^{n-1}$. Hence, there is a continuous u such that for any n, the utility of functions constant on the subintervals of $\mathcal{P}_n$ can be written $U^n = \sum_i u(\mathbf{x}_i)/2^n$. What remains is to consider the limit as $n \to \infty$.

By the interval continuity axiom A5, the widths of all intervals in $\mathcal{P}_n$ go to zero as $n \to \infty$. To see this, suppose it did not. Then for some n there would be two intervals of $\mathcal{P}_n$ such that one has length less than ε times the length of the other; therefore, these two intervals could not be equivalent.

Corresponding to the partition $\mathcal{P}_n$ define $F_n(\cdot)$ to be the function that is of magnitude $1/[2^n(t_i - t_{i-1})]$ on the interval $[t_{i-1}, t_i)$, for each i. Let $P_n(\cdot)$ be the integral of $F_n(\cdot)$. Then U^n can be written as $U^n = \int_0^1 u(\mathbf{x}(t))\, dP_n(t)$. Limit arguments then establish the result. ∎

The requirement that the underlying uncertainty allows refinement into equivalent subsets is quite strong. A finite-state situation, such as in the Ellsberg paradox, does not fit this framework. It is sometimes suggested, however, that in a finite-state world, states can be divided (artificially) by introducing a coin flip. Each state s then becomes two states: (s, head) and (s, tail). Further refinement is obtained by additional coin flips. However, to develop a theorem similar to the above, the independence axiom must be applied to these artificial states, even though rewards do not differ among them. It seems more reasonable to acknowledge that preferences may sometimes be more complex than those represented by expected utility.

Part II
MARKETS UNDER UNCERTAINTY

11.8   The Consumer and Uncertainty

A theory of consumer choice under uncertainty is straightforward now that a preference framework has been developed. This theory posits, just as in the deterministic case, that consumers maximize their preferences subject to whatever budget and other constraints they face. The application of this theory to specific situations can become complex, but on the other hand, this complexity reveals the richness of the theory.

Prices for State-Contingent Claims

The theory of consumer choice under uncertainty uses the concept of state-contingent claims developed in the early part of the chapter. Suppose there are S states and m real commodities. Bundles of state-indexed commodities (equivalently expressed as state-contingent claims to commodities) have the form $(\mathbf{x}_1, \mathbf{x}_2, \ldots, \mathbf{x}_S)$ where each $\mathbf{x}_s$ is an m-vector representing commodities associated with state s.

A price system can be associated with state-indexed commodities. Such a system consists of mS separate prices, one for each commodity in each state; these prices are termed *state-contingent prices*.

An elementary contingent claim is a claim to a single commodity, say j, if and only if a certain single state, say s, occurs. We can denote the price of such an elementary claim by p_{js}. More complex contracts can always be decomposed into a collection of elementary contracts involving a single state and a single commodity. For example, a contract that delivers a specific commodity in either state s or state r is equivalent to two elementary contracts, one delivering in state s and the other in state r. A contract that is equivalent to a linear combination of elementary contingent claims must (under perfect competition with no transaction costs) have a price equal to the same linear combination of elementary prices; otherwise there would be arbitrage opportunities. (If the price did not equal the combination price, an individual could trade this contract for the equivalent bundle of elementary claims and make arbitrarily large profit.) Therefore if bundles contingent on states s and r have corresponding unit prices $\mathbf{p}_s$ and $\mathbf{p}_r$, a combined bundle $(\mathbf{x}_s, \mathbf{x}_r)$ must cost $\mathbf{p}_s \cdot \mathbf{x}_s + \mathbf{p}_r \cdot \mathbf{x}_r$.

Suppose now that there is a set of prices for state-contingent claims to commodities. How does the consumer select a bundle of claims? Naturally, the consumer maximizes preferences subject to a budget constraint, just as in the deterministic case. The only difference is that there are many more commodities. This is the advantage of the state-contingent approach to uncertainty—it reduces the consumer choice problem to the standard one.

The Importance of Weak Independence

The state-contingent model of exchange has great conceptual power, and we shall frequently refer to it as an idealization. In reality, however, few markets for contingent claims exist. More commonly, one purchases actual physical commodities in a *spot market* (a market for commodities to be delivered immediately—on the spot) at prevailing prices. Surprisingly, if a state-contingent claims market exists before uncertainty is resolved and a spot market exists after it is resolved, preference conflicts can arise. Such conflicts disappear if preferences satisfy a weak independence assumption.

To see how the conflict can arise, imagine that you are planning today for tomorrow's consumption. There is uncertainty, characterized by S states of the world, that will be resolved tomorrow. Suppose first that there is a complete market of contingent claims for commodities that will be delivered tomorrow, with prices $\mathbf{p} = (\mathbf{p}_1, \mathbf{p}_2, \ldots, \mathbf{p}_S)$. You have income r to be allocated to this market. According to the theory of choice, you would select the bundle $\mathbf{x} = (\mathbf{x}_1, \mathbf{x}_2, \ldots, \mathbf{x}_S)$ of contingent claims that maximizes your state-indexed preference ordering. Suppose that as a result of this process you purchase the state s contingent bundle $\mathbf{x}_s$ for a cost of $r_s = \mathbf{p}_s \cdot \mathbf{x}_s$.

Alternatively, suppose there is no market for state contingent claims today, but you have to wait until tomorrow to purchase actual commodities on the spot market. Suppose state s occurs, you then have an income of r_s (the amount you would have spent in the other situation on state-s contingent commodities), and prices are again $\mathbf{p}_s$. At this point you would maximize your preference ordering *given that state s had occurred*. This is a preference ordering over just m commodities, and it involves no uncertainty. The original bundle $\mathbf{x}_s$ is feasible (and, in fact, is on the boundary of your budget constraint), but you may wish to select a different bundle, for there is no guarantee that your preferences when you know the state is s agree with your full state-indexed preferences.

If both markets existed, you would have a major conflict! Today you would make a selection of contingent commodities, knowing that tomorrow you would be unhappy with your choice.

An assumption of weak independence together with a consistency assumption avoids this type of conflict. Suppose an individual has preferences for state-indexed commodities that can be represented by a weakly separable utility function of the form

$$U(u_1(\mathbf{x}_1), u_2(\mathbf{x}_2), \ldots, u_S(\mathbf{x}_S)).$$

Then the first problem above (selecting from a full set of contingent claims) can be written

$$\max\ U(u_1(\mathbf{x}_1), u_2(\mathbf{x}_2), \ldots, u_S(\mathbf{x}_S))$$
$$\text{sub to } \mathbf{p}_1 \cdot \mathbf{x}_1 \le r_1$$
$$\mathbf{p}_2 \cdot \mathbf{x}_2 \le r_2$$
$$\vdots$$
$$\mathbf{p}_S \cdot \mathbf{x}_S \le r_S$$
$$r_1 + r_2 + \cdots + r_S \le r.$$

On the other hand, consider the state-s spot market with income r_s (determined by the solution of the above maximization problem) and prices $\mathbf{p}_s$. Suppose, for consistency, the individual has utility u_s. Then in the spot market the individual solves

$$\max\ u_s(\mathbf{x}_s)$$
$$\text{sub to } \mathbf{p}_s \cdot \mathbf{x}_s \le r_s,$$

which yields the same $\mathbf{x}_s$ as the first problem. Hence, if preferences are weakly independent (or utility is weakly separable) with respect to states, and if the preferences conditional on a state are identical to the preferences that hold when that state occurs, there is no preference conflict. Because a preference conflict is troublesome and not likely to be realistic, we shall always assume that preferences have the weak separability property and that the spot preferences are consistent with it.

Note that, in particular, expected-value utility functions are weakly separable. (In fact, they are strongly separable.) However, for much of what follows we require only weak separability (or weak independence).

11.9 The Role of the Securities Market

We have seen that if a complete set of markets for state-contingent commodity claims exists, the consumer's problem under uncertainty exactly parallels the deterministic case. Unfortunately, state-contingent markets are usually *not* complete. This section shows that completeness is not, however, absolutely necessary. Suitable securities markets can provide the essentials of completeness, in equilibrium, with far fewer actual markets.

Suppose an exchange economy consists of n individuals, S states, and m real commodities, each of which is state-indexed. Suppose individual i has income r_i and a weakly separable utility function. Suppose that $\bar{\mathbf{p}}_s$ are the equilibrium prices for state-s contingent claims to commodities. Let $\mathbf{x}_i^* = (\mathbf{x}_{i1}^*, \mathbf{x}_{i2}^*, \ldots, \mathbf{x}_{iS}^*)$ denote the bundle of state-contingent commodities chosen by individual i before the state is known. Individual i determines this bundle by solving

$$\max\ U_i(u_{i1}(\mathbf{x}_{i1}), u_{i2}(\mathbf{x}_{i2}), \ldots, u_{iS}(\mathbf{x}_{iS}))$$

$$\text{sub to}\ \sum_{s=1}^{S} \bar{\mathbf{p}}_s \cdot \mathbf{x}_{is} \leq r_i.$$

This is the complete markets framework discussed above.

As an alternative market structure, suppose that S *security markets* are established, numbered $1, 2, \ldots, S$, to correspond to the various states. Security s pays one unit of account if the true state is revealed to be state s, and it pays zero otherwise. The price for one unit of security s is some value q_s (determined by market conditions). Security s is therefore a claim to one unit of account, contingent on the occurrence of state s. Using these securities, individuals can "invest in" (or bet on) the occurrence of any of the S states. In fact, an individual can purchase different amounts of each of the S securities.

These S security markets are the only markets open before the state is revealed. In particular, there are no markets for contingent commodities. However, after the state is revealed, there are markets for each of the m real commodities. If state s occurs, we set commodity prices to

$$\mathbf{p}_s = \frac{\bar{\mathbf{p}}_s}{q_s},$$

where $\bar{\mathbf{p}}_s$ is the price vector from the complete markets framework. We shall show that this market structure provides an individual with the same range of commodity choice as the complete markets framework.

Note that commodities contingent on state s can be purchased by first buying security s and then using the proceeds of this security, if s occurs, to buy commodities. The total price for state-contingent commodities purchased this way is $q_s \mathbf{p}_s$ because a unit of account in state s costs q_s in the security market and commodities have prices $\mathbf{p}_s$. However, by definition, $q_s \mathbf{p}_s = \bar{\mathbf{p}}_s$, so the net cost is the same as before.

To match the $\mathbf{x}_{is}^*$ of the other framework, the individual must purchase the proper amount of security s. Specifically, individual i must purchase

$$r_{is}^* = \mathbf{p}_s \cdot \mathbf{x}_{is}^*$$

units of the security. The budget constraint for purchase of securities is

$$\sum_{s=1}^{S} q_s r_{is} \leq r_i.$$

The choice r_{is}^* given above satisfies this budget constraint since

$$\sum_{s=1}^{S} q_s r_{is}^* = \sum_{s=1}^{S} q_s \mathbf{p}_s \cdot \mathbf{x}_{is}^* = \sum_{s=1}^{S} \overline{\mathbf{p}}_s \cdot \mathbf{x}_{is}^* \le r_i.$$

Therefore, the individual can duplicate the purchase made in the earlier market structure.

The security prices q_s, $s = 1, 2, \ldots, S$, are determined by market clearing. The total number of the units of account in the system is $r = \sum_{i=1}^{n} r_i$. This must equal the total claims payable when any state s occurs. Therefore we must have

$$r = \sum_{i=1}^{n} r_{is}^*$$

for each $s = 1, 2, \ldots, S$. From the definition of r_{is}^* and $\mathbf{p}_s$, this leads to

$$r = \sum_{i=1}^{n} \mathbf{p}_s \cdot \mathbf{x}_{is}^* = \frac{1}{q_s} \sum_{i=1}^{n} \overline{\mathbf{p}}_s \cdot \mathbf{x}_{is}^*.$$

Hence,

$$q_s = \frac{\sum_{i=1}^{n} \overline{\mathbf{p}}_s \cdot \mathbf{x}_{is}^*}{r}.$$

That is, q_s is the fraction of the total units of account originally committed to state s.

Let us review the whole process. Given the prices q_s and $\mathbf{p}_s$ for $s = 1, 2, \ldots, S$, how does individual i behave? First, he or she purchases r_{is}^* units of security s, for each state s. Then when a particular state s occurs, the proceeds from security s are used to purchase commodities on a prevailing spot market with prices $\mathbf{p}_s$. Because of weak separability, the individual then selects real commodities by solving the problem

$$\max \ u_{is}(\mathbf{x}_{is})$$
$$\text{sub to } \mathbf{p}_s \cdot \mathbf{x}_{is} \le r_{is}^*.$$

This yields the solution $\mathbf{x}_{is}^*$, which is exactly the same as the consumption bundle that would be obtained in the complete markets, contingent-claims structure.

The difference between the two structures is illustrated schematically in Fig. 11.8 for the case of two states and three commodities. Each open circle represents a market. In the state-contingent structure all commodities are treated simultaneously and the system resembles an ordinary static consumer choice problem. In the second structure there are two stages. Securities are purchased in the first stage; then after the state is determined, commodities are purchased with the proceeds from the securities.

The two-stage structure reduces the number of markets that must actually be open. With complete markets formed directly, the total number of markets is mS. In the two-stage structure the number of markets ever opened is only $S + m$.

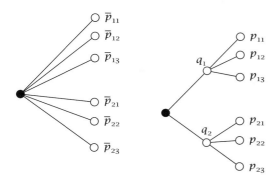

FIGURE 11.8   The role of securities.

Fulfilled Expectations

The equivalence of the securities market solution and the complete markets solution is based on the assumption that consumers correctly estimate future commodity spot prices in the various states. This feature of consumer behavior (or consumer knowledge) is termed *fulfilled expectations.*

Let us consider a general two-period situation in which a decision is made in the first period and the rewards of the decision are determined in the second period through a market. For example, imagine a farmer who plants a crop in the first period and receives a reward based on market price in the second period. To make a decision in the first period using preference theory, something must be assumed about future prices, and this expectation of prices can conceivably be formed in many ways. The farmer, for example, might simply extrapolate from past crop prices in order to estimate future prices. For the decision to be fully rational, however, the price estimation process must itself be rational.

A fulfilled expectations process is *closed* in a special way. Individuals each guess a set of prices for the next period in each of the S possible states. Based on this set of guessed prices, each individual is then able to determine the best action to take in the first period—which for the consumer treated above consists of security purchases, and for the farmer consists of planting decisions. Then in the second period, when the state is revealed, individuals act optimally in the existing spot market, and market clearing conditions determine a set of actual commodity prices. The whole process is closed if the prices that are formed are exactly those that individuals guessed (that is, expected) for the given state. Hence, the expected prices turn out to be correct.

The concept of fulfilled expectations clearly implies some special capabilities of individuals. Either they have deep market intuition or great computing capabilities. Most likely, this condition is not realized in practice. However, like that of perfect markets, the concept of fulfilled expectations is a useful idealization that may not be met exactly but provides a coherent and structured theory.

11.10   A Fuller Model

We add two features to the model of the previous section that make it more realistic.

General Securities

Pure state-contingent securities rarely exist in practice. However, there do exist other securities that have payoffs depending in some way on the state of nature. Individuals may invest in a portfolio of these securities while simultaneously making consumption choices.

Suppose again that there are S states of nature. A *security* is an S-vector with components corresponding to payoffs in each of the S states. Hence we write a security in the form $\mathbf{z} = (z_1, z_2, \ldots, z_S)$, where z_s is the payoff if state s should occur. Security $\mathbf{z}$ has a price $p_{\mathbf{z}}$.

We say that a set of securities is *independent* if it is independent in the usual sense of linear independence in S-dimensional vector space. There can therefore be at most S independent securities in an S-state world.

Suppose a security $\mathbf{z}$ can be expressed as a linear combination of two securities $\mathbf{z}_1$ and $\mathbf{z}_2$, say as $\mathbf{z} = \alpha \mathbf{z}_1 + \beta \mathbf{z}_2$. Suppose the corresponding prices are $p_{\mathbf{z}}, , p_{\mathbf{z}_1}$, and $p_{\mathbf{z}_2}$. Then in a competitive economy with no transactions costs, there must hold $p_{\mathbf{z}} = \alpha p_{\mathbf{z}_1} + \beta p_{\mathbf{z}_2}$. Both $\mathbf{z}$ and $\alpha \mathbf{z}_1 + \beta \mathbf{z}_2$ represent exactly the same payoff pattern, and hence they must have the same price for otherwise someone could make arbitrarily large arbitrage profits by buying $\mathbf{z}$ and selling $\alpha \mathbf{z}_1 + \beta \mathbf{z}_2$ or vice versa. Let $\mathbf{e}_1, \mathbf{e}_2, \ldots, \mathbf{e}_S$ be the elementary securities, with $\mathbf{e}_s$ paying one unit if and only if state s occurs. These elementary securities form a basis for the space of all securities. Suppose the prices of these are q_s, $s = 1, 2, \ldots, S$. It follows immediately that a security $\mathbf{z} = (z_1, z_2, \ldots, z_S)$ must have price

$$p_{\mathbf{z}} = \sum_{s=1}^{S} q_s z_s.$$

The unit risk-free security (or bond) is the one that pays one unit in each state. This bond must have price $\sum_{s=1}^{S} q_s$. Hence, we have

$$r = \frac{1}{\sum_{s=1}^{S} q_s} - 1,$$

where r is the one-period interest rate.

The Two-Period Choice Problem

It is useful to recognize that commitments to future (uncertain) consumption are made at the expense of present consumption. This leads to the introduction of a two-period model. In this model the consumer has an income r that is to be allocated in the first period to consumption goods and purchase of securities that will generate income for purchase of goods in the second period. (The consumer has the option of purchasing the risk-free security, of course.)

The prices $\mathbf{p}_0$ of first-period goods, the prices q_s, $s = 1, 2, \ldots, S$, of elementary securities, and the collection $\mathbf{p}_1, \mathbf{p}_2, \ldots, \mathbf{p}_S$ of second-period state-dependent prices are all known. The consumer's preferences are described by a continuous utility function that is weakly separable with respect to consumption in the first period and with respect to each second-period state. The consumer's problem is therefore

$$\max \ U(u_0(\mathbf{x}_0), u_1(\mathbf{x}_1), u_2(\mathbf{x}_2), \ldots, u_S(\mathbf{x}_S))$$
$$\text{sub to } \mathbf{p}_0 \cdot \mathbf{x}_0 + \sum_{s=1}^{S} q_s r_s \leq r$$
$$\mathbf{p}_s \cdot \mathbf{x}_s \leq r_s, \qquad s = 1, 2, \ldots, S.$$

11.11 **Production and Uncertainty**

Firms are subject to uncertainties just as consumers are. For example, a farm's output depends on uncertain weather, the output of a high-technology firm depends on the uncertain results of research, and the output of a service activity depends on uncertain demand. Production under uncertainty can be analyzed by combining the uncertainty concepts of this chapter with the methods for characterizing firms developed in earlier chapters.

State-Contingent Production

We begin by applying the concept of state-contingent commodities to economies with production.

Consider a two-period model. In the first period firms make production plans and commit resources. In the second period production is completed, but the actual amounts produced depend on the state. Let $\mathbf{y}_0 \in \mathcal{R}^m$ be a vector of commodities selected for the first period. (Typically $\mathbf{y}_0$ is nonpositive, with $-\mathbf{y}_0$ being a vector of input commodities.) If state s occurs, this initial vector leads to a second-period netput $\mathbf{y}_s \in \mathcal{R}^m$. (Typically $\mathbf{y}_s$ is nonnegative and corresponds to output.) Overall, this production plan can be described by the vector $\mathbf{y} = (\mathbf{y}_0, \mathbf{y}_1, \mathbf{y}_2, \ldots, \mathbf{y}_S)$. Such a vector is a complete production plan for the firm under uncertainty. It describes the input and the various possible outputs that can occur as a function of the state. The set $\mathcal{Y}$ of all such vectors is the complete production possibility set. In other words, the production possibility set $\mathcal{Y}$ is a special subset of $m(S + 1)$-dimensional space, the space of all commodities indexed by both period and state.

Example 11.8.   A farmer uses a single input l to produce a crop. The amount of crop produced depends on the weather, which can be either of two states. In particular, the production is $q_1 = l^\alpha$ in state 1 and $q_2 = l^\beta$ in state 2. The production possibility set is therefore the set of vectors $[(-l, 0), (0, q_1), (0, q_2)] \in \mathcal{R}^6$ with $l \geq 0$, $q_1 \leq l^\alpha$, and $q_2 \leq l^\beta$.

The above framework embeds the uncertain situation in the standard theoretical structure for production. To obtain this embedding, in general, it is only necessary to define a complete set of dated and state-contingent commodities. Once we have the standard structure, the conventional theory of the firm can be directly applied.

Suppose there is a price system for all the dated and state-contingent commodities, represented by an $m(S + 1)$-dimensional vector $\mathbf{p}$. Given these prices, the firm will, according to the standard theory of perfect competition, select a netput vector $\mathbf{y} \in \mathcal{Y}$ so as to maximize the profit $\mathbf{p} \cdot \mathbf{y}$. Note that the firm does not need an assessment of state probabilities, nor does it need to define a special objective function. With complete markets, the standard theory of profit maximization carries through.

Equilibrium

An equilibrium can be defined for a two-period, productive, uncertain, private-ownership economy in a way that parallels the deterministic definition. We briefly outline the structure of the economy and the equilibrium here, based on a complete market for state-contingent commodities.

Assume that there are n consumers, m underlying perishable commodities (which cannot be stored from one period to another), K firms, and S states of the world in the second period. Consumer i has an endowment vector $\mathbf{w}_i$ of commodities in the first period and owns a fraction θ_{ik} of firm k. Firm k has a production possibility set $\mathcal{Y}_k$ of the type described above. A netput vector is of the form $\mathbf{y}_k = (\mathbf{y}_{k0}, \mathbf{y}_{k1}, \mathbf{y}_{k2}, \ldots, \mathbf{y}_{kS})$.

In the first period there are markets for both first-period commodities and for state-contingent, second-period commodities. The corresponding prices are $\mathbf{p}_0, \bar{\mathbf{p}}_1, \ldots, \bar{\mathbf{p}}_S$. Each firm k selects a netput vector $\mathbf{y}_k \in \mathcal{Y}_k$ to maximize profit in these markets and distributes the profit to its owners. Each consumer i selects a consumption bundle $\mathbf{x}_i = (\mathbf{x}_{i0}, \mathbf{x}_{i1}, \mathbf{x}_{i2}, \ldots, \mathbf{x}_{iS})$ to maximize utility subject to the budget constraint

$$\mathbf{p}_0 \cdot \mathbf{x}_{i0} + \sum_{s=1}^{S} \bar{\mathbf{p}}_s \cdot \mathbf{x}_{is} \le \mathbf{p}_0 \cdot \mathbf{w}_i + \sum_{k=1}^{K} \theta_{ik} \left\{ \mathbf{p}_0 \cdot \mathbf{y}_{k0} + \sum_{s=1}^{S} \bar{\mathbf{p}}_s \cdot \mathbf{y}_{ks} \right\}.$$

In this economy all market transactions, for both consumers and producers, take place in the first period. The market clearing conditions are

$$\sum_{i=1}^{n} \mathbf{x}_{i0} \le \sum_{i=1}^{n} \mathbf{w}_i + \sum_{k=1}^{K} \mathbf{y}_{k0}$$

$$\sum_{i=1}^{n} \mathbf{x}_{is} = \sum_{k=1}^{K} \mathbf{y}_{ks}, \quad s = 1, 2, \dots S.$$

Since all transactions occur simultaneously, this economy is essentially static and can be treated by the standard Arrow-Debreu framework.

*11.12   Production and Securities

We can combine the results of the previous few sections to obtain a theory of equilibrium with production that comes close to representing actual multiperiod uncertain economies. In this model stock in firms is used in place of elementary state-contingent claims.

The Model

The economy is identical to that at the end of the previous section except for the market structure and the additional assumption that utility functions are weakly separable with respect to states and periods.

In this model there is during the first period a stock market for the shares of each firm. Through this market consumers can trade their initial ownership for a different portfolio. The price of firm k's stock in this market is denoted v_k and is referred to as the initial *value* of the firm. Accordingly, if θ_{ik} is the fraction of the firm initially owned by consumer i, the total value of consumer i's initial stock holdings is $\sum_k \theta_{ik} v_k$. After trading, the consumer may have new holdings t_{ik} with total value $\sum_k t_{ik} v_k$. For market clearing we must have

$$\sum_{i=1}^{n} t_{ik} = \sum_{i=1}^{n} \theta_{ik} = 1 \qquad \text{for } k = 1, 2, \dots, K.$$

There is a market for commodities in the first period, with corresponding prices $\mathbf{p}_0$. Consumers purchase initial-period commodities at these prices. Also each firm k distributes $\mathbf{p} \cdot \mathbf{y}_{k0}$ to the current (new) owners, proportional to their ownership. (This is likely to be negative, since $\mathbf{y}_{k0}$ is most likely nonpositive.) In the second period, after a state s is realized and production is completed, a spot market opens for commodities in that period with prices $\mathbf{p}_s$. Since the model ends in the second period, the firms sell their products and simultaneously distribute all proceeds to the current owners, proportional to their ownership. These proceeds depend on the state (as well as on the production plans).

From the above, it is clear that the consumer faces the budget constraints

$$\mathbf{p}_0 \cdot \mathbf{x}_{i0} + \sum_{k=1}^{K} t_{ik} v_k \leq \mathbf{p}_0 \cdot \mathbf{w}_i + \sum_{k=1}^{K} \theta_{ik} v_k + \sum_{k=1}^{K} t_{ik} \mathbf{p}_0 \cdot \mathbf{y}_{k0}$$

$$\mathbf{p}_s \cdot \mathbf{x}_{is} \leq \sum_{k=1}^{K} t_{ik} \mathbf{p}_s \cdot \mathbf{y}_{ks} \qquad \text{for} \quad s = 1, 2, \dots, S.$$

As before, the market clearing conditions in the two periods are

$$\sum_{i=1}^{n} \mathbf{x}_{i0} = \sum_{i=1}^{n} \mathbf{w}_i + \sum_{k=1}^{K} \mathbf{y}_{k0}$$

$$\sum_{i=1}^{n} \mathbf{x}_{is} = \sum_{k=1}^{K} \mathbf{y}_{ks}, \qquad s = 1, 2, \dots, S.$$

Symbolically, an equilibrium for this model consists of an allocation $\mathbf{X}$ to consumers, a collection $\mathbf{Y}$ of production plans, a set of security portfolios $\mathbf{T}$, a system of spot prices $\mathbf{p}$ for commodities, and a value system $\mathbf{v}$ for the firms. Hence, an equilibrium can be denoted $(\mathbf{X}, \mathbf{Y}, \mathbf{T}, \mathbf{p}, \mathbf{v})$. Consumers act to maximize their utility subject to the constraints above. To fully define an equilibrium, we must describe the operation of the firm; that is, we must describe how $\mathbf{y}_k \in \mathcal{Y}_k$ is chosen.

Spanning Equilibria

The spot value of the output produced by firm k in state s is $\mathbf{p}_s \cdot \mathbf{y}_{ks}$. Let $\mathbf{z}_k$ be the S-dimensional vector with these revenue components $\mathbf{p}_s \cdot \mathbf{y}_{ks}$, $s = 1, 2, \dots, S$. A consumer owning a share of firm k owns a share of the security with payoff $\mathbf{z}_k$. We say that the collection of K vectors $\mathbf{z}_k$, $k = 1, 2, \dots, K$, is *spanning* if it spans S-dimensional space in the usual sense of spanning a vector space, that is, if any arbitrary vector can be expressed as a linear combination of these $\mathbf{z}_k$ vectors.

Note that the initial cost of the state-indexed output vector $\mathbf{z}_k$ is $v_k - \mathbf{p}_0 \cdot \mathbf{y}_{k0}$. That is, it is the value of the firm plus the cost of the inputs. We therefore know the costs of the K securities $\mathbf{z}_k$. The securities may be linearly dependent, so that one can be written as a linear combination of others. If this is the case, we require that the v_k's be chosen so that the costs of the securities are mutually consistent; that is, the cost of a linear combination must equal the corresponding combination of costs, as discussed in Section 11.10. Now, if the $\mathbf{z}_k$'s are spanning and the v_k's are chosen so that the costs are mutually consistent, we can determine an implicit set of prices q_s, $s = 1, 2, \dots, S$, for elementary state-contingent claims that can be used to evaluate any uncertain outcome. In particular, the value of the production plan $(\mathbf{y}_{k0}, \mathbf{y}_{k1}, \ldots, \mathbf{y}_{kS})$, based on the prices q_s, $s = 1, 2, \ldots, S$, would be $v_k = \mathbf{p}_0 \cdot \mathbf{y}_{k0} + \sum_{s=1}^{S} q_s \mathbf{p}_s \cdot \mathbf{y}_{ks}$.

In this model firms are assumed to be price takers with respect to *all* prices, including the implied prices q_s, $s = 1, 2, \ldots, S$. Given these prices, firm k operates in such a way as to maximize its value $\mathbf{p}_0 \cdot \mathbf{y}_{k0} + \sum_{s=1}^{S} q_s \mathbf{p}_s \cdot \mathbf{y}_{ks}$. This is the fundamental operational assumption, replacing (but essentially equivalent to) profit maximization.

A combination $(\mathbf{X}^*, \mathbf{Y}^*, \mathbf{T}^*, \mathbf{p}^*, \mathbf{v}^*)$ is a *spanning equilibrium* if, in addition to the equilibrium conditions for the consumer and the market clearing conditions, the set of corresponding $\mathbf{z}_k^*$'s is spanning and if $\mathbf{y}_k^* \in \mathcal{Y}_k$ maximizes value as computed from the corresponding q_s^*'s. In equilibrium,

$$v_k^* = \mathbf{p}_0^* \cdot \mathbf{y}_{k0}^* + \sum_{s=1}^{S} q_s^* \mathbf{p}_s^* \cdot \mathbf{y}_{ks}^* .$$

The allocation resulting from a spanning equilibrium of this two-period model is identical to that obtained with a complete market of contingent commodities. An intuitive way to see this is the following. Begin with a complete market of state-contingent commodities. Now use the construct of Section 11.9 to implement this equilibrium with a two-stage process: a market for elementary state-contingent claims exists in the first stage, followed by a spot market for commodities in the second stage. Next replace the elementary state-contingent claims by securities on the firms themselves. This is possible because these securities span the securities space. The resulting allocation will be identical to the first one. Furthermore, it is not hard to see that this argument can be reversed, starting with an equilibrium for the two-period model with securities on firms and ending with the complete market equilibrium.

One consequence of the above model is that a proper objective of the firm in situations of uncertainty is maximization of firm value as determined by the securities market. If the spanning assumption holds, all stockholders will unanimously approve this criterion, and the result will be Pareto efficient.

If the spanning assumption does not hold, the situation is far more complex. The problem takes on a game theoretic character, since stockholders might not agree on the criterion. Of course, a lack of spanning by stocks can be remedied by the introduction of additional financial instruments that fill out other dimensions, and indeed, in reality, additional financial instruments do seem to be introduced to move toward this objective.

11.13 Multiperiod Models

Economies lasting more than two periods can be treated by extending the techniques used in the previous section. The starting point for such an extension is a description of how uncertainty unfolds. One such description

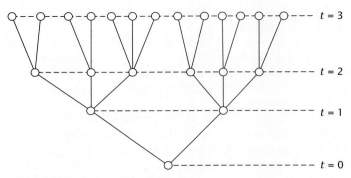

FIGURE 11.9   Uncertainty tree.

is based on an *uncertainty tree*, which shows explicitly how events occur sequentially or how information about the state is revealed. Such a tree is shown in Fig. 11.9 for four time periods including the initial period. The nodes at the top of the tree are states, which are revealed at the final time. Initially it is possible for any state to ultimately occur. At each new time period, the economy progresses upward along a branch of the tree to a node at the next level, limiting the set of states ultimately attainable. We suppose that physical commodities are available for purchase in every node.

The state-contingent commodities framework can be applied to this system. Each commodity is defined by its type and the node in the tree with which it is associated. A complete market would consist of contingent-claim markets for all these commodities. Clearly, the number of such markets required for completeness can be quite large, easily growing geometrically with the number of periods. Suppose, for example, there are T periods, from each node two nodes can occur in the next period, and there are m basic commodity types. Then the total number of markets required for completeness is $m(2^T - 1)$.

Suppose instead that security markets are introduced at each node as in Section 11.9 for the two-period model. Upon reaching any given node, consumers may purchase elementary contingent claims for the nodes that can possibly be reached at the next period. Then, once the next node is determined, consumers cash in the claims and purchase both commodities in the spot market and elementary claims for the following period. The same kind of reasoning used for the two-period model shows that all the relevant degrees of economic freedom inherent in a complete market are preserved by this system, but with fewer total markets. In the case above, for example, only $(m + 2)T - 2$ markets are required.

The number of different securities can be reduced even further by establishing claims contingent on the final state. These securities can be retraded at each time period. Furthermore, under appropriate spanning assumptions, securities of firms can be used in place of these elementary state-contingent claims.

11.14 Exercises

1. (Are uncertain prices preferred?) Suppose there are S states of the world, and state-contingent claims for a single real commodity can be purchased. A consumer has income r and a preference ordering that is symmetric among the S possible claims. That is, the consumer is always indifferent to an interchange of the payoffs of two states. (This would be true, for example, if the consumer used an expected-value utility function with equal state probabilities.) Consider two situations:

(*i*) The prices for state-contingent claims are all equal to a value p.

(*ii*) There are separate prices q_s, $s = 1, 2, \ldots, S$, but the expected value of these prices is equal to p; that is, $p = (1/S) \sum_{s=1}^{S} q_s$.
Which of these situations will the consumer prefer?

2. Reduce the compound lottery shown in Fig. 11.10 to an elementary lottery.

3. (Certain equivalent) Consider a lottery over S states with monetary payoffs. An individual evaluates this lottery with an expected-value utility function u. The *certain equivalent* of the lottery is the payoff amount that if received with certainty would be equivalent to the lottery. Specifically, if the probabilities and payoffs are π_s and y_s, respectively, for $s = 1, 2, \ldots, S$, the certain equivalent is the number x satisfying $u(x) = \sum_{s=1}^{S} \pi_s u(y_s)$. Show that if the individual is risk averse then $x \leq \sum_{s=1}^{S} \pi_s y_s$. That is, x is less than or equal to the expected value of the lottery.

4. (Kelly rule of betting) Assume that a gambler has an expected-value utility function based on the logarithm of wealth and that his current wealth is X_0. He has the opportunity to bet on a proposition that has a probability p of returning double his bet and $(1 - p)$ of returning nothing. What fraction of X_0 should be bet on this proposition?

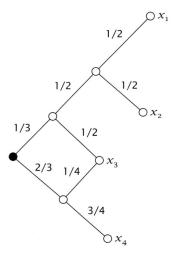

FIGURE 11.10

5. Two individuals each have the expected-value utility function $u(x) = -e^{-x}$. They disagree on the (subjective) probability of occurrence of a certain event E. Individual A believes that the probability of E is α, and B believes it is β. They are related by $\alpha > \beta$. The two decide to form a wager with odds $p : 1$ that the event E will occur. That is, an individual who takes one unit of this bet on the side of E will win 1 unit (net) if E occurs and lose p units if E does not occur. Assuming that p is set to clear the market, what is p and how much is bet?

6. An individual with an expected-value utility function has *constant relative risk aversion* if

$$\frac{u''(x)}{u'(x)} = \frac{-r}{x}.$$

   Find the forms of u satisfying this condition. Hint: Be sure to consider $u(x) = \ln(x)$.

7. A decision maker has expected-value utility function $\sum_{s=1}^{S} p_s u(x_s)$ with $\sum_{s=1}^{S} p_s = 1$, $p_s \geq 0$. Let $\mathbf{z} \in \mathcal{R}^S$ satisfy $\sum_{s=1}^{S} p_s z_s = 0$ and $\sum_{s=1}^{S} p_s z_s^2 = 1$. For the certainty point $\mathbf{x}_0 = (x_0, x_0, \ldots, x_0)$ let $u^0 = u(x_0)$ and define $b(\alpha) = b(\mathbf{x}_0 + \alpha \mathbf{z}, u^0)$ where the function on the right is the certainty benefit. Show that $-b''(0)$ is equal to the Arrow-Pratt risk aversion coefficient, independent of the direction of $\mathbf{z}$.

8. Consider a consumer facing uncertainty. There are $m = 2$ commodities and $S = 2$ states. Let $x_j(s)$ denote the consumption of commodity j in state s. If state s occurs, the consumer has utility function

$$u_s(\mathbf{x}) = x_1(s)^{\alpha_s} x_2(s)^{1-\alpha_s}$$

   for $s = 1, 2$. The consumer's utility for state-contingent commodities is

$$U\big(\mathbf{x}(1), \mathbf{x}(2)\big) = \beta \ln u_1\big(\mathbf{x}(1)\big) + (1 - \beta) \ln u_2\big(\mathbf{x}(2)\big).$$

   Assume that the consumer has initial income Y, which can be allocated to elementary security claims. A spot market for the two physical commodities opens after the state is revealed.

   Given the prices q_1 and q_2 of elementary state-contingent claims and spot prices $p_1(s)$ and $p_2(s)$ of commodities in state s, find

   (a) The amount of each elementary claim the consumer will purchase before the uncertainty is resolved.

   (b) The amounts of commodities purchased in the spot market, depending on the state.

9. Apply the theorem on multiple constraints (Section 5.9) to the consumer's choice problem of Section 11.12 to obtain an alternative interpretation of q_s, $s = 1, 2, \ldots, S$. Note that this theorem can be applied even if $K < S$ but that then the q_s's may differ among individuals.

10. (Prices as probabilities) Consider an exchange economy with a single (representative) consumer who has an expected-value utility function $U = \sum_{s=1}^{S} \pi_s u(\mathbf{x}_s)$, where π_s is the probability that state s will occur.

Assume u is concave. The consumer has endowment $\mathbf{w}$ in every state. Show that the elementary security prices are $q_s = \pi_s$, $s = 1, 2, \ldots, S$.

11. (Prices as average probabilities) Suppose in the security-markets economy of Section 11.9 consumer i has utility function $U_i(\mathbf{x}_1, \mathbf{x}_2, \ldots, \mathbf{x}_S) = \sum_{s=1}^{S} \pi_{is} u(\mathbf{x}_{is})$ and endowment $\beta_i \mathbf{w}$ in each state s. For each i, $\sum_{s=1}^{S} \pi_{is} = 1$. The (homothetic) function u, which is common to all individuals, satisfies $u(t\mathbf{x}) = \log t + u(\mathbf{x})$ for all $t > 0$ (the logarithmic form of a Cobb-Douglas utility, for example). We also have $\sum_{i=1}^{n} \beta_i = 1$. Suppose there is a $\mathbf{p}^* > \mathbf{0}$ such that the unique solution to

$$\max\ u(\mathbf{x})$$
$$\text{sub to } \mathbf{p}^* \cdot \mathbf{x} = 1$$

is $\mathbf{x} = \mathbf{w}$. Show that the equilibrium state-contingent security prices are

$$q_s = \sum_{i=1}^{n} \beta_i \pi_{is}$$

and hence these prices are a weighted average of the (implicit) probabilities used by the individuals.

12. (Expected present benefit) Consider a two-period situation and a consumer who has the expected-value utility function

$$U = u_0(\mathbf{x}_0) + \pi_1 u_1(\mathbf{x}_1) + \pi_2 u_2(\mathbf{x}_2) + \cdots + \pi_S u_S(\mathbf{x}_S).$$

The π's are probabilities, and u is concave. Let $\mathbf{g} \in R_+^m$, $\mathbf{g} \neq \mathbf{0}$, be a commodity bundle from period 0. Define the standard benefit function

$$b(\mathbf{x}, U) = \max\{\beta : u_0(\mathbf{x}_0 - \beta \mathbf{g}) + \sum_{s=1}^{S} u(\mathbf{x}_s) \geq U\}.$$

Also define the state-contingent benefit function

$$\beta(\mathbf{x}_0, \mathbf{x}_s, u) = \max\{u_0(\mathbf{x}_0 - \beta \mathbf{g}) + u(\mathbf{x}_s) \geq u\}.$$

The *expected present benefit* is

$$\hat{b}(\mathbf{x}, u_1, u_2, \cdots, u_S) = \sum_{s=1}^{S} \pi_s \beta(\mathbf{x}_0, \mathbf{x}_s, u_s).$$

(a) Show that

$$b(\mathbf{x}, U) \geq \hat{b}(\mathbf{x}, u_1, u_2, \cdots, u_S).$$

(b) Show that if $\mathbf{x}^* = (\mathbf{x}_0^*, \mathbf{x}_1^*, \mathbf{x}_2^*, \cdots, \mathbf{x}_S^*)$ solves the consumer's problem, then $\mathbf{x}^*$ is zero-maximal for the expected present benefit subject to the consumer's budget constraint.

(c) Apply the above to $U = x_0^{\alpha_0} + \sum_{s=1}^{S} \pi_s x_s^{\alpha_s}$.

13. Suppose there is a single physical commodity (like money) in a two-period model with S states in the final period. The corresponding financial commodities are $x_0, x_1, x_2, \ldots, x_S$. Suppose a consumer has utility function of the quasi-linear form $u(\mathbf{x}) = x_0 + \sum_{s=1}^{S} \pi_s u_s(x_s)$. Show that in this case the expected present benefit function is equal to the actual present benefit. (Refer to Exercise 12.)

14. (Pareto efficiency of spanning equilibrium) Consider a spanning equilibrium $(\mathbf{X}, \mathbf{Y}, \mathbf{T}, \mathbf{p}, \mathbf{v})$, and let q_s, $s = 1, 2, \ldots, S$, be the elementary state-contingent claim prices implied by $\mathbf{v}$. Let $R = \sum_{s=1}^{S} q_s$. Assume that each consumer i has a continuous, locally nonsatiated, weakly separable utility function u_i. Show directly that the spanning equilibrium is Pareto efficient by the following steps:

(a) Write the $S + 1$ budget constraints for consumer i.

(b) Without loss of generality assume that $K = S$, and eliminate the K variables t_{ik}, $k = 1, 2, \ldots, K$, from the budget constraints, leaving one constraint. (Hint: Multiply the sth equation in (a) by q_s and sum the resulting equations.)

(c) Complete the proof by following the standard method for the First Theorem of Welfare Economics.

15. (Incomplete markets example) Consider an economy with $n = 2$ consumers, $m = 1$ commodity, $S = 2$ states, and $K = 1$ firm. A consumption plan is $\mathbf{x} = (x_0, x_1(1), x_1(2))$. Here x_0 denotes initial consumption of an individual and $x_1(s)$, $s = 1, 2$, denotes final-period consumption in state s. The two utility functions are

$$u_i(\mathbf{x}) = \ln(x_0) + \tfrac{1}{2}\ln\left(x_1(1)\right) + \tfrac{1}{2}\ln\left(x_1(2)\right).$$

We assume endowment $\mathbf{w}_i = (1, 0, 0)$ and ownership fraction $\theta_i = \tfrac{1}{2}$ for $i = 1, 2$. The production possibility set of an independent firm is

$$\mathcal{Y} = \left\{\mathbf{y} = \left(y_0, y_1(1), y_1(2)\right) : y_0 \leq 0, \ \mathbf{y}_1 \geq \mathbf{0}, \ \mathbf{y}_1 \cdot \mathbf{y}_1 \leq -y_0\right\},$$

where $\mathbf{y}_1 = (y_1(1), y_1(2))$. Consumers are allowed to participate in spot markets for the commodity and in a market for stock of the firm. Note, however, that $K < S$ and hence the set of markets is incomplete. Set state prices $\mathbf{q} = (1, 1)$ and normalize spot prices by $p_0 = 1$. Show that there is a (nonunique) equilibrium for this economy. Hint: The solution has $\mathbf{p}_1 \cdot \mathbf{p}_1 = \tfrac{8}{3}$.

11.15   References

11.1–11.2   The states-of-the-world approach to uncertainty in economics was developed by Arrow (1953). For good textbook discussions, see Hirshleifer (1970) and Malinvaud (1985).

11.3–11.5   Expected utility theory traces back to Bernoulli (1738). The first axiomatic development of the theory was that of von Neumann and Morgenstern (1944). The proof given in this section is based on Herstein and Milnor (1953). The equivalence of risk aversion for the two approaches to uncertainty was shown by Arrow (1964) for the special case of $p = \tfrac{1}{2}$. The result can actually be generalized to $U(\mathbf{x}_1, \mathbf{x}_2, \ldots, \mathbf{x}_n) = \sum_{i=1}^{n} u_i(\mathbf{x}_i)$. In this case if U is quasi-concave, each of the u_i's, *except possibly one*, must be quasi-concave. For a full study and history of this result see Debreu and Koopmans (1982) and Crouzeix and Lindberg (1986); also see Yaari (1977). For good textbook presentations of expected utility theory, see Kreps (1988) and Hirshleifer and Riley (1992).

11.6-11.7 The relation of subjective probabilities to the tangents of indifference curves is discussed in Yaari (1969). Justification for the use of expected utility with subjective probabilities was developed axiomatically by Savage (1954). The simplified approach of this section was inspired largely by Arrow (1974). See also Drèze (1987) and Luce and Raiffa (1957). For an overview see Machina (1987).

11.8-11.9 The basic idea of incorporating uncertainty with state-contingent claims goes back to Arrow (1953, 1964). See also Debreu (1959). Arrow (1953, 1964) showed that securities markets could be used to reduce the number of markets actually required, starting a long chain of research on markets and uncertainty. For recent work concerned with incomplete markets for uncertainty, see Chae (1988), Cass and Shell (1983), Hart (1975), Green (1977), and Geanakoplos (1990).

11.12 For a survey of models of firm behavior under uncertainty, see Neilsen (1974).

11.13 For multiperiod theory see Duffie (1984).

11.14 Exercise 15 is an example from Duffie and Shafer (1986).

Chapter 12
INFORMATION AND ECONOMICS

Information is closely related to uncertainty. Indeed, roughly speaking, information is what determines the degree of uncertainty one has about an event. For example, today's weather report is information that influences our uncertainty about tomorrow's weather.

Information also provides a framework for explaining how uncertainty changes over time and why different individuals may view a given uncertain situation differently. Important economic issues arise from information changes and from differences in information among individuals, and such issues constitute one of the deepest and most complex parts of microeconomics. This chapter is intended only to be an introduction to this important subject.

12.1 Information Structures

The concept of information can be easily described using the state description of uncertainty. Suppose that there is a set of possible states $\Omega = \{1, 2, \ldots, S\}$. An *information set* H is a subset of Ω. Such a subset represents the specific information held by an individual in the sense that "knowledge of H" means that it is known that the true state lies in H. Hence, for example, $H = \Omega$ represents lack of additional information, since knowledge of H implies only that the true state s is in Ω. At the other extreme, if $H = \{1\}$, knowledge of H implies that the state is $s = 1$. If two information sets H_1 and H_2 satisfy the relation $H_1 \subset H_2$ (with strict containment), we say that H_1 has more information than H_2 or, alternatively, that H_1 is more precise than H_2. This general description is consistent with the notion of information sets introduced in Chapter 8 in the context of games in extensive form.

An *information structure* is a collection of subsets forming a partition of Ω. That is, an information structure is a collection of subsets $H_1, H_2, \ldots, H_m$ that are mutually disjoint but whose union is Ω. An individual with this

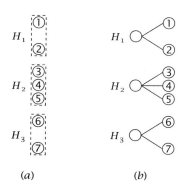

(a) (b)

FIGURE 12.1 Two graphical descriptions of information structures.

information structure knows in which set H_j the true state belongs. For example, if individual A knows B's information structure, A knows the partition $H_1, H_2, \ldots, H_m$, but A does not know which particular information set H_j it is that B knows. (That is, A knows that B knows that the state is in some particular H_j—B knows j, but A does not.) *Perfect information* is the information structure corresponding to the partition $\{1\}, \{2\}, \ldots, \{S\}$. In this case knowledge of which information set in the partition contains the state is equivalent to knowing the state itself. At the other extreme, complete *lack* of information corresponds to the partition Ω consisting of Ω alone, for it is known only that the true state is in Ω.

One information structure is considered to have more information than another if the partition of the first is a refinement of the second, that is, if every set in the partition of the first information structure is a subset of a set of the second (with at least one instance of a strict subset).

An information structure can be represented graphically in two different ways, as shown in Fig. 12.1. In this figure the possible states of nature are represented by a set of S nodes. A partition defining an information structure can be represented by enclosing nodes with dashed lines, as in (a), or alternatively by forming a kind of *super node* that is connected to a set of individual state nodes, as in (b).

Information is often revealed sequentially, in a series of stages. The resulting information flow is captured by a sequence of information structures, that is, by a sequence of partitions. If no information is lost or forgotten as time progresses, the information at one stage is at least as informative as that at the previous stage. This means that the partition at one stage is at least as fine as that at a previous stage. An information structure for a sequential situation can be represented graphically by a tree network as shown in Fig. 12.2. In this figure the initial position, represented by the extreme left node, corresponds to complete lack of information, since it is connected to all final nodes. At the second stage it will be known which of the two next nodes applies, and therefore it will be known whether the state is among the upper half or the lower half of those represented by the final nodes. At the last stage we use the dashed-line representation for

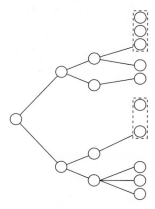

FIGURE 12.2   A sequential information structure.

the partition defining the information structure there. This structure is, of course, identical to that of uncertainty trees used in Section 11.13.

Signals and Information

Information about an uncertain event is often obtained by observing the value of some associated variable. For example, if you were inside a closed office and could not directly observe the weather outside, a report of the outside temperature would give you some information about that weather. You could, for instance, probably improve your estimate of whether or not it was snowing outside. Such information-revealing observations are termed *signals*.

Signals can be easily incorporated into the general information framework. For instance, we could formalize the weather example by first defining several possible weather states. These states would not be just the trivial two states *snowing* and *not snowing,* but would include states corresponding to various combinations of snow conditions and temperature. We might decide on about one hundred possible states. Then when a particular temperature was reported, we could run down our list of states and see which ones have this temperature as a component, thereby obtaining a specific information set corresponding to that report. If we did this separately for every temperature value that might be reported, the collection of sets obtained would represent the information structure corresponding to a temperature report. In this fashion, signals (that is, observations of specific variables) generally convey information and accordingly define information structures.

Probability

If a probability distribution is attributed to the set of possible states of nature, additional information has the effect of changing these probabilities.

Suppose originally there is probability p_s associated with state s, $s = 1, 2, \ldots, S$. Suppose later it becomes known that the true state is in the information set $H \subset \Omega$. The new probabilities are found by simply renormalizing those in H so that they sum to 1. Hence the new probabilities are

$$p'_s = \begin{cases} p_s / \sum_{j \in H} p_j, & s \in H \\ 0 & s \notin H. \end{cases}$$

12.2   Information and Economic Structure

We now examine how the information model presented above is incorporated into the standard framework of economics. In particular, we examine how information is related to individual preferences, to markets, and to individual decision making.

Information and Preferences

In Section 11.8 we pointed out the importance of weak independence of preferences for state-contingent commodities. We extend that discussion here.

Consider the situation depicted in Fig. 12.3a, where a consumer faces uncertainty defined by S states (with $S = 5$ in the figure). The consumer selects a vector $\mathbf{x}_0$ representing current consumption, at the initial time 0, or more generally representing some action that the consumer can take at time 0. In addition, the consumer may select a set of state-contingent commodity levels $\mathbf{x}_s$ for each state $s = 1, 2, \ldots, S$. The choices of $\mathbf{x}_0, \mathbf{x}_1, \mathbf{x}_2, \ldots, \mathbf{x}_S$ are restricted by a budget or other constraint.

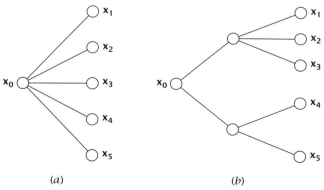

(a)   (b)

FIGURE 12.3   The consumer faces uncertainty.

By the weak independence argument, a consumer's preferences must have the form $U(\mathbf{x}_0, u_1(\mathbf{x}_1), u_2(\mathbf{x}_2), \ldots, u_S(\mathbf{x}_S))$. This implies that the preference ordering for bundles in state s is independent of the ordering of bundles in any other state t. However, we can take the argument a step further. We recognize that if state s occurs, the enjoyment received depends only on $\mathbf{x}_0$ and $\mathbf{x}_s$, so it is the composite $(\mathbf{x}_0, \mathbf{x}_s)$ that represents the true overall bundle if state s occurs. We can then hypothesize that the consumer's ranking of $(\mathbf{x}_0, \mathbf{x}_s)$ is independent of the $(\mathbf{x}_0, \mathbf{x}_t)$. This hypothesis implies that utility takes the form

$$U = U(u_1(\mathbf{x}_0, \mathbf{x}_1), u_2(\mathbf{x}_0, \mathbf{x}_2), \ldots, u_S(\mathbf{x}_0, \mathbf{x}_S)).$$

Next consider the situation shown in Fig. 12.3b, where there is an intermediate information structure. How should the consumer evaluate his or her situation at the intermediate stage? If the consumer is in the top information set, then he or she knows only that the bundle for that set is $(\mathbf{x}_0, \mathbf{x}_1, \mathbf{x}_2, \mathbf{x}_3)$. The consumer may feel that the ordering of this bundle is independent of the bundle that would be obtained in the other information sets. This requirement puts further restrictions on the form of the utility function. In the case shown it implies that the utility must have the form

$$U = U\{f_1(u_1(\mathbf{x}_0, \mathbf{x}_1), u_2(\mathbf{x}_0, \mathbf{x}_2), u_3(\mathbf{x}_0, \mathbf{x}_3)), f_2(u_4(\mathbf{x}_0, \mathbf{x}_4), u_5(\mathbf{x}_0, \mathbf{x}_5))\}.$$

If this argument is extended fully, we would hypothesize that the preference ordering should have the independence property for every conceivable intermediate information structure, so that preferences make sense at any stage. This requirement is precisely equivalent to the definition of strong independence of preferences given in Section 4.6. Hence, under the assumptions of that section we find that utility can be written in the strongly separable form

$$U = u_1(\mathbf{x}_0, \mathbf{x}_1) + u_2(\mathbf{x}_0, \mathbf{x}_2) + \cdots + u_S(\mathbf{x}_0, \mathbf{x}_S).$$

A very important special case, of course, is the expected-value form

$$U = \pi_1 u(\mathbf{x}_0, \mathbf{x}_1) + \pi_2 u(\mathbf{x}_0, \mathbf{x}_2) + \cdots + \pi_S u(\mathbf{x}_0, \mathbf{x}_S),$$

where the π_s's are probabilities.

Information and Markets

When we consider more than a single consumer, we find a strong connection between markets and the value of information. As a concrete example, suppose that consumers A and B each have a chance to win $1,000. The prize will go to either A or B. Hence there are two states s_A and s_B. At stage 0 a market may develop between A and B for contingent claims. For example, they may agree to split the prize equally no matter who wins. Both A and B prefer this to the original situation, where the prize will go entirely to one or the other.

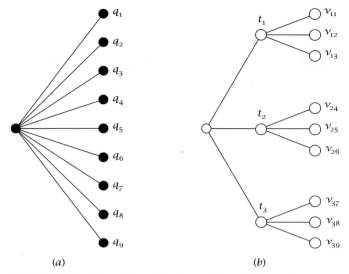

(a) (b)

FIGURE 12.4   The effect of intermediate information.

Now suppose information is revealed early, before the participants have an opportunity to agree on a sharing rule. A and B know who wins before the market is established. There is then no incentive for the market to develop later. If it is known that A wins, A will not give away half of the prize. If we back up and evaluate the situation just before the winner is revealed and know that a market will not be formed, both individuals are worse off than they would be if a market did form. This shows that there are strong incentives for markets to develop before information is revealed.

Next we show how information serves to reduce the requirements for markets. Consider the situations shown in Fig. 12.4a and 12.4b. In Fig. 12.4a there are nine states and nine markets—therefore there is a complete set of markets. Suppose the prices for state contingent claims, paying \$1, are q_s, $s = 1, 2, \ldots, 9$. An individual will allocate an initial income of r among these claims, purchasing r_s units of the contingent claim s. This allocation must satisfy

$$\sum_{s=1}^{9} q_s r_s = r.$$

Next, consider Fig. 12.4b. This figure represents an alternative pattern of information structure, whereby some information about the nine states is revealed at an intermediate point. In this example there are three information sets, each containing three states. It is quite likely that markets will develop for claims contingent on these three sets. We denote the prices of claims by t_1, t_2, and t_3. After the true intermediate information set is revealed, new markets will develop for claims contingent on the states within the information set. There will again be three markets for each information set. We denote the corresponding prices by v_{is} where i indexes the information sets and s indexes the state within an information set.

We set the prices as follows:

$$t_i = \sum_{s \in H_i} q_s .$$

This means that we set the price of a claim to information set H_i equal to the sum of the original prices for claims to states in that set.

We set the prices in the subsequent market equal to

$$v_{is} = \frac{q_s}{t_i} .$$

Note that, overall, the price for a claim to state s in information set H_i is $t_i v_{is} = q_s$, as before. (We can scale all prices t_i by a factor $\alpha > 0$ and all prices v_{is} by $1/\alpha$.)

The consumer can do exactly the same thing with either market structure. For example, the consumer can purchase x_i units of a claim contingent on information set H_i, defined by

$$x_i = \sum_{s \in H_i} \frac{q_s r_s}{t_i} .$$

This satisfies the budget constraint because

$$\sum_{i=1}^{3} t_i x_i = \sum_{s=1}^{9} q_s r_s = r .$$

Subsequently the consumer can purchase r_s units of a claim contingent on state s that is in H_i. This satisfies the budget constraint at the intermediate point because

$$\sum_{s \in H_i} r_s v_{is} = \sum_{s \in H_i} \frac{r_s q_s}{t_i} = x_i .$$

If state s occurs, the consumer will have r_s dollars, just as in the original situation.

In our example the total number of markets required by the two-stage process is only six—three at each stage. This compares with nine in the original situation. Thus the presence of intermediate information reduces the number of markets required. It may seem that the reduction in the number of markets is relatively modest. In fact, however, if additional stages are added, the result can be dramatic. For example, a billion states can be treated completely with only 60 markets! (See Exercise 3.)

Information and Action

Individuals facing uncertainty usually want to incorporate all available information into their decision process. This means that an individual's action is a function of his or her information set. However, allowing action to depend on information leads to tremendous complexity, since different individuals may have different information structures. Suppose individual A observes an information set H in A's information structure. If A's action depends on H, other agents may be able to infer something about H from observation of A's action. Therefore, the information sets available to these other agents depend, through observation of actions, on A's information set. Hence, B's information structure is influenced by A's action, and similarly, A's information structure is influenced by B's action. This phenomenon takes us into a realm of game theory far deeper than anything treated earlier. Indeed, such issues pierce the very edge of current research in microeconomics and game theory. The remainder of this chapter addresses this important issue through examination of examples and special cases.

12.3 Adverse Selection

An important example of asymmetric information is the problem termed *adverse selection*, illustrated classically by the insurance market. As a specific example, consider the market for health insurance. Suppose there is an average health risk in the general population, but the risk differs among individuals. Furthermore, suppose individuals have better information about their own risk class than can be determined by an insurance company. What would happen if a company were to offer insurance at a price designed to break even at the average risk? Those who were in low-risk groups would not purchase the insurance, but those in high-risk groups would. Hence, the average risk in the pool of individuals actually insured would be higher than the average risk of the general population, and as a consequence, the insurance company would lose money. Individuals *select* insurance, and this self-selection is *adverse* to the insurance company. It is clear that the equilibrium price in such a market must be higher than the cost implied by the average population risk, and this implies a lack of efficiency in the insurance market.

The problem of adverse selection can be cast into the information framework of the previous section by use of the graph shown in Fig. 12.5. In

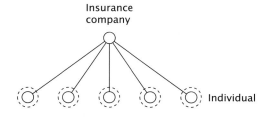

FIGURE 12.5 Information structures for adverse selection.

this figure the states correspond to the different risk classes. The insurance company, when dealing with a particular individual, has no additional information, so its information set is the trivial partition consisting of the single set of all possible states. On the other hand, the information structure of an individual is the fine partition consisting of the separate states. Each individual knows the state exactly.

In general, adverse selection describes a situation where the agents have different information *before* market participation. In the case of insurance, for example, the company and its potential customers have different information before a contract is signed.

Equilibrium

When individuals have different information sets and their decisions interact, the usual process of equilibrium formation can be upset. This is a general theme of this chapter, and the adverse selection situation is a simple illustration of this theme.

To make things concrete, we consider a case where all individuals have equal initial wealth W and identical preferences for wealth. Additionally, rather than a health risk, we assume that all individuals face a strict financial risk: starting with wealth W, they either lose an amount x (which is fixed and identical for all individuals) or lose nothing. Hence, with no insurance, an individual faces two states of wealth: in the first (corresponding to no loss) it is $W_1 = W$, and in the second it is $W_2 = W - x$.

We consider an insurance contract having fixed coverage y and premium h. With this contract the individual will have wealth in the two states of

$$W_1 = W - h, \qquad W_2 = W - h - x + y.$$

Now first, as a point of reference, we assume that all individuals face the same probability of loss, say p. In this case the profit π to an insurance company offering a contract of the form defined above is

$$\pi = p(h - y) + (1 - p)h,$$

where we are neglecting administrative costs and assuming that the law of large numbers is operative so that exactly a fraction p of individuals will incur loss. In a perfectly competitive market with constant returns to scale, as in this industry, the profit must be zero. Hence, we find that $h = py$, which means that the premium exactly equals the expected value of what will be paid back.

Now consider this contract from the viewpoint of a typical individual. The individual's indifference curve over the two states is shown in Fig. 12.6. Without insurance the individual is at the point A in the figure. Purchase of an insurance contract corresponds to movement up a line defined by its price to a point B. If insurance is priced fairly, this line is called the *fair odds*

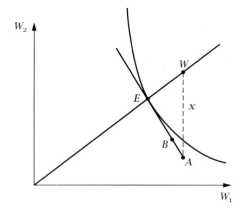

FIGURE 12.6 Equilibrium in insurance market.

line. It will be tangent to an indifference curve at the certainty ray. (The indifference curve must be tangent to the fair odds line or the individual would accept small bets that are unfavorable; see Section 11.6.) Assuming convex preferences, the most preferred level of coverage is at the point E, corresponding to full coverage. In this case, the full-coverage contract is in fact a competitive equilibrium. There is no other contract earning nonnegative profits that is preferred by all individuals.

Now let us relax the assumption that all individuals face the same risk. In particular, let us assume that there are two types of individuals: a fraction λ have a relatively *high* probability p_H of loss and a fraction $(1 - \lambda)$ have a relatively low probability p_L of loss. The potential loss in either case is x, as before. We assume that $p_L < p_H$ and refer to those in the first group as type H (for high risk) and those in the second group as type L (for low risk).

There are potentially two types of equilibria in this market: *pooling equilibria,* in which both types buy the same contract, and *separating equilibria,* in which the two types buy different contracts. We first explore the feasibility of a pooling equilibrium. If everyone purchases the same amount of insurance, the aggregate probability of loss as seen by an insurance company is $\bar{p} = \lambda p_H + (1 - \lambda)p_L$. Hence the condition of zero profit means that the premium h and the coverage y are related by $h = \bar{p}y$. Equivalently, the contract must lie on the line of slope $-(1 - \bar{p})/\bar{p}$ through the original point A, as shown in Fig. 12.7*a.*

We denote by D an arbitrary point on the fair odds line, and we shall test whether it is an equilibrium. We construct the indifference curves of H and L that pass through the point. (These have the relative slopes at the 45° line shown: L is steeper, and H is less steep than the fair odds line.) If the situation is like that of Fig. 12.7*a,* D cannot be a pooling equilibrium because L would prefer to move to a point like B, or even A. On the other hand, if the situation is like that of Fig. 12.7*b,* D is a pooling equilibrium if the insurance company offers only D. This is likely to occur only if the

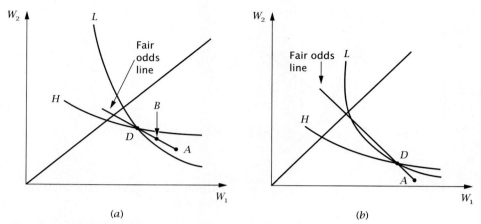

(a)   (b)

FIGURE 12.7   Possibility of a pooling equilibrium.

potential loss is very extreme and the company offers a small amount of insurance.

Now let us explore the feasibility of a separating equilibrium consisting of two contracts, each purchased by a different group. In this case, the zero-profit condition can be maintained if the two contracts each lie on the corresponding fair-odds line through the initial point A. Each type would like to be at the intersection of the respective line and the 45° line, namely, the points B and C in Fig. 12.8. However, if these two contracts were offered, both types would choose point C, producing negative profits to the insurance companies. Hence, the contract designed for the type L individuals must be moved down the fair-odds line to a point where the type H individuals would not shift from B. The appropriate point is shown as D in the figure, which is where the type H indifference curve intersects the type

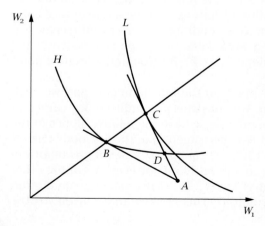

FIGURE 12.8 Separating equilibrium.

L fair odds line. If the contracts corresponding to B and D are offered, with type H selecting B and type L selecting D, then zero profits will be made and there is no incentive for switching. Furthermore, no other preferred pair of points on these fair odds lines are separating.

12.4 Market Signaling

Some of the difficulties associated with adverse selection situations can be overcome by the use of market signals. The signal takes the form of an action that has economic consequences, and observation of the action an agent takes may reveal information that is otherwise hidden. This, in turn, can lead to equilibria that separate classes of individuals.

An example is shown in Fig. 12.9. In part (a) of the figure two types of commodities are to be sold, but the types cannot be distinguished by buyers at the time of sale. The two commodity types might represent different quality grades of otherwise identical commodities (such as in a used-car market) or different productive capacities (as in a labor market). Since the two types cannot be distinguished before purchase, there can be only a single market.

Suppose now that certain actions of the sellers of the commodities can be observed by the buyers, and the costs of these actions depend on the commodity type. An owner of a used car might, for example, choose to have it certified by a mechanic before sale. The certification then serves as a signal and provides a means for partitioning the market. This is illustrated in Fig. 12.9b, where the c_{ij}'s denote the costs of different actions. If the costs are sufficiently different (for example, if certification were much more costly for a poor-quality car than for a good car), the partitioned market may have an equilibrium that separates the two types. In these figures, the seller has complete information and the buyer's information structure is denoted by the dashed lines around the information sets.

We shall explore the phenomenon of market signaling through study of a classic example in this area, which is based on a stylized model of a job

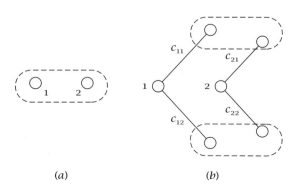

(a)   (b)

FIGURE 12.9 Market signals.

market. This example points out some of the possible results and difficulties associated with market signal equilibria.

Example 12.1 (Job market signaling).   Consider a labor market composed of two types of individuals: type L has low productivity, and type H has high productivity. There is a fraction q of type L and a fraction $(1 - q)$ of type H in the market. For specificity, we assume that productivity is measured by marginal product (that is, the net revenue generated by an additional employee), which is 1 for type L and 2 for type H. The average marginal product is then $q + 2(1 - q) = 2 - q$. If employers are unable to distinguish between types, then the equilibrium wage, paid to workers of both types, will be equal to this average marginal product.

Suppose now that workers are able to obtain education before entering the labor market. The total cost of education (including time, psychic energy, and direct costs) is different for the two types. For type L individuals, the cost of an amount y is $c_L = y$, while for type H individuals it is $c_H = \frac{1}{2}y$.

We now propose a two-level wage rate, and we shall see whether it yields a separating equilibrium. Specifically, suppose that employers select a critical level of education y^*. They pay a wage of 1 to employees with an educational level below y^*, and they pay a wage of 2 to employees with an educational level of y^* or above. Given this wage schedule, individuals will select that level of education that maximizes their net return: wage minus cost of education.

The solution to the individual's optimization problem can be deduced by inspection of Fig. 12.10. The cost curves for the two types are shown, together with the wage schedule. The wage schedule shown assumes that $1 \le y^* \le 2$. It can be easily seen that the maximum of wage minus cost is at $y = 0$ for type L individuals and at $y = y^*$ for type H individuals. It follows that this configuration represents a separating equilibrium.

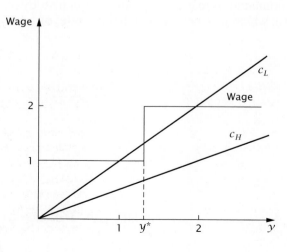

FIGURE   12.10   Signaling equilibrium.

Individuals have no incentive not to adhere to this separating policy; likewise, firms satisfy the zero profit condition since they are paying the marginal product to each employee. Note that the equilibrium is not unique in this case; any y^* satisfying $1 \leq y^* \leq 2$ yields an equilibrium.

The welfare properties of these equilibria are interesting. Note first that the type L individuals are worse off than before, since their wage has been reduced from the average marginal product of $2 - q$ to 1. Note also that the type H individuals are made worse off as y^* is increased, since their wage remains the same but their signaling costs increase. They may also, depending on q, be worse off than they were in the original pooled equilibrium. For example, if $q = \frac{1}{2}$ and $y^* > 1$, then their net wage is $2 - \frac{1}{2}y^* < \frac{3}{2}$. However, in the pooled equilibrium, their wage was $2 - q = \frac{3}{2}$. Producers make zero profit in both cases. This shows that it is possible for the signaling equilibrium to be worse for everyone than the equilibrium without signals. The reason, of course, is that in this model (unlike actual education!) signaling is costly and has no other productive value.

What makes signals work? Basically, if we have a single economic variable, such as labor or cars, it is impossible to form a separating equilibrium. Another variable is needed so that two states in an information set can be distinguished. An insurance policy has two natural variables, premium amount and coverage level, and therefore a separating equilibrium can be constructed. When there is originally only a single variable, a signal can serve as the required second variable.

*12.5 Information Equilibria

As can be imagined, no general equilibrium theorem exists for economies in which agents have arbitrary information structures and information can be deduced from other agents' actions or from prices. The situation is just too complex. However, there is an extension of the standard (Arrow-Debreu) general equilibrium framework that applies when the information structures are not influenced by market action. We present this result in this section. We do not give a formal theorem statement, but instead simply describe the general framework and illustrate it with an example.

Consider an exchange economy with S possible states of nature, m physical commodities, and n individuals. Initially, all individuals have the information structure consisting of all states together; that is, everyone believes that each of the S states is possible. Trading in contingent claims for commodities takes place at this initial stage, but this trade is subject to informational restrictions, discussed below.

The information structures are different at the next stage, with in fact each individual having his or her own information structure. Hence, at this stage, individuals still may not know the state exactly (they only know which of their information sets contains the state), and the individuals may have different information sets. At this stage, physical exchange takes place on the basis of the contingent claims already in force.

Different states may distinguish among individual endowments as well as external factors (such as weather, etc.), but we assume that individuals always know their own endowment in the second stage. That is, each individual's information structure is fine enough that his or her endowment is constant within each information set.

At the initial stage an individual develops a *consumption strategy*, which gives consumption as a function of the state. However, an individual's information structure restricts the form of this strategy. Consumption cannot vary within an information set, since at the second stage, states within this set are indistinguishable (and by definition must not become distinguishable through observation of one's own consumption). It follows that since endowment is also constant within an information set, the physical contingent claims (and actual physical trade) will likewise be constant over an information set—hence, the trade itself does not reveal information.

As in the standard contingent claims model, there are in principle mS contingent commodities in this economy (corresponding to m underlying physical commodities in each of the S states), but separate contracts for each may not actually be traded because of the information constraints. Each consumer selects an mS-dimensional vector of contingent commodities $\mathbf{x}_i = (\mathbf{x}_{i1}, \mathbf{x}_{i2}, \ldots, \mathbf{x}_{iS})$. However, based on the above discussion, $\mathbf{x}_i$ is not selected arbitrarily from $\mathcal{R}_+^{mS}$. Instead, it must be chosen from the set $\mathcal{X}_i$ which is the nonnegative part of the subspace of $\mathcal{R}^{mS}$ induced by the information structure. That is, $\mathbf{x}_{is} = \mathbf{x}_{is'}$ if s and s' are in the same information set. It is because $\mathcal{X}_i$ has this restricted form that the original (Arrow-Debreu) general equilibrium theorem cannot be applied to this economy.

Each individual is assumed to have a preference ordering over the set of consumption strategies. That is, each individual has a preference ordering $\succsim_i$ over the set $\mathcal{X}_i$. This ordering generalizes the concept of an ordering over state-contingent commodities. In a given case, it reflects basic preferences for the underlying commodities in each information set and also the perceived likelihood of these sets.

We can now give a rather straightforward extension of the standard definition of an equilibrium.

Equilibrium.   A *competitive equilibrium* for the economy with information is a pair $(\mathbf{X}^*, \mathbf{p}^*)$ where $\mathbf{X}^* = (\mathbf{x}_1^*, \mathbf{x}_2^*, \ldots, \mathbf{x}_n^*)$ is a vector of individual consumption choices and $\mathbf{p}^*$ is a price vector. These satisfy (for all $i = 1, 2, \ldots, n$)

(a) $\mathbf{x}_i^* \in \mathcal{X}_i$ (individual feasibility).

(b) $\mathbf{p} \cdot \mathbf{x}_i^* \leq \mathbf{p} \cdot \mathbf{w}_i$ (budget constraint).

(c) If $\mathbf{x}_i \in X_i$ and $\mathbf{x}_i \succ_i \mathbf{x}_i^*$, then $\mathbf{p}\cdot\mathbf{x}_i > \mathbf{p}\cdot\mathbf{w}_i$ (optimality).

(d) $\sum_{i=1}^n \mathbf{x}_{is}^* = \sum_{i=1}^n \mathbf{w}_{is}$ for all $s = 1, 2, \ldots, S$ (aggregate feasibility).

The dimension of commodity bundles and prices is mS, since trade involves contingent claims for physical commodities. Some collapsing of dimension may be possible (as illustrated in the example below) because of the restrictions on trade implied by the information structures.

It is possible to show that an equilibrium exists for this type of structure. However, a number of additional technical assumptions must be introduced. Rather than state the full theorem, we present an example that illustrates the nature of such equilibria and how the dimension can collapse.

Example 12.2. Suppose there are two consumers (A and B), two physical commodities, and two states. The endowments of the two physical commodities are shown in the table below.

state	A	B
1	(6,1)	(0,6)
2	(4,1)	(0,6)

Hence, the only difference between the states is A's endowment of the first commodity. We assume that in the second stage, A knows the state exactly (since one knows one's own endowment) but B cannot distinguish between the two states.

There are four contingent-claim commodities: two for each of the two states. The endowments of these can be written as the vectors

$$\mathbf{w}_A = (6, 1, 4, 1)$$
$$\mathbf{w}_B = (0, 6, 0, 6).$$

We assume that both individuals have utility function

$$u(\mathbf{x}) = x_1 x_2 x_3 x_4.$$

Individual A will, as is standard, maximize this subject to the relevant budget constraint. Individual B's maximization problem must have the additional constraints that $x_1 = x_3$ and $x_2 = x_4$.

We claim that an equilibrium price vector is $\mathbf{p} = (1, 1, 2, 1)$. To check this we use the standard formula for the demand function associated with a Cobb-Douglas utility function to compute the corresponding consumption choices

$$\mathbf{x}_A = (4, 4, 2, 4)$$
$$\mathbf{x}_B = (2, 3, 2, 3).$$

Markets clear because, as is easily checked,

$$\mathbf{x}_A + \mathbf{x}_B = \mathbf{w}_A + \mathbf{w}_B = (6, 7, 4, 7).$$

There are some interesting things to note about this equilibrium. First, although individual A has different consumption patterns in the two states, the actual amounts traded with B are identical. A sells two units of commodity 1 and buys three units of commodity 2 in both states. Hence, B cannot infer the actual state from the delivery of goods.

Second, as a consequence of the equality of trades, the original market for contingent claims can be restricted to *sure* contracts. The prices for sure delivery of the two commodities are $(p_1 + p_3) = 3$ and $(p_2 + p_4) = 2$, respectively. Only these two markets and these two prices are needed.

The market structure in such an information equilibrium does not always reduce to only sure contracts, but it typically does reduce to substantially fewer than a full system mS of contingent claims.

Although this framework for information equilibria is an interesting extension of the standard Arrow-Debreu framework, it does have some important limitations. It assumes that one individual cannot observe another's consumption choice, for such observations could convey information not represented by the given information structure. In reality, it is frequently possible to observe the actions of others, and in fact individuals often give information directly if it will help negotiate a trade. Such information violates the assumption of a fixed information structure.

Another problem arises if we relax the assumption that all contracts for trade are negotiated at the beginning. If spot markets are introduced after the information state is known, commodity prices in these markets may not be proportional to the corresponding (earlier) futures prices, and hence these new prices might reveal additional information. This again would violate the assumption of a fixed information structure, and equilibrium may not exist.

12.6   The Principal-Agent Problem

Another important issue in information economics is *moral hazard*. This arises when the reward to one party of a contract depends on the performance of another party, and that performance cannot be monitored. A classic example again occurs in the insurance industry. If a company insures a person against automobile theft, the company hopes that the individual will carry out activities that protect his car against theft, such as locking the car, parking it in a garage, and so forth. On the other hand, once the individual has obtained the insurance, he or she might relax his performance on such matters, thereby increasing the likelihood of theft. It is not practical for the insurance company to monitor the insured's performance, and hence the company faces a moral hazard.

In general, moral hazard represents a situation in which there is a difference of information *after* trading (or contract signing) but before the terms have been fulfilled. This contrasts with adverse selection, in which there is asymmetry of information before trading. The difference in information in a moral hazard problem is associated with control or levels of performance.

What one seeks in such situations is a method for designing contracts or terms of trade that carry incentives for desirable performance levels. These incentives must be indirect, in that they cannot be tied to the performance itself, which cannot be observed, but must be tied to outcomes that are indirectly influenced by performance. For example, in the case of automobile theft insurance, the company may offer a policy that pays only a portion of the replacement cost, so that the individual is still motivated to protect his or her car.

The *principal-agent problem* is a framework for analyzing situations characterized by an asymmetry of information and control and for designing suitable contracts. In this problem one party, the *principal*, is in control at the highest level. The principal can set the terms of communication and payment to the other party, who is the *agent* (or agents, if there are more than one). The agent performs actions and receives compensation according to the terms of a contract with the principal. An essential feature of the principal-agent problem is that the contract specifies compensation as a function of an outcome that can be objectively measured. The outcome is presumably influenced by the agent's actions, but the actions themselves cannot be measured. Hence, the terms of the contract only indirectly reflect action and accordingly can at best provide only indirect incentives to the agent.

There are numerous examples of principal-agent relationships. One example is an insurance company, which is the principal, and an automobile owner, who is the agent. A classic example used frequently in the literature is that of a farm owner, who is the principal, and a tenant farmer, who is the agent. The owner wishes to maximize the profit of the farm, but cannot manage or observe the detailed actions of the tenant farmer. The owner must therefore design a contract, possibly taking the form of a profit-sharing rule, that provides incentive to the tenant farmer and yields the maximum possible net profit to the owner.

Formulation

We formulate a simple, single-agent version of the principal-agent problem. In this version, the agent chooses an action a from the real interval $A = [\underline{a}, \overline{a}]$. The outcome can be any one of N alternatives, which are measured in monetary units. We let $X = \{x_1, x_2, \ldots, x_N\}$ denote these possible outcomes, and without loss of generality we assume that they are ordered from smallest to largest. There is a known probability $p_j(a)$ that outcome j occurs given that the action a is chosen.

The principal has an expected-value utility function over income r, defined by the concave utility function $u(r)$. Similarly, the agent has an expected-value utility function over income r and action a, defined by the function $v(r, a)$, where v is concave with respect to r.

A *contract* between the principal and the agent is a wage schedule $\mathbf{w} = (w_1, w_2, \ldots, w_N)$ with components being the amounts to be paid to the agent if the corresponding outcome occurs. We then compute

$$U(\mathbf{w}, a) = \sum_{j=1}^{N} p_j(a) u(x_j - w_j)$$

$$V(\mathbf{w}, a) = \sum_{j=1}^{N} p_j(a) v(w_j, a),$$

which are the expected utilities to the principal and the agent, respectively, if action a is taken under the contract $\mathbf{w}$.

Since the agent is not a captive of this situation, but rather is free to either accept or reject the contract, it is useful to define the quantity V^*, termed the agent's *reservation utility*. Any contract proposed by the principal will be accepted by the agent if and only if it guarantees the agent an expected utility level of at least this value. (This feature does not really need to be explicitly incorporated, since one could define a nonacceptance action that yields the zero outcome. However, it is often convenient to include the reservation utility constraint explicitly.)

A contract is optimal for the principle if it gives the agent utility of at least V^* and if there is no other such contract producing greater utility for the principal. Formally we have the following.

Principal-agent problem. A contract is optimal for the principal problem if it solves the following program

$$\max_{\mathbf{w}, a} U(\mathbf{w}, a)$$

$$\text{sub to } V(\mathbf{w}, a) \geq V^* \tag{12.1}$$

$$a \in \underset{a' \in A}{\operatorname{argmax}} V(\mathbf{w}, a').$$

Note that the last statement means that the value a solving the program must also solve the agent's problem of maximizing expected utility given the contract $\mathbf{w}$. This is termed the *incentive compatibility* constraint since it implies that the principal must account for the incentives of the agent when selecting a contract $\mathbf{w}$.

First-Order Approach

The incentive compatibility constraint really represents a family of constraints. It can be written as

$$V(\mathbf{w}, a) \geq V(\mathbf{w}, a') \quad \text{for all } a' \in [\underline{a}, \overline{a}].$$

If there were only a finite number of actions rather than a continuum, this family would reduce to a finite set, and the optimization problem (12.1) would be finite-dimensional. However, as formulated above, the problem has an infinite number of constraints.

The first-order approach replaces the argmax constraint by the corresponding first-order necessary condition for a maximum of the agent's problem. Hence, assuming an interior point solution to the agent's problem, the constraint in the principal's problem is replaced by

$$\frac{\partial}{\partial a} V(\mathbf{w}, a) = 0.$$

The principal's optimization problem is then finite-dimensional. This approach obviously has great appeal. If the solution is unique and interior, the first-order approach is indeed valid. However, if the optimal a is not unique, the first-order approach can lead to incorrect solutions.

Example 12.3 (Legal help).   Suppose you are suing someone for damages X that you suffered. You are planning to hire a lawyer, but you would like to make the lawyer's fee depend on the outcome of the case because you realize that once the lawyer is engaged, you face a moral hazard risk with respect to how much effort the lawyer devotes to your case. You decide to use the principal-agent framework to find the optimal fee schedule.

Assume that both you and the lawyer have identical exponential utilities for money

$$u(r) = -e^{-sr}.$$

You also both know that the probability of winning the case is

$$p(a) = \frac{a}{a+1},$$

where a is the time the lawyer devotes to the case. We assume that the lawyer values time at 1 monetary unit per unit of time.

Let w_1 and w_2 be the fee paid if the case is won or lost, respectively. You then formulate your problem as

$$\max_{a, w_1, w_2} \; p(a)u(X - w_1) + (1 - p(a))u(-w_2)$$
$$\text{sub to } \; p(a)u(w_1 - a) + (1 - p(a))u(w_2 - a) \geq u(0)$$
$$a \in \text{argmax} \, \{p(a)u(w_1 - a) + (1 - p(a))u(w_2 - a)\} \, .$$

Let us make a few observations about this formulation. First, the exponential utility function has the property that any baseline level of wealth factors out; therefore it is only necessary to consider incremental wealth levels without reference to a baseline. Second, since the lawyer's time is equivalent to money, the reservation value of utility is $u(0)$. The reservation constraint can be written equivalently as

$$p(a)u(w_1) + (1 - p(a))u(w_2) \geq u(a),$$

which says that the expected utility of the payments received must be at least equal to the opportunity value of the time devoted to the case.

Let $U_1 = u(w_1)$ and $U_2 = u(w_2)$. Using the specific forms for u and p and using the first-order approach to treat the incentive compatibility constraint, the original problem becomes

$$\max_{a,U_1,U_2} \frac{1}{a+1}\left[\frac{-au(X)}{U_1} + \frac{1}{U_2}\right]$$

$$\text{sub to } \frac{1}{a+1}[aU_1 + U_2] \geq -e^{-sa}$$

$$\frac{[(sa+1)(a+1) - a]U_1 + [s(a+1) - 1]U_2}{(a+1)^2} = 0.$$

This problem can be solved for U_1, U_2, and a and the results translated into w_1 and w_2. For large X, the solution will have $w_2 < 0$, which means that the lawyer should agree to *pay you* if he loses the case!

Example 12.4 (Moral hazard equilibrium).   The principal-agent concept can be used in equilibrium form when there are many competing principals. We illustrate this idea with the moral hazard problem in insurance.

Assume that an individual has wealth W and faces a potential loss of x if a certain event occurs (theft, for example). The individual can affect the probability of loss through expenditure z. Hence we write $p(z)$ for the probability of loss. We assume that $p'(z) < 0$, reflecting that the probability of loss decreases as z is increased. Now consider the insurance company as principal and the insured individual as agent. The insurance company proposes a premium schedule $h(y)$ giving the premium as a function of the level y of coverage. The individual responds by selecting the level of effort z and the coverage y.

If the individual purchases insurance in amount y for a premium cost of h, then that individual's expected utility is

$$V = p(z)v(W - z - x + y - h) + (1 - p(z))v(W - z - h),$$

or with $W_1 = W - z - x + y - h$ and $W_2 = W - z - h$,

$$V = p(z)v(W_1) + (1 - p(z))v(W_2).$$

We use the first-order approach to represent the agent's maximization problem. Thus we differentiate with respect to z and y, obtaining

$$p'(z)[v(W_1) - v(W_2)] + p(z)v'(W_1) + (1 - p(z))v'(W_2) = 0 \qquad (12.2)$$

and

$$p(z)v'(W_1)[1 - h'(y)] - (1 - p(z))v'(W_2)h'(y) = 0, \qquad (12.3)$$

the last of which can be written as

$$h'(y) = \frac{p(z)v'(W_1)}{p(z)v'(W_1) + (1 - p(z))v'(W_2)}. \tag{12.4}$$

Now we can solve (12.2) for z in terms of y and h, yielding the choice function $z(y, h)$. Substituting this in (12.4), we can solve for y in terms of h and h'. Hence we obtain $y(h, h')$. Of course, this expression for y can be used above to obtain a function $z(h, h')$.

At the level of the principal we do not maximize to describe equilibrium in the insurance industry, but rather we set profit equal to zero. This requires

$$p(z)y = h(y).$$

If the earlier expressions are substituted, we obtain

$$p(z(h, h'))y(h, h') = h.$$

This is a differential equation for the premium function $h(y)$. Solving this differential equation will give the equilibrium schedule.

This solution will not be the true equilibrium if individuals are free to purchase duplicate policies from various companies without reporting their total coverage when applying for additional coverage; for in this case, if h' were increasing, the individual would purchase a number of small policies to obtain a large aggregate coverage. The above solution, then, basically assumes that there is some mechanism by which multiple policies are ruled out.

The solution also assumes that all individuals are identical and face identical risks. If this is not the case, issues of adverse selection will arise, and an equilibrium of the type found above might not exist. It can be seen that this area presents some exceedingly complex problems.

12.7 The Revelation Principle

Frequently in principal-agent relationships, the agent possesses private information, information that is unknown to the principal but potentially influences the agent's choice of actions. It may be factual information about the environment, and hence about the relation between the agent's effort and the resulting output, or it may be personal information about the agent's utility function, which would influence the agent's response to a proposal by the principal. The principal must account for this (unknown) private information when designing a contract.

The influence of private information of this sort was studied in Section 12.3 under the heading of *adverse selection*. The other informational aspect of a principal-agent relationship, the fact that an agent's actions cannot be directly observed or controlled, is a moral hazard property. Hence, the general principal-agent framework embodies both these basic information phenomena.

When the agent has private information, the principal should try to obtain the information as part of the negotiation process leading to a contract. One way to do this is to simply ask the agent for it. However, the agent, in anticipation of how the information will be used, may have an incentive to misrepresent this information, reporting untruthfully. The principal must accordingly plan for this effect when defining questions and forming a contract.

Formulation

As before, we explicitly consider only the case of a single agent. The development that follows can, however, be extended to the case of multiple agents.

The agent possesses private information that is parameterized by t. The parameter t is called the agent's *type*. (It may be the agent's risk aversion coefficient or a property of the environment.) The parameter t can take values from the set $\{t_1, t_2, \ldots, t_T\}$. The principal has a probability distribution over the agent's types. We let q_t be the probability that the agent's type is t. The agent knows t exactly.

The agent selects an action a from the real interval $[\underline{a}, \overline{a}]$. The outcome can be any one of N possibilities, and these are measured in monetary units. We let $\{x_1, x_2, \ldots, x_N\}$ denote these possible outcomes, ordered from smallest to largest.

The probability that outcome j occurs given action a and type t is $p_j(a, t)$. This probability is known to both the principal and the agent. The principal has an expected-value utility function over income r defined by the concave function $u(r)$. Similarly, the agent has an expected-value utility function over income r, action a, and type t defined by $v(r, a \mid t)$ where v is concave with respect to r.

As before, a contract between the principal and the agent is a wage schedule $\mathbf{w} = (w_1, w_2, \ldots, w_N)$ with components being the amounts paid to the agent if the corresponding outcome occurs.

We now incorporate the possibility of information exchange. Suppose that before announcing a contract, the principal requests a report of the agent's type. The agent reports $\hat{t}$, which may or may not equal the true value t. The principal determines the contract as a function of the report, and we denote this function by $\mathbf{w}(\hat{t})$. The agent, on the other hand, must determine both a report and an action.

To carry out this procedure, the principal must design a contract function $\mathbf{w}(\cdot)$ defined over all contract types. Then if the agent reports $\hat{t}$, the specific contract $\mathbf{w}(\hat{t})$ will be used.

This contract function (the set of possible contracts) is known to the agent. Hence, when asking for a report of the agent's type, the principal is, equivalently, allowing the agent to select one of the specific contracts.

It is difficult to compute the expected utility that the principal receives in such a situation, since it will be a function of both the reported type and the true type.

Truthful Revelation

The principal's problem would be much simpler if it were known that the agent always reported truthfully. Fortunately, things can be arranged so that this happens. This result is termed the *revelation principle*, referring to the fact that the agent will truthfully reveal private information. We show below how this can be guaranteed.

Let $\mathbf{w}(\cdot)$ be a contract function defined over the set of possible types. Given this function and a true type t, the principal can calculate the optimal response of the agent, including the optimal report $\hat{t}$. Accordingly, define the function σ by $\hat{t} = \sigma(t)$, where $\hat{t}$ is the optimal report if t is the true type. Now define a new contract function $\overline{\mathbf{w}}(\cdot)$ by $\overline{\mathbf{w}}(t) = \mathbf{w}(\sigma(t))$. This simply assigns each original contract to its optimal response. The optimal response to this function is by construction $\hat{t} = \overline{t}$.

The idea is illustrated in Fig. 12.11. A contract function is represented by a series of contracts, one for each type. (The figure shows the contracts as continuous curves, but actually they consist of a finite number of values corresponding to the heights of the curves at the outcome values.) The original contract labels are indicated on the left. The optimal responses are indicated on the right. These responses are the indices for the new function $\overline{\mathbf{w}}(\cdot)$. Hence, $\overline{\mathbf{w}}(\cdot)$ is just a reordering of the curves in $\mathbf{w}(\cdot)$ with perhaps some repetitions and omissions. An agent of type t will select the contract that

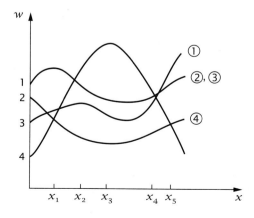

FIGURE 12.11   The revelation principle.

has a t label on the right of the figure. With these labels, type t will always select $\overline{w}(t)$.

The revelation principle shows that anything that can be done with a contract function can be done with one that is incentive compatible with truthful reporting. Hence, in a principal-agent framework the principal can restrict attention to such contract functions.

To be sure that a contract function is compatible with truthful reporting, the principal must explicitly build this relation into the formulation of the optimization problem. However, if this is done and truthful revelation occurs, an expression can be written for the utilities to the principal and agent. The principal must also deduce an action function $a(\cdot)$ such that $a(t)$ is the best action taken by the agent of type t. The utility of the principal corresponding to a contract function $\mathbf{w}(\cdot)$ and action function $a(\cdot)$ is the expected value over types and outcomes; specifically,

$$U(\mathbf{w}(\cdot), a(\cdot)) = \sum_{j=1}^{N} \sum_{t=1}^{T} p_j(a(t), t) q_t \, u(x_j - w_j(t)).$$

The utility of an agent of type $\overline{t}$ is required only for specific choices of $\hat{t}$, which means for specific contracts $\mathbf{w}$ and for specific actions. It is

$$V(\mathbf{w}(\hat{t}), a|\overline{t}) = \sum_{j=1}^{N} p_j(a, \overline{t}) v(w_j(\hat{t}), a|\overline{t}).$$

The principal seeks to solve

$$\max_{\mathbf{w}(\cdot), a(\cdot)} \; U(\mathbf{w}(\cdot), a(\cdot))$$

$$\text{sub to} \; V(\mathbf{w}(t), a(t)|t) \geq \overline{V}(t) \quad \text{for all } t \in T$$

$$(t, a(t)) \in \underset{(\hat{t}, a')}{\operatorname{argmax}} V(\mathbf{w}(\hat{t}), a'|t) \quad \text{for all } t \in T,$$

where $\overline{V}(t)$ is the reservation value of utility if the type is t.

The first constraint is the reservation constraint. Since t is unknown, the principal must ensure that this constraint is satisfied for all t.

The second constraint is the incentive compatibility constraint, and it can be viewed as consisting of two parts. It states that with respect to $\hat{t}$, there is no better report than $\hat{t} = t$, the true type. Again, since the true type is unknown, this must hold for all $t \in T$. With respect to a', the last constraint says that the action $a(t)$ is optimal. In the previous section, only the second of these entered since t was fixed.

As before, the incentive compatibility constraint can be treated as a family of inequalities, or the first-order approach can be applied.

Example 12.5 (Cost-sharing contracts). In the procurement of items involving new technology (such as military aircraft), production costs are often highly uncertain, and hence a fixed-price contract is not appropriate. In an attempt to compensate the contractor adequately while also providing incentives for low-cost production, it is common in such cases for contracts to award profit to the contractor on the basis of total cost.

Let us assume that there is a single potential contractor (that is, this is a sole-source contract). We assume that the cost of the item is unknown, but both the buyer and the contractor agree that the uncertainty in cost can be described by a probability density $f(c)$ where $c \in C$, an interval of the real line. The buyer has an expected-value utility function $u(y)$ for money y, and the contractor has an expected-value utility function $v(y, t)$ for money, where t is a parameter unknown to the buyer. This parameter can take only two possible values t_1 and t_2, which have probabilities q_1 and q_2, respectively (from the buyer's viewpoint). The reservation utilities are $\overline{v}(t_i)$, $i = 1, 2$.

In this case the buyer will design two contracts, indexed by t_1 and t_2. The agent (the contractor) can take no action other than accept at most one of these contracts. The buyer's problem is the following:

$$\max \int_C \sum_{i=1}^{2} u(-\mathbf{w}(c, t_i)) q_i f(c)\, dc$$

$$\text{sub to } \int_C v(\mathbf{w}(c, t_i)|t_i) f(c)\, dc \geq \overline{v}(t_i) \qquad i = 1, 2$$

$$\int_C v(\mathbf{w}(c, t_i)|t_i) f(c)\, dc \geq \int_C v(\mathbf{w}(c, t_j)|t_i) f(c)\, dc \qquad i = 1, 2, \quad j \neq i.$$

The resulting two contracts will be presented to the contractor, who may select either one. For example, suppose t_1 and t_2 correspond to low- and high-risk aversion coefficients, respectively. Both contracts might offer a profit schedule that falls off with increasing total cost. The first contract may offer high initial profit with a steep decrease as cost increases, whereas the second may offer modest initial profit with only slight decrease as cost increases and may have lower expected value. If the true type is t_1, the first will be selected; if the true type is t_2, the second will be selected. By offering this choice, the buyer does not need to guess the contractor's type, nor offer a single contract that is attractive for all types. The result is a more favorable contract for the buyer.

12.8 Exercises

1. (Updating probabilities)   Let $\Omega = \{1, 2, \ldots, S\}$ be a set of states, and suppose an individual initially knows only that the true state is in Ω and that the probabilities of the states are p_s, $s = 1, 2, \ldots, S$. Suppose a signal is received having value y. The conditional probabilities $p(y|s)$, where $s = 1, 2, \ldots, S$ (the probability that y would be the value of the signal, given that the true state is s) are known. Find the new state probabilities that account for receipt of the signal.

2. (Value of information)   Let $\Omega = \{1,2,\ldots,S\}$ be a set of states. Suppose an individual initially has Ω as information structure and assigns probabilities p_s, $s = 1,2,\ldots,S$, to the states. The individual can take action from a set A. Assuming an expected-value utility function, the individual will select a as the solution to

$$\max_{a \in A} \sum_{i=1}^{S} p_i u\,(x_i(a))\,.$$

Denote the corresponding value $V(\Omega)$.

Now suppose the individual can postpone the choice of action until after receiving information. This information changes the information structure to $\mathcal{H} = \{H_1, H_2,\ldots, H_m\}$. Show how the best action for each possible H_i can be computed, and denote the corresponding expected utility $V(H_i)$. Next, show how to compute $V(\mathcal{H})$, which is the expected utility evaluated *before* the particular H_i is revealed. Finally, show that $V(\mathcal{H}) \geq V(\Omega)$.

3. Suppose there are S states. Suppose that intermediate information is available that partitions the states into m information sets each containing the same number of states.

(a) Show that the number of markets required is $m + S/m$.

(b) Show that as $S \to \infty$ the number of markets required when a single intermediate market stage can be as small as $2\sqrt{S}$.

(c) Show that if n intermediate market stages are introduced, the number of markets can be as small as $(n + 1)S^{1/(n+1)}$.

(d) Show that as $S \to \infty$, the number of markets required is $e \cdot \ln S$. Apply this to $S = 1$ billion.

4. Suppose an individual has an expected-value utility function u for money, which is strictly concave and increasing. The individual has wealth W and faces a loss of wealth x with probability p. It is possible to ensure against the loss. The premium (cost) for a policy that pays y in case of loss is py. Show analytically that the individual will select $y = x$.

5. Consider an economy with two consumers, one firm, and the two commodities food and labor. The firm can transform one unit of labor into one unit of food and can scale this process arbitrarily. Individual endowments consist only of labor, but these endowments are uncertain. The table below shows the labor endowments as a function of the three states of the economy.

	Labor	
States of nature	Consumer 1	Consumer 2
1	1	1
2	1	2
3	2	2

All agents know this table, and each consumer knows, in addition, how much labor he or she has.

Six state-indexed commodities can be distinguished, expressed in vector form as $(\text{labor}_1, \text{food}_1, \text{labor}_2, \text{food}_2, \text{labor}_3, \text{food}_3)$, where the subscripts denote states. Both consumers have the same utility function over these commodities, namely,

$$u = 3\left(x^2 + x^4 + x^6\right) + \left(x^1 + x^3 + x^5\right)$$

where the superscripts denote the commodity index as defined above. Each individual also owns one-half of the firm.

(a) Show that an equilibrium of this economy, constrained by the relevant information sets, is

$$\mathbf{p} = (7, 3, 1, 3, 1, 3)$$
$$\mathbf{y} = (-2, 2, -2, 2, -2, 2)$$
$$\mathbf{x}_1 = (0, 1, 0, 1, 1, 1)$$
$$\mathbf{x}_2 = (0, 1, 1, 1, 1, 1).$$

(b) Show that all trades are identical in every state of nature, and conclude that only two prices are actually operative.

6. (Adverse selection for profit) Suppose an individual has wealth W and a concave expected-value utility function u and faces a risk of losing an amount x of wealth with probability p. Only one firm will issue policies for this type of risk. The firm knows the individual's u, W, and x but does not know the probability p of the loss. The firm knows that this probability is either p_1 or p_2 (with $p_1 < p_2$), and it assigns probabilities q_1 and q_2 to these two possibilities.

The firm decides to offer two policy options to the individual. Policy i (for $i = 1, 2$) has premium h_i and pays y_i if the loss occurs. The firm wishes to select h_1, y_1, h_2, and y_2 so that an individual of type i (for $i = 1, 2$) will select policy i and the result will maximize the firm's expected profit.

Formulate the firm's problem as a principal-agent problem. There should be four inequality constraints. Conclude which of these are binding (that is, met with equality).

7. Suppose an agent of a principal can select an action $a \in A$. This action *influences*, but does not uniquely determine, the gross profit that the principal receives. In fact, there are n possible profit levels $q_1, q_2, \ldots, q_n$, and they will occur with corresponding probabilities $p_1(a), p_2(a), \ldots, p_n(a)$, which depend on the agent's choice of a. The agent has utility function $u(a, I)$ depending on a and the income I received from the principal.

The principal can observe the profit q but not the action a and seeks to design an optimal contract. Such a contract is a set of payments $I_1, I_2, \ldots, I_n$ to be paid to the agent, with I_i being paid if q_i occurs. The principal maximizes expected net profit. The agent maximizes expected utility, but has a reservation utility level $\bar{u}$. The corresponding principal-agent problem is

$$\max_{I_1,I_2,\dots,I_n,a^*} \sum_{i=1}^{n} p_i(a^*)[q_i - I_i]$$

$$\text{sub to } \max_{a \in A} \sum_{i=1}^{n} p_i(a)u(a, I_i) = \sum_{i=1}^{n} p_i(a^*)u(a^*, I_i) \geq \overline{u}.$$

(a) Let $C(a^*)$ be the way of least (expected) cost for the principal to ensure that the agent selects action a^*. Then the above problem becomes $\max_{a^*}\{B(a^*) - C(a^*)\}$ where $B(a^*) = \sum_{i=1}^{n} p_i(a^*)q_i$. Write an optimization problem that gives $C(a^*)$.

(b) Now assume that u has the form

$$u(a, I) = G(a) + K(a)V(I),$$

where V is increasing and concave on $(0, \infty)$. Use the variables $v_i = V(I_i)$ instead of I_i and show that the problem in (a) has a convex objective and linear inequality constraints.

8. (Class demonstration)
Preparation: Obtain a few decks of playing cards (one deck is enough for about ten students). You will only use the aces through the sixes. Form pairs of the form $(i, i + 1)$ and of the form $(i + 1, i + 1)$ for $i = 1, 2, \dots, 5$, where the first entry of a pair denotes the value of a red card (heart or diamond) and the second entry denotes the value of a black card (club or spade). Hence, the first possible pair is a red ace and a black two. Be sure that at least one of each possible pair is included; otherwise, the distribution of pairs is arbitrary. (Note that no black aces are used.) Altogether, form as many pairs as one-half the class size. After the pairs are formed, thoroughly mix all cards together.

In class: Students randomly draw one card each. If it is black, it must be turned face up so everyone can see its value. If it is red, its value need not be revealed. Students then form two-person partnerships between red and black cards. The value of a partnership of the form (i, j) is ij. This value must ultimately be divided among the partners; however, the players with red cards need not reveal the true value of their cards until all partnerships have been formed and all agreements made. Hence, it may be advisable to devise contracts that are contingent on the revealed value.

(a) Is there any incentive for players with red cards not to reveal their true value?

(b) Find the theoretical equilibrium contracts and compare with those obtained experimentally.

12.9   References

12.3   For discussion of adverse selection see Rothschild and Stiglitz (1976), and for a textbook discussion see McKenna (1986).

12.4   For the market signaling problem and the job market example, see Spence (1973), and for a somewhat more elaborate model see Kreps and Cho (1987).

12.5 This section is based on Radner (1968).

12.6–12.7 The principal–agent problem was originally formulated in Mirrlees (1975), and Mirrlees (1976). The first-order method is explored in Rogerson (1985). See also Jewitt (1988). The revelation principle was developed largely in Myerson (1979), Myerson (1981), and Myerson (1982). See Brown (1986) for applications of the principal-agent framework to government contracting.

12.8 Exercise 5 is based on an example in Radner (1968). The formulation and example in Exercise 7 are from Grossman and Hart (1983).

Appendix **A**
GENERAL ANALYSIS

This appendix is intended as a reference for the basic mathematical definitions, notations, and relations that are used in the text.

A.1 Sets

A set can be specified in various ways. The most direct way is to list its elements between braces, as $S = \{1, 2, 3, 4\}$. Alternatively, a set can be defined as those elements satisfying some property P, in which case we write $S = \{x : P(x)\}$. For example, the set $S = \{x : x > 0\}$ is the set of all positive real numbers. If x is a member of the set S, we write $x \in S$. If y is not a member of S, we write $y \notin S$.

There are several important operations on sets. The *union* of two sets S and T, denoted $S \cup T$, is the set consisting of all elements that are in S or T. The *intersection* of two sets S and T, denoted $S \cap T$, is the set consisting of all elements that are in both S and T. A set S is a *subset* of T if every element in S is also in T. In this case we write $S \subset T$ or $T \supset S$. The *product* of two sets S and T, denoted $S \times T$, is the set consisting of all ordered pairs (s, t) where $s \in S$ and $t \in T$.

If a and b are real numbers, $[a, b]$ denotes the interval set of real numbers x satisfying $a \le x \le b$. Strict inequality in the definition is indicated through the use of parentheses instead of square brackets. Thus, for example, $(a, b]$ denotes the interval of all x satisfying $a < x \le b$.

For a set S of real numbers, selection of the minimum or maximum value from S is an important operation. We write the minimization operation over S as min S. For example, $\min\{1, 2, 3, 4\} = 1$. Similar notation applies to the maximization operation, abbreviated as max. We also frequently minimize or maximize a real-valued function f over a set S on which it is defined. For example, minimization is written as

$$\min_{x \in S} f(x) \qquad \text{or} \qquad \min \{f(x) : x \in S\}.$$

447

The subset of S where the minimum of f over S is achieved is denoted

$$\operatorname*{argmin}_{x \in S} f(x) \quad \text{or} \quad \operatorname{argmin}\{f(x) : x \in S\}.$$

If the function does not achieve a minimum over S, it is useful to define the *infimum* of f over S as the largest number that is smaller than or equal to $f(x)$ for all $x \in S$. That is, it is the number $m = \max\{m' : m' \le f(x) \text{ for all } x \in S\}$. It may have value $-\infty$. The infimum is denoted

$$\inf_{x \in S} f(x) \quad \text{or} \quad \inf\{f(x) : x \in S\}.$$

Likewise we define the *supremum,* denoted $\sup\{f(x) : x \in S\}$ as the smallest number that is larger than or equal to $f(x)$ for all $x \in S$.

A.2   Vectors and Matrices

The set of all m-tuples with real elements is denoted $\mathcal{R}^m$. It is also called *real m-dimensional space,* and members of $\mathcal{R}^m$ are said to be *m-dimensional vectors.* The subset of $\mathcal{R}^m$ consisting of vectors with nonnegative components is denoted $\mathcal{R}_+^m$ and is called the *nonnegative orthant* in $\mathcal{R}^m$. Likewise, $\mathcal{R}_-^m$ denotes the subset of nonpositive vectors.

An m-tuple of real numbers is frequently written in vector form, represented by a single boldface letter, as $\mathbf{x} = (x_1, x_2, \ldots, x_m)$. An m-tuple of all zeros is denoted $\mathbf{0}$, and an m-tuple of all ones is denoted $\mathbf{1}$.

The individual members of the m-tuple $\mathbf{x}$ are called the *elements* or *components* of $\mathbf{x}$. The *dot product,* or *inner product,* of two vectors $\mathbf{x}$ and $\mathbf{y}$ is $\mathbf{x} \cdot \mathbf{y} = \sum_{i=1}^{m} x_i y_i$.

Inequalities between vectors are expressed in terms of the elements. We write

$$
\begin{aligned}
\mathbf{x} = \mathbf{y} \quad &\text{if } x_i = y_i \quad &&\text{for all } i = 1, 2, \ldots, m \\
\mathbf{x} \ge \mathbf{y} \quad &\text{if } x_i \ge y_i \quad &&\text{for all } i = 1, 2, \ldots, m \\
\mathbf{x} > \mathbf{y} \quad &\text{if } x_i > y_i \quad &&\text{for all } i = 1, 2, \ldots, m.
\end{aligned}
$$

If S and P are sets in $\mathcal{R}^m$, then their *sum* is defined as $S + P = \{\mathbf{x} : \mathbf{x} = \mathbf{s} + \mathbf{p}, \text{ where } \mathbf{s} \in S, \mathbf{p} \in P\}$. If S is a set in $\mathcal{R}^m$ and a is a real number, then $aS = \{\mathbf{x} : \mathbf{x} = a\mathbf{s}, \mathbf{s} \in S\}$.

If $\mathbf{x}_1, \mathbf{x}_2, \ldots, \mathbf{x}_n$ are m-dimensional vectors associated with n individuals, we can form a composite vector of mn dimensions. We typically use a boldface capital letter to denote the composite vector. Thus we write $\mathbf{X} = (\mathbf{x}_1, \mathbf{x}_2, \ldots, \mathbf{x}_n)$ for the corresponding nm-dimensional vector.

Matrices are also denoted by boldface capital letters. Thus we write

$$
\mathbf{A} = \begin{bmatrix}
a_{11} & a_{12} & \cdots & a_{1n} \\
a_{21} & a_{22} & \cdots & a_{2n} \\
\vdots & & & \\
a_{m1} & a_{m2} & \cdots & a_{mn}
\end{bmatrix}
$$

for the matrix $\mathbf{A}$ having m rows and n columns, and such a matrix is said to be $m \times n$. Occasionally, we specify a matrix by the notation $\mathbf{A} = [a_{ij}]$.

The *transpose* of an $m \times n$ matrix $\mathbf{A}$ is the $n \times m$ matrix $\mathbf{A}^{\mathrm{T}}$ with elements $a_{ij}^{\mathrm{T}} = a_{ji}$. An $n \times n$ matrix $\mathbf{A}$ is *symmetric* if $\mathbf{A}^{\mathrm{T}} = \mathbf{A}$. If an $n \times n$ matrix $\mathbf{A}$ has an *inverse*, the inverse is denoted $\mathbf{A}^{-1}$.

A vector $\mathbf{x}$ is often considered to be a matrix with a single column. The corresponding row is $\mathbf{x}^{\mathrm{T}}$. In particular, $\mathbf{x}^{\mathrm{T}}\mathbf{x} = \mathbf{x} \cdot \mathbf{x}$.

A symmetric matrix $\mathbf{A}$ is said to be *positive definite* if $\mathbf{x} \cdot \mathbf{A}\mathbf{x}$ is positive for all nonzero vectors $\mathbf{x}$. Similarly, we define *positive semidefinite, negative definite,* and *negative semidefinite* if $\mathbf{x} \cdot \mathbf{A}\mathbf{x} \geq 0$, $\mathbf{x} \cdot \mathbf{A}\mathbf{x} < 0$, or $\mathbf{x} \cdot \mathbf{A}\mathbf{x} \leq 0$, respectively, for all $\mathbf{x} \neq \mathbf{0}$.

A.3 Topological Concepts

The *norm* of a vector $\mathbf{x} = (x_1, x_2, \ldots, x_m)$ is $||\mathbf{x}|| = \left(\sum_{i=1}^{m} x_i^2\right)^{1/2}$.

A sequence of vectors $\mathbf{x}_0, \mathbf{x}_1, \ldots, \mathbf{x}_k, \ldots$, denoted $\{\mathbf{x}_k\}_{k=0}^{\infty}$ or simply $\{\mathbf{x}_k\}$, is said to *converge* to the limit $\mathbf{x}$ if $||\mathbf{x}_k - \mathbf{x}|| \to 0$ as $k \to \infty$ (that is, if given $\varepsilon > 0$, there is an N such that $k \geq N$ implies $||\mathbf{x}_k - \mathbf{x}|| < \varepsilon$). In this case, we write $\mathbf{x}_k \to \mathbf{x}$.

A point $\mathbf{x}$ is a *limit point* of the sequence $\{\mathbf{x}_k\}$ if there is a subsequence of $\{\mathbf{x}_k\}$ convergent to $\mathbf{x}$. Thus $\mathbf{x}$ is a limit point of $\{\mathbf{x}_k\}$ if there is a subset $\mathcal{K}$ of the positive integers such that $\{\mathbf{x}_k\}_{k \in \mathcal{K}}$ is convergent to $\mathbf{x}$.

A *sphere around* $\mathbf{x}$ is a set of the form $\{\mathbf{y} : ||\mathbf{y} - \mathbf{x}|| < \varepsilon\}$ for some $\varepsilon > 0$.

A subset S of $\mathcal{R}^m$ is *open* if for every point in S there is a sphere centered at that point and contained in S. Equivalently, S is open if for every $\mathbf{x} \in S$ there is an $\varepsilon > 0$ such that $||\mathbf{y} - \mathbf{x}|| < \varepsilon$ implies $\mathbf{y} \in S$. For example, the sphere $\{\mathbf{x} : ||\mathbf{x}|| < 1\}$ is open. The *interior* of any set S in $\mathcal{R}^m$ is the set of points $\mathbf{x} \in S$ that are centers of spheres in S. This set is always open and is denoted $\overset{\circ}{S}$. For example, the interior of the sphere $\{\mathbf{x} : ||\mathbf{x}|| \leq 1\}$ is the open sphere $\{\mathbf{x} : ||\mathbf{x}|| < 1\}$.

A subset P of $\mathcal{R}^m$ is *closed* if every point that is arbitrarily close to P belongs to P. Equivalently, P is closed if $\mathbf{x}_k \to \mathbf{x}$ with $\mathbf{x}_k \in P$ implies that $\mathbf{x} \in P$. For example, the set $\{\mathbf{x} : ||\mathbf{x}|| \leq 1\}$ is closed. The *closure* of a set P in $\mathcal{R}^m$, denoted $\overline{P}$, is the smallest closed set containing P. The *boundary* of a set is that part of the closure that is not contained in the interior.

A subset S of $\mathcal{R}^m$ is *bounded* if it is contained in a sphere of finite radius. If S is closed and bounded, it is *compact*.

Weierstrass' convergence theorem. *If S is compact in $\mathcal{R}^m$ and $\{x_k\}$ is a sequence whose members belong to S, then $\{x_k\}$ has a limit point in S (that is, there is subsequence converging to a point in S).*

A.4   Functions

Let S and P be sets, not necessarily in the same space. A *function f on S with values in P* is denoted $f : S \to P$. It assigns to every $x \in S$ an element $f(x)$ in P. A common case is where $S \subset \mathcal{R}^m$ and $P = \mathcal{R}$, in which case f is said to be a *real-valued* function on $S \subset \mathcal{R}^m$.

A real-valued function f defined on a subset of $\mathcal{R}^m$ is said to be *continuous* at $\mathbf{x}$ if $\mathbf{x}_k \to \mathbf{x}$ implies $f(\mathbf{x}_k) \to f(\mathbf{x})$. Equivalently, f is continuous at $\mathbf{x}$ if given $\varepsilon > 0$ there is a $\delta > 0$ such that $||\mathbf{y} - \mathbf{x}|| < \delta$ implies that $|f(\mathbf{y}) - f(\mathbf{x})| < \varepsilon$.

Suppose $f_1, f_2, \ldots, f_n$ are real-valued functions on a subset S of $\mathcal{R}^m$. The vector function $\mathbf{f} = (f_1, f_2, \ldots, f_n)$ defined by $\mathbf{f}(\mathbf{x}) = (f_1(\mathbf{x}), f_2(\mathbf{x}), \ldots, f_n(\mathbf{x}))$ is a function from S into $\mathcal{R}^n$. Such a vector-valued function is said to be *continuous* if each of its component functions is continuous.

Let f be a real-valued function on $\mathcal{R}^m$ with continuous partial derivatives. We define the *gradient* of f to be the vector

$$\nabla f(\mathbf{x}) = \left[\frac{\partial f(\mathbf{x})}{\partial x_1}, \frac{\partial f(\mathbf{x})}{\partial x_2}, \ldots, \frac{\partial f(\mathbf{x})}{\partial x_m} \right].$$

We sometimes use the alternative notations $f_{\mathbf{x}}(\mathbf{x})$ or $\nabla_{\mathbf{x}} f(\mathbf{x})$ for $\nabla f(\mathbf{x})$.

Suppose f has continuous second partial derivatives. We define the *Hessian* of f at $\mathbf{x}$ to be the $m \times m$ matrix denoted $\nabla^2 f(\mathbf{x})$ or $\mathbf{F}(\mathbf{x})$ as

$$\mathbf{F}(\mathbf{x}) = \left[\frac{\partial^2 f(\mathbf{x})}{\partial x_i \partial x_j} \right].$$

Since

$$\frac{\partial^2 f}{\partial x_i \partial x_j} = \frac{\partial^2 f}{\partial x_j \partial x_i},$$

it is easily seen that the Hessian is symmetric.

A real-valued function f on $\mathcal{R}^m_+$ is said to be *homogeneous of degree k* if $f(t\mathbf{x}) = t^k f(\mathbf{x})$ for all $t > 0$. An important result concerning homogeneous functions is the following:

Euler's theorem.   *If $f : \mathcal{R}^m_+ \to \mathcal{R}$ is continuously differentiable, then f is homogeneous of degree k if and only if*

$$k f(\mathbf{x}) = \sum_{i=1}^{m} \frac{\partial f(\mathbf{x})}{\partial x_i} x_i.$$

Appendix **B**
CONVEXITY

Convexity plays an important role in many aspects of economic theory. This appendix summarizes the main concepts.

B.1   Convex Sets

Convexity.   A set C in $\mathcal{R}^m$ is said to be *convex* if for every $\mathbf{x}_1, \mathbf{x}_2 \in C$ and every real number α, $0 < \alpha < 1$, the point $\alpha\mathbf{x}_1 + (1 - \alpha)\mathbf{x}_2 \in C$.

   Geometrically this definition states that a set is convex if every point on the line segment joining any two points in the set is also in the set. Convexity is illustrated in Fig. B.1.
   Certain set operations preserve convexity, as presented in the following proposition.

Proposition B.1.   *Convex sets in $\mathcal{R}^m$ satisfy the following:*

   (a) If C is a convex set and a is a real number, the set

$$aC = \{\mathbf{x} : \mathbf{x} = a\mathbf{c},\ \mathbf{c} \in C\}$$

   is convex.

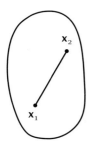

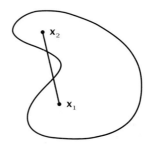

Convex   Nonconvex

FIGURE B.1   Convexity.

451

(*b*) *If C and D are convex sets, the set C + D is convex.*

(*c*) *The intersection of any collection of convex sets is convex.*

B.2   Separating Hyperplanes

Hyperplane.   Let **a** be a nonzero vector in $\mathcal{R}^m$ and let c be a real number. The set

$$H = \{\mathbf{x} \in \mathcal{R}^m : \mathbf{a}\cdot\mathbf{x} = c\}$$

is termed a *hyperplane*.

Geometrically, a hyperplane is an $(m-1)$-dimensional flat surface in $\mathcal{R}^m$. This definition is illustrated in Fig. B.2. The vector **a** and the constant c are not unique, since multiplying both by the same nonzero constant will yield the same set.

A hyperplane can be regarded as dividing the space $\mathcal{R}^m$ into two halves, called half spaces.

Half spaces.   Let **a** be a nonzero vector and c a real number. Corresponding to the hyperplane $H = \{\mathbf{x} : \mathbf{a}\cdot\mathbf{x} = c\}$ are the positive and negative closed half spaces, defined by $H_+ = \{\mathbf{x} : \mathbf{a}\cdot\mathbf{x} \geq c\}$ and $H_- = \{\mathbf{x} : \mathbf{a}\cdot\mathbf{x} \leq c\}$, and the positive and negative open half spaces, defined by $\overset{\circ}{H}_+ = \{\mathbf{x} : \mathbf{a}\cdot\mathbf{x} > c\}$, and $\overset{\circ}{H}_- = \{\mathbf{x} : \mathbf{a}\cdot\mathbf{x} < c\}$.

The theorems below represent the most important results related to convexity. They have strong geometric interpretations and are used frequently

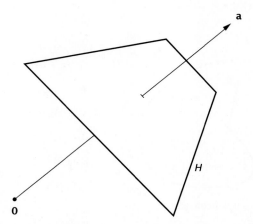

FIGURE B.2   Hyperplane.

in the text. They are the basis for modern duality theory in economics and optimization.

Point separating hyperplane theorem. *Let C be a convex set and let* **y** *be a point exterior to the closure of C. There is a hyperplane containing* **y** *in one of its open half spaces and containing C in its other open half space. Specifically there is a nonzero vector* **a** *and a constant c such that* $\mathbf{a}\cdot\mathbf{y} < c$, *and* $\mathbf{a}\cdot\mathbf{x} > c$ *for all* $\mathbf{x} \in C$.

Proof: Let

$$\delta = \min_{\mathbf{x}\in C} \|\mathbf{x} - \mathbf{y}\| .$$

We need to show that the indicated minimum exists. For this, let $\bar{\mathbf{x}} \in C$ be arbitrary, and define $\bar{\delta} = \|\bar{\mathbf{x}} - \mathbf{y}\|$. The continuous function $f(\mathbf{x}) = \|\mathbf{x} - \mathbf{y}\|$ achieves its minimum over the closed and bounded set defined as the intersection of the closure of C and the sphere of radius $\bar{\delta}$ centered at $\mathbf{y}$ (see Weierstrass' existence theorem in Section C.1). Hence δ is well defined. Since $\mathbf{y}$ is not in the closure of C, we have $\delta > 0$ and there is an $\mathbf{x}_0$ on the boundary of C such that $\|\mathbf{x}_0 - \mathbf{y}\| = \delta$.

We show that $\mathbf{a} = \mathbf{x}_0 - \mathbf{y}$ and $c = \frac{1}{2}\delta^2$ satisfy the conditions of the theorem. Let $\mathbf{x} \in C$. For any α, $0 \le \alpha \le 1$, the point $\mathbf{x}_0 + \alpha(\mathbf{x}-\mathbf{x}_0) \in \bar{C}$, the closure of C, and thus

$$\|\mathbf{x}_0 + \alpha(\mathbf{x} - \mathbf{x}_0) - \mathbf{y}\|^2 \ge \|\mathbf{x}_0 - \mathbf{y}\|^2 .$$

When expanded, this yields

$$2\alpha(\mathbf{x}_0 - \mathbf{y})\cdot(\mathbf{x} - \mathbf{x}_0) + \alpha^2\|\mathbf{x} - \mathbf{x}_0\|^2 \ge 0 .$$

Dividing by α and then letting $\alpha \to 0+$, we find

$$(\mathbf{x}_0 - \mathbf{y})\cdot(\mathbf{x} - \mathbf{x}_0) \ge 0 .$$

This means

$$\begin{aligned}(\mathbf{x}_0 - \mathbf{y})\cdot\mathbf{x} \ge (\mathbf{x}_0 - \mathbf{y})\cdot\mathbf{x}_0 &= (\mathbf{x}_0 - \mathbf{y})\cdot(\mathbf{x}_0 - \mathbf{y}) + (\mathbf{x}_0 - \mathbf{y})\cdot\mathbf{y} \\ &= \delta^2 + (\mathbf{x}_0 - \mathbf{y})\cdot\mathbf{y} .\end{aligned}$$

Hence $\mathbf{a} = \mathbf{x}_0 - \mathbf{y}$ and $c = \frac{1}{2}\delta^2$ satisfy the conditions of the theorem. ∎

Geometrically, this theorem says that given any point **y** outside the closure of a convex set C, there is a hyperplane separating the point **y** and the set C. This theorem is illustrated in Fig. B.3a. The theorem can be extended to include the case where **y** is a boundary point of C.

Supporting hyperplane theorem. *Let C be a convex set and let* **y** *be a boundary point of C. There is a hyperplane containing* **y** *and containing C in one of its closed half spaces.*

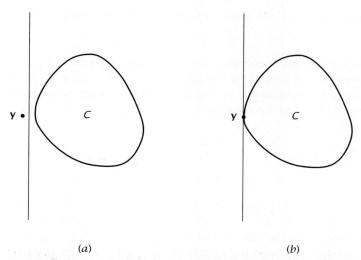

(a)   *(b)*

FIGURE B.3   Hyperplane theorems: (*a*) separating hyperplane; (*b*) supporting hyperplane.

Proof: Let $\{y_k\}$ be a sequence of vectors converging to y such that no y_k is in the closure of C. Let $\{a_k\}$ be a corresponding sequence of vectors constructed according to the point separating hyperplane theorem and normalized so that $\|a_k\| = 1$. For any $x \in C$ we have

$$a_k \cdot y_k < a_k \cdot x.$$

Since $\{a_k\}$ is a bounded sequence, there is (by Weierstrass' convergence theorem, Section A.3) a convergent subsequence $\{a_{k_i}\}$ with limit a. For any $x \in C$, we have

$$a \cdot y = \lim_{i \to \infty} a_{k_i} \cdot y_{k_i} \le \lim_{i \to \infty} a_{k_i} \cdot x = a \cdot x. \quad \blacksquare$$

Finally, it is possible to apply the separating concept to two convex sets.

Separating hyperplane theorem.   *Let C and D be two convex sets such that $C \cap D$ is empty. There is a hyperplane H separating C and D. That is, C is in one closed half space of H, and D is in the other.*

Proof: Consider the set $C - D$. It is convex by Proposition B.1 and $0 \notin C - D$. Therefore by the point separating hyperplane theorem or by the supporting hyperplane theorem (depending on whether 0 is a boundary point of $C - D$), there is a hyperplane separating 0 and $C - D$. It follows that C and D are separated by the hyperplane. $\blacksquare$

A set C is *monotonic* if $c \in C$ implies that $c + n \in C$ for all $n \ge 0$. In many cases one of the convex sets in the above theorems is monotonic. In such a case the separating hyperplane can be defined by a nonnegative vector.

Monotonic separation theorem.   *Let C and D be convex sets such that $C \cap D$ is empty, and suppose that C is monotonic. There is a nonzero vector $\mathbf{p} \geq \mathbf{0}$ and a constant r such that $\mathbf{c} \in C$ implies $\mathbf{p} \cdot \mathbf{c} \geq r$ and $\mathbf{d} \in D$ implies $\mathbf{p} \cdot \mathbf{d} \leq r$.*

Proof: The separating hyperplane theorem gives the existence of a $\mathbf{p}$ and an r that define separation. It remains to prove that $\mathbf{p} \geq \mathbf{0}$. Suppose a component $p_i < 0$. Let $\mathbf{c} \in C$, and let $\mathbf{e}_i$ be the ith unit vector. By monotonicity $\mathbf{c} + \alpha \mathbf{e}_i \in C$ for all $\alpha > 0$. But $\mathbf{p} \cdot (\mathbf{c} + \alpha \mathbf{e}_i)$ can be made arbitrarily large in magnitude but negative, contradicting the separating property. ∎

B.3   Convex and Concave Functions

Convex, concave, quasi-convex, and quasi-concave functions arise frequently in microeconomics. They have a special role in optimization problems.

Concave functions.   Let f be a real-valued function defined on a convex subset C of $\mathcal{R}^m$. Then f is said to be *concave* if for any $\mathbf{x}_1, \mathbf{x}_2 \in C$ and any α, $0 \leq \alpha \leq 1$, there holds

$$f(\alpha \mathbf{x}_1 + (1 - \alpha)\mathbf{x}_2) \geq \alpha f(\mathbf{x}_1) + (1 - \alpha)f(\mathbf{x}_2).$$

If for every $\mathbf{x}_1 \neq \mathbf{x}_2$ and $0 < \alpha < 1$ there holds

$$f(\alpha \mathbf{x}_1 + (1 - \alpha)\mathbf{x}_2) > \alpha f(\mathbf{x}_1) + (1 - \alpha)f(\mathbf{x}_2),$$

then the function is said to be *strictly concave*.

Actually, it can be shown that a function is concave (or strictly concave) if the above corresponding inequality holds for $\alpha = \frac{1}{2}$ and all $\mathbf{x}_1, \mathbf{x}_2 \in C$.

The definition of concave functions is illustrated in Fig. B.4. Geometrically, the definition says that a function is concave if the line segment joining two points on its graph lies below (or at least not above) the function itself.

Convexity for functions is just the opposite of concavity.

Convex functions.   A function g defined on a convex set $S \subset \mathcal{R}^n$ is *convex* if $-g$ is concave.

When concave functions are combined linearly, the result is also concave. Specifically, the following results follow immediately from the definition.

Proposition B.2.   *Concave functions satisfy the following properties:*

   (a) If f is a concave function on a convex set S and c is a positive constant, then cf is concave on S.

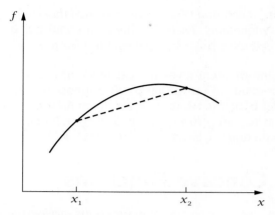

FIGURE B.4   Concave function

(b) *If f and g are concave functions on a convex set S, the function f + g is concave on S.*

For functions that have continuous second partial derivatives, concavity can be related to properties of the function at a single point.

Proposition B.3.   *Let f have continuous second partial derivatives. Let C be a convex set containing an interior point. Then f is concave over C if and only if the Hessian matrix* **F(x)** *of f is negative semidefinite at every point* **x** *in C.*

In economic theory quasi-concave functions are used frequently, especially for the representation of utility functions. Quasi-concavity is somewhat weaker than concavity.

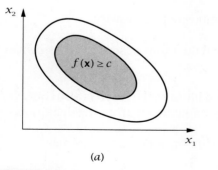

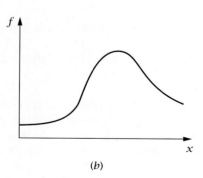

(a)

(b)

FIGURE B.5

Quasi-concavity. Let f be a real-valued function defined on a convex set C in $\mathcal{R}^n$. Then f is *quasi-concave* if the set

$$\{\mathbf{x} : \mathbf{x} \in C, f(\mathbf{x}) \geq c\}$$

is convex for all real numbers c.

The above definition is illustrated in Fig. B.5a. It is easily verified that every concave function is in fact quasi-concave. However, the converse is not necessarily true, as illustrated in Fig. B.5b, which shows a quasi-concave function of one variable that is not concave.

Appendix **C**
OPTIMIZATION

Optimization is a fundamental tool for the development of modern micro-economic analysis. Results of this appendix are used throughout the text.

C.1   Basic Results

The basic optimization problem is that of maximizing (or minimizing) a function over some set. A basic and central result is the existence theorem of Weierstrass.

Weierstrass' existence theorem.   *Let S be a closed and bounded set in $\mathcal{R}^m$, and let f be a continuous function on S. Then f has a maximum on S; that is, there is an $\mathbf{x}^* \in S$ such that $f(\mathbf{x}^*) \geq f(\mathbf{x})$ for all $\mathbf{x} \in S$.*

A point $\mathbf{x}^* \in S$ is a *relative maximum* of f over S if there is an $\varepsilon > 0$ such that $\mathbf{x} \in S$, $||\mathbf{x} - \mathbf{x}^*|| < \varepsilon$, implies that $f(\mathbf{x}) \leq f(\mathbf{x}^*)$. On the other hand, a true overall maximum is called a *global maximum*. Differential conditions typically can only characterize relative maxima or minima.

Equality Constraints

An optimization problem with equality constraints has the form

$$
\begin{aligned}
\max\ & f(\mathbf{x}) \\
\text{sub to}\ & h_1(\mathbf{x}) = 0 \\
& h_2(\mathbf{x}) = 0 \\
& \quad\vdots \\
& h_l(\mathbf{x}) = 0,
\end{aligned}
\tag{C.1}
$$

where *sub to* is an abbreviation for *subject to*. In this problem $\mathbf{x} \in \mathcal{R}^m$ and the functions f and $h_1, h_2, \ldots, h_l$ are real-valued. We have $l \leq m$. Such a problem can have numerous relative maxima.

458

Regularity. A point $\mathbf{x}^*$ satisfying the constraints

$$h_1(\mathbf{x}^*) = 0, \; h_2(\mathbf{x}^*) = 0, \; \ldots, \; h_l(\mathbf{x}^*) = 0$$

is said to be a *regular point* if the gradient vectors

$$\nabla h_1(\mathbf{x}^*), \nabla h_2(\mathbf{x}^*), \ldots, \nabla h_l(\mathbf{x}^*)$$

exist and are linearly independent.

First-Order Conditions

The most important result for constrained optimization problems is the Lagrange multiplier theorem, giving necessary conditions for a point to be a solution.

Lagrange multiplier theorem. *Assume that f and h_i, $i = 1, 2, \ldots, l$ have continuous first partial derivatives. Let $\mathbf{x}^*$ be a relative maximum point for the problem* (C.1) *and suppose $\mathbf{x}^*$ is a regular point of the constraints. There are real numbers (called Lagrange multipliers) $\lambda_1, \lambda_2, \ldots, \lambda_l$ such that*

$$\nabla f(\mathbf{x}^*) - \lambda_1 \nabla h_1(\mathbf{x}^*) - \lambda_2 \nabla h_2(\mathbf{x}^*) - \cdots - \lambda_l \nabla h_l(\mathbf{x}^*) = \mathbf{0},$$

This theorem gives *first-order conditions*, since only first-order derivatives are used. It is often applied by first constructing the *Lagrangian*

$$L(\mathbf{x}, \lambda_1, \lambda_2, \ldots, \lambda_l) = f(\mathbf{x}) - \lambda_1 h_1(\mathbf{x}) - \lambda_2 h_2(\mathbf{x}) - \cdots - \lambda_l h_l(\mathbf{x}).$$

The necessary conditions of the theorem are then expressed as

$$\frac{\partial L(\mathbf{x}, \lambda_1, \lambda_2, \ldots, \lambda_l)}{\partial x_i} = 0, \qquad i = 1, 2, \ldots, m.$$

Second-Order Conditions

If all the functions are twice continuously differentiable, there are also second-order conditions for constrained optimization. We form the Hessian of the Lagrangian

$$\mathbf{L}(\mathbf{x}^*) = \mathbf{F}(\mathbf{x}^*) - \lambda_1 \mathbf{H}_1(\mathbf{x}^*) - \lambda_2 \mathbf{H}_2(\mathbf{x}^*) - \cdots - \lambda_l \mathbf{H}_l(\mathbf{x}^*)$$

where $\mathbf{F}(\mathbf{x}^*)$ and the $\mathbf{H}_i(\mathbf{x}^*)$'s are the Hessians of f and the h_i's, respectively. The λ_i's are the Lagrange multipliers of the first-order conditions. If $\mathbf{x}^*$ is a relative maximum point, a *necessary* condition is that $\mathbf{y} \cdot \mathbf{L}(\mathbf{x}^*)\mathbf{y} \leq 0$ for all $\mathbf{y}$ satisfying $\nabla h_i(\mathbf{x}^*) \cdot \mathbf{y} = 0$ for $i = 1, 2, \ldots, l$. In the case where there are no constraints, this condition means that $\mathbf{F}(\mathbf{x}^*)$ is negative semidefinite.

If $\mathbf{x}^*$ is any point that satisfies the first-order conditions, and if $\mathbf{y} \cdot \mathbf{L}(\mathbf{x}^*)\mathbf{y} < 0$ for all $\mathbf{y} \neq 0$ satisfying $\nabla h_i(\mathbf{x}^*) \cdot \mathbf{y} = 0$ for $i = 1, 2, \ldots, l$, then these conditions are *sufficient* to ensure that $\mathbf{x}^*$ is a local constrained maximum point.

C.2   Linear Programming

A linear program is an optimization problem (either maximization or minimization) having a linear objective function and a set of linear inequality constraints. A *standard form* is

$$
\begin{aligned}
&\min \ \mathbf{c} \cdot \mathbf{x} \\
&\text{sub to } \mathbf{Ax} = \mathbf{b} \\
&\qquad\quad \mathbf{x} \geq \mathbf{0}.
\end{aligned}
\tag{C.2}
$$

In this problem, $\mathbf{x}$ is an n-dimensional vector of unknowns. The vectors $\mathbf{c}$ and $\mathbf{b}$ and the matrix $\mathbf{A}$ are fixed. The vector $\mathbf{c}$ is n-dimensional, and $\mathbf{b}$ is m-dimensional, with $m \leq n$. The matrix $\mathbf{A}$ is therefore $m \times n$.

There is an efficient computational method, the *simplex method*, that determines the optimal solution, if there is one, or determines whether the program is infeasible or unbounded. Hence, linear programs are considered *solved* in the sense that solution is generally routine.

C.3   General Nonlinear Problems

A general nonlinear programming problem has the form

$$
\begin{aligned}
&\max \ f(\mathbf{x}) \\
&\text{sub to } \ h_1(\mathbf{x}) = 0, \quad g_1(\mathbf{x}) \leq 0 \\
&\qquad\qquad h_2(\mathbf{x}) = 0, \quad g_2(\mathbf{x}) \leq 0 \\
&\qquad\qquad \quad \vdots \qquad\qquad\quad \vdots \\
&\qquad\qquad h_l(\mathbf{x}) = 0, \quad g_p(\mathbf{x}) \leq 0.
\end{aligned}
\tag{C.3}
$$

At a feasible point $\mathbf{x} \in \mathcal{R}^m$ any one of the inequality constraints may be satisfied with equality, in which case that constraint is said to be *active,* or it may be satisfied with strict inequality, in which case it is said to be *inactive.* The active constraints can then essentially be regarded as equality constraints. Hence the generalization of regularity is the following:

Regularity.   Let $\mathbf{x}^*$ be a point satisfying the constraints in (C.3), and let J be the set of indices j for which $g_j(\mathbf{x}^*) = 0$. Then $\mathbf{x}^*$ is a *regular point* of the constraints if the gradient vectors $\nabla h_i(\mathbf{x}^*)$, $i = 1, 2, \ldots, l$, and $\nabla g_j(\mathbf{x}^*)$, $j \in J$, are linearly independent.

The Lagrange multiplier theorem can be extended as well. Basically, when there are inequality constraints the Lagrange multiplier of any inactive constraint must be zero. The Lagrange multipliers of an active inequality constraint must be positive (or at least nonnegative).

Kuhn-Tucker theorem. *Let f, h_i, $i = 1, 2, \ldots, m$, and g_j, $j = 1, 2, \ldots, p$, have continuous second partial derivatives. Let $\mathbf{x}^*$ be a relative maximum for the nonlinear program* (C.3) *and suppose $\mathbf{x}^*$ is a regular point of the constraints. There are real numbers $\lambda_1, \lambda_2, \ldots, \lambda_m$ and $\mu_1 \geq 0, \mu_2 \geq 0, \ldots, \mu_p \geq 0$ such that*

$$\nabla f(\mathbf{x}^*) - \sum_{i=1}^{m} \lambda_i \nabla h_i(\mathbf{x}^*) - \sum_{j=1}^{p} \mu_j \nabla g_j(\mathbf{x}^*) = \mathbf{0}$$

and

$$\mu_j g_j(\mathbf{x}^*) = 0, \qquad j = 1, 2, \ldots, p.$$

An important special case is a problem defined by

$$\max \ f(\mathbf{x})$$
$$\text{sub to } g_j(\mathbf{x}) \leq 0 \quad j = 1, 2, \ldots, m, \tag{C.4}$$

where f is concave and each g_j is convex. The constraint set defined by the inequalities is itself convex. The first-order conditions for a relative maximum are then *sufficient* for a global minimum.

Proposition C.1. *Suppose $\mathbf{x}^*$ satisfies the Kuhn-Tucker conditions for the problem* (C.4) *where f is concave and each g_j is convex. Then $\mathbf{x}^*$ is a global solution to* (C.4).

C.4 Parameterized Optimization Problems

Consider the function defined by

$$V(\mathbf{a}) \ = \ \max_{\mathbf{x} \in X} \ f(\mathbf{x}, \mathbf{a})$$
$$\text{sub to } h_1(\mathbf{x}, \mathbf{a}) = 0, \qquad g_1(\mathbf{x}, \mathbf{a}) \leq 0$$
$$h_2(\mathbf{x}, \mathbf{a}) = 0, \qquad g_2(\mathbf{x}, \mathbf{a}) \leq 0 \tag{C.5}$$
$$\vdots \qquad\qquad \vdots$$
$$h_l(\mathbf{x}, \mathbf{a}) = 0, \qquad g_p(\mathbf{x}, \mathbf{a}) \leq 0,$$

for $\mathbf{a} \in A \subset \mathcal{R}^r$. V is defined by an optimization problem parameterized by the vector $\mathbf{a}$.

The following important result shows that V is continuous under certain elementary assumptions on the functions defining the parameterized optimization problem.

Proposition C.2. *Suppose the set X is closed and bounded and the functions f, h_i, and g_j are continuous with respect to $\mathbf{x}$ and $\mathbf{a}$. Suppose also that for all $\mathbf{a} \in A$ there is an $\mathbf{x}$ satisfying $h_i(\mathbf{x}, \mathbf{a}) = 0$, $i = 1, 2, \ldots, l$, and $g_i(\mathbf{x}, \mathbf{a}) \leq 0$, $i = 1, 2, \ldots, p$. Then $V(\mathbf{a})$ defined by* (C.5) *is continuous on A.*

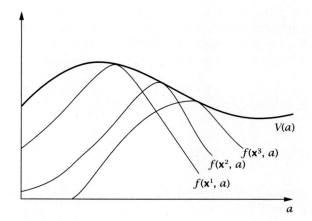

FIGURE C.1 The enve-
lope theorem.

In some cases the solution to (C.5) is unique for each **a**. Then it is meaningful to define the solution function **x**(**a**). The proposition below states that
this function is continuous.

Proposition C.3. *Suppose all the conditions of Proposition C.2 hold, and in
addition the solution* **x**(**a**) *to* (C.5) *is unique for each* **a** $\in$ *A. Then* **x**(**a**) *is continuous with respect to* **a**.

A most important result concerning parameterized problems is the *envelope theorem*. The idea is illustrated in Fig. C.1, where a family of functions is shown, each being of the form $f(\mathbf{x}^0, a)$ where $\mathbf{x}^0$ is fixed and a is
variable. The function $V(a) = \max_{\mathbf{x}} f(\mathbf{x}, a)$ is found by holding a fixed and
maximizing over **x**. In the figure this corresponds to selecting the function
f of maximum height at a. It is then evident that the curve $V(a)$ is the envelope of the original family. The envelope theorem shows how to find the
derivative of the envelope.

We consider the case of a single parameter and equality constraints. That
is,

$$V(a) \; = \; \max \; f(\mathbf{x}, a)$$
$$\text{sub to } h_i(\mathbf{x}, a) = 0, \qquad i = 1, 2, \ldots, l. \tag{C.6}$$

Envelope theorem. *Suppose for $a = a_0$ the problem* (C.6) *has a solution
point* $\mathbf{x}_0 = \mathbf{x}(a_0)$ *that is a regular point of the constraints. Let* $\lambda_1, \lambda_2, \ldots, \lambda_l$ *be
the corresponding Lagrange multipliers. Define the Lagrangian*

$$L(\mathbf{x}, a) = f(\mathbf{x}, a) - \sum_{i=1}^{l} \lambda_i h_i(\mathbf{x}, a).$$

Then

$$\frac{dV}{da}\bigg|_{a_0} = \frac{\partial L(\mathbf{x}, a)}{\partial da}\bigg|_{a_0}$$

Proof: We have the identity

$$h_i(\mathbf{x}(a), a) = 0, \qquad i = 1, 2, \ldots, l.$$

Differentiation with respect to a yields

$$\nabla_\mathbf{x} h_i(\mathbf{x}(a), a) \cdot \frac{d\mathbf{x}(a)}{da} + \frac{\partial h_i(\mathbf{x}(a), a)}{\partial a} = 0.$$

Multiplying the ith equation by λ_i and summing, we have at a_0

$$\sum_{i=1}^m \lambda_i \nabla_\mathbf{x} h_i(\mathbf{x}_0, a_0) \cdot \frac{d\mathbf{x}(a_0)}{da} + \lambda_i \frac{\partial h_i(\mathbf{x}_0, a_0)}{\partial a} = 0. \qquad (C.7)$$

At a_0 we also have from the first-order conditions

$$\nabla_\mathbf{x} f(\mathbf{x}_0, a_0) - \sum_{i=1}^m \lambda_i \nabla_\mathbf{x} h_i(\mathbf{x}_0, a_0) = 0. \qquad (C.8)$$

Now by definition

$$V(a) = f(\mathbf{x}(a), a).$$

Therefore

$$\frac{dV(a)}{da} = \nabla_\mathbf{x} f(\mathbf{x}(a), a) \cdot \frac{d\mathbf{x}(a)}{da} + \frac{\partial f(\mathbf{x}(a), a)}{\partial a}.$$

Substituting from (C.7) and (C.8), we obtain

$$\frac{dV}{da}\bigg|_{a_0} = \frac{\partial f(\mathbf{x}_0, a_0)}{\partial a} - \sum_{i=1}^m \lambda_i \frac{\partial h_i(\mathbf{x}_0, a_0)}{\partial a}$$

$$= \frac{\partial L(\mathbf{x}_0, a_0)}{\partial a}. \quad \blacksquare$$

Appendix **D**
COMPARATIVE STATICS

An important product of economic theory is the ability to compute changes in economic variables, such as quantities produced or consumed, as a function of changes in the economic environment, such as prices or levels of available resources. The computation is usually carried out through study of small changes, using derivatives of the functions involved. In microeconomics the underlying relation between the variables describing the external environment and the variables determined by economic action is often defined by an optimization problem. This appendix gives an overview of some comparative statics results for such problems.

There are two main approaches to comparative statics of optimization. One is based on duality relations. It requires that the problem have special structure, but fortunately this structure is quite common in economic theory. The second is more general, but of course also more complex.

D.1   Duality

Consider the function V defined by an optimization problem as

$$V(\mathbf{p}) = \max_{\mathbf{x}} \ \mathbf{p} \cdot \mathbf{x}$$

$$\text{sub to } \mathbf{x} \in S.$$

This problem has duality form because the parameters $\mathbf{p}$ of the problem are of the same dimension as the vector $\mathbf{x}$ and the two appear together as a dot product. We shall refer to $\mathbf{p}$ as a price vector.

The first thing to note is that the function $V(\mathbf{p})$ is homogeneous of degree one and convex with respect to $\mathbf{p}$. These facts are easy to prove.

The solution to the optimization problem is denoted $\mathbf{x}(\mathbf{p})$. We shall assume that this is a well-defined (single-valued) function.

By the envelope theorem (Appendix C) we have $\mathbf{x}(\mathbf{p}) = \nabla V(\mathbf{p})$, or, equivalently,

$$x_i(\mathbf{p}) = \frac{\partial V(\mathbf{p})}{\partial p_i}.$$

Differentiating the above we have

$$\frac{\partial x_i(\mathbf{p})}{\partial p_j} = \frac{\partial^2 V(\mathbf{p})}{\partial p_i \partial p_j}.$$

This is the main *quantitative* result for comparative statics from the duality viewpoint.

Since the function V is convex, it is known that the matrix

$$\mathbf{V} = \left[\frac{\partial^2 V(\mathbf{p})}{\partial p_i \partial p_j} \right]$$

is symmetric and positive semidefinite (see Appendixes B and C). Therefore we immediately conclude the following comparative statics results.

1. *The own-price effect is nonnegative.* That is,

$$\frac{\partial x_i(\mathbf{p})}{\partial p_i} \geq 0.$$

This follows from the fact that the diagonal terms of the matrix $\mathbf{V}$ must be nonpositive.

2. *Cross effects are symmetric.* That is, for all i and j

$$\frac{\partial x_i(\mathbf{p})}{\partial p_j} = \frac{\partial x_j(\mathbf{p})}{\partial p_i}.$$

This follows from the fact that the matrix $\mathbf{V}$ is symmetric.

3. *The average price effect is nonnegative.* That is,

$$\mathbf{dp} \cdot \mathbf{dx} \geq 0.$$

This follows from $\mathbf{dx} = \mathbf{V}\,\mathbf{dp}$ and hence $\mathbf{dp} \cdot \mathbf{dx} = \mathbf{dp} \cdot \mathbf{V}\,\mathbf{dp}$, which is nonnegative because $\mathbf{V}$ is positive semidefinite.

In the text these results can be applied directly (with a change of sign if min is used instead of max) to the conditional factor demand (Chapter 2), the unconditional factor demand (Chapter 3), and the compensated demand function (Chapter 5).

D.2   General Unconstrained Problems

Consider the unconstrained parameterized optimization problem defined by

$$\max_{\mathbf{x}} \; f(\mathbf{x}, \mathbf{a}),$$

where $\mathbf{a}$ is a vector of parameters. If $\mathbf{x}^*$ is a solution corresponding to $\mathbf{a}^*$, the first-order necessary conditions are

$$\nabla_{\mathbf{x}} f(\mathbf{x}^*, \mathbf{a}^*) = \mathbf{0}. \tag{D.1}$$

As **a** varies we obtain new solutions; the result is a function **x(a)**. We form the differential of (D.1) at a solution $\mathbf{x}^*, \mathbf{a}^*$, obtaining

$$\mathbf{F}\, d\mathbf{x} + \mathbf{A}\, d\mathbf{a} = \mathbf{0},$$

where $\mathbf{F} = \nabla_{\mathbf{xx}} f(\mathbf{x}^*, \mathbf{a}^*)$ and $\mathbf{A} = \nabla_{\mathbf{xa}} f(\mathbf{x}^*, \mathbf{a}^*)$. Hence we obtain

$$d\mathbf{x} = -\mathbf{F}^{-1}\mathbf{A}\, d\mathbf{a}.$$

The above equation is the *quantitative* expression of comparative statics. It enables one to calculate the small change in **x** due to a small change in **a**.

Since $\mathbf{x}^*$ is a maximum point, we know that **F** is a negative semidefinite matrix (see Appendix C). Hence we find the main *qualitative* result of comparative statics:

$$d\mathbf{a}\cdot\mathbf{A}\, d\mathbf{x} = -d\mathbf{a}\cdot\mathbf{A}\mathbf{F}^{-1}\mathbf{A}\, d\mathbf{a} \geq 0. \tag{D.2}$$

As a special case suppose x and a are one-dimensional and $\partial^2 f/(\partial x \partial a) > 0$. Then we can conclude from (D.2) that the sign of dx is the same as the sign of da.

A similar analysis can be carried out for problems with constraints, although the mathematics is a bit more complex.

Appendix **E**
POINT-TO-SET MAPPINGS

Suppose $X \subset \mathcal{R}^n$ and $Y \subset \mathcal{R}^m$ are sets. A *point-to-set mapping* $\mathbf{T}$ from X to Y assigns to every point $\mathbf{x} \in X$ a subset $\mathbf{T}(\mathbf{x})$ of Y. The set $\mathbf{T}(\mathbf{x})$ is called the image of $\mathbf{x}$. The definition of a point-to-set mapping is illustrated in Fig. E.1.

Point-to-set mappings arise frequently in economic theory, especially in the context of optimization problems. For example, suppose $f(\mathbf{x}, \mathbf{z})$ is a function on $X \times Z$. For each $\mathbf{x} \in X$ consider the set of points $\mathbf{z}$ that maximize $f(\mathbf{x}, \mathbf{z})$. Since in general the maximization is not unique, there will be a set of $\mathbf{z}$'s that achieve the maximum. A point-to-set mapping is therefore defined by

$$\mathbf{z}(\mathbf{x}) = \operatorname*{argmax}_{\mathbf{z} \in Z} \, f(\mathbf{x}, \mathbf{z}).$$

As with ordinary point-to-point mappings, it is important to have a concept of continuity for point-to-set mappings. The following definition is the one that is most important for the text.

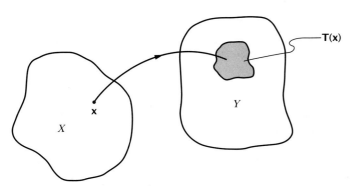

FIGURE E.1   A point-to-set mapping.

467

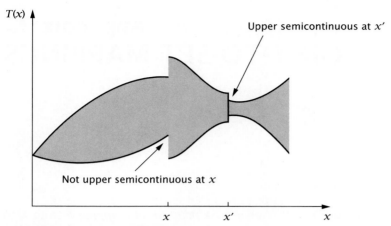

FIGURE E.2   Upper semicontinuity.

Upper semicontinuity.   Let $\mathbf{T} : X \to Y$ be a point-to-set mapping from X into Y and assume that Y is compact.[1] $\mathbf{T}$ is *upper semicontinuous* at $\mathbf{x}$ if for any sequences $\{\mathbf{x}_k\}$ and $\{\mathbf{y}_k\}$ from X and Y, respectively, such that $\mathbf{x}_k \to \mathbf{x}$, $\mathbf{y}_k \in \mathbf{T}(\mathbf{x}_k)$, and $\mathbf{y}_k \to \mathbf{y} \in Y$, it follows that $\mathbf{y} \in \mathbf{T}(\mathbf{x})$.

The definition is best visualized in terms of the graph of the mapping, as shown in Fig. E.2. (The graph of $\mathbf{T}$ is the set of points in $X \times Y$ of the form $(\mathbf{x}, \mathbf{y})$ with $\mathbf{x} \in X$, $\mathbf{y} \in \mathbf{T}(\mathbf{x})$.) The definition says that $\mathbf{T}$ is upper semicontinuous at $\mathbf{x}$ if whenever a sequence of points in the graph converges to a point of the form $(\mathbf{x}, \mathbf{y})$, it follows that $\mathbf{y} \in \mathbf{T}(\mathbf{x})$.

If a point-to-set mapping is upper semicontinuous at each $\mathbf{x} \in X$, we say simply that the mapping is *upper semicontinuous.* A point-to-set mapping is upper semicontinuous at each point if and only if the graph of the mapping is a closed subset of $X \times Y$.

The point-to-set mapping

$$\mathbf{T}(\mathbf{x}) = \operatorname*{argmax}_{\mathbf{z} \in Z} f(\mathbf{x}, \mathbf{z})$$

is upper semicontinuous if f is continuous and Z is compact.

A central result concerning point-to-set mappings is the Kakutani fixed point theorem. It is used extensively in equilibrium theory.

Kakutani fixed point theorem.   *Let* $\mathbf{T}$ *be an upper semicontinuous point-to-set mapping of a compact convex set* S *into itself such that for each* $\mathbf{x} \in S$ *the image* $\mathbf{T}(\mathbf{x})$ *is compact and convex. Then there is a point* $\mathbf{x}^* \in S$ *such that* $\mathbf{x}^* \in \mathbf{T}(\mathbf{x}^*)$.

---

[1] More generally, if Y is not necessarily compact, the property of this definition is called *closedness* of $\mathbf{T}$ at $\mathbf{x}$. The general definition of upper semicontinuity differs from the one given here if Y is not compact, but the usage in the definition here is common.

BIBLIOGRAPHY

Afriat, S. N. (1987) *Logic of Choice and Economic Theory,* Clarendon Press, Oxford.

Allais, M. (1943) *A la Recherche d'une Discipline Economique Première Partie, L'Economie Pure,* Atliers Industria, vol. 1, Paris. Second edition published as *Traité d'Economie Pure,* Imprimerie Nationale of Centre National de la Recherche Scientific, 1952, 5 volumes.

Allais, M. (1981, 1989) *La Théorie Générale des Surplus,* Presses Universitaires de Grenoble 1989. Originally published in 1981 in the *Revue Économies et Sociétés* of l'Institute des Sciences Mathématiques et Économiques Appliqueés.

Arrow, K. J. (1951) "An Extension of the Basic Theorems of Classical Welfare Economics," in *Proceedings of the Second Berkeley Symposium on Mathematical Statistics and Probability,* ed. J. Neyman, 507–532, University of California Press, Berkeley and Los Angeles.

Arrow, K. J. (1951, 1963) *Social Choice and Individual Values,* 1st ed., Yale University Press, New Haven, 1951; 2nd ed., John Wiley and Sons, New York, 1963.

Arrow, K. J. (1953, 1964) "The Role of Securities in the Optimal Allocation of Risk-Bearing," *Rev. Econ. Stud., 31* (April 1964) 91–96. Originally published in 1953 as "Le rôle de valeurs Doursièrs pour la répartition de la meilleure des risques," *Econométrie,* Paris, Centre National de la Research Scientifique, 41–48.

Arrow, K. J. (1969) "The Organization of Economic Activity: Issues Pertinent to the Choice of Market versus Non-Market Allocation," in *The Analysis and Evaluation of Public Expenditures: The PPB System,* 47–64, Joint Economic Committee of the Congress of the United States, Washington, D.C.

Arrow, K. J. (1974) *Essays in the Theory of Risk-Bearing,* North Holland, Amsterdam, chapter 2.

Arrow, K. J., and F. H. Hahn (1971) *General Competitive Analysis,* Holden-Day, San Francisco.

Arvanitidis, N. V., et al. (1972) "A Computer Simulation Model for Flood Plain Development," part 1, Institute of Water Resources, IWR 72-1 (1972), Department of the Army.

Aumann, R. J. (1967) "A Survey of Cooperative Games without Side Payments," in *Essays in Mathematical Economics,* ed. M. Shubik, 3–27, Princeton University Press, Princeton, New Jersey.

Balasko, Y. (1988) *Foundations of the Theory of General Equilibrium,* Academic Press, Boston.

Barone, E. (1908) "Il Ministro della Produzione nello Stato Collettivista," *Giornale degli Economisti,* July, 276-293 and 391-414.

Bator, F. M. (1958) "The Anatomy of Market Failure," *Quarterly Journal of Economics, 72* 351-379.

Bernoulli, D. (1738) "Specimen theoriae novae de mensura sortis," *Commentarii Academiae Scientiarium Imperiales Petropolitanae, 5* 175-192. See *Econometrica, 12* (1954) 23-36, for an English translation by L. Sommer.

Black, D. (1948) "On the Rationale of Group Decision Making," *Journal of Political Economy, 56* 23-24.

Black, D. (1958) *The Theory of Committees and Elections,* Cambridge University Press, London.

Blackorby, C., D. Primont, and R. R. Russell (1978) *Duality, Separability and Functional Structure: Theory and Economic Applications,* Elsevier North Holland, New York.

Brown, P. C. (1986) "Competitive Procurement Contracting When Risk-Preferences Are Uncertain," *Math. Modelling, 7* 285-299.

Brucker, S. M., and S. E. Hastings (1984) "An Interindustry Analysis of Delaware's Economy," Bulletin No. 452, Agricultural Experiment Station, University of Delaware, Newark, March 1984.

Buchanan, J. M. (1965) "An Economic Theory of Clubs," *Econometrica, 32* 1-14.

Buchanan, J. M., and W. C. Stubblebine (1962) "Externality," *Economica, 29* 371-384.

Cass, D., and K. Shell (1983) "Do Sunspots Matter?" *Journal of Political Economy, 91* 193-227.

Chae, S. (1988) "Existence of Competitive Equilibrium with Incomplete Markets," *Journal of Economic Theory, 44* 179-188.

Chamberlain, E. H. (1950) *The Theory of Monopolistic Competition,* Harvard University Press, Cambridge, Mass.

Chipman, J. S., and J. C. Moore (1980) "Compensating Variation, Consumer's Surplus, and Welfare," *American Economic Review, 70* (December) 933-949.

Clarke, E. H. (1971) "Multipart Pricing of Public Goods," *Public Choice, 11* 17-33.

Coase, R. H. (1960) "The Problem of Social Cost," *Journal of Law and Economics, 3* 1-44.

Cook, P. J. (1972) "A One-Line Proof of the Slutsky Equation," *American Economic Review, 62* 139.

Cooter, R. D. (1980) "How the Law Circumvents Starrett's Nonconvexity," *Journal of Economic Theory, 22* 499-504.

Cornes, R., and T. Sandler (1986) *The Theory of Externalities, Public Goods, and Club Goods,* Cambridge University Press, Cambridge, England.

Cournot, A. (1838, 1897) *Recherches sur les Principes Mathematiques de la Théorie des Richesses,* Hachette, Paris. English translation by N. T. Bacon (1897) *Researches into the Mathematical Principles of the Theory of Wealth,* Macmillan, New York.

Crouzeix, J. P., and P. O. Lindberg (1986) "Additively Decomposed Quasiconvex Functions," *Mathematical Programming, 35* 42-57.

de La Grandville, O. (1989) "In Quest of the Slutsky Diamond," *American Economic Review, 79* 468-481.

Dasgupta, P. S., and G. M. Heal (1979) *Economic Theory and Exhaustible Resources,* Cambridge University Press, Cambridge, England.

Deaton, A. (1979) "The Distance Function in Consumer Behavior with Applications to Index Numbers and Optimal Taxation," *Review of Economic Studies, 46* 391–405.

Deaton, A., and J. Muellbauer (1980) *Economics and Consumer Behavior,* Cambridge University Press, Cambridge, England.

Debreu, G. (1951) "The Coefficient of Resource Utilization," *Econometrica, 19* 273–292.

Debreu, G. (1952) "A Social Equilibrium Existence Theorem," *Proceedings of the National Academy of Sciences, 38* 886–893.

Debreu, G. (1959) *Theory of Value,* John Wiley and Sons, New York.

Debreu, G. (1960) "Topological Methods in Cardinal Utility Theory," in *Mathematical Methods in the Social Sciences,* ed. K. J. Arrow, S. Karlin, and P. Suppes, 16–26, Stanford University Press, Stanford.

Debreu, G. (1982) "Existence of Competitive Equilibrium," chapter 15 in *Handbook of Mathematical Economics,* vol. 2, ed. K. J. Arrow and M. D. Intriligator, North Holland, Amsterdam.

Debreu, G., and T. C. Koopmans (1982) "Additively Decomposed Quasiconvex Functions," *Mathematical Programming, 24* 1–38.

Debreu, G., and H. E. Scarf (1963) "A Limit Theorem on the Core of an Economy," *International Economic Review, 4* 235–246.

Denzau, A. T., and R. P. Parks (1983) "Existence of Voting-Market Equilibria," *Journal of Economic Theory, 30* 243–265.

Diamond, P., and M. Rothschild, editors (1978) *Uncertainty in Economics,* Academic Press, Orlando, Florida.

Dierker, E., and J. Lenninghaus (1986) "Surplus Maximization and Pareto Optimality," chapter 9 in *Contributions to Mathematical Economics,* ed. W. Hildebrand and A. Mas-Colell, 143–166, North Holland, Amsterdam.

Diewert, W. E. (1982) "Duality Approaches to Microeconomic Theory," chapter 12 in *Handbook of Mathematical Economics,* vol. 2, ed. K. J. Arrow and M. D. Intriligator, North Holland, Amsterdam.

Dorfman, R., P. A. Samuelson, and R. M. Solow (1958) *Linear Programming and Economic Analysis,* McGraw-Hill, New York.

Drèze, J. H. (1987) *Essays on Economic Decisions under Uncertainty,* Cambridge University Press, Cambridge, England.

Duffie, J. D. (1984) *Advances in General Equilibrium Theory,* Ph.D. Dissertation (May), Department of Engineering-Economic Systems, Stanford University.

Duffie, J. D., and W. Shafer (1986) "Equilibrium and the Role of the Firm in Incomplete Markets," Research Paper No. 915, Graduate School of Business, Stanford University.

Dupuit, J. (1844) "De la Measure de l'Utilité des Travaux Publics," *Annales des Ponts and Chaussées,* 2^c serie, 2e semestre 1844, Mémoires et Documents, n° 116, t.VIII, pp. 332–375. Translated in 1952 as "On the Measurement of the Utility of Public Works," *International Economic Papers.*

Eaves, B. C. (1985) "Finite Solution of Pure Trade Markets with Cobb-Douglas Utilities," *Math. Prog. Study, 23* 226–239 (North Holland).

Edgeworth, F. Y. (1881, 1932) *Mathematical Psychics,* Kegan Paul, London (1881). Reprinted as *Mathematical Psychics,* London School of Economics (1932).

Feldman, A. M. (1980) *Welfare Economics and Social Choice Theory,* Kluwer Nijhoff, Boston.

Fishburn, P. C. (1970) *Utility Theory for Decision Making,* John Wiley and Sons, New York.

Fisher, F. M. (1989) "Games Economists Play: A Noncooperative View," *Rand Journal of Economics, 20* (Spring) 113-124.

Foley, D. K. (1970) "Lindahl's Solution and the Core of an Economy with Public Goods," *Econometrica, 38* (January) 66-72.

Friedman, J. W. (1986) *Game Theory with Applications to Economics,* Oxford University Press, New York.

Geanakoplos, J. (1990) "An Introduction to General Equilibrium with Incomplete Asset Markets," *Journal of Mathematical Economics, 19* 1-38.

Gibbard, A. (1973) "Manipulation of Voting Schemes: A General Result," *Econometrica, 41* 587-601.

Gorman, T. (1953) "Community Preference Fields," *Econometrica, 21* 63-80.

Graaff, J. de V. (1967) *Theoretical Welfare Economics,* Cambridge University Press, Cambridge, England.

Gramlich, E. M. (1981) *Benefit-Cost Analysis of Government Programs,* Prentice Hall, Englewood Cliffs, New Jersey.

Green, J. (1977) "The Non-Existence of Informational Equilibria," *Review of Economic Studies, 44* 451-463.

Greenberg, J., and B. Shitovitz (1988) "Consistent Voting Rules for Competitive Local Public Goods Economies," *Journal of Economic Theory, 46* 223-236.

Grossman, S. J., and O. Hart (1983) "An Analysis of the Principal-Agent Problem," *Econometrica, 51* (January) 7-45.

Groves, T. (1973) "Incentives in Teams," *Econometrica, 41* (July) 617-631.

Groves, T., and J. Ledyard (1977) "Optimal Allocation of Public Goods: A Solution to the 'Free Rider' Problem," *Econometrica, 45* (May) 783-809.

Groves, T., and M. Loeb (1975) "Incentives and Public Inputs," *Journal of Public Economics, 4* 211-226.

Guttman, J. (1978) "Understanding Collective Action: Matching Behavior," *American Economic Review Papers and Proceedings, 68* 251-255.

Hammond, P. J. (1990) "Theoretical Progress in Public Economics: A Provocative Assessment," *Oxford Economic Papers, 42* 6-33.

Hart, O. D. (1975) "On the Optimality of Equilibrium When the Market Structure Is Incomplete," *Journal of Economic Theory, 11* 418-443.

Hausman, J. A. (1981) "Exact Consumer's Surplus and Deadweight Loss," *American Economic Review, 71* 662-676.

Herstein, I. N., and J. Milnor (1953) "An Axiomatic Approach to Measurable Utility," *Econometrica, 21* (April) 291-297.

Hicks, J. R. (1939) "Foundations of Welfare Economics," *Economic Journal, 49* 696-712.

Hicks, J. R. (1946) *Value and Capital,* Clarendon Press, Oxford, England.

Hicks, J. R. (1956) *A Revision of Demand Theory,* Oxford University Press, London.

Hirshleifer, J. (1970) *Investment, Interest, and Capital,* Prentice Hall, Englewood Cliffs, New Jersey.

Hirshleifer, J. (1984) *Price Theory and Applications,* 3rd edition, Prentice Hall, Englewood Cliffs, New Jersey.

Hirshleifer, J., and J. G. Riley (1992) *The Analytics of Uncertainty and Information,* Cambridge University Press, Cambridge, England.

Hotelling, H. (1929) "Stability in Competition," *Economic Journal, 39* 41-57.

Hotelling, H. (1932) "Edgeworth's Taxation Paradox and the Nature of Demand and Supply Function," *Journal of Political Economy, 40* 577-616.

Houthakker, H. S. (1950) "Revealed Preference and the Utility Function," *Economica, 17* 159-174.

Hurwicz, L. (1979a) "On Allocations Attainable through Nash Equilibria," *Journal of Economic Theory, 21* 140-165.

Hurwicz, L. (1979b) "Outcome Functions Yielding Walrasian and Lindahl Allocations at Nash Equilibrium Points," *Review of Economic Studies, 46* 217-225.

Hurwicz, L., and M. K. Richter (1979) "Ville Axioms and Consumer Theory," *Econometrica, 47* 603-619.

Hurwicz, L., and H. Uzawa (1971) "On the Integrability of Demand Functions," in *Preferences, Utility, and Demand,* ed. J. Chipman, L. Hurwicz, M. K. Richter, and H. F. Sonnenschein, 114-148, Harcourt Brace Jovanovich, New York.

Jewitt, I. (1988) "Justifying the First-Order Approach to Principal-Agent Problems," *Econometrica, 56* 1177-1190.

Kalai, E., A. Postlewaighte, and J. Roberts (1979) "A Group Incentive Compatible Mechanism Yielding Core Allocations," *Journal of Economic Theory, 20* 13-22.

Kaldor, N. (1939) "Welfare Propositions of Economics and Interpersonal Comparisons of Utility," *Economic Journal, 49* 549-552.

Kaplan, R. S. (1984) *Advanced Management Accounting,* Prentice Hall, Englewood Cliffs, New Jersey.

Katzner, D. W. (1970) *Static Demand Theory,* Macmillan, New York.

Keeney, R. L., and H. Raiffa (1976) *Decisions with Multiple Objectives: Preferences and Value Tradeoffs,* John Wiley and Sons, New York.

Kelly, J. S. (1978) *Arrow Impossibility Theorems,* Academic Press, New York.

Khilstrom, R., A. Mas-Colell, and H. Sonnenschein (1976) "The Demand Theory of the Weak Axiom of Revealed Preference," *Econometrica, 44* 971-978.

Kim, K. H., and F. W. Roush (1983) *Competitive Economics: Equilibrium and Arbitration,* North Holland, Amsterdam.

Koopmans, T. C. (1957) "Allocation of Resources and the Price System," *Three Essays on the State of Economic Science,* McGraw-Hill, New York.

Krantz, D. H., R. D. Luce, P. Suppes, and A. Tversky (1971) *Foundations of Measurement,* vol. 1, Academic Press, New York.

Kreps, D. M. (1988) *Notes on the Theory of Choice,* Westview Press, Boulder.

Kreps, D. M. (1990) *A Course in Microeconomic Theory,* Princeton University Press, Princeton, New Jersey.

Kreps, D. M., and I.-K. Cho (1987) "Signalling Games and Stable Equilibria," *Quarterly Journal of Economics, 102* 179-221.

Lancaster, K. (1968) *Mathematical Economics,* Macmillan, New York.

Lemke, C. E. (1965) "Bimatrix Equilibrium Points and Mathematical Programming," *Management Science, 11* 681-689.

Lemke, C. E., and J. T. Howson, Jr. (1964) "Equilibrium Points of Bimatrix Games," *SIAM Journal of Applied Math, 12* 413-423.

Leontief, W. W. (1941) *The Structure of the American Economy, 1919-1939,* 1st ed., Oxford University Press, New York.

Leontief, W. W. (1966) *Input-Output Economics,* Oxford University Press, New York.

Lindahl, E. (1919) "Just Taxation—A Positive Solution," ("Die Gerechtigkeit der Besteuerung" (Lund), translated and reprinted in *Classics in the Theory of Public Finance,* ed. R. A. Musgrave and A. T. Peacock, 168-176, MacMillan, London, 1958.

Luce, R. D., and H. Raiffa (1957) *Games and Decisions,* John Wiley and Sons, New York.

Luenberger, D. G. (1968) "Quasi-Convex Programming," *SIAM Journal on Applied Mathematics, 16* 1090-1095.

Luenberger, D. G. (1969) *Optimization by Vector Space Methods,* John Wiley and Sons, New York.

Luenberger, D. G. (1984) *Linear and Nonlinear Programming,* 2nd ed., Addison-Wesley, Reading, Mass.

Luenberger, D. G. (1992a) "Benefit Functions and Duality," *Journal of Mathematical Economics, 21* 461-481.

Luenberger, D. G. (1992b) "New Optimality Principles for Economic Efficiency and Equilibrium," *Journal of Optimization Theory and Applications, 75* 221-264.

Luenberger, D. G. (1994a) "Dual Pareto Efficiency," *Journal of Economic Theory, 62* 70-85.

Luenberger, D. G. (1994b) "Optimality and the Theory of Value," *Journal of Economic Theory, 63* 147-169.

Luenberger, D. G. (1994c) "Externalities and Benefits," *Journal of Mathematical Economics* (to appear).

Luenberger, D. G. (1994d) "Welfare from a Benefit Viewpoint," Working Paper, Department of Engineering–Economic Systems, Stanford University. (To appear in *Economic Theory.*)

Luenberger, D. G., and R. R. Maxfield (1995) "Computing Economic Equilibria Using Benefit and Surplus Functions," *Computational Economics* (to appear).

Machina, M. J. (1987) "Choice under Uncertainty: Problems Solved and Unsolved," *Economic Perspectives, 1* 121-154.

Malinvaud, E. (1985) *Lectures on Microeconomic Theory,* revised ed., North Holland, Amsterdam.

McKenna, C. J. (1986) *The Economics of Uncertainty,* Oxford University Press, New York.

McKenzie, L. (1959) "On the Existence of General Equilibrium for a Competitive Market," *Econometrica, 27* 54-71.

McKenzie, G. W., and D. Ulph (1986) "Exact Welfare Measures," *Economic Perspectives, 4* 1-43.

Meade, J. E. (1952) "External Economies and Diseconomies in a Competitive Situation," *Economic Journal, 62* 54-67.

Miller, R. E., and P. D. Blair (1985) *Input-Output Analysis: Foundations and Extensions,* Prentice Hall, Englewood Cliffs, New Jersey.

Milleron, J.-C. (1968) *Duality in Consumer Behavior Analysis,* reprint, Institute National de La Statistique et des Etudes Economiques, Paris.

Mirrlees, J. A. (1975) "The Theory of Moral Hazard and Unobservable Behavior— Part I," mimeo, Nuffield College, Oxford.

Mirrlees, J. A. (1976) "The Optimal Structure of Incentives and Authority within an Organization," *Bell Journal of Economics,* Spring, 105-131.

Myerson, R. B. (1979) "Incentive Compatibility and the Bargaining Problem," *Econometrica, 47* 61-73.

Myerson, R. B. (1981) "Optimal Auction Design," *Mathematics of Operations Research, 6* 58-73.

Myerson, R. B. (1982) "Optimal Coordination Mechanisms in Generalized Principal-Agent Problems," *Journal of Mathematical Economics, 10* 67-81.

Nadiri, M. I. (1982) "Producer's Theory," chapter 10 in *Handbook of Mathematical Economics,* vol. 2, ed. K. J. Arrow and M. D. Intriligator, North Holland, Amsterdam.

Nakayama, M. (1980) "Optimal Provision of Public Goods through Nash Equilibria," *Journal of Economic Theory, 23* 334-347.

Nash, J. F. (1951) "Non-Cooperative Games," *Annals of Mathematics, 54* 286-295.

Nash, J. F. (1954) "Equilibrium States in *N*-Person Games," *Proceedings of the National Academy of Sciences, 36* 48-49.

Negishi, T. (1960) "Welfare Economics and Existence of an Equilibrium for a Competitive Economy," *Metroeconomica, 12* 92-97.

Neilsen, N. C. (1974) *The Firm as an Intermediary between Consumers and Production Functions under Uncertainty,* Ph.D. Dissertation, Graduate School of Business, Stanford University.

Nicholson, W. (1985) *Microeconomic Theory,* 3rd ed., Dryden, Chicago.

Owen, G. (1982) *Game Theory,* 2nd ed., Academic Press, New York.

Pareto, V. (1906, 1971) *Manuale d'Economia Politica,* Societa Editrice, Milan (1906). 1st and 2nd eds., English translation: *Manual of Political Economy,* translated by A. S. Schwier, ed. A. S. Schwier and A. N. Page, A. M. Kelley, New York (1971).

Pearce, D. W., and C. A. Nash (1981) *The Social Appraisal of Projects: A Text in Cost-Benefit Analysis,* Halsted Press, John Wiley and Sons, New York.

Phlips, L. (1983a) *Applied Consumption Analysis,* revised and enlarged edition, North Holland, Amsterdam.

Phlips, L. (1983b) *The Economics of Price Discrimination,* Cambridge University Press, Cambridge, England.

Pigou, A. C. (1920) *The Economics of Welfare,* Part 2, MacMillan, London.

Quirk, J. P. (1982) *Intermediate Microeconomics,* 2nd ed., Science Research Associates, Chicago.

Quirk, J. P., and Saposnik, R. (1968) *Introduction to General Equilibrium Theory and Welfare Economics,* McGraw-Hill, New York.

Radner, R. (1968) "Competitive Equilibrium under Uncertainty," *Econometrica, 36* 31-58. Also in Diamond and Rothschild (1978).

Radner, R. (1993) "A Note on the Theory of Cost-Benefit Analysis in the Small," in *Capital, Investment, and Development,* ed. K. Basu, M. K. Majumdar, and T. Mitra, 129-141, Basil Blackwell, Oxford.

Rawls, J. (1971) *A Theory of Justice,* Harvard University Press, Cambridge, Mass.

Richter, M. K. (1976) "Revealed Preference Theory," *Econometrica, 34* 635-645.

Roberts, J. D. (1974) "The Lindahl Solution for Economies with Public Goods," *Journal of Public Economics, 3* 23-42.

Robinson, J. (1934) "What Is Perfect Competition?" *Quarterly Journal of Economics, 49* 104-120.

Rogerson, W. P. (1985) "The First-Order Approach to Principal-Agent Problems," *Econometrica, 53* 1357-1367.

Rothschild, M., and J. Stiglitz (1976) "Equilibrium in Competitive Insurance Markets: An Essay on the Economics of Imperfect Information," *Quarterly Journal of Economics, 90* 629-650. Also in Diamond and Rothschild (1978).

Roy, R. (1942) *De l'utilité,* Hermann, Paris.

Samuelson, P. A. (1938) "A Note on the Pure Theory of Consumer's Behavior," *Econometrica, 5* 61-71, 353-354.

Samuelson, P. A. (1947) *Foundations of Economic Analysis,* Harvard University Press, Cambridge, Massachusetts.

Samuelson, P. A. (1954) "The Pure Theory of Public Expenditure," *Review of Economics and Statistics, 36* 387-389.

Satterthwaite, M. A. (1975) "Strategy-Proofness and Arrow's Conditions: Existence and Correspondence Theorems for Voting Procedures and Social Welfare Functions," *Journal of Economic Theory, 10* 187-217.

Savage, L. J. (1954, 1972) *The Foundations of Statistics,* John Wiley, New York, 1954. Reprinted second edition, Dover, New York, 1972.

Scarf, H. E. (1982) "The Computation of Equilibrium Prices: An Exposition," chapter 21 of *Handbook of Mathematical Economics,* vol. 2, ed. K. J. Arrow and M. D. Intriligator, North Holland, Amsterdam.

Scherer, F. M. (1980) *Industrial Market Structure and Economic Performance,* 2nd ed., Rand McNally, Chicago.

Schotter, A., and G. Schwödiauer (1980) "Economics and the Theory of Games: A Survey," *Journal of Economic Literature, 18* 479-527.

Scitovsky, T. (1941) "A Note on Welfare Propositions in Economics," *Review of Economic Studies, 9* 77-88.

Selten, R. (1975) "Reexamination of the Perfectness Concept for Equilibrium Points in Extensive Games," *International Journal of Game Theory, 4* 25-55.

Sen, A. K. (1970) *Collective Choice and Social Welfare,* Holden Day, San Francisco.

Sen, A. (1973) *On Economic Inequality,* Clarendon Press, Oxford.

Shephard, R. (1953) *Cost and Production Functions,* Princeton University Press, Princeton, New Jersey.

Shubik, M. (1982) *Game Theory in the Social Sciences--Concepts and Solutions,* MIT Press, Cambridge, Mass.

Slutsky, E. E. (1952) "On the Theory of the Budget of the Consumer," reprinted in *American Economic Review, Readings in Price Theory,* 27-56, Irwin, Homewood, Illinois.

Slutsky, S. (1977) "A Voting Model for the Allocation of Public Goods: Existence of an Equilibrium," *Journal of Economic Theory, 14,* 299-325.

Spence, M. A. (1973) "Job Market Signaling," *Quarterly Journal of Economics, 87* 355-374. Also in Diamond and Rothschild (1978).

Starrett, D. A. (1972) "Fundamental Nonconvexities in the Theory of Externalities," *Journal of Economic Theory, 4* 180-199.

Takayama, A. (1974) *Mathematical Economics,* Dryden Press, Hinsdale, Illinois.

Thomas, L. C. (1984) *Games, Theory, and Applications,* Ellis Howard, Chichester, England.

Varian, H. R. (1992) *Microeconomic Analysis,* 3rd ed., W. W. Norton and Company, New York.

Vartia, Y. (1983) "Efficient Methods of Measuring Welfare Change and Compensated Income in Terms of Demand Functions," *Econometrica, 51* 79-98.

Vickrey, W. (1961) "Counterspeculation, Auctions, and Competitive Sealed Tenders," *Journal of Finance, 16* 8-37.

Ville, J. (1951–1952) "The Existence Conditions of a Total Utility Function," *Review of Economic Studies, 19,* 123-128.

von Neumann, J., and O. Morgenstern (1944) *Theory of Games and Economic Behavior,* Princeton University Press, Princeton, New Jersey.

Wald, A. (1936, 1951) "Über einge Gleichungssysteme der mathematischen Ökonomie," *Zeitschrift für Nationalökonomie, 7* (1936) 637-670. English translation by A. Wald, "On Some Systems of Equations of Mathematical Economies," *Econometrica, 19* (1951) 368-403.

Walras, L. (1874, 1877) *Eléments d'économie politique pure.* L. Corbaz, Lausanne. English translation by William Jaffé, *Elements of Pure Economics,* Allen and Unwin, London (1954).

Weddepohl, N. H. (1972) "Duality and Equilibrium," *Zeitschrift für Nationalökonomie, 32* 163-187.

Wicksell, K. (1896) "Ein Neues Prinzip der Gerechten Besteuerung," in *Finanztheoretische Untersuchungen,* Jena. Translated as "A New Theory of Just Taxation," in *Classics in the Theory of Public Finance,* ed. R. A. Musgrave and A. T. Peacock, MacMillan, London (1958) 72-118.

Willig, R. (1976) "Consumer Surplus without Apology," *American Economic Review, 66* 589-597.

Wilson, R. B. (1993) *Nonlinear Pricing,* Oxford University Press, New York.

Yaari, M. E. (1969) "Some Remarks on Measures of Risk Aversion and Their Uses," *Journal of Economic Theory, 1* 315-329. Also in Diamond and Rothschild (1978).

Yaari, M. E. (1977) "A Note on Separability and Quasi-Concavity," *Econometrica, 43* 1183-1186.

INDEX